PRINCIPLES
OF
EUROPEAN UNION
LAW

By

Ralph H. Folsom
Professor of Law
University of San Diego

CONCISE HORNBOOK SERIES®

Mat #40273241

Concise Hornbook Series, *WESTLAW* and West Group are
registered trademarks used herein under license.

© 2005 Thomson/West
610 Opperman Drive
P.O. Box 64526
St. Paul, MN 55164–0526
1–800–328–9352

ISBN 0–314–15469–8

TEXT IS PRINTED ON 10% POST
CONSUMER RECYCLED PAPER

Preface

Principles of European Union Law is part of the West Group's Concise Hornbook series. Its coverage goes well beyond that found in Folsom's *European Union Law in a Nutshell*. *Principles* adds citations and more detail than the Nutshell permits. It is an advanced study guide for students and professionals seeking to understand the law of the world's largest common market.

Chapter One presents the history, growth and future of the European Union. Chapters Two and Three focus on critical EU processes, law-making and litigation. Without an understanding of these processes, it is nearly impossible to function as a lawyer working with European Union law.

Chapter Four covers the bedrock "Four Freedoms:" free movement of goods, services, capital and people. Chapter Five contains a broad selection of internal EU policies, ranging from taxation to agriculture. The European Union's complex external trade relations law (of special interest to North Americans) is analyzed in Chapter Six.

Chapter Seven concludes with an extended coverage of European Union business competition law, typically the area of "first contact" for traders and investors.

Appendix I contains the consolidated version of the Treaty on European Union (TEU). Appendix II consists of the consolidated version of the Treaty establishing the European Community (Treaty of Rome). Both Appendices are current through the amendments made by the Treaty of Nice (2003).

Many thanks to San Diego-based Anne-Celine Woelk of the Paris Bar (LLM King's College) for her cite checking. This is the first edition of *Principles of European Union Law.* Your comments and suggestions for the next edition are welcomed.

PROF. RALPH H. FOSOM

rfolsom@sandiego.edu

*

Summary of Contents

*

Table of Contents

*

PRINCIPLES
OF
EUROPEAN UNION
LAW

*

Chapter 1

THE HISTORY, GROWTH AND FUTURE OF THE EUROPEAN UNION

Table of Sections

---

§ 1.0   A Timeline of European Integration

A timeline presenting major developments in European integration follows:

1948 — Benelux Customs Union Treaty

1949 — COMECON Treaty (Eastern Europe, Soviet Union)

1951 — European Coal and Steel Community ("Treaty of Paris")

1957 — European Economic Community (EEC) ("Treaty of Rome")
European Atomic Energy Community Treaty (EURATOM)

1959 — European Free Trade Area Treaty (EFTA)

1968 — EEC Customs Union fully operative

1973 — Britain and Denmark switch from EFTA to EEC; Ireland joins EEC; Remaining EFTA states sign industrial free trade treaties with EEC

1979 — Direct elections to European Parliament

1981 — Greece joins EEC

1983 — Greenland "withdraws" from EEC

1986 — Spain and Portugal join EEC, Portugal leaves EFTA

1987 — Single European Act amends Treaty of Rome to initiate campaign for a Community without internal frontiers

1990 — East Germany merged into Community via reunification process

1991 — COMECON defunct; trade relations with Central Europe develop rapidly

1993 — Maastricht Treaty on European Union (EU) ratified and operational, EEC officially becomes EC

1994 — European Monetary Institute established

1995 — Austria, Finland, and Sweden join EU, Norway votes no again

1999 — Amsterdam Treaty ratified and operational

1999 — Common currency (EURO) managed by European Central Bank commences with 11 members

2003 — Treaty of Nice ratified and operational, draft Constitution for Europe released

2004 — Cyprus, Estonia, Slovenia, Poland, Hungary, the Czech Republic, Slovakia, Latvia, Lithuania, Malta join EU

2006 — Projected ratification of Constitution for Europe

2007 — Accession of Bulgaria, Romania expected, possibly also Croatia

War, twice in the Twentieth Century and for ages previously, has plagued the European continent. The desire for peace after World War II helps explain the beginnings of European integration. As Allied control of West Germany declined in the late 1940s, the return of Germany's basic war industries became a prominent issue. Coal and steel, in particular, were seen as essential to warmaking potential on the Continent. Many feared that if these basic industries were left in national hands, future wars between traditional enemies might emerge. Winston Churchill, in his famous Zurich speech of 1946, urged the establishment of a United States of Europe. He meant that there should be a partnership between France and Germany. The United Kingdom would simply act as a friend and sponsor of this partnership but would not participate. France, especially, was concerned about what it often called "the German problem." The solution that emerged in 1951 was the creation of the European Coal and Steel Community (ECSC).

§ 1.1   Treaty of Paris (1951)

The Coal and Steel Community was the first of Western Europe's major treaties of integration. The basic theory behind this development was that war would be more difficult to pursue if European institutions empowered with substantial regulatory authority controlled the coal and steel industries. Known as the Schuman Plan after Robert Schuman, the Foreign Minister of France, the ECSC was opened for membership in 1950. Although addressed to much of Europe, only France, West Germany, Italy and the three Benelux countries (Belgium, Luxembourg and The Netherlands) joined by signing the Treaty of Paris in April of 1951. West Germany and Italy, of course, were still politically weak from the aftermath of World War II. The Benelux countries, though often united in perspective, were not significantly influential to the development of the European Coal and Steel Community. Thus, the Community essentially represented French ideas and these ideas permeated its founding treaty.

The Treaty of Paris is a complicated document. It is very detailed and legalistic, what the French call a "traité-loi." Its regulatory approaches to the coal and steel industries are diverse. On the one hand, there are provisions which permit substantial European control over prices, the level of subsidies, investment incentives, production levels, transportation rates, discriminatory and restrictive trade practices, employment and industrial structure. These controls represent a regime of French "dirigisme." At the same time, other provisions of the Treaty of Paris contemplate freer trade and more competitive coal and steel markets with only occasional governmental intervention. Over the years, regulation of the coal and steel industries in the ECSC has gone through different cycles but predominantly followed the French regime.

The Treaty of Paris remains the legal basis for European Union law governing these two industries. However, the Treaty of Paris expired near the end of the year 2002. At that time the coal and steel industries were subsumed under the much broader and more economically significant Treaty of Rome of 1957 which established the European Economic Community (EEC) for an "unlimited period" of time.[1]

1.   Article 312, Treaty of Rome.

Lasting Regional Institutions

The most critical features of the Treaty of Paris were those establishing regional institutions for the governance of coal and steel. Here the French perspective that new institutions were required, to which substantial power would be conveyed by national governments, prevailed. The willingness to transfer control over coal and steel to European institutions seems even more remarkable when the prevalence of government ownership of companies in those industries is taken into account. In contrast, the British at that time were of the view that governance of coal and steel in the pursuit of peace did not require the establishment of numerous powerful European institutions. Thus it is in the Treaty of Paris that the four fundamental institutions of the European Union originate: The Council of Ministers, the Commission, the Court of Justice, and the Parliament.

These institutions are sometimes referred to as *supranational* in character although this term is no longer in fashion. They are neither national nor international (*i.e.,* intergovernmental). Within the limits of the treaties empowering them, they exercise sovereignty. It is to the ECSC institutions that responsibility for the establishment and operation of a free trade area and regulation of coal and steel was given. Indeed, some powers granted the Commission (initially called the High Authority) by the Treaty of Paris are not to be found in the subsequent Treaty of Rome. For example, the Commission is given the power to levy taxes directly on coal and steel enterprises. This is a power that is generally absent from the Treaty of Rome. Each of the four major institutions of the European Union will be reviewed subsequently. For now, it is worth noting that their origins strongly reflected the French view that only European institutions could solve "the German problem."

§ 1.2 Treaty of Rome (1957)

As the post-war economies of Europe revitalized, it became increasingly evident that France and Britain were vying for leadership of Western Europe. Each had its own vision of how to proceed beyond the limited European Coal and Steel Community with which Britain became loosely "associated" in the mid–1950s. The British maintained that a free trade area, as distinct from more advanced forms of integration such as a customs union, a common market, an economic community or an economic union, was all that was required for economic integration in Western Europe.

Competing Alternatives for European Integration

The major difference between a free trade area and a customs union is the presence of a common external tariff in the latter.

Common market treaties additionally provide for the free movement of what economists call the "factors of production:" capital, labor, enterprise and technology. Economic communities seek to coordinate or harmonize economic policies important to the functioning of the common market, *e.g.* transport, taxation, monetary matters and government subsidies. Economic unions embrace a more or less complete harmonization or coordination of national policies related to the economy of the union. The difference between a treaty establishing an economic community and one creating an economic union is in the number and importance of integrated national policies.

Britain continued to believe regional integration could be achieved with a minimum of European governance and a maximum of retention of national sovereignty. France, on the other hand, generally envisioned a broader economic community modeled and implemented on the basic design provided by the Treaty of Paris, although even it had begun to express reservations about the degree of power vested in the ECSC. France had the support and could point to the successful integration of the Benelux countries. Belgium, Luxembourg and The Netherlands had signed a Customs Union Treaty in January of 1948. By the middle of the 1950s, the Benelux Nations were close to agreement on a comprehensive economic union. Benelux integration was already providing substantial economic growth to its member nations. Though not as heavily ladened with European institutions as the Coal and Steel Community, the Benelux union served as a pacesetter for wider European economic integration. To a limited degree, this remains true. The Treaty of Rome expressly permits the existence and completion of the Benelux Union to the extent that its objectives are not attained through the European Union.[1]

In June of 1955 a conference of the foreign ministers of the European Coal and Steel Community held in Messina, Italy and responding to a Benelux memorandum authorized an intergovernmental committee to study and report on the prospects for a Western European common market and peaceful use of atomic energy. This committee, still heavily influenced by French perspectives but increasingly subject to a resurgent West Germany, laid the foundations for the Treaty of Rome establishing the European Economic Community in 1957. The Committee was led by a dynamic Belgian, Paul–Henri Spaak. Its report is sometimes referred to as the Spaak Plan, and focuses on the fusion of markets. Adoption of the Committee's report and its embodiment in the Treaty of Rome was influenced by another dynamic Frenchman long an advocate of

§ 1.2   1. Article 306, Treaty of Rome.

European integration. Jean Monnet organized a pressure group known as the Action Committee for the United States of Europe.

EURATOM

At the same time, by separate treaty in 1957, a third European community was created. This is the European Atomic Energy Community (EURATOM). EURATOM is a very specialized community focused on joint research and peaceful development of atomic energy. Its Supply Agency owns all fissionable materials located within the member states not intended for defense requirements. About 35 percent of all electricity, and 14 percent of all European Union energy needs are now supplied by nuclear plants. EURATOM has joined the Treaty on the Non–Proliferation of Nuclear Weapons. In the Chernobyl aftermath, renewed attention has been paid to EURATOM safety standards and the Court of Justice has held that the Commission's advisory opinion must be obtained prior to approval of the final plans for radioactive effluent disposal.[2] Nevertheless, EURATOM is the least significant of the three European communities.

The Treaty of Rome and the EURATOM Treaty follow the institutional pattern of the Treaty of Paris. Each of these three treaties empowers a Council of Ministers, a Commission (called High Authority in the ECSC Treaty), an Assembly (Parliament) and a Court of Justice. This led to an unnecessary and confusing institutional structure which was remedied in part by merging the Court and Parliament in 1957 and later by the so-called "Merger Treaty" of 1967. Since then, there has been one Council, one Commission, one Parliament and one Court, all staffed by the same people. Each of these European Union institutions, however, derives its power and authority from the terms and conditions of whatever treaty it is acting under. In other words, the treaties were not merged, only their institutions. Thus, when the Commission acts on coal and steel matters, the legality of its actions is measured by the Treaty of Paris. When the Council legislates on atomic energy, the EURATOM treaty controls, and so forth.[3] Given the scope of the Treaty of Rome establishing the EEC, the institutions of the Union most often operate under its terms and implementing protocols and legislation.

Treaty of Rome

The Treaty of Rome that established the European Economic Community in 1957 remains the penultimate source of European Union law. In November 1993, the Treaty of Rome was officially

---

2. Saarland v. Minister for Industry, Posts, Telecommunications and Tourism (1988) Eur.Comm.Rep. 5013.

3. *See* Article 305, Treaty of Rome.

renamed the Treaty establishing the European Community. Dropping the word "Economic" from its title was symbolic of the expanded political, social and other non-economic roles of the Community in European affairs. At the same time, the Maastricht Treaty on European Union (TEU) was superimposed over the Treaty of Rome (thereby adding certain common provisions as well as coverage of foreign and security policy and justice and home affairs). The resulting document is titled the "Treaty on European Union together with the Treaty establishing the European Community."

Some have analogized the Treaty of Rome to a constitution. Certainly it is the founding document of the European Community, which is the principal pillar of The European Union. The European Court of Justice has, of late, referred to the Treaty of Rome as the "constitutional charter of a Community based on the rule of law[4]." Under this charter, the member states have limited their sovereignty in ever widening fields of law. Unlike the Coal and Steel Treaty, the Treaty of Rome is open-ended in much of its language, a "traité-cadre" or "traité de procédure" in French terms. It provides the framework and process upon which to build Regional Europe. When compared with the narrowness of the Treaty of Paris establishing the European Coal and Steel Community in 1951, the Treaty of Rome is breathtaking in scope.

The Treaty of Rome commences with some fundamental principles. These principles elaborate upon the goal of establishing a common market throughout the member states. The Treaty lists the activities to achieve its objectives. This listing is found in Article 3 and includes the elimination of customs duties and quotas on internal trade, the establishment of a common external tariff and trade policy towards third countries, the free movement of persons, services and capital, the adoption of common policies on agriculture and transportation, the institution of a "system" of nondistorted competition within the Common Market, and the approximation of member state laws.

Treaty on European Union

In 1993, the Treaty of Rome was amended substantially by the Treaty on European Union (TEU). Since the failure of the "Plan Fouchet" in 1962, European integration has gained momentum and is now finally given a more openly political prospect. With the TEU, the European Union (EU) rests on separate pillars: the EC, a common foreign and defense policy, and cooperation regarding justice and home affairs. Only the first of these three components falls within the scope of the Treaty of Rome, but the maintenance

---

4. Re Draft Treaty on European Eco-   nomic Area (1991) ECJ Opinion 1/91.

of the European Community is by far the most significant of the Union's three pillars. The choice between a federative and a confederative approach to the EU has not been definitively made, but the will to establish a united Europe is leading to a closer political integration.

The tasks of the Union now embrace creation of an economic and monetary union with emphasis upon price stability. The listing of activities in pursuit of that goal was expanded in 1993 to include environmental, social, research and development, trans-European network, health, education, development aid, consumer protection, energy, civil protection, internal market, visas and other policy endeavors of the European Union. Article 4 details the ambitious program of economic and monetary union launched by the TEU. Article 5, on the other hand, seeks to limit Union activities to those areas where the results are best achieved at the European (versus national) level. This is known as the "subsidiarity principle" and is the subject of intense controversy.

Though the Treaty of Rome as drafted in 1957 was much less dirigiste than the Coal and Steel Treaty, Britain once again abstained from membership because of the nature and extent of the European controls over the economy. Britain, too, was still preoccupied with its empire-based trade relations. Europe was important, but it had not yet become critical to British trading interests.

§ 1.3 EFTA (1959) and COMECON

Early United States support for European integration came through the Marshall Plan which was distributed through the Organization for European Economic Cooperation. This organization had no real political power, but successfully mediated some differences in national economic policies prevalent during the late 1940s. By 1957, the cold war between the United States and the Soviet Union was evident. This caused the United States to be generally supportive of the EEC initiative under the theory that a united Europe would present a stronger defense to Soviet aggression.

The Soviets, in turn, increasingly emphasized Eastern European integration through the Council for Mutual Economic Assistance (COMECON). This effort, commenced in 1949, was basically seen as a counterweight to the developments in Western European integration. Locked behind the Iron Curtain, the countries of Eastern Europe found themselves producing whatever the Soviet economic plans required. In exchange, they mostly received subsidized oil and other basic resources.

European Free Trade Area (EFTA)

The fragmentation of Europe's economy during the 1950s became even more accentuated by the emergence of another competing organization. Led by Britain, many of the fringe or traditionally neutral nations of Western Europe organized themselves into the European Free Trade Association (EFTA) in 1959. Austria, Denmark, Iceland, Norway, Portugal, Sweden and Switzerland joined this undertaking. With eight nations, essentially surrounding the core six nations who created the EEC in 1957, Britain felt that it had contained French influence and ideas in the economic sphere. True to British philosophy, the EFTA Treaty was very limited in scope. It applied only to free trade in industrial goods, omitting coverage of agriculture, transport, labor, capital, technology and services to mention only a few areas fully incorporated into the Treaty of Rome. Moreover, the British view on the nature of the governmental institutions required to achieve industrial free trade prevailed. A single institution, the EFTA Council, was created. Since it normally followed a unanimous voting principle, each of the member states retained a veto over new policy developments within the EFTA group. The surrender of national sovereignties to EFTA was minimized.

Thus, by 1960, Europe was economically allied in three major trade groups. France and an increasingly powerful West Germany led Italy and the Benelux states in the European Coal and Steel and Economic Communities. Britain and its partners were loosely integrated through the European Free Trade Association. And the whole of Eastern Europe came under the sway of Soviet dominance through COMECON. In addition, Finland became associated with EFTA and Greece and Turkey were associated with the EEC. Only Spain under Franco remained an economic outcast. More than a decade passed before major shifts in these alliances occurred.

§ 1.4   The Treaty of Rome, the GATT and the Customs Union Dilemma

The General Agreement on Tariffs and Trade (GATT), adopted in 1947 and much amended and interpreted since then, governs many features of the free world trading system. Over 100 nations, including those of the European Union, now adhere to the GATT and a host of "Uruguay Round" agreements administered by the World Trade Organization. In 1957, when the Treaty of Rome was signed, the United States, Britain and other GATT members protested that the Treaty was not in accord with the terms of Article 24 of the GATT.

GATT Article 24

Article 24 permits contracting parties to enter into free trade area and customs union agreements of a fixed or evolutionary character. The premise here is that regional economic groups can be viewed as gradual steps (second-best alternatives) along the road to freer, less discriminatory *world* trade. All regional forms of economic integration are inherently discriminatory in their trade impact. As nonuniversalized trade preferences, they tend to simultaneously *create* trade among member states and *divert* trade between member states and the rest of the world. Thus, while trade creation may represent an improvement in the allocation of scarce world resources, trade diversion may generate an opposite result.

With free trade areas, diversionary trade effects are usually not distinct because of the absence of a common trade wall against outsiders. Trade diversion nonetheless occurs. "Rules of origin" in free trade area treaties keep third-party imports from seeking the lowest tariff or highest quota state and then exploiting the trade advantages within a free trade area. Under rules of origin, free trade areas are "free" only for goods substantially originating therein. This causes member state goods to be preferred over goods from other states. Rules of origin within a free trade area can be as trade diversionary as a common trade policy in other forms of regional economic integration. This appears to be true in the case of NAFTA, for example.

With customs unions, common markets, economic communities and economic unions, trade diversion is more obvious given a common trade policy for third-party states. In these circumstances the resulting "trade creation" and "trade diversion" effects are known generally in economic literature as the "customs union dilemma."[1] In light of the discussion of rules of origin in free trade areas, it might be better to call this the "dilemma of regional economic integration."

Article 24 attempts to manage the internal trade-creating and external trade-diverting effects of regional economic groups. Free trade area and custom union proposals must run the gauntlet of a formal GATT (now WTO) approval procedure during which "binding" recommendations are possible to bring the proposals into conformity with Article 24. Such recommendations might deal with Article 24 requirements for the elimination of internal tariffs and other restrictive regulations of commerce on "substantially all" products originating in a customs union or free trade area. Or they might deal with Article 24 requirements that common external

§ 1.4   *Issue* (1950).
1. See J. Viner, *The Customs Union*

tariffs not be "on the whole higher or more restrictive" in effect than the general incidence of prior existing national tariffs. The broad purpose of Article 24, acknowledged therein, is to facilitate trade among the GATT contracting parties and not to raise trade barriers.

Article 24 and European Integration

It is through this GATT approval mechanism that most regional economic treaties, including those of Western Europe, have passed *without* substantial modification. Only the EFTA Treaty seems to have come genuinely close to meeting the terms of Article 24. The GATT, not the regional economic treaties, most often has given way. With the European Coal and Steel Community only two products were involved. Clearly no case could be made for its compliance with the requirement of elimination of internal trade barriers on "substantially all" products. Hence, the GATT members, passing over Article 24's own waiver proviso for proposals leading to a customs union or a free trade area "in the sense of Article 24," reverted to Article 25. That article allows a two-thirds vote by the contracting parties to waive any GATT obligation.

During passage through the GATT of the Treaty of Rome, many "violations" of the letter and spirit of Article 24 were cited by nonmembers. The derivation of the common external tariff by arithmetically averaging existing national tariffs was challenged as more restrictive of trade than previous arrangements. Such averaging on a given product fails to take account of differing national import volumes. If a product was faced originally with a lower than average national tariff and a larger than average national demand, the new average tariff is clearly more "restrictive" of imports than before. Averaging in high tariffs of countries of low demand quite plausibly created more restrictions on third-party trade. If so, the letter and spirit of Article 24 were breached.

The economic association of Overseas Territories (mainly former French, Dutch, and Belgian colonies) with the EEC also raised considerable difficulty under Article 24. The Community argued that these "association" agreements were free trade areas in the long run, while the GATT officials viewed them as rather open efforts at purely preferential tariff status. Similar problems arose later in the GATT review of the multitude of "evolving" free trade area treaties with Mediterranean nations. In 1975, the openly preferential and discriminatory Lomé Convention negotiated between the European Community and forty-six African, Pacific and Caribbean nations (including many former colonies) challenged the evolutionary character of Community "free trade areas" with developing states. Once again it was the GATT and not the European Community that gave way. In fairness, since 2000 the Cotonou

Agreement at least pledges the EU and its Lomé partners to reciprocal free trade principles.

Despite these and other arguments, the Treaty of Rome passed through the GATT study and review committees without final resolution of its legal status under Article 24. Postponement of these issues became permanent. GATT attempts—through the law-yer-like conditions of Article 24 to maximize trade creation and minimize trade diversion—must be seen in the European context as generally inadequate. Treaty terms became negotiable demands that were not accepted.

§ 1.5   EFTA and the EEC Reconciled (1973)

During the 1960s, Britain began to come to grips with the loss of its empire. Although special trading relations were often pre-served with former colonies through the Commonwealth network, it became increasingly apparent that Britain's economic future lay more in Europe than Africa, Asia or the Caribbean. Moreover, the EEC had helped to spur a phenomenal economic recovery on the Continent at a time when many were questioning the competitive-ness of British industry. For these reasons, and others, Britain began to seek membership as early as 1961 (only two years after the formation of EFTA). France under the leadership of Charles De Gaulle would have none of it. Since the Treaty of Rome provided (as the Treaty on European Union still does) that all new member-ships require a unanimous Council vote, France was effectively able to veto the British application. It was not until the resignation of De Gaulle in 1969 that the British were able in due course to secure membership in the EEC.

New Members (1973)

Agreement on the terms of British accession (including with-drawal from EFTA and the elimination of trade preferences with major Commonwealth nations) was reached in 1971, with an effec-tive date of January, 1973. The switch from EFTA to the EEC by Britain under Conservative Party leadership was undertaken with an ambivalence that continues to be evident. It was only with reluctance that the British accepted the surrenders of sovereignty inherent in the Treaty of Rome. From 1973 onwards, more and more of the economic life of the United Kingdom would be gov-erned by the four institutions of the European Community (now Union). British reluctance to join the Common Market was re-played in a 1975 national referendum under a Labor Party govern-ment. Approximately 60 percent of the populace voted to remain a member of the Community.

Denmark also switched sides in 1973. Norway was scheduled to become a member of the EEC at that time, and the terms of its membership had been negotiated, but the people of Norway rejected the Community in a national referendum. The rejection had a lot to do with the requirements of the Common Fisheries Policy which would have unacceptably opened Norwegian waters to fishermen from the Continent, Britain and Ireland (which followed the British lead into the Community in 1973). This Policy also regulates the type and number of fish that can be caught in EU waters, significantly subsidizes the fishing industry, and protects it from foreign competition.

In addition to the expansion of the EEC to nine members, 1973 brought an even greater degree of European economic integration. Although EFTA remained intact, each of the remaining EFTA nations signed bilateral trade treaties with the expanded Community. These treaties governed trade relations between all EFTA nations and the Community until 1994. They essentially provide for industrial free trade. Thus the 1973 enlargement of the European Economic Community was the catalyst for the most wide-scale and comprehensive effort at Western European integration yet to take place, the reconciliation of the EFTA and EEC trading alliances. This was an historic watershed in European economic integration.

New Members (1980s)

During the 1980s there was a strong trend toward increased membership in and expansion of the European Community (now Union). The only exception to this trend was the "withdrawal" of Greenland in 1983. Greenland had been admitted with Denmark in 1973, but voted in a home rule referendum (essentially rejecting the Common Fisheries Policy) to withdraw. It is now associated with the EU as an overseas territory of Denmark. Greece joined in 1981 and Portugal and Spain became members in 1986. Portugal left the EFTA group, and Spain finally overcame the yoke of General Franco.

§ 1.6   The European Economic Area, EU–Swiss Agreements

Expanded relations between the European Community (now Union) and the seven remaining EFTA states (Iceland, Norway, Sweden, Finland, Switzerland, Austria and Lechtenstein) have been under negotiation since the mid–1980s. These negotiations envisioned closer economic relations short of membership. Late in 1991, a linkage of the two groups in what is called a European Economic Area (EEA) was agreed. The EEA generally embraces Union law on free movement of goods, services, persons and capital. But integration on agricultural, fisheries and tax policy is excluded and the

EFTA nations will retain their own border controls, tariffs, currencies and external trade policies. Antidumping measures, countervailing duties and illicit commercial practices law will not be applied to EEA trade. Political and defense union is also excluded from the EEA agreement.

The EEA agreement reached in October of 1991 envisioned the creation of a number of inter-regional organizations vested with law-making and dispute settlement powers. These included an EEA Council, an EEA Joint Committee (EU parallel is the Committee of Permanent Representatives), an EEA Court of Justice and Court of First Instance, an EEA Joint Parliamentary Committee, an EEA Consultative Committee (EU parallel is Economic and Social Committee), and an EFTA Surveillance Authority (EU parallel is the Commission). The latter will focus on EFTA application of EU competition law.

Judicial Authority

In December of 1991, the European Court of Justice (ECJ) issued an opinion that the EEA Courts were not compatible with the Treaty of Rome.[1] The Court was particularly concerned with its own supremacy as the final arbiter of Community law. This sent the negotiators back to the drawing board on dispute settlement. A revised EEA agreement was concluded early in 1992 with a scheduled effective date of January 1, 1993. The ECJ found this agreement compatible with the Treaty of Rome.[2]

As revised, the European Economic Area agreement provides for a new EFTA Court of Justice. In all cases of disparate jurisprudence, the EEA creates a "Joint Committee" consisting of EU and EFTA political representatives. This Committee will not have judicial powers. It will review conflict on the EEA between the ECJ and the EFTA Court, but exercise no control over them. If the case law diverges and the Joint Committee fails to reach a solution, correction procedures may be invoked. Under these procedures, the European Court of Justice upon request issues an Opinion on the matter. This Opinion presumably would be followed by the EFTA party to the dispute. Courts in EFTA nations may request an advisory decision by the ECJ when EFTA law is identical to Union law. Presumably, again, this decision would be binding. If the dispute is not referred to the ECJ, either party may take "safeguard measures." If these measures do not resolve the matter, then either party may ultimately refer the dispute to binding arbitration.

§ 1.6   **2.** Opinion 1/92 (April 10, 1992).
1. 1 Opinion 1/91 (Dec. 14, 1991).

Swiss Rejection of EEA

The revised EEA agreement had to be ratified by the European Parliament as well as all EU and EFTA nations. Perhaps not surprisingly, the Swiss rejected the EEA in a national referendum held in December 1992. This rejection casts doubt upon the Swiss membership request, but it did not cause the EEA to falter. Subsequent negotiations in 1993 produced a still further revised agreement minus Switzerland. This version of the EEA then made the required rounds of ratification, and came into force January 1, 1994. Today it applies only to Iceland, Lichtenstein and Norway. A series of bilateral 1999 EU agreements with Switzerland cover free movement of persons, transport, agriculture, procurement and mutual recognition. In 2004, additional EU–Swiss agreements were reached on taxation of savings, fighting fraud, Swiss participation in the Schegen Accord, trade in processed agricultural goods, environmental cooperation, media programs and avoidance of double taxation on pensioners.

§ 1.7   Growth in Membership

New Members (1990s)

One reason for the Union's advancement of the EEA and reluctance to accept new members was its intensive internal focus on the 1992 campaign for a fully integrated common market. Other reasons involve the practical problems associated with governance of a regional organization with substantial numbers of nations. With 12 member states, the EU found it difficult to arrive at a consensus and move forward towards further integration without substantially overriding national interests. A community with more members would presumably be all that more difficult to govern. Nevertheless, membership in the European Union for all EFTA states that want it is a foregone conclusion.

The Maastricht Summit accords (December, 1991) opened the door to new membership, and negotiations with Austria, Sweden, Finland and Norway began in earnest in 1993. Accession agreements for these countries were concluded early in 1994 and ratification by the European Parliament was obtained in May of that year. Each of these countries scheduled a national referendum on membership in the EU. The Austrians voted by a 2 to 1 margin to join. The Finns and Swedes also ratified accession, but Norway once again voted no. Membership took effect January 1, 1995.

It has always been a rule, at times unwritten, that EU members and applicants must support democratic governments. This principle was applied to Greece during the coup by the colonels in the late 1960s and early 1970s. The Community suspended trade relations with Greece during this period and the coup certainly delayed admission of that country. The commitment of the Community (now Union) to governance by representative democracy, the rule of law, social justice and respect for human rights was formalized in 1977 under a Declaration on Democracy by the heads of all the member state governments. At the same time, the Council, Commission and Parliament issued a Joint Declaration on Fundamental Rights to much the same effect. More recently, new applicants are said to have to embrace the ever expanding body of regional legislation and case law, the "acquis communautaire." Short of exceptions or postponements negotiated through "accession treaties," this is true.

With 15 member states, the European Union in 1995 became a powerful and lucrative economic market. Its aggregate population and gross domestic product exceeded that of the United States and Canada, which implemented a Free Trade Agreement in 1989. The addition of Mexico and the emergence of a North American Free Trade Area in 1994 were just some of the continuing repercussions of the need to compete with the European Union in the global marketplace.[1]

Membership Criteria

At the Copenhagen Summit in June of 1993, the European Council set the following membership criteria for Central and Eastern countries:

(1) stable democracies based upon a rule of law, human rights and protection of minorities;

(2) market economies able to compete with the EU; and

(3) the ability to make full commitments to EU political, monetary and economic union ("acquis communautaire").

Turkey has been associated with the EU as a trade ally since 1963. Relations were suspended during the military takeover of Turkey from 1981 to 1986. Turkey formally applied for membership in 1987 but has been kept under study since then. In the Fall of 2004, the Commission recommended opening "full" EU membership negotiations with Turkey. Apart from concerns about the stability of democracy in Turkey, Greek and Greek Cypriot membership in the Union would seem to make admission unlikely. Furthermore, membership is limited by the Treaty on European Union to "European states".[2] Morocco's "application" was politely rejected because it is not a European nation. Turkey's application presents difficult questions about its status in Europe and the

1. See R. Folsom, *NAFTA and Free Trade in the Americas in a Nutshell.*

2. Article 49, Treaty on European Union.

meaning of the Treaty. Does "European" only have geographic implications or is there an expectation that members must also be culturally or religiously European?

There has been an incorporation of what was East Germany into the Union through the reunification process. The accession of East Germany to the Union renewed concerns over the role of Germany in Europe. Instead of four large member states (France, West Germany, Italy and the United Kingdom) of roughly equal populations, united Germany has substantially more people and potentially much more economic clout than any other member of the Union. This caused anxieties about keeping that country well anchored by European institutions.

New Members (2004)

Starting in 1997, following the Commission's recommendations and a series of association agreements (Europe agreements), the European Union commenced negotiations for membership with Cyprus, Estonia, Slovenia, Poland, Hungary, the Czech Republic, Malta, Romania, Bulgaria, Lithuania, Latvia and Slovakia. Long in the making, accession agreements for all but Bulgaria and Romania were finalized late in 2002 with entry for the ten new member states definitively scheduled for May 1, 2004. Particularly sensitive issues such as full participation in agricultural subsidies and free movement of workers were finessed with extended periods. Nine of the 2004 member states ratified accession in national referendums, with only Greek Cyprus not holding a plebiscite. Romania and Bulgaria are expected to join in 2007, possibly also with Croatia.

§ 1.8 Europe Without Internal Frontiers (1992)

The campaign for a European Community without internal frontiers by the end of 1992 was the product of Commission studies in the mid–1980s which concluded that a hardening of the trade arteries of Europe had occurred. The Community was perceived to be stagnating relative to the advancing economies of North America and East Asia. Various projections of the wealth that could be generated from a truly common market for Western Europe suggested the need to revitalize the region. A "white paper" drafted under the leadership of Lord Cockfield of Britain and issued by the Commission in 1985 became the blueprint for the 1992 campaign.

The Commission's white paper identified three types of barriers to a Europe without internal frontiers—physical, technical and fiscal. Physical barriers occur at the borders. For goods, they included national trade quotas, health checks, agricultural monetary compensation amount charges, statistical collections and transport controls. For people, physical barriers concern clearing immigrations, security checks and customs. Technical barriers mostly involve national standards and rules for goods, services, capital and labor which operate to inhibit free movement among the member states. Medical and surgical equipment and pharmaceuticals provide traditional examples of markets restrained by technical trade barriers. Fiscal barriers identified in the Commission's 1985 white paper centered on different value-added and excise taxation levels and the corresponding need for tax collections at borders. There were, for example, wide value-added tax (VAT) differences on auto sales within the Common Market.

The Commission estimated that removal of all of these barriers could save the Community upwards of 100 billion ECUs (European Currency Units) in direct costs. In addition, another roughly 100 billion ECUs could be gained as price reductions and increased efficiency and competition took hold. Overall, the Commission projected an increase in the Community's gross domestic product of between 4.5 to 7 percent, a reduction in consumer prices of between 6 to 4.5 percent, 1.75 to 5 million new jobs, and enhanced public sector and external trade balances. These figures were thus said to represent "the costs of non-Europe."

Single European Act

Major amendments to the Treaty of Rome were undertaken in the Single European Act (SEA) which became effective in 1987. Amendments to the Treaty can occur by Commission or member state proposal to the Council which calls an intergovernmental conference to unanimously determine their content. The amendments are not effective until ratified by all the member states in accordance with their respective constitutional requirements.[1] Proposals originating in the Commission's 1985 white paper on a Europe without internal frontiers were embodied in the Single European Act. The SEA amendments not only expanded the competence of the European Community institutions, but also sought to accelerate the speed of integration by relying more heavily on qualified majority (not unanimous) voting principles in Council decision-making.

The Single European Act envisioned the adoption of 282 new legislative measures designed to fully integrate the goods, services and capital markets by the end of 1992. Nearly all of these measures and others were adopted by the Council.[2] Implementation at the national level has proceeded more slowly and is still a

§ 1.8

1. Article 48, Treaty on European Union.

2. See Section 2.14.

concern, especially regarding insurance, investment advisors and procurement.

Realization of the goal of a Europe without internal frontiers *for people* has proved harder to achieve. Most members agreed to remove their internal frontier controls on people under the 1990 "Schengen Accord." This accord is the product of intergovernmental agreement, not EU legislation. It is not expected that Ireland and the United Kingdom will participate, but non-members Norway and Iceland do. The Schengen Accord covers such sensitive issues as visas, asylum, immigration, gun controls, extradition and police rights of "hot pursuit." The main points of contention were cross-border traffic of immigrants and criminals, especially terrorists and drug dealers. These issues were resolved largely by promises of greater intergovernmental cooperation, notably through computer linkages. Much of the substance of the Schengen Accord was incorporated into the Treaty of Rome by the Amsterdam Treaty of 1999 (below).

§ 1.9 The Maastricht Treaty on European Union (1993), Opt–Out Rights

Well before the realization of a Europe without internal frontiers under the Single European Act, Community and national leaders were forging another momentous round of European integration. These efforts bore fruit in the December 1991 summit meeting of the European Council in Maastricht, The Netherlands, where the "Treaty on European Union" (TEU) was signed. The Maastricht agreement, like the Single European Act, significantly amends the Treaty of Rome. Furthermore, it adds what amount to side agreements on a common foreign and security policy[1] and cooperation regarding justice and home affairs. These two new pillars of the EU are to grow in importance as integration deepens. Like the Single European Act's provisions on foreign policy, these side agreements do not amend the Treaty of Rome and stand on their own as separate international agreements. As such, they are not subject to the judicial review of the Court of Justice.

The most important Maastricht amendments to the Treaty of Rome concern the ambiguous principle of "subsidiarity"[2] and economic and monetary integration, notably a detailed timetable for the convergence of national economies and creation of a common currency.[3] Other significant amendments include the conveyance to Parliament of a limited legislative and international agreements' veto, a power to conduct inquiries into maladministration of the

---

§ 1.9

1. *See* Section 1.13.

2. *See* Section 2.0.

3. *See* Section 4.16.

EU, and a right to reject Commission appointments and new member state applicants.[4] The TEU also adds new Articles on cooperation regarding education, health and culture, the development of European Union citizenship rights and a formal commitment to respect the rights protected by the European Human Rights Convention,[5] expanded economic aid to the least developed members (the "cohesion fund"),[6] authorization of the Court of Justice to sanction delinquent member state governments by fines and penalties,[7] and a Social Protocol (Britain excepted).[8] The TEU formally authorizes Union legislation on consumer protection, industrial policy, energy, tourism, visas and coordinated police action, largely by qualified majority voting which is also extended to transportation and most environmental law.[9]

Ratification and Opt–Out Rights

The ink was no sooner dry on the Treaty on European Union when Denmark's voters by a slim margin rejected ratification in June 1992. Ireland and France (by an equally slim margin) ratified the TEU in national referenda and by year's end the Maastricht agreement had been ratified in all but Denmark and the United Kingdom. After concessions to Denmark were made at the December 1992 Edinburgh summit of the European Council, a new referendum was scheduled for May 1993. Denmark obtained confirmation of its right to opt out of a common currency and new rights to opt out of the TEU provisions on common defense, European citizenship and home and justice affairs. Europe a la carte carried the day, a harbinger for the ongoing membership negotiations with Austria, Sweden, Finland and Norway. The Danes ultimately approved Maastricht, and a bitter Parliamentary battle in Britain brought similar results in August of 1993. After a constitutional challenge to ratification failed in Germany, the Treaty on European Union became effective November 1, 1993.

The following chart presents the major "opt-out" rights under Maastricht of various member states:

United Kingdom	— Social Protocol, Single Currency, Schengen Accord (Internal border controls over people).
Ireland	— Schengen Accord.
Denmark	— Schengen Accord, Single Currency, Defense, Justice and Home Affairs,

---

4. *See* Section 2.2.

5. *See* Section 2.12.

6. *See* Section 5.12.

7. *See* Section 3.9.

8. *See* Section 5.19.

9. *See* Section 2.7.

European Citizenship.

It should be noted that the United Kingdom under the Labour Party administration of Prime Minister Blair opted into the region's Social Policy and the Social Protocol has been repealed.

§ 1.10   The Amsterdam Treaty (1999)

The Maastricht Treaty on European Union of 1993 called for another round of intergovernmental negotiations to revise both the TEU and the Treaty of Rome. Late in 1997, these negotiations bore fruit in the Amsterdam Treaty, which then faced national referenda and court challenges during the ratification process.

The Amsterdam Treaty is in many respects best known for what it did *not* accomplish, namely major institutional and agricultural policy reforms in anticipation of European Union membership expansions. The Treaty did significantly extend Parliament's co-decision legislative powers, and institutionalized procedures to deal with "serious and persistent" member state violations of democracy, human rights and the rule of law. It authorized legislative action to secure "freedom, security and justice" (an effective transfer of much of the TEU justice and home affairs power), including asylum, extradition and the essentials of the Schengen Accord, all subject to Court of Justice review but also British, Danish and Irish opt outs. Additional legislative powers cover employment incentives, public health, fraud prevention, customs cooperation, transparency principles and social policy (formerly the Social Protocol). A complex provision on "flexibility" seeks to allow, subject to detailed controls but generally not (after Nice) vetoes, a minimum of eight member states to establish "closer cooperation" than others. This provision appears to reflect the realities of less than comprehensive participation in existing policies and programs such as defense, the common currency, the Schengen Accord and the like. Lastly, the Amsterdam Treaty adds a special protocol on the principles of subsidiarity and proportionality, and attempts to secure greater support for common foreign and security policies.

§ 1.11   The Treaty of Nice (2003)

With the Amsterdam Treaty in place, and new memberships looming, yet another round of intergovernmental negotiations was swiftly commenced. By 2001, the Treaty of Nice was signed and sent on its way for national ratifications. Like the Amsterdam Treaty and its predecessors, Nice amends the Treaty of Rome, notably extending qualified majority legislative voting in the Council, authorizing the creation of specialized "judicial panels" attached to the Court of First Instance, and increasing the possibility of closer cooperation ("flexibility") by less than the Union's full membership. More significantly, the Enlargement Protocol to the Treaty of Nice establishes the rules of governance once the ten (eventually twelve) new members accede to the European Union. These byzantine institutional changes for the European Council, Commission, Parliament and Courts are covered in Chapters Two and Three. Lastly, a Charter of Fundamental Rights was "proclaimed" at Nice, but not made binding as a matter of law, and therefore not subject to ratification. See Chapter Three.

Ratification of the Treaty of Nice and its Enlargement Protocol ran into unexpected opposition in Ireland. Often cited as a model of how the European Union can benefit small countries, Irish law mandates a national referendum on EU ratifications. In the first vote, admittedly a low turnout, the Irish people soundly rejected the Treaty of Nice. Fear of loss of regional benefits to the economically struggling new members may have been critical to this surprising result. A year later, in 2002, after a major persuasion campaign by the Irish government and no provision for "opt-outs," the people voted "yes" on Nice by a wide margin. Shortly thereafter, the accession of the new member states to the European Union was finalized.

§ 1.12 Political Union

Economic integration has outstripped the Union's political growth. Many suggest that the European Union suffers from a "democratic deficit." How long can governance of the Union postpone its rendezvous with democracy? The predominance of the Council has become increasingly embarrassing and intolerable. Incremental changes have prevailed. But what will be the end result? One vision of the future has the Council of Ministers becoming an "upper house" like the United States Senate to the House of Representatives, though most probably with more power. In this scenario, the Commission becomes the Executive Branch of EU government. It could have a directly elected President who then appoints a Cabinet with Parliamentary or Council approval. The variations on these themes are endless, as the Convention on the Future of Europe (below) found out.

Another vision of the future was adopted, way before its time, in 1984 by the Parliament. In its "Draft Treaty establishing European Union" (Spinnelli Report), the Parliament showed strong federalist proclivities. This Treaty would have totally replaced the Treaty of Rome. The law-making powers of the Council would be shifted to the Parliament and Commission with limited member state ability to block new policy initiatives. There would also be serious sanctions on member states who persistently breach their EU duties. The Court of Justice would get the power to appeal decisions of national courts. A common monetary system, a common citizenship and effective protection of fundamental human rights were also part of Parliament's vision of European Union. In contrast, the draft Constitution for Europe (below) looks timid.

§ 1.13   Foreign and Security Policy

The Foreign Ministers of the member states regularly meet and seek to coordinate EU foreign policy and security matters. These ministers have their own secretariat in Brussels to monitor and implement common foreign policy positions. Junior staff members supervise much of this work through what is called the European Political Committee. The Commission is represented at all meetings of this Committee and the Foreign Ministers. The Parliament, however, is merely briefed after the fact about these meetings and is for the most part limited to asking questions of the Foreign Ministers.

The heads of state and government also meet twice a year in what is called "the European Council," as distinct from the Council of Ministers. The President of the Commission participates in meetings of the European Council. These meetings have increased the degree of foreign policy cooperation (known as "political cooperation") within the Union, but not without criticism. The European Council and the Foreign Ministers' meetings function outside the Treaty of Rome and its various policy making mandates and voting procedures, including consultation, cooperation or co-decision with Parliament. Hence, foreign policy coordination is purely intergovernmental in nature, and does not involve supranational EU mandates. It is said that *"une forme originale de diplomatie concertée"* now exists.

Foreign policy cooperation has been a part of Union affairs since 1970 and was formally recognized in Article 30 of the Single European Act of 1987. Unlike most SEA provisions, this article did not amend the Treaty of Rome. It stood on its own as a separate international agreement and, to a large extent, codified the existing foreign policy cooperation procedures. Except for a duty of information and consultation, the SEA did not create any new obligations for the member states. However, the somewhat bumpy road to increased cooperation in the area of foreign policy is slowly setting up the embryo of a genuine European foreign policy.

Common Policies and Joint Actions

Under the Maastricht Treaty on European Union, a Common Foreign and Security Policy (CFSP) was established. Although not very different from the political cooperation already in place, it symbolizes Europe's growing ambitions. The European Council, together with the Union's institutions are the EU's unique institutional framework that can act both in the foreign policy and common security areas. Intergovernmental political cooperation and the Union are not kept apart, even if the Union's institutions hold different powers under the CFSP. The CFSP includes the whole scope of foreign and security policy and is given a large number of goals among which are: international peacekeeping and the preservation of the Union's principles and interests outside of the Union. It is recognized, however, that the CFSP is not yet granted many means of practical intervention.

Under the Maastricht and Amsterdam Treaties, the Union's national foreign ministers decide which areas of foreign and security policy merit "joint action," a "common position," or a "common strategy." The details of such activities are now generally set by those ministers acting by qualified majority voting or with the "constructive abstention" of some members. This type of political cooperation remains outside the framework of the Treaty of Rome and is considered a separate "pillar" of the Union.

The net result is that the European Union increasingly but erratically speaks with a single voice on foreign affairs. This has been evident regarding political developments in Central Europe, the Middle East (much less so on the Iraq War), Cyprus, South Africa, Rwanda, Angola, Iran (especially to condemn the threats against Salman Rushdie), Burma, Cambodia, and Afghanistan. However, the remarkable disunity and dithering displayed by EU nations over the break-up and ethnic cleansings in Yugoslavia casts a long shadow over the political cooperation goals of the Union. The increasing involvement of the European Union in world politics also makes it more difficult for traditionally neutral nations like Austria, Sweden and Ireland. Already there are arguments over whether it is possible to segregate the Union's economic and political spheres for membership purposes.

§ 1.14 Defense

In the early years of the Coal and Steel Community, a European Defense Community (EDC) treaty was drafted and nearly adopted. It failed when the French National Assembly refused to ratify it in 1954. Under this proposal, a European army would have been placed under the control of a European Ministry of Defense functioning within the North Atlantic Treaty Organization (NATO) alliance. The institutional structure of the EDC would have been similar to that employed in the Coal and Steel Community. The rejection by the French National Assembly was led by the Gaullists and the French Communist Party who quite simply did not want to surrender sovereignty over the French army, even if this meant that the West Germans could re-arm on their own. Following a British initiative, however, a looser confederation for military purposes was established in 1954 through the Western European Union (WEU). It was under this Union that West Germany and Italy re-armed and were integrated into the NATO alliance. In 2000, the WEU transferred its principal activities to the European Union despite the fact that not all EU members belong to the WEU.

The vision of a common defense policy has started to become a reality. At the 1991 Maastricht Summit, agreement was achieved on language explicitly stating that defense cooperation is expected of member states. Moreover, the Western European Union is to serve as the bridge between the Union and NATO. The Maastricht Treaty on European Union referred to the "eventual framing" of a common defense policy to be implemented through the WEU as another separate "pillar" of the Union. The Amsterdam Treaty altered this language to "progressive framing," a subtle change in Euro-speak meant to convey progress. In 1992, the WEU defense and foreign ministers issued the "Petersburg Declaration." This Declaration affirms the ongoing efforts to develop a new Franco–German military brigade. By 2003, EU-led forces of 50,000–60,000 persons were ready for deployment in peace and rescue operations. A Military Committee and Staff have been created.

The integration of Europe's defense may be the ultimate in politically sensitive issues. Neutrality, the NATO alliance and a host of national interests stand in the way of a common defense policy for the European Union. Transfers of sovereignty over war, peace, military forces, military weapons, and military command are momentous issues not only for the member states, but the world.

§ 1.15   The Convention on the Future of Europe and its Draft Constitution

The growth in membership in the European Union raises fundamental issues of governance. The Nice Enlargement Protocol offers patchwork solutions, but will they measure up to the task? Less than a year after signing on to the Nice Treaty, the heads of state meeting at the Laeken Summit of the European Council established the 105–member Convention on the Future of Europe. Popularly referred to as a "constitutional convention," this body's very existence recognized that the traditional means of governance as revised by the Enlargement Protocol may not be up to the task.

Members of the Convention were drawn from national governments and parliaments, the European Parliament, and Commission. The 12 future member states had nonvoting observer status at the Convention. Chaired by former French President Valery Giscard d'Estaing and driven by an inner 12–member presidium, the Convention became a focal point for change. Lobbying on all fronts was intense, running from strong federalists to states rights' advocates. In June of 2003, the Convention released its draft Treaty establishing a Constitution for Europe, some 260 pages of complex text merging the Rome, Maastricht TEU and EURATOM treaties. The draft went under review by the EU member states, which unanimously signed off on a final version in June of 2004. The Constitution will need individual ratification in all 25 member states, about ten of which (Ireland and Denmark, for example) will hold referendums. Optimists suggest that the Constitution will take effect by 2006. Pessimists believe it will (and should) end up in a waste bin.

Proposed Constitution for Europe

The proposed Constitution is already the subject of conflicting sometimes bizarre interpretations. The Union's Charter of Fundamental Rights ("declared" at Nice) becomes binding EU law, but may apply only to EU institutions, personnel and law. The principle of "subsidiarity" (see Chapter 2) is retained, but subordinated to broad Union objectives. Most policy areas are to be "shared" with the member states, which nevertheless essentially retain vetoes over foreign policy, social security, taxation and defense. No doubt the proposed EU "Foreign Minister," President of the European Council, and EU Armaments Agency will have a tough time. Qualified majority voting disappears as the triple legislative majority system (see Chapter 2) adopted under the Nice Treaty is reduced to a double majority in the Council of Ministers to enact law: 55 percent of the member states representing at least 65 percent of the Union's population, but not until 2009. By 2014, the Commission is "shrunk" to two-thirds the number of member states. Member states for the first time can withdraw from Union, but they can also be "suspended" by their fellow members. If ratification of the final version of the Constitution is not unanimous, but 20 member states have ratified it, the European Council will "review the situation." Climb aboard, this promises to be an interesting ride.

Chapter 2

LAW–MAKING IN THE EUROPEAN UNION

Table of Sections

§ 2.0 Introduction—The Principle of Subsidiarity and the Power to Legislate

The European Union has been creating law at a dazzling speed. It is almost impossible to function on EU matters without an understanding of the region's law-making institutions and procedures. Once these are understood, attorneys, executives and others can seek to influence the development of European law in ways which reflect their interests.

Primary and Secondary Law

The two remaining treaties of the European communities (the EC and EURATOM) and the Maastricht Treaty on European Union

27

are the "primary" sources of European law. The EU treaties have had a common set of institutions since 1967. These are the Council of Ministers, the Commission, the Parliament and the Court of Justice (to which the Court of First Instance was attached in 1989). These institutions, supplemented by national legislatures, courts and tribunals, have been busy generating a remarkably vast and complex body of "secondary" law. Some legislative acts are adopted directly at the EU level, but much of it is enacted by national governments under the "direction" of the Union. Similarly, some (and the most important) of the case law of the EU is created by decisions of the European Court of Justice or Court of First Instance, but much development of law also occurs in the national courts acting in many instances with "advisory rulings" from the Court of Justice. European Union secondary law also includes international obligations, often undertaken through "mixed" EU and national negotiations and ratifications.

Legislative Powers

The starting point for a basic understanding of law-making is, as always, the founding treaties. The Treaty of Rome is premised upon the idea of a regional government of limited or derived powers (compétences d'attribution). That is to say, the Treaty does not convey a general power to create law. European Union law-making is either specifically authorized or dependent upon the terms of Article 308. That article permits action if "necessary to attain, in the course of the operation of the common market, one of the objectives of the Community and this Treaty has not provided the necessary powers."

Article 308 has been used rather extensively, and in ways which suggest that there are relatively few limits upon what the Union can legislate, or negotiate by way of international agreements, once a political consensus has been reached to move forward. For example, Article 308 was widely used as the legal basis for environmental programs well prior to the Single European Act amendments that specifically authorize action in this field. In the early years, the Court of Justice had slowly been fashioning a doctrine of *implied* powers under the Treaty of Rome, most notably concerning external relations' powers.[1] However, the Court of Justice has more recently been retreating from the doctrine of implied powers.[2]

---

§ 2.0

1. *See* Fédération Charbonnìee de Belgique v. High Authority (1955–56) Eur.Comm.Rep. 245; Germany v. Commission (1987) Eur.Comm.Rep. 3203 (Immigration of External Workers);

Commission v. Council (1971) Eur. Comm.Rep. 263 (*ERTA*).

2. *See* Opinion 1/94 (1994) Eur. Comm.Rep. I 5267 (WTO). But see Spain v. Council (1995) Eur.Comm.Rep. I–1985 (medicinal product certificates

The Treaty on European Union (TEU) added provisions to the Treaty of Rome authorizing the Union to support and encourage cooperation among the member states regarding education, vocational training, cultural affairs and public health. These provisions basically reserve to the member states basic policy decision-making in these areas. The Union is placed in a subordinate supporting role, a clear attempt at demarcating the limits of its legislative powers. This approach, while novel, is consistent with the broader principle of "subsidiarity" enshrined in the Treaty of Rome by the TEU. It is interesting to note that Parliament is given a veto over EU action on education, cultural affairs and public health, but not vocational training.

Subsidiarity

The Treaty on European Union (Maastricht) and to a lesser extent the Single European Act (1987) formalized a "subsidiarity" principle. The Amsterdam Treaty of 1999 added a Protocol on the application of the principles of subsidiarity and proportionality. This much debated principle holds that the Union can act in areas where it does not *exclusively* have power only if the member states cannot sufficiently achieve the objectives, i.e., "by reason of scale or effects [the] proposed action [can] be better achieved by the Community." In all cases, European Union action must not go beyond what is necessary to achieve the objectives of the Treaty of Rome (proportionality principle).[3] Thus subsidiarity is a kind of "states' rights" amendment intended to limit the growth of regional government in Europe. An inter-institutional agreement by the Council, Commission and European Parliament on the application of subsidiarity principles by all EU institutions has been negotiated. Subsidiarity guidelines were adopted by the European Council in December of 1992[4] and a Protocol on the Application of the Principles of Subsidiarity and Proportionality was adopted in conjunction with the 1999 Amsterdam Treaty. The Commission regularly reviews proposed and existing legislation in light of the subsidiarity principle. This has caused a number of legislative proposals and acts to be withdrawn or amended. Under the Subsidiarity Protocol, moreover, if a third or more of the *national* Parliaments give reasoned opinions that a proposal breaches the subsidiarity principle, the Commission must undertake a reconsideration.

The European Council takes the position that EU subsidiarity principles do not have direct effect in the member state legal

upheld as implied internal market power).

3. Article 5, Treaty of Rome.

4. *Guidelines* on Subsidiarity (Conclusions of the Presidency—Edinburgh, December 12, 1992).

systems.[5] If this is correct, subsidiarity issues cannot be raised in litigation before member state courts and tribunals.[6] However, interpretation of these principles and review of compliance by European Union institutions are subject to judicial review before the Court of Justice through challenges initiated by a member state or another EU institution.[7] It is the Court, therefore, that will ultimately determine whether and to what degree subsidiarity will limit governance by the European Union, a task it has undertaken gingerly.[8] Should subsidiarity preclude Union action, member states are still required to ensure fulfillment of their Treaty of Rome obligations and abstain from measures that could jeopardize the objectives of that treaty.[9]

Although variations do occur from treaty to treaty, the Union's legislative, administrative and judicial processes are generally similar. Unless otherwise indicated, the analysis in this chapter is drawn from the Treaty of Rome establishing the European Community. A review of the diagrams may assist the reader in understanding the text that follows, particularly the law-making institutions.

§ 2.1   Legislation—Directives and Regulations

Legislative and Nonlegislative Acts

There are two primary types of legislative acts, directives and regulations. These should be distinguished from declarations, resolutions, guidelines, notices, policy statements, recommendations, opinions and individual decisions which rarely involve legislative acts. These predominantly "soft law" sources can, however, be used to interpret related national or regional law. Article 249 of the Treaty of Rome clarifies the powers of the Council of Ministers and the Commission, in accordance with the Treaty, to make regulations and issue directives. EC regulations are similar in form to administrative regulations commonly found in North America. EC directives, on the other hand, have no obvious parallel. The Court of Justice has repeatedly affirmed that both regulations and directives must state the "reasons" on which they are based.[1]

5. *See* Conclusions of the Presidency, Edinburgh Summit, Dec. 12, 1992, Annex 1 to Part A.

6. *See* Section 3.1.

7. *See* Sections 3.8, 3.9 and 3.10.

8. For decisions deferential to EU legislative powers and recitals of need, see Germany v. Parliament and Council (1997) Eur.Comm.Rep. I–2405 (deposit-guarantee schemes), United Kingdom v. Council (1995) Eur.Comm.Rep. I–5755

(working time), Netherlands v. Parliament and Council (2001) Eur. Comm.Rep. I-07079 (Oct. 9, 2001) (biotech) and The Queen v. Secretary for Health, 2002 Eur.Comm.Rep. I–11453 (tobacco).

9. Article 10, Treaty of Rome.

§ 2.1

1. Germany v. Commission (1963) Eur.Comm.Rep. 63.

A directive establishes Union policy. It is then left to the member states to implement the directive in whatever way is appropriate to their national legal system. This may require a new statute, a Presidential decree, an administrative act or even a constitutional amendment. Sometimes it may require no action at all. As Article 249 indicates, a directive is "binding as to the result to be achieved" but "leave[s] to the national authorities the choice of form and methods." The vast majority of the legislative acts of the single market campaign are directives. All directives contain time limits for national implementation. The more controversial the policy, the longer the likely allotment of time. But if, at the end of the deadline, the directive is not transposed into national law, some of its dispositions may under the doctrine of "direct effect" be binding nevertheless. This doctrine is discussed in Section 3.1.

The Council does not always act through directives and regulations. At times, especially when the heads of state and government meet in the European Council, it issues "declarations" or "resolutions." Council resolutions and declarations are used when a political but not necessarily a legislative consensus has been reached. For example, the 1981 Council resolution on the adoption of Community passports with uniform characteristics fits this mold.[2] This symbolic resolution has been fully implemented, adding significantly to the consciousness of the European Union among its citizens. Plans are afoot to gradually convert to European Union passports. Another example is the Council's Declaration on Democracy (1977), which "codifies" the longstanding tradition that no European state can join or remain associated with the EU without a pluralistic, democratic form of government. A third example is the formulation of foreign policy resolutions by the European Council.

Legislative Procedures

The Commission's civil servants initiate the process of legislation by drafting proposals which the Council of Ministers (from the governments of the member states) has the power to adopt into law. Although the Council may request the Commission to submit legislative proposals,[3] it cannot force the Commission to do so except by way of litigation before the Court of Justice nor draft legislative proposals itself. This makes the Commission the focal point of lobbying activities. The Commission's legislative proposals are always influenced by what it believes the Council will accept. The Council, however, has the right to amend legislative proposals by unanimous vote. Readers will immediately note that the European Parliament does not have the power to propose legislation, nor the power to enact it! Parliament's role has traditionally been

---

2.   Official Journal C241/1 (1981).   **3.**   Article 208, Treaty of Rome.

consultative. It is the source of proposed amendments when the so-called "cooperation" procedure applies. These absences of Parliamentary power are so fundamental that many observers decry a "democratic deficit" in the European Union. This deficit has been minimally remedied by conveying limited "co-decision" powers to Parliament. These powers amount to a Parliamentary right to veto selected legislative proposals. Parliament's role in law-making is detailed in Section 2.2.

The Treaty on European Union created an advisory Committee of the Regions.[4] This Committee is composed of representatives of regional and local bodies throughout the Union. Like the Economic and Social Committee, it must be consulted on certain types of Union action. Moreover, it is free to render an opinion without prior request. The Committee of the Regions appears chiefly to be an attempt at bringing local officials into the regional legislative and decision-making processes.

§ 2.2   The   Parliament—Consultation,   Cooperation and Co-decision

The European Parliament (first called the Assembly in the treaties) was originally composed of representatives appointed by member state governments. In other words, the people's representation was indirect, although the Members of the European Parliament (MEPs) had to be serving in their national parliaments. Since 1979, universal suffrage is employed to directly elect the representatives of the citizens of the Union to their Parliament.

Under the Treaty of Nice Enlargement Protocol, there are 99 MEPs from united Germany, 72 from Britain, France and Italy, 50 from Poland and Spain, 25 from Holland, 22 from Belgium, Greece and Portugal, 20 from the Czech Republic and Hungary, 18 from Sweden, 17 from Austria and Bulgaria, 13 from Denmark and Finland, 12 from Lithuania and Ireland, 8 from Latvia, 7 from Slovenia, 6 from Luxembourg, Cyprus and Estonia and 5 MEPs from Malta. These numbers correspond roughly to the populations of each country. A cap of 732 MEPs has been established, with pro rata MEP allocations expected when Bulgaria and Romania join in 2007. MEPs serve 5–year terms, and are presently divided into transnational political groups.

The European Parliament is a kaleidoscope of European politics. For example, there are groupings of Socialists, Christian Democrats, the Greens, the European Democratic Alliance, the Technical Group of the European Right, the Left Unity Group, the Rainbow Group and non-affiliated MEPs. Even these groupings fail to capture the full picture of diversity as the Socialists often realize

---

4. *See* Articles 263–267, Treaty of   Rome.

once they start talking to each other. Since it takes majority votes to pass a measure in Parliament, alliances are essential. There are numerous standing Parliamentary Committees. Each is responsible for reviewing and reporting on legislative proposals within its expertise, such as agriculture, external relations, etc. In addition, unofficially allied groups of MEPs with special interests in particular areas of development (*e.g.*, the European Monetary System and the internal market) have been formed. These groups are quite influential in proposing legislative amendments under the cooperation and co-decision procedures discussed below.

The member states have fulfilled their obligations under the Treaty of Rome for direct elections. In 1998 they enacted "uniform procedures" for these elections. European Union MEPs these days cannot also be representatives in their national parliaments. Some commentators have suggested that this leads to an estrangement between European Union and national politicians. The member states have failed to decide where the Parliament is located. Presently, Parliament's plenary sessions are held in Strasbourg, its committee meetings in Brussels and its secretariat is in Luxembourg.[1] Each nation has vied for a permanent assignment of the European Parliament to it. And the member states have sued to protect their existing allocations.[2] One suspects that this litigation reflects the economic more than the political value associated with Parliament and its expense-account-spending members.

Legislative Powers

With direct elections, the impetus toward greater Parliamentary input into the legislative process has magnified. Traditionally, the Parliament has a right to be consulted and to give an "opinion" as part of the Union's legislative process. That opinion is not binding upon the Commission or Council, but it can prove increasingly awkward if it is disregarded. For example, in 1980 the Court of Justice held that the Council acts illegally if it legislates without waiting for the Parliament's opinion.[3] Left unanswered is how long Parliament may delay giving an opinion when merely consulted on legislation. If the Council amends the Commission's legislative proposal substantively, the Parliament has the right to be consulted

§ 2.2

1. The European Council affirmed these allocations in a formal decision taken at the 1992 Edinburgh Summit.

2. *See* Luxembourg v. Parliament (1983) Eur.Comm.Rep. 255 (Parliament may hold all plenary sessions in Strasbourg); France v. Parliament (1988) Eur.Comm.Rep. 4821 (Parliament may hold exceptional plenary sessions in Brussels); Luxembourg v. Parliament (1984) Eur.Comm.Rep. 1945 (Parliament could not transfer secretariat from Luxembourg); Luxembourg v. European Parliament (1991) Eur.Comm.Rep. I–5643 (refusal to annul increased Parliamentary staffing in Brussels).

3. Roquette Frères SA v. Council (1980) Eur.Comm.Rep. 3333.

and to issue a second opinion.[4] Since 1977, a "conciliation procedure" is used whenever the Council departs from an opinion of the Parliament on proposed legislation of importance to the Union's income or expenses. This procedure was instituted by a Joint Declaration of the Parliament, Council and Commission.[5]

An important step forward towards democratic governance was taken in the Single European Act of 1987. Article 252 of the Treaty of Rome created a "cooperation procedure" which gave the Parliament more of a voice on selected legislation. Basically, when the Treaty required adherence to this procedure, the Parliament could reject or seek to amend the Council's "common position" on a legislative proposal from the Commission. One early study indicated that Parliament introduced nearly 1,000 amendments after the cooperation procedure was adopted in 1987. Of these, 72 percent were accepted by the Commission and 42 percent ultimately adopted by the Council. The "cooperation procedure" applied selectively. Most significantly, it applied to nearly all internal market measures following the Single European Act of 1987. With the development of the cooperation procedure, and success in persuading the Commission and Council to adopt its amendments, Parliament became a second center of legislative lobbying.

The European Parliament also acquired significant powers under the Maastricht Treaty on European Union. On legislation, under what is called the "co-decision" procedure of Article 251 (formerly 189b), it has what amounts to a legislative veto over selected matters if conciliation through direct negotiations with the Council cannot be achieved. Co-decision after Maastricht applied to single market, education, culture, health, consumer protection, environmental, transportation and research affairs. Parliament in fact first exercised its veto rights over a biotechnology directive, out of concern about potential human cloning and, in 2001, against a corporate takeover directive which did not allow for "poison pill" defenses. *Thus, three distinct European legislative processes resulted in 1993, each defined in terms of the role Parliament plays: consultative, cooperative and co-decisional.*

The Amsterdam Treaty of 1999 and the Nice Treaty of 2003 mandated co-decision in many additional legislative areas. Only European Monetary Union matters remain subject to the cooperation procedure. Parliament still cannot draft or initiate legislation, but its veto power ensures influence and a sparingly used negative power over legislative outcomes. Most conciliation committees formed under the co-decision procedure have reached legislative

---

4. ACF Chemiefarma v. Commission (1970) Eur.Comm.Rep. 661; European Parliament v. Council (1992) Eur. Comm.Rep. I–4193 Case C–295/90.

5. Official Journal C98/1 (1975).

compromises satisfactory to the Council and Parliament. Such compromises reduce the power of the Commission in Europe's law-making process. Even so, the European Parliament as a legislative institution is still waiting to come of age.

Ancillary Powers

Other powers of the European Parliament should be noted. First, it can put written and oral questions to the Council and the Commission on virtually any Union matter, legislative or otherwise. This prerogative mostly has a nuisance and information gathering value. Absent forceful persuasion, it is not terribly influential. Second, Article 201 of the Treaty of Rome gives the Parliament the power to "censure" the Commission by a two-thirds vote. A motion of censure would require all Commissioners to resign, but the member states acting in common accord (not the Parliament) get to choose the new Commissioners. These could conceivably be the very persons just censured. Parliament cannot selectively censure one Commissioner, nor can it censure the Council of Ministers at all. A motion of censure has at times been threatened by Parliament, but never adopted. Third, the Parliament can initiate a lawsuit against the Council or Commission under Article 232 of the Treaty of Rome for failure to act. Parliament did exactly this when it sued the Council over the failure to implement a Common Transport Policy as required by the Treaty. The Court of Justice ruled that the Council had failed to act, but denied the Parliament a remedy given the imprecise nature of the Council's obligation to act.[6] Neverthe-less, the Council has since undertaken a number of reforms in the transport sector.[7]

Fourth, since the Maastricht Treaty, the European Parliament has more say in the choice of the Commissioners. As a first step, the Parliament's advice is to be sought before the new President of the Commission is chosen. For example, in the 1990s, the choice of the Commission's new President to replace legendary Jacques De-lors resulted in a bitter fight. Belgian Prime Minister Jean–Luc Dehaene was heavily favored and had gained approval from most Member States before he was vetoed by Britain's John Major, who desperately needed to reinvigorate his image domestically, causing considerable tensions with the other EU members. Ultimately, Jacques Santer, Luxembourg's former Prime Minister was chosen, but he was nearly vetoed by the Parliament. Besides the debate over the appointment of Mr. Santer, this was seen also as a sign of independence and the MEP's arrival as a more fully-fledged legisla-tive branch of the Union.

6. European Parliament v. Council   **7.** *See* Chapter 4.
(1985) Eur.Comm.Rep. 1513.

The Parliament has selected other litigation alternatives. It can intervene as an interested party in cases pending before the Court, which it did quite successfully when challenging a regulation enacted by the Council without its consultation and opinion.[8] But it does not appear to have a right to file briefs in Article 234 litigation.[9] Since the Nice Treaty (2003), it can litigate the legality of acts of the Commission or Council under Article 230 even if its own prerogatives are not at stake.

Parliament's powers were expanded in 1993 by The Maastricht Treaty on European Union. If an international agreement touches upon a co-decisional area, or has institutional or budgetary implications, Parliament must approve.[10] The Parliament also gets a veto over the nomination of the Commissioners and their President and may create committees to inquiry into alleged "contraventions or maladministration" of Union law.[11] One-fourth of the members of the Parliament must request the creation of such committee. Issues of this kind may come to Parliament's attention from citizens through a new petitioning procedure to the Parliament or to its new Ombudsman.[12] Since the Parliament must further assent to new member states, yet another veto power is established by the Treaty on European Union.

§ 2.3 Budgetary Legislation

The Coal and Steel Community is financed exclusively by taxes levied against producers. The European Economic Community was originally financed by contributions from the member states. This created a fiscally dependent relationship. Since 1971, the Community (now Union) is funded through its "own resources," but still dependent upon the member states for their collection and transfer. The Union's income is now principally derived from the common external tariff, agricultural levies on imports, a small but growing portion of the value-added tax (VAT) collected in every state, and an assessment based upon the gross domestic product (GDP) of the member states. Some countries (like Germany) are habitually net payors to the Union budget. Others (like Ireland) are always net payees receiving funds under the Union's various common policies. Britain, initially a large net payor, negotiated a special rebate agreement in 1984 which now annually returns substantial sums to it from EU revenues.

Article 268 of the Treaty of Rome requires a balanced Union budget. This requirement has been met by increasing the level of Union revenues and, occasionally, reducing (agricultural) expendi-

8. Roquette Frères SA v. Council (1980) Eur.Comm.Rep. 3333.

9. *See* Chapter 3.

10. *See* Article 300, Treaty of Rome.

11. *See* Article 193, Treaty of Rome.

12. *See* Article 195, Treaty of Rome.

tures. Revenue-raising decisions are undertaken by the heads of state and government acting through the European Council. In other words, Parliament lacks the power to tax. Control over the spending of these resources, however, is another area where the Parliament has sought to acquire power.

Budgetary Procedures

The budgetary process is outlined in Article 272 of the Treaty of Rome. The Commission creates a preliminary draft budget which it forwards to the Council of Ministers. The Council revises it and then sends a draft budget to the Parliament. The Parliament can reject the draft budget in its entirety, something it did in 1979 and 1984. Article 272 gives the Parliament the power to propose changes in the budget regarding matters "necessarily resulting from this Treaty or from acts adopted in accordance therewith." This has increased Parliamentary influence over "compulsory expenditures" (mostly agricultural subsidies), but the Council has the final word.

Since 1975, Parliament has had ultimate control by way of amendment over "non-compulsory" EU expenditures, about 25 percent of the budget. As a practical matter, this gives the Parliament influence over expenditures in many of the new and important policy areas of the Union. However, Parliamentary amendments to the Council's draft budget cannot exceed the maximum rate of increase allowed under Article 272(9).[1] This maximum involves a complex calculation by the Commission of EU inflation and gross domestic product (GDP) rates as well as national budget variations. Parliament, at the end of a laborious process with multiple communications to the Council, adopts the final budget.

Parliament and the Council of Ministers often quarrel over creation of the budget, with Parliament prevailing more and more. Parliament and the Council review how the Commission has implemented the budget. The Court of Justice has indicated that the Commission's power to implement the budget does not include making decisions which are legislative in character.[2] Upon Council recommendation, Parliament gives the Commission a "discharge" of its budgetary duties.[3] The Court of Auditors[4] assists the Parliament and Council in these tasks, which are reasonably routine. In 1982, however, Parliament refused to discharge the Commission, resulting in tighter controls thereafter. Parliament's power over the

§ 2.3

1. Council v. European Parliament (1986) Eur.Comm.Rep. 288.

2. Commission v. Council (1989) Eur.Comm.Rep. 1425 (Erasmus).

3. Article 275, Treaty of Rome.

4. The Court of Auditors was formally recognized by the Treaty on European Union. *See* Articles 246–248, Treaty of Rome. This "court" serves as a watchdog over Union financial affairs.

purse is increasing and its President reportedly remarked: "As long as Parliament does not have more power in other fields, there will be conflicts on the budget."

§ 2.4 Which Council?

EU Council

The foregoing analysis of the legislative process illustrates the dominant role given by the Treaty of Rome to "the Council" in EU affairs. The Council of the European Union as an institution is a bit of a moving target. The EU Council consists of representatives of the governments of the member states. Thus, there are presently 25 (27 in 2007 with the accession of Bulgaria and Romania) Council members. However, the people who comprise the Council change according to the topic at hand. The national ministers of foreign affairs, agriculture, economy and finance (Ecofin), social affairs, environment, etc. are sent to Brussels to confer and vote on EU matters within their competence. Several different Council meetings can take place at once. Some refer to the Ecofin Council, the Environment Council, the Agriculture Council and so forth in order to differentiate the various EU Councils. The Presidency of these Councils rotates among the member states every six months and a certain amount of competition has emerged to see who can achieve the most under their Presidency. It is from all these meetings that the legislation of the European Union pours forth.

The EU Council is greatly assisted in their work by a Committee of Permanent Representatives known as COREPER. The Committee is comprised of high-ranking national civil servants and based in Brussels. COREPER in turn consults extensively with a large number of "working groups" composed of other national civil servants with expertise in areas of Union concern. Thus, by the time a legislative proposal from the Commission reaches the Council for a vote, the proposal has been thoroughly reviewed by COREPER and the appropriate working groups. If there is no controversy, the proposal is scheduled as an "A point" on the Council's agenda and virtually certain to be adopted. If no agreement is reached within COREPER, the proposal becomes a "B point" on the agenda which means that the Council of Ministers will discuss and debate its merits. In 1992, the European Council agreed to make all formal votes of the Council of Ministers public. Moreover, by unanimous vote, the Council of Ministers may decide to televise or openly debate legislative initiatives. These changes are part of a broader program aimed at greater institutional "transparency" and less bureaucratic secrecy.

European Council

Then there is the "European Council." With growth, legislative and other decisions have inevitably become more political and thus more difficult. A new institution has emerged to keep the EU moving, mostly forward but arguably (at times) backward. The European Council consists of the heads of the state or government of the member nations, a kind of ultimate Council of Ministers. The heads of state have met twice a year since 1974 to formulate broad policy guidelines or initiatives for the Union. For example, the European Council has shown leadership on direct elections to Parliament, the European Monetary System, new memberships and innovative legislative agendas. Its meetings are sometimes called "summits," and Article 2 of the Single European Act of 1987 formally recognizes their existence.

European Council summits (though sometimes fractious) have generally proved to be quite successful. They have greatly facilitated the development of common foreign and security policy positions, and are expected to do likewise on justice and internal affairs under the Maastricht Treaty on European Union. Although these meetings are undertaken in close consultation with the EU Commission and Parliament, they are not subject to the procedural rules of the Treaty of Rome. For example, whereas the Council of Ministers must seek the opinion, cooperate or co-decide with the Parliament on legislative acts, the European Council need not do so. Whether the European Council can be subjected to judicial review by the Court of Justice is most unclear. This is the case despite the fact that European Council pronouncements (*e.g.* the Social Charter in 1989,[1]) may have important legal implications for the Union. Some fear that the European Council's ability to operate outside the Treaty of Rome may exacerbate the Union's "democratic deficit."

§ 2.5   Voting Procedures of the Council

The voting procedures of the Council of Ministers and the European Council are critical to an understanding of law-making in the European Union. The Treaty of Rome provides for simple majority voting unless otherwise specified. However, nearly all the voting rules of the Treaty do specify otherwise. The exceptions thus become the rule. The point of contention is always whether unanimous or "qualified majority" voting is required. Unanimous voting has the practical effect of giving each member state a veto over legislation and policy developments. If a consensus cannot be reached, the minority always seeks shelter under the Treaty of Rome for unanimous voting. The Treaty, however, has only a

1. *See* Chapter 5.

limited number of such mandates. A partial list of the Treaty of Rome's unanimous voting requirements is provided below, notably on tax and social security matters.

Qualified Majority Voting Rules

Much of the voting in the EU Council now takes place on a "qualified majority" basis. The rules that define this procedure are given in Article 205. Under the Nice Treaty Enlargement Protocol for 27 member states there will be a total of 345 votes, with Germany, France, Italy and Britain having 29 qualified majority votes each. Spain and Poland will have 27 votes, Romania 14 votes, the Netherlands 13 votes, and Belgium, Greece, Portugal, the Czech Republic and Hungary 12 votes. Austria, Sweden and Bulgaria will have 10 votes, Denmark, Ireland, Finland, Slovakia and Lithuania 7 votes, Luxembourg, Latvia, Slovenia, Estonia and Cyprus 4 votes, and Malta has 3 qualified majority votes.

To adopt legislation by qualified majority, 258 votes starting in 2005 (255 after 2007) must be cast in favor by a majority of the member states (for measures requiring a proposal from the Commission) *or* two-thirds of the members (for all other measures). In addition, the qualified majority must when challenged by a member state constitute 62 percent of the total EU population. In the interim between 25 member states (2004) and 27 member states (2007, adding Romania and Bulgaria), proportionate adjustments to these voting rules will be made. Thus, compared with the law prior to the Treaty of Nice Enlargement Protocol, two demanding rules have been added: (1) The majority or two-thirds member state requirement; and (2) the percentage of population challenge requirement. The third requirement, the qualified majority vote count, has been tightened by slightly raising the percentage of votes needed to pass legislation. Byzantine hardly seems adequate to describe the new "triple majority" rules on qualified majority voting.

Note that under these rules, the "Big Six" cannot prevail without some support from smaller nations. Put conversely, if the little nations stick together, they can block anything. Over the years, as the Community grew from 6 to 9 to 10 to 12 to 15 to 25 to 27 members, these political dynamics have always been preserved in the qualified majority voting rules. Other "blocking minorities" can emerge on North–South and East–West lines.

Demise of the Luxembourg Accord

Treaty of Rome terms notwithstanding, a special agreement known as the "Luxembourg Accord" has in the past led to unanimous voting. In 1965, France under General de Gaulle walked out of a Council of Ministers meeting in a dispute over revenue and budgetary policy. Many believe that the real reason for the dispute was the fact that qualified majority voting was due to come into force in 1966. This was the major crisis of the early years of the Community of six. A compromise agreement was reached, which when "very important interests" are at stake, committed the Council to reaching solutions by consensus if at all possible. The Luxembourg accord then proceeds to express disagreement over what is to be done if a consensus cannot be reached. The French delegation took the view that discussions must continue until unanimity is achieved. The five other delegations took the position that the Treaty rules apply and a decision by qualified majority vote must follow.

For many years, the Luxembourg accord was followed under the French perspective. Qualified majority voting was almost non-existent. Surprisingly, there was no challenge by the Commission before the Court of Justice to this breach of the Treaty's terms. Arguably, the Council was not acting in accordance with an essential procedural requirement of the Treaty. If so, the Commission could have brought suit under Article 173. As the Community grew to twelve member states, it became more and more difficult for the Council to arrive at a consensus. New legislation and new policy initiatives floundered as institutional and trade arteries hardened.

The Commission, recognizing the economic costs involved (especially vis-a-vis Europe's competitive position with North America and Japan), proposed in its "white paper" of 1985 a return and indeed expansion of qualified majority voting. These proposals bore fruit in the Single European Act of 1987. This Act amended the Treaty of Rome extensively. It was the authority for all single market legislation, and much of that legislation was adopted by qualified majority vote. Moreover, the Act amended the Treaty in a few instances to change unanimous voting requirements to qualified majority. The Maastricht Treaty on European Union, the Amsterdam Treaty of 1999 and the Nice Treaty of 2003 made similar changes. The net result, operationally speaking, has been the demise of the French perspective to the Luxembourg accord. Unanimity is still sought, sometimes at great lengths, but qualified majority voting prevails. A partial list of the Treaty of Rome provisions specifying qualified majority voting follows in Section 2.7.

§ 2.6 Unanimous Voting Requirements

The Treaty of Rome and Treaty on European Union indicate that the EU Council needs a unanimous vote to act on following matters. All references are to the Articles as renumbered by the Amsterdam Treaty.

Article 23(1) (TEU)	— common foreign and security policy
Article 24 (TEU)	— id; international agreements
Article 34 (TEU)	— police and judicial cooperation in criminal matters
Article 42 (TEU)	— id; shift of matters to Treaty of Rome, Title IV
Article 49 (TEU)	— new members
Article 13 (begin Treaty of Rome)	— discrimination based on sex, racial or ethnic origin, religion or belief disability, age or sexual orientation
Article 18	— right of residence
Article 19	— voting and candidate rights
Article 22	— new citizenship rights
Article 67	—— most visa, asylum and immigration matters
Article 88(2)	— state subsidy exceptions
Article 93	— taxation
Article 94	— harmonization of national laws
Article 95	— internal market tax, free movement of persons and employment legislation
Article 159	— economic and social cohesion
Article 175s(2)	— environmental taxes, land use planning, water resources, energy supplies
Article 187	— association of overseas territories and countries
Article 190(4)	— Parliamentary election rules
Article 202	— delegation of powers to Commission
Article 207	— appointment of Council's Secretary General
Article 213	— number of members of Commission
Article 215	— decision not to replace Commission member
Articles 221, 222	— increase in ECJ, AG members
Article 225	— creation of Court of First Instance, rules of procedure
Article 245	— Court of Justice rules of procedure and statute
Article 247	— appointment of Court of Auditors
Article 250	— unanimous legislative acts
Article 258	— appointment of Economic and Social Committee
Article 263	— appointment of Committee of Regions
Article 269	— budget finances
Article 279	— financial controls
Article 290	— language rules
Article 296	— military material free trade exceptions list

Article 299(2)	— application of specific Treaty articles to French overseas departments
Article 300	— international agreements in areas with unanimous internal voting requirements
Article 308	— general power to act when necessary to Treaty objectives
Article 310	— association agreements (trade treaties)

The significance of unanimous voting requirements was driven home in 1997 by British "non-cooperation" in regional affairs as a protest against blockage of its beef and cattle exports in the wake of the outbreak of "Mad Cow disease." British non-cooperation lasted about a month before a gradual removal of the ban on British beef was agreed. During that month, regional matters requiring a unanimous vote were held in suspended animation pending resolution of the dispute.

§ 2.7   Qualified Majority Voting

The Treaty of Rome and Treaty on European Union authorize qualified majority voting within the EU Council regarding the following areas. All references are to Articles as renumbered by the Amsterdam Treaty.

Article 7(TEU)	— sanctions for serious and persistent breach of Treaty obligations
Article 23(2) (TEU)	— foreign and security policy joint actions, common positions and their implementation
Article 34(2)(c) (TEU)	— implementation of police and judicial cooperation decisions
Article 40 (TEU)	— authorization of cooperation by selected member states on police and judicial matters (flexibility)
Article 11 (begin Treaty of Rome)	— authorization of cooperation by selected member states in most Treaty of Rome areas (flexibility)
Article 12	— nondiscrimination on grounds of nationality
Article 14	— implementation of community-wide collective bargaining agreements
Article 26	— creation of common external tariff
Article 37	— agriculture
Articles 40, 42	— free movement of workers, social security
Articles 44–46	— right of establishment
Article 47	— mutual recognition of diplomas
Articles 49, 52	— freedom to provide services
Articles 57, 59, 60	— free movement of capital

Articles 66, 67	— selected visa, asylum and immigration matters
Articles 71, 79	— road, rail and waterway transport
Article 80	— sea and air transport
Article 83	— competition law
Article 89	— state subsidies
Articles 95	— internal market legislation except taxation, free movement of persons and employment
Article 96	— distortions of competition
Article 99	— broad economic guidelines, surveillance and recommendations to member states
Article 100	— emergency economic conditions
Articles 102, 103	— public finance prohibitions
Article 104	— excessive deficit sanctions
Article 106	— harmonization of coinage
Article 107	— ESCB statute and affairs
Article 111	— ECU exchange rates
Article 114	— Economic and Financial Committee
Articles 119, 120	— balance of payments crises
Articles 121, 122	— meeting of conditions for common currency and derogations
Articles 128, 129	— employment recommendations and incentives
Articles 132–133	— common external commercial policy
Article 135	— customs cooperation
Article 137(2)	— occupational health and safety
Article 141	— equal pay, opportunities and treatment
Article 148	— European Social Fund
Article 149	— education
Article 150	— vocational training
Article 151	— cultural affairs
Article 152	— public health
Article 153	— consumer protection
Article 157	— industrial competitiveness
Article 156	— trans-European energy, transport and telecommunications networks
Article 161	— coordination of structural funds
Article 162	— Regional Development Fund
Articles 166, 172	— research and development
Article 175	— environment
Article 181a	— cooperation with third countries
Article 179	— assistance to developing nations
Article 195	— Ombudsman regulations
Article 210	— salaries
Article 251	— co-decision legislative procedure
Article 252	— cooperative legislative procedure
Articles 273, 273	— budget proposals, emergency budgets

Article 276	— discharge of Commission budget duties
Article 280	— prevention of fraud
Article 283	— staff regulations
Article 285	— statistical studies
Article 286	— personal data privacy
Article 300	— international agreements
Article 301	— trade embargoes
Article 309	— suspensions of treaty rights

§ 2.8   Diagrams of Legislation

CONSULTATION – ASSENT PROCEDURE

Chart 1

Economic and Social Committee and Committee of the Regions
opinions are not required in all cases and not in the assent procedure

Chart 2

COOPERATION PROCEDURE

CO-DECISION PROCEDURE:
AMSTERDAM TREATY

Chart 3

Commission Proposal to EP and Council

EP takes no action

Council adopts Act (QM)

EP amends (AM)

Council Common Position

EP Second Reading three months

EP rejects the common position (AM)

EP amends (AM)

Council accepts Act adopted (QM)

EP agrees or takes no action

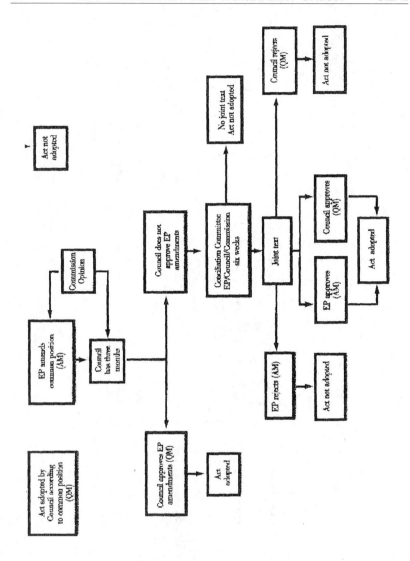

§ 2.9 Which Voting Procedure?—The Legal Basis of Legislation

With the revival of qualified majority voting in the Council, one critical question is the source of authority under the Treaty of Rome for legislative action. For example, when nontariff trade barriers (NTBs) are removed via the traditional harmonization process, Article 94 mandates a unanimous vote. But if an NTB can be dealt with as part of the 1992 campaign for an internal market without frontiers, Article 95 stipulates a qualified majority in most cases. Naturally, the Council (composed of government representatives) and the member states favor interpretations that result in unanimous voting and greater retention of national sovereignty.[1] Naturally, the Parliament favors interpretations that require use of the cooperation and co-decision legislative procedures. Most of the latter areas correspond with qualified majority voting rules. Naturally, countries with "opt outs" favor interpretations which preserve those rights.

The Commission, as the independent "guardian of the treaties," favors interpretations that promote integration and particularly the internal market campaign. It thus tends to side with Parliament in disputes over the source of power for EU legislative enactments. But it did not do this when proposing post-Chernobyl safety legislation under EURATOM instead of Article 95 of the Treaty of Rome. This had the effect of avoiding Parliamentary cooperation procedures. The Parliament subsequently sued the Council before the European Court, which ruled its challenge to the EURATOM safety legislation admissible under Article 230, but denied relief on the merits.[2]

Article 308, "Necessary" Legislative Powers

Legislative authority issues came to a head in a Commission prosecution against the Council initiated on the very day that the Single European Act was signed.[3] In this case, the Court of Justice ruled that the Council violated Article 253 by failing to clearly state the legal basis for regulations implementing the generalized system of tariff preferences (GSP) for goods originating in the developing world. More importantly, the Court held that the Council enacted the regulations on the wrong legal basis. Both of these violations, which were longstanding Council practices, amounted to unlawful failures to act in accordance with the Treaty of Rome.

The Commission had proposed adoption of the GSP regulations under the common external commercial policy provisions, specifically Article 133 which employs qualified majority voting. The Council replaced this proposal with vague language simply referring to "the

§ 2.9

1. *See* United Kingdom v. Council (1988) Eur.Comm.Rep. 855 (beef hormones directive validly adopted by qualified majority vote under Article 43, unanimous vote under Article 100 not required). For other decisions favoring qualified majority voting in disputes over the legal basis of Community legislation, *see* United Kingdom v. Council (1988) Eur.Comm.Rep. 905, Commission v. Council (1989) Eur.Comm.Rep. 3743, Greece v. Council (1990) Eur. Comm.Rep. 1527, Commission v. Council (1989) Eur.Comm.Rep. 1425.

2. European Parliament v. Council (1991) Eur.Comm.Rep. 4529 (Case 70/88).

3. Commission v. Council (1987) Eur.Comm.Rep. 1493. For other major cases on determining the legal basis of legislation, see Commission v. Council, 1991 Eur.Comm.Rep. I–2867 (titanium dioxide), Commission v. Council, 1993 Eur.Comm.Rep. I–939 (waste disposal), United Kingdom v. Council, 1996 Eur. Comm.Rep. I–5755 (working time), and Spain v. Council, 2001 Eur.Comm.Rep. I–779 (Danube Convention).

Treaty" as the legal basis for its acts. In court, the Council explained that this reference was really to Article 133 *and* Article 308. Article 308 authorizes legislation necessary to achieve objectives for which specific enabling powers are otherwise not found in the Treaty of Rome. Article 308 had been previously used by the Council as the legal basis for a number of innovative programs and laws, including the Monetary Cooperation Fund, the Center for Development of Vocational Training, the Foundation for the Improvement of Living and Working Conditions, and environmental, research and development and energy legislation. It had also been used in areas where the Treaty contains other provisions, including agriculture, the customs union, services, the right of establishment and (as in the GSP case) external commercial policy.

Article 308 legislation must be enacted by a unanimous Council vote and does not require cooperation with Parliament. By ruling that Article 133 alone was the proper legal basis for GSP regulations, the Court nullified the Council's unanimous decision and reaffirmed its power to subject Council actions to judicial review. The Commission now has more leeway when proposing legislation for which the Treaty stipulates qualified majority voting under what has become known as the "center of gravity" test.[4] And the Council is clearly limited in its use of Article 308 to situations where no other authority to act is found in the Treaty of Rome, as amended by the Single European Act and the Maastricht Treaty on European Union. This doctrine has even been held to require the Council to adopt legislation under the general principle of equal treatment established in Article 12 rather than Article 308.[5]

§ 2.10 The Commission as an Institution and Law–Maker

The pivotal role of the Commission in the law-making process of the European Union should be evident. It alone drafts legislative proposals. As the GSP litigation makes clear, the Commission can also prosecute when proper legislative procedures are not followed. Furthermore, in certain areas (notably agriculture and competition law), the Commission has been delegated by the Council the authority to issue implementing regulations and decisions that establish law.[1] These acts detail administrative rules rather than create new or broad policies. Thus the Council establishes the "target

4. *See* Commission v. Council (1993) Eur.Comm.Rep. I–939 (Case C–155/91) (waste disposal directive properly based on Article 175 not 95); Germany v. Parliament and Council (2000) Eur. Comm.Rep. I–8419 (tobacco advertising directive could not be based on Article 95).

5. *See* Parliament v. Council (1992) Eur.Comm.Rep. I–04193 (Case C–295/90) (student residence rights).

§ 2.10

1. Articles 202, 211, Treaty of Rome.

prices" for agriculture, but the Commission issues thousands of regulations aimed at actually realizing these goals. The Commission has also promulgated an important series of "group exemption" regulations under competition law.[2] These cover franchising, patent licensing, exclusive dealing and a variety of other business agreements. Lastly, the Commission is authorized by Article 86 of the Treaty of Rome to issue (on its own initiative) directives addressed to member states regarding public enterprises.[3] This authority avoids the usual Union legislative process.

When exercising law-making powers conferred upon it by the Council, the Commission must first consult various committees. These requirements are known as the "comitology" rules of the Council.[4] These rules, in essence, allow the Council to actively monitor the Commission as a law-maker. In most cases, they vest a power of reversal or modification in the Council.

The Commissioners

Who and what is the European Commission? Under the Nice Treaty Enlargement Protocol, there will initially be 25 then 27 Commissioners, one from each member state. Germany, France, Italy, Britain and Spain will give up their second Commissioners. Moreover, after the accession of Romania and Bulgaria in 2007, it has been agreed that the EU Council, acting unanimously, will reduce the number of Commissioners and establish a rotation system to "reflect satisfactorily the demographic and geographical range" of the member states. Commissioners are appointed by a qualified majority o the EU Council subject to Parliament's approval for five-year renewable terms. The President of the Commission is similarly appointed by the European Council and Parliament. Great pains are taken to ensure the independence of Commissioners from their home governments. Article 213 stipulates that Commissioners must be chosen on the basis of competence and their independence must be "beyond doubt." Any breach of this trust by Commissioners could lead to compulsory retirement, or since the Nice Treaty, dismissal by the President of the Commission.

Unlike the Ministers of the Council, Commissioners are not supposed to function as representatives of their nations. Over the years, in large measure, this has been true. Indeed, Prime Minister Thatcher once failed to renew a British Commissioner's appointment because he had "gone native." Sent over to Brussels in a stormy period when the Prime Minister was quite hostile to Union developments, this Commissioner proceeded to act independently, too independently as it turned out. His non-renewal, however,

2. *See* Chapter 7.
3. *See* Chapter 7.

4. Council Decision No. 87/373, Official Journal L197/33 (1987).

broke with a longstanding tradition of regular reappointments for competent Commissioners. Renewal decisions have thus become more politicized in recent years and Commissioners no doubt look over their shoulders towards home as their four year terms begin to expire.

Policy Portfolios

Each Commissioner supervises one or more "Directorate–Generals" or departments of the Commission. These "portfolios" are determined by the President of the Commission. Each Directorate–General (DG) has a Director–General of a nationality different than that of its supervising Commissioner. Each DG has a specific allocation of administrative, legislative drafting and law enforcement duties. Each DG has a staff of highly paid Eurocrats selected in part to ensure national diversity. The staff regulations officially refer to a "geographical distribution" (quotas) of employees based upon the populations of the various member states. Acts performed by Commissioners and their staff in official capacity are immune from legal proceedings in national courts.[5] Union employees are also exempt from national income taxation, although they pay a nominal tax.[6] The DGs which correspond roughly to the main divisions of the treaties. Many consider that there are an excessive and inefficient number of governmental departments. And some DGs, like environment and external relations, are seriously understaffed while others (especially personnel and information) seem grossly overstaffed. The number of Directorates–General changes periodically as do their assignments. Ordinarily, these include Directorates for:

External Relations

Economic and Financial Affairs

Industry

Competition

Employment, Industrial Relations and Social Affairs

Agriculture

Transport

Development

Personnel and Administration

Information, Communication, Culture, Audiovisual

Environment, Nuclear Safety and Civil Protection

5. Sayag v. Leduc (1968) Eur. Comm.Rep. 395.

6. Hamblet v. Belgium (1960) Eur. Comm.Rep. 559 (official's salary cannot be used when calculating income of spouse).

Science, Research and Development

Telecommunications, Information Market and Exploitation of Research

Fisheries

Internal Market and Financial Services

Regional Policies and Cohesion

Energy

Credit and Investment

Budgets

Financial Control

Customs Union and Indirect Taxation

Education Training and Youth

Enterprise Policy, Distributive Trades, Tourism and Cooperatives

Consumer Policy and Consumer Health

Each Commissioner also supervises a personal staff, known as a cabinet. Critics maintain that there has been excessive growth in the size and power of cabinets. These staff members have been known to override the advice of the various Directors–General and generally isolate their Commissioners from professional civil servant input. Defenders of these trends maintain that some of the DGs have been less than competent, and that the Commissioners need another, less bureaucratic perspective. The truth no doubt lies somewhere in between. Just as there are energetic and effective Commissioners, Directors–General and cabinets, none of these offices is immune from the deadwood syndrome.

Voting Procedures

The Treaty of Rome also establishes voting rules for the Commission. Simple majority votes prevail. As a matter of custom, considerable deference is usually given to the Commissioner in charge of a DG when legislative or other proposals are being reviewed by the Commission as a whole. This is sometimes achieved by circulating files with proposed actions which are implemented unless objections are shortly received. Individual Commissioners can be delegated authority to act for the body on routine matters. For example, when the Commissioner on Agriculture adopts new regulations, these are likely to involve such delegation.

Other Commission Tasks

The Commission performs a number of functions in addition to those concerning Community law-making. The most important of these include its prosecutorial powers against individuals and enterprises for breach of EU law, and against member states for failure to adhere to their treaty obligations.[7] The Commission also administers the EU budget and publishes a general and a series of specific annual reports (*e.g.*, on competition policy), all of which are a good way to survey Union affairs. The Commission negotiates the Union's international trade and other agreements.[8] However, the Commission's representative power in this field can be contested. In a judgment rendered in 1994, the Court of Justice determined that the antitrust agreement signed between the Commission and the United States Government should have been concluded by the Council of Ministers.[9] The agreement was challenged on the basis of Article 228 of the Treaty of Rome by France (with the support of Spain and The Netherlands). Article 228 gives the Council the competence to conclude international agreements. Following the Court's decision, the agreement needed to be approved by the Council which presented no difficulty since the substance of the agreement was never questioned. This case has emphasized the necessity to settle questions related to responsibilities within the EU, particularly in light of more recent concerns over the Commission's exact competence in GATT/WTO negotiations.[10]

§ 2.11   The Court of Justice as a Law–Maker

United States students of law and attorneys are familiar (if not always comfortable) with the law-making role of American courts. This perspective is a product of the common-law tradition inherited from England made explicit by the teachings of American realists. Such awareness is less present in European legal communities for a variety of reasons. One important factor is the pre-dominance of the civil law tradition on the Continent. This tradition, with its heavy reliance upon abstract inductive (not deductive) reasoning, tends to obscure rather than illuminate the way in which judges on the Continent do in fact make law. Like their common-law counterparts, European judges must often fill in legislative gaps and arrive at conclusions based upon broadly worded legal language. Anyone who has ever read a "Code" knows that it invites, indeed often requires, law-making by judges. Nevertheless, the mystique that judges only apply the law, not create it, weighs heavily in the minds of many Europeans.

It is against this background that the law-making achievements of the European Court of Justice take on a truly remarkable

7.   *See* Chapters 2 and 7.

8.   *See* Chapter 6.

9.   France v. EC Commission (1994) Eur.Comm.Rep.   I–03641   (Case   C–327/91).

10.   Opinion   1/94   (1994)   Eur. Comm.Rep. I–5267 (WTO).

significance. There are presently 25 (27 in 2007) justices on the Court, one from each member nation plus (traditionally when an odd number was required) a rotating justice. Thus, only two or perhaps three are trained in the common law. All are prominent jurists who serve six year terms by appointment of the member states acting in common accord. The Court was created by the Treaty of Paris in 1951 establishing the Coal and Steel Community. At that time neither Britain nor Ireland was a member. Its procedures and methods (but not its mentality) remain solidly based upon civil law, especially French law, traditions.[1]

The Court of Justice emerged in the earliest years as a powerful law-maker. In part, this role was thrust upon it by the open-ended, constitutional language of the Treaty of Rome. This is noticeably less true of the ECSC and EURATOM treaties. In part, also, the Court simply embraced the role, drawing power and influence to it while constantly pushing Europe forward through its "integrationist jurisprudence." The supremacy doctrine[2] and the "doctrine of direct effect"[3] have been called the twin pillars of this jurisprudence. No less potentially significant are the rules of interpretation requiring national courts to construe their laws so as to facilitate Union policies and the general principles of law articulated by the Court.

§ 2.12 General Principles of Law—Fundamental Rights

The law-making role of the Court of Justice is evident when it recognizes general principles of law, a kind of common law of the Common Market. This is similar to what occurs when the Court finds the general principles of tort liability common to the member states as required by Article 288.[1] However, there is no other express Treaty authorization for the development by the Court of general principles of EU law. Article 220 does oblige the Court to ensure that "the law" is observed when interpreting and applying the Treaty of Rome. In different contexts, as part of "the law," the Court has recognized a right of legitimate expectation,[2] a right to be heard,[3] the duty to respect fundamental human rights,[4] a right to equality of treatment,[5] and a duty to employ means that are

§ 2.11

1. *See* Chapter 3.

2. *See* § 2.13.

3. *See* Chapter 3.

§ 2.12

1. *See* Chapter 3.

2. Töpfer v. Commission (1978) Eur. Comm.Rep. 1019.

3. Transocean Marine Paint Association v. Commission (1974) Eur. Comm.Rep. 1063.

4. Rutuli v. Minister for the Interior (1975) Eur.Comm.Rep. 1219.

5. Louwage v. Commission (1974) Eur.Comm.Rep. 81.

proportional (not excessive) to the end sought (proportionality principle).[6] It is important to note that the Court can and has declared legislation invalid if it fails to adhere to general principles of law. Thus these principles, as articulated by the Court of Justice, are a *higher* source of law capable of overriding legal acts of the European Union.[7]

Other general principles of European Union law recognized by the Court of Justice include contractual certainty,[8] legal certainty,[9] the right to engage in trade union activities,[10] and protection against artibitrary or disproportionate governmental intervention in private activities.[11] A limited attorney-client privilege of confidentiality has been recognized by the Court of Justice as a general principle of law applicable to Union proceedings. This right, however, only applies to external EU-licensed counsel.[12] A limited doctor-patient right of confidentiality has also been acknowledged by the Court.[13]

Legal Certainty

A good example of the way in which ECJ-recognized general principles of law can permeate Union affairs is presented by the principle of legal certainty. This principle means that Union acts must be clear, precise and predictable to those subject to them.[14] Legal certainty has been invoked in connection with Union competition, agricultural, customs, and social security law so as to protect individuals and their rights. For example, social security notices to workers in other member states must be in a language the worker can understand.[15] In general, legal certainty bars the adoption of retroactive legislation.[16] And the Court's decisions can, in the name of legal certainty, apply only prospectively.[17] ECJ decisions other-

---

6. Internationale Handelsgessels-chaft MBH v. Einfuhr–Und Vorratsstelle Für Getreide Und Futtermittel (1970) Eur.Comm.Rep. 1125; Buitoni SA v. FORMA (1979) Eur.Comm.Rep. 677; United Kingdom v. Council (1996) Eur. Comm.Rep. I–5755.

7. *See* Regina v. Intervention Board (1985) Eur.Comm.Rep. 2889 (principle of proportionality invalidates Community regulation).

8. Brasserie de Haecht v. Wilkin–Janssen (1973) Eur.Comm.Rep. 77.

9. Openbaar Ministerie v. Bout (1982) Eur.Comm.Rep. 381.

10. Union Syndicale, Massa and Kortner v. Council (1974) Eur. Comm.Rep. 917.

11. *See* Roquette Frères SA and Directeur général de la concurrence, 2002 Eur.Comm.Rep. I–9011.

12. AM & S v. Commission (1982) Eur.Comm.Rep. 1575.

13. M v. Commission (1980) Eur. Comm.Rep. 1797.

14. Ireland v. Commission (1987) Eur.Comm.Rep. 5041; Administration des Douanes v. SA Gondrand Frères (1981) Eur.Comm.Rep. 1931.

15. Re Farrauto (1975) Eur. Comm.Rep. 157.

16. Re Racke (1979) Eur.Comm.Rep. 69; Amylum v. Council (1982) Eur. Comm.Rep. 3107.

17. Defrenne v. Sabena (1976) Eur. Comm.Rep. 455; Blaizot v. University of Liege (1988) Eur.Comm.Rep. 379.

wise are taken to represent what was always the correct law and thus retroactively date back to the creation of the law under consideration.[18]

Fundamental Rights Doctrine

The Court's decisions in the field of fundamental rights also draw upon the different constitutional traditions of the member states.[19] The Court, in this respect, does not see itself as merely replicating human rights found in common at the national levels. It is instead "inspired" by these traditions to create of its own accord a European Union law of fundamental human rights and freedoms.[20] EU human rights are not absolute and public interest exceptions not disturbing "the substance" of those rights may be allowed.[21] One interesting and sensitive issue is the possible supremacy of Union law on fundamental rights over national rights.

Finally, the Treaty of Rome is not completely devoid of human rights protections. Article 12, for example, establishes the fundamental principle of non-discrimination on grounds of nationality, including corporate nationality. This principle has been frequently invoked in litigation, very often to set aside national rules embodying such discrimination.[22] Discrimination on grounds of nationality by private parties acting within the scope of the Treaty of Rome is also prohibited.[23] Furthermore, Article 12 applies to the Community and its institutions.[24] The principle of non-discrimination on grounds of nationality applies to covert activities.[25] Speaking generally, the Court of Justice has ruled that Article 12 requires comparable situations not to be treated differently and different situations not to be treated in the same way, unless such treatment is objectively justified (permissible differentiation).[26]

Other provisions of the Treaty of Rome also touch upon fundamental human rights. These include the right to challenge Council or Commission action taken in breach of essential procedural

---

18. Ammistrazione delle Finanze v. Denkavit Italiana (1980) Eur. Comm.Rep. 1205; Procureur de la République v. Waterkeyn (1982) Eur. Comm.Rep. 4337.

19. Stauder v. City of Ulm (1969) Eur.Comm.Rep. 419. This approach was codified in Article 6 of the Treaty on European Union.

20. Internationale Handelsgesellschaft mbH v. Einfuhr-und Vorratsstelle für Getreide und Futtermittel (1970) Eur.Comm.Rep. 1125.

21. Nold v. Commission (1974) Eur. Comm.Rep. 491.

22. See Patrick v. Ministre des Affaires Culturelles (1977) Eur.Comm.Rep. 1199; Knoors v. Secretary of State for Economic Affairs (1979) Eur.Comm.Rep. 339; Cowan v. Trésor Public (1989) Eur. Comm.Rep. 195.

23. Walrave and Koch v. Association Union Cycliste Internationale (1974) Eur.Comm.Rep. 1405.

24. Italy v. Commission (1963) Eur. Comm.Rep. 165.

25. Sotgiu v. Deutsche Bundespost (1974) Eur.Comm.Rep. 153.

26. Sermide v. Cassa Conguaglio Zucchero (1984) Eur.Comm.Rep. 4209.

requirements[27] and equal pay for equal work.[28] In addition, Article 295 provides that the Treaty shall not prejudice the rules of the member states governing property ownership. However, this has not stopped the Commission and Council from extensively regulating agricultural land.[29] And the Court of Justice has significantly limited the exercise of intellectual property rights when they inhibit internal trade.[30]

European Human Rights Convention

In the *Rutuli* decision, the Court recognized the relevance and drew upon the European Convention for the Protection of Human Rights and Fundamental Freedoms (1950). In other decisions, the Court of Justice drew upon Article 10 of the European Convention as support for freedom of expression within Union broadcasting law,[31] and Article 6 for the right to a fair hearing.[32] This Convention has been ratified by every EU member state. The Commission has repeatedly proposed that European Union accede to the Human Rights Convention. This would mean that the Union itself would be bound by the catalogue of human rights enumerated in it. These include property, privacy, fair trial, equal treatment, religious, associational and trade or professional rights. If the European Union acceded to the Convention's "right of individual petition," EU citizens would be able to file complaints with the European Commission on Human Rights in Strasbourg, France against acts of the Union's institutions. The European Court of Human Rights in Strasbourg ultimately decides upon such complaints.[33] Article 6 of the Maastricht Treaty on European Union requires the Union to respect fundamental rights as guaranteed by the Human Rights convention, but stops short of actual accession to it.[34] Article 6 also affirms that the Union is founded on principles of liberty, democracy, respect for human rights and fundamental freedoms, and the rule of law.

Neither the Commission nor the Court of Human Rights are Community institutions. They operate in a broader European sphere, and this may explain the reluctance of the Council to accede to the Human Rights Convention. The Human Rights Court could

27. *See* Chapter 3.

28. *See* Chapter 5.

29. Hauer v. Land Rheinland–Pfalz (1979) Eur.Comm.Rep. 3727 (planting of new wine grapes barred).

30. *See* Chapter 4.

31. Elliniki Radiophona Tiléorassi (ERT) AE v. Dimotiki Etairia Pliroforissis (DEP) + Anor (1991) Eur. Comm.Rep. I–2925 Case (C–260/89).

32. Pecastaing 1980 Eur.Comm.Rep. 691.

33. *See* Matthews v. United Kingdom, 28 Eur.Human Rights Rep. 461 (Feb. 18, 1999) (absence of elections to European Parliament in Gibraltar violates Convention).

34. *See* Connolly v. Commission (2001) Eur.Comm.Rep. I–1611 (freedom of expression recognized).

become the supreme arbiter of Union law on human rights, diminishing the role of the European Court of Justice. For its part, the European Commission on Human Rights has rejected complaints concerning Union actions because the EU is not party to the Human Rights Convention.[35] However, if the complaint were to involve the responsibility of all EU member states, such an application might be entertained by the Human Rights Commission.[36] Americans should particularly note the ruling of the Human Rights Court that extradition of criminals who face a possible death sentence and the "death row phenomenon" in the United States amounts to torture or an inhumane or degrading treatment or punishment in breach of the Convention.[37]

EU Charter of Fundamental Rights

In 2000, a Charter of Fundamental Rights was "proclaimed" (but not made legally binding) by the European Council. The Charter focuses on dignity, freedoms, equality, solidarity, citizens rights and justice as its fundamental values. Its scope is far ranging: the death penalty is forbidden, as is "the reproductive cloning of human beings." Privacy rights, freedom of expression, the rights to work, health care and education, broad antidiscrimination rights (including against sexual orientation), the rights of children and the elderly, and the right to "cultural diversity" are recognized. Access to documents,[38] petitioning rights, a fair trial and criminal procedure rights, and a general ban against "abuse of rights," are also enshrined. The Charter's relationship to the European Human Rights Convention is intended to be consistent, allowing for the possibility of higher levels of protection. Many critics have cited the inability of the ECJ and CFI to enforce the Charter as its principle flaw.

§ 2.13　Supremacy Doctrine

None of the European Union treaties addresses the question of what to do when national and Union law are in conflict. There is no supremacy clause analogous to that found in the United States constitution. The issue is absolutely critical to the success or failure of European Union law in all its manifestations; the founding treaties, directives, regulations, ECJ and CFI decisions, international obligations, the general principles of Union law, etc. Its omission from the treaties was perhaps necessary to secure their passage

---

35. Re European School in Brussels 1986–2 Common Mkt.L.Rep. 57.

36. See Dufay v. European Parliament (1987) Eur.Comm.Rep. 1561 (suggesting that exhaustion of EU remedies is a precondition to Human Rights Convention applications).

37. Re Soering (1989) Eur. Ct.Hum.Rgts. 161.

38. See Article 255, Treaty of Rome and Regulation 1049/2001, O.J.L. 145/43 (May 31, 2001).

through various national parliaments. But the issue did not disappear, it was merely left to the European Court to resolve.

In a very famous 1964 decision, the Court ruled that it simply had to be the case that Community law is supreme.[1] The Court reasoned that the whole of the Common Market edifice would be at risk if national laws at variance with regional law could be retained or enacted:

> The transfer by the states from their domestic legal systems to the Community legal system of the rights and obligations arising under the Treaty carries with it a permanent limitation of their sovereign rights, against which a subsequent unilateral act incompatible with the concept of the Community cannot prevail.

Invalidity of National Laws

Under its supremacy doctrine, the European Court of Justice has (effectively speaking) invalidated countless national laws as in conflict with EU law. It is conceivable that such laws could retain validity in cases not involving a conflict, although this would be a rare event. Supremacy notwithstanding, one of the Declarations to the 1993 Maastricht Accord indicates that European Union does not prevent member states from maintaining or introducing more stringent law on working conditions, social policy, consumer protection and the environment, provided those laws are compatible with the Treaty of Rome. This Declaration is consistent with the relevant provisions of the Treaty of Rome on these subjects.

Repeal or amendment of conflicting national law is a duty of the member states that can be reviewed by the Court of Justice in further legal proceedings.[2] An alternative growing in use and encouraged by the European Court is creative judicial interpretation by national courts so as to incorporate Union law requirements and avoid conflicts.[3] For quite some time after *Costa v. ENEL,* and even somewhat today, national courts, legislatures and executives have resented the supremacy doctrine. They adhere, in the end, to this judge-made law because of their mutual interest in the success of the Union enterprise and their respect for the rule of law by its prestigious Court.

National Constitutional Rights and Supremacy

One especially sensitive point has been the conflict of national constitutional rights and EU law. Unlike Britain, many Continental

---

§ 2.13

1. Costa v. ENEL (1964) Eur. Comm.Rep. 585.

2. Commission v. France (1981) Eur. Comm.Rep. 2299.

3. Von Colson and Kamann v. Land Nordrhein–Westfalen (1984) Eur. Comm.Rep. 1891.

states have written constitutions and some have specialized courts or tribunals vested with exclusive powers of constitutional interpretation. Both Germany and Italy, for example, have such "constitutional courts." The Court of Justice has explicitly ruled that *every* national court or tribunal must apply EU law in its entirety so to set aside *any* conflicting provision of national law. This duty arises out of European Union law.[4]

In France, implementation of this duty by its highest courts has been mixed. The Conseil d'Etat (but not the Cour de Cassation) ordinarily has not invalidated French law when in conflict with EU law because it (under French law) is not empowered to review the constitutionality of administrative acts. The Conseil d'Etat does not acknowledge EU law as a source of review power and duty.[5] But there are signs that the Conseil d'Etat has come in from the cold on supremacy.[6]

The German and Italian constitutional courts also initially refused to strike down inconsistent national law.[7] Indeed, the Bundesverfassungsgericht went so far as to review and find EU law deficient as against German constitutional protections for human rights. Both courts have retreated from their initial positions. Practically speaking, they have accepted the supremacy doctrine of the European Court and their duty to set aside contrary national law.[8] In the human rights area, however, neither has fully given up its review powers when Union law is challenged.[9] Recently, in a case where Irish constitutional restraints on the advertising of the availability of abortion services in Britain were challenged as incompatible with the Treaty of Rome, there were signs within the Irish Supreme Court that supremacy might not prevail.[10]

4. Nold v. Commission (1974) Eur. Comm.Rep. 491; Ammistrazione delle Finanze v. Simmenthal Spa (1978) Eur. Comm.Rep. 629.

5. Re Syndicat Général des Fabricants de Semoules de France (1970) Common Mkt.L.Rep. 395 (Conseil d'Etat); Compare Administration de Douanes v. Société Café Jacques Vabre (1975) Common Mkt.L.Rep. 367 (Cour de Cassation adheres to EU law supremacy).

6. *See* Re Application of R. Nicolo (1990) 1 Common Mkt.L.Rep. 173 (supremacy of EU law acknowledged when Conseil d'Etat functions as an electoral court); Re Maurice Boisdet (1991) 1 Common Mkt.L.Rep. 3.

7. *See* Frontini et al v. Ministero delle Finanze (1974) 2 Common Mkt.

L.Rep. 386; Solange I (1974) 2 Common Mkt.L.Rep. 551.

8. *See* Solange II (1988) 25 Common Mkt.L.Rep. 201; Granital Spa v. Administrazione delle Finanze (1984) translated in 21 Common Mkt.L.Rev. 756. *But see* Wunsche Handelsgellschaft (1987) 3 Common Mkt.L.Rep. 225 (suggesting German constitutional court will not review EU legislation against German human rights standards because of Community law developments in ECJ cases).

9. Solange II, supra; Fragd Spa v. Amministrazione delle Finanze (1989) reported in Caja, 27 Common Mkt. L.Rev. 83.

10. *See* Society for the Protection of Unborn Children (Ireland) Ltd. v. Grogan (1990) Common Mkt.L.Rep. 689.

The collision and reconciliation of the European Court's supremacy doctrine with national constitutions illustrates an essential feature of the Union's legal system. The efficacy of the system depends heavily upon the willingness of national judges to acknowledge and adhere to EU law, in particular to adhere to the European Court's interpretation of that law. This dependency has meant that the outer limits of the Court's authority and credibility are really to be found amongst the national judiciaries. On supremacy, the European Court has largely prevailed. Indeed, even in Britain where issues of supremacy are hypersensitive, the House of Lords has indicated:

> If the supremacy ... of Community law over the national law of Member States was not always inherent in the EEC Treaty it was certainly well established in the jurisprudence of the European Court of Justice long before the United Kingdom joined the Community. ...Under the terms of the [European Communities] Act of 1972 it has always been clear that it was the duty of a United Kingdom court, when delivering final judgment, to override any rule of national law found to be in conflict with any directly enforceable rule of Community law. ...Thus there is nothing in any way novel in according supremacy to rules of Community law in those areas to which they apply ... [11]

In other areas, notably the question of giving "direct effect" to EU directives,[12] the process of education and persuasion continues.

§ 2.14 Single Market Legislation: 1992–Plus at a Glance

Article 94 of the Treaty of Rome empowers the Council of Ministers, acting on Commission proposals, to issue directives for the "approximation" (better known as "harmonization" or "coordination") of national laws directly affecting the establishment or operation of the Common Market. Such directives must be adopted unanimously within the Council. Since a vast number of national laws affect the Common Market, the potential scope of Article 94 is very broad. This scope, over the years since 1957, was not fully exploited principally because of the unanimous Council voting requirement. Indeed, by 1986 with a Union of twelve nations, innovative legislation under Article 94 became quite difficult to obtain. That is why one major thrust of the 1987 Single European Act was the inclusion of Article 95. It specifies qualified majority voting in the Council of Ministers for much of the single market

---

11. Regina v. Secretary of State for Transport (Factortame) (1991) 1 All Eng.Rep. 70 (Lord Bridge).

12. *See* Chapter 3.

legislative agenda. Qualified majority voting procedures also apply to directives used to harmonize national laws (*e.g.,* subsidies) distorting the conditions of competition in the Common Market.

Harmonization of national laws of concern to the Common Market is critical to advancing European Union integration. Harmonization can, for example, remove many of the barriers to free movement discussed in Chapter 4, including those expressly permitted by Article 30 and the *Dassonville/Cassis* and *Keck* line of cases. It can do the same for the public security exceptions to the free movement of workers and the self-employed, as well as to the freedom to provide services across borders, discussed in Chapter 4 as well. Harmonization is critical to removal of the tax and NTB frontiers within the Union which were a central focus of the campaign for a Europe without internal frontiers. See Chapter 5. In addition, harmonization can reach out to areas not specifically treated in the Treaty of Rome but which are of consequence to the functioning of the Common Market. A good example is government procurement law covered in Section 5.4.

By 1992, the European Union had implemented 282 regulations and directives to create a Single Internal Market. Many of these laws address nontariff trade barriers. Plus, during the remainder of the decade the EU adopted several hundred additional laws related to market integration that were not formally part of the 1992 program. The listing below is representative of the scope of European Union legislation undertaken to create a common market.

In standards, testing and certification

Harmonization of standards for:

Simple pressure vessels

Toys

Construction products

Machine safety

Agricultural & forestry tractors

Cosmetics

Quick frozen foods

Flavorings

Food emulsifiers

Food preservatives

Jams

Fruit juices

Food inspection

Definition of spirited beverages & aromatised wines

Coffee extracts & chicory extracts

Food additives

Materials & articles in contact with food

Tower cranes (noise)

Household appliances (noise)

Tire pressure gauges

Hydraulic diggers (noise)

Detergents

Lawn mowers (noise)

Radio interferences

Automobiles, trucks, and motorcycles and their emissions

Liquid fertilizers & secondary fertilizers

Weighing instruments

Gas appliances

Personal protection equipment

Global Approach to Testing & Certification

Infant formula

Mutual Recognition of Tests

New rules for harmonizing packing, labelling and processing requirements

Ingredients for food & beverages

Irradiation

Nutritional labelling

Classification, packaging, & labelling of dangerous preparations

Extraction solvents

Harmonization of regulations for the health industry (including marketing)

Medical specialties

High technology medicines

Veterinary medicinal products

Active implantable medical devices

Pharmaceuticals

Medical devices

In-vitro diagnostics

Changes in government procurement regulations

Coordination of procedures on the award of public works & supply contracts

Extension of E.C. law to telecommunications, utilities, transport; services

Harmonization of regulation of services

Mutual Funds

Broadcasting

Tourism

Air transport

Electronic payment cards

Information services

Life & nonlife insurance

Banking

Securities

Maritime transport

Road passenger transport

Road Haulage

Railways

Liberalization of capital movements

Long-term capital, stocks

Short-term capital

Consumer protection regulations

Misleading definitions of products

Indication of prices

Liability of defective products

Consumer Protection Policy

Consumers Consultative Council

General Product Safety

Harmonization of taxation

Value added taxes

Excise taxes on alcohol, tobacco, and other

Harmonization of laws regulating company behavior

Trademarks

Accounting operations across borders

Protection of computer programs

Transaction taxes

Company law

Mergers & acquisitions

Copyrights

Cross border mergers

Bankruptcy

Harmonization of veterinary & phytosanitary controls

Antibiotic residues

Bovine animals and meat

Porcine animals and meat

Plant health

Fish & fish products

Live poultry, poultry meat and hatching eggs

Pesticide residues in fruit & vegetables

Pesticide residues in animal origin products

Elimination and simplification of national transit documents and procedures for intra-EU trade

Introduction of the Single Administrative Document (SAD)

Abolition of customs presentation charges

Elimination of customs formalities & the introduction of common border posts

Harmonization of rules pertaining to the free movement of labor and the professions within the EU

Mutual recognition of higher educational diplomas

Comparability of vocational training qualifications

Specific training in general medical practice

Training of engineers

Activities in the field of pharmacy

Activities related to commercial agents

Income taxation provisions

Elimination of burdensome requirements related to residence permits

Autos

Speed limitation devices

External projections of rear panel

Masses and dimensions

Field of vision of motor vehicles

Rear view mirrors of motor vehicles

Braking devices

Engine power of motor vehicles

Roadworthiness

Side guards

Indicator lamps

Light and light signalling

Type approval for sound levels

Headlamps

Marker lamps

Rear fog lamps

Safety belts and restraint systems

Tires

Spray suppression devices

Safety glazing of autos

Health and Safety/Social Charter

Banning of certain chemical agents from workers

Safety and health of workers

Minimum safety & health at the workplace: physical plant design

Work equipment used at the workplace

Right of residence

Worker protection from risks to exposure of carcinogens

Handling heavy loads/risk of back injury

Worker protection from risks to exposure to biological agents

Worker protection from risks to exposure to asbestos

Employers obligation to inform employees of conditions for contracts or employment relationship

Social Security Schemes

Workers with fixed-duration or temporary employment relationship

Safety signs at work

Exposure to noise at work

Right of residence for EC workers not yet or no longer employed

Charter of Fundamental Social Rights

Organization of working time

Protection at work of pregnant women who have given birth

Operational protection of outside workers

Safety and health at temporary or mobile work sites

Mobility improvement of workers

Safety and health workers in extraction industries

Protection of workers from radioactive waste

Freedom of movement of workers

European Agency for Safety and Health at Work

Employee participation and enterprise

Energy

Transit of electricity through grids

Natural gas through grids

Promotion of energy efficiency (SAVE Program)

Efficiency of hot-water boilers with liquid or gaseous fuels

Sulphur content of gasoil

Environment

PCB's

Asbestos

Shipments of hazardous waste

Pollution caused by waste from titanium oxide

Limitation of sulphur dioxide and particulates

Genetically Modified Organisms

Freedom of Information on the Environment

Waste

Lead content of petrol

Urban waste water treatment

Substances that deplete the ozone layer

Civil liability for damage caused by waste

Substances discharged into the aquatic environment

European Environment Monitoring and Information Network

Control of the environmental risks of existing substances

Eco-labelling

Pollution caused by nitrates in the waters

Waste landfills

Packaging and packaging waste

Telecommunications

Legal protection of micro circuits

Type approval of terminal equipment

Introduction of ISDN

Standardization on information technology and telecommunications

Competition in telecom terminal equipment

Information Services Market

Information technology and telecom in health care

Telecom Services with Open Network Provisions

Visual Display Units

Competition for telecommunications services

Trans European Networks

Radio Paging equipment/frequency bands

Computer programs

Digital European cordless telecommunications

Development of a common market on telecom services

Green Paper for telecom services and equipment

Development of an Audiovisual Industry

Personal data and information security

Public digital telecommunications networks

Open Network Provision to leased lines

Frequency bands of digital short-range (DSSR)

Satellite Broadcasting and Cable Transmission

International Telephone Access Codes in the EC

Computer Reservation Services

Chapter 3

LITIGATING EUROPEAN UNION LAW

Table of Sections

§ 3.0 Introduction

There has been an explosive growth in litigation of European Union law. The bulk of this growth has taken place in national courts and tribunals. These bodies are vested with wide (but not final) authority to resolve EU legal issues. For example, contracts disputes can raise a host of Union law questions. Is an exclusive dealing distribution contract enforceable as a matter of competition law? Can goods to which a sales contract applies be freely traded in the Common Market? Is payment for sales across borders protected by EU law? Does an employment contract fail to provide equal pay for equal work? Can employees be terminated because of their nationality? May patent licensing agreements contain grant-back clauses? Can franchisees be limited to certain geographic markets? What joint ventures can be established for research and development purposes?

70

Administrative decisions present another fertile field of European law litigation. When can customs officers seize goods in transit between member states? When can they collect money in such situations? When can immigrations authorities keep workers from other member states out? When can they deport them? When can professional licensing boards deny the applications of citizens of Union nations? Can national authorities deny EU nationals the right to establish a restaurant? Can they require residency or work permits? What about the families of all these persons? What about pensions, social security, health insurance and other job-related benefits for resident EU workers? These listings only scratch the surface of EU law litigation in national courts and tribunals.

The explosion in litigation must be qualified. Not all areas of European Union law fall within the jurisdiction of the European Court of Justice (ECJ) and its judicial doctrine. For example, to the extent that the nations involved rely upon intergovernmental conventions to reach their goals, these agreements do not follow the typical litigation patterns described below. Such conventions will have their own dispute settlement mechanisms unless they specifically convey jurisdiction to the ECJ. For example, the "Brussels Convention" on jurisdiction and enforcement of civil and commercial judgments makes such a conveyance. Moreover, commencing with the 1987 Single European Act amendments to the Treaty of Rome, certain areas of European Union activity are undertaken outside the normal legislative and litigative frameworks of the Union. More such exclusions, where intergovernmental procedures predominate, were added by the 1993 Maastricht Treaty on European Union and the Amsterdam Treaty of 1999, although the latter treaty and the Treaty of Nice of 2003 also removed certain exclusions. Consequently, at this point, some EU foreign and security policy matters and some EU actions on justice and home affairs do not fall within the litigation system analyzed in this chapter.

§ 3.1 Direct Effects Doctrine

The right to commence litigation in national forums must be given to the plaintiff by national law. In other words, European Union law has not (as yet) been interpreted to create national causes of action.[1] What it does do, according to the "direct effects doctrine," is give litigants the right to raise many issues ("Euro-defenses" and "Euro-offenses") in national courts and tribunals. In doing so, individuals often function as guardians of the Treaty of Rome (like the Commission). Americans might analogize this role

1. *See* Wöhrmann v. Commission, 1962 Eur.Comm.Rep. 501 (Plea of ille-gality does not amount to an independent cause of action).

to that of "private attorneys general," a law enforcement technique adopted in a number of United States statutes. The Court of Justice has noted that the vigilance of private litigants enforcing their rights is an important element in the Union's legal system.[2]

The direct effects doctrine is, to a very large degree, a product of the jurisprudence of the European Court of Justice. It can apply to EU treaties, directives, regulations, decisions and international agreements. When any of these measures are of direct effect, this impact generally commences from the date of its entry into force.[3] But the direct effects doctrine is not automatically applied. For example, although the General Agreement on Tariffs and Trade (GATT) is binding upon the Union and its member states, it has typically been construed by the Court not to have direct legal effects.[4] Likewise, WTO agreements are unlikely to have direct effect.[5] Both the Council of Ministers and the European Council tend to issue resolutions or declarations when there is a political consensus but no desire to adopt legislation. For the most part, the Court of Justice has held such acts incapable of creating direct legal effects in the member states.[6]

Regulations

The legal effects of regulations are the easiest to understand. Article 189 of the Treaty of Rome provides that regulations are "directly applicable in all member states." In other words, regulations have immediate, unconditional legal effect without any need for national implementation. They are law in the member states from the moment of issuance, binding upon all individuals, business organizations and governments.[7] For litigants, when regulations are applicable, they control the outcome. This is true under the supremacy doctrine even in the face of contrary national law.[8]

2. Van Gend en Loos v. Nederlandse Administratie der Belastingen (1963) Eur.Comm.Rep. 585.

3. Ammistrazione delle Finanze v. Salumi (1980) Eur.Comm.Rep. 1237.

4. *See* International Fruit Company Produktschap voor Groenten en Fruit (1972) Eur.Comm.Rep. 1219; FEDIOL v. Commission (1989) Eur.Comm.Rep. 1781 (Case 70/87); Germany v. Council (1994) Eur.Comm.Rep. I–4973 (bananas). *Compare* Bresciani v. Amministrazione della Finanze (1976) Eur. Comm.Rep. 129 (Yaoundé Convention trade agreements directly effective and thus override conflicting national law); Hauptzollamt Mainz v. Kupferberg (1982) Eur.Comm.Rep. 3641 (EC–Portugal Free Trade Agreement has direct effect).

5. Portuguese Republic v. Council, (1998) Eur.Comm.Rep. I–7379. *See* Schieving–Nijstad Vof v. Groeneveld (2001) Eur.Comm.Rep. I–5851.

6. Pubblico Ministero v. Manghera (1976) Eur.Comm.Rep. 91; Schülter v. Hauptzollamt Lörrach (1973) Eur. Comm.Rep. 1135.

7. *See, e.g.,* Politi SAS v. Ministry of Finance of the Italian Republic (1971) Eur.Comm.Rep. 1039; Fratelli Zerbone SNC v. Amministrazione delle Finanze (1978) Eur.Comm.Rep. 99.

8. *See* Chapter 2. *See especially* Variola v. Amministrazione delle Finanze dello Stato (1973) Eur.Comm.Rep. 981 (no member state legislation necessary or permissible after EU regulation).

Directives

Directives are more difficult to understand. Article 249 does *not* specify that they shall have "direct applicability." In part, their design prohibits this. Directives are addressed to member states, instructing them to implement (in whatever way is required) certain Union policies within a fixed timetable. These policies do not become law in the member states until implemented or, if timely implementation does not follow, until the European Court rules that the directive is of "direct effect." Some national courts, notably in France, have opposed this judge-made doctrine.[9]

Not all directives have direct effect. The Court of Justice has selectively ruled that only those directives that establish clear and unconditional legal norms and do not leave normative discretion to the member states are of direct effect.[10] Once the ECJ has decided that a European Union directive has direct effect, litigants can rely on it to the full extent of its application to member states, public service entities,[11] and local governments.[12] Litigants can challenge contrary national law, including defective implementing measures if required, and can challenge criminal laws.[13]

Interpretative Duties

Unlike regulations, directives cannot be used to challenge private activities. Thus it is said that directives do not have "horizontal" direct effects.[14] Even so, the Court of Justice has held that in applying national law the national courts and tribunals are required by Article 10 of the Treaty of Rome to interpret their law in light of the wording and purposes of all EU directives.[15] National law must be interpreted in the light of regional directives even if the directive has not yet been implemented.[16] Some commentators

9. *See especially* In re Cohn–Bendit (1978) 1979 Common Mkt.L.Rep. 702 (French Conseil d'Etat); German Federal Tax Court (Bundesfinanzhof) V.B. 51/80 (July 16, 1980), *reversed on appeal* In re Application of Frau Kloppenburg (1988) 3 Comm.Mkt.L.Rep. 1 (Fed.Constit.Ct.1987).

10. Van Duyn v. Home Office (1974) Eur.Comm.Rep. 1337; Becker v. Finanzamt Münster-Innenstadt (1982) Eur. Comm.Rep. 53.

11. Foster v. British Gas (1990) 1 Eur.Comm.Rep. 3313.

12. Fratelli Costanzo v. Milano (1989) Eur.Comm.Rep. 1839.

13. Pubblico Ministero v. Ratti (1979) Eur.Comm.Rep. 1629; Criminal Proceedings against Bordessa (1995) Eur.Comm.Rep. I–361.

14. Marshall v. Southampton and South West Hampshire Area Health Authority (teaching) (1986) Eur.Comm. Rep. 723. Faccini Dori v. RECREB SRL (1994) Eur.Comm.Rep. I–3325 (consumer contract rights denied because of state failure to timely implement directive).

15. *See* Von Colson v. Land Nordrhein–Westfalen (1984) Eur. Comm.Rep. 1891; Oberkreisdirektor des Kreises Borken v. Moormann (1988) Eur.Comm.Rep. 4869; Lister v. Forth Dry Dock Engineering Co., 1 All Eng. Rep. 1194 (House of Lords, 1989) (*Von Colson* principles followed in employee rights case).

16. Marleasing SA v. La Comercial Internacional de Alimentación SA (1990) 1 Eur.Comm.Rep. 4135 (*Compare* Duke have characterized these duties as involving the "indirect effect" of directives.

The obligation to interpret national law in view of EU directives "is limited by the general principles of law which form part of Union law and in particular the principles of legal certainty and non-retroactivity."[17] Even so, in considerable private litigation before the tribunals and courts of member states, directives will be given effect through judicial interpretations of national law. This is likely to have the same practical impact as would adoption of a "horizontal" direct effects doctrine at the regional level. Moreover, it has been argued that Article 10 mandates that *all* provisions of national law (not just those touched by Union directives) must be interpreted in conformity with all European Union law (not just directives).[18] If this argument becomes binding law, the doctrine of direct effects will reach a zenith which few would have ever dreamed.

§ 3.2 Directly Effective Treaty Provisions

The third major category of directly effective law originates in the treaties establishing the EURATOM and EC communities. The Court of Justice has ruled that parts of these treaties are capable of having immediate, binding legal effect in the member states. Here again the Court has been selective, sorting out which treaty provisions establish clear, unconditional and nondiscretionary legal norms. Those many articles of the treaties that are largely aspirational, procedural or written as guidelines for the exercise of member state discretion are unlikely to have direct effect.[1]

The Court of Justice has consistently refused to view the treaties as merely creating obligations among the contracting states. Citing Article 234, the Court finds acknowledgment that the Treaty of Rome was intended to have effect in national legal regimes.

> The conclusion to be drawn ... is that the Community constitutes a new legal order of international law for the benefit of which the States have limited their sovereign rights, albeit within limited fields, and the subjects of which comprise not

v. GEC Reliance, 1 All Eng.Rep. 626 (House of Lords, 1988) (*Von Colson* principles not followed in equal treatment case)).

17. Case 80/86, Officier van Justitie v. Kolpinghuis Nijmegen (1987) Eur. Comm.Rep. 3969.

18. *See* Barber v. Guardian Boyal Exchange Assurance Group (1990) 1 Eur.Comm.Rep. 1889 (Advocate General's Opinion). See also Grimaldi v. Fonds

des Maladies Professionnelles (1990) Eur.Comm.Rep. I–04407 (Case 322/88) (EU Recommendations have indirect effect).

§ 3.2

1. *See* Spa Salgoil v. Italian Ministry for Foreign Trade (1968) Eur. Comm.Rep. 453 (Articles 33(1) and (2) discretionary and not directly effective).

only Member States but also their nationals. Independently of the legislation of Member States, Community law therefore not only imposes obligations on individuals but is also intended to confer upon them rights which become part of their legal heritage. These rights arise not only where they are expressly granted by the Treaty, but also by reason of obligations which the Treaty imposes in a clearly defined way upon individuals as well as upon the Member States and the institutions of the Community.[2]

Once the Court has held a Treaty term directly effective in the member states, litigants before national courts and tribunals can rely fully upon it. They can, under the supremacy doctrine, use it to set aside contradictory national law. Like regulations, directly effective Treaty of Rome provisions can apply horizontally to private parties.[3] This follows, in the court's view, because national courts are an arm of the states that signed the Treaty and therefore bound to apply the law in all cases. The same logic has not been carried over to directives.[4]

Directly Effective Treaty Provisions

The following is a partial list of the articles of the Treaty of Rome that have been held directly effective by the European Court of Justice. Many of these decisions are qualified.

Article 12	— no discrimination on grounds of nationality
Articles 23–24	— customs union free trade rules
Article 25	— no internal customs duties or measures of equivalent effect
Article 28	— no internal trade quotas or measures of equivalent effect
Article 30	— no disguised restraints on internal trade
Article 31	— state trading monopolies cannot discriminate between nationals
Article 39	— free movement and employment of workers without nationality discriminations
Article 43	— right of establishment for self-employed
Article 49(1)	— freedom to provide services across borders
Article 50(3)	— national treatment of cross-border service providers

2. Van Gend en Loos v. Nederlandse Administratie der Belastingen (1963) Eur.Comm.Rep. 1.

3. Defrenne v. Sabena (1976) Eur. Comm.Rep. 455.

4. Marshall v. Southampton and South West Hampshire Area Health Authority (teaching) (1986) Eur. Comm.Rep. 723.

Articles 56, 57, 58 — current payments and capital transfers

Articles 72, 75, 76 — transport discriminations prohibited

Articles 81, 86, 86 — competition law prohibitions

Articles 87(1), 88(3) — state subsidies cannot distort competition without Commission approval

Article 90 — national treatment on taxation of goods

Article 91 — no excessive tax rebates upon exports

Article 141 — equal pay for equal work, equal treatment

Article 294 — no discrimination on capital participation in companies

The following Treaty of Rome provisions have generally been held *not* to have direct legal effect. Again, many of these ECJ decisions are qualified.

Articles 2, 3 — general tasks and objectives

Article 10 — member state obligations to facilitate and not jeopardize Treaty of Rome

Article 88 — state subsidies

Article 97 — harmonization of laws

Article 108 — balance of payments

Article 293 — negotiation of certain conventions

§ 3.3   National Legal Remedies for Directly Effective Law

Directly effective European Union law conveys at the national level immediate legal rights and obligations. What remedies can be secured in national courts and tribunals when European law has these effects? The Treaty of Rome does not provide a ready answer. In general, the Court of Justice has held that directly effective rights must be enforceable in the national courts by means of remedies that are real, effective and non-discriminatory.[1] Interim or preliminary judicial and administrative remedies may be required to protect directly effective rights when national *or* Union law is challenged.[2] The precise determination of those remedies is a matter for the national courts to decide. For example, one British court issued a notable interim order requiring public authorities to prom-

---

§ 3.3

1. Rewe Zentralfinanz v. Landwirtschaftskammer Saarland (1976) Eur. Comm.Rep. 1989; Amministrazione delle Finanze v. San Giorgio (1983) Eur. Comm.Rep. 3595; Marshall v. Southampton and South West Hampshire Area Health Authority (1993) Eur. Comm.Rep. I–4367 (Case C–271/91).

2. Regina v. Secretary of State for Transport (1990) Eur.Comm.Rep. I–2433 (Case C–213/89); Zuckerfabrik Süderdithmarschen v. Hauptzollamt Itzehoe (1991) Eur.Comm.Rep. I–415 (Cases 143/88 and C–92/89).

ise to pay damages if that country's Sunday trading bans ultimately were found invalid under Union law as the "price" for interlocutory injunctions sought by the authorities against Sunday traders.[3]

In Britain, the Court of Appeal ruled that a failure on the part of the government to adhere to Treaty of Rome obligations does *not* give rise to an action for damages even when directly effective rights are involved.[4] This litigation was commenced by French turkey producers who lost sales when Britain imposed import restraints, allegedly for animal health reasons. The Court of Justice had previously ruled that the restraints were unlawful under Article 31 as measures of equivalent effect to quotas. The British restraints were not subject to the animal health exception created by Article 30 because they were economically motivated, *i.e.* they were disguised restraints on internal free trade. The plaintiffs in *Bourgoin* apparently could have obtained injunctive relief had Britain continued to impose its restrictions after the European Court's decision.[5]

There was some question whether *Bourgoin* meets the general criteria of the Court of Justice for real, effective and nondiscriminatory national legal remedies when directly effective EU rights are at stake. The case was settled before reaching the House of Lords by payment to Bourgoin of 3.5 million Pounds Sterling for damages, costs and interest by the UK government. Similar remedial issues have been litigated in Britain concerning directly effective European Union competition law.[6] In contrast, the French Conseil d'Etat has awarded damages against the French government for harm caused by a breach of Union law.[7] Dutch law also permits such recoveries,[8] as does Spanish law.[9]

Member State Liability for Damages

In a major decision, *Francovich*, the Court of Justice has ruled that member state liability for damages to individuals caused by the state's infringement of Union law is inherent in the scheme of the Treaty of Rome.[10] This obligation follows from member state duties

3. Kirklees BC v. Wickes Building Supplies, 4 All Eng.Rep. 240 (Court of Appeal, 1991). *See* Tarfaen Borough Council v. B & Q PLC Ltd. (1989) Eur. Comm.Rep. 3851.

4. Bourgoin SA v. Ministry of Agriculture, Fisheries and Food (1985) 3 All Eng.Rep. 585, (1986) 1 Common Mkt. L.Rep. 267.

5. Commission v. United Kingdom (1982) Eur.Comm.Rep. 2793. *Accord,* Regina v. Secretary of State for Transport (1990) 3 Common Mkt.L.Rep. 375 (House of Lords).

6. Articles 81 and 82, *infra* Chapter 7.

7. Ministre du Commerce Extérieur v. Alivar (March 23, 1984).

8. Roussel Laboratories (Hague District Court, July 18, 1984).

9. *See* Canal Satélite Digital, Case 1/46/1999 (Spanish Tribunal Supremo, June 12, 2003).

10. Francovich + Ors v. Italian Republic (1991) Eur.Comm.Rep. I–5357 (Cases C–6 and C–9/90).

under Article 10 to ensure fulfillment of EU law. The case involved an Italian failure to implement a directly effective EU directive on employee benefits in the event of insolvency. Whether or not the unimplemented directive is of direct effect does not matter, and faulty implementation or retention of contrary domestic law also gives rise to state liability whenever three conditions are met: (1) the law infringed is intended to confer individual rights; (2) the infringement is sufficiently serious; and (3) there is a direct causal link between the breach and damages sustained.[11] Member state liability for damages generally tracks Community tort liability under Article 288[12] and extends to administrative as well as legislative acts and omissions.[13] In a second major decision, *Kobler*, the Court of Justice has indicated that it is possible for individuals to sue member states for damages when *national courts* exceptionally breach EU law.[14] The Commission has also challenged member state judicial interpretations that run contrary to EU law.[15]

In the absence of precise European Union rules on remedies for directly effective legal rights, the results vary from country to country and context to context. Many cases involve the question of repayment of custom duties, customs charges and taxes paid to governments under national laws that are invalidated by Union law. Others concern national laws implementing EU law which is subsequently invalidated by the Court of Justice.[16] The Court has reiterated in these decisions that the means of recovery for monies unlawfully paid to governments are controlled by national law. Thus, statutes of limitations,[17] the forum, interest on the amounts paid and related issues are national legal questions. The Court has also reiterated that procedural hurdles which discriminate against recoveries based upon EU rights when measured against procedures for similar domestic recoveries do not satisfy the requirements of the Treaty of Rome.[18] And, in general, national rules on recovery of unlawful payments to governments cannot have the practical result of making it impossible to recover such sums.[19]

---

11. Brasserie du Pecheur SA v. Germany, joined Cases C–46, 48/93 (1996) Eur. Comm. Rep. I–1029.

12. *See* Section 3.10.

13. R. v. Ministry of Agriculture, Fisheries and Food (Hedley Lomas) (1996) Eur.Comm.Rep. I–2553.

14. Köbler v. Austrian Republic (2003) Eur.Comm.Rep. I–00000 (Case C–224/01).

15. Commission v. Italy, 2003 Eur. Comm.Rep. I–8003.

16. Deville v. Administration des Impôts (1988) Eur.Comm.Rep. 3513. *See* Marshall v. Southhampton and South-

West Hampshire Area Health Authority (1993) Eur.Comm.Rep. 4367 (equal treatment remedies).

17. *But see* Emmott v. Minister for Social Welfare (1991) Eur.Comm.Rep. 4269 (national statutes of limitations do not run until member state has fulfilled Directive duties).

18. Express Dairy Foods Ltd. v. Intervention Board for Agricultural Produce (1980) Eur.Comm.Rep. 1887.

19. *Compare* Re Jules Borker (1980) Eur.Comm.Rep. 1975 (Bar Council of Cour de Paris not a tribunal preliminary ruling request rejected); with Broekmeu-

§ 3.4   Article 234—Referrals by National Courts and Preliminary ECJ Rulings

The European Court of Justice derived its doctrine of directly effective law partly from Article 234 of the Treaty of Rome. This article is the linchpin that joins the national legal systems of the member states to the European Court.

Article 234 vests jurisdiction in the European Court to give "preliminary rulings" (sometimes called "advisory rulings") on the interpretation of the Treaty, the validity and interpretation of acts by the Union's institutions and other matters. These rulings occur when national courts or tribunals (faced with an issue of Union law) request them. Professional bodies may or may not constitute "tribunals of a member state" for these purposes.[1] Since the Treaty of Nice (2003), the ECJ has the power to allow some Article 234 cases to go to the Court of First Instance (below).

Discretionary References

Article 234 requests or "references" are discretionary with the judges of the lower-level courts and tribunals of the member states. They cannot be initiated as a matter of right by litigants, nor by arbitrators designated by contract to resolve a dispute when those arbitrators are not functioning as a court or tribunal of a member state.[2] This is a particularly notable decision because ever increasing numbers of business disputes are being taken to binding arbitration. The only recourse for review of an arbitrator's interpretation of Union law is through ancillary or enforcement proceedings in the national courts.

Whenever a national court considers a reference necessary to enable judgment, it may seek the advice of the European Court by posing questions to it. It may do so even when the European Court or a higher national court has already ruled on the question of EU law at hand. In other words, the common law doctrine of binding precedent does not remove the discretion of lower courts to invoke Article 234.[3] Similarly, the fact that appeals are mandatory under

len v. Huisgarts Registratie Commissie (1981) Eur.Comm.Rep. 2311 (Dutch Appeals Committee for General Medicine is a tribunal of the state; request accepted).

§ 3.4

1. Nordsee v. Reederei Mond (1982) Eur.Comm.Rep. 1095 (German arbitration court reference rejected). *See* Corbiau v. Administration des Contributions (1993) Eur.Comm.Rep. I–1277 (Case C–24/92) (Luxembourg Director of

Taxes cannot refer questions under Article 234).

2. Nordsee v. Reederei Mond (1982) Eur.Comm.Rep. 1095 (German arbitration ciourt reference rejected). *See* Corbiau v. Administration des Contributions (1993) Eur.Comm.Rep. I–1277 (Case C–24/92) (Luxembourg Director of Taxes cannot refer questions under Article 234).

3. Rheinmühlen–Düsseldorf v. Einfuhr-und Vorratsstelle für Getreide und Futtermittel (1974) Eur.Comm.Rep. 33.

national law does not block utilization of Article 234 references to the ECJ if the lower court believes such a reference is necessary to enable it to give judgment.[4]

In practice, lower courts refer EU law issues to the ECJ quite regularly. However, these referral decisions may be subject to an interlocutory appeal within the national legal system.[5] Such an appeal will not ordinarily require the ECJ to suspend its review of and decision on the reference.[6] But if the appeal of the referral has the effect under national law of suspending the referral decision, then the Court of Justice will suspend its Article 234 proceeding.[7] Thus, in most cases, the national interlocutory appeal of the referral decision and the ECJ's Article 234 proceeding will move forward simultaneously. Should the decision to refer be reversed on appeal, the Court of Justice will terminate its proceeding and not rule under Article 234.[8]

Assuming the request comes from a proper national court or tribunal, the European Court of Justice cannot refuse the reference, even when it has already ruled on the EU legal issue.[9] Once underway, the Commission almost always files a written brief expressing its opinion in Article 234 proceedings. The government of the member state whose court or tribunal is the source of the reference typically does so as well. Private parties "interested" in the questions being referred may not intervene.[10] After a preliminary ruling of the European Court is secured, the national court is obliged to implement that ruling in its final judgment.[11] The ruling is also binding on appeal of that judgment, and (at a minimum) persuasive in courts of other nations.[12]

Validity of EU and National Laws

The discretion of national courts to refer EU law questions to the European Court is largely removed whenever the question is

But see to the contrary Duke v. GEC Reliance Systems Ltd. (1987) 2 Common Mkt.L.Rep. 24 (English Court of Appeal).

4. Mecanarte–Metalurgica da Lagoa Lda v. Chefe do Servico da Conferencia final da Alfandega do Porto (1991) Eur. Comm.Rep. I–3277 (Case C–348/89).

5. Rheinmühlen–Düsseldorf v. Einfuhr-und Vorratsstelle für Getreide und Futtermittel (1974) Eur.Comm.Rep. 33. *But see* Campus Oil Ltd. v. Minister for Industry and Energy (1984) 1 Common Mkt.L.Rep. 479 (Irish Supreme Court, 1983) (Article 234 references not subject to interlocutory appeal under Irish law).

6. *Id.*

7. SA Chanel v. Cepeha Handels Maatschappij NV (1970) Eur.Comm.Rep. 404.

8. Rheinmühlen, *supra.*

9. Re Da Costa en Schaake (1963) Eur.Comm.Rep. 11.

10. Biogen Inc. v. Smithkline Beecham Biological S.A. (1996) Eur.Comm. Rep. I–717.

11. Rewe Zentralfinanz v. Landwirtschaftskammer Saarland (1976) Eur. Comm.Rep. 1989.

12. International Chemical Corp. v. Amministrazione delle Finanze (1983) Eur.Comm.Rep. 119; SpA Int'l Chemical Corp. v. Amministrazione delle Finanze dello Stato (1981) Eur.Comm.Rep. 1191.

one of the *invalidity* (not interpretation) of Union law. Such invalidity is ordinarily retrospective, nullifying EU law *ab initio*.[13] The Court of Justice has ruled that only it and not the national courts can determine the invalidity of an EU legal measure. The Court reasoned that divergent invalidity determinations could place the unity of the Union's legal order in jeopardy and detract from the general principle of legal certainty. However, national courts can declare EU legislation valid and proceed accordingly.[14]

There is a dispute as to whether the European Court can pronounce without request upon the effects of an invalid Union measure, *e.g.* whether monies paid previously can be recovered. The Court asserts the power to spell out the consequences of its invalidity rulings under Article 234.[15] It draws upon the analogy to Article 231 of the Treaty of Rome which conveys to the ECJ the power to determine the effects of decisions made in the context of Article 230 challenges to Council, Commission, Parliamentary or other EU action.[16] The highest French courts are split as to the duty to follow the Court's Article 234 rulings on the consequences of invalid Union law. The Cour de Cassation adheres, while the Conseil d'Etat rejects. The Conseil d'Etat limits adherence to ECJ rulings to the scope of the questions posed by the national courts. The Court's rulings on repayment in *Roquette* were treated as gratuitous and uncontrolling since not requested.[17] This dispute illustrates, more generally, the distinct tendency on the part of the European Court not to see itself confined by the limits of the questions posed by national forums under Article 234. Rarely, however, has such a hostile national response been received upon delivery of the ruling.

On questions of the validity of *national* laws under the EU legal regime, the lower courts retain complete discretion to use the Article 234 reference procedure, or to immediately set aside national laws under the supremacy doctrine.[18] Genuine disputes as to the compatibility of the national law of another member state may be referred to the European Court under Article 234. The Court will provide criteria for interpreting Union law so as to enable the referring court to solve the legal problem it faces. For example, in one decision on reference from a German court, by implication the European Court suggested that an Italian law conflicted with Directive 76/768 on cosmetics.[19] Nevertheless, the Court's prelimi-

---

13. Roquette Frères SA v. Hauptzollamt Geldern (1994) Eur.Comm.Rep. I–01445 (Case C–228/92). *See* Firma Foto–Frost v. Hauptzollamt Lübeck-Ost (1987) Eur.Comm.Rep. 4199.

14. *Id.*

15. Roquette v. French Customs (1980) Eur.Comm.Rep. 2917.

16. *See* § 3.7.

17. Conseil d'Etat (1985) Rec. des Décisions 233.

18. *See* § 2.12.

19. Kommanditgesellschaft Eau de Cologne et al. v. Provide SRI (1989) Eur. Comm.Rep. 3891.

nary ruling jurisdiction cannot be invoked through "sham litigation" where there is no genuine dispute before the national court, only a desire to challenge the validity of national law.[20] Purely hypothetical questions, and questions the ECJ believes are not connected to the underlying dispute, will not be answered by Court when responding under Article 234.[21] The Court of Justice has also begun to reject Article 234 references that fail to provide adequate factual and legal information to enable it to respond.

Mandatory References

In the early years of the European Community, lower courts and tribunals in the member states hesitated to invoke the preliminary ruling procedure of Article 234. In some cases, this was a matter of ignorance, in others a matter of national pride. Over the years, Article 234 references of EU law issues have risen dramatically. Today, they amount to about half of the Court's caseload. Article 234 references are undertaken not only out of need for advice, but also a growing sense of judicial cooperation in the Union. Absent such cooperation, there is a great risk that different interpretations of European law would proliferate among member state forums.

For the lower courts, Article 234 references are discretionary. For courts of last resort (no appeal as a matter of right), Article 234 *requires* a reference to the European Court except in interlocutory proceedings.[22] This requirement insures that the European Court will have the last and supreme word on EU legal issues. Thus, if a litigant is willing to exhaust his or her national judicial remedies, access to the European Court is supposed to be guaranteed. In many instances, this is exactly what happens. In others, the doctrine of "acte clair" has been invoked so as to avoid mandatory Article 234 references.

§ 3.5 Acte Clair

"Acte clair" originates in the French law. It posits that appeals need not be taken whenever the law and result in the case at hand are clear. Appeals in such circumstances are wasteful of judicial and litigant time and energy. The problem in the European Union context, of course, is that differences of opinion as to the clarity of EU law will often exist. If abused by national courts of last resort,

---

20. Foglia v. Novello (1980) Eur. Comm.Rep. 745; (1981) Eur.Comm.Rep. 3045.

21. *See* Wienand Meilicke v. ADV/ ORGA F.A. Meyer AG (1992) Eur. Comm.Rep. I–04871 (Case C–83/91); Manuel José Lourenço Dìiaz v. Director da Alfânndega do Porto (1992) Eur. Comm.Rep. I–04673 (Case C–343/90); Re der Weduwe (2002) Eur.Comm.Rep. I–11319 (Case C–153/00).

22. Hoffmann La–Roche v. Centrafarm (1977) Eur.Comm.Rep. 957.

acte clair could break rather than occasionally remove the linchpin of Article 234.

Entreprises Garoche Case

The *Entreprises Garoche* case provides a good example of French invocation of acte clair so as to totally avoid an Article 234 reference. A Dutch boat builder entered into a three-year exclusive dealing agreement with a French agent concerning France, Belgium, Switzerland, Monaco, and Corsica. The Dutch builder undertook to refrain from selling in these territories directly or indirectly through agents. Shortly thereafter he sold two boats through an Italian dealer to two customers domiciled in Monaco. The French agent sued for breach of the exclusive dealing contract. The Tribunal de Commerce de Paris awarded him damages.

The Cour d'Appel de Paris and then the Cour de Cassation held that the contract was void under Articles 81(1) and (2) (formerly 85) of the Treaty of Rome and not subject (for lack of notification to the Commission) to individual exemption under Article 81(3). Furthermore, the contract was outside the protection afforded by group exemption Regulation 67/67 because the isolation of national markets from other distributors resulted in high prices being charged by the French agent and hence did not allow consumers "a fair share of the resulting benefit." Thus the principle of the illegality under Article 81(1) of absolute territorial protection clauses prevailed.[1] Moreover, the direct effect of EU competition law in the French courts was not in doubt. The Dutch builder could rely on it as a matter of right.

None of these three French courts found it necessary to refer any of the issues in *Entreprises Garoche* to the European Court of Justice. Both the Tribunal de Commerce and the Cour d'Appel invoked the acte clair doctrine while noting that their decisions were subject to appeal and hence not mandatorily referable. The Cour de Cassation, from which no appeal lies under the French legal system, agreed that the dispute was fundamentally centered on an interpretation of Article 3 of Regulation 67/67. That Regulation was clear to the highest French court in light of a 1971 European Court of Justice opinion dealing with it. Consequently a "fresh interpretation" by way of reference in 1973 to the European Court was not required.[2] Although it is difficult to criticize the actual results of the *Garoche* case in the French courts, their application of acte clair illustrates how dependent European Union law is on national courts and national legal principles.

---

§ 3.5

1. *See* Chapter 7.

2. Entreprises Garoche v. Société Striker Boats (1973) 1974 Common Mkt. L.Rep. 469.

CILFIT Case

Despite an initial annoyance at French invocations of acte clair,[3] courts in other member states soon became converts. By 1982, when the European Court ruled definitively on the validity of this practice, it was faced with widespread but not particularly abusive utilization of acte clair. In *CILFIT*, the Italian Corte Suprema di Cassazione made a mandatory referral of the acte clair issue to the European Court. That is to say, the question it posed to the European Court was whether it was absolutely obliged to refer all issues of interpretation of EU law to the Court. The European Court deferentially incorporated acte clair into Union law as a gloss on the otherwise straightforward language of Article 234. In doing so, however, it was able to spell out the terms and conditions for its invocation:

> The correct application of Community law may be so obvious as to leave no scope for any reasonable doubt as to the manner in which the question raised is to be resolved. Before it comes to the conclusion that such is the case, the national court or tribunal must be convinced that the matter is equally obvious to the courts of the other Member States and to the Court of Justice. Only if those conditions are satisfied may the national court or tribunal refrain from submitting the question to the Court of Justice and take upon itself the responsibility for resolving it. . . .

> It must be borne in mind that Community legislation is drafted in several languages and that the different language versions are all equally authentic. An interpretation of a provision of Community law thus involves a comparison of the different language versions. . . . Even where the different language versions are entirely in accord with one another, Community law uses terminology which is peculiar to it. Furthermore, it must be emphasized that legal concepts do not necessarily have the same meaning in Community law and in the law of the various Member States.[4]

§ 3.6   Multiple Official Languages

In *CILFIT*, the European Court issues a reminder of the problems of language in interpreting European Union law. The Coal and Steel Treaty sought to avoid these problems by making French the only official language of that treaty.[1] Since the 2004

---

3.   *See especially* Re Société des Pé-troles Shell–Barre (1964) Common Mkt. L.Rep. 462 (Conseil d'Etat).

4.   CILFIT v. Ministro della Santa (1982) Eur.Comm.Rep. 3415.

§ 3.6

1.   1Article 100 of the Treaty of Paris.

enlargement, there are over 20 official EU languages. Each working language can be consulted on questions of interpretation. However, with Treaty of Rome terms (such as Article 234) it is important to remember that English was *not* an official language prior to 1973 when the British joined. Thus, with reference to older legal documents *and* the Treaty of Rome, French, German, Dutch or Italian versions are arguably more authoritative. The French version is considered the most authoritative of all because the Treaty of Rome was originally drafted in French. At a minimum, reference to different versions will promote greater understanding of European law. Attorneys practicing EU law routinely consult different language versions of European regulations, directives, decisions and treaties.

The European Court of Justice, when confronted with linguistic difficulties, has stressed the need to reconcile different official texts without giving preference to any one language.[2] Difficulties of this kind are minimized in the foreign policy arena (which operates outside the Treaty of Rome)[3] by using only English and French in the European Council. To the same effect, in Court of Justice or Court of First Instance proceedings, the plaintiff generally gets to choose the official language of the case unless the defendant is from or is a member state (in which case the language of that member state prevails). When Article 234 proceedings are involved, the language of the nation whose court or tribunal is making the reference is official. The official language of the case is used in the pleadings, documents and oral hearings.

The Court's decision will be published in all working Union languages but only the language of the case is authentic. By custom, French is the internal working language of the Court of Justice. This means that judgments are debated and drafted in French. All other versions are translations, even when French is not the language of the case. Parliament, the Commission and the Court in public session, on the other hand, are a veritable babble of languages with simultaneous translations occurring. There are over 200 different possible pairs of official languages.

§ 3.7 Articles 230 and 232—Challenging Regional Institutions

In *CILFIT*, the Court of Justice also warned against the transferability of legal concepts within the Union. Article 230 of the Treaty of Rome provides a good example of these kinds of problems.

Article 230 gives the Court the power to review the legality of acts of the Council of Ministers, Commission, European Central

---

2. Regina v. Bouchereau (1977) Eur. Comm.Rep. 425.   **3.** *See* Chapter 8.

Bank, acts jointly undertaken by the Parliament and Council, and acts of Parliament intended to produce legal effects on third parties. In unusual circumstances, individual acts of Parliament may also be challenged.[1] Acts which are merely preparatory, such as the commencement of a competition law investigation by the Commission, cannot be challenged.[2] To be challengeable, the "legal interests" of those under investigation must have been affected.[3] Member states, the Commission or Council, and directly concerned individuals may challenge regulations, directives or enforcement decisions on specified grounds. Prior to the Maastricht Treaty on European Union, Parliament had no express authority to challenge Council or Commission action under Article 230. Now it and the future European Central Bank may make Article 230 challenges for the purpose of protecting their prerogatives. No challenges may be brought against Council or Commission recommendations or opinions, but "soft" legal instruments (communications, instructions) that impose legal burdens or obligations can be challenged.

Challenging Acts

There are four grounds for challenging (often called "appealing") acts of Union institutions. These are specified in Article 230 and originate in French administrative law governing "action en recours pour excès de pouvoir." The same grounds apply to challenges under Article 230, which concern failures to act as required by the Treaty of Rome ("action en carence"). The four grounds are:

(1) lack of competence (*i.e., ultra vires,* or lack of jurisdiction or authority to act)[4];

(2) infringement of an essential procedure ("administrative due process")[5];

(3) infringement of the Treaty of Rome or any related rule of law (including general principles of EU law[6] and international law); and

(4) misuse of powers.

Each of these grounds for challenging acts or failures to act has been extensively and uniquely developed in the jurisprudence of the

§ 3.7

1. Les Verts v. Parliament (1986) Eur.Comm.Rep. 1339.

2. IBM Corp. v. Commission (1981) Eur.Comm.Rep. 2639.

3. *Id.*

4. *See* the discussion of "legal bases" for legislative acts in Section 2.9.

5. Article 253. *See, e.g.,* Transocean Marine Paint Assn. v. Commission,

(1974) Eur.Comm.Rep. 1063; Germany v. Commission (1963) Eur.Comm.Rep. 63.

6. *See, e.g.,* Bela–Mühle Josef Bergmann v. Grows–Farm GmbH (1977) Eur.Comm.Rep. 1211 (principle of equal treatment voids agricultural regulation). The general principles of Community law are discussed in Section 2.12.

European Court. For example, the term "misuse of powers" in Article 230 originated in the French administrative law concept of *détournement de pouvoir*. Research on and an understanding of French administrative law thus becomes important to Article 230.[7] Misuse of powers is a term of art in British administrative law which is narrower than the U.S. concept of abuse of administrative discretion. The original French concept is generally limited to situations of "subjective wrong" as when public institutions or personnel use their powers for personal benefit, such as to favor a relative or for financial gain. Thus the concept of *détournement de pouvoir* does not transfer easily from French into British or United States law and language. Moreover, as *CILFIT* suggests, the Court of Justice is entirely free to develop its own doctrine in this area independent of its French origins.[8]

Article 230 litigation must be brought within two months of the publication of the act that is being challenged or its notification to the appellant (in the absence of notice, two months from the day when that person had knowledge of it), as the case may be. Article 231 authorizes the Court to declare acts of Union institutions null and void if the appeal is well founded. This explains why Article 230 litigation is sometimes referred to as "actions for annulment." Regulations may be partially or fully annulled, or retain validity until replaced, at the Court's discretion.[9] Article 230 cannot be used to challenge the validity of national legislation.[10]

Challenging Failures To Act

Challenges for failure to act under Article 232 can only be brought if the relevant EU institution has first been called upon to act, and only if it fails to "define its position" within two months thereafter. This definition is not necessarily an act that can itself be challenged under Article 230.[11] The challenge for failure to act may then be brought in two additional months provided the institution's duty to act was owed to the plaintiff.[12] If an Article 232 challenge is well founded, Article 233 in essence authorizes the Court to order action by the institution. In both Article 230 and 232 litigation, Article 231 imposes a duty on the EU institution, as appropriate, to "take the necessary measures to comply with the judgment of the Court of Justice."

7. *See* ASSIDER v. High Authority (1954–56) Eur.Comm.Rep. 63 (Advocate–General's opinion).

8. *See* Guiffrida v. Council (1976) Eur.Comm.Rep. 1395 (sham competition for EC job is misuse of power).

9. Article 231(2); Commission v. Council (1989) Eur.Comm.Rep. 259.

10. Oleificio Borelli v. Commission (1992) Eur.Comm.Rep. I–06313 (Case C–97/91).

11. GEMA v. Commission (1979) Eur.Comm.Rep. 3173.

12. Lord Bethell v. Commission (1982) Eur.Comm.Rep. 2277.

§ 3.8 Articles 230 and 232–Standing to Challenge Regional Institutions, Pleas of Illegality

Standing Issues

One limitation on Article 230 actions before the Court concerns the appeal rights of natural and legal persons. Such persons may only challenge decisions addressed to them, or regulations or decisions addressed to others which are of "direct and individual concern" to them. The Court has for the most part narrowly construed the concept of "directly concerned individuals" so as to effectively limit the number of private challenges capable of being raised under Articles 230.[1] However, in the competition law area where private interests are at stake when individual exemptions are issued by the Commission,[2] the Court has been more liberal in its allowance of challenges by concerned third parties.[3] Jurisdiction to hear competition law challenges by private parties to Commission actions in the competition field has been transferred since 1989 to the European Court of First Instance. The selectively liberal approach to Article 230 standing has also been followed regarding Commission decisions on antidumping duties, internal state aids, countervailable subsidies applicable to Union imports, and illicit commercial practices of non-member nations.[4]

The "direct and individual concern" requirement and the four grounds for appeal found in Article 230 are repeated in Article 232 which governs the failure of an EU institution to undertake actions required by the Treaty of Rome or other Union law. Actions by individuals and enterprises under Article 232 challenge the failure to address an act to the appellant. They cannot be used to compel

---

§ 3.8

1. *See, e.g.,* Commission v. Jégo-Quéré & Cie SA, 2004 Eur.Comm.Rep. I–2365; Union de Pequenos Agricultores v. Council (2002) Eur.Comm.Rep. I–06677 (Case C–50/00); France v. Comafrica SpA and Dole (1999) Eur. Comm.Rep. I–185; Confédération Nationale des Producteurs de Fruits et Legumes (1962) Eur.Comm.Rep. 471; Calpak SpA v. Commission (1980) Eur. Comm.Rep.1949; Union Deutsche Lebensmittelwerke v. Commission (1987) Eur.Comm.Rep. 2265. *But see* Les Verts v. Parliament (1986) Eur.Comm.Rep. 1339 (political group has standing to challenge electoral budget decision).

2. *See* Chapter 7.

3. Metro SB–Grossmärkte GmbH & Co. KG v. Commission (1977) Eur. Comm.Rep. 1875 (complainant allowed to challenge).

4. Phillip Morris Holland v. Commission (1980) Eur.Comm.Rep. 2671 (prospective recipient of state aid may challenge denial of authorization by Commission); COFAZ SA v. Commission (1986) Eur.Comm.Rep. 391 (complainant allowed to challenge aid authorization by Commission); Allied Corp. v. Commission (1984) Eur.Comm.Rep. 1005 (named exporters may challenge imposition of dumping duties); Timex Corp. v. Council and Commission (1985) Eur.Comm.Rep. 849 (complainant may challenge antidumping decisions); FEDIOL v. Commission (1983) Eur. Comm.Rep. 2913 (complainant may challenge countervailing duties decision); FEDIOL v. Commission (1989) Eur.Comm.Rep. 1781 (Case 70/87) (complainant may challenge illicit commercial practices decision).

discretionary Commission acts, such as Article 226 prosecutions of member states or competition law prosecutions of anticompetitive airline practices.[5]

Pleas of Illegality

The expiration of the two months period for challenges to acts under Article 230 is not a firm statute of limitations. Article 184 allows any party to a proceeding where a regulation is in issue to plead the grounds for challenge specified in Article 230 in order to claim its inapplicability before the Court of Justice. This means, as a practical matter, that European Union regulations can be challenged at any time by what is called a "plea of illegality." Moreover, the European Court has extended this plea to directives, decisions and other acts of the Union institutions.[6] Private parties may thus wait until the implementation of Union law is of immediate concern to them without losing an ability to test the legality of that law. Pleas of illegality are frequently made in EU torts and contracts litigation, and can be made before national courts and tribunals which must refer such issues to the Court of Justice.[7] Pleas of illegality are not allowed if the complainant had standing to challenge the act of the Union under Article 230 but failed to do so in a timely manner.[8] Under this approach, it is unclear whether member states can plea illegality since they always have Article 230 standing.[9]

Institutional Litigation

Articles 230 and 232 have spawned an interesting series of institutional litigations. In these cases, the Council, Commission and Parliament end up suing each before the European Court of Justice. These suits reflect the struggle for power and influence among these institutions. One major limitation upon them had been the absence of a general authority for Parliamentary suits under Article 230 against Council or Commission acts.[10] Prior to the Nice Treaty of Treaty of 2003, such suits could only be filed only when Parliamentary legislative prerogatives were at stake.[11] The Nice Treaty removed that limitation.

5. Alfons Lütticke GmbH v. Commission (1966) Eur.Comm.Rep. 19; Lord Bethell v. Commission (1982) Eur. Comm.Rep. 2277.

6. Simmenthal v. Commission (1979) Eur.Comm.Rep. 777.

7. Universität Hamburg v. HZA Hamburg–Kehrwieder (1983) Eur. Comm.Rep. 2771; Foto Frost v. HZA Lubeck Ost (1987) Eur.Comm.Rep. 4199.

8. Simmenthal v. Commission (1977) Eur.Comm.Rep. 777.

9. *See* Italy v. Commission (1966) Eur.Comm.Rep. 389; Commission v. Belgium (1978) Eur.Comm.Rep. 1881.

10. European Parliament v. Council (1988) Eur.Comm.Rep. 5615 (Comitology).

11. European Parliament v. Council (1990) Eur.Comm.Rep. 2041 (Chernobyl). Article 173, Treaty of Rome as amended by TEU.

The Parliament is authorized by the Treaty of Rome to file Article 232 suits when the Council or Commission has failed to act. The Parliament successfully sued the Council over its failure to act in accordance with Treaty obligations to implement a Common Transport Policy.[12] The Council in turn has successfully sued the Parliament for excessive budgetary allocations.[13] The Commission has challenged the Council frequently before the European Court. Sometimes several institutions gang up on one. For example, the Commission (with Council and Parliamentary support) successfully challenged the European Central Bank's creation of an independent anti-fraud unit.[14] Some of its most important victories concern the proper "legal basis" for Community legislation and international agreements.[15]

Articles 230 and 232 also provide the member states with the means to challenge the Commission. This is the reverse of the type of litigation that flows from Article 226 prosecutions of member states by the Commission.[16] Member state challenges of legislative acts by the Council seem likely to rise as more qualified majority voting occurs, and the minority seeks legal redress.[17]

§ 3.9   Article 226—Commission Prosecutions of Member States

Article 226 authorizes the Commission (alone) to bring an action before the Court of Justice against member states that have failed to fulfill their obligations under the Treaty of Rome. This authority is reinforced by some basic normative rules of the Treaty. In Article 10, the member states undertake to adopt "all appropriate measures" to ensure the fulfillment of obligations arising out of the Treaty of Rome or resulting from action taken by the institutions of the Union. They "shall facilitate" achievement of its tasks and "shall abstain" from jeopardizing its objectives. These fundamental principles have frequently been the subject of litigation as the Commission seeks to enforce member state duties under European law. Although it has not yet done so, it appears that the Commission could prosecute a member state *court* for failure to

---

12. European Parliament v. Council (1985) Eur.Comm.Rep. 1513.

13. Council v. European Parliament (1986) Eur.Comm.Rep. 288.

14. Commission v. European Central Bank, 2003 Eur.Comm.Rep. I–1651.

15. Commission v. Council (1989) Eur.Comm.Rep. 1493 (GSP preferences); (1971) Eur.Comm.Rep. 263 (the *ERTA* decision).

16. *See, e.g.,* Germany v. Commission (1987) Eur.Comm.Rep. 3203 (lack of competence to act); Ireland v. Commission (1987) Eur.Comm.Rep. 5041 (violation of EU law); Netherlands v. Commission (1971) Eur.Comm.Rep. 639 (failure to act). The Council can likewise be challenged by the member states under Articles 230 and 232. *See* United Kingdom v. Council (1988) Eur. Comm.Rep. 855 (infringement of essential procedural requirement).

17. *See* Chapter 2.

fulfill its treaty obligations (*e.g.*, mandatory Article 234 references). Government passivity in the face of private conduct (angry French farmer blockades) creating obstacles to internal trade has been successfully prosecuted.[1] Informal promises to comply with EU regulations can be prosecuted, in this case repeatedly over decades against France.[2]

The Commission's prosecutorial powers under Article 226 must be distinguished from its ability in selected other circumstances to "directly" file actions against member states before the Court of Justice. Such direct actions do not involve the lengthy procedures described below in connection with Article 226 prosecutions. The Commission is authorized to sue the member states "directly" when they infringe Union rules on government subsidies to enterprises.[3] This can also be done when the member states "improperly" invoke Article 30 exceptions to single market legislation adopted by qualified majority voting in the Council of Ministers.[4]

Procedures and Penalties

Prior to commencing any Article 226 prosecutions before the Court of Justice, the Commission first delivers notice and the member state may submit a reply. Hundreds of such infringement notices are issued annually. The next stage involves issuance by the Commission of a reasoned opinion setting time limits for compliance. These time limits must be reasonable.[5] The member state can submit a reply if it wishes. When a member state claims to have conformed to the opinion within the stipulated time limits, the burden of proof shifts to the Commission to prove otherwise.[6] Negotiations may ensue at any time, and settlements frequently result. Almost 80 percent of all formal proceedings under Article 226 are settled.

If no settlement is reached, the Commission commences suit before the Court of Justice. Compliance after this point does not moot or remove the suit.[7] The most common type of Article 226 enforcement action actually filed with the Court of Justice concerns member state failures to implement directives. Constitutional, political or legal problems are unacceptable excuses for such failures.[8]

§ 3.9

1. *See* Commission v. France, 1997 Eur.Comm.Rep. I–6959. *See* Regulation 2679/98.

2. Commission v. France (1974) Eur. Comm.Rep. 359; Commission v. France (1996) Eur.Comm.Rep. I–1307 (French merchant seaman).

3. *See* Chapter 5.

4. *See* Chapter 4.

5. Commission v. Belgium (1988) Eur.Comm.Rep. 305.

6. Commission v. Italy (1973) Eur. Comm.Rep. 101; Commission v. Italy (1987) 3 Common Mkt.L.Rep. 483.

7. Commission v. Italy (1988) 2 Common Mkt.L.Rep. 951.

8. Commission v. Italy (1979) Eur. Comm.Rep. 771; Commission v. Belgium (1980) Eur.Comm.Rep. 1473 (Type approval directives).

Nor is the failure of other member states to implement the directive.[9] All Article 226 prosecutions are discretionary with the Commission and cannot be forced by individual complaints.[10]

Article 228 specifically requires member states to take the measures necessary to remedy failures identified by the Court in Article 226 proceedings. Prior to 1993, there were no obvious means by which the Court could enforce its judgments under Article 226 against member states. This contrasted with the power of the Court and the Commission in some areas of Community law to levy fines and penalties against individuals and corporations. Such fines and penalties can be collected in judgments enforced in the national courts.[11] To compel a member state to follow Union law, the Commission had little alternative but to bring yet another enforcement proceeding for determination before the Court. It has actually done this on occasion.[12] However, the Maastricht Treaty on European Union authorized the ECJ to levy fines and penalties against member states that do not take the measures necessary to remedy their Treaty of Rome failures.[13] Private litigants may also remedy member state failures, functioning in effect as attorneys general of Union law.[14]

The unwillingness of member states to carry out Court rulings under Article 226 is a problem. It could test the very fabric of the Rome Treaty. In 2002, for example, the Commission commenced 1604 infringement proceedings against member states. An additional enforcement option would be to allow the Court to authorize the withholding of EU subsidies and benefits from nonconforming states. Sanctions of this kind were possible under the Coal and Steel Treaty by joint Commission and Council action.[15]

Article 239 allows member states to submit (by special agreement) disputes concerning the Treaty of Rome to the European Court. In Article 292, the member states have agreed not to submit such disputes to any method of settlement other than those of the Treaty. Article 227 authorizes member states to prosecute each other before the European Court for failure to fulfill Treaty obligations. For diplomatic and institutional reasons, these options are

---

9. Commission v. France (1979) Eur. Comm.Rep. 2729; Commission v. Blanguernon (1990) Eur.Comm.Rep. I–00083 (Case C–38/89).

10. Alfons Lütticke GmbH v. Commission (1966) Eur.Comm.Rep. 19.

11. Article 256, Treaty of Rome.

12. Commission v. Italy (1972) Eur. Comm.Rep. 527; Commission v. France (1979) Eur.Comm.Rep. 2729; Commis-

sion v. Italy (1993) Eur.Comm.Rep. I–00191 (Case C–101/91).

13. See Commission v. Greece (2000) Eur.Comm.Rep. I–5047 (rubbish tip II).

14. See Minister for Fisheries v. Schoenenberg (1978) Eur.Comm.Rep. 473 (Irish law invalid); Meijer v. Department of Trade (1979) Eur.Comm.Rep. 1387 (British law invalid).

15. See Article 88 of Treaty of Paris.

almost never pursued.[16] The preferred approach is to persuasively complain to the Commission and then allow it to commence an Article 226 prosecution. Article 227 supports this approach by mandating a cooling off period of three months during which the Commission considers the arguments of both member states and issues a reasoned opinion.

§ 3.10   Contract and Tort Litigation—Court of First Instance

Article 281 of the Treaty of Rome provides that the European Community (not the European Union) is a legal person. As such, it can sue and be sued like most corporations or governments. These disputes can involve employees of the Community, parties with whom it has contracted and those who are victims of its negligence or other tortious behavior.

The Treaty of Rome conveys exclusive jurisdiction to the Court of Justice over employment and noncontractual liability disputes.[1] It also can function as an arbitrator pursuant to dispute settlement clauses of contracts.[2] Contract disputes involving the Community may otherwise be entertained in the national courts.[3] The contractual liability is governed by the law applicable to the contract in question.[4]

Court of First Instance

Much of the work of the Court of Justice in employment and noncontractual liability litigation is now handled by the European Court of First Instance (CFI). This court was authorized by 1987 Single European Act amendments to the Treaty of Rome found in Article 225. The CFI is "attached" to the European Court of Justice and its jurisdiction is generally limited to direct actions or proceedings by individuals or legal persons. Thus the Court of First Instance cannot hear Article 226 prosecutions of member states by the Commission, Article 230 references of EU legal issues from national courts, nor Article 230 or 232 challenges to EU institutional acts or failures to act when these are initiated by member states or Union institutions. It can hear such challenges and related "pleas of illegality" when they are privately initiated, for example, in the business competition law area.[5]

---

16. *But see* Ireland v. France (1977) Case 58/77 (withdrawn); France v. United Kingdom (1979) Eur.Comm.Rep. 2923 (fisheries dispute).

§ 3.10

1. Articles 235 and 236, Treaty of Rome.

2. Article 238, Treaty of Rome.

3. Article 240, Treaty of Rome.

4. Article 288, Treaty of Rome.

5. *See* Chapter 7.

In 1993, the Council extended the jurisdiction of the CFI to all direct actions brought by natural or legal persons except antidumping cases.[6] In 1994, antidumping and countervailing duty cases were also brought within the scope of the jurisdiction of the CFI. The CFI has additionally been granted jurisdiction over Community trademark disputes arising out of the Office for Harmonization in the Internal Market (OHIM). It is widely perceived that the CFI is now overloaded, and the Nice Treaty anticipates an offloading of staff and perhaps other areas to specialized "judicial panels," for which the CFI would function as an appeals court.

The purpose, in general, behind creation of the Court of First Instance (CFI) was to relieve the Court of Justice of some of its caseload. It commenced doing this in November of 1989. However, there is a right of appeal on points of law from the CFI to the Court of Justice. Article 51 of the Council Decision establishing the CFI indicates that such appeals lie on the grounds of lack of competence, procedural failures that adversely affect the appellants' interests, and infringement of Union law by the CFI. Any failure by the CFI to follow prior ECJ decisions could amount to such an infringement. To distinguish between the judgments of these Union courts, some law reporters now prefix Court of Justice case numbers with a "C" (Case C–213/89) (Court) and Court of First Instance cases with a "T" (Case T–81/90) (Tribunal). In the official European Court Reports, ECJ judgment page numbers are preceded by "I-." CFI judgment page numbers are preceded by "II-."

Noncontractual Liability

The Court of First Instance is partially heir to an interesting body of law on noncontractual (tort) liability created by the Court of Justice. In this area, the Court's role as a law-maker was fully anticipated by the Treaty of Rome. Article 288 provides that the noncontractual liability of the European Community is governed by the "general principles common to the laws of the member states." Under these principles, the Community is obliged to "make good any damage caused by its institutions or servants in the performance of their duties." For example, the negligent disclosure by the Commission of the identity of an informant who was a former employee of a company subject to EU competition law sanctions was an actionable tort.[7] In this case, a Swiss informant was arrested, held in solitary confinement, interrogated, and convicted under Swiss law for economic espionage. While in prison, his wife was interrogated by Swiss police officers and then committed suicide.

6. Council Decision 93/350, O.J. 1993 L144/21.

7. Adams v. Commission (1985) Eur. Comm.Rep. 3539. *See* Article 214 of the

Treaty of Rome creating an EU duty of confidentiality.

The European Court of Justice, and now the Court of First Instance when damages are sought in litigation properly before it, has had to determine just what general principles of noncontractual liability are common to the laws of the member states. At first, of course, there were only six civil law states to consider. Now there are twelve, including two common law jurisdictions. The Court of Justice has ruled that Article 288 does not require adherence to the highest common denominator of liability law in the member states. Rather, the Court's duty is to track down in the national laws the elements or measures necessary to create liability principles which are fair and viable.[8] Such principles can include no-fault under the EC and EURATOM treaties.[9]

It is now generally recognized that the Community is liable in noncontractual cases whenever its tortious conduct causes actual damages.[10] Such conduct includes faults of its officers and agents committed within the scope of their duties, including negligence, bad faith, and intentional misconduct. Drawing from French administrative law, the Court has also recognized torts resembling "faute de service." These liabilities occur when the Community fails to function in the reasonably efficient manner expected of a well run government even if such a fault cannot be traced to negligence or misconduct by specific officials.[11]

Tortious conduct giving rise to liability also includes unlawful legal measures, *e.g.*, EU regulations and directives, and unlawful failures to adopt such measures. The "plea of illegality" is used to challenge such activities. At first, the Court of Justice held that damages actions on these bases could only be pursued if successful challenges had been previously undertaken under Articles 230 or 232.[12] In a good demonstration of its willingness to reverse itself, the Court has since held the opposite.[13] Similarly, private parties need not challenge the validity of EU acts in national litigation prior to seeking damages relief before the Court. Here again the Court of Justice reversed its initial ruling to the contrary in the interest of the "proper administration of justice . . . and procedural efficiency."[14]

---

8. Plaumann & Co. v. Commission (1963) Eur.Comm.Rep. 95.

9. *See* Article 40 of the Treaty of Paris mandating a finding of fault in coal and steel cases.

10. Alfons Lütticke GmbH v. Commission (1971) Eur.Comm.Rep. 325.

11. *See* Compagnie Continentale France v. Council (1975) Eur. Comm.Rep. 117.

12. Plaumann & Co. v. Commission (1963) Eur.Comm.Rep. 95.

13. Alfons Lütticke, supra; Aktien–Zuckerfabrik Schöppenstedt v. Council (1971) Eur.Comm.Rep. 975.

14. Merkur–Aussenhandels GmbH v. Commission (1973) Eur.Comm.Rep. 1055.

Nevertheless, the chances of obtaining individual damages relief for legislative acts of the European Union are not great. The Court has limited this possibility to manifest and grave disregard by EU institutions of the limits of their powers amounting to a breach of superior rules of law protecting individuals.[15] This is known as the "*Schöppenstedt* formula." And when directives are implemented at the national level in ways which cause damages, national remedies (if available and effective) must first be pursued.[16] Directives that partly harmonize an area of law intended for total harmonization are not actionable even if discriminatory.[17]

§ 3.11 Judicial Practice and Procedure

The structure and procedures of the European Court of Justice (ECJ) and the Court of First Instance (CFI) are quite similar. Each presently has, for example, 25 (27 in 2007) judges who serve six-year renewable terms upon appointment by the member states acting in common accord. There is one judge from each member state, plus (traditionally when an odd number was required) an additional judge who rotates from the five largest member states. The Court of First Instance does not, however, have Advocates–General (discussed below) appointed to it, although members of the Court may serve in that role. Moreover, the CFI only sits in six chambers of three to five judges. The Court of Justice is also divided into chambers, but may sit *en banc* or as a "grand chamber" of 11 judges when cases are brought before it by member states or Union institutions, and in many Article 234 preliminary rulings. Some case reporters now identify the Court's opinions by chamber number. To an American, the Court's most distinguishing features are its emphasis on written (versus oral) procedures, the dominance of the Court (not the parties) over development of the evidence, and the absence of dissenting opinions.

Proceedings

The Protocol on the Statute of the Court of Justice annexed to the Treaty of Rome and the Courts' Rules of Procedure (approved by the Council) establish a two-part proceeding. The written part commences with an application to the Court's registrar and designation of an agent or legal representative. This designation must occur. In other words, litigants may not represent themselves before the Court. Any lawyer entitled to practice before a national

15. Bayerische HNL Vermehrungsbetriebe GmbH & Co. KG v. Council and Commission (1978) Eur.Comm.Rep. 1209; Amylum NV v. Council and Commission (1979) Eur.Comm.Rep. 3497.

16. Krohn & Co. Import–Export GmbH v. Commission (1986) Eur.

Comm.Rep. 753; Asteris AE + Ors v. Hellenic Republic (1990) Eur. Comm.Rep. 5515.

17. Les Assurances du Crédit S.A. v. Council and Commission (1991) Eur. Comm.Rep. I–01799 (Case C–63/89).

court of a member state may act before the Court of Justice or Court of First Instance. The application serves as a "complaint" for notice purposes and thereby limits (in most cases) the issues and evidence that can be raised in the proceeding. Its filing also triggers the assignment of a reporting judge (juge rapporteur) and an Advocate–General to the case. The fact of the application and a summary of the issues presented is published in the Official Journal.

The application is also sent to the respondent who has one month to file a written "defense." Plaintiff may then reply, to which the defendant may submit a rejoinder. All of these written submissions to the court resemble full evidentiary and legal briefs more than pleadings. When the Article 234 preliminary ruling procedure is being used, the parties, member states, the Commission and (where appropriate) the Council may submit written briefs to the Court. The Parliament does not appear to have this right of submission, but the member states and the EU institutions (including Parliament) always have a right to intervene in cases before the Court. Individuals and enterprises with an interest in the litigation have the same right. Trade and professional associations, consumer groups and unions have been particularly active as intervenors.

At the discretion of the Court, a preliminary inquiry may be held. The Court (typically acting through the reporting judge) can pose questions to the litigants. The role of a court in posing questions is part of the civil law tradition which predominates on the Court. It is a procedure that most common law students familiar with a more adversarial system will find a bit unusual. The Court also has the power to examine witnesses, call experts and generally develop the evidence before it. Limited rights of cross-examination are allowed to counsel when this occurs.

The second part of the proceeding before the Court is oral. The Court first hears the views of the reporting judge in charge of the case and then counsel for both sides. At the end of the oral procedure, the Court of Justice hears the *Advocate–General,* a special lawyer employed by the Union to analyze and evaluate all cases before the Court and give public opinions on the proper result under EU law. Americans are typically unfamiliar with the role of an Advocate–General since there is no parallel in United States procedure. The closest parallel is the French Commissaire du Gouvernement at the Conseil d'Etat. The Advocate–General does not represent anyone and is a kind of permanent *amicus curiae* on behalf of justice.

There are presently nine Advocates–General (AG) appointed for six-year terms to the Court of Justice by the member states acting in common accord. Four of the AG come from the largest member states, and the others "represent" the remaining states. Their opinions are often much more informative than those of the Court in any given case. Whereas the Advocate–General is willing to spin out various hypotheticals and consider the broader ramifications of the legal principles at issue, the Court tends to write its opinions in a terse and summary fashion. It should be stressed that lawyers working with EU law commonly use the opinions of the Advocate–General in their practice to forecast future developments and to better understand the judgments issued by the Court. Some of the most controversial cases in European Union law have involved instances where the Court has declined to agree with the opinions of the Advocate–General.[1]

Judgments

The Court's judgment is drafted in French by the reporting judge. This draft is then discussed by the full court or chamber. The Court's decision is rendered *without dissent* in the language of the case. The absence of dissenting opinions shelters the judges from nationalistic pressures and critics. But it also makes analysis of opinions and projection of trends in the case law more difficult.

Costs are normally borne by the losing party. Costs, for these purposes, generally include the Court's expenses, witnesses and experts, travel and subsistence of the parties to the Court's proceedings, and reasonable legal fees.[2] The Court's assessment powers on costs are wide, and substantial litigation over costs has ensued. However, most litigation results in a settlement agreement as between the parties on payment of costs. The loser must also pay the costs of intervenors who have supported the successful litigant.[3] The Court may make cash legal aid awards in appropriate cases and in the absence of national legal aid.[4]

Litigation brought before the Court of Justice does not automatically suspend the act being challenged. It continues to operate pending the Court's decision. The Court (*i.e.,* the President of the Court) may order suspension when it considers this necessary, along with any "interim measures." This is done only in exceptional circumstances of harm to the applicant.[5] Pecuniary judgments of

---

§ 3.11

1. *See* Van Gend en Loos v. Nederlandse Administratie der Belastingen (1963) Eur.Comm.Rep. 1; Consten and Grundig v. Commission (1966) Eur. Comm.Rep. 299; Defrenne v. Sabena (1976) Eur.Comm.Rep. 455; Commission v. Council (1971) Eur.Comm.Rep. 263 (*ERTA*).

2. *See* Article 72 of the ECJ Rules of Procedure.

3. Hoogovens v. High Authority (1962) Eur.Comm.Rep. 253.

4. Lee v. Minister for Agriculture (1980) Eur.Comm.Rep. 1495 (Article 234 reference in a civil case from Ireland).

5. United Kingdom v. Commission (1996) Eur.Comm.Rep. I–3903 (interim ban on British beef upheld in "mad cow" crisis); NTN Toyo Bearing Co. Ltd. v. Council (1977) Eur.Comm.Rep. 1721;

the Court against persons (not member states) are enforceable under the terms of Article 256 of the Treaty of Rome. Once authenticated, the Court's judgment is enforced according to the ordinary judgment-creditor procedures of the member state where it is executed.

The Rules of Procedure for the Court of Justice permit revisions of Court judgments.[6] No revision can occur more than ten years after judgment, and requests for revisions must be submitted within three months of the knowledge of new facts of decisive importance justifying revision. Such facts must have originally been unknown to both the Court and the litigant.[7] Moreover, if the information could have been easily obtained during litigation, no revision of judgment will be allowed.[8]

Article 102 of the Rules of Procedure permits requests for interpretation of Court judgments when there are "difficulties" as to its meaning or scope. Such requests can be made by the parties or any Union institution with an interest in the judgment. They are granted when the effect of the judgment on the parties is uncertain, not when the consequences for others are at issue.[9] Finally, third parties may seek reconsideration of Court judgments which will cause them damage. Requests for reconsideration must be made within two months of judgment, and the applicant must demonstrate no prior notice of the litigation.[10]

§ 3.12   Jurisdiction and Enforcement of Civil and Commercial Judgments

The 1968 Jurisdiction and Enforcement of Judgments Convention (Brussels Convention) regulates jurisdiction among the member states and facilitates enforcement of civil and commercial judgments of the courts of the member states in each others' courts. In other words, the Brussels Convention introduces "full faith and credit" principles to the European Union. Much of its substance is reproduced in the Lugano Convention on Jurisdiction and Enforcement of Judgments in Civil and Commercial Matters (1988). The Lugano Convention extends these principles to all ratifying EFTA countries, such as Switzerland.

Commission v. Ireland (1977) Eur. Comm.Rep. 1411.

6. Articles 92–94.

7. Acciaieria di Roma v. High Authority (1960) Eur.Comm.Rep. 165.

8. Fonderie Acciarierie Giovanni Mandelli v. Commission (1971) Eur. Comm.Rep. 1.

9. High Authority and European Court v. Collotti (1965) Eur.Comm.Rep. 275.

10. Re Breedband (1962) Eur. Comm.Rep. 145.

The Brussels Convention was converted for all but Denmark from an international agreement into legislation by Council Regulation 44/2001. A number of amendments were added at that time. In addition, Regulation 1348/2000 establishes speedy and reliable means for service of civil or commercial process. Regulation 1206/2001 facilitates the cross-border taking of evidence in civil and commercial matters. These regulations take the 1965 and 1970 Hague Conventions as their inspirations.

It is important to remember that the Brussels Convention and Regulation 44/2001 govern jurisdiction as well as enforcement of national court judgments. This means, as a practical matter, that it applies from the outset of the litigation once a jurisdictional challenge is raised and not just after judgment has been reached. Interpreting the Brussels Convention and the Regulation thus initially is the task of national trial courts. One elementary issue is the scope of applicability of the Convention to "civil and commercial matters."[1] The Convention does not define these terms, except by exclusion. Most revenue, customs and administrative litigation along with legal status, capacity, matrimonial property, wills, succession, bankruptcy, social security and arbitration matters are not covered by the Brussels Convention. In 1998, however, a separate EU Convention on Jurisdiction, Recognition and Enforcement of Judgments in Matrimonial matters was concluded.[2] In 2000, Regulation 1346/2000 established jurisdictional, procedural and recognition rules for insolvency proceedings.

The ECJ has adopted an independent approach to the meaning of civil and commercial matters drawn from the Convention's purposes and the general principles of relevant law found in the member states. Special attention has been given to the original six civil law jurisdictions and their distinction between public and private law. Thus, most exercises of public authority by administrative bodies do not fall within the Convention.[3] Marital dissolution property settlements are not covered by the Convention,[4] but suits against estates by third parties over title to realty are.[5] Employment contracts fall within its scope.[6] The Convention's rules of jurisdiction thus mandate classification of the litigation in terms of the exclusions to civil and commercial matters.

§ 3.12

1. Brussels Convention, Article 1.

2. O.J. C221 (July 16, 1998).

3. *See* Lufttransportunternehmen GmbH & Co. K.G. v. Eurocontrol (1976) Eur.Comm.Rep. 1541 (recovery of route charges); Netherlands v. Rüffer (1980) Eur.Comm.Rep. 3807.

4. de Cavel v. de Cavel (1979) Eur. Comm.Rep. 1055.

5. CHW v. GJH (1982) Eur. Comm.Rep. 1189.

6. Sanicentral v. Collin (1979) Eur. Comm.Rep. 3423.

Jurisdiction

The Brussels Convention and Regulation 44/2001 apply to all persons who are domiciled in a member state even if they are not citizens thereof. Thus, a United States-owned subsidiary incorporated in an EU state benefits from the Convention whereas its parent would not. This coverage is important regarding the application of so-called "exorbitant jurisdiction" (below) and enforcement of judgments derived therefrom which will *not* apply to the subsidiary but will apply to the parent. Furthermore, generally speaking, defendants are to be sued where they are domiciled. The concept of "domicile" is thus critical. As the Convention does not define it, this is left to national law. National courts must be satisfied that jurisdiction is taken in accordance with the Convention.[7] Co-defendants may be sued in non-domiciliary jurisdictions so closely connected that expediency requires suit to avoid the risk of irreconcilable judgments.[8]

Persons may be sued in forums outside their state of domicile only if the Convention/Regulation so provides. It is unclear whether this approach effectively negates the British tradition of *forum non conveniens*. The Convention provides for a number of special jurisdictions as alternatives to domicile. Contract disputes can ordinarily be litigated where the "place" of performance of the obligation occurs as determined by the law controlling the contract.[9] This includes disputes as to the existence of contracts.[10] Regulation 44/2001 replacing the Brussels Convention renders the place of performance of the obligation as that agreed, or in the case of sale of goods, the place of delivery of the goods, or in the case of provision of services, the place of provision. Special new rules govern employment contracts and favor employees.[11]Torts may be litigated at the place where the event or damage occurred.[12] This has been construed to mean either the place where the defendant acted (*e.g.*, manufactured a product) or where the injury was suffered.

7. Group Josi Reinsurance Company SA v. Universal General Insurance Co (2000) Eur.Comm.Rep. I–5925; Duijnstee v. Goderbauer (1983) Eur.Comm.Rep. 3663. *See* Brussels Convention, Article 19.

8. Regulation 44/2001, Article 6.

9. Industrie Tessilli Italiana Como v. Dunlop A.G. (1976) Eur.Comm.Rep. 1473. *See also* Ivenel v. Schwab (1982) Eur.Comm.Rep. 1891 (commercial agency contracts also where work performed) and Leathertex v. Bodetex (1999) Eur. Comm.Rep. I–6747 (commercial agency)

10. Effer v. Kantner (1982) Eur. Comm.Rep. 825.

11. Regulaton 44/2001, Articles 18–21; *See* Mulrox IBC Ltd. V. Hendrick Geels (1993) Eur.Comm.Rep. I–4075 (employment contract place of performance is where employee works).

12. Dumez France SA and Tacoba SARL v. Hessiche Landesbank, (1990) Eur.Comm.Rep. I–49; Handelskerij G.J. Bier B.V. v. Mines de Potasse d'Alsace (1976) Eur.Comm.Rep. 1735; Bier B.V. v. Mines de Potasse d'Alsace SA (1976) Eur.Comm.Rep. 1735.

The contract rules of the Brussels Convention does not apply to damages' actions between manufacturers and purchasers of their products with whom they have no privity of contract, even when the chain of sale is through wholly-owned subsidiaries.[13] Such actions are ordinarily governed by the rules applicable to noncontractual (tortious) liability. If there are several contractual obligations in question, the national court must distinguish between principal and secondary obligations. In one case, a German architect sued a Dutch client over fees for plans for construction of buildings located in Germany. The principal obligation at issue was payment, not the plans or construction, which could be pursued in the courts of the Netherlands where the fees were to be paid. However, employment and consumer contracts come under special provisions designed to protect the weaker party. For example, the focus may be upon the place of work and not the place of the payment obligation when that would favor employees.

Civil damages or restitution flowing from criminal acts are to be litigated in the forum of the crime. Cases involving branches, agencies or other establishments may be pursued where the branch, agency or other establishment is located or in the domicile of the principal. The mere appointment of a commercial agent does not appear to trigger this rule.[14] Suits for recovery of family and other support obligations ("maintenance") may be brought where the creditor is domiciled or "habitually resident," another undefined term.[15] Additional Convention/Regulation rules for jurisdiction which operate as alternatives to the general rule of suit where the defendant is domiciled have been created for trusts, admiralty, insurance (policy-holder, insured and beneficiary domicile options)[16] and consumer contracts (consumer domicile). The rules on jurisdiction favor only ordinary consumers, not business consumers.[17] Consumers, for these purposes, are economically weaker and less experienced private persons not engaged in commercial or professional activities. A German company trading currency futures could not, therefore, benefit from the consumer domicile option of the Brussels Convention in its suit against a New York broker.[18]

In a few areas, the Brussels Convention and Regulation 44/2001 convey exclusive jurisdiction to specified courts regardless

---

13. Jacob Handle & Co. GmbH v. Traitements Mécano-chimiques des Surfaces (1992) Eur.Comm.Rep. I–03967 (Case C–26/91).

14. Blanckaert v. Willems & Trost (1981) Eur.Comm.Rep. 819.

15. See Delvaux v. Commission (1976) Eur.Comm.Rep. 167.

16. Regulation 44/2001, Article 9(1).

17. Société Bertrand v. Paul Ott KG (1978) Eur.Comm.Rep. 1431.

18. Shearson Lehmann Hutton Inc. v. TUB Treuhandgesellschaft für Vermögenverwaltungs und Beteiligungen mbH (1993) Eur.Comm.Rep. I–139 (Case C–89/91).

of domicile or party agreement on choice of forum.[19] These concern real property, company validity, public register, intellectual property validity, and enforcement of judgment litigations. As exceptions to the general rule, they have been narrowly construed. For example, although disputes between landlords and tenants (including unpaid rent)[20] are treated as subject to exclusive jurisdictional rules under the Convention, disputes between tenants and sub-tenants are not.[21]

The Brussels Convention and Regulation 44/2001 deny enforcement by EU domiciliaries against EU domiciliaries of certain judgments deemed to be based on "exorbitant jurisdiction" (*e.g.* jurisdiction based solely on citizenship or asset-based *in personam* jurisdiction). But, in a discriminatory measure of importance, it permits EU domiciliaries to enforce judgments based upon exorbitant jurisdiction against non-EU domiciliaries.[22] Thus, a North American trader with assets somewhere in the Union could find itself at the wrong end of such discrimination. Other grounds for denial of enforcement of a judgment that is subject to the Brussels Convention include public policy, violation of defendant's procedural rights (service, notice), and the existence of an irreconcilable judgment of the enforcement court or another court (even one of a nation not party to the Brussels Convention).

Article 21 of the Brussels Convention provides that when the same cause of action is being litigated before the courts of two member states, the second court to be seised with litigation must stay or dismiss the proceeding pending resolution of the jurisdiction of the first court seised. This is the case even if the defendant is not domiciled in a member state, such as when the defendant is a U.S. insurance carrier.[23] Likewise, even a court designated by the parties must await resolution of the first court's jurisdiction.[24] It is in this sense that the doctrine of *forum non conveniens* is said to be precluded by the Brussels Convention.

Party Autonomy

Article 17 of the Brussels Convention affirms party autonomy to choose in writing a dispute settlement forum. This freedom does not apply regarding the insurance, consumer contract and exclusive jurisdiction areas. The Convention's affirmation of party autonomy

19. Brussels Convention Article 16; Regulation 44/2001, Article 22.

20. Rösler v. Rottwinckel (1985) Eur.Comm.Rep. 99 (Case 241/83).

21. Sanders v. van der Putte (1977) Eur.Comm.Rep. 2383. *See* Dansommer A/S v. Götz (2000) Eur.Comm.Rep. I–393 (tour operator and tenancy).

22. *See* Article 28(1), Brussels Convention.

23. Overseas Union Insurance v. New Hampshire Insurance (1991) Eur. Comm.Rep.I–03317 (Case C–351/89).

24. Erich Gasser GmbH v. MISAT (2003) Eur.Comm.Rep. I–00000 (Case C–116/02).

will override national rules contrary to such autonomy, even in the employment area. Article 17 has been construed rather narrowly and party awareness and appreciation of the significance of choice of forum clauses must be proved. There must be, in other words, informed written consent. Company statute clauses adopted by shareholders designating jurisdiction can meet these criteria.[25] However, when international trade contracts are involved, compliance with custom and practice is sufficient to enforce the choice of forum.[26] The parties may avoid the stringency of Article 17 by designating determinative issues (*e.g.,* place of performance of contracts) in their contract. The chosen place of performance will have jurisdiction.[27] Such choices notwithstanding, if a party appears in another forum other than to contest jurisdiction, acquiescence to that forum will allow the litigation to proceed.[28]

Article 17 permits parties from outside the Community to join in the selection of a member state court without fear of an exercise of jurisdiction elsewhere (*e.g.,* the place of performance) in the EU. Article 17 also provides that if any judicial forum selection was concluded for the benefit of only one party, *that* party may sue elsewhere. The idea of permitting the sole beneficiary of what some might see as an adhesion clause to escape from its forum selection obligations has not been found compelling.[29]

Recognition and Enforcement

The regulatory regime governing jurisdiction established in the Brussels Convention and Regulation 44/2001 makes recognition and enforcement of subsequent civil and commercial judgments in the EU nearly automatic. This is true for money and non-money judgments, settlements and authentications. Moreover, recognition and enforcement of national court judgments falling within the jurisdictional scope of the Convention occurs regardless of the nationality or domicile of the parties. To facilitate use of the Convention, *full* legal aid in the enforcing state must be given to anyone who obtained full *or* partial legal aid in the source state.

25. Powell Duffryn v. Wolfgang Peteriet (1992) Eur.Comm.Rep. I–01745 (Case 214/89).

26. *See, e.g.,* Estasis Solotti v. RuWa (1976) Eur.Comm.Rep. 1831 (placement of choice of court clause on reverse side of offer insufficient); Galeries Segoura SPRL v. Rahim Bonakdarian (1976) Eur.Comm.Rep. 1851; MS Tilly Russ (1984) Eur.Comm.Rep. 02417 (Case 71/83); Berghoefer GmbH v. ASA SA (1986) Eur.Comm.Rep. 02699 (Case 221/84).

27. Zelger v. Salinitri (1980) Eur. Comm.Rep. 89.

28. Elefanten Schuh v. Jacqmain (1981) Eur.Comm.Rep. 1671; Spitzley v. Sommer (1985) Eur.Comm.Rep. 00787 (Case 48/84).

29. *See* Anterist v. Crédit Lyonnais (1986) Eur.Comm.Rep. 1951 (selection of bank's domicile court insufficient proof of intent to benefit bank exclusively).

Recognition (but not enforcement)[30] of the judgment is possible as soon as it is enforceable in its state of origin, even if appeals or further review are pending or available.

The *ex parte* enforcement procedures of the Brussels Convention and Regulation 44/2001 are exclusive and must be undertaken "without delay."[31] This means that no collateral attack by the parties to the judgment may occur in another EU state and that the successful plaintiff must adhere to Convention procedures even if there are alternative means at less cost of obtaining enforcement.[32] National courts are prohibited from charging a sliding scale of fees.

To obtain enforcement, the applicant need only provide supporting documentation on the original judgment and its enforceability under the law of the state of origin and, if required, translations. At this stage, the defendant is not summoned to appear. The decision on grant or denial of recognition and enforcement must be notified to the defendant and can be appealed by the losing party. The defendant may also appeal on points of law. But there is a presumption of recognition for judgments falling within the Convention which can only be rebutted on the grounds set out in Articles 27 and 28. The enforcing court may issue whatever interim protective relief measures it deems necessary to secure assets while appeals are pending even if such protection is not generally available under national law.[33]

There are five grounds under Articles 27 and 28 (as modified by Regualtion 44/2001) for refusing full or partial recognition and enforcement of judgments under the Brussels Convention. These are reviewed *ex parte* by the enforcing court, subject to appeal, and include:

- Public policy (but not as applied to Convention's jurisdictional rules).[34]

- Protection of defendants' rights (*e.g.* service, opportunity to be heard and adequate time to prepare a defense).[35]

- Irreconcilable conflict with an existing judgment in the enforcing state.

30. *See* Industrial Diamond Supplies v. Riva (1977) Eur.Comm.Rep. 2175.

31. Brussels Convention, Article 34.

32. DeWolf v. Cox (1976) Eur. Comm.Rep. 1759.

33. Capeloni and Anor v. Pelkmans (1985) Eur.Comm.Rep. 3147 (Case 119/84).

34. Rohr v. Ossberger (1981) Eur. Comm.Rep. 2431. *See* Krombach v. Bam-bersk (2000) Eur.Comm.Rep. I–1935 (denial of fair hearing violates public policy).

35. *See* Klomps v. Michel (1981) Eur. Comm.Rep. 1593; Pendy Plastic Products B.V. v. Pluspunkt Handelsgesellschaft mbH (1982) Eur.Comm.Rep. 2723; Debaecker and Plouvier v. Bouwman (1986) Eur.Comm.Rep. 01779 (Case 49/84).

- Conflict with an earlier judgment between the same parties and on the same cause of action in a state not party to the Convention.

- An agreement with a third party nation not to enforce judgments based upon exorbitant jurisdiction.

Since recognition and enforcement will be granted absent an *existing* judgment to the contrary in the enforcing state, the Convention essentially gives *res judicata* effect to civil and commercial judgments throughout the European Union. But this does not mean that third party creditors interested in the enforcement because it might affect their own claims may not seek independent legal redress rescinding execution of an enforcement order under the Convention.[36] Proper service of process under the law of the country of the defendant is a prerequisite to enforcement of a default commercial judgment even when the defendant becomes aware by other means of the lawsuit and could have taken advantage of procedural rights in the courts of the judgment country.[37]

36. *See* Deutsche Genossenschafts-bank v. Brasserie du Pêcheur (1985) Eur.Comm.Rep. 1981 (Case 148/84). (Case C–123/91).

37. Minalmet GmbH v. Brandeis Ltd. (1992) Eur.Comm.Rep. I–5661

Chapter 4

FREE MOVEMENT OF GOODS, SERVICES, CAPITAL AND PEOPLE

Table of Sections

§ 4.0 Introduction

This chapter concerns the free movement of goods, trade in agriculture, transport and the free movement of persons, services and capital. The implementation since 1957 of free movement has been a slow and not entirely successful process. Indeed, as the 1992 campaign for a fully integrated market illustrated, considerable amendment and rejuvenation of the Treaty of Rome has been required. The Single European Act of 1987 amended the Treaty of Rome to establish the goal of creating a Europe genuinely "without internal frontiers," leaving customs and other controls solely to points of entry. The target for the completion of this task was the end of December 1992. Hundreds of new legislative acts were adopted in its pursuit,[1] with substantial progress on all fronts.

§ 4.1   Free Movement of People—EU Citizenship

The Union has increasingly focused its attention on the creation of what it calls a "People's Europe." This focus is multidimensional. It includes traditional free movement rights of workers, the self-employed and their families,[1] and of professionals and others operating in the services sector.[2] The "People's Europe" has been expanded to include general rights to reside anywhere in the EU for nonworkers, such as students, the retired and persons who are independently wealthy.[3] The Maastricht Treaty on European Union formally introduced the idea of European citizenship into EU law and brought with it a selected bundle of civil rights. These include the right to run for office and vote wherever resident in local and European Parliament elections, and the right to be represented abroad diplomatically by other member state consular or embassy services.[4] European Community passports have replaced national passports, and driving licenses have been standardized. In 2004, EU health insurance cards were introduced to facilitate access to "necessary" care when traveling in other member states.

Schengen Accord

Dismantling border controls over the free movement of people within the European Union, a goal of the 1992 campaign for a Europe without internal frontiers, has not proven to be an easy task. The Benelux states, Germany, Italy, Spain, Greece, Portugal and France agreed to remove their internal frontier controls on people under the 1990 "Schengen Accord." This accord is the product of intergovernmental agreement, not EU legislation. As such, the Schengen Accord was an early harbinger of what is often called a "two-speed" Union or "Europe à la carte." At this writing, only Ireland and the United Kingdom do not participate. The ten new member states entering in 2004 will be transitioned into the Schengen Accord and the right of free movement for their peoples is delayed until 2011.

The Schengen Accord covers such sensitive issues as visas, asylum, immigration, gun controls,[5] extradition and police rights of "hot pursuit." The main points of contention were cross-border

§ 4.0

1. *See* "1992–Plus at a Glance" in § 2.14.

§ 4.1

1. *See* Section 4.10.

2. *See* Sections 4.11, 4.12, 4.13, 4.14.

3. *See* Section 4.9.

4. *Id.*

5. *See* Council Directive 91/477.

traffic of immigrants and criminals, especially terrorists and drug dealers.[6] These issues were resolved largely by promises of greater intergovernmental cooperation. In December of 1990, for example, the Council reached agreement on a directive that will make drug money laundering a crime in all member states. In addition, the member states have reached agreement on an External Borders Convention covering mutual recognition of visas and a limited right of free movement for non–EU nationals legally resident in Union states. Substantial ratification of the Dublin Asylum Convention by Union states also promises greater uniformity in that area.

Justice and Home Affairs

One new focus of the Maastricht Treaty on European Union, established as a separate "pillar" outside the Treaty of Rome, is cooperation on justice and home affairs. The member states have committed their interior ministries to coordinate their laws on asylum, immigration, frontier controls, crime, customs, terrorism and drugs. Under the Amsterdam Treaty of 1999, much of the Schengen Accord and other European policies on visas, asylum,[7] immigration and free movement of persons were brought under the Treaty of Rome (Title IV), subject to opt out rights for Denmark, Britain and Ireland. This transfer had the notable effect of conveying jurisdiction in these areas to the European Court of Justice. The separate pillar on justice and home affairs was essentially reduced to police and judicial cooperation in criminal matters (e.g., the EUROPOL Convention and EURO warrant), but opened to the possibility of ECJ judicial review.

§ 4.2   Free Movement of Goods

The free movement of goods within the European Union is based upon the creation of a customs union. Under this union, the member states have eliminated customs duties among themselves.[1] They have established a common customs tariff for their trade with the rest of the world.[2] Quantitative restrictions (quotas) on trade between member states are also prohibited, except in emergency and other limited situations.[3] The right of free movement applies to goods that originate in the Common Market and to those that have lawfully entered it and are said to be in "free circulation."[4]

6. *See* Council Regulation 900/92.

7. *See* Directives 2003/9 and 2004/83 creating minimum standards for receiving asylum seekers and Regulation 343/2003 ("Dublin II" asylum review rules).

§ 4.2

1. Article 25, Treaty of Rome.

2. *See* Chapter 6.

3. Articles 28–31, Treaty of Rome.

4. Articles 23 and 24, Treaty of Rome.

Measures of Equivalent Effect

The establishment of the customs union has been a major accomplishment, though not without difficulties. The member states not only committed themselves to the elimination of tariffs and quotas on internal trade, but also to the elimination of "measures of equivalent effect."[5] The elastic legal concept of measures of equivalent effect has been interpreted broadly by the European Court of Justice and the Commission to prohibit a wide range of trade restraints, such as administrative fees charged at borders which are the equivalent of import or export tariffs.[6] Charges of equivalent effect to a tariff must be distinguished from internal taxes that are applicable to imported and domestic goods. The latter must be levied in a nondiscriminatory and nonprotective manner (Article 90), while the former are prohibited entirely (Articles 23, 25). There has been a considerable amount of litigation over this distinction.[7]

The elasticity of the concept of measures of an equivalent effect is even more pronounced in the Court's judgments relating to quotas. This jurisprudence draws upon an early Commission directive (no longer applicable) of extraordinary scope.[8] In this directive, the Commission undertook a lengthy listing of practices that it considered illegal measures of equivalent effect to quotas. It is still occasionally referenced in Commission and Court of Justice decisions. The directive's focus was on national rules that discriminate against imports or simply restrain internal Community trade.

Cassis Formula

This "effects test" soon found support from the ECJ. In a famous case, the Court of Justice ruled that Belgium could not block the importation of Scotch whiskey via France because of the absence of a British certificate of origin as required by Belgian customs law.[9] The Court of Justice held that any national rule directly or indirectly, actually or potentially capable of hindering internal trade is generally forbidden as a measure of equivalent effect. However, *if* European Union law has not devel-

---

5. *See especially* Articles 25, 28 and 29 of Treaty of Rome.

6. Sociaal Fonds v. SA Ch. Brachfield (1969) Eur.Comm.Rep. 211; Rewe Zentralfinanz v. Landwirtschaftskammer Westfalen–Lippe (1973) Eur.Comm.Rep. 1039; Commission v. Italy (1969) Eur. Comm.Rep. 193. *But see* Commission v. Germany (1988) Eur.Comm.Rep. 5427 (border fees to cover costs of inspections required by EU law may be lawful).

7. *See* Chapter 5. *See e.g.*, Industria Gomma, Articoli Vari v. Ente Nazionale

ENCC (1975) Eur.Comm.Rep. 699; Humblot v. Directeur des Services Fiscaux (1985) Eur.Comm.Rep. 1367 (tax on goods not domestically produced invalid).

8. Commission Directive 70/50 on the Abolition of Measures which have an Effect Equivalent to Quantitative Restrictions, 1970 O.J. L13/29 (Special Edition) (I), p. 17.

9. Procureur du Roi v. Dassonville (1974) Eur.Comm.Rep. 837.

oped appropriate rules in the area concerned (here designations of origin), the member states may enact "reasonable" and "proportional" (no broader than necessary) regulations to ensure that the public is not harmed.[10] This is commonly called the "*Cassis* formula." Products meeting reasonable national criteria, the *Cassis* opinion continues, may be freely traded elsewhere in the Union.[11] This is the origin of the innovative "mutual reciprocity" principle used in significant parts of the legislative campaign for a Europe without internal frontiers.

The *Cassis* decision suggests use of a Rule of Reason analysis for national fiscal regulations, public health measures, laws governing the fairness of commercial transactions and consumer protection. Environmental protection and occupational safety laws of the member states have been similarly treated. Under this approach, for example, a Danish "bottle bill" requiring use of approved soft drink and beer containers was held disproportionately restrictive of internal trade. The use of only approved containers was therefore unreasonable.[12] However, the Danes' argument that a deposit and return system was environmentally necessary prevailed. This was (absent the approved container rules) a reasonable restraint on internal trade recognized by the Court under the *Cassis* formula for analyzing compelling state interests. Likewise, a Belgian law prohibiting the importation of general wastes from neighboring countries was found reasonable and not in breach of Community free trade principles.[13]

There are cases which suggest that "cultural interests" may justify national restrictions on European Union trade. For example, British, French and Belgian bans on Sunday retail trading have survived initial scrutiny under the *Cassis* formula.[14] British prohibitions of sales of sex articles, except by licensed sex shops, are EU compatible[15] and French legislation prohibiting the sale or rental of cassettes within one year of a film's debut also survived such scrutiny under the *Cassis* formula.[16] National laws prohibiting sales

---

10. *See* the "Cassis de Dijon" case, Rewe Zentral AG v. Bundesmonopolverwaltung für Branntwein (1979) Eur. Comm.Rep. 649 (German *minimum* alcoholic beverage rule not reasonable). *See also* Commission Communication, O.J. C256/2 (March 10, 1980).

11. *See* the Commission Communication Concerning the *Cassis* Case, O.J. C256/2 (March 10, 1980).

12. Commission v. Denmark (1988) Eur.Comm.Rep. 4607.

13. Commission v. Belgium (1992) Eur.Comm.Rep. I–4431 (Case C–2/90).

14. Torfaen Borough Council v. B+Q PLC Ltd. (1989) Eur.Comm.Rep.

3851; UDS v. Sidef Conforma & Ors (1991) Eur.Comm.Rep. 997 (Case C–312/89); Re Marchandise & Ors (1991) Eur.Comm.Rep. I–1027 (Case C–332/89); Reading Borough Council v. Payless DIY Ltd + Ors (1992) Eur.Comm.Rep. I–6493 (Case C–304/90).

15. Quietlynn Ltd. v. Southend Borough Council (1990) 1 Eur.Comm.Rep. 3051.

16. Cinéthéque SA v. Fédération Nationale des Cinémas Francais (1985) Eur.Comm.Rep. 2605.

below cost, when applied without discrimination as between imports and domestic products, are not considered to affect trade between the member states. In the remarkable *Keck* decision signaling a jurisprudential retreat, the ECJ ruled that "selling arrangements" may not be challenged under Article 30 and the traditional *Cassis* formula.[17] Deceptive trade practices laws ordinarily do not amount to "selling arrangements,"[18] but national laws regulating sales outlets[19] and advertising[20] may.

In recent years, member state regulations capable of being characterized as governing "marketing modalities" or "selling arrangements" have sought shelter under *Keck*. For example, the French prohibition of televised advertising (intended to favor printed media) of the distribution of goods escaped the rule of reason analysis of *Cassis* in this manner, but the Swedish ban on magazine ads for alcoholic beverages did not since it discriminated against market access by imports. Some commentators see in *Keck* and its progeny an unarticulated attempt by the Court to take subsidiarity seriously. Others are just baffled by its newly found tolerance for trade distorting national marketing laws. But the Court of Justice has poignantly refused to extend *Keck* to the marketing of services.

Under *Cassis* national rules requiring country of origin or "foreign origin" labels have fallen as measures of effect equivalent to quotas.[21] Likewise, the selective "Quality Produce from Germany" label fell to free trade principles.[22] So have various restrictive national procurement laws, including a "voluntary" campaign to "Buy Irish."[23] Minimum and maximum retail pricing controls can also run afoul of the Court's expansive interpretation of measures of equivalent effect.[24] Compulsory patent licensing can amount to a measure of equivalent effect nullified by operation of Union law. Where demand for the patented product was satisfied by imports from another member state, the U.K. could not compulsorily re-

---

17. *See* Re Keck and Mithouard (1993) Eur.Comm.Rep. I–6097 (Cases C–267/91, C–268/91).

18. Verband Sozialer Wettbewerb v. Clinique Laboratories (1994) Eur. Comm.Rep. I–317.

19. Commission v. Greece (1995) Eur.Comm.Rep. I–1621.

20. Societe d'Importation Edouard Leclerc–Siplec v. TFI Publicite (1995) Eur.Comm. I–179. *Compare* Konsumertombusmannen (KO) v. Gourmet International Products ABS, (GIP) (2001) Eur.Comm.Rep. I–6493.

21. Commission v. Ireland (1981) Eur.Comm.Rep. 1625; Commission v. United Kingdom (1985) Eur.Comm.Rep. 1202.

22. Commission v. Germany (2002) Eur.Comm.Rep. I–9977 (Case C–325/00).

23. Commission v. Ireland (1988) Eur.Comm.Rep. 4929 (product standards); Commission v. Ireland (1982) Eur.Comm.Rep. 4005 (Buy Irish). *But see* Apple and Pear Development Council (1983) Eur.Comm.Rep. 4083 (permissible promotion of local agricultural products).

24. Re Ricardo Tasca (1976) Eur. Comm.Rep. 291; Openbaar Ministerie v. Van Tiggele (1978) Eur.Comm.Rep. 25.

quire manufacturing within its jurisdiction.[25] Member states may not impose linguistic labelling requirements so as to block trade and competition in foodstuffs. In one case, a Belgian law requiring Dutch labels in Flemish areas was nullified as in conflict with the Treaty of Rome.[26] These cases vividly illustrate the extent to which litigants are invoking the Treaty of Rome and the *Cassis* formula in attempts at overcoming commercially restrictive national laws.

The Court has made it clear that all of the Rule of Reason justifications for national regulatory laws are temporary. Adoption of Common Market legislation in any of these areas would eliminate national authority to regulate trading conditions under *Dassonville*, *Cassis* and (presumably) *Keck*.[27] These judicial mandates, none of which are specified in the Treaty of Rome, vividly illustrate the powers of the Court of Justice to expansively interpret the Treaty and rule on the validity under EU law of national legislation affecting internal trade in goods.

§ 4.3   Article 30 and the Problem of Nontariff Trade Barriers

The provisions of the Treaty of Rome dealing with the establishment of the customs union do not adequately address the problem of nontariff trade barriers (NTBs). As in the world community, the major trade barrier within the European Union has become NTBs. To some extent, in the absence of a harmonizing directive completely occupying the field,[1] this is authorized. Article 30 of the Treaty of Rome permits national restraints on imports and exports justified on the grounds of:

(1) public morality, public policy ("ordre public") or public security;

(2) the protection of health and life of humans, animals or plants;

(3) the protection of national treasures possessing artistic, historical or archeological value;[2] and

25. Commission v. United Kingdom (1992) Eur.Comm.Rep. I–0829 (Case C–30/90).

26. Piageme ASBL v. Peeters BVBA (1991) Eur.Comm.Rep. I–2971 (Case C–369/89).

27. Oberkreisdirektor des Kreises Borken v. Moormann B.V. (1988) Eur. Comm.Rep. 4869.

§ 4.3

1. *See* Firma Eau de Cologne v. Provide (1989) Eur.Comm.Rep. 3891 and Pubblico Ministero v. Ratti (1979) Eur. Comm.Rep. 1629 (Article 30 preempted by EC directives). *But see* Article 95 of the Treaty of Rome regarding internal market directives where member states retain certain Article 30 prerogatives (discussed in Section 4.4) and cases allowing member states to "supplement" EU directives on the basis of genuine need, including Ministère Public v. Grunert (1980) Eur.Comm.Rep. 1827, In re Motte (1985) Eur.Comm.Rep. 3887, Ministère Public v. Muller (1986) Eur. Comm.Rep. 1511, Ministére Public v. Bellon (1990) Eur.Comm.Rep. 4683.

2. *See* Council Directive 93/7 securing the right of return of national cultural treasures removed unlawfully after Dec. 31, 1992.

(4) the protection of industrial or commercial property.

Article 30 amounts, within certain limits, to an authorization of nontariff trade barriers among the EU nations. This "public interest" authorization exists in addition to, but somewhat overlaps with, the Rule of Reason exception formulated under Article 28 in *Dassonville* and *Cassis* above. However, in a sentence much construed by the European Court of Justice, Article 30 continues with the following language: "Such prohibitions or restrictions shall not, however, constitute a means of arbitrary discrimination or a disguised restriction on trade between member states."

Case Law

In a wide range of decisions, the Court of Justice has interpreted Article 30 in a manner which generally limits the ability of member states to impose NTB barriers to internal Union trade. Britain, for example, may use its criminal law under the public morality exception to seize pornographic goods made in Holland that it outlaws,[3] but not inflatable sex dolls from Germany which could be lawfully produced in the United Kingdom.[4] Germany cannot stop the importation of beer (e.g., Heineken's from Holland) which fails to meet its purity standards.[5] This case makes wonderful reading as the Germans, seeking to invoke the public health exception of Article 30, argue all manner of ills that may befall their populace if free trade in beer is allowed. Equally interesting are the unsuccessful Italian health protection arguments against free trade in pasta made from common (not durum) wheat,[6]and the similar failure of French standards' arguments against free trade in foie gras. But a state may obtain whatever information it requires from importers to evaluate public health risks associated with food products containing additives that are freely traded elsewhere in the Common Market. This does not mean that an importer of muesli bars to which vitamins have been added must prove the product healthful, rather that the member state seeking to bar the imports must have an objective reason for keeping them out of its market.[7] Assuming such a reason exists, the trade restraint may not be disproportionate to the public health goal.[8] A notable 2002 ECJ opinion invalidated a French public health ban on U.K. beef

3. Regina v. Henn and Darby (1979) Eur.Comm.Rep. 3795.

4. Conegate Ltd. v. H.M. Customs and Excise (1986) Eur.Comm.Rep. 1007.

5. Commission v. Germany (1987) Eur.Comm.Rep. 1227. *But see* Aragonesa de Publicidad Exterior SA (APESA) + Anor v. Departamento de Sanidad y Seguridad Social (1991) Eur.Comm.Rep. I–4151 (Cases C–1/90 and C–176/90) (advertising ban applied to strong alcoholic beverages can be justified on public health grounds).

6. Re Drei Glocken GmbH and Criminal Proceedings against Zoni (1988) Eur.Comm.Rep. 4233, 4285.

7. Officer van Justitie v. Sandoz BV (1983) Eur.Comm.Rep. 2245.

8. Commission v. United Kingdom (UHT Milk) (1983) Eur.Comm.Rep. 203.

imports maintained after a Commission decision to return to free trade following the "mad cow" outbreak.[9]

Public security measures adopted under Article 30 can include external as well as internal security. In one case, the validity of national CoCom restrictions on the export of strategic goods to the U.S.S.R. was noted.[10] An unusual case under the public security exception contained in Article 30 involved Irish petroleum products' restraints.[11] The Irish argued that oil is an exceptional product always triggering national security interests. Less expansively, the Court acknowledged that maintaining minimum oil supplies did fall within the ambit of Article 30. The public policy exception under Article 30 has been construed along French lines (ordre public). Only genuine threats to fundamental societal interests are covered.[12] Consumer protection (though a legitimate rationale for trade restraints under *Dassonville* and *Cassis*), does not fall within the public policy exception of Article 30.[13] Permitting environmental protesters to block the Brenner Pass for 30 hours is acceptable public policy in support of fundamental assembly and expression rights.[14]

§ 4.4   Intellectual Property Rights as Trade Barriers

A truly remarkable body of case law has developed around the authority granted national governments in Article 30 to protect industrial or commercial property ("intellectual property") by restraining imports and exports. These cases run the full gamut from protection of trademarks and copyrights to protection of patents and know-how. There is a close link between this body of case law and that developed under Article 81 concerning restraints on competition.[1]

Trade restraints involving intellectual property arise out of the fact that such rights are nationally granted. Owners of intellectual property rights within the Union are free under most traditional law to block the unauthorized importation of goods into national markets. There is a strong tendency for national infringement lawsuits to serve as vehicles for the division of the Common

9. National Farmers' Union v. Secrétariat Général (2002) Eur.Comm.Rep. I–9079.

10. Ministre des Finances v. Richardt (1991) Eur.Comm.Rep. I–4621 (Case C–367/89).

11. *See* Regina v. Thompson (1978) Eur.Comm.Rep. 2247 (coinage).

12. Campus Oil Ltd. v. Minister for Industry and Energy (1984) Eur. Comm.Rep. 2727.

13. Kohl KG v. Ringelhan and Rennett SA (1984) Eur.Comm.Rep. 3651; Silhouette International v. Hartlauer, (1998) Eur.Comm.Rep.I–4799 (Austrian manufacturer's trademark rights block imports of its sunglasses from Bulgaria).

14. Schmidberger v. Austria (2003) Eur.Comm.Rep. I–5659 (Case C–112/00).

§ 4.4

1. *See* Chapter 7.

Market. Although considerable energy has been spent by the Commission on developing Common Market rights that would provide an alternative to national intellectual property rights, not all of these proposals have been fully implemented. However, late in 1993, the Council reached agreement on a Common Market trademark regime and the Council adopted Directive 89/104, which harmonize member state laws governing trademarks.[2] As a result, for example, the United Kingdom enacted the Trade Marks Act of 1994. The Court of Justice has ruled that goods bearing trademarks registered somewhere in the EU may be freely circulated marked with an "R" in a circle after the trademark. National law on unfair competition cannot be used to impede trade in such goods on the grounds that the mark in question is not registered in the country of sale.[3] In the copyright field, several directives have harmonized European law, perhaps most importantly on copyrights for computer software (No. 91/250).

Exhaustion Doctrine

The European Court of Justice has addressed these problems under Article 30 and generally resolved against the exercise of national intellectual property rights in ways which inhibit free trade inside the Union. In many of these decisions, the Court acknowledges the existence of the right to block trade in infringing goods, but holds that the *exercise* of that right is subordinate to the Treaty of Rome. The Court has also fashioned a doctrine which treats national intellectual property rights as having been *exhausted* once the goods to which they apply are freely sold on the market.[4] One of the few exceptions to this doctrine is broadcast performing rights which the Court considers incapable of exhaustion.[5] Records, CDs and cassettes embodying such rights are, however, subject to the exhaustion doctrine once released into the market.[6] Such goods often end up in the hands of third parties who then ship them into another member state.

The practical effect of many of the rulings of the Court of Justice is to remove the ability of the owners of the relevant intellectual property rights from successfully pursuing infringement actions in national courts.[7] When intellectual property rights have a

---

2. *See* § 5.25.

3. Pall Corp. v. P.J. Dalhausen (1990) Eur.Comm.Rep. I–4827 (Case C–238/89).

4. *See*, regarding trademarks, Van Doren + Q. GmbH v. Lifestyle Sports (2003) Eur.Comm.Rep. I–3051 (Case C–244/00).

5. *See* Coditel v. Ciné Vog Films SA (1980) Eur.Comm.Rep. 881; (1982) Eur. Comm.Rep. 3381.

6. Musik–Vertrieb membran Gmbh v. GEMA (1981) Eur.Comm.Rep. 147.

7. *See, e.g.,* Administration des douanes v. Rioglass SA and Transremar SL (2003) Eur.Comm.Rep. I–3711 (Case C–115/02).

single proprietor and have been placed on goods by consent, as when a licensor authorizes their use in other EU countries, then infringement actions to protect against parallel imports of the goods to which the rights apply are usually denied. This may not be the case, however, when voluntary trademark assignments that are not anticompetitive are involved. In such cases, the ECJ has demonstrated some concern for consumer confusion when trade in parallel goods occurs.

It is only when intellectual property rights do not have a single proprietor (thus sharing a "common origin") or the requisite consent is absent that they stand a chance of being upheld so as to stop trade in infringing products.[8] Compulsory licensing of patents, for example, does not involve consensual marketing of products. Patent rights may therefore be used to block trade in goods produced under such a license.[9] But careful repackaging and resale of goods subject to a common or even different trademark may occur against the objections of the owner of the mark.[10] And compulsory licensing cannot be conditioned upon import bans applicable to the beneficiary licensee. Such bans offend the free movement of goods law of the EU and unfairly create investment incentives.[11]

Centrafarm Case

An excellent example of the application of the judicial doctrine developed by the Court of Justice in the intellectual property field under Article 36 can be found in the *Centrafarm* case.[12] The United States pharmaceutical company, Sterling Drug, owned the British and Dutch patents and trademarks relating to "Negram." Subsidiaries of Sterling Drug in Britain and Holland had been respectively assigned the British and Dutch trademark rights to Negram. Owing in part to price controls in the UK, a substantial difference in cost for Negram emerged as between the two countries. Centrafarm was an independent Dutch importer of Negram from the UK and Germany. Sterling Drug and its subsidiaries brought infringement

8. *See* CNL–Sucal v. HAG (1990) Eur.Comm.Rep. I–3711 (Case C–10/89) (wartime expropriation of trademark removes common origin). *See also* Terrapin (Overseas) Ltd. v. Terranova Industrie CA Kapferer & Co. (1976) Eur. Comm.Rep. 1039.

9. Pharmon BV. v. Hoechst AG (1985) Eur.Comm.Rep. 2281.

10. Hoffman–LaRoche & Co. AG v. Centrafarm Vertriebsgesellschaft Pharmazeutischer Erzeugnisse mgH (1978) Eur.Comm.Rep. 1132; Pfizer, Inc. v. Eurim–Pharm GmbH (1981) Eur. Comm.Rep. 2913; Bristol–Myers Squibb & Orrs v. Paranova (1996) Eur. Comm.Rep. I–3457; Pharmacia & Upjohn v. Paranova (1999) Eur.Comm.Rep. I–6927; Boehringer Ingelheim KG v. Swingward Ltd and Douelhurst Ltd (2002) Eur.Comm.Rep. I–3759 (Case C–143/00); Merck, Sharp + Dohme GmbH v. Paranova Pharmazeutica (2002) Eur. Comm.Rep. I–3703 (Case C–443/99).

11. Generics (UK) Ltd. v. Smith, Kline & French Laboratories, Ltd. (1992) Eur.Comm.Rep. I–5335 (Case C–191/90).

12. Centrafarm BV v. Sterling Drug Inc. (1974) Eur.Comm.Rep. 1147.

actions in the Dutch courts under their national patent and trade-mark rights seeking an injunction against Centrafarm's importation of Negram into The Netherlands.

The Court of Justice held that the intellectual property rights of Sterling Drug and its subsidiaries could not be exercised in a way which blocked EU trade in "parallel goods." In the Court's view, the exception established in Article 36 for the protection of industrial and commercial property covers only those rights that were specifically intended to be conveyed by the grant of national patents and trademarks. Blocking trade in parallel goods after they have been put on the market with the consent of a common owner, thus exhausting the rights in question, was not intended to be part of the package of benefits conveyed. If Sterling Drug succeeded, an arbitrary discrimination or disguised restriction on Union trade would be achieved in breach of the language which qualifies Article 36. Thus the European Court of Justice ruled in favor of the free movement of goods within the Common Market even when that negates clearly existing national legal remedies.

While the goal of creation of the Common Market can override national intellectual property rights when internal trade is concerned, these rights apply fully to the importation of goods from outside the European Union.[13] North American exporters of goods allegedly subject to rights owned by Europeans may therefore find entry into the EU challenged by infringement actions in national courts. This is notably true regarding trade in gray market goods.[14] Levi Strauss successfully cited *Silhouette* to keep low-price (made in the USA) Levi's out of the EU.

§ 4.5   NTBs and the Single Market

Nontariff trade barrier problems were the principal focus of the campaign for a fully integrated Common Market. It is estimated that the retention of customs frontiers, even in the absence of tariffs and quotas, costs the Union approximately 11 billion dollars a year. Many new legislative acts have been adopted, or are in progress, which target NTB trade problems inside the EU.[1] There are basically two different methodologies being employed. When possible, a common European Union standard is adopted. For example, legislation on auto pollution requirements adopts this methodology. Products meeting these standards may be freely

---

13. *See* E.M.I. Records Ltd. v. CBS United Kingdom Ltd. (1976) Eur. Comm.Rep. 811.

14. Silhouette International v. Hartlauer (1998) Eur.Comm.Rep. I–4799 (Case C–355/96); Zino Davidoff SA v. A + G Imports Ltd. (2001) Eur.

Comm.Rep. I–8691 (Cases C–414/99 to 416/99).

§ 4.5

1. *See* "1992–Plus at a Glance" in § 2.14.

traded in the Common Market. Traditionally, this approach (called "harmonization") has required the formation of a consensus within the Union as to the appropriate level of protection. Once adopted, harmonized standards must be followed.[2] This approach can be deceptive, however. Some harmonization directives contain a list of options from which member states may choose when implementing those directives.[3] In practice, this leads to differentiated national laws on the same so-called harmonized subject. Furthermore, in certain areas (notably the environment and occupational health and safety), the Treaty of Rome and certain directives[4] expressly indicate that member states may adopt laws that are more demanding than the Union's legislation. The result is, again, less than complete harmonization.

Under Article 95, added by the Single European Act of 1987, most single market legislation was adopted by qualified majority voting in the Council of Ministers. Notable exceptions requiring a unanimous vote included new laws on taxation, employment and free movement of persons. However, if a 1992 measure was adopted by a qualified majority, the public interest exceptions to free internal trade specified in Article 30 apply.[5] This may provide an escape clause for member states that were outvoted in the Council on single market legislation. Indeed, Article 95 extends the scope of Article 30 to include "major needs" relating to national protection of the working or natural environments. The Commission must be notified of any member state use of such an exception, which it or another member state can then challenge directly before the European Court as an "improper use." In doing so, the Commission need not adhere to the lengthy procedures used with Article 226 prosecutions of member states.[6]

Harmonization Principles

Many efforts at the harmonization of European environmental, health and safety, standards and certification, and related law have been undertaken. Nearly all of these are supposed to be based upon "high levels of protection."[7] Some have criticized what they see as the "least common denominator" results of harmonization of national laws under the campaign for a Europe without internal frontiers. One example involves the safety of toys. Directive 88/378

---

2. Pubblico Ministero v. Ratti (1979) Eur.Comm.Rep. 1629 (dangerous solvents); Commission v. United Kingdom (1988) Eur.Comm.Rep. 3921 (dim-dip lighting); Kemilkaieinspektionen v. Toolex Alpha (2000) Eur.Comm.Rep. I–5681 (dangerous substances).

3. *See* the discussion of products liability in Chapter 5.

4. *See* Buet v. Ministere Public (1989) Eur.Comm.Rep. 1235; Queen v. Secretary of State for Health (1993) Eur. Comm.Rep. I–3545.

5. *See* § 4.3.

6. *See* Chapter 3.

7. Article 95, Treaty of Rome.

permits toys to be sold throughout the Common Market if they satisfy "essential requirements." These requirements are broadly worded in terms of flammability, toxicity, etc. There are two ways to meet these requirements: (1) produce a toy in accordance with CEN standards (drawn up by experts); or (2) produce a toy that otherwise meets the essential safety requirements. Local language labeling requirements necessary for purchaser comprehension have generally, though not always, been upheld.[8]

The least common denominator criticism may be even more appropriate to the second legislative methodology utilized in the internal market campaign. The second approach is based on the *Cassis* principle of mutual reciprocity.[9] Under this "new" minimalist approach, EU legislation requires member states to recognize the laws of other member states and deem them acceptable for purposes of the operation of the Common Market.[10] For example, major legislation has been adopted in the area of professional services.[11] By mutual recognition of higher education diplomas based upon at least three years of courses, virtually all professionals have now obtained legal rights to move freely within the Union in pursuit of their careers. This is a remarkable achievement.

§ 4.6 Product Standards and Testing

An important part of the battle against nontariff trade barriers (NTBs) in the European Union involves product testing and standards. More than half of the legislation involved in the single market campaign concerned such issues. Since 1969, there has been a standstill agreement among the EU states to avoid the introduction of new technical barriers to trade. A 1983 directive (No. 83/89) requires member states to notify the Commission of proposed new technical regulations and product standards. The Commission can enjoin the introduction of such national rules for up to one year if it believes that a Union standard should be developed,[1] and failures to notify can invalidate national rules.[2] The goal is to move from different sets of regulatory approvals to one unified Union system embodying essential requirements on health, safety, the environment and consumer protection. Goods that meet these essential requirements will bear an "CE mark" and can be freely traded.

---

8. *See* Piageme & Orrs v. Peeters (1995) Eur.Comm.Rep. I–2955; Colim v. Bigg's Continent Noord (1999) Eur. Comm.Rep. I–3175.

9. *See* § 4.2.

10. *See, e.g.,* Council Resolution on a New Approach to Technical Harmonization and Standards, 1985 O.J. C136/1.

11. *See* Council Directive 89/48. Council Directive 92/51 expanded the

mutual recognition of diplomas to cover post-secondary and secondary education and training.

§ 4.6

1. Council Directive 83/169. *See* Directives 98/34, 98/48 (extension to on-line services).

2. CIA Security International v. Signalson (1996) Eur.Comm.Rep. I–2201.

Manufacturers will self-certify their compliance with relevant EU standards. Design and production process standards generally follow the ISO 9000 series on quality management and assurance. Firms must maintain a technical file documenting compliance and produce the file upon request by national authorities.

Standards Bodies

Private regional standards bodies have been playing a critical role in the development of this system. These include the European Committee for Standardization (CEN), the European Committee for Electrotechnical Standardization (CENELEC), and the European Telecommunications Standards Institute (ETSI). Groups like these have been officially delegated the responsibility for creating thousands of technical product standards. They have been turning out some 150 common standards each year. For example, directives on the safety of toys, construction products and electromagnetic compatibility have been issued.[3] These directives adopt the so-called "new approach" of setting broad, exclusive standards at the Union level which if voluntarily met guarantee access to every member state market. Under the "old approach", which still applies to most standards for processed foods, motor vehicles, chemicals and pharmaceuticals, EU legislation on standards is binding law. The technical specifications and testing protocols of these directives must be followed and (unlike the new approach) the member states may add requirements to them. Under either approach, goods meeting Union standards will bear a CE mark.[4] North American producers have frequently complained that their ability to be heard by European standards' bodies is limited. They have had little influence on EU product standards to which they must conform in order to sell freely in the Common Market.

Testing and Certification

Testing and certification of products is another part of the 1992 campaign. The main concern of North American companies is that recognition of U.S., Canadian and Mexican tests be granted by the European Union. In the past, many North American exporters have had to have their goods retested for Union purposes. The EU is generally committed to a resolution of such issues under what it calls a "global approach" to product standards and testing. This involves creation of a regional system for authorizing certification and testing under common rules and procedures.[5] In negotiations undertaken as part of the Uruguay Round on revising the Standards Code of the GATT, the EU gave its commitment to giving

3. *See* Council Directives 88/378, 89/106 and 89/336.

4. *See* Council Directive 93/68.

5. Council Resolution Dec. 21, 1989, O.J. C10 (Jan. 16, 1990).

recognition to "equivalent technical regulations" of other nations, and to avoidance of unnecessary obstacles to trade. A Department of Commercial official has concluded:

> While it may not be the least cost route, the most straightforward means to certify compliance with EC legal health and safety requirements is to follow European standards and testing procedures. Incompatibility between North American and European standards, testing procedures, quality assessment systems, and certifications can mean additional testing costs for U.S. exporters who want to qualify their products for sale in the EC market.[6]

In 1991, the United States and the European Union issued a nonbinding joint communiqué on product standards and certification procedures. Each side states its commitment to using international consensus standards in their legal régimes. This commitment will apparently extend to private sector product standard bodies. Regarding certification, the EU indicates that testing facilities located outside its borders will be able to obtain "Notified Body" (official) status for purpose of applying the many new EU product standards. Such facilities may include subcontractors of official Notified Bodies.

Product Standards Legislation

The following is a partial list of major EC product standard laws. Occupational health and safety laws are covered in Chapter 5.

Transport

- Directives 70/156, 87/358, 92/53 (approval of motor vehicles)
- Directives 70/311, 92/62 (steering equipment)
- Directives 71/127, 88/321 (rear view mirrors)
- Directives 71/320, 88/194 92/54 (motor vehicle braking)
- Directives 77/143, 92/55 (motor vehicle exhaust)
- Directives 80/1269, 88/195 (motor vehicle engine power)
- Directives 85/3, 88/214 (truck weights and dimensions)
- Directive 86/217 (tire pressure gauges)
- Directives 88/366, 90/360 (motor vehicle field of vision)
- Directives 88/449, 91/225 (roadworthiness tests for motor vehicles)
- Directive 89/173 (tractor weights and dimensions)

---

6. Duesterberg, "Federal Government Response to the EC 1992 Challenge in Standards, Testing and Certification," *Business America* (Feb. 24, 1992). *See* Hagigh, "Obtaining EC Product Approvals after 1992," *Id.* at p. 30.

- Directives 89/277, 89/278, 89/516, 89/517, 89/518 (motor vehicle lamps and signals)
- Directive 89/297 (motor vehicle side guards)
- Directives 89/459, 92/23 (motor vehicle tires)
- Directives 90/638, 90/629 (motor vehicle safety belts)
- Directive 91/226 (motor vehicle spray suppression)
- Directive 92/22 (motor vehicle safety glass)
- Directive 92/24 (motor vehicle speed limitation devices)
- Directives 93/29–93/34 (2 and 3 wheel vehicles)

Consumer Goods

- Directive 73/23 (low voltage electrical appliances)
- Directive 87/404 (simple pressure vessels)
- Directive 88/378 (toy safety)
- Directives 89/336, 92/31 (radio electromagnetic incompatibility)
- Directive 92/42 (hot water heaters)
- Directive 92/75 (energy consumption appliance labels)

Industrial Goods

- Directive 86/663 (self-propelled industrial trucks)
- Directives 87/402, 89/681, 88/465, 89/173, 89/682, 89/680 (tractors)
- Directive 87/405 (tower cranes-sound)
- Directives 88/571, 90/487 (dangerous electrical equipment)
- Directive 89/106 (construction products)
- Directive 89/240 (test methods for industrial trucks)
- Directive 89/392 (machine safety)
    - Directive 2004/22 (measuring instruments)

Miscellaneous

- Directives 84/529, 90/486 (electrically operated lifts)
- Directive 90/384 (non-automatic weighing instruments)
- Directive 90/396 (gas appliances)
- Directive 92/38 (satellite broadcasting of television signals)

§ 4.7   Pharmaceutical and Medical Products

A surprising number of European Union directives and other legislative acts focus on harmonization and mutual recognition of the law governing pharmaceuticals and other medical products. These acts focus primarily on product registration, research, manufacturing, pricing and advertising.

Legislative Digest

The following is a partial list of major EU legislation in the pharmaceuticals and medicinal products area:

- Directive 65/65 (proprietary medicinal products) as particularly amended by Directives 75/319, 91/356, 92/73
- Directive 75/318 (medicinal standards and protocols)
- Directive 78/25 (coloring)
- Directives 81/851, 92/18 (veterinary medicinal products)
- Directive 81/852, 92/74 (veterinary standards and protocols)
- Directive 84/539 (electro-medical equipment)
- Directive 86/609 (protection of animals)
- Directives 87/18, 88/320 (good laboratory practices)
- Directive 89/105 (transparency of pricing measures)
- Directive 89/342 (immunologicals)
- Directive 89/343 (radiopharmaceuticals)
- Directive 89/381 (blood products)
- Directive 89/341 (generics)
- Directive 90/385 (medical implants)
- Directive 92/27 (labelling and information)
- Directive 92/28 (advertising)
- Directive 92/26 (prescriptions)
- Directive 92/25 (wholesale practices)
- Directive 93/39 (medicinal product standards and testing)
- Regulation 2309/93 (biotechnology products)
  - Directive 98/8 (biocidal products)
  - Directive 2001/83 (medicinal products)
  - Directive 2002/98 (blood products)
  - Regulation 726/2004 (medicinal products authorization)

Directive 92/28 restricts pharmaceutical advertising. There is a ban on advertising prescription drugs to the general public. The advertising of over-the-counter medicines must be clear and not misleading. The gift of free samples to medical doctors is also restrained, as is the sponsorship of conferences by pharmaceutical companies. Directive 92/27 requires the listing of pharmaceutical ingredients and proper usage on a label. Detailed information on precautions and possible side effects is also mandatory.

The Court of Justice has clarified the dividing line between cosmetic and medicinal products.[1] Products which by presentation or by function are used with a view towards restoring, correcting or modifying physiological functions are medicinal and must be authorized by state authorities. Cosmetic products are subject to a separate series of EU directives[2] which do not generally require authorization. In the *Upjohn* litigation, the Court was concerned with a hair growth product that was treated as a medicinal by one company and a cosmetic by another. The Court took a broad view of the definition of "medicinals" found in Directive 65/65, emphasizing that mere representation of the product for physiological functions suffices to bring the product under state authorization requirements. Likewise, herbal teas advertised as having therapeutic qualities even though there is no scientific basis for such claims were "medicinal products" falling under Directive 65/65 and subject to national regulation.[3] Germany's classification of *all* vitamins as medicinals was ruled an invalid trade barrier,[4] whereas Denmark's regulation of the marketing of foods to which vitamins or minerals are added was a legitimate public health control.[5]

Trade Issues

Free trade in medicinal products has been a contentious area. One leading Court of Justice opinion struck down a German law requiring import certificates for medicinal products that were repackaged.[6] The importer has a duty to see that medicinals are packaged and marketed in accordance with national law. Repackaging of pharmaceuticals traded across state borders is both legal and common.[7] At present, national monopolies granted to pharmacists over the sale of medicinal products have survived scrutiny as trade barriers under Treaty of Rome examinations by the Court of Justice. National courts must decide whether such monopolies are necessary consumer protection laws and whether their goals might not be achieved by less restrictive means.[8] Mail ordering of medici-

§ 4.7

1. The Upjohn Co. + Anor v. Farzoo Inc. + Anor (1991) Eur.Comm.Rep. I–1703 (Case C–112/89); Re Monteil + Anor (1991) Eur.Comm.Rep. I–1547 (Case C–60/89). *See* Council Directive 65/65.

2. *See* Council Directives 76/768, 92/7, 93/35.

3. Re Ter Vaart (1992) Eur. Comm.Rep. I–5485 (Case C–219/91).

4. Commission v. Germany (2004) Eur.Comm.Rep. I–00000 (Case 387/99).

5. Commission v. Denmark (2003) Eur.Comm.Rep. 9693 (Case C–192/01).

6. Freistaat Bayern v. Eurim–Pharm GmbH (1991) Eur.Comm.Rep. I–1747 (Case C–347/89).

7. *See* Section 4.4.

8. Re Delattre (1991) Eur. Comm.Rep. I–1487 (Case 369/88).

nals is protected by free trade principles and Directive 2001/83.[9]

Evaluation Agency

Council Regulation 2309/93 created the European Agency for the Evaluation of Medicinal Products to evaluate and authorize technologically advanced medicinal products, notably those derived from biotechnology, intended for use in humans or food-producing animals. Prescription drug companies can seek EU-wide "centralized" marketing approval from this agency,[10] or individually obtain "decentralized" national approvals. If Union authorization is not required, all national authorizations for the marketing of medicinal products must be mutually recognized and such products may be freely traded in the EU. Support for such mutual recognition is derived from the harmonization of standards for medicinal products and their testing.[11] Centralized marketing technique approvals bind parallel importers.[12] Similar treatment and free trade in authorized veterinary products has also been accomplished.[13]

§ 4.8 Food Products

Another area where the European Union has been especially active legislatively is food products. These laws focus on labelling, product contents, additives and packaging. In 2002, the European Food Safety Authority was created in response to "mad cow" and other food crises.

Legislative Digest

The following is a partial list of major EU legislation in the foodstuffs area:

• Directives 64/54, 85/585 (preservatives)

• Directives 74/329, 86/102, 89/393 (emulsifiers, etc.)

• Directive 79/112 (labelling and advertising)

• Directives 79/581, 88/315 (pricing of foodstuffs)

• Directive 80/777 (natural mineral waters)

• Directive 85/373 (coffee extracts)

• Directive 86/197 (alcoholic strength labels)

• Directive 88/314 (pricing of non-foodstuffs)

---

9. Deutscher Apothekerverband eV v. DocMorris NV (2003) Eur.Comm.Rep. I-___ (Case C-322/01).

10. *See* Regulations 1084/2003 and 1085/2003, Council Directive 2003/63.

11. *See especially* Council Directive 93/39.

12. *See* Aventis Pharma Deutschland GmbH v. Kohlpharma GmbH (2002) Eur.Comm.Rep. I-7761 (Case C-433/00).

13. Council Directive 93/40.

- Directive 88/344 (extraction solvents)
- Directives 88/388, 91/71 (flavorings)
- Directive 88/593 (fruit jams)
- Directives 89/107, 90/612 (food additives)
- Directive 89/108 (quick-frozen food)
- Directive 89/109 (materials coming into contact with food)
- Directive 89/394 (fruit juices)
- Directive 89/396 (lot identification)
- Directive 89/397 (official control of food)
- Directive 89/398 (particular nutritional uses)
- Directive 89/347 (egg products)
- Regulation 1576/89 (spirit drinks)
- Directives 90/128, 93/9 (plastic materials coming into contact with food)
  - Directive 90/220 (GMOs)
- Directive 90/496 (nutritional labelling)
- Directive 90/642 (pesticide residues)
- Directive 91/321 (infant formulae)
- Directives 91/325, 91/326, 91/410, 91/442 (classification, packaging and labelling of dangerous substances)
- Directives 91/492, 91/493 (fish products)
- Directives 91/494, 91/495, 91/497 (poultry and meat products)
- Regulation 2092/91 (organic foods)
- Regulation 315/93 (food contaminants)
- Directive 93/43 (food hygiene)
  - Directive 96/5 (cereals and baby foods)
  - Directive 97/41 (maximum food pesticides)
  - Directive 2000/13 (food labels)
  - Directive 2000/36 (chocolate)
  - Directive 2001/01 (preserved meats)
  - Regulation 466/2001 (contaminants)
  - Directive 2002/16 (food packaging)
  - Regulation 2092/91 (organic foods)
  - Directive 2003/60 (pesticides)

Labels

Directive 79/112 requires the following information to be listed on all food packaging labels: (1) the name under which the product is sold; (2) the list of ingredients; (3) the net quantity; (4) the "use by" date of minimum durability; (5) any special storage conditions or conditions of use; (6) the name or business name and address of the manufacturer or the packager, or of the seller established within the Union; (7) the place of origin, especially where labels might mislead the consumer; and (8) instructions for use when it would be impossible to make appropriate use of the foodstuff in the absence of such instructions. Manufacturers have the responsibility to identify and label all "health risks." The nutritional value of a product must be designated on the package. Nutrition labelling refers to statements regarding energy value, or any of the following nutrients: protein, carbohydrates, fat, fiber, sodium, and assorted vitamins and minerals. Statements that include phrases such as "provides, provides at a reduced rate, or does not provide" refer to health risk in a foodstuff. The manufacturer has the responsibility to insure that products are worthy of energy value claims. The indication of minimum durability is not required on fresh fruits, vegetables, wines, beverages containing greater than ten percent alcohol, baked goods and pastries consumed within a 24–hour period, vinegar, cooking salt, solid sugar, and confectionery products consisting of flavored sugars.

Ingredients which are present in packages must be listed in a clear, concise manner in languages expected to be easily understood by national customers. Food and beverage products must be labeled with a list of ingredients and alcohol content percentages. Directive 89/396 requires lot marks on all packaged foods distributed throughout the EU. Lot marks are designated by the placement of the letter "L" on the package. It is said that the new lot marking directive will have a major impact on the U.S. food sector, where food does not generally bear this type of marking. The directive also mandates a special format in which foods are date marked. This format differs from the one currently used in the United States. In 1992, the Council adopted two additional regulations on food labelling and food quality. The first concerns use of protected geographical indications (PGIs) and protected designations of origin (PDOs) on foodstuffs, excepting wine and spirits. This regulation seeks to keep generic names from being so registered. The second regulation deals with certificates of specific character for foodstuffs meeting EU criteria and specifications. Registration and Union inspection requirements for such certificates focus on the use of traditional raw materials or processing techniques.

Trade Issues

The Court of Justice has vigorously promoted free internal trade in foodstuffs. Member state food standards may not generally impede the flow of food products across borders in the absence of identifiable health and safety risks. The Court has repeatedly decided that consumer protection goals are adequately met by use of informative labelling regarding food ingredients,[1] characteristics and origin. Such labelling may be required by national law, but free movement of foodstuffs may not otherwise be impeded. This line of reasoning originated in the famous *Cassis de Dijon* case[2] involving German *minimum* alcoholic content controls as applied to French liquors. Thus, absent bona fide health and safety concerns,[3] each member state must ordinarily recognize the food product standards of other member states. Principles of mutual recognition also underlie much of the EU foodstuffs legislation outlined above.

§ 4.9 General Rights of Residence

A general right is accorded EU nationals to move freely for purposes of residence throughout the Union and benefits students, retirees and the populace at large.[1] This right should be distinguished from the free movement rights of workers discussed in the next section. The chief concern about a general right of residence is coverage for health and social welfare purposes, and a possible run towards those states with more generous programs. Council Directive 90/364 (effective in 1992) extends a general right of residence to all member state nationals of independent means and their families (including co-habitants) provided they do not become a burden on the public finances of the host country. Spouses and dependent children (even those who are *not* EU nationals) are entitled to work in the country where the non-working EU spouse has taken up residence. These principles also apply to employees and the self-employed who have retired.[2]

All EU nationals and their families seeking to exercise their right of residence in another member state must demonstrate sufficient financial resources and health insurance coverage. "Sufficiency" for these purposes connotes resources in excess of the level which would trigger social assistance in the host state. Retired

§ 4.8

1. *See,* e.g., Commission v. Spain, 2003 Eur.Comm.Rep. I–469 (chocolate).

2. REWE v. Bundesmonopolverwaltung für Branntwein (1979) Eur. Comm.Rep. 649. *See, particularly,* Baumbast and R. v. Secretary of State for the Home Department, 2002 Eur. Comm.Rep. I–7091.

3. *See, e.g.,* Gilli and Andres (1980) Eur.Comm.Rep. 2071; Commission v. Italy, 2003 Eur.Comm.Rep. I–6445 (approval of caffeine-added beverages not justified).

§ 4.9

1. *See* Article 18(1), Treaty of Rome and Directive 2004/38.

2. Council Directive 90/365.

persons must prove that they receive a disability, retirement or old age pension meeting this criterion. Students have a general right of residence for educational purposes throughout the Union provided they can show sufficient resources, health insurance and enrollment in the host state. The student's family (but not co-habitant) may accompany him or her and work in that state.[3] The student's enrollment must be his or her principal purpose for residing in the host country. All general rights of residence are subject to exceptions based upon public policy, health or safety.[4]

Students

Students seeking vocational training in another member state cannot be subjected to discriminatory tuition fees not charged to nationals.[5] In one decision, the Court of Justice took a broad view of "vocational training" under Article 151 of the Treaty of Rome. Any form of education which prepares for qualification in a particular trade, profession or employment is included. This is the case regardless of age or the level of the training, and even if the study program involves some general education. A French national, for example, was therefore entitled to train in strip cartoon arts without paying special fees at a Belgian city academy.

Students also benefit from an EU initiative first known as ERASMUS, now SOCRATES. This program supports "vocational" student mobility and enrollment rights, even when research is primarily involved.[6] University education is treated as vocational by the Court of Justice. Tens of thousands of students are now exchanged under this program each year. It has been extended to students from EFTA and many Central European countries. Articles 149 to 150 of the Rome Treaty were amended by the 1993 Maastricht Accord to authorize cooperative EU action and "incentive measures" on education, vocational training, youth, cultural and public health affairs. The Amsterdam Treaty of 1999 added employment incentives to this authority. These provisions explicitly rule out harmonization by Union mandate in these fields and thus reflect the growing trend toward "subsidiarity."[7]

§ 4.10   Free Movement of Workers, the Self–Employed and Their Families

The foundations of the Union in the Treaty of Rome concern the free movement of persons, services and capital. These are often

---

3. Council Directive 90/366.

4. *See* the discussion of these issues in connection with workers' rights in the next section.

5. Gravier v. City of Liège (1985) Eur.Comm.Rep. 593. *Accord,* Raulin v. Minister of Education and Science

(1992) Eur.Comm.Rep. I–1027 (Case C–357/89).

6. *See* Commission v. Council (1989) Eur.Comm.Rep. 1425 (ERASMUS).

7. *See* Section 2.0.

referred to in economic literature as the "factors of production." Their inclusion in the Treaty of Rome distinguishes the Treaty from others which merely create customs unions.

Freedom of movement for workers is secured in Article 39, and by an extensive range of legislative acts which have implemented this right. Whereas, for example, North Americans must obtain work permits in order to undertake employment within the European Union, this is not required of citizens and legally resident aliens of the member states.[1] They may seek employment on the same basis as nationals of the EU state where the job is located. In other words, workers from Union countries enjoy "national treatment."[2] This right has caused renewed interest by North Americans in becoming "dual nationals." Irish and Italian "laws of return" generally permit emigrants born in Europe *and* their children or grandchildren to obtain Irish and Italian citizenship. British subjects who are patrials may generally do likewise. And German law on nationality applies to *descendants* of persons who were German citizens or German nationals, with a special preference for refugees of Nazism. Although the U.S. government discourages dual citizenship status for Americans, the benefits of being an EU national under the Treaty of Rome makes this status quite attractive. Dual nationals with one EU citizenship may not be denied their Union rights by another member state whose law gives precedence to their country of habitual residence. In this case, an Argentinian/Italian was entitled to reside and enter business in Spain.[3] But British Overseas Citizens may be denied UK residency rights.[4]

Social Advantages

The right of expatriate European Union workers to bring their families,[5] obtain social services, housing, education and pensions in a nondiscriminatory manner is all provided in a wealth of EU law on "social advantages." There is no Union social security system. Rather, the Union assures equal treatment of claims made against national systems covering health care, old age, taxation, housing, unemployment, family benefits, and workers' compensation.[6] The

§ 4.10

1. Vander Elst v. Office des Migrations Internationales (1994) Eur. Comm.Rep. I–3803.

2. Council Regulation 1612/68; Commission v. France (1974) Eur. Comm.Rep. 359. (French citizenship quota for crews on ships invalid).

3. Micheleitti & ORS v. Delegación del Gobierno en Cantabria (1992) Eur. Comm.Rep. I–4239 (Case C–369/90).

4. Queen v. Secretary of State (Kaur) (2001) Eur.Comm.Rep. I–1237.

5. *See especially* Baumbast v. Secretary of State for the Home Department (2002) Eur.Comm.Rep. I–7091 (spousal and child rights post-divorce/separation). *See also* The Netherlands v. Reed (1986) Eur.Comm.Rep. 1283 (companions; Re Humer (2002) Eur.Comm.Rep. I–1205) (Case C–255/99) (children's rights).

6. *See, e.g.* Regina v. Warry (1977) Eur.Comm.Rep. 2085 (health care); Frilli v. Belgium (1972) Eur.Comm.Rep. 457 (old age); DiPaolo v. Office National de l'Emploi (1977) Eur.Comm.Rep. 315

exercise of the right of free movement by EU workers cannot be subject to the issuance of restrictive residency or entrance permits.[7] They can be required within a reasonable time to report their presence to the host member state.[8] A valid identity card from their home state is all that is required to prove a worker's right to reside elsewhere in the Union.[9] Part-time and probationary workers (such as teachers seeking licensure) are included, as are the unemployed who actively seek work.[10] However, a six months limitation on the right to enter another member state in search of work is reasonable and not contrary to free movement law under the Treaty of Rome.[11] In one decision, the European Court of Justice struck down a longstanding Greek law restricting ownership of land to Greeks as contrary to free movement rights of the Treaty of Rome.[12] In another widely known decision, free movement rights were extended to professional athletes.[13]

Free Movement Exceptions

The only blanket exception to the regime of free movement of workers is established in Article 39(4) of the Treaty of Rome. Employment in the "public service" of member states is exempted. The public service, for these purposes, involves jobs with official authority, including the judiciary, the police, defense forces and tax inspectors.[14] Licensed attorneys fall outside the public service, even though they may be required in order to litigate in national courts.[15] Municipal positions are also included when there is participation in the exercise of public power, which was the case for example in Brussels with the city architect but not city hospital

(unemployment); Reina v. Landeskredit-bank Baden–Württemberg (1982) Eur. Comm.Rep. 33 (family benefits); Pennartz v. Caisse Primaire d'Assurance Maladie des Alpes–Maritimes (1979) Eur.Comm.Rep. 2411 (workers' compensation); Finanzamt Köln-Alstadt v. Schumacker (1995) Eur.Comm.Rep. I–225 (taxation); Commission v. Italy (1988) Eur.Comm.Rep. 29 (housing loans).

7. Rutuli v. Minister for the Interior (1975) Eur.Comm.Rep. 1219; State v. Royer (1976) Eur.Comm.Rep. 497; Regina v. Pieck (1980) Eur.Comm.Rep. 2171; Lawrie–Blum v. Land Baden–Württe,berg (1986) Eur.Com.Rep. 2121; Clean Car Auto Service v. Landeshauptmann Von Wien (1998) Eur.Comm.Rep. I–2521.

8. Re Watson and Belman (1976) Eur.Comm.Rep. 1185.

9. Giagounidis v. City of Reutlingen (1991) Eur.Comm.Rep. I–1069 (Case C–376/89).

10. Lawrie Blum v. Land Baden–Württemberg (1986) Eur.Comm.Rep. 2121; Kempf v. Staatssecretaris van Justitie (1986) Eur.Comm.Rep. 1741; Lair v. Universitat Hanover, (1988) Eur. Comm.Rep. 3161; Regina v. Antonissen (1991) Eur.Comm.Rep. I–0745 (Case C–292/89).

11. Regina v. Antonissen (1991) Eur. Comm.Rep. I–0745 (Case C–292/89).

12. Commission v. Greece (1989) Eur.Comm.Rep. 1461.

13. Union Royale Belge des Societes de Football v. Bosman (1995) Eur. Comm.Rep. I–4921.

14. Sotgiu v. Deutsche Bundespost (1974) Eur.Comm.Rep. 153.

15. Reyners v. Belgium (1974) Eur. Comm.Rep. 631.

nurses.[16] Secondary school teachers are not part of the public service. Such positions are therefore open to Union competition,[17] but may be subject to language requirements.[18]

Member states may restrict the free movement of workers from other Union nations on grounds of public policy (ordre public), public security or public health.[19] These provisions have been litigated extensively. In a long series of decisions, the European Court has evolved rules which limit the power of EU states to expel or deny admission to workers whose past conduct is objectionable. Only when that conduct is effectively combatted if engaged in by its own nationals may restraints on expatriate Union workers be applied.[20] Public policy reasons for limiting the free movement rights of EU workers must be based on the existence of a genuine and serious threat affecting fundamental societal interests.[21] Past criminal convictions, alone, are insufficient.

Reverse Discrimination

The Common Market law prohibiting discrimination against workers from member states does not reach national laws that discriminate against a country's own citizens regarding free movement and employment. In other words, "reverse discrimination" can occur where EU law protects the rights of workers from other states but national law denies similar rights to workers of that nation.[22] In one reverse discrimination case, the right of Italy to prosecute the Italian biotherapists and planotherapists for unauthorized medical practice was upheld notwithstanding EU right of establishment law on diploma recognition and medical doctors.[23] Conversely, when a worker has exercised the right to employment elsewhere in the Union, he or she is entitled to rely on the Treaty of Rome upon returning home.[24]

16. Commission v. Belgium (1982) Eur.Comm.Rep. 1845.

17. Bleis v. Ministère de l'Education Nationale (1992) Eur.Comm.Rep. I–5627 (Case C–4/91). Allue v. Universita di Venezia (1989) Eur.Comm.Rep. 1591.

18. Groener v. Minister for Education (1989) Eur.Comm.Rep. 3967. *Compare* Angonese v. Cassa di Risparmio di Bolzano (2000) Eur.Comm.Rep. I–4139.

19. Article 39(3), Treaty of Rome; Council Directive 64/221.

20. *Compare* Van Duyn v. Home Office (1974) Eur.Comm.Rep. 1337 (denial of right of Church of Scientology secretary from Holland to work in U.K. upheld) with Adoui and Cornuaille v. Belgium (1982) Eur.Comm.Rep. 1665 (denial of right of French waitresses suspected of prostitution to work in Belgium invalid).

21. Regina v. Bouchereau (1977) Eur.Comm.Rep. 1989.

22. Regina v. Saunders (1979) Eur. Comm.Rep. 1129; Moser v. Land Baden–Württemberg (1984) Eur.Comm.Rep. 2539; Scholz v. Opera Universitaria di Cagliari (1999) Eur.Comm.Rep. I–505.

23. Re Nino (1990) Eur.Comm.Rep. I–3537 (Cases C–54/88, C–91/88, C–14/89).

24. Knoors v. Secretary of State for Economic Affairs (1979) Eur.Comm.Rep. 399.

In the early years of the European Community, many Italian workers moved north into the factories of West Germany and to a lesser extent France as the rebuilding of the European economy took place. Membership in the EU was eagerly sought in later years by Greece, Portugal and Spain so as to acquire these rights for their expatriate workers. Prior to membership, Greek, Portugese and Spanish workers were subject to much less liberal national laws on guest workers. These national laws continue for the most part to govern the rights of the large number of Turkish and Slavic employees in Germany, North Africans in France and Commonwealth citizens in Britain. Special employment rights (but not national treatment) have been given to Turkish workers in the Union under the "Ankara Agreement" which acknowledges Turkey's associate status with the European Union.[25]

§ 4.11 Right of Establishment—Professionals; Lawyers

The right to go into business as a self-employed person or through agencies, branches or subsidiaries in another member state is secured by Article 52 of the Treaty of Rome. This is known as the "right of establishment." Many Union entrepreneurs, for example, have used this right to open restaurants throughout the EU. The right of self-establishment carries with it nearly the same bundle of national treatment rights and exceptions associated with employed workers.[1] It is also subject to the *Cassis* formula.

Implementation of the right of establishment for professionals is anticipated in Article 57 by the issuance of Union legislation mutually recognizing diplomas and national licenses. Medical doctors, dentists, veterinarians, architects, insurance agents, nurses, midwives, pharmacists and others have benefited from these provisions and the substantial implementing law that now accompanies them. For example, the Council in 1982 adopted directives about freedom to supply services in the case of travel agents, tour operators, air brokers, freight forwarders, ship brokers, air cargo agents, shipping agents, and hairdressers. It has been relatively easy to deal with those liberal professions (*e.g.,* medicine and allied professions) in which diplomas and other evidence of formal qualification relate to equivalent competence in the same skill. It did, however, take 17 years to negotiate the directive on free movement of veterinarians. And litigation over the implementation of these

---

25. For a case exploring the rights of Turkish workers in the EU under that country's association agreement with the Union, *see* Kus v. Landeshauptstadt Wiesbaden (1992) Eur.Comm.Rep. I–6781 (Case C–237/91).

§ 4.11

1. *See* The Council's General Program for the Abolition of Restrictions on Freedom of Establishment (1962).

directives continues. For example, it took a Commission prosecution to remove the French requirement that doctors and dentists give up their home country professional registrations before being licensed in France.[2]

Diploma Directives

Typically, European Union law on the right of establishment creates minimum professional training standards which, if met, will result in mutual recognition. Substantial variations in training may trigger special admissions requirements, such as time in practice, an adaptation period or an aptitude test.[3] A major single market directive applies this approach to virtually all EU professionals receiving diplomas based upon a minimum of three years of study.[4] A subsequent directive requires mutual recognition of certificates and diplomas awarded for less than three years study,[5] which has been construed to apply to one-year masters degree (LLMs).[6] Mutual recognition in this instance means that access is gained to host country professional bodies. This is different from the home country licensing method of mutual recognition used for banking, insurance and investment advisors.[7] Even in the absence of such legislation, professional disqualification on grounds of nationality is prohibited.[8] When an EU directive establishes practical training requirements for mutual recognition purposes, the host state must give credit for home state training taken in academic courses. In this case, a German-trained architect received credit and was entitled to practice in Belgium.[9]

Legal Profession

Considerable difficulty has been encountered in lifting restrictions within member states on the freedom to provide legal services. For example, within the legal profession there may be only a small amount of training or required knowledge held in common by a "lawyer" from a civil law jurisdiction (*e.g.,* an avocat from France) and a "lawyer" from a common law jurisdiction (*e.g.,* a solicitor from England). As a result, the initial directive relating to

2. Commission v. France (1986) 1 Common Mkt.L.Rep. 57.

3. *See* Commission v. Italy, 2002 Eur.Comm.Rep. I–2235.

4. Council Directive 89/48. *See* Burbaud v. Ministere de l'Emploi et la Solidarite (2003) Eur.Comm.Rep. I–00000 (Case C–285/01) (hospital administrator's diploma).

5. Council Directive 92/51.

6. Kraus v. Land Baden–Württemberg (1993) Eur.Comm.Rep. I–1663.

7. *See* § 4.12.

8. Patrick v. Ministre des Affaires Culturelles (1977) Eur.Comm.Rep. 1199 (architects).

9. Bauer v. Conseil National de l'Ordre des Architectes (1992) Eur. Comm.Rep. I–2797 (Case C–166/191). *See* Commission v. Spain (2000) Eur. Comm.Rep. I–10375 (architects' activities); Josef Corsten (2000) Eur. Comm.Rep. I–7919 (self-employed architect lays floors, no duty to register as skilled trade).

lawyers' services took a delicate approach to the question of freedom to provide legal services and stops short of dealing with a right of establishment.[10] This 1977 directive allows a lawyer from one member state, under that lawyer's national title (*e.g.*, abogado, rechtsanwalt, barrister), to temporarily provide services in other member states. This includes the right to appear in court without retaining local co-counsel unless representation by counsel is mandatory under national laws.[11] Once retained, a local lawyer need not actually conduct the litigation. It is sufficient that the local attorney is retained to "act in conjunction with" the proceedings.[12] But the EU legal services directive cannot be used so as to circumvent national rules on professional ethics, particularly where a dual nationality lawyer has been disbarred and then moves to another state.[13]

Right of Establishment for Lawyers

Directive 77/249 gave rise to lawyer identity cards issued under the auspices of *Commission Consultative des Barreaux Européens* (C.C.B.E.), which has been charged to propose a specific directive about a right of establishment for lawyers. However, the mutual recognition of diplomas accomplished in Council Directive 89/48 applies to lawyers.[14] The maximum adaptation or training period allowed under this directive is three years. In 1997, the long-awaited right of establishment directive was adopted.[15] It mirrors much of the prior law, but makes it easier (than under the diploma directive) to join the local bar after three years of practice under home country title in the host state.

The C.C.B.E. adopted a common Code of Conduct for lawyers in 1988. It is hoped that this Code will ultimately become binding in all member states. It seeks to harmonize rules of conduct on confidentiality, conflicts of interest, segregation of client funds and malpractice insurance. In other areas, the Code does not harmonize, but rather provides choice of law rules to resolve conflicting national approaches to advertising, contingent fees and membership on boards of directors. The host country rules in these areas will apply to lawyers providing services across borders under Directive 77/249. Home country rules apply as to general fee ar-

---

10. *See* Council Directive 77/249.

11. Commission v. Germany (1988) Eur.Comm.Rep. 1123.

12. Commission v. France (1991) Eur.Comm.Rep. I–3591 (Case C–294/89).

13. Gullung v. Conseil de l'Ordre des Avocats (Colmar) (1988) Eur.Comm.Rep. 111.

14. *See* Morgenbesser v. Consiglio dell'Ordine degli avvocati di Genova

(2003) Eur.Comm.Rep. I-___ (Case C–313/01) (French maitrisse en droit degree must be recognized in Italy which has no equivalent).

15. Council Directive 98/5. Unsuccessfully challenged in Luxembourg v. Parliament and Council (2000) Eur. Comm.Rep. I–9131.

rangements. Some EU jurisdictions (e.g., Germany) allow multi-professional practices, but a Dutch ban on practicing law in full partnership with accountants was upheld primarily because of the absence of strict codes of ethics for accountants.[16]

Admission to the practice of law is still governed by the rules of the legal profession of each member state. Several European Court judgments have upheld the right of lawyer applicants to be free from discrimination on grounds of nationality, residence or retention of the right to practice in home jurisdictions.[17] For example, a Greek lawyer who had a doctorate in German law and had worked for some time advising on Greek and EU law in Munich was denied admission to the German bar. On appeal, the Court of Justice held that Article 52 obligates member states not to impede the movement of lawyers in the Union. The member state must compare an applicant's specific qualifications with those detailed by national law. Only if the applicant does not meet all the necessary qualifications may the host state require additional courses or training.[18] By joining the bar in another EU country, lawyers acquire the right to establish themselves in more than one nation. The multinational law firm, pioneered by Baker and McKenzie in the United States, has relatively few regional counterparts in the practice of European Union law. Slowly, however, attorneys from member states are establishing affiliations and sometimes partnerships which reflect and service the economic, political and social integration of Europe. These "European law firms" often compete with existing branches of United States multinational firms for the lucrative practice of EU law.

In professional fields, the real barrier to movement of people across borders is language. In some instances, linguistic requirements for jobs are lawful despite their negative impact on free movement rights.[19] As much as the Union may succeed in its campaign for truly establishing an integrated market, the language barriers within the EU will remain. Although younger generations are increasingly multilingual, a professional who cannot speak to his or her clients or students is unlikely to succeed in another member state.

---

16. Wouters v. The General Council of the Dutch Order of Advocates (2002) Eur.Comm.Rep. I–1577.

17. Reyners v. Belgium (1974) Eur. Comm.Rep. 631; Thieffry v. Conseil de l'Ordre des Avocats de Paris (1977) Eur. Comm.Rep. 765; Van Binsbergen v. Bestuur van de Bedrijfsvereniging voor de Metaalnijverheid (1974) Eur. Comm.Rep. 1299; Gebhard v. Consiglio Dell'Ordine Degli Avocati di Milano (1995) Eur.Comm.Rep. I–4165.

18. Vlassopoulou v. Ministerum fuer Justiz, Bundes und Europaangelegenheiten, 1991 Eur.Comm.Rep. I–4087 (Case C–340/89).

19. *See* Groener v. Minister for Education (1989) Eur.Comm.Rep. 3967. (Irish required for vocational teaching job); Haim v. Kassenzahrartzliche Vereinigung (2000) Eur.Comm.Rep. I–5123 (German required to practice dentistry).

§ 4.12 Freedom to Provide and Receive Services Across Borders

The freedom of nonresidents to provide services within other parts of the Union is another part of the foundations of the Treaty of Rome.[1] The freedom to provide services (including tourism) implies a right to receive and pay for them by going to the country of their source.[2] Free movement to receive unavailable or just better medical care is protected, along with reimbursement rights.[3], commercial, craft and professional services are included within this right, which is usually not dependent upon establishment or registration in the country where the service is rendered.[4] In other words, the freedom to provide or receive services across borders entails a limited right of temporary entry into another member state.

The Council has adopted a general program for the abolition of national restrictions on the freedom to provide services across Union borders. This freedom is subject to the same public policy, public security and public health exceptions applied to workers and the self-employed.[5] The Council's program has slowly been implemented by a series of legislative acts applicable to professional and nonprofessional services. As with the right of self-establishment, discrimination based upon the nationality or nonresidence of the service provider is generally prohibited even if no implementing EU law has been adopted.[6]

In parallel with law developed in connection with the free movement of goods, the Court of Justice in *van Binsbergen* indicated that EU governments may require providers of services from other states to adhere to professional public interest rules under the *Cassis* formula. These rules must be applied equally to all professionals operating in the nation, and only if necessary to ensure that the out-of-state professional does not escape them by

§ 4.12

1. Articles 49 and 50, Treaty of Rome.

2. Luisi and Carbone v. Ministero del Tesoro (1984) Eur.Comm.Rep. 377; Cowan v. Le Trésor Public (1986) Eur. Comm.Rep. 195 (British tourist entitled to French criminal injury compensation); Society for the Protection of Unborn Children Ireland v. Grogan (1991) Eur.Comm.Rep. I-a4685 (abortion services).

3. *See, e.g.,* Muller–Faure v. Onderlinge Waarborg–Maatschappij OZ, 2003 Eur.Comm.Rep. I–4509.

4. Proceedings against Corsten (2000) Eur.Comm.Rep. I–7919 (Oct. 3,

2000) (skilled trades); Säger v. Dennemeyer + Co. (1991) Eur.Comm.Rep. I–4221 (patent agents); Commission v. France (1991) Eur.Comm.Rep. I–659 (tour guides); Commission v. Germany (1986) Eur.Comm.Rep. 3755; Ministère Public v. van Wasemael (1979) Eur. Comm.Rep. 35 (employment agencies).

5. Article 66, Treaty of Rome.

6. Van Binsbergen v. Bestuur van de Bedrijfsvereniging voor de Metaalnijverheid (1974) Eur.Comm.Rep. 1299 (legal representation); Coenen v. Sociaal Economische Raad (1975) Eur.Comm.Rep. 1547 (insurance intermediary).

reason of establishment elsewhere. In other words, if the professional rules (*e.g.,* ethics) of the country in which the service provider is established are equivalent, then application of the rules of the country where the service is provided does not follow. Following *Cassis*, and notably not *Keck*, the Court of Justice has affirmed member state marketing controls over the sale of lottery tickets (social policy and fraud interests)[7] and over "cold calling" solicitations for commodities futures.[8] Telemarketing in most other areas is forbidden, except with prior consumer consent, under a 1977 directive.

Financial Services

Bankers, investment advisors and insurance companies have long awaited the arrival of a truly common market. Their right of establishment in other member states has existed for some time. The right to provide services across borders without establishing local subsidiaries was forcefully reaffirmed by the Court of Justice in 1986.[9] This decision largely rejected a German requirement that all insurers servicing the German market be located and established there. Legislative initiatives undertaken in connection with the single market campaign promise to create genuinely competitive cross-border European markets for banking,[10] investment[11] and insurance[12] services. Licensing of insurance and investment service companies and banks meeting minimum capital, solvency ratio and other EU requirements as implemented in member state laws will be done on a "one-stop" home country basis. Banks, for example, cannot maintain individual equity positions in non-financial entities in excess of 15 percent of their capital funds, and the total value of such holdings cannot exceed 50 percent of those funds.[13] They can participate and service securities transactions and issues, financial leasing and trade for their own accounts. The investment services directive requires home country supervision of the "good repute" and "suitability" of managers and controlling shareholders.[14]

Member states must ordinarily recognize home country licenses and the principle of home country control. For example, Council Directive 89/646 ("the Second Banking Directive") employs the home country single license procedure to liberalize banking services throughout the Union. However, host states retain the right to

---

7. Her Majesty's Customs and Excise v. Schindler (1994) Eur.Comm.Rep. I–1039.

8. Alpine Investments v. Minister Van Financien (1995) Eur.Comm.Rep. I–1141.

9. Commission v. Germany (1986) Eur.Comm.Rep. 3755.

10. *See* Section 4.13.

11. *See* Section 4.15.

12. *See* Section 4.14.

13. Council Directive 89/646.

14. *See* Commission v. Italy (1996) Eur.Commm.Rep. I–2691 (incorporation rule for stockbrokers breaches freedom of establishment).

regulate a bank's liquidity and supervise it through monetary policy and in the name of the "general good." Similarly, no additional insurance permits or requirements may be imposed by host countries when large industrial risks (sophisticated purchasers) are involved. However, when the public at large is concerned (general risk), host country rules still apply.[15] Major auto and life insurance directives employing one-stop licensing principles were adopted late in 1990.[16] The auto insurance directive reproduces the large versus general risk distinctions found in the Second Non–Life Insurance Directive. Host country controls over general risk auto insurance policies are retained until 1995. Host country permits are also required when life insurers from other member states actively solicit business.

Reciprocity and the United States

Unless there is "effective market access" under United States law for European firms, U.S. companies entering the Europe after 1992 may be unable to obtain the benefits of common service markets. This problem is generally referred to as the "reciprocity requirement" of EU legislation. It is this kind of requirement that gave the campaign for a Europe without internal frontiers the stigma of increasing the degree of external trade barriers. Many outsiders, in rhetoric which sometimes seems excessive, refer to the development of a "Fortress Europe" mentality and threat to world trading relations.

There was a rush by non-EU bankers, investment advisors and insurers to get established in the Union before January 1, 1993 in order to qualify for home country licenses. North Americans and others outside the Union have been particularly concerned about certain features of the new legislation mandating effective access in foreign markets for European companies before non-Union firms may benefit from the liberalization of services within the Common Market. Since state and federal laws governing banking, investment services and insurance are quite restrictive, and in no sense can it be said that one license permits a company to operate throughout the United States, one result of European integration has arguably been reform of U.S. regulatory legislation. Since 1994 the United States has noticeably relaxed its rules on interstate banking and largely repealed the Glass–Steagall Act limitations on universal banking.

§ 4.13 Banking

This section focuses on major European Union legislation on banking, capital movements and consumer credit. These include:

---

15. Council Directive 88/357 ("the Second Non–Life Insurance Directive").

16. Council Directives 90/619 (life insurance) and 90/618 (auto insurance).

- First Banking Directive 77/780.

- Second Banking Directive 89/646.

- Consumer Credit Directives 87/102, 90/88.

- Money Laundering Directive 91/308.

- Large Exposures of Credit Institutions Directive 92/121.

- Own Funds (Capital Requirements) Directive 89/299 as amended by Directive 92/16.

- Solvency Ratios Directive 89/647.

- Capital Movements Directive 88/361.

- Deposit Guarantee Schemes Directive 94/19.

Banking Directives

Community regulation of banks originated with the First Banking Directive,[1] adopted by the Council of Ministers in 1977. This directive harmonized the conditions for the exercise of the right of establishment by "credit institutions." Such institutions are defined as undertakings "whose business is to receive deposits and other repayable funds from the public and to grant credits for its own account."[2] To exercise the right of establishment under the First Banking Directive two basic conditions were imposed. At least two persons of good repute and experience had to be running the credit institution which itself had to possess separate and adequate minimum own funds (capital base). These are minimum EU banking standards. Member States can, and frequently do, impose stricter requirements.

The preamble to the First Banking Directive states that "the rules governing branches of credit institutions having their head office outside the Union [*e.g.*, U.S. banks] should be analogous in all Member States." The Directive requires that such branches should not be treated more favorably by the different member states than the branches of EU credit institutions. The Second Banking Directive amended the First.[3] It enables authorized credit institutions relying on a "single license" from home state governments to carry on banking activities throughout the EU via branches or cross-border services. Authorization from the host State is not needed.[4] The provisions of the Second Banking Directive were implemented in all Member States by January 1, 1993.

§ 4.13

1. Council Directive 77/780.

2. Council Directive 77/780, Article 1.

3. Council Directive 89/646.

4. *See* Societe Civile Immobiliere Parodi v. Banque H. Albert de Bary (1997) Eur.Com.Rep. I–3899.

The combined minimum requirements for a single license as a "credit institution" under the Second and the First Banking Directives are as follows: (1) Capital of at least 5 million ECUs or, in exceptional circumstances, 1 million ECUs; (2) management by two persons of good repute and sufficient experience; (3) submission of a business plan, including an organizational structure; and (4) suitable major shareholders (holders of 10 percent or more of the shares or voting rights or those who may exercise "significant influence"). Member states may impose more demanding requirements on their own credit institutions. Such requirements cannot, however, be imposed on credit institutions authorized in other member states. Some commentators have suggested that this provides an incentive to seek out the home state jurisdiction with the least demanding requirements. A credit institution with a single license will be entitled to carry on all of the activities listed in the Directives throughout the Union even if the regulations of the host state prohibit domestic credit institutions from doing so.

A credit institution's single license authorization may cover traditional banking activities, such as deposit-taking and lending. It may also permit lease financing, transmission services, payment services, loan guarantees and commitments, money market trading, futures and options, exchange and interest rate services, participation in securities issues, underwriting, corporate finance, merger and acquisition services, portfolio management and advice, credit reference services and custodial services. If a credit institution wishes to establish a branch elsewhere in the Union, it must notify its home state of its intention and supply the following information: (1) The relevant member state where it intends to establish a branch; (2) a business plan; (3) the address in the host state; and (4) the names of the managers of the branch. In most cases, the home state banking authority must forward within three months this information (together with the amount of the bank's capital base, its solvency ration and details of any deposit guarantee scheme) to the competent authority of the host state. The host state then has two months in which to "prepare for the supervision of the credit institution." It may impose conditions on the activities of the branch "if necessary" in the interest of the "general good."

When providing cross-border services the credit institution has to first notify the authorities of its home state. The home state then has a month within which to send notice to the host state. Host state authorities are entitled to take "appropriate measures" to prevent or punish banking irregularities committed within their territories. For example, restrictions may be placed by host states on the advertising of financial services.

Mergers and acquisitions are also regulated by the Banking Directives. Anyone intending to acquire a "qualifying holding" (a direct or indirect holding representing 10 percent or more of the capital or voting rights) or increase a qualifying holding so that either the proportion of voting rights or capital held reaches thresholds of 20, 33 or 50 percent must inform the home state. These authorities have up to three months to oppose the acquisition if not satisfied as to the acquirer's suitability. "Suitability" is assessed in terms of the ability to provide sound and prudent management of a credit institution. Similar restrictions will cover the disposal or reduction of a qualifying holding. All credit institutions will be required to disclose the details of qualifying holdings to their home states. Sanctions can include the suspension of voting rights.

Credit institutions also have two limits imposed on their shareholdings in other entities. Holdings in businesses that are neither credit institutions nor financial institutions are generally restricted to 10 percent of its own funds. The aggregate value of all such participations is limited to 50 percent of the capital base. The supervision of a credit institution, e.g., on accounting and internal controls, is the responsibility of the home state. The host state authority shares responsibility with the home state for supervising the liquidity of branches within its territory. The host state authority also has complete responsibility for monetary policy measures.

Host state regulation on the grounds of general good is covered in the Second Banking Directive. The preamble states that a host state may "require compliance" with specific provisions of its national laws and regulations where these are for the general good, provided that such provisions are compatible with Union law, intended to protect the general good and do not duplicate equivalent rules under the legislation or regulation of the home member state. This authorization only applies to "unlisted" activities (those activities not covered by the single license) of credit institutions of member states and all activities of noncredit institutions.

Regarding "listed" activities the member states must ensure that there are no obstacles to carrying on activities receiving mutual recognition in the same manner as in the home member state, as long as the latter do not conflict with legal provisions protecting the general good in the host member state. Thus, pending harmonization of "general good" rules, there will be considerable scope for divergent host state general good laws. For example, though credit institutions are expressly granted the right to advertise their services through all available means of communication in host states, such advertising is subject to rules adopted in the interests of the general good governing the form and the content of such advertising. There is no provision for the "mutual recognition" of advertising rules and consequently host state regulations will apply when necessary to protect unsophisticated customers.

Credit institutions from outside the EU that incorporate and obtain a single license under the provisions of the Second Banking Directive will be free to enjoy its benefits. Branches of non-EU banks cannot obtain those benefits. However, a "reciprocity" test must be satisfied before non-EU financial institutions can take full advantage of the new regime. The original reciprocity provisions of the Second Banking Directive were amended following criticism from outside the Union. The United States especially feared that these provisions would be interpreted to require "mirror-image reciprocity". Since the Glass–Steagall Act prohibits banks in the U.S. from engaging in securities business and as U.S. banking laws have traditionally prohibited cross-border branching, mirror-image reciprocity would not have been possible.

The Second Banking Directive on "reciprocity" stipulates that: (1) Member states notify the Commission when they have authorized or allowed acquisitions by banks owned (directly or indirectly) by outsiders; (2) member states inform the Commission of difficulties encountered by their banks in establishing or carrying on activities in countries outside the Union; (3) the Commission report to the Council whether EU banks are being granted equivalent market access in non-EU countries and receiving national treatment (effective market access and national treatment will be viewed in terms of initial entry as well as subsequent operations and acquisitions); (4) if the Commission considers that a Union bank is not being so treated, it may initiate negotiations with the country concerned. The Commission can also require member states to limit or suspend both requests for banking authorizations and the acquisition of shares in Union banks. Neither restraint can continue for more than three months unless authorized by the Council. Non–EU banking subsidiaries located in the Community at the time the Commission and Council take retaliatory action are grandfathered such that these limitations and suspensions cannot apply to their creation of subsidiaries or acquisitions.

One practitioner has reached the following conclusions regarding the Banking Directives:

> The implementation of the Second Banking Directive and the concept of a single license should mean that U.S. banks are able to benefit from relatively greater economies of scale through selling a wider array of services in a larger geographic market. Banks will have the opportunity to reduce their operating costs by, for instance, consolidating their management or their back-office operations. The chance to sell cross-border services, or to set up a branch that has standardized reporting and accounting requirements and which does not need to be independently capitalized, should also reduce costs. However, the corollary of creating a greater competitive environment is

that it may bring operating and profit margins down. In order to get the benefit of a single license, a U.S. bank will have to set up a subsidiary in a Member State which must obtain authorization from that Member State to act as a credit institution. Unfortunately this may involve higher costs than just operating through a branch network, for example, higher tax and capital costs.[5]

Capital Requirements

The capital requirements directives of the EU are based on the Basle Report on the International Convergence of Capital Measurement and Capital Standards produced by the Committee on Banking Regulations and Supervisory Practices meeting at the Bank for International Settlements in Basle, Switzerland in July 1988. Capital requirements addressed to credit risk are set out in the Own Funds Directive and the Solvency Ratio Directive. The Own Funds Directive[6] was adopted by the Council in April 1989 and the Solvency Ratio Directive in December 1989.[7] These two Directives, along with the Second Banking Directive, were brought into force by the Member States January 1, 1993. Directive 92/121 provides for the monitoring and control of large exposures of credit institutions. No exposure to a client or a group of connected clients may exceed 25 percent of the institutions own funds.

The Own Funds Directive seeks to set minimum EU standards. It stipulates the maximum number of items that can be included in a bank's capital base and the maximum level of the qualifying amounts for each of those items. Each member state has discretion over which capital base items they use and whether to adopt a lower ceiling for the qualifying amounts than that specified in the Own Funds Directive. The Directive acknowledges a distinction between types of own funds like the Basle Report's distinction between Tier 1 and Tier 2 capital. This distinction is expressed using the terminology of "original own funds" and "additional own funds". The difference in quality between original and additional own funds is reflected in the respective proportions of these two elements of aggregate own funds. Thus, additional own funds must not exceed original own funds, and certain items of additional own funds must not exceed 50 percent of original own funds.

The Own Funds Directive allows inclusion of the following items as "own funds": (1) Paid up share capital, plus share premium accounts but excluding cumulative preference shares; (2) re-

5. Travers, "Banking and Capital Movements," in Folsom, Lake and Nanda (eds.), *European Community Law After 1992: A Practical Guide for Lawyers*

Outside the Common Market (Kluwer, 1992).

6. Council Directive 89/299.

7. Council Directive 89/647.

serves and profits carried forward from the year end profit and loss account; (3) revaluation reserves; (4) funds for general banking risks (See Directive 91/633); (5) certain value adjustments; (6) selected other items; (7) securities of indeterminate duration and other selected instruments; (8) the commitments of the members cooperative societies and the joint and several commitments of the borrowers of funds; and (9) fixed term cumulative preference shares and certain subordinated capital. The items set out in paragraphs (1) and (2) constitute original own funds. The funds for general banking risks referred to in paragraph (4) are provisionally included in own funds without restriction but subject to review. This means that the items set out in paragraph (3) and paragraphs (5) to (9) constitute additional own funds, the level of which must be limited by reference to the amount of original own funds.

The total of a credit institution's additional own funds must not exceed 100 percent of the amount of the original own funds having first deducted, at book value, any of its own shares, the value of intangible assets such as goodwill and material losses for the current financial year. In addition, the aggregate amount of the items referred to in paragraphs (8) and (9) above must not exceed 50 percent of original own funds after the same deductions. There is a general requirement that the items listed in paragraphs (1) to (4) must be available to a credit institution for unrestricted and immediate use to cover risks and losses as soon as they occur. The amounts being brought into account for the purposes of calculating own funds under these headings must be net of any foreseeable tax charge at the time of calculation or be adjusted to take into account any such tax charge.

The Solvency Ratio Directive requires banks to maintain capital at levels equal to a certain proportion of assets. The credit institution's own funds, as calculated in accordance with the Own Funds Directive, constitute the numerator, the denominator being total assets and off-balance sheet items which have been risk-adjusted. This is then expressed as a percentage. The target ratio is 8 percent. The provisions of the Solvency Ratio Directive are another attempt to set minimum EU standards. The solvency ratio must be calculated not less than twice a year and the solvency ratio of a credit institution with subsidiaries is generally calculated on a consolidated basis.

Money Laundering

A Money Laundering Directive[8] reinforces the commitments made by member states to the United Nations Convention against the illicit traffic in narcotic drugs and psychotropic substances

---

8. Council Directive 91/308, extend-   ed and revised by Directive 2001/97.

(Vienna, 1988) and the Council of Europe Convention on laundering, tracing, seizure and confiscation of proceeds of crime (Strasbourg November 1990). The Money Laundering Directive focuses on civil, not criminal, law. Member states must ensure that laundering of money derived from criminal activity (not just drug trafficking) is prohibited. They must ensure that banks and other financial institutions (including insurance companies) clearly identify their customers before entering into business relations. Any transaction or series of transactions amounting to 15,000 ECUs or more necessitates an investigation into the customer's identity. Credit and financial institutions have to carry out such an investigation even when the amount involved is lower if there is any suspicion of money laundering. The information obtained has to be kept for 5 years from the date following the end of the relationship with the customer or, in the case of transactions, 5 years from the date of execution of the transaction.

Credit and financial institutions have to provide information about money laundering to the relevant authorities. They have to establish appropriate internal monitoring procedures to ensure that the necessary information is obtained. A suspect transaction cannot be carried out until the relevant authorities have been informed. The authorities may order the credit or financial institution not to execute that transaction. There is an exception for those cases where to delay in executing a transaction might alert the suspected launderers to the existence of an investigation. In those cases the transaction can be executed and the relevant authorities informed afterwards. In any event, the institution concerned must not tell its customer of any of this. The Directive requires the member states to enact legislation entitling employees and directors of banks, insurance companies and other relevant financial institutions to disclose customer information without liability. Member states are not precluded from adopting stricter provisions.

Directive 97/5 on cross-border credit transfers sets minimum information standards, maximum transfer time limits, and identification requirements.

§ 4.14 Insurance

This section focuses on major European Union laws on insurance. These laws include:

- First Non-life Insurance Directive 73/239

- Second Non-life Insurance Directive 88/357

- Third Non-life Insurance Directive 92/49

- First Life Insurance Directive 79/267

- Second Life Insurance Directive 90/619

- Third Life Insurance Directive 92/96
- Insurance Agents and Brokers Directive 77/92
- Reinsurance Directives 64/225 and 78/473
- Auto Insurance Directive 90/232

Non-Life Insurance Directives

The First Non-life Insurance Directive was adopted in 1973. It establishes common rules on admission to the insurance business, requirements for undertaking such business and withdrawal from the offering of insurance. This first directive covers insurance for accidents, sickness, transport, general liability, and credit and sure-tyship. National export credit insurance operations are excluded from its coverage. Any insurance company that wants to establish itself in another member state must obtain a license from that state. In other words, the First Non-life Insurance Directive did not establish a single insurance licensing system. It merely established minimum criteria that must be fulfilled in order to obtain national authorizations in host states. Under this directive, insurance companies seeking to do business in other member states must provide the national authorities with a variety of information based upon their home country operations. Such information concerns the types of insurance they are authorized to write, solvency and financial resources. The application must also provide a "scheme of operation" which details the financial structure of the company. If the national authorities refuse to permit an insurance company based in another EU country to undertake business in their jurisdiction, that company must be given a right of judicial review. Notably, this right is not extended to insurance companies from outside the Union, *e.g.,* the United States.

In order to qualify to do business, non-EU insurance companies must be entitled to undertake insurance under their national laws and be approved by the relevant national authorities. Although the Union may agree with non-Union countries to specific provisions concerning insurance companies, including reciprocity, the First Non-life Insurance Directive does not mandate reciprocity. This directive was supplemented by Directive 73/240 which facilitates the right of insurance companies to establish themselves anywhere inside the Union under national treatment conditions. Host states may demand proof of good standing and the absence of prior bankruptcies, but such proof can be provided through home country documentation.

The Second Non-life Insurance Directive was adopted in 1988. This directive builds upon the first, and makes an important distinction between large risk and mass risk insurance business. Mass risk business relates largely to private individuals and is not governed by the Second Non-life Insurance Directive. Large risks are covered, and these are defined to include policy holders with balance sheets of approximately 12 million ECUs, net turnovers of 24 million ECUs and 500 employees. Starting January 1993 these thresholds were lowered by 50 percent. The effect of this reduction will be to expand the scope of the Second Non-life Insurance Directive. Insurance companies are free to provide their services across borders anywhere inside the European Union as regards large risks. For these purposes, as in the banking area, home country licensing and control principles have been adopted. Host country licensing and controls continue in effect for mass risk insurance.

The Third Non-life Insurance Directive was implemented in most member states on July 1, 1994. This directive completes the internal market with respect to non-life insurance. Home country licensing and control are extended for all coverages, including individual consumers. This directive, together with others concerning insurance accounts, seeks to insure a sound financial basis for all European Union insurance companies. It specifically regulates the types of assets that may be used as technical reserves by insurance companies. Member states are able to require that their contract law continue to apply to mass risk insurance issued for their territory. However, contracts concerning large risks will enjoy complete freedom as to choice of law. Various national requirements regarding compulsory insurance are continued throughout the non-life insurance directives and made subject to notification requirements to the national authorities. Special directives are aimed at eliminating particularly restrictive German legal requirements concern credit insurance and suretyship insurance,[1] as well as legal expenses insurance.[2] Directive 2002/13 raises the solvency margin requirements of non-life insurance firms.

Life Insurance Directives

The First Life Insurance Directive was adopted in 1979. This directive focuses on the right to establish insurance subsidiaries in other member states, including rules on admission, doing business and withdrawal. It harmonizes financial guaranties connected with life insurance and the requirements for authorization of the right to sell such insurance. The First Life Insurance Directive prohibits simultaneous operation of life and non-life insurance businesses by one company. However, there is a grandfather clause retaining such rights for companies existing as of 1979. For such companies, certain segregation requirements are established. Minimal rules on

---

§ 4.14

1. Council Directive 87/343.

2. Council Directive 87/344.

technical reserves and solvency margins are also established. Insurance companies from outside the Union are generally permitted in the EU if they meet their home country legal and administrative requirements for life insurance companies. No mandatory reciprocity rule is enacted in the First Life Insurance Directive, although reciprocal agreements with third countries is anticipated by the directive.

The Second Life Insurance Directive was adopted in 1990. This directive generally follows the positions taken in the Second Non-life Insurance Directive. It focuses on cross frontier provision of insurance services. Companies can sell life insurance across borders subject only to home country licensing controls as long as the policyholder has taken the initiative to obtain the policy. This is referred to as a "passive sale." When the company has approached potential policyholders in other member states (active sales), local authorities must be notified and the host country rules will generally apply except in cases of group coverage. The passive sales permission contained in the Second Life Insurance Directive does not apply for three years when brokers are employed in the host country (even if the client has approached the broker on his or her own initiative). This means that host country rules will govern such passive sales through brokers until roughly the end of 1993. In all cases where passive sales are made across borders, the insurance company must provide a certificate of solvency and a certificate listing the classes of insurance it is licensed to offer in its home country. These certificates must be presented to the host country authorities. In addition, the home country must certify that it does not object to the provision of cross-frontier insurance by one of its companies.

The Third Life Insurance Directive was implemented in most member states on July 1, 1994. As in the non-life insurance area, this directive allows companies to operate freely throughout the Union on the basis of home country rules that adhere to limited standards of consumer protection established at the European Union level. The conditions for allowing such freedom to provide services are provided for by further harmonization of provisions relating to the prudential supervision of insurers. Each member state must recognize the insurance supervisory systems of others as equally prudential.

The reduced requirement to obtain only a single authorization, sometimes called a "single passport", available following the implementation of the Third Insurance Directives, is not available to the pure re-insurers or small mutual associations excluded by the First Insurance Directive. Non–EU insurers with their head offices outside the Union, yet with branches in member states, will not be able to take advantage of the "single passport" situation. However, it will apply to subsidiaries of such insurers set up in a member state. While the financial supervision of a company with a head office in a member state is primarily carried out by the "home" member state under the Third Insurance Directives, the host state authorities retain power to prevent persons entering into certain types of contract and to prohibit advertising where it is considered to accord with the common good. Mergers and acquisitions in the insurance industry are regulated under this directive, and each insurer may be required to notify its premiums and reserves to the member states. Directive 2002/12 increases the solvency margins required of life insurers.

The so-called BCCI directive (No. 92/121), prompted by a number of recent cases of fraud (particularly the Bank of Credit and Commerce International case), requires that where a financial undertaking is part of a group sufficient information relating to the group must be provided so as to allow the group to be supervised effectively.

Brokers

Insurance brokers and agents are subject to general European Union rules regarding their licensure. These predominantly concern commercial or professional knowledge. The relevant rules are established in Council Directive 77/92. Reinsurance and coinsurance are the subject of two Council Directives, 64/225 and 78/473. These directives extend the right of establishment and freedom to provide services in the reinsurance and coinsurance fields. Participation in such activities is now exclusively governed by the Union rules as administered by national insurance regulatory authorities. In 1990, the Council adopted Directive 90/618 concerning motor vehicle liability insurance. This directive was the successor to Council Directives 72/166 and 84/5. It coordinates national laws on the level and content of compulsory civil liability insurance for automobiles. Commission Regulation 3932/92 creates a competition law group exemption for insurance industry agreements, decisions and concerted practices. Cooperation between insurance companies regarding statistical compilations of claims, amounts paid and risks taken that is intended to facilitate mortality tables and common risk premium tariffs is allowed provided the companies are not identified. The Regulation permits creation and distribution of optional standard policy conditions for direct insurance and common profit realization models. Co-insurance and co-reinsurance groups for specified risk categories are also exempted from Article 81 for up to 10 and 15 percent of the market respectively.

§ 4.15   Investment Services

The Council has adopted two directives intended to integrate investment services under a single home state licensing regime similar to that adopted for banking. These are the Investment Services Directive and the Capital Adequacy Directive, both effective January 1, 1996.[1] The Investment Services Directive (ISD) creates minimum standards for authorization of investment firms and advisors by member state authorities and stock exchanges. All persons whose regular occupation or business is the provision of investment services to third parties on a professional basis fall within the directive. The ISD divides responsibilities for supervision between the home and host states. The home state will be responsible throughout the Union for authorization and prudential supervision of the firm, with the host state being responsible for applying conduct of business rules and other rules to be made in the "general good"; these rules will apply only to the business which the firm carries on in the host state. Home state authorization will, therefore, allow investment firms to obtain membership in the stock and electronic trading exchanges of all other member states subject only to business conduct and "general good" regulation by the host state. There will be no need to become "established" in the host country, but branches may be opened there. Such branches will, however, be subject to the prudential supervision of the firm's home state. This prudential supervision will include fitness and properness, administrative and accounting methods, holding and protection of client securities and funds and conflicts of interest. Trade in commodities is not governed by the ISD.

One controversial aspect of Union law on investment services concerns the "transparency" of stock markets. Minimum disclosure duties are established for stock exchanges such that investors will have all commercially useful and accessible information relevant to stock trading, including price movements and share volumes. Only in unusual circumstances may these duties be suspended (*e.g.,* very large transactions, illiquid trades and very small markets).

The Capital Adequacy Directive (CAD) requires minimum capitalization for investment firms to which CAD applies. A minimum requirement of 125,000 EUROs applies to investment firms which provide investment services and operate from investor instructions, including holding client funds and securities, but which do not deal for their own account or underwrite issues. This requirement is reduced for investment firms which are not permitted to hold client funds and securities, to deal for their own account or to underwrite issues. For all other investment firms the requirement is 730,000 EUROs. An additional minimum of 25 per cent (thirteen weeks) of the preceding year's fixed overhead costs must be maintained. Furthermore, the CAD directive details minimum capital requirements for market risk exposure. These rules apply to both investment companies *and* banks or other credit institutions trading securities. They cover position, settlement, counterparty, foreign-exchange and other risks undertaken in their "trading books." The broad thrust of the EU investment services directives is to place banks and investment firms on an equal footing as regards single licensing and capital adequacy controls in securities trading. National restraints upon the direct trading of securities by banks had to be removed by 1999. As under the Union's banking legislation, existing U.S. and other third party investment advisors are grandfathered in their European operations. New licenses to non-Union advisors are subject to a review of foreign country treatment of EU counterparts.

§ 4.16   Capital Movements, the European Monetary System and A Common Currency

The Treaty of Rome is also concerned with the free movement of money. "Current payments" associated with import/export transactions in goods and services, as well as wage remittances, are routinely made and protected by Articles 73 and 106. This includes money taken abroad to make payment for tourist, medical, educational or business travel services.[1] But it does not include the unsubstantiated export of banknotes.[2]

The free movement of *capital* goals of the Treaty of Rome have been much delayed. In fairness, the Treaty initially just required member states to be "as liberal as possible" in granting exchange control authorizations for investment capital transfers. This provision acknowledged the sensitivity of the member states' concerns about disequilibriums in balance of payments and currency values.[3] It was not until the implementation of the single market campaign that new legislative acts of the Union firmly entrenched the right of individuals and companies to move capital across borders without substantial limitation.[4] This approach was strongly reaffirmed by Maastricht amendments to the Treaty of Rome Article 56 prohibiting "all restrictions on the movement of capital" inside the EU *and* as between the EU and third party nations.[5] This blanket right is

---

§ 4.16

1. Luisi and Carbone v. Ministero del Tesoro (1984) Eur.Comm.Rep. 377. *See* Criminal Proceedings against Sanz de Lera (1995) Eur.Comm.Rep. I–4821 (prior declarations but not prior authorizations permissible).

2. Re Casati (1981) Eur.Comm.Rep. 2595.

3. Articles 56–60, Treaty of Rome.

4. Council Directive 88/361.

5. *See* Svensson v. Ministre du Logement (1995) Eur.Comm.Rep. I–3955 (denial of interest rate subsidy indirectly restricts free movement of capital); Association Eglise de Scientologie de Paris v. The Prime Minister (2000) Eur. Comm.Rep. I–1335 (French prior authorization for investments too indefinite, contrary to free movement of capital rights); In re Trummer and Mayer (1999) Eur.Comm.Rep. I–1661 (Austrian mortgage registration national currency rule invalid).

subject to existing third party restraints regarding investment, real estate, financial services and securities. Also permitted are restraints to prevent "infringements of national law" (taxation especially)[6] and for reasons of public policy or security.[7]

European Monetary System

The capital movements legislation, combined with the various banking and investment services reforms and Maastricht amendments, promises to bring forth a remarkable new financial sector in the European Union. In moving toward monetary union, the member states created the European Monetary System (EMS). When the EMS was established in 1979, member states deposited 20 percent of their gold and dollar assets with the European Monetary Cooperation Fund in exchange for an equivalent amount of European Currency Units (ECUs). This fund is used as a non-cash means of settlement between central banks undertaking exchange rate support.

The legal basis for the European Monetary System and European Currency Units was substantially advanced by the addition to the Treaty of Rome of Article 98 in the Single European Act of 1987. This article committed the member states to further development of the EMS and ECU, recognized the cooperation of the central banks in management of the system, but specifically required further amendment of the Treaty if "institutional changes" were required. In other words, a common currency managed by a central bank system was *not* part of the campaign for a Europe without internal frontiers. Draft plans for such developments surfaced in the Commission using the U.S. Federal Reserve Board as a model. Britain, always concerned about losses of economic sovereignty (what greater loss is there?), proposed an alternative known as the "hard ECU." This proposal would have retained the national currencies but added the hard ECU as competitor of each, letting the marketplace in most instances decide which currency it preferred.

In December of 1989, the European Council (outvoting Britain) approved a three stage approach to economic and monetary union (EMU). Stage One began July 1, 1990. Its focus was on expanding the power and influence of the Committee of Central Bank Governors over monetary affairs. This Committee was a kind of EuroFed in embryo. It was primarily engaged in "multilateral surveillance." Stage One also sought greater economic policy coordination and convergence among the member states.

6. *See* Sandoz v. Finanzlandeskirektion (1999) Eur.Comm.Rep. 7041 (Austrian tax not justified).

7. *See Svensson* and *Scientologie de Paris* cited above. *See also* In re Albore (2000) Eur.Comm.Rep. I–5965 (July 13, 2000) (real estate and security).

Stage Two anticipated the creation of a European Union central banking system, but functioned with the existing national currencies in the context of the EMS and ERM. Stage Two was a learning and transition period. In October of 1990, it was agreed (save Britain) that Stage Two would commence January 1, 1994. This deadline was actually met, and the European Monetary Institute was installed in Frankfurt. It was the precursor to the European Central Bank. Stage Three involved the replacement of the national currencies with a single currency, the EURO, managed by a European Central Bank. In December of 1991, agreement was reached at Maastricht to implement Stage Three no later than Jan. 1, 1999 with a minimum of seven states. Britain and Denmark reserved a right to opt out of Stage Three.

All member states had to meet strict economic convergence criteria on inflation rates, government deficits, long-term interest rates and currency fluctuations. To join the third stage, a country was supposed to have an inflation rate not greater than 1.5 percent of the average of the three lowest member state rates, long-term interest rates no higher than 2 percent above the average of the three lowest, a budget deficit less than 3 percent of gross domestic product (GDP), a total public indebtedness of less than 60 percent of GDP, and no devaluation within the ERM during the prior two years. These criteria will likewise govern admission of the new member states from Central Europe into the EURO zone.

European Central Bank

It was also agreed at Maastricht that in the third stage the European Central Bank (ECB) and the European System of Central Banks (ECSB) would start operations. The ECB and ECSB are governed by an executive board of six persons appointed by the member states and the governors of the national central banks. The ECB and the ECSB are independent of any other European institution and in theory free from member state influence. Their primary responsibility is to maintain price stability, specifically keeping price inflation below two percent per year. In contrast, the U.S. Federal Reserve has three primary responsibilities: maximum employment, stable prices and moderate long-term interest rates.

The main functions of the ECB and ECSB are: (1) define and implement regional monetary policy; (2) conduct foreign exchange operations; (3) hold and manage the official foreign reserves of the member states; and (4) supervise the payments systems. The ECB has the exclusive right to authorize the issue of bank notes within the Common Market and must set interest rates to principally achieve price stability. The Court of Justice may review the legality of ECB decisions. The ECB works closely with the Ecofin Council's broad guidelines for economic policy, such as keeping national budget deficits below 3 percent of GDP in all but exceptional circumstances (2 percent decline in annual GDP). If the Ecofin considers a national government's policy to be inconsistent with that of the region, it can recommend changes including budget cuts. If appropriate national action does not follow such a warning, the Ecofin can require a government to disclose the relevant information with its bond issues, block European Investment Bank credits, mandate punitive interest-free deposits, or levy fines and penalties. By 2004, half the Eurozone states were under threat of sanctions for failure to comply with the 3 percent budget deficit rule, which does not appear to be enforceable before the Court of Justice.[8]

EURO Zone

The economic performance of member states in 1997 became the test for admission to the economic and monetary union. Since both France and Germany had trouble meeting the admissions criteria, this opened a window for much more marginal states such as Belgium, Italy and Spain to join immediately. Greece also subsequently qualified for the EURO zone. As expected, Denmark, Britain and Sweden opted out of initial participation in the common currency. The Danes did so by voting No in a year 2000 national referendum. The Swedes voted similarly in 2003.

On January 1, 1999, the participating states fixed the exchange rates between the EURO and their national currencies. National notes and coins were removed from the market by July 2002 as the EURO was installed. The EURO has been used for most commercial banking, foreign exchange and public debt purposes since 1999. It has also been adopted (voluntarily) by the world's securities markets, and by Monaco, San Marino, the Vatican, Andorra, Montenegro and Kosovo.

The arrival of the EURO has important implications for the United States and the dollar. For decades, the dollar has been the world's leading currency, although its dominance has been declining since the early 1980s. Use of the Deutsche Mark and Yen in commercial and financial transactions, and in savings and reserves, had been steadily rising. The EURO is likely to continue the dollar's decline in all of these markets. It is certainly the hope of many Europeans that they have successfully created a rival to the dollar.

§ 4.17 Common Transport Policy

The Union's common transport policy is another objective that the Treaty of Rome outlines. Despite its critical role in the free movement of goods and people within the Common Market, trans-

---

8. See Commission v. Council (2004) Eur.Comm.Rep. I–00000 (Case C–27/04).

portation is an area in which the Treaty's aspirations have long remained unfulfilled. Trade restraints in road, rail and air transportation within the European Union abound. Indeed, the level of frustration with the lack of integration in this field is reflected in a lawsuit filed by the Parliament against the Council before the European Court of Justice seeking to force the Council to fully implement the Treaty's goals for a more common and integrated transportation market.[1] The Court found that there had been a "failure to act" by the Council which had to be remedied within a reasonable time. There have been important reforms in the transportation field since then.

Road Transport

After much delay, progress has been made in road transportation. Legislation has been issued to abolish discriminations arising from different (but still regulated) rates and from conditions applied to like goods in like circumstances. European Union law also deals with common rules for international road carriage, restrictions upon drivers' hours, and installation of tachygraphs that record such hours. The latter requirement caused a furor in Britain because it stopped drivers from "moonlighting" extra runs.[2] Differences among the Member States about road taxes, safety requirements, noise levels, and truck weights and dimensions have been mostly resolved. In 1988, a Council directive vastly increased the number Union authorizations of interstate carriage of goods. Since 1993, such authorizations are unlimited, though subject to qualitative licensing controls.[3] Another Council Regulation removes restraints on motor carriers hauling goods inside other member states (cabotage).[4] At least in this area, the Council has seriously addressed its obligations under the 1985 Court of Justice judgment of inaction.

Maritime Transport

Council Regulations 4055–58/86 on maritime transport services move in the same direction (especially by removing so-called national flag reservations), but fail to deal with "cabotage" (transport within one EU state). European Union competition law rules apply, as do its antidumping rules.[5] This represents the first application of dumping law in the services sector.

§ 4.17

1. European Parliament v. Council (1985) Eur.Comm.Rep. 1513.

2. Commission v. United Kingdom (1979) Eur.Comm.Rep. 419.

3. Council Directive 1841/88.

4. Council Regulation 2454/92.

5. *See* Chapters 6 and 7.

Air Transport

Air transport has been a tougher nut to crack. Market-sharing, profit pooling and other restrictive cartel practices have long victimized Europe's flying public. Not surprisingly, many of the Union's airlines are governmentally owned. In the so-called "Nouvelles Frontières" case, the Court of Justice struck a blow for greater competition and consumer benefit by legitimizing EU and national law enforcement actions against restrictive airline practices.[6] Price fixing by air carriers and state approvals of rates (including on flights to and from the Union) are unlawful unless specifically exempted by the Commission.[7]

Since these decisions, Commission threats of prosecutions combined with new legislation deregulating the market have made some headway at flying friendlier skies in Europe. These laws are known as the First (1987) and Second (1990) Air Transport Liberalization Packages. For example, the old system that allowed any carrier on a route to veto low-fare proposals by other airlines was replaced by the "double disapproval" rule. It now takes disapproval by two civil air authorities to negate low-fare proposals. Moreover, the right of governments to oppose the introduction of new fares and market access was limited.[8] The Commission (after winning a major case before the Court of Justice)[9] has also announced an intention to take over from the member states the responsibility for negotiating international air-traffic agreements. Traditionally, these agreements have been bilaterally undertaken at the national level.

Early in 1992, the Council adopted the Third Package of Liberalization measures on air transport.[10] Under this package, airlines have substantial freedom to set ticket prices, operating throughout the Union under a single license issued by national authorities employing common EU financial and safety criteria. Each airline is able to acquire freight and passengers in other EU nations (cabotage rights). National authorities may regulate flights and prices to and from non-member countries, and within their internal markets. National authorities may also intervene if they deem Union fares unreasonably low or high, with the airline

6. Ministère Public v. Asjes (1986) Eur.Comm.Rep. 1425. *See* Council Directives 3975/87 and 3976/87.

7. Ahmed Saeed Flugreisen v. Zentrale zur Bekämpfung unlauteren Wettbewerbs (1989) Eur.Comm.Rep. 838.

8. *See* Council Directives 87/601 (tariffs), 87/602 (market access) and Council Regulations 3975/87, 3976/87 on competition law. Taken together, these measures are sometimes referred to as the

"First Package of Liberalization." The "Second Package" created more flexibility on fares and market access. *See* Council Regulations 2432/90 (tariffs) and 2343/90 (market access).

9. Commission v. Belgium, 2002 Eur. Comm.Rep. I–9681.

10. *See* Council Directives 2407/92, 2408/92 and 2409/92.

retaining a right to appeal such interventions to the Commission. Late in 1992, the Council issued a series of additional regulations on airline license criteria, market access, consumer protection and competition.[11] Although it employs a four-year transition period, the Third Package of Liberalization had an immediate impact. Sparked by Lufthansa's price-cutting, airline rate competition has improved. Discounter Ryanair for example is successfully adapting the Southwest Airlines formula to the EU market.

The Treaty on European Union added a number of provisions to the Treaty of Rome intended to foster the growth of trans-European networks, including transportation.[12] Special emphasis is placed on inter-operability and access issues.

Transport Legislation

The following is a partial list of major EU transport laws regarding fares and market access. Technical laws covering vehicle and operator safety are omitted.

- Regulation 4055/86 (freedom to provide maritime services)
- Regulation 4056/86 (maritime services and competition law)
- Regulation 4057/86 (unfair maritime pricing)[13]
- Regulation 4058/86 (ocean cargoes)
- Directive 87/601 and Regulation 2342/90 (scheduled airfares)
- Directive 87/602 and Regulation 2343/90 (air passenger sharing and market access)
- Regulations 3975/87, 2344/90 (competition law and airlines)
- Regulation 4060/87 (road and inland waterway border controls)
- Regulation 1841/88 (road transport quotas)
- Regulation 2671/88 (coordination of airline capacity, revenues, tariffs and slot allocations at airports)
- Regulation 4058/89 (road carrier rates)
- Regulations 4059/89, 296/91 (provision of intrastate services by nonresident road carriers)
- Directive 91/224 (combined railroad carriage)
- Regulation 294/91 (air cargo services)
- Regulation 2454/92 (road transport services by nonresident carriers)
  - Directives 96/26, 98/76 (road haulers, licenses)

11. Council Regulations 2407–2411/92.

12. *See* Article 154.

13. *See* "The Hyundai Case," O.J. 1989 L4/1; Council Regulation 15/89 (unfair maritime services result in special duties).

- Directive 96/48 (high-speed rail)
- Directive 99/62 (road tolls)
- Directive 2002/15 (working time, road transport)
- Regulation 411/2004 (competition rules apply to airlines)
- Decision 2004/96 (U.S. commitments to protect personal data of air travelers)
- Directive 2004/49 (railway safety)
- Directive 2004/54 (road tunnel safety)
- Regulation 549/2004 (air travel/safety framework)

Chapter 5

EUROPEAN UNION BUSINESS LAW

Table of Sections

§ 5.0 Introduction

Some of the most dramatic surrenders of national sovereignty to EU institutions occur in the business law area. If a common market is to result, many national economic policies must be coordinated or conformed to uniform standards. Thus the Treaty of Rome seeks to minimize the trade distorting impact of national economic laws. Taxation is an excellent and perhaps the most difficult example.

§ 5.1 VAT and Excise Taxation, Savings Taxation

If each government were to legislate freely and differently on taxation, the operation of the Common Market would clearly be affected. Article 90 of the Treaty of Rome forbids discriminatory or protective taxation based on nationality or the origin of products. The goal of this article is to prohibit the use of tax laws as a trade barrier and ensure that goods which compete are equally taxed. The practical effect of Article 90 is to convey substantial powers of judicial review over national tax law and policy to the European Court. France, for example, has repeatedly found its annual car taxes under such review. France based this tax on a power rating scale the practical effect of which was to tax all French autos at a lesser rate than some imports. This tax system was twice held invalid under Article 90 of the Treaty of Rome.[1] A Greek tax on imported cars not applied domestically also ran afoul of Article 90.[2] So too did an Italian tax on bananas.[3]

Value-Added Taxes

Sales taxes and what the Europeans refer to as "turnover taxes" can also have a trade distorting impact. Each member state now has a turnover tax generally referred to as the value-added tax (VAT). This was not always the case. Britain, for example, had to switch from a sales tax to a VAT upon joining the EU. The VAT is a cumulative multistage tax system encountered in virtually every transaction of goods *or services* throughout the Union. United States attorneys might ponder what their clients' reactions would be if they added service taxes to their fees. The Sixth VAT Directive[4] adopted in 1977 was particularly notable. It established a uniform basis for VAT assessment within the EU governing territorial application, taxable transactions, the place of taxable transaction, chargeable events and the chargeability of the tax, applicable rates and exemptions, deductions, and persons liable for VAT and their obligations.

§ 5.1

1. Hamblot v. Directeur des Services Fiscaux (1985) Eur.Comm.Rep. 1367; Re Feldain (1987) Eur.Comm.Rep. 3536. *See*, more recently, De Danske Bilimportorer v. Skatteministeriet, 2003 Eur. Comm.Rep. I–6065.

2. Commission v. Hellenic Republic (1990) Eur.Comm.Rep. I–1567 (Case C–105/92). *Accord*, Commission v. Greece (1997) Eur.Comm.Rep. I–5981.

3. Commission v. Italy (1987) Eur. Comm.Rep. 2013.

4. Council Directive 77/388.

Although harmonization has been achieved as to the nature of the required tax system, the VAT, differing levels of VAT taxation within the Union continue to distort trade relations. Britain, for example, has generally charged one uniform VAT rate of 15 to 17.5 percent but zero rated a number of "necessities." Italy, on the other hand, had three levels of VAT with luxuries taxed at times as high as 38 percent. Furthermore, each country established tax collection points at its borders in order to assure the collection of the proper amount of VAT for particular products in accordance with national law (the "destination principle"). These "tax frontiers" probably represented the most significant nontariff trade barrier in the Union prior to 1993.

Many considered the ability of the European Union to achieve a consensus as to the proper levels of VAT and excise taxation, or at least to reduce the degree of differences in such taxation among the member states, to be the litmus test of the campaign for a fully integrated market. Late in 1992, the Council formally agreed to the Commission's proposed interim VAT system scheduled to last through 1996. Agreement was reached on alignment of VAT rates. At this point, Denmark and Sweden have the highest 25 percent VAT rates with Luxembourg the lowest at 15 percent. Since 2003, VAT is collected on Internet sales and services, including digital downloads. The tax frontiers have been eliminated by imposing VAT reporting and collection duties on importers and exporters using the destination principle on VAT rates. Customers must obtain a VAT registration number which must be given to their cross-border suppliers. The suppliers will report these numbers and transactions to the relevant national tax authorities, all of whom are electronically linked.

The harmonization of VAT rules inside the Union has had a wide ranging impact. Regarding the taxation of boats, for example, it used to be that a buyer or importer for personal use could gain VAT exemption by exporting the boat every 6 to 12 months to another country. This was commonly done. However, a 6–month VAT exemption limit for the entire Union has been imposed since 1993. This means that VAT exemption can be had only by leaving the EU for 6 months, a much more difficult requirement given European geography and most boater preferences.

Excise Taxes

Excise duties are an obvious example of the potential for trade distortion through taxation. Excise taxes on imported liquor, for example, must be levied at the same rate, on the same basis and by the same methods as domestic competitors. Low alcohol, cheap wines imported into Britain thus could not be taxed more than beer.[5] Nor could France discriminate in taxation of wine versus grain spirits.[6] But the prohibition against discriminatory internal taxation does not apply where there are no similar or competing national products.[7]

The excise tax frontier has been eliminated by moving to a system of interlinked bonded warehouses between which goods can move easily. To help prevent smuggling from low-tax to high-tax member states, the Council agreed to "presumption of fraud" limits on duty-paid imports. These limits are 110 liters of beer, 90 liters of wine, 800 cigarettes, and 10 liters of spirits. An individual must prove, if challenged by a customs official, that imports above these limits are for private consumption rather than for resale. The UK, Denmark and Ireland, countries which have high excise tax rates, have indicated they will definitely use the presumption.

As with the VAT, excise taxation will continue to follow the destination principle.[8] The Commission hopes to move to taxation on the basis of origin principles. Under the destination method, goods are shipped within the Common Market net of tax and incur VAT upon entry into the importing country. An origin-based system would apply VAT to exported goods before they are shipped, thus collecting tax revenues in the country where the value was added.

Tax Enforcement, Savings Taxation

As a supplement to the extensive tax treaty network among members of the Union on tax enforcement, the Council adopted the 1977 Tax Authorities Mutual Assistance Directive. The Directive provides for information exchange between the tax authorities of the Union's member states. It requires information sharing when a reduction of tax in one member state is likely to give rise to an increase in tax in another. The Directive covers the VAT, income taxation, capital gains and the sale of property, but does not affect excise duties. All information exchanged is held in confidence. A 1990 directive sought to extend the Mutual Assistance Directive to inheritance and gift taxes. It also sought to remove administrative and legal barriers to cross-border disclosure and enforcement, including a proposed agreement to override secrecy laws in cases of alleged tax fraud. Luxembourg vetoed the proposal, illustrating the need for unanimous Council votes on tax legislation. Luxembourg was especially concerned with the degree of disclosure required of banks. Council Directive 2003/48 addresses taxation of interest

5. Commission v. United Kingdom ("Wine and Beer") (1983) Eur. Comm.Rep. 2265.

6. Commission v. France (1980) Eur. Comm.Rep. 347.

7. Commission v. Denmark (1990) Eur.Comm.Rep. 4509 (Case C–47/88).

8. Council Directive 92/12.

income of nonresidents by promoting the exchange of tax information and withholding, nonmember Switzerland included. This directive is expected to particularly hit Germans with bank accounts in Luxembourg and Switzerland, but also covers Monaco, Lichtenstein, Andorra and San Marino. Directive 2003/49 eliminates taxes levied in source countries on interest and royalty payments between associated companies.

§ 5.2   Corporate Taxation

There are wide variations on corporate income tax levels among the EU member states, which low-tax countries like Ireland view as essential to attract foreign investment. Harmonization of corporate taxes has been proposed, but the unanimous voting rules for tax legislation make such proposals difficult to enact. Business tax rules that discriminate on nationality grounds may breach the right of establishment secured by Article 43 of the Treaty of Rome. In one decision, the Court of Justice invalidated French tax rules that denied tax credits to shareholders of branches operated in France by companies from other member states.[1] These credits were generally available to domestic enterprises, including French subsidiaries of foreign firms. The Court found such discrimination to violate Article 43. The principal opposition to the French tax rules came from the insurance sector. Another decision involving banking affirms the right of private parties to challenge national tax laws that are discriminatory as applied to deposits obtained by persons from other member states.[2] The right to be free from discrimination on grounds of nationality has also been extended to corporations doing business in other EU jurisdictions, particularly in cases of tax liability discrimination between local and "nonresident" companies. In one notable application, the U.K. was required to make tax refunds to non-resident enterprises on the same basis as to British corporations.[3]

The Council has also been active in the corporate tax area, focusing particularly on double taxation issues. A 1969 Directive abolished stamp duties on securities.[4] It also created a limited tax rate band for capital formation, share issuance, and other asset contributions. However, the transfer of profits between two companies having a common shareholder can be subject to capital taxation[5] and branch offices equipped with equipment and personnel

§ 5.2

1. Commission v. France (1986) Eur. Comm.Rep. 273.

2. *See* Van Eycke v. A.S.P.A. (1988) Eur.Comm.Rep. 1469 (Case 267/86).

3. Regina v. Inland Revenue Commissions (1993) Eur.Comm.Rep. I–04017 (Case 330/91).

4. Council Directive 69/335.

5. Weber Haus v. Finanzamt Freiburg–Land (1992) Eur.Comm.Rep. (Case C–49/91).

engaging in their own activities can benefit from a reduction in capital taxation.[6] Share transfers between unlimited liability shareholders and limited liability shareholders are not subject to capital duties.[7] Transactions subject to capital duty are taxable only in the member state where the effective center of management is located. For those without a company center in the Union, the member state of the company's registered office is the taxing jurisdiction.

The Council adopted directives in 1990 on the taxation of cross-border mergers,[8] the taxation of dividends paid by subsidiaries to parent companies,[9] and a five-year "trial" convention on arbitration of transfer pricing tax disputes between member states.[10] Additional directives on taxation of interest and royalties as between parent and subsidiary companies, and the allocation of losses as between them are expected to follow. Nevertheless, there are substantial differences among the member states on corporate taxation. One tax practitioner has summarized these differences as follows:

> The Netherlands, Luxembourg and Spain have wholly unintegrated classical structures. Greece and Portugal have partial integration with respect to dividends at the corporate level, the former through dividend deductions and the latter through a split-rate system. The remaining seven States provide relief for dividend taxation at the shareholder level under some form of imputation or credit system. Rates are also widely divergent, with basic rates on undistributed profits ranging up from zero to 56%, imputation credits up to 56.25%, and withholding tax rates on distributed profits from zero to 50%.

> The taxation of dividends, interest and royalties which are paid from one member state to another currently bears no relationship to the underlying corporation tax or to withholding tax paid elsewhere. As a result, the combined corporate taxes borne by particular dividend streams within the EC may vary considerably from one country to another. Imputation credits, moreover, generally are not extended to shareholders in other EC States and the treatment of foreign source income differs markedly from country to country. Further, while some countries tax foreign source income but give a credit for underlying taxes paid elsewhere, others will exempt the income from further taxation under provisions of domestic law or treaty arrangements. Treatment of income arising from branch opera-

6. Commerz–Credit–Bank v. Finanzamt Saarbrücken (1992) Eur. Comm.Rep. I–05225 (Case C–50/91).

7. Finanzamt Kassel–Goethestrasse v. Kommanditgesellschaft Viesmann (1993) Eur.Comm.Rep. I–00971 (Case C–280–91).

8. Council Directive 90/434.

9. Council Directive 90/435.

10. Convention 90/463.

tions also may differ from that applied to dividends from subsidiaries.[11]

Mergers Taxation

The 1990 Mergers Taxation Directive facilitates corporate transfers and reorganizations without immediate tax costs by eliminating tax on any capital gains, allowing cross-border transfer of tax exempt reserves, and allowing transfer and carryforward of unutilized tax losses. Depreciation and any future gains or losses on the transferred assets are calculated by applying the transferor's basis. The member state that has allowed the deferral of tax retains the power to tax any profits on the ultimate disposition of the relevant assets. It also continues to tax the ongoing business operations in that member state after the transfer. The Mergers Taxation Directive applies only to transactions between companies in the Union. The companies must therefore be residents and subject to tax in a member state. The directive applies to mergers, divisions, share exchanges and asset transfers. These transactions include most stock-for-stock acquisitions, corporate combinations, divisions and liquidations. However, shareholders of the transferor company may only receive stock in most cases. In limited circumstances, an additional cash or property "boot" may be allowed. A member state may deny or withdraw these tax benefits if it determines that a principal objective of the underlying transaction is tax avoidance or evasion. The absence of valid commercial purpose may give rise to a presumption that the transaction was motivated by tax evasion or tax avoidance. Tax relief may also be denied if a company reorganizes to avoid worker participation obligations.

Parent-Subsidiary Taxation

The 1990 Parent–Subsidiary Taxation Directive removes withholding on profits distributed by subsidiaries to parent companies in different member states. Likewise, the member states of parent companies may not tax distributions of profits received from subsidiaries. The directive took effect Jan. 1, 1992 and applies to companies that are resident for tax purposes and subject to corporate tax in a member state. Dividends paid to a parent company or a stockholder outside the EU are subject to the ordinary tax rules. A parent company exists if it has held 25 percent of the capital or voting rights of a company resident and subject to tax in another member state for at least two years. A parent's member state will not generally tax distributed profits received from a subsidiary except upon liquidation. The parent's member state may, alterna-

---

11. Rich and Wilson, "EC Taxation in 1992" in Folsom, Lake and Nanda (eds.), *European Community Law After* *1992: A Practical Guide for Lawyers Outside the Common Market* (Kluwer, 1992).

tively, tax the profits distributed to the parent. But it must allow a credit (the "deemed-paid credit") for the corporation tax paid by the subsidiary. Each member state of a parent company may disallow deductions against the taxable profits of the parent for any costs or losses relating to the holding or disposing of stock in the subsidiary. Moreover, profits distributed by a subsidiary to a parent company are withholding tax exempt provided the parent company holds a minimum of 25 percent of the subsidiary's capital.

Transfer Pricing

The 1990 Transfer Pricing Arbitration Convention adopts an "arm's length" standard to govern dealings between related entities in two states, an enterprise in one state with its permanent establishment in another member state, or an entity of one state with a permanent establishment in a third country of an entity of a second state. If the tax authorities are unable to agree within two years, an *advisory* commission delivers an opinion on the case. This advisory commission will be composed of an equal number of representatives of the competent tax authorities and an "uneven number of independent persons of standing" appointed by mutual agreement. The tax authorities must reach a decision within six months of the advisory commission's opinion. The authorities are bound by the opinion unless they subsequently reach a mutually agreeable alternative. Double taxation is deemed to have been eliminated when either the profits included are only taxed in one state or the taxable charge in one state is reduced by an amount equal to the tax chargeable in the other state. Businesses liable for a "serious penalty" (defined by national rules) because of transfer pricing violations have no recourse to the Arbitration Convention. The Convention does not limit any pre-existing rights under current bilateral double taxation treaties.

§ 5.3   Government Subsidies

The Union's competition policy is a natural consequence of its Common Market. The dismantling of internal tariffs, quotas, and measures of equivalent effect opens up traditionally sheltered national markets to competition through trade in goods and services. Having created the playing field, so to speak, the Treaty of Rome seeks through its rules on competition to ensure that the field is as level as possible for all who participate. These rules are of two basic types: business competition (*i.e.*, antitrust) and government subsidies. The business competition rules of the Union originate in Articles 81–86 of the Treaty of Rome. They are of such enormous importance to all who do business with the Community that Chapter 7 is devoted exclusively to them.

Subsidies by governments are one of the most intractable of world and Common Market trade problems. In the first place, there are subsidies everywhere. For example, most tax laws (including the Internal Revenue Code) are littered with subsidies. Secondly, identification and calculation of the amount of subsidy can be extremely difficult. The EU, like the GATT/WTO, has spent years just cataloging subsidies. As early as 1988 the Commission concluded that the member states spent approximately 100 billion ECUs annually on state subsidies. This amounted to about $2,000 per person engaged in manufacturing. Much of this aid goes to "crisis industries" that are declining, but a reasonable amount is targeted at growth sectors, technology development and general support. Moreover, subsidies are almost endemic where the member states own or are heavily invested in enterprises. Some enterprises have been acquired by governments out of bankruptcy in order to save jobs. Some have been established for strategic, prestige or capital requirement reasons. Others have simply been nationalized as a matter of social policy. In recent years, there has been a trend (but not a stampede) towards privatization of enterprises owned by EU governments. Neither nationalization nor privatization is mandated or controlled by the Treaty of Rome.[1]

The Commission has taken the position that any action by a member state as an owner that is different from what a private investor would do can violate the subsidy or competition law[2] rules of the Treaty of Rome. Such actions may include cash payments, debt write-offs, acceptance of rates of return that are below market, implied or express guarantees of loans, cheap financing, new equity capital in circumstances a private investor would avoid and dividend waivers. In adopting this position, the Commission is relying heavily upon Article 87 of the Treaty of Rome.

Treaty Provisions

Article 87(1) declares incompatible with the Common Market every national "aid" (subsidy) that distorts or threatens to distort competition by favoring certain businesses or goods. For example, state aids intended to benefit workers but implemented through a reduction in public charges to textile corporations in Italy were caught within Article 87(1). The impact of the subsidy, not its purposes, determines its character.[3] French textile industry aids financed partly by import levies were similarly prohibited because of their discriminatory impact.[4] Though the money may be private

---

§ 5.3

1. Costa v. ENEL (1964) Eur. Comm.Rep. 585 (Italian nationalization of electricity companies).

2. *See* Chapter 7.

3. Italy v. Commission (1974) Eur. Comm.Rep. 709.

4. France v. Commission (1970) Eur. Comm.Rep. 487.

in origin, a state aid exists when that money is distributed through a public body.[5] Provision of subsidies through state-owned enterprises are also caught.[6] Investment subsidies that strengthen the position of a company in the Common Market fall within Article 87(1) as threats to the distortion of competition.[7]

Article 87(2) declares the following subsidies *compatible* with the Treaty of Rome: (a) social aid granted to individuals without discrimination as to the origin of goods; (b) natural disaster aid; and (c) economic aid to East Germany (a reservation now mooted by German unification).[8] Furthermore, Article 87(3) lists a number of aids which *may* be compatible with the Common Market if approved by the Commission. These include regional subsidies to promote development in areas of high unemployment or abnormally low standards of living, subsidies for important projects of common European interest and subsidies to remedy serious disturbances in the economy of a member state. Also included are subsidies to facilitate the development of certain economic activities or areas (*e.g.* shipbuilding) provided they do not adversely affect trading conditions to an extent contrary to the common interest. Finally, any subsidy may be lawful if approved by the Council acting by qualified majority vote.

Enforcement

The Commission is charged in Article 88 with keeping all state aids under "constant review," which it does mostly by way of a reporting system. The duty of member state governments to report on the provision of subsidies to industry has been repeatedly upheld by the European Court.[9] If a subsidy is not compatible with the Common Market per Article 87 or is being misused, the Commission may render a decision to that effect against the member state unless the Council unanimously approves of the aid. Such Commission decisions terminate the ability to receive further state aid payments.[10] Absent compliance, the Commission can enforce its decision by bringing an action *directly* before the European Court of Justice. The Commission need not follow the more deliberate procedures established in Article 226 for ordinary prosecutions of member states not adhering to their EU obligations.[11]

5. Commission v. France (1985) Eur. Comm.Rep. 439.

6. Italy v. Commission (1991) Eur. Comm.Rep. I–01433 (Cases C–303/88, C–305/89).

7. Philip Morris Holland BV v. Commission (1980) Eur.Comm.Rep. 2671.

8. *See* Germany v. Commission (2000) Eur.Comm.Rep. I–6857 (state aids for small businesses in former East Germany not 87(2) exempt).

9. France v. Commission (1990) Eur. Comm.Rep. I–00307 (Case 301/87).

10. Capolongo v. Azienda Agricola Maya (1973) Eur.Comm.Rep. 611.

11. *See, e.g.,* Commission v. United Kingdom (1977) Eur.Comm.Rep. 921; Commission v. Germany (1973) Eur. Comm.Rep. 813.

Enterprises sometimes sue the Commission for failure to act against state subsidies. In one case, a French pasta maker sued the Commission for damages under Article 228 of the Treaty of Rome as a result of its failure to act against Italian subsidies to domestic pasta manufacturers. Holding that a causal link had not been established between the Commission's failure to act and the French company's damages, the Court of Justice agreed that the case was rightly dismissed.[12] The final assessment of the compatibility of subsidies with the Treaty of Rome is the exclusive responsibility of the Commission. National courts involved in subsidies litigation because of the direct effect of Article 88(3) operate in a different capacity. Their job is to protect individual rights, not to determine the legality of state subsidies.[13]

Certain patterns have emerged in the Union's law on state subsidies. Regional development aids are generally supported, especially since the Single European Act of 1987 made elimination of regional economic disparities a priority. The whole of Greece, Portugal and Ireland, for example, are now treated as underdeveloped regions for subsidy law purposes.[14] Indeed, the Union itself engages in the same subsidies under its Regional Policy[15] Sectoral industrial aids to ease unemployment and modernize smokestack industries (coal, steel, textiles, shipbuilding) have generally been allowed. Production and marketing subsidies have generally been disallowed. Research and technological development subsidies, especially for energy saving projects, often pass muster. Since environmental protection subsidies violate the polluter must pay principle of the Union's Environmental Policy, such subsidies are not frequently approved.

The Commission's role relative to national subsidies has gradually changed over the years from prosecutorial watchdog against discriminatory and anticompetitive aids to coordinator of national subsidy policies and levels. In this capacity, the Commission can find itself negotiating specific subsidy amounts or refunds with national governments, *e.g.,* French subsidies to state-owned Renault and Air France. The power of prosecution under Article 87 remains. No member state, for example, may match another nation's subsidy.[16] The Court of Justice has affirmed the power of the Commission to order refunds of offending national subsidies.[17] The

---

12. Bertrand v. Commission (1976) Eur.Comm.Rep. 1.

13. Fédération Nationale du Commerce Exterieur des Produits Alimentaires + Ors v. France (1992) Eur. Comm.Rep. I–05505 (Case C–354/90).

14. *See* Official Journal C 212/2.

15. *See* § 5.12.

16. Steinike und Weinlig v. Germany (1977) Eur.Comm.Rep. 595.

17. Commission v. Germany (1973) Eur.Comm.Rep. 813; Commission v. Belgium (1988) 2 Common Mkt.L.Rep. 258 (failure of timely repayment is breach of Treaty obligations).

Commission can order suspensions in national aid payments until prior illegal aid is repaid.[18] Many have suggested authorizing the Commission to levy fines and penalties against member states that fail to adhere to European Union law on subsidies.

§ 5.4 Procurement

Every government, at whatever level, tends to favor local producers when spending the taxpayers' money. Various "Buy American" laws permeate much of the military and civil procurement of the federal, state and local governments in the United States. The governments of the European Union nations are no different. Nevertheless, through a long series of harmonizing directives issued by the Council and aggressive decisions of the European Court, the effects of Buy French, Buy Greek and Buy Greater London Council types of laws are slowly being overcome. For example, the Court's opinion in the *Buy Irish* case struck down a program of public advertisements urging consumers to voluntarily buy only goods marked with a "Guaranteed Irish" symbol. This program combined private and governmental funds and officials. It was declared a measure of equivalent effect to a quota hindering EU trade in breach of Article 28.[1] Public supply contracts that establish regional preferences, in this case the Mezzogiorno of Italy, violate Article 28 and the principles of free internal Community trade. Such preferences cannot be justified under Article 30, nor as a state aid under Article 87.[2]

Procurement Directives

The Council has issued a series of directives intended to open up government procurement to competitive bids from all Union enterprises. The first focus of this effort was on tendering procedures for public works projects.[3] Discriminations on the basis of nationality which amount to the equivalent of trade quotas are prohibited under an early 1969 directive. Discriminatory procedural rules concerning the award of public works and construction contracts are standardized in a 1971 directive. These public works directives apply to contracts exceeding one million ECUs.

The second focus of the effort to combat discriminatory government procurement patterns is on supply contracts for goods and services to member governments, their regional and local subdivi-

---

18. Deggendorf GmbH (1997) Eur. Comm.Rep. I–02549 (Case 91/391).

§ 5.4

1. Commission v. Ireland (1982) Eur. Comm.Rep. 4005.

2. DuPont de Nemours Italiana SpA v. Unita Sanitaria Locale No. 2 di Carrara (1990) Eur.Comm.Rep. I–00884 (Case C–21/88).

3. Council Directive 71/305 amended by Directive 89/440 and consolidated in Directive 93/37.

sions, public agencies and the like. A 1977 directive requires most public supply contracts to be announced in advance in the Official Journal.[4] The announcement must also include the criteria for selection of bidders or suppliers, which may not be discriminatory. This directive does not apply to purchases of military supplies, but covers purchases of nonmilitary supplies used by military forces. Certain national governmental monopolies, *e.g.,* water, gas and electricity, were excluded from its application. A 1980 directive amended these rules to bring them into conformity with the 1979 GATT Code on Government Procurement, to which the EU is a party. A 1994 GATT Code on Procurement awaits full implementation. The GATT Code liberalizes government procurement rules on an international basis. The 1980 directive, nevertheless, maintained a margin of preference for EU enterprises seeking governmental supply contracts within the Union.

The early procurement legislation did not live up to expectations. Purchasing entities and public authorities undertaking construction projects continued to give preference to domestic suppliers and contractors. A survey revealed the most common and serious breaches of Union procurement rules: (1) failure to advertise contracts in the *Official Journal;* (2) abuse of the exceptions permitting single tendering; (3) discriminatory administrative, financial or technical requirements in tenders, especially the insistence on compliance with national standards even when EU law does not allow this; (4) illegal disqualification or elimination of bidders or applicants from other Member States, for example by discriminatory selection criteria; and (5) discrimination at the award stage.

It was reported in late 1986 that approximately 98 percent of all procurement contracts went to national suppliers. Single tendering (unpublicized, noncompetitive contract awards) and selective supplier arrangements (unpublicized, selectively competitive contract awards) continue to hurt Union efforts at overcoming buy-local preferences. Other problems exist with exemptions from EU procurement law for special needs such as "speed of delivery," "security" and "particular specifications." Procedural and substantive reforms of the existing directives were developed by the Commission in 1986. These reforms covered notice requirements, longer bid periods, publication of contract awards (who won), use of European specification standards (not national standards), and reduction of exemption industries (energy, transport, water and

4. Council Directive 77/62 amended by Directives 80/767, 88/295 and consoli-   dated in Directive 93/36.

telecommunications). A legislative simplification of EU procurement rules was accomplished in Directives 2004/17 and 2004/18.

Buy EU

Reform of procurement rules was part of the unified internal market campaign. Early in 1988, the Council adopted a directive tightening up the procedural aspects of the Union's procurement rules so as to reduce single tendering.[5] Under another 1988 directive, public construction bidding was similarly reformed. Council Directives 89/665 and 92/59 coordinated member state remedies for review of the award of public supply and public works contracts. Council Directive 92/50 extends the Union's open procurement rules and procedures to public service contracts in excess of 200,000 ECU, excepting research and development and property contracts. In 1990, a directive was adopted which in 1993 opened up public contracts to EU firms in the Union's telecommunications, energy, transport and water industries.[6] This directive contains a controversial "Buy EU" clause which allows public authorities to dismiss bids with less than 50 percent Union content, and gives EU suppliers a minimum margin of preference of 3 percent. Late in 1991, the United States threatened to retaliate against the Buy EU rules of this directive by unilaterally imposing trade sanctions on EU goods imported into the U.S. market. This threat was announced under Title VII of the Omnibus Trade and Competitiveness Act of 1988. The EU responded by first pointing out the greater degree of procurement preferences accorded under Buy American law.

Negotiations on this issue outside the Uruguay Round led in 1993 to a compromise Memorandum of Understanding. The EU agreed not to discriminate against U.S. suppliers, goods or services, and to open certain energy contracts.[7] The U.S. agreed to waive certain federal "Buy American" provisions as applied to bids of EU origin and to try to persuade the states to do likewise. No agreement was reached regarding telecommunications procurement. This led first to U.S. procurement sanctions,[8] followed by EU retaliation.[9] Germany, however, seemingly broke ranks with the Union by negotiating a bilateral telecommunications agreement with the U.S. This resulted in the suspension of the U.S. sanctions as applied to Germany and much consternation within the European Union. Since 1995, Europe and the United States have participated fully in the WTO Procurement Agreement. This has helped reduce transatlantic trade and procurement tensions.

---

5. *See* Council Directives 89/665, 89/440.

6. *See* Council Directives 90/531, 92/13 consolidated in Directive 93/38.

7. Council Decision 93/323.

8. Executive Order 12845.

9. Council Regulation 141/93.

§ 5.5   Products Liability

Products liability law is one field where the Union acted before the single market campaign to harmonize national rules. Prior to the EU products liability directive, the rules of law on products liability of the individual member states varied greatly. Traditional negligence liability with plaintiff's burden of proof was the rule in Italy, Portugal, Spain and Greece. A presumption of liability shifting the burden of proof to the defendant which bordered on strict products liability governed in Germany, Denmark, the Netherlands, the United Kingdom and Ireland. Absolute strict liability, creating a presumption liability that could not be overcome, was the rule in France, Belgium and Luxembourg.

Strict Liability

Council Directive 85/374 established, for all member states, a regime of strict (no-fault) defective products liability. The injured person is required to prove damages, the defect and a causal relationship between defect and damage. The term "product" applies to "all movables, with the exception of primary agricultural products and games, even though incorporated into another movable or into an immovable" and specifically includes electricity. Both new and used products are covered. However, the evaluation of whether a product is defective takes place at the time when the "producer" has most recently put the product into circulation. Manufacturers of components are treated as such producers. Producers also include manufacturers of finished products, suppliers of raw materials or component parts and persons who, by putting names, trademarks or other distinguishing features on products, present themselves as producers. Licensors are not generally treated as producers but their licensees are. Thus, department stores and commercial chains will be regarded as producers if they sell products manufactured by others under their own names without referring to actual origin. They will be jointly and severally liable with the actual producer. However, if a department store has had a product specially made under the designation "specially manufactured for ... by ... ," the department store should not be regarded as a "producer."

Any person who imports products into the Union for distribution in the course of business is deemed a producer. This rule only concerns persons who import products into the Union, not persons who import from one member state to another. The importer's intentions at the time of importation are crucial. If the product was originally imported in the course of business, the importer will be regarded as a producer even if the product is later dedicated to personal use. An importer who originally imported the product for personal use, but later decides to use the product commercially, does not become a producer. The burden of proof that the product is not imported in the course of business rests with the importer. Whether the doctrine of strict products liability applies to retailers is decided by each member state.

A product is defective "when it does not provide the safety which a person is entitled to expect." It is not the injured person's expectations that control, but rather the normal expectations of purchasers of such products. The reasonable expected use of the product is determined when evaluating defects of production, design or the lack of adequate warnings or instruction. The gravity of the potential injury, the probability of the occurrence of injury, and the consumer's awareness of the danger are analyzed to determine whether adequate warnings or instruction have been given.

Exceptions and Defenses

The exception for "primary agricultural products" includes fish products but excludes all products that "have undergone initial processing." The line between primary and initially processed products thus becomes quite important and will no doubt be subjected to judicial interpretation. Moreover, member states can elect to include primary agricultural products under their strict liability regime. Luxembourg appears to be the only nation to do so to date. The Products Liability Directive does not apply to services. However, if a defective product is used when rendering services, the producer may be held strictly liable for any damages. The person rendering services will only be liable if he or she has acted with negligence.

Strict liability is tempered by certain defenses, notably the "state-of-the-art" defense which excludes liability if the manufacturer could not have discovered the defect when the product was made. However, the member states have the option of omitting this defense, which (to date) only Luxembourg has done. The British version of this defense, implemented in the 1987 Consumer Protection Act, was unsuccessfully challenged as too broad by the Commission before the European Court of Justice.[1] Strict liability is also tempered in the award of damages by contributory negligence principles. The calculation and types of damages that may be recovered and damages caps are largely left to national law. Thus the award of "pain and suffering" or punitive damages is under member state control, as is the imposition of total limits on recovery. Germany, Greece and Portugal have set such total limits. A three-year statute of limitations ordinarily applies, and a ten-year

§ 5.5   (1997) Eur.Comm.Rep. I–2649.
1. Commission v. United Kingdom

absolute bar on liability is established in the Council directive on products liability.

For some EU nations, such as Ireland and Spain, this directive mandated a fundamental switch away from liability systems grounded entirely in negligence principles. France, on the other hand, considered the directive too generous to manufacturers. All three were pursued by the Commission for their implementation failures.[2] Nevertheless, Americans who have studied the painstaking manner in which strict products liability doctrine was crafted in state courts are often surprised by the sweeping implementation of comparable law in the European Union. One explanation lies in the goal of free movement and a desire to equalize the risks of liability (and the insurance costs) that most often accompany the distribution of goods to the public. There is, also, greater acceptance in Europe of the need to compensate accident victims regardless of fault. Moreover, the absence of a well financed plaintiff's bar, contingency legal fees, juries and rules that require each party to pay their own legal costs (*i.e.*, the loser generally pays in Europe) have made products liability litigation infrequent. These factors facilitated the passage of the products liability directive and its implementation by the member states. The Products Liability Directive has, with certain adaptations, been extended to the EFTA countries (excluding Switzerland and Liechtenstein) by virtue of its inclusion in the Annex to the European Economic Area Agreement which came into force on January 1, 1994.

§ 5.6   Consumer Protection and Credit

The European Union has had a consumer protection and information policy since 1975. Its consumer protection role was recognized in TEU amendments to the Treaty of Rome.[1] The member states, however, may enact more stringent protective measures provided they are compatible with the Treaty of Rome.[2] In addition to products liability (above), EU law covers health and safety product labelling and manufacturing. Foodstuffs, cosmetics, detergents, vehicles, textiles, toys, dangerous substances, medicines, fertilizers, pesticides and animal feed are some of the areas now governed by Union consumer protection law. There is, for example, a directive which fixes the maximum level of pesticide residues on fruits and vegetables.[3] The Commission operates an information exchange network on products that present grave and immediate

---

2. *See, e.g.,* Commission v. French Republic (2002) Eur.Comm.Rep. I–03827 (Case 52/00).

§ 5.6

1. *See* Article 153, Treaty of Rome.

2. *Id.*

3. Council Directive 76/895 (amended by Directive 90/642).

danger to consumers. The source member state notifies the Commission of the hazard, and the Commission forwards this information to the other member states.

All products dangerous to humans or the environment are subject to the Union's *dangerous substances directives.*[4] This includes explosives, flammable, toxic and carcinogenic substances. No such products are to be allowed on the market until after a review of their "forseeable risks" and "unfavorable effects" by national authorities. Child-resistant packaging is ordinarily required as is labelling using a common "CE" black on orange-yellow symbol. Any special risks associated with the product and safety advice must be spelled out on the label. Dangerous substances meeting the terms and conditions of this directive may be freely traded within the Union, each nation relying on the authorities of all other EU countries to implement the directive as to manufacturers within their borders.

An EU *product safety directive* has also been adopted Council Directive 92/59 revised by Directive 2001/95 applies to all products not subject to more specific Union law on safety. Suppliers may place only safe products on the market. A safe product does not present any risk, or only risks considered acceptable and consistent with a high standard of protection. In assessing the acceptability of risk, the product's intended or reasonably foreseeable use must be evaluated. The supplier must give the user sufficient information to assess acceptable risks and to monitor the safety of the product. Suppliers will be deemed to meet the general safety requirement if they comply with Union standards or (in their absence) member state safety requirements. The directive requires member states to have the power to impose sanctions for violations, including the power to ban products from the market, but it does not require that consumers be given a damages remedy for unsafe products.

Council Directive 93/13 covers *unfair terms in standardized consumer* contracts concluded after Dec. 31, 1994. Such terms do not bind consumers, and the member states are obliged to take effective measures to ensure their discard by suppliers and sellers. Consumer groups must be allowed to proceed before courts or authorities involved with determinations of unfairness in consumer contracts of general use. Standardized contract terms are considered "unfair" if they evidence bad faith and cause a significant imbalance in the parties' rights and obligations under the contract.[5] A nonexhaustive list of examples of unfair terms is annexed to the directive. These examples include liability limits, seller rights to

---

4. Council Directive 67/548.

5. *See* Oceano Grupo Editorial SA v. Murciano Quintero (2000) Eur.

Comm.Rep. I–04941 (June 27, 2000) (encyclopedia sales, choice of distant court forum clause).

unilaterally alter the contract without good cause and restraints upon consumer legal remedies. Member states remain free to provide for higher levels of consumer protection against unfair terms in standardized contracts.

Consumer Credit

The Council has adopted two important *consumer credit directives*. Directive 87/102 seeks to insure that consumers receive precise information from creditors as to the true costs of credit. "Consumers" for these purposes do not include business customers. "Creditors," on the other hand, must be acting in the course of a trade, business or profession. The directive applies to "credit agreements" involving loans or deferred payment, but not installment contracts. Leasing agreements, charge cards and other selected contracts are exempted. Directive 90/88 establishes an annual percentage rate of charge (APR) disclosure requirement. These directives are discussed in Section 4.12 on banking.

Directive 99/44 concerns the sale of consumer goods and associated guarantees. Basically, the seller must deliver goods conforming to the contract of sale. If nonconformity is discovered within two years, the consumer generally is entitled to free repair or replacement, a price adjustment or contract recision. Final sellers in turn have recourse against producers and intermediate sellers. Directive 98/27 mandates the availability of injunctive relief in connection with eleven consumer rights directives, including for example misleading advertising (see Section 5.7), medicinal products advertising, unfair contract terms, time shares, distance sales, package travel, product guarantees and off premise sales.

Consumer Protection Legislation

The following is a partial list of major EU consumer protection laws (note that E-commerce and "distance selling" are covered in Sections 5.26—5.30):

- Directive 67/548 (classification, packaging and labelling of dangerous substances) as amended by Directives 88/379, 91/325, 91/326, 93/18, 93/21, 94/410

- Directive 79/112 (labelling, presentation and advertising of foodstuffs)

- Directives 79/530, 92/75 (labelling of energy consumption of household appliances)

- Directive 79/581 (selling price and price per unit of foodstuffs)

- Directive 80/232 (nominal quantities and nominal capacities for pre-packaged products)

- Directive 84/450 (misleading advertising)

- Directive 85/577 (off premise selling)[6]
- Directive 85/610 (use of asbestos)
- Directives 87/102 and 90/88 (consumer credit)
- Directive 87/357 (dangerous imitation products)
- Directive 87/404 (simple pressure vessels)
- Directive 88/314 (selling price and price per unit of non-food products)
- Directive 88/378 (toy safety)
- Directive 89/622 (labelling of tobacco products)
- Directive 90/239 (tar yield limits for cigarettes)
- Directive 90/314 (package holidays)
- Directive 91/442 (child resistant fastenings)
- Directive 92/59 (product safety)
- Directive 93/13 (unfair standard contract terms)
- Directive 94/47 (time shares)
- Directive 97/7 (distance selling)
- Directive 98/27 (injunctive relief)
- Directive 99/44 (guarantees)
- Directive 2002/65 (distance selling of consumer financial services)
- Directive 2003/15 (cosmetics)

§ 5.7 Advertising

European Union law has touched upon advertising in a variety of ways. Cigarette advertising, for example, is banned in television broadcasts. Tobacco advertising is broadly banned.[1] The EU Broadcasting directive[2] regulates advertising aimed at children. Directives also exist on the advertising of foodstuffs,[3] medicinal products,[4] dangerous substances,[5] and consumer credit.[6] A general directive on misleading advertising was adopted in 1984.[7] This directive indicates that advertising is misleading if it deceives or is likely to deceive consumers *and* is likely to affect their economic behavior or

---

6. Faccini Dori v. Recreb Srl, (1994) Eur.Comm.Rep. I–3325 (implications of Italian failure to implement directive on time); *See* Re Di Pinto (1991) Eur. Comm.Rep. I–495 (Case–361/89) (door-to-door solicitation of advertising contracts not covered).

§ 5.7

1. Council Directive 2003/33 replacing annulled Directive 98/43.

2. *See* § 5.14 and Konsumentbudsmannen v. De Agostini (Svenska) Forlag (1997) Eur.Comm.Rep. I–3843 (Swedish rules on childrens' ads unenforceable).

3. Council Directive 79/112.

4. Council Directive 92/28.

5. Council Directive 92/32.

6. Council Directive 87/102.

7. Council Directive 84/450.

injure a competitor. Thus, the directive is intended to protect competitors as well as consumers. Advertising of gray market autos as new, subject to the warranty of the manufacturer, and less expensive than those sold by established dealers was not false or misleading.[8] Cross-border broadcasters are subject to home and host nation rules on misleading ads.[9]

Each member state is required to establish adequate means for monitoring and controlling misleading advertising. This may involve impartial administrative controls or legal proceedings. Self-regulatory controls by trade associations and the like are permissible but must not replace legal or administrative remedies. Such remedies must include cease and desist orders and the power to require corrective statements. All advertisers can be required to provide evidence of the accuracy of any factual claims they make. Comparative advertising is included.[10]

The Commission has proposed an amendment to this directive that would permit comparative advertising. National legislation prohibiting conspicuous or eye-catching comparative ads violates the Union's free trade rules. In this decision, the ECJ nullified a German law as applied to advertising by a French cosmetics company.[11]

§ 5.8 Securities

Article 294 of the Treaty of Rome creates a right of national treatment as regards participation in the capital of profit-making companies. In other words, discrimination based upon nationality cannot be practiced when it comes to corporate capital. In addition, several important EU directives have been adopted in the securities field. These concern admission of securities to stock exchange listings,[1] the issuance of a prospectus,[2] and regular information disclosures by publicly traded companies.[3] Some commentators have suggested that the net result of these directives will be a "Common Market Prospectus." Once approved by a member state, a prospec-

8. Procureur de la République v. X (1992) Eur.Comm.Rep. I–131 (Case C–373/90).

9. Konsumentbudsmannen v. De Agostini (Svenska) Forlag (1997) Eur. Comm.Rep. I–3843.

10. Council Directive 97/55 amending Directive 84/450. *See* Pippig Augenoptik GmbH v. Hartlauer Handelsgesellschaft mbH (2003) Eur.Comm.Rep. I–03095 (Case 44/01) (reviewing lawful comparative advertising).

11. Schutzverband gegen Unwesen in der Wirtschaft v. Yves Rocher GmbH (1993) Eur.Comm.Rep. 02361 (Case C–126/91).

§ 5.8

1. Council Directives 79/279, 80/390, 87/345, 90/211, 03/34.

2. Council Directive 89/298, 03/34.

3. Council Directives 79/279, 82/121.

tus conforming to EU rules can be used throughout the Community subject to minimal additional disclosure requirements.[4]

Early Securities Law Directives

The 1989 Prospectus Directive[5] created prospectus requirements for nearly all transferable securities publicly offered within a member state. The directive exempted Eurosecurities (equities and bonds) that are not the "subject of a generalized campaign of advertising or canvassing." The directive was inapplicable to offers of securities to a "restricted circle of persons." Government securities, securities offered in connection with a takeover bid or merger and certain debt securities were also exempt. The Prospective Directive contained a mutual recognition clause. When public offerings are made within short intervals in two or more member states, a prospectus prepared and approved in accordance with EU law must be recognized and accepted in all member states. An additional mutual recognition directive adopted in 1990 further integrated the listing and public offering processes.[6] In 2003, a New Prospectus Directive (No. 03/34, discussed below) was adopted, repealing the 1989 Prospectus Directive.

The 1979 Listing Conditions Directive[7] established minimum conditions for the admission of securities to a stock exchange listing in the EU. These conditions concerned the size of the issuer, its history and the distribution of its shares in the market. The directive created reporting obligations for issuers of listed securities. It provided that if shares of a non-EU company are not listed in the issuer's home country or principal market, they could not generally be listed in a Union country. However, if the national authorities are satisfied that the absence of a listing "is not due to the need to protect investors," an EU listing could follow. Non–EU issuers were required to meet the minimum conditions and obligations of the 1979 Listing Conditions Directive.

The 1980 Listing Particulars Directive[8] coordinated member state disclosure requirements. Member states had to ensure that securities listings in their territories were accompanied by the release of a disclosure document ("listing particulars"). This document was akin to an SEC registration statement and had to enable investors to make an "informed assessment" of the financial position and prospects of the issuer. This directive thus imposed a general obligation to disclose material facts in the listing application. The Listing Particulars Directive allowed a member state to

---

4. See especially Council Directives 80/390 (as amended May 30, 1994) and 2003/34.

5. Council Directive 89/298.

6. Council Directive 90/211.

7. Council Directive 79/279.

8. Council Directive 80/390.

create exemptions, such as an exemption for securities for which the issuer released an equivalent disclosure document during the preceding year. The directive detailed debt and equity disclosure requirements. These particulars could not be published until they were approved by the national authorities. They could be published either by insertion in newspapers or as a brochure available to the public. The directive did *not* require disclosure documents to be delivered to investors when securities are purchased. Directive 94/18 amended the Listing Particulars Directive giving further flexibility regarding secondary listings and transfers from second tier markets. It provided that, where securities are admitted to listing in one member state and the issuer wishes to list them in another, that member state may grant an exemption from the obligation to produce new listing particulars. The directive also contained a further exemption allowing a waiver of the requirement to produce listing particulars where an issuer wants to transfer from a second tier market to the official list in the same member state.

A 1987 Directive[9] applied when applications are made to list securities on two or more exchanges located in the European Union. The listing particulars in such cases follow home state rules and are approved by home state authorities. Other member states had to recognize these documents without requiring approval by their authorities and without requiring additional information. This 1987 directive allowed EU countries to restrict mutual recognition to listing particulars of issuers having registered offices in a member state. In 2003, the New Prospectus Directive 03/04 replaced the Listing Particulars Directive.

New Prospectus Directive

The New Prospectus Directive (No. 2003/34) covers all securities offered to the public or admitted to trading on a regulated market. The prospectus must provide all necessary information for investors to make informed assessments in an "easily analyzable and comprehensible form." Either a single or "subdivided" prospectus can be used. A subdivided prospectus consists of three documents: (1) a registration; (2) a securities note; and (3) a summary note. Once a subdivided prospectus is approved, the registration is valid for 12 months. Thus only the security and summary notes need to be revised in subsequent offerings. The prospectus must be prepared according to International Accounting Standards.

Home country registration by issuers of securities results in sending notices of approval to host state authorities who are bound

---

9. Council Directive 87/345.

to honor them. Translation requirements are minimized. Exemptions cover government bonds, small issues and qualified sophisticated buyers. The prior "mutual reciprocity" approach is abandoned. That said, an EU-wide securities and exchange commission has not been created, and whether the New Prospectus Directive will gain marketplace adherents remains to be seen.

Mutual and Pension Funds

Council Directive 85/611 on open-end investment companies ("unit trusts" or mutual funds) was implemented in 1985. It allows marketing in other member states based upon home country authorization meeting the minimum EU standards of the directive. There is no "reciprocity rule" in the Unit Trust Directive that might hinder North American mutual fund companies wishing to operate in Europe. The Unit Trust Directive controls the structure, obligations, investment policies and disclosure obligations of unit trusts and investment companies. With certain exceptions, such entities may only invest in transferable securities listed on an EU stock exchange, traded on a regulated market in a member state, or traded on an approved exchange or regulated market in a nonmember state. Unit trusts and investment companies must repurchase or redeem units from holders upon request. It is currently proposed that this Directive be amended to extend its scope by widening the permitted investments and amending certain definitions in order to allow a common approach in all directives covering the financial services and banking sectors. Directive 2001/107 regulates the prudential management and access to markets of UCITs.

Council Directive 2003/41 concerns pension funds. High levels of protection for members and beneficiaries are required. Cross-border administration of pension schemes is facilitated using mutual recognition principles along with customized investment strategies following the "prudent person principle." Whether to use pay-as-you-go or funded pension schemes is left to member state discretion.

Market Abuses and Inside Trading

In 1988, the Council adopted an "anti-raider" directive requiring disclosure of the acquisition or disposal of 10 percent or more of a publicly listed company.[10] Securities "market abuses," including stock buy-back programs, are covered in Directive 2003/6. Market manipulations and public disclosure of inside information, along with investment recommendations and disclosure of conflicts of interest, also fall within its scope.

10. Council Directive 88/627.

Until 1988, only three of the member states had laws regulating insider trading. Nevertheless, a directive on insider trading was finalized in 1989,[11] and now contained in Directive 2003/6. This directive prohibits trading on the basis of inside information "with full knowledge of the facts" by primary and secondary insiders. Specifically, this prohibition applies to any person who possesses inside information from membership in the structure of the issuer, share ownership, or access to information through employment, professional or other duties. Persons who possess inside information, the source of which "could not be other than" one of the previously enumerated persons, are also covered. Disclosure of inside information to third parties outside the normal course of employment or professional duties, and procurement of securities by others on the basis of such information is prohibited. Inside information is defined as nonpublic information "of a precise nature" which if made public would be "likely to have a significant effect on the price" of securities.

Many perceive that EU insider trading law closely parallels U.S. securities law principles. However, unlike U.S. law, the European Union directive only applies to securities traded on markets regulated by "public bodies" that operate regularly and are accessible directly or indirectly to the public. The directive specifically permits member states to exclude transactions without a professional intermediary undertaken outside a regulated market. One concern with the directive is that it allows member states to choose which types of penalties apply to insider trading violations. These directives were extended with certain adaptations to EFTA countries (except Switzerland and Liechtenstein) by virtue of their inclusion in the Annex to the European Economic Area Agreement which came into force on January 1, 1994.

In September of 1991, the United States Securities and Exchange Commission (SEC) and the Commission signed a joint communiqué intended to improve bilateral and multilateral cooperation in the securities law field. Information exchange, cooperative approaches to financial integrity of issuers and securities market oversight are covered by this communiqué.

§ 5.9 Company Law

Article 293 of the Treaty of Rome obliges member states to enter into negotiations with each other about equal protection of citizens, abolition of double taxation, mutual recognition of firms and companies, the possibility of international mergers, and simplification of enforcement of judgments. Article 293 was the backdrop against which member states signed in 1968 a Convention on

---

11. Council Directive 89/592, re- placed by Directive 2003/16.

Mutual Recognition of Companies and Other Bodies Corporate. This Convention sought to ensure that Treaty benefits extend to such legal personae. Unfortunately, it never achieved full ratification by the member states. Article 43 on the right of establishment entitles companies based in one member state to set up agencies, branches or subsidiaries in other member states, even when this avoids paid-in capital requirements.[1] In the absence of an EU convention on legal personalities, nothing in the right of establishment permits a company to freely transfer its place of incorporation (seat) and administrative center to another member state without home state permission where that is required. In this case, the British Daily Mail newspaper sought to change to Dutch citizenship to take advantage of lower taxes.[2]

However, two recent decisions of the European Court of Justice, *Überseering*[3] and *Inspire Art*,[4] hold that a company formed under the laws of one member state of the European Union may move or establish its entire operations to or in any other member state. The other member state may not impose any restrictions on or deny the legal capacity of such a company even if there is no connection to the member state in which it was formed other than statutory registration. The Court explicitly clarified that it does not constitute an abuse of the principle of freedom of establishment if the purpose is to circumvent the application of the stricter company laws of the member state in which the company is operating through its branch by forming the company in another member state with more liberal laws. It further stated that all questions relating to the company's status (liability of limited partners and managing directors, capital requirements etc.) must be governed by the law of incorporation of the company. It is widely thought that these decisions will avoid restrictive Germany company law rules by incorporation in other EU jurisdictions.

Company Law Directives

The Council has adopted a number of non-controversial coordination directives under Article 44 advancing Union company law. These in theory seek to avoid the race to the bottom problems associated with Delaware corporate law in the United States. The first directive sets out requirements for disclosure, validity and nullity of share capital companies. The ECJ has ruled that the listing of grounds for nullifying the formation of a company found

§ 5.9

1. Centros v. Erhvervs–OG Selskabsstyrelsen (1999) Eur.Comm.Rep. II–1459.

2. Re Daily Mail (1988) Eur. Comm.Rep. 5483.

3. (2002) Eur.Comm.Rep. 00000 (May 11, 2002).

4. (2003) Eur.Comm.Rep. 00000 (Sept. 30, 2003) (Case 167/01).

in the First Company Law Directive 68/151 exhausts all such possibilities. Grounds for nullification based upon the Spanish Civil Code requirement of "causa" could not be utilized since that Code must be construed in conformity with Directive 68/151.[5] The second deals with the classification, subscription and maintenance of capital of public and large companies. Increases in share capital must be approved by company shareholders with preemptive rights preserved.[6] This obligation is derived from Article 25 of the Second Company Law Directive, which has direct effect in Union law.[7] Companies are generally forbidden from acquiring their own shares. Governmental acts authorizing increases in company capital to ensure survival which prejudice the preemptive rights of shareholders are impermissible under Directive 77/91.[8] The Second Company Law Directive was amended in late 1992 to close a loophole by prohibiting parent companies from buying through subsidiaries more than 10 percent of their own shares when faced with hostile takeovers.[9]

The Third Company Law Directive concerns the internal merger of public companies. Modern procedures for mergers with related and unrelated companies are established. Asset and liability acquisitions and new company formations are allowed. Shareholder rights are specified. The sixth directive governs sales of assets of public companies, including certain shareholder, creditor and workers' rights. The fourth standardizes the treatment of annual accounts (*e.g.,* in their presentation, content, valuation and publication). It requires public presentation of a "true and fair view" of company assets, liabilities, finances, profits and losses. Small and medium-sized firms can publish abridged accounts. All companies must present comparable figures for the preceding year. Valuation of assets and liabilities must be prudent, consistent and reflect the company as a going concern. The fourth directive even details the notes that must accompany annual accounts. In addition, shareholders must be given a report by management annually on the development of the business, future plans, research activities and company purchases of its own shares. There is a permissive provision relating to inflation or current cost accounting. There is some doubt about the degree of relation to similar requirements of the

---

5. Marleasing SA v. La Comercial Internacional de Alimentación SA. (1990) 1 Eur.Comm.Rep. 4135. Regarding the first directive, *see also* Daihatsu Handler v. Daihatsu Deutschland (1997) Eur. Comm.Rep. II–6843; Commission v. Germany (1998) Eur.Comm.Rep. II–5449.

6. Karella & Anor v. Greek Minister for Industry, Energy and Technology (1991) Eur.Comm.Rep. I–2691 (Cases C–19 and C–20/90).

7. *Id.* Regarding the second directive, *see also* Siemens v. Nold (1996) Eur.Comm.Rep. I–6017; Pafitis v. Trapeza Kentrikis Ellados (1996) Eur. Comm.Rep. I–1347.

8. Kerafina–Keramische und Finanz Holding AG & Anor v. Hellenic Republic (1992) Eur.Comm.Rep. I–5699 (Cases C–234/91, C–135/91).

9. *See* Council Directive 92/101.

United Kingdom accounting bodies or "generally accepted accounting practices" in the United States. Directive 2001/65 spells out "fair value" accounting rules, notably for derivatives. Regulation 1606/2002 mandated use of International Accounting Standards by publicly traded companies.

The Sixth Company Law Directive adopted in 1982 complements the third directive and addresses the division or "scission" of public limited companies, where they wind up without liquidation. The seventh concerns requirements for consolidated accounts of groups of companies. Consolidated accounts must follow the rules of the fourth directive as supplemented by the seventh. Consolidated accounts are required if an EU firm has legal or *de facto* control over other companies through majority shareholdings, appointment or removal power over management in a subsidiary, the right to exercise dominant influence, or the possibility of shareholder agreements conveying majority voting rights. Consolidated accounts must treat the group as a single enterprise regarding transactions among the companies. The Eighth Company Law Directive provides certain minimum standards and qualifications for auditors of company accounts.

Works Councils

Several controversial proposals for company law directives are in varying stages of evolution. These include a fifth directive on company structure and administration which has been long delayed due to differing views about the functions of single and two-tier boards of directors and officers, and worker representation at these levels. Another controversial topic (the "Vredeling proposal") would have required substantial information sharing between companies and their employees. The 1994 "works council" Directive 94/45 requires councils in companies with more than 1000 employees operating with 150 employees in at least two member states. Workers must be given information on and an opportunity to respond to a broad range of topics including the firm's economic and financial situation, employment, work methods and mergers and layoffs. But the information can be withheld when disclosure might "seriously harm" the functioning of the company or be "prejudicial" to it. Thousands of works councils now operate with little controversy. Directive 94/45 applies to parent companies located outside the EU.[10]

Other less controversial directives are also planned. The ninth directive concerns liability on the part of parent companies for the debts of subsidiaries they effectively control. The tenth directive

---

10. Gesamtbetriebsrat der Kühne + Nagel AG + Co. KG v. Kühne + Nagel   AG + Co. KG (2004) Eur.Comm.Rep. I–00000 (Case 440/00).

deals with cross-border company mergers. The eleventh (adopted in 1989) involves disclosure by branches operating in other EU states, and the twelfth (also adopted in 1989) affects single member private limited liability companies. Hostile takeovers, a sensitive area, are the subject of the thirteenth proposed company law directive. This directive to require equal treatment of shareholders and specify permissible defensive measures was denied in 2001 by a tie vote in Parliament. It was finally adopted as Directive 2004/25.

Status of Company Law Directives

The following directory gives the status of European Union company law directives.

First Council Directive (Adopted) 68/151

Second Council Directive (Adopted) 77/91

Third Council Directive (Adopted) 78/855

Fourth Council Directive (Adopted) 78/660

Fifth Council Directive (Proposed) (see Works Council Directive 94/45)

Sixth Council Directive (Adopted) 82/89

Seventh Council Directive (Adopted) 83/349

Eighth Council Directive (Adopted) 84/253

Ninth Council Directive (Adopted) 2004/25

Tenth Council Directive (Proposed)

Eleventh Council Directive (Adopted) 89/666

Twelfth Council Directive (Adopted) 89/667

Thirteenth Council Directive (Adopted) 2004/25

§ 5.10   European Companies and Partnerships

Partnerships

Innovative company law proposals include those for a European Company Statute (SE) and a European Economic Interest Grouping (EEIG). The former is intended to create a regional corporate entity, overcoming the transnational problems associated with existing methods of incorporation within member states. The EEIG, adopted by Council Regulation in 1985, is a vehicle with legal capacity formed in the manner of an international partnership of member state companies. It draws its inspiration from French *groupement d'intérêt économique*. The EEIG is prohibited from offering proprietary interests to the public and is a nonprofit enterprise. Limited liability is not obtained. The EEIG is intended for small or medium sized research and development or marketing ventures. Utilization of EEIG has been relatively low, in part because of perceptions of uncertainty about their tax status. The EEIG should be "tax transparent," *i.e.,* the EEIG does not pay taxes. All its profits and losses pass directly to its members.

European Company (SE)

An amended proposal for a European Company was submitted by the Commission to the Council in August 1989. Nineteen years had passed since the submission of the first proposal in 1970, and 14 years since the last amended proposal in 1975. In that period, considerable harmonization had been accomplished by way of directives. Finally, late in 2001, a European Company Statute was finalized, taking effect in 2004. Forming a European Company ("Societas Europeae" or SE) is optional. An SE operates on a European-wide basis governed by EU law. A regulation establishes its company law rules, while a directive covers worker involvement in SE. Under the Statute, an SE registered in one member state can freely move its registered office to another. SEs may be privately or publicly traded companies. SE, at least in theory, will remove the need for costly networks of subsidiaries throughout the European Union. Large legal and administrative cost savings are expected to be realized. SE must be registered in the member state where it has its administrative head office, and the Statute does not significantly alter applicable taxation.

Regarding worker participation, the issue that held up the SE proposal for over 30 years, the first duty is to try negotiate agreement on employee involvement. Failing that, Standard Principles attached to the directive require regular reports, consultation and information exchange between management and worker representatives. Such reports must detail business plans, production and sales, management changes, mergers, divestments, potential closures and layoffs, and the implications of all this to workers. In the case of a European Company created by merger, the Standard Principles apply when at least 25 percent of the employees had the right to participate before the merger. However, member states need *not* implement the directive on participation for SEs created by mergers, but if so the SE can be registered only if an agreement with the employees is reached, or when no employees were covered by participation rules before the SE was created.

§ 5.11 Environmental Policy

For many years, environmental law was a stepchild of the European Union. The Treaty of Rome of 1957 did not expressly authorize or anticipate such a policy. Clearly, however, differing national standards on the environment can have a substantial impact on the functioning of the Common Market. As environmental politics (remember the Green Party) and consciousness came of age in Western Europe, initial environmental efforts rested on Article 94 (harmonization) and Article 308, the Treaty's "necessary and proper" powers clause. The first Environmental Action Program commenced in 1973. The Union is now embarked on its sixth such program covering 2001–2010. Hundreds of environmental legislative acts have been adopted. The Commission has noted at length, however, that there are serious problems with national implementation (or the lack thereof) of regional environmental law.

Policy Principles

The Single European Act of 1987 added Articles 174–176 to the Treaty of Rome. These articles firmly establish environmental policy as an important domain of the Union. Indeed, Article 174(2) makes environmental protection requirements a mandatory component of *all* European Union policies. One of the overriding legal principles of EU environmental policy is that the polluter shall pay.[1] This may mean that national governments are limited in their ability to grant subsidies for environmental protection purposes.[2] Another key principle is that member states may adopt more demanding environmental requirements, provided they are compatible with the Treaty of Rome.[3] Still another important touchstone is that environmental policy must be based on the "precautionary principle."[4]

The procedures for adoption of European Union environmental legislation and the conclusion of international environmental agreements are unusually detailed. Article 174(3) requires the Union to consider available scientific and technical data, the environmental conditions in the regions of the EU, the potential benefits and costs of regional action or inaction, the economic and social development of the EU as a whole, and balanced development of its regions when preparing environmental policy.

There are two basic thrusts to the Union's environmental policy. The first is the establishment of minimum quality standards (*e.g.,* drinking water). The second involves specific emission and waste controls (*e.g.,* the discharge of pollutants into surface and ground water). On emission controls, the Union has proceeded slowly, industry by industry, after first identifying priority problems. The first water emissions directives involve mercury and cadmium discharges. EU rules govern the biodegradability of deter-

---

§ 5.11

1. Article 174(2), Treaty of Rome. *See* Directive 2004/35.

2. *See* Commission Guidelines on State Aids for Environmental Protection, O.J. C 37/3 (Feb. 3, 2001).

3. *Id.* Article 176, Treaty of Rome. *See* Commission v. Denmark (1988) Eur. Comm.Rep. 4607 (Danish bottle bill generally upheld).

4. *Id.* Article 174(2), Treaty of Rome.

gents and the sulphur content of liquid fuels.[5] Among the first air pollution directives, auto emissions and lead content in gasoline have had a high priority. Since 1989, Union law requires all member states to introduce lead-free gasoline into their markets and leaded gas is reduced to a minimum content as are sulfur-free fuels.[6] But there is no requirement, as yet, that all new cars use lead-free gasoline.

Waste Controls

Waste control directives have targeted oil, PCB and PCT discharges as priorities. Waste management issues have frequently come before the Court of Justice. For example, an Italian municipal ban on the sale and use of plastic carrying bags was upheld as consistent with Directive 75/442 on waste materials.[7] French law implementing the waste oil directive could not deny the right of oil companies to export wastes to an approved recycling center in another member state.[8] Similarly, existing Community directives meant that Belgium could not ban the disposal of hazardous waste.[9] But it could prohibit, in the name of environmental protection, importation of general waste products from neighboring countries.[10]

A strict liability directive for damages caused by commercial waste was proposed as part of the single market campaign. The producer (or transporter if negligent) would be strictly liable to individuals and public authorities for personal and property damages. If the producer of the waste cannot be found, holders or disposers will be strictly liable. When compared with the liability of companies under U.S. "superfund" legislation, however, the EU proposal may impose noticeably lower costs on industry. It is now thought unlikely that it will ever be adopted in the form of the original draft. This is the result primarily of EU cost-benefit limitations on cleanup liability and the absence of any duty to pay governments for damages to natural resources. Commentators have noted that a competitive handicap may follow for United States companies.

Labels, Audits, Impacts and Information

Questions arose as to under litigation is whether innovative German packaging laws comport with EU environmental and trade

5. Commission v. Italy (1980) Eur. Comm.Rep. 1099 and 1115.

6. Directive 2003/17.

7. Enichem Base v. Commune di Cinisello Balsamo (1989) Eur. Comm.Rep. 2491.

8. Syndicat National des Fabricants Raffineurs d'Huile de Graissage v. Groupement d'Intérêt Economique "Inter–Huiles" (1983) Eur.Comm.Rep. 555.

See also Procureur de la Republique v. Association de Defense des Bruleurs d'Huiles Usagees (ADBHU) (1995) Eur. Comm.Rep. 531 (internal French waste oil collection system upheld).

9. Commission v. Belgium (1992) Eur.Comm.Rep. I–04431 (Case C–2/90).

10. *Id.*

policy. These laws require acceptance for recycling of transport packaging, secondary packaging (*e.g.,* boxes), and all sales packaging including cans, plastic containers, foil, etc. The duty to take back sales packaging will not apply to manufacturers, distributors and retailers who participate in the "green dot" program. This program involves regular collection of sales packaging at consumers' homes or collection centers. Green dots may appear on products when a company's system meets prescribed quotas for collection and recycling. By 1995, 80 percent of all packaging materials had to be collected and no less than 80 percent of those materials recycled or reused. Germany's early packaging laws served to stimulate a major environmental directive (No. 94/62 amended No. 2004/12). It requires recovery of at least 60 percent of all packaging by weight of which a minimum of 55 percent must be recycled.[11] Member states, like Germany, may exceed these targets assuming distortions of the regional market are avoided. The directive also requires compliance with certain packaging standards. Directive 2000/53 follows the same path on recycling end-of-life vehicles.

An *eco-labelling* system to enable consumers to identify environmentally less harmful products has been approved.[12] Using a "cradle to grave" approach, products will be evaluated for their impact on the environment throughout their lifespan. Products less damaging to the environment will receive the eco-label logo, a flower with the stars as petals enclosing the EU's Greek-style "E" symbol. Consumer trade, industry and environmental organizations will be consulted on the stringency of the criteria products must meet for the award. Final decisions will be taken by a regulatory committee of the member states on the basis of Commission proposals. All products will be eligible for the labelling system except beverages, foodstuffs, pharmaceuticals and dangerous substances. National eco-labelling plans will coexist with the EU system. Participation in the system will be voluntary, but shifts in consumer preferences to environmentally friendly products may spur use of the logo for competitive reasons.

The Commission created an *eco-auditing* system for much of European industry in 1991. This voluntary system was adopted by the Council of Ministers in 1993 as part of a broader "eco-management" scheme.[13] Companies may participate on a site-by-site basis by adopting a company environmental policy, conducting an environmental review, introducing an environmental management system, executing an environmental audit, setting environmental performance objectives and preparing an environmental statement

---

11. *See* Commission v. Luxembourg (2003) Eur.Comm.Rep. I–1553 (recovery includes incineration at waste plants with energy recovery).

12. Council Regulation 880/92, revised Regulation 1980/2000.

13. Council Regulation 1836/93.

after the audit. All of these requirements must be verified by an independent, accredited environmental "verifier." Monitoring and reporting on subsequent environmental conditions are regularly required. The "benefits" of participation, apart from public opinion, include registration and publication of the participants by national and EU governments and by the company (but the fact of participation may not be used in advertising or on product packaging). The Commission originally sought a mandatory eco-auditing system. It is conceivable that experience with this voluntary scheme may lead ultimately to that result.

A 1985 Council Directive[14] creates an *environmental impact assessment* requirement for environmentally significant development projects. The Directive aims to "identify, describe and assess in an appropriate manner ... the direct and indirect effects" of such projects on humans, fauna, flora, soil, water, air, climate, landscape, material assets and cultural heritage. The directive requires developers to provide national authorities with detailed information relating to the project. Such information includes: (1) a description of the project, including information on its site, design, processes and wastes; (2) an outline of the "main alternatives" considered; (3) a description of "the measures envisaged to prevent, reduce and where possible offset any significant adverse effects on the environment"; and (4) a "non-technical" summary. The EU Environmental Impact Directive does not create substantive environmental protection standards. Rather, it establishes development permission procedures to promote public review at the national level of environmental consequences.[15]

Similarly, the Directive on the Freedom of Access of Information on the Environment[16] obliges the member states to create procedures for citizens to obtain *environmental information*. Under this directive, national authorities must allow access to "any available information ... on the state of water, air, soil, fauna, flora and natural sites and on activities ... or measures adversely affecting, or likely so to affect these, and on activities or measures designed to protect these." However, national authorities may refuse to provide information where the request may affect foreign relations, national security, public security, commercial and industrial confidentiality, and the information, if disclosed, could increase the likelihood of environmental damage.

14. Council Directive 85/337. *See also* Council Directive 2001/42 (impact assessment of plans and programs).

15. *See* World Wildlife Fund v. Autonome Provinz Bozen (1999) Eur. Comm.Rep. I–5613.

16. Council Directive 90/313 replaced by Directive 2003/4.

International Environmental Agreements

Cooperation within international organizations on the environment is shared between the Union and its member states "within their respective spheres of competence."[17] EU adoption of international environmental accords is subject to the same procedures regularly used for trade treaties.[18] One important indicator of just how sensitive the environmental field is within the Union is provided by Article 175. Under the SEA that article required a unanimous Council vote before any legislative or international action on the environment could be undertaken, specifically reserving to the Council the decision as to when qualified majority voting could be used. Most other authority added to the Treaty of Rome in 1987 by the Single European Act prescribed qualified majority voting.[19] This divergence led to litigation over the proper legal basis for EU environmental legislation. The Court of Justice upheld use of Article 95 (internal market measures) with its qualified majority voting and Parliamentary cooperation rules.[20] The Maastricht European Union Treaty alters the SEA to provide regular Parliamentary cooperation on environmental legislation and general use of qualified majority voting by Council in this field.

Europe is rapidly making up for lost time and forging ahead in some areas of environmental protection. For example, regarding fluorocarbons and the ozone layer, the Commission has started using "voluntary agreements" with industry. The Commission reached such an agreement with the Federation of European Aerosol Manufacturers in 1989 committing the industry to a 90 percent reduction in the use of CFCs by 1991. This agreement was confirmed in Commission Recommendation 89/349, an act without legal force. Similar results have been achieved on the use of styrofoam in the refrigeration industry. The Commission has also proposed taxing sources of CFCs, carbon dioxide and aircraft noise.

The European Parliament has been a supporter of stronger environmental policies, backing up its commitment with new budgetary allocations and by promoting the creation of a European Environmental Agency. Its initial task will be to function as an information clearinghouse. A general directive on freedom of access to information on the environment has been passed.[21] The EU has also concluded a large number of international environmental agreements, including the Basel Convention on Transboundary

---

17. Article 174(5), Treaty of Rome.

18. *See* Chapter 6.

19. *Compare* Articles 95 and 138, Treaty of Rome.

20. Commission v. Council (1991) Eur.Comm.Rep. I–2867 (Case C–300/89)

(Titanium Dioxide). *But see* Commission v. Council (1993) Eur.Comm.Rep. I–939 (Case C–155/91) (waste management directive properly adopted under Article 130S).

21. Council Directive 90/313.

Movements of Hazardous Wastes, the Bonn Agreement on the Prevention of Pollution of the North Sea, the Rotterdam Convention on Hazardous Chemicals, and the Washington Convention [against] International Trade in Endangered Species of Wild Flora and Fauna. The Council adopted a Resolution in 1993 tightening supervision and control of shipments of waste into and from the Union. This Resolution transposes the Basel Convention into EU law. One particularly innovative environmental agreement to which the Union is a party is the Barcelona Convention on the Mediterranean Sea. This Convention obligates the signatories to select from a menu of options on improvement and protection of the Mediterranean. The EU has implemented the Arhus Convention on public participation in environmental decision-making.[22]

Environmental Legislation

The following is a partial listing of major European Community environmental laws:

1. Water

- Directive 73/404 (detergents) (replaced by Regulation 648/2004)
- Directive 75/440 (surface drinking water)
- Directive 76/160 (bathing water)
- Directive 76/464 (discharge of dangerous substances into the aquatic environment)
- Directive 78/659 (fish water)
- Directive 79/869 (measuring methods)
- Directive 79/923 (shellfish water)
- Directive 80/68 (groundwater)
- Directive 80/778 (water quality for consumption)[23]
- Directives 82/176, 84/156 (mercury discharges)
- Directive 83/513 (cadmium discharges)
- Directive 84/491 (hexachlorocyclohexane)
- Directive 91/271 (municipal waste water treatment)
- Directive 91/676 (agricultural nitrates)
- Directive 98/8 (biocides)
- Directive 98/83 (drinking water)

---

22. Council Directive 2003/35.

23. *See* Commission v. Germany (1992) Eur.Comm.Rep. I–05973 (Case C–237/90) and Commission v. United Kingdom (1992) Eur.Comm.Rep. I–06103 (Case C–337/89) for findings that Germany and U.K. failed to adequately implement Directive 80/778.

2. Air Pollution

- Directives 70/220, 88/76, 88/436, 89/458, 91/441, 93/59 (motor vehicles)
- Directive 75/516 (sulphur content in liquid fuels)
- Directives 78/1015, 89/235 (motorcycle exhaust)
- Directives 80/779, 89/427 (sulphur dioxide and particles)
- Directive 82/884 (lead in the air)
- Directive 84/360 (air pollution of industrial plants)
- Directives 84/429, 89/369 (municipal waste incineration plants)
- Directive 85/203 (nitrogen dioxide)
- Directives 85/210, 87/416 (lead content of petrol)
- Directive 87/217 (asbestos)
- Directives 88/77, 91/542 (diesel emissions)
- Directive 88/436 (diesel auto engines)
- Directives 88/609, 2001/80 (large combustion plants)
- Directive 89/369 (municipal incinerators)
- Directive 89/629 (noise emissions from civil aircraft)
- Regulation 3322/88 (CFCs)
- Regulation 594/91 (ozone depleting substances)
- Directive 92/72 (ozone air pollution)
- Directive 93/76 (carbon dioxide emissions)
- Directive 93/389 (monitor greenhouse gases)
- Directive 96/62 (air quality assessment)
- Directive 1999/30 (air pollutants)
- Regulation 2037/2000 (ozone depletion)
- Directive 2000/69 (benzene and carbon monoxide)
- Directive 2001/80 (combustion plants)
- Directive 2001/81 (air pollutants)
- Directive 2003/87 (omissions trading)

3. Waste Pollution

- Directive 75/439 (waste oils)
- Directives 75/442, 91/156 (framework for waste management)
- Directives 76/403, 96/59 (PCBs and PCTs)
- Directives 78/176, 82/883 (titanium dioxide)
- Directives 78/319, 91/689 (toxic wastes)
- Directive 84/631 (transborder shipment of hazardous waste)

- Directive 85/339 (beverage containers)
- Directive 86/278 (sewage sludge)
- Directives 90/245, 90/667 (veterinary waste)
- Directive 91/157 (batteries)
- Directive 91/271 (urban waste water treatment)
- Directive 91/689 (hazardous waste)
- Regulation 259/93 (waste shipments)
- Directive 96/59 (PCBs and PCTs)
- Directive 1999/31 (landfills)
- Directive 2000/53 (end-of-life vehicles)
- Directive 2002/95 (hazardous electrical/electronics)
- Directive 2002/96 (waste electrical/electronics equipment)
- Directive 2003/11 (dangerous substances)
- Regulation 2003/2003 (fertilizers)
- Regulation 2004/12 (packaging waste)

4. Noise Pollution

- Directive 70/157 (motor vehicles)
- Directives 78/1015, 89/235 (motorcycles)
- Directive 80/51 (aircraft)
- Directives 84/538, 87/252, 88/180 (lawn mowers)
- Directive 86/594 (household appliances)
- Directives 86/662, 89/514 (hydraulic diggers)
- Directive 2000/14 (outdoor equipment)
- Directive 2002/49 (outdoor noise)
- Directive 2003/10 (noise at work)

5. Conservation

- Directive 92/43 (natural habitats, wild fauna and flora)
- Directive 2001/77 (renewable energy)

§ 5.12 Regional Policy

The Treaty of Rome is premised upon the opening of national markets to competitive trade. The Treaty, especially as amended by the Single European Act in 1987, recognizes that some areas of the Union will not succeed under these conditions. These "less developed" parts of the EU benefit from the Regional Policy. Since 1987, the basic provisions on Regional Policy are located in Articles 158–

162 of the Treaty of Rome under the title "economic and social cohesion."

The Regional Policy operates in conjunction with other programs, notably in agriculture, the Social Fund and coal and steel, to facilitate the growth and development of its poorer parts. The Mezzogiorno in Southern Italy was an early target for regional aid which now extends to most of Portugal, Greece and Ireland, as well as parts of the remaining member states. Some aid comes in the form of Union authorization for national subsidies. Other aid comes directly from the nonprofit European Investment Bank (EIB). The EIB is funded by the Union and the capital market. It has financed a large number of regional development projects.

Article 158 commits the Union to the goal of reducing the disparities between its regions and the "backwardness" of its least-favored regions. A region is least-favored if its per capita GDP is less than 50 percent of the EU average. A major step toward this goal accomplished by the Single European Act was formal recognition of the European Regional Development Fund. This fund has operated since 1975 in addition to, and coordinated with, those that function under the Union's Common Agricultural Policy and its Social Policy.[1] The Regional Development Fund targets structural adjustment and conversion of declining industrial regions with aid grants. Its monies have gone a long way toward convincing the poorer regions of the Union that the campaign for a fully integrated market will bring some benefit to them. Regional development has often become the grease that insures a unanimous vote whenever needed to move the Common Market closer to a full reality.

Expanded economic aid to the least developed members of the Union was accomplished under the "cohesion funds" of the Maastricht Treaty on European Union and the European Economic Area agreement with the EFTA states (less Switzerland). Extensive and difficult negotiations over retention of such funds preceded the 2004 expansion in membership of the European Union which took in numerous states less developed than even the poorest EU member. Countries like Poland, Latvia and Slovakia (for example) are going to receive substantial regional development funds, possibly at the expense of Spain, Greece and Ireland (for example).

§ 5.13 Energy

Despite the specificity of the EURATOM and ECSC treaties, and the oil shocks of the 1970s, it is hard to say that the European Union has developed a viable all-encompassing energy policy. One reason is that Europe is energy poor. Those EU states with oil and gas (Britain and Holland especially) are not keen to be obliged to share these resources in a crisis with their fellow members. Neither would, one suspects, Norway. Common ground has been reached on minimum 90–day crude oil reserves,[1] funding for alternative fuels and energy efficiency, and defense of the massive Siberian natural gas pipeline project from early Reagan administration ("evil empire") attacks. The exclusive French government trading monopoly over petroleum products was finally eliminated in accordance with Article 37 of the Treaty of Rome.[2] And cheap energy subsidies through state enterprises to industry have frequently been condemned by the Commission and Court of Justice.[3] Directives intended to promote greater electricity and gas price competition have also been adopted.[4]

The Council has adopted Resolutions on Energy Objectives. The primary objective is to limit oil dependency to about 40 percent of the Union's total energy needs (down from 60 percent in 1973), and 15 percent of its electricity requirements. In practice, this has mostly meant more subsidies for coal and nuclear power production. However, Directive 2001/77 mandates increased utilization of renewable energy sources, Directive 2003/96 harmonizes taxation of energy products, and Directive 2004/8 promotes co-generation of energy. In 1990, the Union initiated a European Energy Charter. This charter is open to all European nations. Its goals are security of energy supplies, energy efficiency, and safety and environmental protection. The Treaty on European Union added a number of provisions to the Treaty of Rome intended to foster the growth of trans-European networks, including energy.[5] Special emphasis is placed on inter-operability and access issues.

§ 5.14 Broadcasting

The launch of the European satellite EUTELSAT in 1983 made transborder broadcasting possible. July 1994 saw the Russian Federation enlist as a full member of the EUTELSAT organization and it is likely that other Eastern Bloc nations will also join in the future. In March 1989 the Council of Europe (not an EU institution) agreed on a Transborder Television Convention. The Council's twenty-two members will permit transmission of programs by cable or satellite throughout their countries. A common set of minimum broadcasting rules govern free expression, rights of response, sponsorship, pornography, violence and incitement to racial hatred. Advertising is regulated by content (tobacco, alcohol and medicine), duration (normally not to exceed 12 minutes per hour), and impact

§ 5.13

1. Council Directive 72/425.

2. Cullet v. Centre Leclerc Toulouse (1985) Eur.Comm.Rep. 305.

3. See Commission v. Netherlands (1988) Eur.Comm.Rep. 281.

4. See Council Directives 90/377, 90/547, 91/296.

5. See Article 154, Treaty of Rome.

(the program's integrity and its producer's rights must be preserved). The Convention came into effect on May 1, 1993.

Broadcasting Directive

The European Union Council of Ministers laid the basis for a statutory framework for the free movement of audiovisual programs throughout the European Union with its "Television Without Frontiers" Broadcasting Directive.[1] The Broadcasting Directive has recently been extended to the EFTA countries (with the exception of Liechtenstein and Switzerland). In short, each state must admit television broadcast from the others. The regulation of the control of the content of those broadcasts is generally left to home state control, subject to various harmonizing rules concerning rights of reply, protection of minors and advertising and sponsorship.

The Broadcasting Directive provides that "when practicable", broadcasters (many of which are government-owned) should reserve a majority of their time for programs of European (not just Union) origin.[2] This is more restrictive than meets the eye because broadcast time devoted to news, sports events, games, advertising and teletext services is *excluded* when measuring compliance. Moreover, no member state may reduce the percentage of broadcast time allotted to European works from that which existed in 1988. The rules of origin for television programs focus on producer citizenship and production costs, not cultural contents. A work is "European" if it is made by producers in a member state, supervised and actually controlled by producers there or the contribution of EU co-producers to the cost is "preponderant".

The Broadcasting Directive, when first proposed, contained an absolute requirement of more than 50 percent European broadcasting content. Intense lobbying by the United States, a major exporter of films and TV shows to Europe, introduced the "when practicable" limitation. Nevertheless, the long term goal of broadcasting European television productions at least half the time is clearly stated. Many U.S. firms have moved quickly into EU co-productions intended to qualify as European under the Broadcasting Directive. There is a view that the "as practicable" exception has been used (and abused) as a loophole. It is believed that plans will shortly be presented by the Audiovisual Commissioner backed by the Commission President to force European broadcasters to adhere to the majority of European programs requirement by abolishing the "when practicable" requirement. In addition, proposals will be put

§ 5.14
1. Council Directive 89/552.

2. Article 6 of Directive 89/552.

forward to extend the ambit of the Broadcasting Directive to interactive services such as "teleshopping".

The Broadcasting Directive is supported by decisions of the European Court of Justice that television signals constitute the provision of a "service" and thus come within the Treaty of Rome.[3] The Commission decision to waive EU competition laws to permit European broadcasters to bid collectively for the right to broadcast large sporting events illustrates the concern of the EU institutions to balance the strict application of competition laws with the wider benefit which may result in a particular case.

U.S. Reaction

The Broadcasting Directive was one of the few early single market campaign laws to attract headlines in the United States. The entertainment industry is America's second largest source of export earnings after military products and technology. The broadcasting and the banking directives caused the United States business community to wake up and become proactive in the European Union. They have been supported by Congressional resolutions denouncing the Broadcasting Directive, and repeated statements by the United States Trade Representative (USTR) that it is the "enemy of free trade". In 1991, the USTR put the European Union on a "priority watchlist" of nations whose intellectual property practices are suspect by U.S. standards. This was done under the "Special 301" trade sanction provisions of Section 182 of the Trade Act of 1974. The USTR is monitoring national implementation of the Broadcasting Directive within the EU to determine whether, and to what degree, American programs are denied access. Since France, Italy, the United Kingdom, Spain and Portugal have already enacted broadcast quotas and the Uruguay Round of the GATT did not produce an agreement on trade in media products, the potential for Section 301 retaliation and exacerbation of the dispute between the U.S. and the EU exists.

Most balanced observers note that the Broadcasting Directive reflects the sense of cultural invasion that many Europeans resent and associate with more than just television, *e.g.*, a McDonald's on every corner. Generally, however, the fear of losing cultural identity within Europe is diminishing as younger generations are educated, travel, intermarry and take up work around the Union. The beginnings of a European "melting pot" are evident, but concern about the cultural influence of "outsiders" is growing and Europe

3. Italy v. Saatchi (1974) Eur. Comm.Rep. 409; Re Debauve (1980) Eur.Comm.Rep. 833. See Commission v. The Netherlands (1991) Eur.Comm.Rep. (Case C–353/89) (requirement that national broadcasting organizations commission material from Dutch companies violates Article 59 freedom to provide services).

will always be multicultural. These trends affect not only American broadcasters but also Japanese exporters, and the racial and ethnic minorities of the Union.

Other EU Broadcasting Policies

The deadline for national implementation of Directive 93/83 on Satellite Broadcasting and Cable Transmission was January 1, 1995. That Directive deals with the application of copyright to cable and satellite broadcasts. The thrust of the directive is to view broadcasts as being carried out in one nation only for copyright purposes, as opposed to each receiving country. However, the test employed to determine which country is the relevant one for copyright differs from that employed under the "television without frontiers" directive and the resulting position is that different laws may apply to broadcasters in respect of each sphere. Directive 93/83 also answers the question of where permission must be obtained for broadcasts into the EU from outside its borders, while a minimum level of protection is required throughout the EU itself.

In order to promote the development of audiovisual activities the European Union has created two major sources of financial support—an Action Plan to introduce advanced television services in Europe and a Media Program. An important basis for future developments arose from the publication in 1994 of the Commission's Green Paper on Audiovisual Policy, which sets out the various options available and invites consultation at a wider level. Finally, the aim of promoting media pluralism in the European Union Internal Market has been recognized by its institutions for some time,[4] the underlying objective being to ensure diversity of information for the public and respect for freedom of expression.

§ 5.15   Computer Software and Databases

Software Directive

In 1991, the Council adopted Directive 91/250 regarding computer software. Article 1 of the Software Directive requires member states to protect computer programs by copyright as literary works within the meaning of the Berne Convention of the Protection of Literary and Artistic Work. "Computer programs," although not specifically defined, are deemed to include preparatory design material. Protection applies to the expression of any form of a computer program. Ideas and principles which underlie any element of a computer program, including those which underlie its interfaces,

---

4. European Parliament resolution of 15th February 1990 OJ No. C68, 19/3/1990, pp. 137–138 and 16th September 1992 A3–0153/92/Corr.; Commission communication Com (90)78 and Green Paper COM (92)480 of 23rd December 1992.

are not protected. A computer program is protected if it is original in the sense that it is the author's own intellectual creation. This test for originality accords with the approach taken in the U.S. concerning telephone directories. No other criteria (aesthetic or qualitative) are to be applied to determine its eligibility for protection.

The Software Directive was the subject of fierce industry lobbying in 1990, the two opposing camps being ECIS (the European Committee for Interoperable Systems) which had a liberal "open systems" outlook on matters such as decompilation/reverse-engineering, and SAGE (the Software Action Group for Europe) which represented the big manufacturers' interests in proprietary architectures by seeking copyright protection for interface specifications. The final form of the Directive issued in May 1991 was more or less a victory for ECIS. The Directive was due to have been implemented by each member state by January 1, 1993: only the UK, Italy and Denmark met the deadline. Other member states (such as the Netherlands, Luxembourg, Belgium, and Portugal) were in breach of their obligations and the Commission commenced proceedings against them.

Article 4 of the Directive indicates, subject to the provisions of Articles 5 and 6, that the exclusive rights of the holder include the right to do or to authorize: (1) The permanent or temporary reproduction of a computer program by any means and in any form, in part or in whole (insofar as loading, displaying, running, transmission or storage of the computer program necessitate reproduction, such acts are subject to authorization); (2) the translation, adaptation, arrangement or other alteration of a computer program and the reproduction of the results without prejudice to the rights of the person who alters the program; and (3) any form of distribution to the public, including rental of the original computer program or copies. Following the ECJ principle of exhaustion of rights, the first commercial exploitation in the Union of a copy of a program exhausts the right to control any further distribution within the Union of that copy, with the exception of the right to control further rental of the program or copies of it.

Article 5 of the Directive creates exceptions to the rights conveyed in Article 4 in the absence of specific contractual provisions to the contrary. To the extent reproduction is required to load, display, transmit or store the program in order to use it as intended, such reproduction does not require a separate authorization from the holder. The making of a back-up copy (or more than one) by a lawful user may not be prevented by contract insofar as backup(s) are necessary for use of the program by the lawful user. In general, there is a right to "observe, study, or test the functioning of the program in order to determine the ideas and principles which underlie any element of the program" provided such observation, study or test is made in the course of permitted loading, displaying, running, transmission or storage.

Decompilation

Article 6 of the Directive deals with decompilation, also known as reverse engineering. Authorization is not required where the reproduction of the code and translation of its form are indispensable to obtaining information necessary to achieve the interoperability of an independently created computer program with other programs. However, the following conditions must be met: (1) These acts must be performed by the licensee or by another person having a right to use a copy of a program or on their behalf by a person authorized to do so; (2) the information necessary to achieve interoperability must not previously have been readily available to those persons; and (3) the acts are confined to the parts of the original program which are necessary to achieve interoperability. It remains to be seen how these tests will be applied in the courts of each member state.

Moreover, decompilation is not permitted if the information obtained through its application is to be: (1) Used for goals other than achieving the interoperability of the independently created program; (2) given to others, except when necessary for the interoperability of the independently created computer program; or (3) used for the development, production or marketing of a computer program substantially similar in its expression or for any other act that infringes copyright. Lastly, in accordance with the provisions of the Berne Convention, Article 6 may not be interpreted in such a way as to allow its application to be used in a manner which reasonably prejudices the holder's legitimate interests or conflicts with a normal exploitation of the computer program.

It has been suggested that the decompilation provisions of the EU directive will change traditional software licensing clauses. The traditional clause "Licensee agrees not to cause or permit the reverse engineering, disassembly or decompilation of the Licensed Program" will have to be redrafted to something like:

> Licensee shall not decompile the Licensed Program, except to the extent necessary to achieve interoperability of the Licensed Program with an independently created program, whenever the information necessary to achieve such interoperability has not been made readily available by Licensor to Licensee upon Licensee's written request. Such decompilation acts shall be restricted to the parts of the Licensed Program that are necessary to achieve interoperability. In no event may Licensee

subcontract such decompilation to a third party without Licensor's prior written authorization.[1]

The same practitioner suggests that a clause more adapted to the spirit of the directive would be the following:

> Licensee shall not cause or permit decompilation of the Licensed Program, except to the extent necessary to achieve interoperability of the Licensed Program with an independently created program, whenever the information necessary to achieve such interoperability has not been made readily available by Licensor to Licensee upon Licensee's written request. Such decompilation acts shall be restricted to the parts of the Licensed Program that are necessary to achieve interoperability.[2]

Remedies

The Directive provides for special measures of protection even if such acts are not "infringement" according to national copyright laws in the Union. Such measures are listed in Article 7 of the Directive. These include: (1) Any act putting into circulation or possession for commercial purposes a copy of a computer program while knowing, or having reason to believe, that it is an infringing copy; and (2) any act putting into circulation or possession for commercial purposes any means singularly intended to facilitate the unauthorized removal or circumvention of any technical device which may have been applied to protect a computer program.

Databases

Directive 96/9 concerns legal protection of databases. It creates exclusive rights to databases not otherwise copyrightable.

§ 5.16 Telecommunications

An imposing array of European Union law is making its impact in the telecommunications field. This section summarizes on some of the leading directives and developments, including

• Telecommunications Services Directive 90/388 (now Directive 2002/77).

• Open Network Provision Directives 90/387, 98/10.

• Terminal Equipment Directives 88/301 and 91/263.

---

§ 5.15

1. *See* Bertone, "The EEC Directive on Computer Software," in Folsom, Lake and Nanda (eds.), *European Community Law After 1992: A Practical*

Guide for Lawyers Outside the Common Market (Kluwer, 1992).

2. *Id.*

Other particularly noteworthy developments include the Commission's 1991 Guidelines on applying competition law to the telecommunications industry[1] and a public sector procurement directive which applies, in part, to telecommunications.[2] The Treaty on European Union added a number of provisions to the Treaty of Rome intended to foster the growth of trans-European networks, including telecommunications.[3] Special emphasis is placed on interoperability and access issues.[4] A telecoms package of 2002 overhauled the regulatory framework for the industry,[5] notably leading to application of data privacy rules.[6]

Telecommunications Services

Telecommunications by phone, fax, telex and computers go to the heart of modern service-oriented economies. The European Union has recognized this and taken steps under its 1992 campaign to integrate and improve its telecommunications network. In 1990, the Council finalized the "Open Network Provision" framework directive. This legislation harmonizes the conditions of access and use of public telecommunications networks. Commission Directive 88/301 (issued under Article 90) deregulates the sale and servicing of telecommunications equipment. France failed when it challenged the authority of the Commission to issue this directive before the European Court.[7] Council Directives 90/387 and 98/10 eliminate public monopolies over all but voice telephones and infrastructure ownership. Private sector companies may move freely into electronic mail, interactive communications, data transmission and the like. U.S. firms are particularly thought to have competitive advantages that will benefit them under the new EU telecommunications regime. In addition, there is every reason to believe from the case law of the European Court that state monopolies in the telecommunications area will be required to abandon discriminatory national practices. This case law is partly based upon the freedom to provide services across borders, and partly upon competition law.[8]

§ 5.16

1. O.J.C. 233/2 (Sept. 6, 1991).

2. Directive 90/531. *See* Section 5.4.

3. *See* Article 154, Treaty of Rome.

4. *See* Directive 97/33.

5. *See* Commission IP/02/2002 (Feb. 14, 2002).

6. Directive 2002/58.

7. France v. Commission (1991) 1 Eur.Comm.Rep. 1223.

8. *See* Procureur du Roi v. Debauve (1980) Eur.Comm.Rep. 833 (ban on television advertising); Italy v. Commission ("British Telecom") (1985) Eur. Comm.Rep. 873 (use of leased lines for customer service upheld); Bond van Adverteerders v. The Netherlands (1988) Eur.Comm.Rep. 2085 (discriminatory cross-border advertising restraints); Régie des Télégraphes et des Téléphones v. SA "GB–INNO–BM" (1991) Eur. Comm.Rep. I–05981 (Case C–18/88) (public network operator's specifications for phone sets and compliance monitoring violate Treaty of Rome where operator competes with other phone suppliers); Commission v. Netherlands (1991) Eur.Comm.Rep. I–04069 (Case C–353/89) (Dutch requirement that broadcasters receive significant part of pro-

The Commission Directive on Competition on the Markets for Telecommunications Services 90/388 (now Directive 2002/77) ("The Services Directive") permits member states to retain monopolies over "voice telephony." Voice telephony is defined as the commercial provision for the public of the "direct transport and switching of speech in real-time between public switched network termination points, enabling any user to use equipment connected to such a network termination point in order to communicate with another termination point." In contrast, the member states are obligated to "withdraw all special or exclusive rights for the supply of telecommunications services other than voice telephony and ... ensure that any operator is entitled to supply such telecommunications services ... [and] ensure that the conditions for the grant of Licenses [if any] are objective, non-discriminatory and transparent...." Moreover, starting in 1993, member states will no longer be able to prohibit the offering of leased line capacity for circuit or packet-switched data services for resale to the public. Leased lines must be made available within a reasonable period and without unjustified restrictions or charges. Technical interfaces must be published and unwarranted or discriminatory restrictions on the processing of signals before transmission or after their reception are prohibited. The Services Directive also requires member states to have an independent agency control licenses, specifications, frequency allocations and surveillance of usage conditions. Lastly, the Services Directive regulates the termination of telecommunications contracts. The Court of Justice upheld the issuance by the Commission of the Services Directive under Article 90/(3).[9]

One commentator has reached the following conclusions about the Services Directive:

Despite the pro-competition language, in some respects the Services Directives further entrenches the control of the Postal Telegraph and Telecommunications Administrations (PTTs) and as a practical matter impedes competition. For example, it relies upon analog technology in presuming that voice telephony, which it reserves to the monopoly, is technologically distinguishable from data, which it opens to competition. In fact, digital technology does not distinguish between voice and data.

---

gramming from Dutch companies violates Article 59); Elliniki Radiophonia Tileorassi v. Dimotiki Etairia Pliroforissis (1991) Eur.Comm.Rep. I–2925 (Case C–260/89) (single state broadcasting monopoly over domestic TV and retransmissions of EC programs amounts to discriminatory and excessive breach of Article 59); Commission v. Belgium (1992) Eur.Comm.Rep. I–06757 (Case C–211/91) (language, prior authorization and culturally reserved television program rules violate Treaty of Rome); Procureur du Roi v. Lagauche & Ors (1994) Eur.Comm.Rep. I–05267 (Cases C–46/90 and C–93/91) (radio apparatus approval rules precluded by EU directive).

9. Spain, Belgium & Italy v. Commission (1992) Eur.Com.Rep. I–5833 (Cases C–271/90, 281–90).

Therefore, by allowing the PTTs to keep control over private lines for voice and also allowing the PTTs to define the scope of that control, the Services Directive has reinforced a significant barrier to the development of competition even in data. Likewise, the separation of regulation from operations, although recognized as a step in the right direction, cannot by itself safeguard against PTTs unwarranted control as long as the PTTs can impose tariff restrictions on the purpose for which circuits are used.[10]

ONP Directive

Council Directive 90/387 on the Establishment of the Internal Market for Telecommunications Services Through the Implementation of Open Network Provision ("ONP Directive") is intended to "provide a legal framework for the medium to long-term harmonization of the conditions for telecommunications services provision." The ONP Directive concerns the harmonization of conditions for open and efficient access to and use of public telecommunications networks and services. This is to be accomplished by slowly harmonizing technical interfaces and service features under standards adopted by the European Telecommunications Standards Institute ("ETSI"). Service providers who comply with those standards fulfill the relevant essential technical and service requirements and telecommunications organizations that comply fulfill the requirements of open and efficient access. Adoption of ETSI standards will thus provide access to telecommunications networks and markets throughout the European Union.

The ONP Directive applies to leased lines, packet-and circuit-switched data services, Integrated Services Digital Network (ISDN) voice telephony service, telex services, mobile services, new types of access to the network (such as to the circuits connecting subscriber premises to the public network exchange), and access to broadbank networks. It arguably reduces the opportunity for PTT abuse of their dual function status as exclusive providers of networks and services and as competing providers of nonexclusive services and equipment. However, the ONP Directive indicates that "reasons of general public interest" will restrict access when "essential requirements" are involved. Essential requirements concern noneconomic reasons which may cause a member state to restrict access to the public telecommunications network or public telecommunications services. These reasons include security of network operations, maintenance of network integrity, and in justified cases, interopera-

---

10. Beatson, "An Introduction to Telecommunications Law in the European Community," in Folsom, Lake and Nanda (eds.), *European Community Law* *After 1992: A Practical Guide for Lawyers Outside the Common Market* (Kluwer, 1992).

bility of services and data protection. The ONP Directive specifies the following "framework" for its implementation by the member states:

Open Network Provision conditions shall be drawn up in such a way as to facilitate the service providers' and users' freedom of action without unduly limiting the telecommunications organizations' responsibilities for the functions of the network and the best possible condition of communications channels.

Terminal Equipment Directive

Commission Directive 88/301 on Competition on the Markets in Telecommunications Terminal Equipment ("Terminal Equipment Directive") seeks to create a Union-wide terminal equipment market.[11] The Terminal Equipment Directive recognizes that "the last decades have seen considerable technical developments in networks, and the pace of development has been especially striking in the areas of terminal equipment." The Directive provides for a gradual elimination of PTT monopolies over terminal equipment. The Directive requires the publication of specifications and approval procedures for such equipment. The goal is to "make transparent the characteristics of the termination points of the network to which the terminal equipment is to be connected." Council Directive 91/263 on the Approximation of Laws of the Member States Concerning Telecommunications Terminal Equipment Including the Mutual Recognition of their Conformity ("the Standards Directive") seeks to harmonize interfaces and promote "mutual recognition of type approval." Access to the network without sacrificing its integrity is the focus of this directive. The Standards Directive establishes procedures for certification, testing, marking, quality assurance and product surveillance.

§ 5.17   Research and Development

One important thrust of the Single European Act of 1987 was promotion of more research and technological development. The European Union strongly perceived itself to be falling behind the United States and Japan in these areas. The result was eleven new articles in the Treaty of Rome, Articles 163–173. The opening sentence of Article 163 establishes the goals of strengthening the scientific and technological bases of European industry and encouraging it to become more competitive at the international level. This is to be achieved not only through coordination of national activities and a program of generous Union grants, but also via the continuing single market campaign. When less than all the EU

---

11. The Commission's authority to issue this directive under Article 86 of the Treaty of Rome has been upheld.   French Republic v. Commission (1993) Eur.Comm.Rep. I–01223 (Case 202/88).

states participate in Union-sponsored research and development, the Council has the power to decide to what degree the resulting knowledge must be shared. To encourage commercial enterprises and research organizations across the EU to collaborate on R & D projects, without fear of challenge on the basis of competition law, the Council adopted Regulation 418/85, known as the R & D Block Exemption, which like the other block exemptions contains "white lists" and "black lists" of restrictions.

In 1987, the Council of Ministers adopted the Framework Program for Community Research and Development. This framework focuses on eight areas; the quality of life, information and communication, modernization of industry, exploitation and optimum use of geological resources, energy, development, marine resources and improved European science and technology cooperation. Some research is done at the Union's own Joint Research Center. Other research is sponsored through national institutes and universities. Many of the Union's research and development programs are known by acronyms such as ESPRIT (information technologies), RACE (advanced communications), DRIVE (road transport informatics and telecommunications), DELTA (learning technologies), and JET (nuclear fusion). Participation by United States companies in EU research programs has been limited.

§ 5.18 Occupational Health and Safety

The Treaty of Rome is dominated by economic affairs. Nevertheless, the Union has always sought to provide for some of the concerns of the human beings who are impacted by the winds of economic change. Articles 136–148 of the Treaty of Rome establish the Social Policy of the European Union. These articles seek to improve working conditions and standards of living on a harmonized basis throughout the Union. The right of EU nationals to move freely to take up employment has previously been discussed in Chapter 4 in connection with the foundations of the Treaty. The Union's social policy builds upon this basic right. Article 144, for example, led to the enactment of social security legislation by the EU to insure coverage for those who exercise their right to move freely to work.

A major impetus came in 1987 with the addition of Article 138 by the Single European Act. This article focuses on health and safety in the working environment. Acting by a qualified majority vote, the Council in cooperation with the Parliament is empowered to issue directives establishing minimum requirements in this field. It has already done so, for example, on visual display units, heavy load handling and exposure to biological agents and carcinogens. More generally, Council directives now establish minimum safety and health requirements for most workplaces, equipment used by workers, and protective devices.[1] Article 138 specifically requires such directives to avoid imposing administrative, financial and legal constraints that would hold back the creation and development of small and medium-sized enterprises. Like the 1987 Treaty amendments creating the Environmental Policy, Article 138 allows member states to maintain or introduce more stringent legal rules on working conditions, provided these are compatible with the Treaty of Rome.

Perhaps the most well known occupational law is the "Working Time" Directive 93/104, now 2003/96. Its controversial legal basis is discussed in Section 5.18. The directive requires rest periods, maximum 48 weeks, a minimum of four weeks of paid leave, maximum eight-hour night shifts, but contains a variety of "public sector" exceptions. It continues to generate controversy.[2]

Health and Safety Legislation

The following is a partial list of major European Union occupational health and safety laws:

- Directives 77/576, 92/58 (safety signs)
- Directives 83/477, 91/382 (asbestos)
- Directives 80/1107, 88/364 (chemical agents)
- Directive 89/391 (the workplace framework directive)
- Directive 89/654 (physical plant design)
- Directive 89/655 (equipment used by workers)
- Directive 89/656 (protective equipment)
- Directive 89/665 (use of machines, equipment and installations)
- Directives 89/686, 89/328 (personal protective equipment)
- Directives 90/219, 90/220 (biotechnology)
- Directive 90/269 (heavy loads)
- Directive 90/276 (visual display units)
- Directive 90/394 (carcinogens)
- Directives 80/1107, 90/679 (biological agents)
- Directive 91/368 (machinery risks)
- Directive 92/57 (construction sites)
- Directive 92/85 (pregnant workers)

§ 5.18

1. *See* Council Directives 89/654, 655, 656.

2. *See* Queen v. Secretary of State of Trade ex parte Bectu, (2001) Eur. Comm.Rep. I–04881 (June 26, 2001) (minimum employment period invalid); Sindicato de Medicos v. Conselleria de Sanidad de la Generalidad Valenciana (2000) Eur.Comm.Rep. I–07963 (Oct. 3, 2000) (application to doctors on call).

- Directive 92/91 (drilling for minerals)
- Directive 93/88 (exposure to biological agents)
- Directive 93/04 (working time)
- Directive 94/33 (children at work)
- Regulation 2062/94 (European Agency for Safety and Health at Work)
- Directive 2002/15 (working time for road transport)
- Directive 2002/44 (vibration)
- Directive 2003/10 (noise at work)

§ 5.19   Social Policy

Articles 146–148 create the European Social Fund. This fund comes out of the Union budget. It is used to pay up to 50 percent of the costs of the member states under their vocational retraining and worker resettlement programs.[1] EU rules have substantially harmonized these programs. Unemployment compensation is also funded when plants are converted to other production for workers who are temporarily suspended or suffer a reduction in working hours. They retain the same wage levels pending full reemployment. Commission Decision 83/516 extended the operation of the European Social Fund to promoting employment among those under age 25, women who wish to return to work, the handicapped, migrants and their families, and the long-term unemployed.

Social Charter

The 1992 campaign had a social dimension. Labor unions were especially concerned about the prospect of "social dumping," the relocation of companies to EU states with weaker unions and lower wages. There is no regional legislation on minimum wages, and none is expected in the near future. The Union's response to these concerns led to the Charter of Fundamental Social Rights For Workers, adopted in 1989 by 11 member states less Britain through the European Council. The Charter proclaims the following fundamental social rights for workers:

(1) freedom of movement and choice of occupations;

(2) fair remuneration (sufficient to have a decent standard of living);

(3) improved living and working conditions (*e.g.*, paid leave);

(4) adequate social security benefits;

§ 5.19   1.   Article 148, Treaty of Rome.

(5) free association in unions, including the right *not* to join, and the right to strike;

(6) non-discriminatory access to vocational training;

(7) equal treatment for women and men;

(8) development of rights to access to information, and rights of consultation and participation;

(9) satisfactory health and safety conditions at work;

(10) for the young, a minimum employment age of 15, substantial limitations on night work for those under 18, and start-up vocational training rights;

(11) for retirees, the right to assistance "as needed" and a decent standard of living; and

(12) for the disabled, assistance to integrate socially and professionally.

The Charter was to be implemented immediately by the member states in "accordance with national practices." In addition, for each item listed above, Union legislation was anticipated by the end of 1992. Adoption of this legislation was slow chiefly because of Britain's veto power in the Council over employment matters under the Single European Act. The Commission, however, drafted a number of Social Action Program legislative measures. One such measure guaranteeing *minimum* maternity leave benefits of 14 weeks at statutory sick pay rates was adopted by the Council of Ministers in November of 1992.[2] A woman's employment cannot be terminated because she is pregnant. In addition, pregnant women are entitled to switch from night work, exempted from work detrimental to their health, and entitled to take paid leave for pre-natal check-ups. This directive is expected to require substantial improvements to existing legislation in Ireland, Portugal and the United Kingdom. Unpaid parental leave rights are detailed in Directive 96/34.

Social Protocol

In December 1991 at the Maastricht Summit agreement was reached, save Britain, on a "social policy protocol" allowing the EU to enact laws by qualified majority vote governing many areas which bridge workers' interests and company operations. Some suggested that the "social protocol" would have been more accurately labeled a "workers' rights protocol". It focused on working environment issues including conditions of labor, health and safety, disclosure of information, sex discrimination, and worker consulta-

---

2. Council Directive 92/85.

tion. The "social protocol" thus overlapped considerably with the Social Charter.

Despite its repeated opposition to development of a "social dimension," the United Kingdom under Conservative rule adopted or implemented over half of the measures noted in the Social Charter. What the Conservatives consistently objected to were rules relating directly to the employee-employer relationship, not worker benefits such as pregnancy leave or health or safety measures. Nevertheless, the Court of Justice repeatedly ruled against Britain in litigation challenging the adequacy of its implementation of worker-related directives (e.g., on collective redundancies (mass layoffs) and transfers of enterprises). And, in a major decision, the Court ruled over vehement objection that the "working time" directive (No. 93/104 now 2003/88) was properly adopted by qualified majority vote on the basis of Article 138's authorization of worker health and safety law.[3] This ruling had the practical effect of avoiding Britain's Social Protocol opt out rights. The directive creates, inter alia, a minimum right to four weeks of paid vacation. Subsequently, the United Kingdom under the Labour Party administration of Prime Minister Blair opted into the region's Social Policy and the 1999 Amsterdam Treaty repealed the Social Protocol.

Social Policy

As amended, Articles 136–145 of the Treaty of Rome (the "social chapter") embrace social goals reflecting the Social Charter. There is express authority for EU legislation on worker health and safety, work conditions, information and consultation of workers, and gender equality, mostly using qualified majority voting and co-decision Parliamentary powers. However, there is no authorization for EU action on matters of pay, and rights of association, strike and lock-out. EU legislation can occur by unanimous vote on social security, co-determination, worker protection upon termination, and employment of third country nationals.

One business lawyer has reached the following conclusions regarding the emerging social policy of the European Community:

> From the perspective of the corporation based outside of Europe, the future of EC employment, or "social," regulation— that is, the blueprint set out in the Charter, the Social Action Program, and the Commission's 1990–1991 package of draft instruments—looks expensive. European workers already receive from their employers some of the highest pay and benefit levels in the world. Once the Social Action Program's 47 called-

---

3. United Kingdom v. Council (1996) Eur.Comm.Rep. I–5755.

for instruments are in place, continental European workers' pay and benefit levels will probably rise even higher.

Certain Charter rights, once implemented, will directly raise employers' marginal costs of employing workers. For example, the second right, to "fair pay," could directly raise wages—both in low-paying service industries and, via the "equitable reference wage" concept, in every other industry, as well. The third right, to "improved working conditions," could raise employers' payroll costs, if the Council implements the already-tabled proposals to extend benefits and protections to part-time and temporary workers, and to force employers to enter "indefinite" lengthy, written individual employment contracts with even non-union workers. The sixth right, to vocational training, would, if implemented, force employers (and even unions) to create and pay for career-long job training programs. And the ninth right, to expanded health and safety protections, would impose new work-procedure restrictions on certain EC employers.

Other Charter rights, if implemented, could even more radically raise corporations' costs of employing Europeans; these are the rights which would affect legal liability and the structure of EC labor law. For example, the Charter's fifth right, to EC-level collective bargaining, could raise costs of employment in less economically-developed member states, as wages and benefit levels were negotiated EC-wide. The Charter's seventh right, for equal treatment between the sexes, might raise costs for corporations found to have preferred men over women in employment or pay, and, under an already-approved directive, would raise some employers' costs as regards pregnant women. If implemented, the Charter's eighth right, to worker consultation and participation, would also raise costs—to the extent that business decisions made with labor's input are less beneficial to the "bottom line" than are decisions which management makes alone.

Other Charter rights, once implemented, will most likely be EC-funded. These rights will necessarily raise employers' costs, too, if only by the incremental amount by which the EC must raise taxes to fund them. Such guarantees include the Charter's eleventh, twelfth, and thirteenth rights, to expand social programs for youth, the aged, and the disabled.

Fortunately, certain other aspects of the "social Europe" agenda will actually *benefit* employers based outside the EC. For starters, the Charter's first right, guaranteeing free movement of workers, will continue to streamline intra-European personnel transfers, thereby making personnel "immigration" matters cheaper—an important benefit for companies with trans-European operations.

Additionally, the "social Europe" program sends some positive signals to certain employers based outside the EC—particularly U.S.-based employers—through what it *omits*. The Charter and the Social Action Program are silent on several areas in which U.S. employers bear heavy domestic burdens; most notable is the virtual absence of anti-discrimination law. The EC's proposed protections for the young, the aged, and the disabled do not seem headed toward the extensive U.S. regulation of employment decisions arguably involving age or handicap, such as under the Age Discrimination in Employment Act, the Rehabilitation Act of 1973, the Americans with Disabilities Act, and analogous state laws.

Similarly, although much of the Charter and Social Action Program aims at guaranteeing increased benefits for workers, nothing in the documents raises the specter of benefit plan liability analogous to U.S. law under the Employment Retirement Income Security Act. And nothing in the Charter or Social Action Program approaches the magnitude of U.S. prohibitions, under Title VII and related state laws, against race, nationality, and religious discrimination. Thus, U.S.-based employers, at least, can take solace in that the "social Europe" program, while indisputedly pro-employee, will not create for European workers causes of action on which to sue employers anything analogous to the grounds for liability which haunt companies in the 1990's U.S.[4]

§ 5.20 Employment Law

Apart from gender discrimination in employment relations,[1] the Union has undertaken relatively little by way of employment law. There are, however, some notable directives governing mass lay-offs, employee rights upon insolvency and business transfers, and contractual disclosure duties.

Mass Lay-offs

Council Directive 75/129 amended in 1992 and republished as Directive 98/59 concerns mass lay-offs (collective redundancies). Any private business[2] employing more than 20 workers intending to

---

4. Dowling, "Employment Matters and the Social Charter," in Folsom, Lake and Nanda (eds.), *European Community Law After 1992: A Practical Guide for Lawyers Outside the Common Market* (Kluwer, 1992).

§ 5.20

1. *See* Section 5.21.

2. *See* Commission v. United Kingdom (1994) Eur.Comm.Rep. I–2479 (limited applicability to businesses with trade unions invalid).

dismiss designated numbers of employees for general economic reasons must give 30 days notice with "all relevant information" to those employees or their representatives.[3] For businesses with less than 100 workers, this duty is triggered when 10 employees are to be laid off. For businesses with 100 to 300 employees, the trigger is 10 percent of those employed. For firms with over 300 employees, the trigger is the dismissal of 30 or more employees. Consultations on possible reductions in the lay-offs and mitigation of them follow, ordinarily with public authorities included. More demanding national rules concerning mass lay-offs are allowed and in some countries, notably Germany, have been enacted. By 1992 amendment, this directive applies when the dismissal decision is made by parent companies of the employer located in another member state.[4]

Employee Rights in Business Transfers

Council Directive 77/187 ensures certain employee "acquired rights" when there are "transfers" of for profit and nonprofit[5] businesses or parts thereof,[6] including mergers and acquisitions but not judicial insolvency proceedings.[7] The test of whether a "transfer" occurred is the continuance of the business as a "going concern."[8] This includes lease transfers[9] but not replacement contractors.[10]

Council Directive 77/187 amended in 1998 and republished as Directive 2001/23 requires advance notice of qualified transfers along with an analysis of the implications for workers. All employees working for businesses whose assets are transferred retain their existing terms and conditions of employment, and accrued service rights. Collective agreements are also preserved. No dismissal of employees may occur except for economic, technical or organizational reasons that change workforce needs.[11] Any substantial

---

3. *See* Dansk Metalarbejderforbund v. H. Nielsen & Son (1985) Eur. Comm.Rep. 553 (mandatory notice does not create 30–day pay rights).

4. Directive 92/56, now Directive 98/59.

5. Commission v. United Kingdom (1994) Eur.Comm.Rep. I–2435 (nonprofits).

6. *See* Botzen v. Rotterdamsche Droogdok Maatschappij BV (1985) Eur. Comm.Rep. 519 (partial transfer).

7. *See* D'Urso & Ors v. Ercole Marelli Elettromeccanica (EMG) & Ors (1991) Eur.Comm.Rep. I–4105 (Case C–362/89) (employee transfer rights adhere in civil receivership proceedings when business continues to operate until transfer oc-

curs); Abels v. Administrative Board, Case 135/83 (1985) (judicial insolvency not covered).

8. Bork Int'l A/S v. Foreningen of Arbejdsledere (1988) Eur.Comm.Rep. 3057; Spijkers v. Benedik Abattoir CV (1986) Eur.Comm.Rep. 119.

9. Foreningen of Arbejdsledere v. Daddy's Dance Hall A/S (1988) Eur. Comm.Rep. 739.

10. Suzen v. Zehnacker Gebaudereinigung (1997) Eur.Comm.Rep. I–1259.

11. *See especially* Litster v. Forth Dry Dock, 1 All Eng.Rep. 1134 (1989) (House of Lords).

change in working conditions harmful to employees is treated as a constructive dismissal and the rights of employees under Directive 77/187 cannot be waived by contract or otherwise.[12] Employee rights protected by Directive 77/187 extend to transfers of employment which amount to a contracting out for services previously managed internally.[13] But such transfers cannot force employees to remain with their new employers.[14] Pension benefits are *not* covered and they do not automatically transfer. However, more favorable national law on employee "acquired rights" is allowed. This directive often means that companies seeking to purchase shares or assets of European firms must also consult and negotiate with unions if there is any future possibility of a reduction in staff or rationalization of operations.

Pay Claims in Insolvencies

Council Directive 80/987 requires member states to guarantee certain employee back pay claims against insolvent employers.[15] Such claims do not include employer contributions due under national social security or company pension schemes. More generally, a Bankruptcy Convention has been proposed. Council Directive 91/533 requires employers to disclose in writing "essential" information applicable to employment contracts or relationships. Such information includes party identification, place and nature of work, commencement date, duration, annual leave entitlements, notice requirements, pay and method of payment, length of working day and any relevant collective agreements. Special disclosures apply when employees are sent abroad.

Terms of Employment Disclosure

Directive 91/533 requires employers to provide employees with written terms of their employment, including a job description, period of employment, paid leave, remuneration and benefits, and any relevant collective agreements.[16] Directive 96/71 requires companies posting workers to other member states to generally adhere to host state rules on minimum pay, benefits (except pensions), work periods, paid leave and health and safety at work. Directive 96/34 grants unpaid parental leave rights of three months, with a

---

12. Foreningen of Arbejdsledere v. Daddy's Dance Hall A/S (1988) Eur. Comm.Rep. 739.

13. Watson Rask & Anor v. ISS Kantineservices A/S (1992) Eur.Comm.Rep. I–05755 (Case C–209/91).

14. Katsikas & ORS v. Konstantinidis & ORS (1992) Eur.Comm.Rep. 06577 (Cases C–132, 138, 139/91).

15. *See* Everson & Anor v. Secretary of Stat for Trade (1999) Eur.Comm.Rep. I–8903 (UK guaranty fund covers Irish branch workers).

16. *See* Lange v. Georg Schunemann (2001) Eur.Comm.Rep. I–01061 (Feb. 8, 2001) (overtime included).

right vested in employees of one year or more to return to the same job (if possible) or similar work.

§ 5.21 Equal Pay and Equal Treatment

Article 141 is probably the most prominent element in the Union's social policy. It is derived from International Labor Organization Convention No. 100 which three member states, including France, had adopted by 1957. The French were rightfully proud of this tradition of non-discrimination between the sexes on pay. They also appreciated that gender-based inequality in pay in other member states could harm the ability of their companies to compete. Article 141 thus enshrines the principle that men and women shall receive equal pay for equal work. For these purposes, "pay" is defined in Article 141 to mean wages or salary, and any other consideration in cash or kind, received directly or indirectly respecting employment. "Equal pay without discrimination based on sex" means that piece rate payment must be calculated on the same units of measurement and that time rates must be equal for the same job.

Equal Pay, Comparable Worth

Article 141 has been the subject of voluminous EU legislation and litigation. It applies, quite appropriately, to the Union as an employer.[1] Early on, the Court of Justice decided that Article 141 on equal pay for equal work is directly effective EU law.[2] This decision allowed individuals throughout the Union to challenge pay discrimination in public and private sector jobs. The ruling in *Defrenne* was applied prospectively by the Court of Justice so as to avoid large numbers of lawsuits for back pay. In *Defrenne,* a flight attendant for Sabena Airlines was able to allege illegal discrimination in pay and pension benefits (as a form of deferred pay) to stewards and stewardesses on the basis of EU law before a Belgian work tribunal. Indeed, European Union law in this area enshrines the principle of "comparable worth," a most controversial issue in United States employment law. Furthermore, women who are paid less than men performing work of less worth may claim relief under Article 141.[3] The hard question is how to determine what constitutes "equal work" requiring equal pay under Article 141 or what "women's work" is worth more than that being done by men (again requiring pay adjustments). For example, does secretarial work equal custodial work? Is the work of an airline attendant worth

§ 5.21

1. Sabbatini, née Bertoni v. European Parliament (1972) Eur.Comm.Rep. 345; Razzouk v. Commission (1984) Eur. Comm.Rep. 1509 (working conditions).

2. Defrenne v. Sabena (1976) Eur. Comm.Rep. 455.

3. Murphy v. An Bord Telecom Eireann (1988) Eur.Comm.Rep. 673.

more than that of an airline mechanic? What about speech therapists (mostly women) and pharmacists (mostly men).[4]

Council Directive 75/117 complements Article 141. It makes the principle of equal pay apply to work of *equal value* (to the employer). This mandates establishment of non-discriminatory job classifications to measure the comparable worth of one job with another. The Commission successfully enforced Directive 75/117 in a prosecution before the European Court of Justice against the United Kingdom. The Sex Discrimination Act of 1975, adopted expressly to fulfill Article 141 obligations, did not meet EU standards because employers could block the introduction of job classification systems.[5] Danish law's failure to cover nonunionized workers also breached the equal pay directive.[6] But its implementation under German law, notably by constitutional provisions, sufficed to meet Union standards.[7]

In determining equal or greater values, most states favor a job content approach. Content is determined through job evaluation systems which use factor analysis. For example, in Great Britain a job is broken down into various components such as skill, responsibility, physical requirements, mental requirements, and working conditions. Points or grades are awarded in each of these categories and totaled to determine the value of the job. Different factors may be balanced against each other. In Ireland, the demand of physical work can be balanced against the concentration required in particular skills. This is known as the "total package" approach. The equal job content approach relies on comparisons. This raises the question of which jobs should be deemed to be suitable for comparison. The member states have taken different approaches to this question. In Britain the comparison must be drawn from the same business establishment. In contrast, the Irish Anti–Discrimination Pay Act provides for "comparisons in the same place," and "place" includes a city, town or locality. This approach is designed to ensure that legitimate regional differences in pay are not disturbed.

Defenses

Employer defenses also vary from member state to member state. In Ireland, employers may justify a variation if they can show "grounds other than sex" for a disputed variation in pay. In Britain, employers will succeed if they can prove a "genuine material factor which is not the difference of sex." In Germany, the employer can prove that "material reasons unrelated to a particular

4. *See* Enderby v. Frenchay Health Authority (1993) Eur.Comm.Rep. I–5535.

5. Commission v. United Kingdom (1982) Eur.Comm.Rep. 2601.

6. Commission v. Denmark (1986) 1 Common Mkt.L.Rep. 44.

7. Commission v. Germany (1986) 2 Common Mkt.L.Rep. 588.

sex" justify the differential. A further consideration in the implementation of equal pay laws has been the existence of pre-existing wage schedules set by collective agreement. In Britain and Italy, courts have held that collective agreements relating to pay cannot be changed or altered except where direct discrimination can be shown.

The burden of proving "objectively justified economic grounds" to warrant pay differentials is on the employer.[8] When a woman succeeds a man in a particular position within a company (here a warehouse manager), she is entitled to equal pay absent a satisfactory explanation not based upon gender.[9] The same may be true of part-time (female) workers doing the same job as full-time (male) workers.[10] Free travel to railway employees upon retirement cannot go only to men.[11] And "pay" includes retirement benefits paid upon involuntary dismissal, which cannot be discriminatory.[12] But a protocol adopted at the 1991 Maastricht Summit makes this ruling prospective only. Pay also includes employer-paid pension benefits which cannot be for men only.[13] In this decision the Court refused to remove the retroactive effect of its judgment suggesting that *Defrenne* was adequate notice of the direct effect of Article 141 upon employers. Mobility, special training and seniority may be objectively justifiable grounds for pay discrimination.[14]

Equal Treatment

The principle of equal pay for equal work has been extended by Council Directive to *equal treatment* regarding access to employment, vocational training, promotions, and working conditions (*e.g.* retirement deadlines).[15] This directive prohibits discrimination based upon sex, family or marital status and extends to the self-employed.[16] Equal treatment is limited by three exceptions. Member states may distinguish between men and women if: (1) sex is a determining factor in ability to perform the work; (2) the provision protects women; or (3) the provision promotes equal opportunity for men and women. Discrimination is also permitted in "occupational activities" for which workers of only one sex are appropriate. Equal treatment must be extended to small and household busi-

---

8. Council Directive 97/80.

9. McCarthays Ltd. v. Smith (1980) Eur.Comm.Rep. 1275.

10. Jenkins v. Kingsgate (Clothing Productions) Ltd. (1981) Eur. Comm.Rep. 911.

11. Garland v. British Rail Engineering, Ltd. (1982) Eur.Comm.Rep. 359.

12. Barber v. The Guardian Royal Exchange Assurance Group (1990) 1 Eur.Comm.Rep. 1889.

13. Worringham and Humphreys v. Lloyds Bank Ltd. (1981) Eur.Comm.Rep. 767.

14. Union of Commercial and Clerical Employees v. Danish Employers Assn. *ex parte* Danfoss, 1989 Eur. Comm.Rep. 3199.

15. Council Directive 76/207 (issued under Article 308).

16. Council Directive 86/613.

nesses.[17] Dutch Law compulsorily retiring women at age 60 and men at age 65 violated the directive.[18] Women cannot be refused employment because they are pregnant even if the employer will suffer financial losses during maternity leave.[19] Maternity and adoption leave benefits for women, however, need not be extended to men.[20] The dismissal of a woman because of repeated absences owing to sickness is lawful provided the same absences would lead to the dismissal of men.[21] General prohibitions against night work by women but not men violate equal treatment Directive 76/207. The French government failed to justify this criminal law on any special grounds.[22]

Equality also governs social security entitlements[23] such as disability or caring for the disabled pay.[24] Social security benefits cannot be based upon marital status.[25] Women police officers cannot be denied arms when men are not, even in the interest of "public safety" and "national security."[26] Women chefs can be denied entry to special combat units,[27] but general military exclusions are prohibited.[28] Equal treatment requires the elimination of preferences based upon gender in laws governing collectively bargained employment agreements.[29] In addition, the Council adopted a declaration in December 1991 endorsing the Commission's recommended Code of Practice on sexual harassment. This Code rejects sexual harassment as contrary to EU equal treatment law. Council Directive 2002/73 codifies this approach, emphasizing protection of employee

17. Commission v. United Kingdom (1983) Eur.Comm.Rep. 3431.

18. Beets–Proper v. Van Lanschot Bankiers NV (1986) Eur.Comm.Rep. 773. See Council Directive 86/378 (equal treatment regarding pensions).

19. Dekker v. Stichting Vormingscentrum voor Jong Volwassenen Plus (1990) Eur.Comm.Rep. 3941 (Case C–177–88).

20. Hoffmann v. Barmer Ersatzkasse (1984) Eur.Comm.Rep. 3047; Commission v. Italy (1983) Eur.Comm.Rep. 3273 (adoption leave benefits).

21. Hertz and Aldi Marked (1990) Eur.Comm.Rep. 4047 (Case C–179/88).

22. Ministère Public v. Stoeckel (1991) Eur.Comm.Rep. 4047 (Case C–345–89).

23. Council Directive 79/7. An important exception allows state pension schemes to retain different retirement ages for men and women. See Regina v. Secretary of State for Social Security (1992) Eur.Comm.Rep. II–285 (Case C–9/91) and Article 7(1)(a) of Directive

79/7. But severe disablement allowances (SDA) and invalid care cannot be provided on the basis of different ages. Secretary of State for Social Security v. Thomas and Ors (1993) Eur.Comm.Rep. II–237 (Case C–328/91). Compare Regina Virginia Hepple v. Adjudication Officer (2000) Eur.Comm.Rep. I–3701 (accident victims' reduced earnings allowance nondiscriminatory).

24. Drake v. Chief Adjudication Officer (1986) Eur.Comm.Rep. 1995.

25. Id.

26. Johnston v. Chief Constable (1986) Eur.Comm.Rep. 1651. See generally Articles 296–298, Treaty of Rome.

27. Sirdar v. The Army Board and Secretary of State for Defence (1999) Eur.Comm.Rep. I–7043.

28. Kreil v. Federal Republic of Germany (2000) Eur.Comm.Rep. I–69.

29. Commission v. France (1988) Eur.Comm.Rep. 6315 (Case 312/86) (preferences for women must be removed).

dignity. But both the equal pay and equal treatment directives fail to cover significant categories of women workers; part-time, temporary and home workers.[30] Additional EU legislation in these areas can be expected.

Affirmative Action

Predictably, questions of "affirmative action" have arisen in the context of Article 141 law. A controversial decision of the Court of Justice invalidated a Bremen regulation giving women of equal qualifications priority over men where women made up less than half the relevant civil service staff. While not strictly a quota, the Court found that Bremen had exceeded the limits of the equal treatment directive in promoting equality of opportunity.[31] Specific reservation of University professorships for women in Sweden likewise fell upon ECJ review.[32] Sweden now uses increasing targets for women in full professorships. Article 141(4) of Treaty of Rome, as amended by the Amsterdam Treaty in 1999, attempts to address such issues. It allows member states to maintain or adopt "measures for specific advantages" in order to make it "easier" for the "underrepresented sex" to pursue vocational activity or to prevent or compensate for "disadvantages" in professional careers. That said, the Swedish university post reservations still fell upon ECJ review.

Gender and Other Discrimination

Although Article 141 on equal pay is directly effective law binding upon public and private employers throughout the Union (*Defrenne*), it is not yet clear to what degree the equal treatment directives cited above have that effect. Clearly these directives are binding on the member states and public corporations as employers.[33] The private sector must comply after national implementing legislation is adopted, but if that legislation is deficient the only remedy may be prosecution of the member state by the Commission.[34] There is a trend within the jurisprudence of the Court of

---

30. *See* Jenkins v. Kingsgate Ltd. (1981) Eur.Comm.Rep. 911 (part-time workers paid less, and though largely female, no EC law violation). *Compare* Bilka–Kaufhaus v. Weber (1986) Eur. Comm.Rep. 1607 (employer must show objectively justified economic grounds to pay part-timers less).

31. Kalanke v. Freie Hansestadt Bremen (1995) Eur.Comm.Rep. I–3051. *Compare* permissible advantages upheld in Marschall v. Land Nordrhein Westfalen (1997) Eur.Comm.Rep. I–6363; Badeck v. Hessischer Ministerpräsident (2000) Eur.Comm.Rep. I–1875.

32. Abrahamsson and Anderson v. Fogelgvist (2000) Eur.Comm.Rep. I–5539.

33. *See especially* Marshall v. Southampton and South–West Hampshire Area Health Authority (Teaching) (1986) Eur.Comm.Rep. 723 (discriminatory retirement ages unlawful); Foster v. British Gas (1990) 1 Eur.Comm.Rep. 3313.

34. *See* Duke v. GEC Reliance Ltd. (1988) All Eng.Rep. 626 (discriminatory retirement ages lawful).

Justice towards recognition of a broad human right of equality before the law. This is evidenced in a number of Article 141 cases, reliance upon the European Human Rights Convention in developing general principles of EU law,[35] and in revised Articles 2, 3 and 13 of the Treaty of Rome (1999), which suggests that the private sector will eventually be bound by all European Union legislation on equal pay and equal treatment even in the absence of or in spite of national implementing law.[36]

Transsexuals[37] and homosexuals have begun to benefit from this trend. But the Court notably refused to require equal employer travel benefits for same sex partners under Article 141 law,[38] and likewise the Court of First Instance refused to recognize homosexual partnerships as the equivalent of marriage for household allowance purposes.[39] Revisions of the 1976 equal treatment directive emphasizing an approach called "gender mainstreaming" are in progress. Directive 2000/43 broadly provides for equal treatment irrespective of racial or ethnic origin. Directive 2000/78 more narrowly prohibits employment discrimination on grounds of religion or belief, disability, age or sexual orientation.

§ 5.22 European Investment Bank

The European Investment Bank (EIB) has a separate legal personality within the Union. A Protocol on the EIB which governs the structure and functioning of the bank, was annexed to the Treaty of Rome. The task of the EIB is to contribute "to the balance and stable development of the Common Market in the interests of the Community". The bank has played a major role in funding regional development projects within the Union and external development projects under the Lomé Convention and other EU trade arrangements.

The Board of Governors of the EIB consists of the Ministers of Finance of the member states. This board oversees the bank's capital resources and loan activities. In general, EIB loans are only made to private EU entities when other sources of financing are also available and the member state where the investment is located guarantees the loan. However, the EIB is not restricted to activities within the Union. Article 18 of the Protocol empowers the Board of Governors to permit the granting of loans for investment

---

35. *See* Section 2.12.

36. *See* Section 3.1 (discussion of duty of national courts to interpret national law in furtherance of EU directives).

37. P. v. S. (1996) Eur.Comm.Rep. I–2143; K.B. v. National Health Services

Pensions Agency (2004) Eur.Comm.Rep. I–00000 (Case No. C–117/01).

38. Grant v. South–West Trains Ltd. (1998) Eur.Comm.Rep. I–621.

39. *See* D. and Sweden v. Council (2001) Eur.Comm.Rep. I–04319 (May 31, 2001).

projects to be carried out outside the territories of the Member States.

The EIB acts on a non-profit making basis, and may involve itself in three types of projects:

(1) projects for development of less developed regions;

(2) projects for the modernization or conversion of undertakings or for the development of new activities required by the progressive establishment of the common market; and

(3) projects of common interest to several members.

In (1) and (3) above, the projects must be "of a size and nature that they cannot be entirely financed by the various means available in the individual Member States", before the EIB will consider acting. The European Investment Bank has raised substantial sums in the international money markets.

§ 5.23 Common Agricultural Policy

The Treaty of Rome establishes the basic principles governing what is perhaps the most controversial of all Union policies, the Common Agricultural Program (CAP). The inclusion of agricultural trade in the Treaty of Rome was a critical element to the politics of the Union and remains largely without precedent in other regional economic treaties throughout the world. For many reasons, including the desire for self-sufficiency in food and the protection of farmers, free trade in agricultural products is an extremely sensitive issue. When the Common Market was established in 1957, France and Italy had substantial farming communities, many of which were family based and politically powerful. Both countries envisioned that free trade in agricultural products could threaten the livelihoods of these people. The solution, as outlined in the Treaty of Rome, was to set up a "common organization of agricultural markets."

The objectives of the CAP stated in the Treaty of Rome include the increase of productivity, the maintenance of a fair standard of living for the agricultural community, the stabilization of markets, and the provision of consumer goods at reasonable prices. It has not proved possible to accommodate all of these objectives. Consumer interests have generally lost out to farmers' incomes and trading company profits. Target prices for some commodities (*e.g.,* sugar, dairy products and grain) are established and supported through Union market purchases at "intervention levels". "Variable import levies" (tariffs) are periodically changed to ensure that cheaper imports do not disrupt CAP prices. External protection of this type is also extended to meat and eggs. Fruit, vegetables and wine are subject to quality controls which limit their flow into the market.

Wine and agricultural products are subject to regulated designations of origin,[1] Rioja wine from Spain[2] and Feta cheese from Greece,[3] for examples. Such regulations do not extend to generic food names, such as Edam,[4] jenerver (gin)[5] and Emmenthal,[6] which can be freely traded with proper labels indicating variations in product qualities.

Regulatory Controls

In recent years, perhaps the most controversial "common organization" has been for bananas. The Europeans import bananas under a complex quota system adopted in 1993 that favors former colonies and dependencies. Internally and externally those affected have gone bananas over this regulation. Several challenges originating from Germany failed before the European Court of Justice, but in the end the United States, Mexico, Ecuador, Guatemala and Honduras prevailed in the World Trade Organization. After suffering "authorized retaliation" in the form of tariffs on EU exports, the Europeans have promised to adjust their "common organization" for bananas by replacing its quotas with nonpreferential tariffs. The European Agricultural Guidance and Guarantee Fund (better known by its French initials as FEOGA) channels the Union agricultural budget into export refunds, intervention purchases, storage, and structural adjustment. Agricultural policy regulations cannot discriminate against like or substitute products. But the bias towards producers, not consumers, in the CAP has been consistently upheld by the Court of Justice.[7]

Agricultural goods, like industrial products, can trigger free movement litigation. These issues are often raised under Articles 28–30 covered in Chapter 4. In one case, for example, the Court of Justice suggested that British animal health regulations were a disguised restraint on Union trade in poultry and eggs.[8] As with industrial goods, if the real aim is to block imports, such regulations are unlawful measures of equivalent effect to a quota. On the other hand, the United Kingdom could establish a Pear and Apple

§ 5.23

1. Regulation 823/87 (wine) and Regulation 2081/92 (agricultural products).

2. See Belgium v. Spain (2000) Eur.Comm.Rep. 23.

3. See Denmark v. Commission (1999) Eur.Comm.Rep. I–1541.

4. Ministere Public v. Deserbais (1988) Eur.Comm.Rep. 4907.

5. Criminal proceedings against Miro BV (1985) Eur.Comm.Rep. 3731.

6. Criminal proceedings against Guimont (2000) Eur.Comm.Rep. I–10663 (Dec. 5, 2000).

7. Germany v. Commission (1963) Eur.Comm.Rep. 131; Balkan–Import–Export GmbH v. Hauptzollamt Berlin–Packhof (1973) Eur.Comm.Rep. 1091 (CAP measures valid unless "obviously unreasonable" consumer prices produced). *See* Article 34(3), Treaty of Rome

8. Commission v. United Kingdom (1982) Eur.Comm.Rep. 2793 (Newcastle disease).

Development Council for purposes of technical advice, promotional campaigns (not intended to discourage competitive imports), and common quality standards for its members. But it could not impose a mandatory fee to finance such activities.[9]

Apart from variable tariff protection, CAP quality control regulations can serve to keep foreign agricultural products from entering the European Union market. For example, the ban on beef hormones adopted by qualified majority vote in the late 1980s stirred opposition internally.[10] In the United States, the beef hormones legislation was vehemently opposed by the White House, but accepted by the renegade Texas Department of Agriculture which offered as much hormone-free beef to the Union as it would buy. The Texas offer delighted the EU Commissioner on Agriculture who rarely has a U.S. ally and is said to have wired: "I accept."

A veritable maze of legislation and case law governs the CAP. For many years, special agricultural "monetary compensation amounts" (MCAs) have been collected at national borders, greatly contributing to the failure to achieve a Europe without internal trade frontiers. It was not until 1987 that firm arrangements were realized to dismantle the MCA system. In most years, the net effect of the CAP is to raise food prices in the EU substantially above world price levels. The CAP has meant that agriculture is heavily subsidized. Indeed, it continues to consume the lion's share of the Union budget and at times seems like a spending policy that is out of control.

The Common Agricultural Policy does include a variety of "structural" programs intended to reduce the size of the farm population, increase the efficiency of its production, and hold down prices. These programs have involved retirement incentives, land reallocations, and training for other occupations. There has been a gradual reduction in the number of EU farmers over the years. In 1988, the Council adopted rules designed ultimately to reduce agricultural expenditures by linking total expenditures to the Union's rate of economic growth, establishing automatic price cuts when production ceilings are reached, and creating land set-aside and early retirement programs for farmers.

France and Italy, in the early years of the EU, became major beneficiaries of CAP subsidies. West Germany, with a minimal agricultural sector, was the primary payor under the program. It, in turn, principally benefitted from the custom union provisions establishing free trade in industrial goods. Hence a basic tradeoff was established in 1957 by the Treaty of Rome. France and Italy would

---

9. The Apple and Pear Development Council v. K.J. Lewis, Ltd. (1983) Eur. Comm.Rep. 4083.

10. United Kingdom v. Council (1988) Eur.Comm.Rep. 855.

receive substantial agricultural subsidies out of the regional budget while West Germany gained access for its industrial goods to their markets. Germany now holds a 25 percent share of internal EU trade. Britain, like Germany, sees itself as a net payor under the CAP. It has repeatedly been able to negotiate special compensatory adjustments as a consequence. Greece, Spain, Portugal and Ireland, on the other hand, looked forward eagerly to membership as a means to CAP subsidies. These countries, along with unified Germany, Austria, Sweden and Finland (whose agricultural subsidies were actually *reduced* upon joining the CAP), are often the least efficient producers of agricultural products. As such, they stand to lose the most if the CAP is substantially replaced by market forces.

International Ramifications

In the main like the United States, the European Union seems unable to stabilize the level of its agricultural subsidies. This results in overproduction ("butter mountains," "wine lakes") and frequent commodity trade wars. A significant amount of fraud to obtain CAP subsidy payments has occurred. In 1989, the House of Lords Select Committee on the European Community released a scathing report on subsidy abuses entitled "Fraud Against the Community." Others legitimately farm marginal land with lots of fertilizer. The excess produce is stored, used in social welfare programs and frequently "dumped" in cheap sales abroad.

Despite its incredible cost, the CAP remains one of the political and economic cornerstones of the Union. External protests from North America notwithstanding, the CAP is unlikely to disappear. The provocative question much debated in the Uruguay Round of GATT negotiations is whether a mutually satisfiable reduction in the level of North American and European Union subsidies to agriculture can actually be achieved. In 1992 the Council of Agricultural Ministers agreed as an internal matter to cuts in support prices of 29 percent for cereals, 15 percent for beef and 5 percent for butter. Farmers received direct payments representing the income lost from the price cuts. Further price cuts and direct payments were agreed in 1999. It was hoped that these reductions would reduce EU export subsidies on agricultural goods and international trade tensions. They also supported the argument that the extraordinary level of European subsidization of agriculture was simply not sustainable in cost nor EU politics.

European Union agricultural trade restraints are of enormous consequence to North American exporters. Equally significant are EU "export refunds" on agricultural commodities, refunds that affect the opportunities of North American exporters in other parts of the world. The United States has consistently argued (at times successfully) that these refunds violate the GATT rules on subsidies, while at the same time increasing its own export subsidies on agricultural goods. The result has been an agricultural "trade war" between the U.S. and the EU. Each side has sought to outspend the other on agricultural export subsidies in a market that has been wonderful to buyers. Major attempts at a resolution or at least diminishment of the agricultural trade war were undertaken in the Uruguay Round of GATT negotiations during the late 1980s and early 1990s. Late in 1992, both sides announced the resolution of a number of longstanding subsidies' disputes (notably on oilseeds) and a compromise on the contested Uruguay Round agricultural trade issues. Agreement was reached on 20 percent mutual reduction in internal farm supports and a 21 percent mutual reduction on export subsidies measured on a volume basis over 6 years using a 1986–90 base period. After a year of French protests and further negotiations, this agreement was formally incorporated into the WTO accords.

Tensions between Europe and the United States on agricultural trade have of late diminished (though hardly disappeared), but the U.S. Farm Bill of 2002 threatens to reignite them. The really big issue looming on the CAP horizon is enlargement of the European Union to include Hungary and Poland, among others. Each enlargement of the Union plugs more farmers into the extraordinary CAP subsidy system and the ten new members admitted in 2004 will gain full payments by 2013. The Amsterdam and Nice Treaties notably failed to resolve ongoing disputes over agricultural reform. A last minute deal in 2002 capped costs at their 2006 level plus 1 percent a year starting in 2007. In theory this will force a gradual winding down of CAP subsidies. Efforts are being made to de-couple CAP subsidies from production levels, notably for cotton, tobacco and olive oil. Meanwhile, one wonders just how much longer European taxpayers will continue to pay for the CAP.

§ 5.24   Common Fisheries Policy

Unlike agriculture, the Union is a net importer of fish and fish products. Nevertheless, a "common organization" for the fisheries' market in the EU has also been created.[1] Following the lead of other nations, the Union extended its exclusive economic zone to 200 miles offshore in 1977. The most controversial feature of the Common Fisheries Policy (CFP) is the requirement that member states open their waters beyond six (sometimes twelve) miles to each other's fishing fleets to the limit of a "total allowable catch (TAC)" fixed by the Council. The TACs and related technical measures (*e.g.,* minimum fish net sizes) are basically conservation

§ 5.24
1.   Council Regulation 2796/81.

measures. TACs have even been zero for the evanescent herring in extreme years.

Each TAC is divided into member state fishing quotas by the nations where the fish are found. Those states are authorized to close a fishery when a quota is exhausted. Fishery quotas are exchangeable as between the member states. Each state is required to record all landings or transfers at sea which are deducted from the country quotas. Commission review and inspection of these records and decisions is undertaken to ensure compliance with Fisheries Policy rules. Numerous cases have come before the European Court of Justice enforcing rights of entry and challenging discriminatory quotas.[2] Even the practice of "quota hopping" by registering boats under the national laws of other member states must be tolerated.[3]

The Fisheries Policy was initiated by the original six EC states in 1970 in anticipation of the enlargement to include fishery-rich nations (for whom it has become part of the price of membership). This helps explain why many people in nations like Norway and Iceland shudder at the prospect of joining the Union. The Common Fisheries Policy also governs the marketing and price of fish in the EU. The Commission sets "official withdrawal prices" for various types of fish. These prices act as a floor to the market. When they are reached, fish producers can withdraw up to twenty percent of their catch and receive Union subsidies. Fish withdrawn in this manner cannot be used for human consumption. As in the agricultural area, the EU can grant export refunds to aid the sale of fish abroad, and it can protect the withdrawal price levels by limiting imports. Structural relief measures have emphasized reductions in the Union's fishing fleet and subsidies for fish farming. The European Union has numerous international fishery agreements, including one with the United States which primarily accesses U.S. waters and "surplus fish" to EU boats while opening the Common Market to American exports.[4]

§ 5.25   Intellectual Property Rights

All of the European Union member states are parties to the Paris Convention on the Protection of Industrial Property (1883). The expression "industrial property" is now usually replaced by "intellectual property." This means that each of them grants national treatment rights to citizens of other member states regarding patents and trademarks. The Paris Convention also gives appli-

2. Commission v. Ireland (1978) Eur. Comm.Rep. 417; Regina v. Kirk (1984) Eur.Comm.Rep. 2689; Commission v. United Kingdom (1992) Eur.Comm.Rep. I–05785 (Case C–279/89).

3. Regina v. Secretary of State for Transport (1990) Eur.Comm.Rep. I–02433 (Case C–213/89).

4. *See* Council Decision 91/309.

cants a one year right of priority to apply in other states for patent rights and a six months right of priority for trademark rights. These priority rights date from the initial home country application. Thus the Paris Convention achieved limited harmonization of EU patent and trademark law.

Patents and Designs

The 1973 European Patent Convention (EPC)[1] established the European Patent Office (EPO) in Munich. It allows applicants to simultaneously apply for national patent rights in any of the contracting countries. These include all of the EU nations, plus a number of other European states. The applicant must meet the requirements for patentability established by the EPC. Challenges to patentability decisions by the EPO can be made within 9 months after granting of the patent. Thereafter, challenges must be made in national courts subject to national patent laws. The EPC basically presents a one-stop opportunity to obtain a basket of national patents in Europe. It does not foreclose the option of individual national patent applications.

The 1975 Community Patent Convention (CPC) still has not come into force.[2] The CPC will allow applications for a Common Market patent valid in any contracting state. The CPC does not, however, permit patenting of biotechnology inventions, although this may well be amended following eventual ratification. A Common Market patent may be granted, revoked or transferred throughout the Union as a whole. Licenses for part of the Union will be possible. It will be an alternative to (but not a replacement for) national patent rights. The CPC should be contrasted with the bundle of national rights obtained through the EPC. However, the CPC will require its signatories to harmonize national patent laws to conform to the Convention's rules on infringement, litigation procedures, exhaustion of rights and other issues. It will create a new Court of Patent Appeals.

Biotechnology patents are mandated by Council Directive 98/44, provided industrial application is possible. The human body and its genes are not patentable, nor are processes for cloning human beings or uses of human embryos for industrial or commercial purposes. Plant variety rights are established in Regulation 2100/94.

The protection of semiconductor topographies is regulated by Council Directive 87/54. This directive was adopted in response to U.S. requirements of reciprocity before EU nationals can obtain comparable U.S. rights under the Semiconductor Chip Protection

Act of 1984. Topographies that are original ("not commonplace") are protected for ten years. This protection includes the right to prohibit reproduction of the topography and its commercial exploitation. But exclusivity is not preserved when reverse engineering occurs or a semiconductor product is put on the market by consent. The European Union has not signed the Washington Treaty on protection of microcircuits.

After years of debate, Council Directive 98/71 harmonized national rules on design rights, an area of intellectual property rights law with diverse coverage throughout the EU. Design rights are possible for jewelry, cars, furniture, consumer electronics, machinery, tools, spare auto parts and other products. Such rights last from five to 25 years, and may be used to preclude Common Market trade.[3]

Trademarks

Late in 1993, the Council adopted a regulation creating "Community Trademarks." Businesses operating in the European Common Market may now elect to process applications for such marks through the Union's new Trademark Office in Alicante, Spain. This presents a streamlined alternative to seeking national trademark registration, in each member state. Any words or symbols[4] capable of distinguishing goods or services are registrable even if exclusively descriptive.[5] Colors may also be distinctive.[6] Community Trademarks may be opposed whenever there is a likelihood of confusion,[7] there are prior national registrations of the marks that have been genuinely used, or various nonregistrable grounds (e.g., genericism)[8] are present. Community Trademarks are valid for 10 years and may be renewed. Any failure to use a Community mark for 5 years can cause protection to be withdrawn. Hundreds of thousands of Community marks have been issued, many to U.S. businesses. There is a Board of Appeal within the Trademark Office, followed

3. *See* Consorzio Italiano v. Regie Nationale des Usines Renau H (1988) Eur.Comm.Rep. 6039.

4. *See* Proctor & Gamble v. OHIM (2000) Eur.Comm.Rep. II–00265 (Feb. 16, 2000) (shape of soap bar not registrable); Phillips Electronics NV v. Remington Consumer Products Ltd. (2002) Eur.Comm.Rep. I–5475 (3D shapes).

5. *See* Wrigley v. OHIM (2003) Eur. Comm.Rep. I–00000 (Case C–191/01) (Doublemint gum possibly registrable); Proctor + Gamble Co. v. OHIM (2001) Eur.Comm.Rep. I–6251 (Baby–Dry possibly registrable). *Compare* Best Buy Concepts v. OHIM (2003) Eur. Comm.Rep. II–00000 (Case T–220/01)

(Best Buy rejected as descriptive mark); Eurcool Logistik GmbH v. OHIM (2002) Eur.Comm.Rep. II–00683 (Case T–34/00) (Lite not registrable).

6. Libertel Groep BV v. Benelux Merkenbureau (2003) Eur.Comm.Rep. I–03793 (Case C–104/01).

7. *See* Sabel v. Puma (1997) Eur. Comm.Rep. I–6191; Lloyd v. Schuhfabrik Meyer v. Klijsen Handel (1999) Eur.Comm.Rep. I–3819 (reasonably well informed and reasonably observant consumer standard).

8. *See* DVK v. OHIM (2000) Eur. Comm.Rep. II–00001 (Jan. 12, 2000).

by what have been numerous appeals to the European Court of First Instance.

In addition, the Council has adopted Directive 89/104. This directive seeks to harmonize some aspects of EU trademark law, but not trademark registration procedures. A summary of its highlights follows. The directive applies to individual trademarks, service marks, collective marks, and guarantee or certification marks which are the subject of a registration or an application for registration in the member states. It does not cover trademark rights acquired through use, which is possible in Italy, Ireland and the United Kingdom. A trademark may consist of any "sign" capable of being represented graphically. This includes words, personal names, designs, letters, numerals, and the shape of goods or their packaging, provided that such signs are capable of distinguishing the goods or services of one firm from those of others. It may therefore include such things as musical jingles or screen layouts/user interfaces for computer programs (in each case to the extent that third party rights are not infringed).

Article 3 distinguishes between absolute grounds for refusal or invalidity of marks (*e.g.,* marks devoid of distinctive character, contrary to public policy or accepted principles of morality) and relative grounds (*e.g.,* a sign of high symbolic value, particularly a religious symbol). Allowance is made for registered marks which acquire a distinctive character through use. Member states are also permitted to continue to refuse registration on grounds already in force prior to adoption of the directive. Article 4 provides that registration of a mark which is identical or confusingly similar to one registered nationally or as a regional trademark, or a well known but unregistered mark, is not allowed.

A common set of infringement criteria are contemplated in Article 5 of the directive. These criteria include presentation of the use of registered trademarks on different classes of goods if detrimental to the distinctive character of the mark. Article 7 provides that the principle of the exhaustion of rights applies.[9] Licensing of marks for limited use or for limited areas is generally permissible. Article 9 states that where a proprietor for an earlier trademark has acquiesced for a period of five successive years to the use of a later trademark registered in good faith in that member state while being aware of such use, he or she is no longer entitled to apply for a declaration that the trademark is invalid or to oppose the use of the later trademark. This provision resembles adverse possession. Furthermore, trademark rights can be revoked if the owner has not

---

9. *See* § 4.5 for a discussion of the principle of exhaustion of intellectual   property rights.

put the mark to genuine use for five years absent valid reasons for non-use. Use of the mark on exported goods will meet the genuine use requirement.

Copyrights

In November of 1992, the Council adopted Directive 92/100 on minimum 50–year rental and lending rights for copyrighted works. This directive requires the member states to provide authors' and producers' rights to allow or prohibit the rental or lending of original or copied copyrighted works, such as records, videos or films. The concepts of "rental" and "lending" are broadly defined to include any "direct or indirect economic or commercial advantage." Libraries that loan such works to the public at charges which do not exceed operating costs are not deemed to have an "advantage" and therefore are not caught within Directive 92/100. The member states may override a refusal to lend for cultural promotion and other activities provided they remunerate the rights' holder, but cannot override a refusal to rent. Even when there is an assignment of rental rights to record or film producers, the original holder retains an equitable right to remuneration that cannot be waived. Performers and broadcasters obtain exclusive rights to authorize or deny the fixation of their works and their reproduction and distribution. When broadcasters use sound recordings, a mandatory remuneration scheme is triggered with the funds shared between the record producers and the performers. A number of exceptions to these exclusive rights may be granted, including private, reportorial, teaching, scientific and ephemeral use.

Late in 1993, the Council adopted Directive 93/83 in order to harmonize copyright and related rights for satellite and cable TV transmissions. The primary goal is to insure payment for the holders of such rights. For satellites, commencing in 1995, broadcast rights must be obtained in the country of origin not destination. Prior contracts must be adapted to this rule by the end of 1999. For cable TV, broadcast rights must be negotiated through cooperative bodies representing various categories of rights holders. Unreasonable refusals by broadcasters to retransmit programs by cable were arbitrated until 2003.

The Council also adopted Directive 93/98 in order to harmonize the duration of copyrights and related rights (e.g. photographs and posthumous works). As from July 1, 1995, all works subject to copyright protection in the Union will last for 70 years after the death of the author. The term is 50 years for neighboring rights. For audiovisual and cinematic works, there was some dispute about who is "the author." Copyright protection for these works will extend for 70 years from the death of the last survivor of the following persons: the principal director, the author of the script, the author of the dialogue and the composer of the music. Directive 2001/84 harmonizes the law of monetary resale rights for artists ("droit de suite").

Directive 2001/29 draws upon the WIPO Copyright Treaty of 1996 and corresponds to the U.S. Digital Millennium Copyright Act of 1998. The Directive is Internet driven, and outlaws possession, making or providing all tools capable of circumventing technological measures intended to protect copyrighted material. In other words, "hackers" beware. Likewise, tampering with copyright management information (that is to say, encryption devices) is prohibited under Directive 2001/29. Remedies may vary among the member states, but must be "effective." Some EU members have enacted criminal sanctions, others have limited relief to damages.

TRIPs

The European Union adheres to the WTO Agreement on Trade–Related Intellectual Property Rights (TRIPs), thereby generating substantial uniformity in intellectual property law. The TRIPs Code covers the gamut of intellectual property. On copyrights, there is protection for computer programs and databases, rental authorization controls for owners fo compute software and should recordings, a 50–year motion picture and sound recording copyright term, and a general obligation to comply with the Berne Convention (except for its provisions on moral rights).

On patents, the Paris Convention (1967) prevails, product and process patents are to be available for pharmaceuticals and agricultural chemicals, limits are placed on compulsory licensing, and a general 20–year patent term from the date of application is created. United States law, which previously granted 17 year patents from the date of issuance, has been amended to conform. For trademarks, internationally prominent marks receive enhanced protection, the linking of local marks with foreign trademarks is prohibited, service marks become registrable, and compulsory licensing is banned. In addition, trade secret protection is assisted by TRIPs rules enabling owners to prevent unauthorized use or disclosure. Integrated circuits are covered by rules intended to improve upon the Washington Treaty. Lastly, industrial designs and geographic indicators of alcoholic beverages (e.g., Canadian Whiskey) are also part of the TRIPs regime.

Infringement and anticounterfeiting remedies are included in the TRIPs, for both domestic and international trade protection. There are specific provisions governing injunctions, damages, customs seizures, and discovery of evidence. Directive 3295/94 implements the Union's remedies against counterfeit and infringing goods, but criminal sanctions are not mandatory.[10] A broad directive on enforcement of intellectual property rights was adopted in 2004.[11] It concerns evidence, injunctions, seizure, damages and related remedies.

§ 5.26   Electronic Commerce Initiative*

The European Union began considering the advent of the "Information Society," and the need to establish a Pan–European information technology infrastructure with the 1994 white paper on "Growth, Competitiveness and Employment: the Challenges and Courses for Entering into the XXIst Century" prepared by former European Commission Vice–President Martin Bangemann. The Bangemann Report led to the establishment of an Information Society Project (now Promotion) Office within the EU,[1] and a series of actions plans to promote the Information Society in Europe. These plans were intended to formulate strategies to change the existing regulatory and legal framework, technical infrastructure, and the cultural attitudes necessary to promote the Information Society. This led most recently to the eEurope Initiative to further accelerate the development of an European Information Society.[2]

The EU efforts to coherently address the impact of technology on European society as a whole results in a very different approach to many of the issues raised by E–Commerce than that seen in the United States for example. It is an approach which is inherently multinational, and characterized by a conscious effort to harmonize or approximate legal rules throughout the different member countries in the EU. At the same time it is an approach which also consciously seeks to identify and remove barriers to the development of E–Commerce and other Information Society services. Although only one aspect of the broader European Information Society initiatives, measures related to E–Commerce have been central to the various EU action plans. These measures include the 1997 European Initiative on Electronic Commerce,[3] which focused on primarily on developing infrastructure and protecting consumers' economic and legal interests; the related 1997 Distance Selling

---

10. Criminal proceedings against X (2004) Eur.Comm.Rep. I–00000 (Case C–60/02).

11. Directive 2004/48.

§ 5.26

* Sections 5.26 through 5.30 were prepared by Professor Andy Spanogle of George Washington University National Law Center.

1. See "Europe's Europe's Way to the Information Society—An Action Plan," COM(94) 347 final, 19.07.1994.

2. "eEurope—An Information Society for All," COM(99) 687 final, 8.12.1999.

3. "A European Initiative on Electronic Commerce," COM(97) 157 final, 16.6.1997.

Directive;[4] the 1999 Electronic Signature Directive;[5] and most recently the Electronic Commerce Directive in 2000.[6] There are also several other important measures aimed at particular issues, such as Privacy Directives,[7] which have a significant impact upon online transactions but which would not themselves be considered as "enabling" legislation for E–Commerce transactions.

§ 5.27 Distance Selling*

The Distance Selling Directive is intended to promote European consumer confidence in E–Commerce, by guaranteeing that the local consumer protection laws will apply to contracts concluded at a distance.[1] By relying on the protections of local laws, presumably concerns over the nature and amount of information provided by sellers, the privacy accorded to information provided by consumers, aggressive marketing techniques, and payment fraud resulting from online transactions would be ameliorated. The Directive, however, applies to all types of contracts concluded by any means where the supplier and consumer are not in each others physical presence including those created by mail, telephone, videophone, radio, fax, and email, for example, and is not confined just to online transactions.[2] Each member state in the EU was required to implement the Directive's requirements in their national law, in this manner the various national laws on distance contracts through the EU "approximate" one another and achieve the same objectives.[3]

The Directive imposes a number of requirements. Certain types of technologies, such as automated calling machines or faxes, may not be used for unsolicited marketing without prior consent, and others may not be employed over the consumer's objection.[4] Prior

---

4. Directive 1997/7/EC of the European Parliament and of the Council of 20 May 1997 on the Protection of Consumers in respect of Distance Contracts, *Official Journal L 144, 04/06/1997.*

5. Directive 1999/93/EC of the European Parliament and of the Council of 13 December 1999 on a Community framework for Electronic Signatures, *Official Journal L 013, 19/01/2000.*

6. Directive 2000/31/EC of the European Parliament and of the Council of 8 June 2000 on certain legal aspects of information society services, in particular electronic commerce, in the Internal Market, *Official Journal L 178, 17/07/2000.*

7. Directive 95/46/EC of 24 October 1995 on the protection of individuals with regard to the processing of personal data and on the free movement of such data., *Official Journal L 281,*

23.11.1995. See Directive 2002/58 on privacy in electronic communications.

§ 5.27

* Sections 5.26 through 5.30 were prepared by Professor Andy Spanogle of George Washington University National Law Center.

1. Directive 1997/7/EC of the European Parliament and of the Council of 20 May 1997 on the Protection of Consumers in respect of Distance Contracts, *Official Journal L 144, 04/06/1997.* Directive 2002/65 governs distance selling of consumer financial services such as credit cards, banking, investment funds and pension plans.

2. *Id.,* Art. 2 & Annex 1.

3. *Id.,* Art. 15. EU member nations were given until the end of 2000 to implement the Directive.

4. *Id.,* Art. 10.

to concluding the contract, consumers are to be provided with certain information in "clear and comprehensible form" covering a variety of basic details about the supplier; the cost, terms, and conditions of the transactions; and, significantly, the consumer's right to withdraw or cancel the transaction.[5] This information must be provided either in writing or in some other "durable" media accessible to the consumer prior to delivery or completion of performance of the contract.[6] Orders placed through distance selling must ordinarily be filled within 30 days.[7] Consumers are typically given 7 business days to withdraw from a distance contract for any reason, with no penalty, and the consumer's reimbursement following withdrawal must be processed within 30 days.[8] If the supplier failed to provide the requisite information in advance of the transaction, the time period for the consumer to exercise this right of withdrawal expands to three months.[9]

Not all distance selling transactions are covered however. There are exemptions for financial services contracts, auctions, immovable property, sales of everyday consumable goods by door-to-door sales agents; accommodation, transport, catering or leisure services for specific dates, and vending machines.[10] Additionally, absent agreement, the consumer's right of withdrawal does not apply to services begun before the expiration of the withdrawal period; commodities whose price fluctuates in financial markets beyond the control of the supplier; certain custom produced/ personalized goods; audio/video/software products unsealed by the consumer; periodicals; gaming or lottery services.[11]

Thus, while not exclusively aimed at E–Commerce, the Distance Selling Directive imposes a number of specific requirements on E–Merchants who will be selling to consumers within the EU. These requirements will affect the nature of the transactions conducted with consumers in Europe, the manner in which they are conducted, and even the design of the online systems by which they are accomplished.

§ 5.28   Electronic Signatures*

The Electronic Signature Directive,[1] like the Distance Selling Directive, is aimed at harmonizing the national law among the

5. *Id.*, Art. 4.

6. *Id.*, Art. 5.

7. *Id.*, Art. 7.

8. *Id.*, Art. 6.

9. *Id.*

10. *Id.*, Art. 3.

11. *Id.*, Art. 6(3).

§ 5.28

* Sections 5.26 through 5.30 were prepared by Professor Andy Spanogle of George Washington University National Law Center.

1. Directive 1999/93/EC of the European Parliament and of the Council of 13 December 1999 on a Community various member states. The Directive was intended to create a single common legal framework for electronic signatures within the EU.[2] An electronic signature is defined as any "data in electronic form which are attached to or logically associated with other electronic data and which serve as a method of authentication."[3] This definition is intended to be technologically neutral, and to apply to any and all forms of electronic signatures. However, the Directive expressly states that it is *not* intended to address national or European legal requirements as to the form or use of documents, nor the conclusion or validity of contracts.[4] It was issued in an effort simply to forestall the proliferation of different standards for electronic signatures and services related to providing such signatures at a time when several nations were considering different approaches and technologies.

The Directive establishes that a signature may not be denied legal effect of validity solely on the grounds that it is in electronic form.[5] Additionally, member states within the EU are prohibited from imposing obligations which would restrict the free flow of electronic signature services across national borders.[6] In accord with the emphasis on consumer protection in many European measures, the Directive imposes a number of obligations upon general providers of electronic signature services, but not upon those who use electronic signature technologies within their own closed or proprietary systems.[7] In particular, Certification Service Providers (CSPs), those who provide an "electronic attestation which links signature-verification data to a person and confirms the identity of that person," are to be supervised and regulated in the country where they are established[8] and are liable for the certifications they issue.[9] The establishment of national voluntary accreditation schemes to bolster public confidence in electronic signatures is encouraged,[10] and intended to promote the cross border acceptability of electronic signatures and their accompanying certifications.[11]

§ 5.29   Electronic Commerce*

Based upon the aims and objectives stated in the 1997 Initia-

framework for Electronic Signatures, *Official Journal L 013, 19/01/2000.*

2. *Id.,* Art. 1.
3. *Id.,* Art. 2.
4. *Id.,* Art. 1.
5. *Id.,* Art. 5.
6. *Id.,* Art. 4.
7. *Id.,* Preamble (16).
8. *Id.,* Art. 3.

9. *Id.,* Art. 6.
10. *Id.,* Art. 3.
11. *Id.,* Art. 7.

§ 5.29

* Sections 5.26 through 5.30 were prepared by Professor Andy Spanogle of George Washington University National Law Center.

tive,[1] the Electronic Commerce Directive[2] endeavors to establish a more certain and comprehensive legal framework to generally enable E–Commerce transactions within the member states of the EU. As such, the Directive covers a number of issue areas beyond merely electronic contracting,[3] such as rules regarding the establishment of service providers,[4] information to be provided by service providers,[5] information to be provided in connection with commercial communications such as advertising or direct marketing,[6] liabilities of Internet intermediaries,[7] online dispute resolution processes,[8] and the general role of national authorities.[9]

Service Providers

There is a general "right of establishment" guaranteed by the treaties establishing the European Union. The Directive clarifies that electronic service providers are "established" where they effectively pursue an "economic activity using a fixed establishment for an indefinite period. The presence and use of the technical means and technologies required to provide the service do not, in themselves, constitute an establishment of the provider."[10] It then continues to generally prohibit member states from requiring prior-authorization to establish electronic service provider operations, or from imposing other requirements which do not generally apply to the same services or operations conducted by other means.[11] However, the use of "codes of conduct" or other voluntary measures established at the Community level with input from appropriate trade, professional, and consumer associations is encouraged.[12] Deviations from the "country or origin" and "mutual recognition" principles which underlie the Directive are permitted for public policy purposes such as crime prevention, combating hate crimes, the protection of minors, and the protection of public health. However, any such measures which are imposed must be necessary, proportionate to their objective, and the European Commission has been notified.[13]

Additionally, the Electronic Commerce Directive complements the notice/disclosure provisions of the Distance Selling Directive by

1. "A European Initiative on Electronic Commerce," COM(97) 157 final, 16.6.1997.

2. Directive 2000/31/EC of the European Parliament and of the Council of 8 June 2000 on certain legal aspects of information society services, in particular electronic commerce, in the Internal Market, *Official Journal* L 178, 17/07/2000.

3. *Id.*, § 3.

4. *Id.*, § 1.

5. *Id.*

6. *Id.*, § 2.

7. *Id.*, § 4.

8. *Id.*, Ch. IV.

9. *Id.*

10. *Id.*, Art. 2.

11. *Id.*, Art. 4.

12. *Id.*, Art. 16.

13. *Id.*, Art. 3.

requiring that electronic service providers make "easily, directly, and permanently available" certain information such as its name, physical address, email address, a VAT or similar registrations, and any supervisory or professional regulatory bodies to which it might be subject—and that any pricing information which is provided must be clear and unambiguous.[14]

"Commercial communications"[15] are recognized as an integral part of any Information Society service, and also subject to special requirements. Advertising, direct marketing and similar communications must be clearly identified as "commercial communications" and identified as to their origin, and any conditions attached to promotional offers must be clearly identifiable and easily accessible.[16] Moreover, unsolicited email solicitations must be "identifiable clearly and unambiguously as such as soon as it is received" and service providers using unsolicited email are required to comply with opt-out registers.[17] Regulated professions, such as lawyers or accountants, are specifically authorized to use electronic commercial communications but remain subject to the rules applicable to their professions.[18]

Service providers who are merely passive conduits for Information Society services supplied by others are generally insulated from any liability, so long as they did not initiate or modify the transmission or the content of the communication, nor select the recipient of the transmission.[19] This immunity specifically extends to caching operations, or the "automatic, intermediate, and temporary storage" of information,[20] hosting operations,[21] or any obligation to engage in general monitoring of the service user's activities.[22] However, nothing in the Directive precludes member states within the EU from requiring that service providers inform the authorities of illegal activities which do come to their attention, or from acting to terminate or prevent an infringement in accordance with local judicial or administrative processes.[23]

Means for resolving disputes arising out of the provision of Information Society services are also addressed. In addition to encouraging the formulation of EU-wide voluntary codes of conduct,[24] the member states are directed to ensure that appropriate

---

14. *Id.*, Art. 5.

15. The Directive generally defines "commercial communications" as "any form of communication designed to promote, directly or indirectly, the goods, services, or image of a company, organization, or person or pursuing a commercial, industrial or craft activity or exercising a regulated profession." *Id.*, Art. 2.

16. *Id.*, Art. 6.

17. *Id.*, Art. 7.

18. *Id.*, Art. 8.

19. *Id.*, Art. 12.

20. *Id.*, Art. 13.

21. *Id.*, Art. 14.

22. *Id.*, Art. 15.

23. *Id.*, Art 12(3); 13(2); 14(3); 15(2).

24. *Id.*, Art. 16.

means for alternative dispute resolution processes exist—both off-line and online—particularly for consumer disputes.[25] The member states are also directed to facilitate cross-border cooperation and promote the effective investigation and legal redress of infringements or violations throughout the EU.[26]

Electronic Contracts

At the heart of this framework, however, are the provisions enabling the formation of electronic contracts. Although brief, these provisions are significant in providing a firm basis for E–Commerce, and expanding upon the foundation established in the Electronic Signature Directive. In Article 9, the Electronic Commerce Directive states that the "Member States shall ensure that their legal system allows contracts to be formed by electronic means."[27] It then continues to specify that national laws should neither create obstacles to the contractual process, nor impede the effectiveness or validity of contracts formed by electronic means.[28] Only four categories are exempted from this mandate: contracts which must be registered with a public authority (e.g., real estate transfers), contracts requiring the use of a notary or similar public authority, contracts governed by family law, or contracts governed by the law of succession.[29] Even within these categories, member states wishing to derogate from the general obligations of Article 9 must notify the Commission, and justify their continued exemption every five years.[30]

Additionally, when contracts are to be concluded electronically, the E–Merchant must clearly and unambiguously explain—in advance—the languages in which the contract will be available, the steps involved to form the contract, precisely who will fulfill the contract, and the means for correcting any order entry errors. This information must be made available in a manner in which it may be stored and reproduced. The Directive imposes these requirements on all electronic contracts, except those concluded "exclusively" by means of individual communications such as email.[31] Moreover, the Directive also requires that the receipt of orders placed electronically must be acknowledged "without undue delay and by electronic means," and specifically rejects the "mailbox rule" by stating that both orders and acknowledgments are "received" when they are accessible to the recipient.[32] These requirements ordinarily apply equally to consumers and those pursuing a trade, business, or profession—although those who are not consumers may agree to

25. *Id.*, Art. 17.

26. *Id.*, Arts. 18–20.

27. *Id.*, Art. 9.

28. *Id.*

29. *Id.*, Art. 9(2).

30. *Id.*, Art. 9(3).

31. *Id.*, Art. 10.

32. *Id.*, Art. 11.

dispense with receiving the required information or order acknowl-edgments.[33]

Thus, reflecting the more comprehensive approach which comes from having a regional authority such as the European Union, the enabling legislation in the EU strives to facilitate the formation of electronic contracts—but does so in the broader con-text of its efforts to accelerate the formation of an Information Society. Accordingly, it attempts to integrate the issues associated with E–Commerce within its plans for an eEurope.

§ 5.30 Personal Data Protection and E–Privacy

The European Union has adopted a personal data protection directive that applies to international electronic commerce. Council Directive 95/46 (effective October 1998) requires each member EU state to protect the processing of personal data. Under this di-rective, any information relating to natural persons must be secure, current, relevant and not excessive in content. In most cases, personal data may be processed only with the consent of the individual involved. Processing data revealing racial or ethnic ori-gin, political opinions, religious beliefs, philosophical or ethical persuasion, and health or sexual life is rarely permitted without written consent. Posting phone numbers, working conditions and hobbies of persons on an Internet page constitutes processing of personal data within the Directive.[1]

Directive 2002/58 concerns privacy and personal data protec-tion in electronic communications including mobile, fixed and Inter-net communications. Effective November 2003, the Directive con-tains a Union-wide ban on sending spam to individuals as well as restraints on installing "cookies" on personal computers.

Individual Rights

Directive 95/46 guarantees individual access to processed infor-mation and notice of its use. Individuals may object at any time to the legitimacy of personal data processing. They may also demand erasure without cost of personal data before it is disclosed to or used by third parties for direct mail marketing. Data processors are required to make extensive disclosures to individuals and to govern-ments. Such disclosure duties, for example, apply to virtually all web sites that invite registration. National authorities are empow-ered where appropriate to access, erase or block information held

33. *Id.*, Arts. 10(1), 11(1).　　　(Swedish criminal prosecution).

§ 5.30
1. Re Bodil Lindqvist (2003) Eur. Comm.Rep. I–00000 (Case C–101/01)

by data processors. Private civil liability and public penalty remedies are administered under member state laws, which allow electronic commerce consumers to sue in their countries of residence.

Data Transfers, U.S. Safe Harbors

Article 25 of Directive 95/46 mandates a prohibition against the transfer of personal data to non-member states (like those of North America) that fail to ensure an "adequate level of protection." Hence the adequacy of United States laws offering personal data protection is generally at issue. Exemptions from this scrutiny exist for "unambiguous" consent, when the data is necessary for contract performance between individuals and data processors (e.g., billing), the transfer is legally required or serves "important public interests," the transfer is necessary to protect the individual's "vital interests," or the transfer comes from an open, public register.

Practically speaking, Directive 95/46 governs most global businesses since it is very difficult to segregate European Union data from that collected elsewhere. Both online and offline data processors fall within its scope. The directive's impact has been felt, for example, in restrictive orders denying U.S. direct mail companies access to European mailing lists. More broadly, the European Commission and the U.S. Department of Commerce have sought to defuse the potentially explosive issue of the "adequacy" of U.S. law on personal data privacy. Early in 2000, agreement was reached to create a "safe harbor" for U.S. firms from EU data privacy litigation or prosecution. To obtain such immunity, U.S. data processors can: (1) formally agree to be subject to regulatory oversight in a member EU state; (2) sign up with a U.S. self-regulating privacy group that is supervised by the U.S. Federal Trade Commission or the Department of Transportation; (3) demonstrate to European satisfaction that relevant U.S. laws are comparable to Directive 95/46; or (4) agree to refer privacy disputes to a European panel of data protection authorities. Financial services (including insurance) are not covered by these safe harbor provisions. In 2002, the European Union adopted standardized financial services contracts that subject U.S. data processors to European jurisdiction.

A growing number of U.S. companies (Microsoft included) have signed up with self-regulatory privacy groups (such as BBBOnline) to obtain shelter from Directive 95/46. Some U.S. companies (e.g., Amazon.com) assert that they are in compliance. Others (e.g., DoubleClick.com) have selectively curtailed their use of "cookies" to track online users. Some seem blissfully unaware of the scope and intensity of Directive 95/46.

Chapter 6

EXTERNAL TRADE AND CUSTOMS LAW

Table of Sections

§ 6.0   Introduction—Common Customs Code

The provisions of the Treaty of Rome which deal specifically with trade between the European Union and third countries are Articles 131–134. These articles vest in the European Union control over external commercial relations. This is referred to as the Union's "common commercial policy," and it covers both imports and exports. Article 133 provides some illustrative examples of the wide scope of this policy, including tariffs, quotas, trade agreements, export controls, dumping and subsidies. For example, its common rules on exports[1] generally authorize free exportation of Union products, subject to security (oil and defense) and environmental exceptions. The Common Commercial Policy can also in-

§ 6.0   1934/82.

1. *See* Council Regulations 2603/69,

246

volve the application of international boycott sanctions.[2] The Treaty on European Union added provisions to the Treaty of Rome intended to promote cooperation among the member states and the Union on aid to developing nations.[3]

The European Court of Justice has ruled that the member states cannot enact external commercial policy laws without "specific authorization."[4] In this field, the Union should be supreme. Operationally speaking, however, this is not always the case. This is illustrated by the discussion of national import quotas, voluntary export restraints and "mixed" trade agreements that follows. Surrendering national sovereignty over external commercial relations is a most sensitive area.

Customs Union

As regards customs law which is invariably involved in any trade transaction with the Union the relevant provisions are Articles 23–27 of the Treaty of Rome. The basic principle is that the EU is a customs union[5] with a directly applicable[6]prohibition of customs duties and measures having an equivalent effect on internal trade. The EU also has a common customs tariff. Thus, once goods have cleared customs in any member state they are released for free circulation, moving freely throughout the Union without incurring any further tariffs or any other equivalent charges. Such equivalent charges are understood to comprise any pecuniary charge, however small and whatever its designation and mode of application, which is imposed unilaterally on domestic or foreign goods by reason of the fact that they cross a frontier, and which is not a customs duty in the strict sense.[7] Thus products originating in third countries enjoy the same status as goods originating in a member state for purposes of internal trade. In addition, U.S. exporters to any of the member states will pay the same customs duties, regardless of the port of entry. This is different from NAFTA arrangements, which

---

2. Article 301, Treaty of Rome. *See* Bosphorus Hava Yollari Turzim Ve Ticaret AS v. Minister for Transport, Energy and Communication (1996) Eur. Comm.Rep. I–3953 (Serbia boycott).

3. *See* Articles 177–181.

4. Criel and Schou v. Procureur de la République (1976) Eur.Comm.Rep. 1921.

5. *See* Article XXIV(8)(a) GATT 1994:

"A customs union shall be understood to mean the substitution of a single customs territory for two or more customs territories, so that

(i) duties and other restrictive regulations of commerce ... are eliminated with respect to substantially all the

trade between the constituent territories of the union or at last with respect to substantially all the trade in products originating in such territories, and

(ii) ..., substantially the same duties and other regulations of commerce are applied by each of the member of the union to the trade of territories not included in the Union".

6. Van Gend & Loos v. Nederlandse administratie der belastingen (1963) Eur.Comm.Rep. 1, 13.

7. Commission v. Italy (1969) Eur. Comm.Rep. 193, 201.

only establish a free trade area,[8] without a common external tariff, exclusively for products originating in NAFTA.

Customs Code

The customs law of the EU had been dispersed and shattered in some 25 individual directives and regulations. In a major codification effort all these texts were consolidated and further developed in a Common Customs Code which entered into force on Jan. 1, 1994.[9] This Code includes coverage of customs clearance procedures, customs warehouses and free trade zones, duty free entry for processing and re-export (inward processing arrangement), duty free entry of components of Union origin that have been processed abroad (outward processing arrangement), classification, valuation, origin, payment and customs' bonds. Judicial review of decisions of the national customs authorities must be allowed by a national court capable of referring questions of EU law to the European Court of Justice under Article 234 of the Treaty of Rome.[10] The EU follows the 1999 Kyoto Convention on modernized customs procedures.

§ 6.1 Common Customs Law: Tariffs, Classification, Valuation, Origin and Quotas

Tariffs

The Common Customs Tariff (CCT), now called the Combined Nomenclature (CN), has been steadily reduced over the years as a result of the GATT tariff Rounds. After the Tokyo Round (1978), EU tariffs on manufactured goods dropped on average to about 8 percent.[1] Under the Uruguay Round WTO regime[2] it dropped even further: On aggregate the weighted average Union tariff on industrial products was cut from 6.8 to 4.1 percent, a reduction of 37 percent. In some sectors (construction equipment, medical and pharmaceutical equipment, furniture, steel, agricultural equipment, paper, toys, beer and spirits) duties will disappear entirely. Member

---

8. *See* Article XXIV(8)(b) GATT 1994.

"A free-trade area shall be understood to mean a group of two or more customs territories in which the duties and other restrictive regulations of commerce ... are eliminated on substantially all the trade between the constituent territories in products originating in such territories."

9. Council Regulation 2913/92, O.J. L 302/1 (October 19, 1992); implementing provisions have been promulgated by Commission Regulation 2454/93, O.J. L 253/1 (October 11, 1993) as amended

last by Commission Regulation 2193/94, O.J. L 235/6 (September 9, 1994).

10. Article 243, Common Customs Code.

§ 6.1

1. *See* Council Regulation 2658/87 (Schedule of Customs Duties).

2. Agreement establishing the World Trade Organization, Annex 1A (Multilateral Agreements on Trade in Goods) No. 1 (General Agreement on Tariffs and Trade 1994) Schedule LXXX (European Communities).

states may not alter the common customs tariff by unilaterally imposing additional duties.[3] The CN is supplemented by tariff rate quotas, tariff preferences, antidumping and other special duties, all of which are reported in the "Taric." All of these duties are established by EU law, but it is the member states that apply the rules and collect Union tariffs. These revenues are forwarded by the national customs' services to the Commission less a 10 percent administrative charge. Litigation concerning European Union customs law therefore tends to originate in national tribunals as importers dispute classification, valuation and origin issues. These EU law issues are then typically referenced to the Court of Justice for resolution under Article 234.

The Combined Nomenclature details a tariff schedule that makes two fundamental distinctions. Goods admitted into the Common Market are subject to either "Autonomous" or "Conventional" duties. The Autonomous Duties represent the original 1968 CCT tariffs and are higher than the Conventional Duties which are the Union's current most-favored-nation (MFN) tariffs as negotiated within the GATT. For most exports to the EU, including nearly all those from the United States and Canada, the MFN rates of duty are applied. The various duty free entry programs to which the Union subscribes[4] will almost never apply to goods originating in either Canada or the United States.

New members are usually phased into the EU customs union rules and tariffs over a transitional period. Portugal and Spain, for example, were only fully aligned at the end of 1992. The new member states which joined the Union in 1995, however, were immediately integrated into the customs union. The ten new members joining in 2004 will be phased into the customs union over an extended period of years.

The common customs law of the European Union also includes regulations targeting counterfeit goods. Such goods may not be imported into the Union, nor freely circulated within it. They are subject to seizure by national customs authorities. The definition of counterfeit goods contained in this regulation refers to goods bearing marks without authorization. Thus the regulation does not apply to trade in "gray market goods" (those produced abroad under license). The Union also operates a computerized, encoded data network known as the Customs Information System (CIS) to help combat fraud and illegal trading (especially in drugs). Customs officials at all points of entry and exit may communicate with each other, central authorities and the Commission.

---

3. Sociaal Fonds voor de Diamant Arbeiders v. NG Indiamex (1973) Eur. Comm.Rep. 1609.

4. *See* Sections 6.2, 6.9, 6.10.

Classification

The European Union follows in its customs classification system,[5] the International Convention on the Harmonized Commodity Description and Coding System of June 14, 1983[6] elaborated by the Customs Cooperation Council, which is presently applied by roughly 100 countries representing more than 80 percent of world trade. This generally corresponds to the classifications found in the Harmonized Tariff System (HTS) adopted by the United States in 1988. Starting in 1993, the Union instituted a binding tariff classification system based upon mutual recognition of classification decisions made by national customs authorities. Whenever an importer requests and obtains such a binding tariff information ("BTI"; Articles 11–12 Common Customs Code), it applies to imports of the same product in all other member states. This process will reduce the number of divergent tariff classifications, particularly regarding trade sensitive textiles and electronics.

Nevertheless there are recurrent instances where despite the general obligation to interpret the Combined Nomenclature uniformly the national authorities stick to their traditional views.[7] This results in products being classified differently depending on the member state where the release for free circulation is applied for. It is advisable, therefore, to check whether a particular product should not be imported via another member state when problems arise due to an unfavorable interpretation of the Combined Nomenclature by a national customs administration. The purpose of a binding tariff information is not just that if presented upon import the customs authorities are bound by it, but also that there may not be any post-clearance recovery of duties in case of an incorrect classification or a change of classification. Thus the BTI, if used, offers substantial protection for an importer. It is issued upon request and is subject to judicial review by the competent judicial authorities of the member state[8].

Valuation

The valuation of goods for purposes of assessing the CN is presently done according to the GATT/WTO Customs Valuation Code.[9] This means that in most instances arms-length transaction value is the basis for tariff assessments, subject to various adjust-

---

5. Council Regulations 1445/72, 2658/87.

6. Council Decision 87/369, O.J. L 198/1 (July 20, 1987).

7. *See, e.g.,* Peacock AG v. Hauptzollamt Paderborn (2000) Eur.Comm.Rep. I–08947 (Oct. 19, 2000).

8. Article 243, Common Customs Code.

9. Articles 28–36, Common Customs Code; the Customs Valuation Code was been revised during the Uruguay Round Negotiations.

ments.[10] One notable difference between EU and U.S. implementation of the Valuation Code concerns international freight and insurance charges. Unlike the United States, the Union includes such charges in the customs value of goods subject to its common external tariff. Purchasing agents' commission are not included in customs values for purposes of collecting the common external tariff[11] nor are export permit or quota charges[12] (irrespective of whether the quota is traded legally[13] and unless the charges concern quotas obtained from third parties[14]), weighing charges,[15] and separately invoiced intra-Union transport charges.[16] A leading case discusses when computer software is part of the value of imported "goods" subject to the common customs tariff.[17]

That a careful analysis of the Union law and an appropriate structuring of export transactions is required with regard to customs value questions is particularly true in the case of licensing fees. Article 32(1)(c) Common Customs Code provides that such fees have to be added to the price paid or payable if the buyer must pay them as a condition of sale of the imported goods and to the extent that they are not yet included in the price. This means that, e.g. in the case of fees paid in respect of the right to use a trademark, such fee may only be added to the price if

— the goods are resold in the same state or after minor processing,

— the goods are marketed under the trademark, and

— the buyer is not free to obtain the goods from other suppliers unrelated to the seller.[18]

In cases where the licensing fees do not have to be added to the price it is essential that the fees are invoiced separately.

---

10. *See* Hauptzollamt Hamburg–Ericus v. Van Houten International GmbH (1986) Eur.Comm.Rep. 447 (Costs of weighing imports on arrival excluded from transaction value); Hauptzollamt Schweinfurt v. Mainfrucht Obstverwertung (1985) Eur.Comm.Rep. 3909 (Costs of internal EC transport that are separately invoiced excluded).

11. Hauptzollamt Karlstruhe v. Gerbr Hepp & Co Kg (1991) Eur. Comm.Rep. 4319 (Case 299/90); Hans Sommer GmbH & Co. KG v. Hauptzollamt Bremen (2000) Eur.Comm.Rep. I–08989 (Oct. 19, 2000).

12. Ospig Texilgesellschaft KG W. Ahlers v. Hauptzollamt Bremen–Ost (1984) Eur.Comm.Rep. 609; Malt (1990) Eur.Comm.Rep. 1482.

13. Ospig Textil–Gesellschaft W. Ahlers GmbH & Co. KG v. Hauptzollamt

Bremen–Freihafen (1994) Eur. Comm.Rep. I–1963 (Case C–29/93).

14. Klaus Thierschmidt GmbH v. Hauptzollamt Essen (1994) I–3905 (Case C–340/93).

15. Hauptzollamt Hamburg–Ericus v. Van Houten International GmbH (1986) Eur.Comm.Rep. 447.

16. Hauptzollamt Schweinfurt v. Mainfrucht Obstverwertung (1985) Eur. Comm.Rep. 3909.

17. *See* Brown Boveri & CIE AG v. Hauptzollamt Mannheim (1991) Eur. Comm.Rep. 1884 (Case C–79/89); *see now* Article 167, Commission Regulation 2913/92.

18. Article 159, Commission Regulation 2913/92.

Origin

As a general matter, the Union determines the origin of goods in accordance with the 1973 Kyoto Convention[19], which has not been ratified by the United States. According to the Common Customs Code a product originates either in the country where it was wholly obtained or produced[20] or—in case of a production process involving raw materials or semi-finished products from various countries—where the last, substantial, economically justified processing or working took place in an enterprise equipped for that purpose and resulting in the manufacture of a new product or representing an import stage of manufacture.[21]

This is usually the case where a change in the tariff heading occurs (CTH-text), i.e. where the finished product is to be classified in another heading of the Combined Nomenclature as compared to the classification of the raw materials or of the semi-finished products. A process is "economically justified" if it adds value or provides commercial advantages. A process or operation is "substantial," for these purposes, only if the resulting product has its own properties and composition.[22] Cleaning, grinding, grading, and packaging a raw material do not meet this standard.[23] If the CTH technical approach to origin is insufficient, a "value added" analysis is pursued. This analysis focuses on the value added to the product in the claimed country of origin. Ten percent is insufficient to confer country of origin status.[24]

Specific "rules of origin" exist for semiconductors,[25] photocopiers,[26] radio and television receivers,[27] tape recorders,[28] and ball bearings[29] as well as a number of other products.[30] Most of these specific rules of origin relate to EU dumping law.[31] Rules of origin are critical to duty free or preferential entry of goods from Cotonou Convention, Mediterranean Basin or GSP developing nations as well as from EFTA countries or countries of Central and Eastern

---

19. Council Decision 75/199, O.J. L 100/1 (April 21, 1975) and O.J. L 166/1 (April 21, 1977).

20. Article 23, Common Customs Code.

21. Article 24, Common Customs Code.

22. Gesellschaft für Überseehandel v. Handelskammer Hamburg (1977) Eur.Comm.Rep. 41.

23. *Id.*

24. Brother International GmbH v. Hauptzollamt Giessen (1989) Eur. Comm.Rep. 4253.

25. Council Regulation 288/89.

26. Council Regulation 2071/89.

27. Council Regulation 2632/70.

28. Council Regulation 861/71.

29. Council Regulation 1836/78.

30. Eggs (Council Regulation 2448/90), spare parts (Council Regulation 37/70), meat and meat products (Council Regulation 3620/90), clothing, shoes and textiles (Council Regulation 1365/91), ceramics (Council Regulation 2025/73) and grape juice (Council Regulation 2883/90).

31. *See* § 6.5.

Europe.[32] Generally speaking, the rules of origin associated with these programs focus on changes in tariff headings as the determining factor. But many unique product-specific rules of origin are also created, and these often stress value added approaches. The most generous of these rules of origin apply to Cotonou exports to the EU where, for example, any Union contribution may be counted as from a Cotonou nation for purposes of value added calculations, so-called cumulation.

Special rules of origin and EU content requirements apply to high-technology products like printed circuit boards, integrated circuits and the like. These rules often have the purpose and effect of transferring technology and production to the European Union. Processed EFTA exports originate therein, and may be freely traded to the EU under rules that emphasize a change in tariff heading. The many variations on the origin of goods contained in Union law and EU trade agreements make these rules particularly complex. A product from one country that fails to meet one of the specialized or preferential rules of origin governing such entry into the Common Market will be judged under the general rule of origin discussed above.

Quotas

Until the completion of the internal market on January 1, 1993 a complicated system of import quotas for individual member states existed for various products, notably for automobiles from Japan as well as bananas. The elimination of controls at the Union's internal borders necessitated a harmonization of all European Union import and customs quotas. Regrettably this has not always resulted in a liberalized access to the EU market, but in a number of cases the Union has introduced new regimes which make it more difficult to export to the European Union. A particularly prominent example is the Common Market Organization for bananas,[33] which although incompatible with the GATT according to the findings of GATT/WTO panels, was upheld by the European Court of Justice.[34] It resulted in a discriminatory foreclosure of the Union market for Latin American bananas which before could be imported freely into Germany and the Benelux countries. Since the exporters of bananas most adversely affected by the EU regime of trade restraints are U.S. multinationals, the United States was authorized by the WTO to retaliate against EU exports and did so by imposing substantial tariffs. Finally, in 2001, settlement of the "bananas dispute" was reached, with the EU promising to replace its quotas with a nonpreferential tariff scheme.

32. *See* §§ 6.2, 6.9 and 6.10.

33. Council Regulation 404/93 and Commission Regulation 1442/93.

34. Germany v. Council (1994) Eur. Comm.Rep. I–4973 (Case C–280/93).

§ 6.2   Generalized Tariff Preferences (GSP)

The European Union participates in the generalized system of tariff preferences (GSP) initiated within the GATT to give duty free access to industrial markets for selected goods coming from the developing world. This policy is implemented in the common customs tariff regulations.[1] The Central European countries were added to the Union's GSP list for the interim period between the collapse of the Communist regimes and the entry into force of the free trade and economic association agreements concluded with the EU.[2] The countries of the former USSR are GSP beneficiaries until any free-trade agreement with them comes into force, and provided they undertake to open their markets to developing-country exports. South Africa became a beneficiary as of 1995.

Approximately 150 non-European developing nations now benefit from the GSP trade preferences of the EU, including China. Goods from the Four Dragons of East Asia (South Korea, Taiwan, Hong Kong and Singapore) still qualify. South Korean goods were disqualified between 1987 and 1991 because of inadequate intellectual property protection in that nation. In contrast, the Four Dragons were "graduated" (*i.e.,* no longer treated as developing nations) out of the United States' GSP program in 1989. Burma was suspended from the EU program in 1997 for human rights concerns. In 2001, the EU began phasing in complete duty free access for the world's poorest 48 countries. Special duty free preferences are granted to developing countries who combat illegal drug production. Pakistan received this status, over strenuous objections by India before the World Trade Organization. The WTO Appellate Body upheld the EU scheme in 2004.

The European Union system of generalized tariff preferences is selectively applied when about 130 "sensitive products" are involved. In other words, there are limitations (quotas and tariff ceilings) on duty free access to the Common Market if the goods compete with Union manufacturers. However, these GSP limitations do not apply to products already receiving duty free access under the Cotonou Convention or the Union's Mediterranean Policy.[3] Thus, nations that are covered by the latter trade rules still obtain some margin of preference over other third world GSP beneficiaries.

A revised GSP regime entered into force in 1995. A solidarity mechanism was introduced and applicable in exceptional circumstances: Beneficiary countries whose exports of products covered by

§ 6.2

1. *See* O.J. 1993 C–169/1.

2. GSP status has also been granted to the successor states of former Yugoslavia.

3. *See* §§ 6.9, 6.10.

the GSP in a given sector exceed 25 percent of all beneficiaries' exports of those products in that sector will be excluded from GSP entitlement for that sector irrespective of their level of development.[4] In addition sector/country graduation was introduced on the basis of relative specialization (ratio of a beneficiary country's share of total Union imports in a given sector), coupled with a development weighing (development index, combining a country's per capita income and the level of its exports as compared with those of the Union). Both mechanisms were phased in gradually to keep within the framework of overall neutrality. Preferences for Hong Kong, Singapore, South Korea and the Gulf Cooperation Council (GCC) states[5] were limited to half the margin applied in 1995. In no case may the application of both mechanisms result in a more favorable level of preferential access than that applied in 1993. For sensitive products, lists limit the preferential duty to 80 percent, respectively 40 percent of the most-favoured nation (MFN) duty.

§ 6.3 Escape Clause Proceedings and Voluntary Trade Restraints

European Union commercial policy regulations establish common rules for imports and exports. These rules authorize "escape clause" measures to curb exports in the face of shortages, or to curb surging imports that threaten serious injury to similar EU products.[1] Special rules apply to escape clause proceedings when the imports are from state-trading countries.[2] European Union escape clause law on imports is derived from Article XIX of the GATT and the WTO Safeguards Agreement (1994). The counterparts in U.S. law are found in Sections 201 and 406 of the Trade Act of 1974.[3] Use of escape clause relief triggers a duty to compensate WTO trade partners.

The protective measures authorized by the EU escape clause regulations may include tariffs, quotas, and more controversially, agreements with exporting nations to voluntarily control the flow of certain goods into the Union *or* particular EU nations. Such "voluntary export restraints" (VERs) have been used by the Union on consumer electronics, machine tools, food products and steel imports. The Union itself has "voluntarily" restrained the export of steel to the United States. After much effort, and adherence to the WTO escape clause agreement, Europe has greatly reduced its dependence upon VERs as a means of protection against import

---

4. Commission Document COM (94) 337 final of September 19, 1994.

5. Saudi Arabia, Qatar, United Arab Emirates, Kuwait, Bahrain.

§ 6.3

1. Council Regulation 3285/94.

2. *Id.*

3. 319 U.S.C.A. §§ 2261, 2436.

competition. Unlike the United States, Europe has generally re-
frained from frequent invocation of escape clause relief.

§ 6.4 Foreign Country Trade Barriers

Another area of the Common Commercial Policy was commenced in 1984 in response to efforts (ultimately withdrawn) by
the Reagan Administration at limiting participation of European
licensees of United States technology in the Siberian natural gas
pipeline project. This was sometimes called the "new commercial
policy" and is now embodied in the Trade Barriers Regulation No.
3286/94. It covers situations not subject to escape clause, dumping
or subsidy proceedings.[1] Regulation 3286/94 concerns "obstacles to
trade" by foreign *countries* and roughly approximates Section 301
of the U.S. Trade Act of 1974.[2]

When countries engage in practices that are incompatible with
international agreement (e.g., the GATT/WTO agreements), adversely affect a petitioner's trade and it is in the Union's interest to
take action, the EU may undertake international dispute settlement procedures and (possibly) retaliatory measures. The latter can
include raising tariffs, suspending trade concessions or imposing
quotas. Private parties can file "market access" complaints with
the Commission to initiate examination of alleged obstacles to
trade. Negative decisions by the Commission may be appealed to
the Court of Justice.[3]

§ 6.5 Antidumping Duties

Another part of the Common Commercial Policy concerns
unfair trading practices applied to goods exported to the Union.
The two most important areas of law here concern dumping and
subsidies.[1] Similar rules apply to unfair shipping services used to
bring goods to the Union.[2] In recent years, European Union use of
antidumping proceedings to protect its market has risen substantially. Nearly half of these proceedings involve goods from nonmarket economy states (NMEs). Apart from NMEs, Japanese and
United States exports have most frequently been involved in Union
antidumping proceedings. Many of these proceedings are settled by
promises of the exporters to raise prices and refrain from "dumping." The standing of most exporters and complainants to challenge
EU dumping decisions has been affirmed by the European Court.[3]

§ 6.4

1. *See* §§ 6.3, 6.5 and 6.6.

2. 19 U.S.C.A. § 2411.

3. FEDIOL v. Commission (1989)
Eur.Comm.Rep. 1781.

§ 6.5

1. Council Regulations 384/94 and
3284/96.

2. Council Regulation 4057/86.

3. Allied Corp. v. Commission (1984)
Eur.Comm.Rep. 1005 (named exporters

Such persons would otherwise lack any possible judicial remedy. Importers, on the other hand, have remedies in the national courts of the member states and are therefore generally unable to challenge EU dumping decisions directly before the European Court.[4] However, importers who are end-users of the product in question and seriously affected by the antidumping duties may challenge antidumping determinations under Article 230.[5]

Dumping involves selling abroad at a price that is less than the price used to sell the same goods at home (the "normal" or "fair" value). To be unlawful, dumping must threaten or cause material injury to an industry in the export market, the market where prices are lower. Dumping is recognized by most of the trading world as an unfair practice (akin to price discrimination as an antitrust offense). Dumping is the subject of a special GATT/WTO code which establishes the basic parameters for determining when dumping exists, what constitutes material injury and the remedy of antidumping tariffs.[6] Such tariffs can amount to the margin of the dump, *i.e.,* the difference in the price charged at home and (say) the European Union.

Dumping Determinations

"Normal value" under Union dumping law is first defined as the comparable price actually paid or payable in the ordinary course of trade for the like product intended for consumption in the exporting country or country of origin. The Commission usually considers all sales made in the period under investigation (typically 12 months). It requires that the domestic sales exceed 5 percent of the export sales in order to be considered to be representative and this threshold has been upheld by the European Court of Justice.[7] However, only sales made in the ordinary course of business enter into the calculation. Transactions between related or compensated parties may not be considered in the ordinary course of trade unless the Commission believes they are comparable to arms-length dealings. Sales below cost, for example, are regularly excluded from the Commission's determination of normal value and may trigger "constructed value" determinations if they exceed 20 percent of the sales under consideration.

may challenge imposition of dumping duties); Timex Corp. v. Council and Commission (1985) Eur.Comm.Rep. 849 (complainant may challenge antidumping decisions).

4. Alusuisse Italia v. Council and Commission (1982) Eur.Comm.Rep. 3463.

5. Extramet v. Council (1991) Eur. Comm.Rep. 2527 (Case C–49/88); Nash-

ua Corp. v. Commission (1990) 1 Eur. Comm.Rep. 719.

6. *See* the Agreement on Implementation of Article VI of the GATT (1979) (Antidumping Code) and the Agreement on Implementation of Article VI of the General Agreement on Tariffs and Trade 1994 (WTO Antidumping Code).

7. Goldstar v. Council (1992) Eur. Comm.Rep. I–677.

If there are no sales of the like product in the ordinary course of trade on the domestic market of the exporting country or such sales are inadequate to permit a proper comparison, the Commission turns to (1) the "comparable price" of the product as exported to another surrogate country or (2) its constructed value. The constructed value methodology is often used. It involves calculation of production costs plus a reasonable profit. The costs of production include materials, components and manufacturing costs, as well as sales, administrative and other general expenses. The Commission need not follow the exporter's accountings in making these calculations, but must give priority to the records kept by the producers/exporters and to actual data in determining costs. In addition the Commission makes adjustments for start-up operations. A profit margin of 10 percent is used.

If the goods are from nonmarket economies, a status some Central and East European countries have finally escaped, the Commission has three options for determining normal value. These are utilization of a price derived from the sale of a like product in a market country, a constructed value price based on the costs of a producer in a market country or (if needed) the price actually paid in the Union adjusted to include a reasonable profit margin. The choice of the "market economy third country" for purposes of normal value determination has to be based on sufficient reasons and objections of parties to the investigation have to be taken into account if they are substantiated. The failure to take them into consideration will result in the quashing of the Regulation imposing antidumping duties by the European Court of Justice[8].

Once a normal value for the goods is established by the Commission, the export price is determined. This is defined as the price actually paid or payable for the product sold for export to the Union. Relatively speaking, this calculation is less controversial except when the producer sells through its own subsidiary. In such cases the Commission practice has been to calculate the export price on the basis of the price at which the good is first resold to an independent buyer, and deductions (adjustments) are made both for direct and indirect expenses. The normal value, however, is adjusted only for costs which are directly related to the sales. As a result, the export price is necessarily inferior to the normal value. This asymmetrical approach has repeatedly been upheld by the European Court of Justice[9]. In addition, certain adjustments must be made to the normal value and export prices so calculated. These adjust-

8. Nölle v. Hauptzollamt Bremen–Freihafen (1991) Eur.Comm.Rep. 5163.

9. Nippon Seiles v. Council (1987) Eur.Comm.Rep. 1923; Canon and others v. Council (1988) Eur.Comm.Rep. 5731;

Matsushita Electric v. Council (1992) Eur.Comm.Rep. I–1409; Matsushita Electric Industrial Co. Ltd. (1993) I–04981 (Case C–104/90).

ments reflect differences in physical attributes, import charges, indirect taxes and selling expenses. The object of making these adjustments is to arrive at comparable "ex-factory" price calculations.

The EU dumping margin is the difference between the adjusted normal value and the adjusted export price. It is established by the Union institutions by comparing a weighted average normal value with individual export transactions,[10] thus excluding so called negative dumping margins, i.e. the effect of export sales above the normal value upon the calculation of a weighted average export price. This dumping margin ultimately determines the maximum extra duty the EU importer must pay provided there also is material injury to an EU industry and the Commission decides that imposing the duty would be in the Union's interest. This "public interest" determination typically pits EU consumer interests against industrial interests. The manufacturers usually win out, but occasionally the consumers' interest in lower-priced imports prevails.[11]

Dumping Duties

A de-minimis dumping margin of 2 percent is required to establish injury. Similarly if the volume of imports is less than 3 percent of imports of the like product the investigation has to be terminated immediately—unless countries which individually account for less than 3 percent of these imports collectively account for more than 7 percent. This may entice producers in the future to direct complaints against as many countries as possible. The precise amount of the antidumping duty is supposed to represent only that which is necessary to remove the injury. European Union dumping duties are imposed prospectively, applying in most cases to all future imports during the next five years.

The EU authorities have a wide discretion to impose different forms of duty. These may be:

(a) a specific duty (i.e. fixed amount per unit of product imported);

(b) an ad valorem duty; or

(c) a minimum floor price (i.e. if the exporter sells below the minimum price, the difference between such a price and the minimum price is collected as duty).

In theory, the minimum price approach should be the most appropriate since the object is to eliminate the injury caused by dumping, not to punish the dumpers. In fact, ad valorem duties are

---

10. Upheld by the European Court of Justice in NTN Tokyo (1987) Eur. Comm.Rep. 1854.

11. *See* Commission Dec. May 22, 1990 O.J. L138/48 (May 31, 1990) (photo albums).

the most common as they are more difficult to evade and much easier to administer, particularly when there is a range of types of the dumped product. Ad valorem duties are chosen because the payment of duties cannot be avoided simply by the exporter raising ex-factory export prices so that the imports are no longer dumped (though the importer may be able to claim a refund or seek to have the duty reviewed in such circumstances). The Antidumping Regulation contains specific anti-absorption provisions which prevent the exporter from bearing the duty by reducing export prices so that the retail price is unaffected. If this occurs, the Union authorities may impose an additional duty, to compensate for the amount borne by the exporter.

Undertakings or commitments are commonly offered by exporters during the course of anti-dumping investigations. Indeed more than half of the investigations commenced by the Commission are resolved in this way. To be acceptable, the effect of the undertaking must be that either the dumping margin or the injurious effect of it is eliminated. An undertaking usually involves an upward revision of prices, though exceptionally an undertaking to limit exports may be accepted. In deciding whether to accept an undertaking, the previous violation of an enterprise may also be taken into account. However, as indicated above in the section on duties, the acceptance of undertakings can also be subject to political considerations; for instance, several years ago the Council of Ministers rejected a Commission proposal that a procedure be terminated in this way in the light of the then prevailing trading relations with Japan. Although the Commission may suggest undertakings, the fact that they are not offered may not prejudice the case; but if dumping continues, the Commission may treat that as evidence that a threat of injury is more likely to lead to material injury.

Investigations

The antidumping investigation will cover a period of not less than six months immediately prior to the initiation of the proceeding and will normally be concluded either by termination or definitive action within one year. Some cases, however, take very much longer. In the course of an investigation, the Commission may seek all necessary information from, and examine and verify the records of importers, exporters, traders, agents, producers, trade associations and organizations. Investigations in third countries can take place only if the firms concerned consent and their government has been notified and does not object. The member states may send officials to assist in such investigations. Within the Union, the Commission will obtain assistance from the member states, in particular to carry out checks and inspections of importers, traders and EU producers. Although the Commission does not have the power to obtain the information it requires if an enterprise, within or outside the Union, does not wish to cooperate, findings will be made on the basis of the facts available. Hence anti-dumping duties may be imposed on producers who refuse to cooperate on the basis of the allegations set forth in the complaint[12] or on the basis of the dumping found against other producers and at the highest rate imposed on those other producers[13] or even higher.[14]

As part of the investigation, the Commission will send questionnaires to producers/exporters, importers and Union producers known to it. The normal time period in which to respond to the questionnaire is 37 days but an extension can be requested. The purpose of the questionnaires is to collect all the necessary information to determine normal value, export price and adjustments in order to enable a comparison to be made. In addition, some information relating to injury will be gleaned from the questionnaires. Apart from the questionnaire, the most important step in an anti-dumping proceeding will be the verification visit by Commission officials to the company, which usually takes two to three days. The aim is to compare the answers on the questionnaire with the company's books to ensure that the information supplied is both correct and complete. Answers may be rejected if the officials are not satisfied that they are consistent with the business records. It is important for the company to be able to show how each figure in the questionnaire was arrived at, and all materials used in the preparation of the answers should be kept.

All information obtained or received by the Commission can be used solely for the purpose for which it was requested. It cannot be passed to other Commission departments, such as the Directorate–General for Competition.[15] Confidential treatment can be requested with an indication why the information is confidential, and a non-confidential summary, or statement of reasons why the information is not susceptible to summary, should be provided. This summary is intended for supply to other parties to the proceedings. Failure to submit a summary, where summary is possible, or the unwarranted claiming of confidentiality coupled with an unwillingness to author-

12. Video cassette recorders originating in Korea and Japan, O.J. L 57/55 (27.2.1989); Compact disk players originating in Japan and Korea; O.J. L 13/21 (16.1.1990).

13. Large electrolytic aluminum capacitors originating in Japan, O.J. L 152/22 (June 4, 1992).

14. Electronic weighing scales originating in Singapore and Korea, O.J. L 112/20 (May 6, 1993).

15. But see for limits of confidentiality provisions the caselaw relating to the confidentiality rule in Regulation 17 on competition law infringement investigations, Dirección General de Defensa de la Competencia v. Asuciación Española de Banca Privada and others (1992) Eur. Comm.Rep. I–4785; Samenwerkende Elektriciteitsproductiebedrijven NV v. Commission (1994) I–01911 (Case C–36/92).

ize disclosure in generalized or summary form, will result in the information being disregarded. Even in the absence of a request for confidentiality, information will be treated as confidential if its disclosure is likely to have a significantly adverse effect on the supplier or the source of the information.

Judicial Review

Since March 1994 the Court of First Instance (CFI) has jurisdiction over antidumping matters and the European Court of Justice is only competent to hear appeals against the CFI judgments. The Court of Justice had restricted its control to manifest errors of appraisal and abuse of power. It had thus granted the Union institutions an extremely wide margin of discretion. The reasoning underlying this approach was that the imposition of antidumping duties involves a difficult appraisal of complex economic issues. Finally it should be mentioned that successful litigation before the European Court in antidumping matters opens the way to a claim for damages under Article 288(2) of the Treaty of Rome.[16]

Although much of the EU law on antidumping duties is consistent with the GATT/WTO code, and therefore generally conforms to United States law on the subject,[17] some interesting twists have been applied. One of the most controversial is the so-called "screwdriver plant regulation" aimed mostly at Japanese exporters.[18] These exporters, when faced with antidumping duties on top of the common customs tariff, began to assemble consumer electronics and other products inside the Union using Japanese made components plus a screwdriver. The net effect of the Union's regulatory response is to reimpose dumping duties on these products unless at least 40 percent of the components originate outside the source country (Japan). Similar results have been achieved in certain cases when the Japanese export goods assembled in United States to the EU.[19] In the photocopiers case, the goods had actually qualified as American for purposes of U.S. procurement rules. This origin was rejected by the European Union. The Japanese successfully challenged the screwdriver regulation within the GATT.[20] The Union has indicated that its anti-circumvention rules will remain in effect.

16. Case T–167/94 (formerly Case C–326/93), Nölle v. EEC.

17. 19 U.S.C.A. § 1673.

18. *See* Council Regulation 1761/87 and Article 13(10) of Regulation 4057/86.

19. *See* Council Regulation 3205/88 (photocopiers) (assembly does not involve a substantial operation or process so as to alter origin of goods). *Accord,* Brother International GmbH v. Hauptzollamt Giessen (1989) Eur.Comm.Rep. 4253 (Case 26/88) (suggesting typewriters assembled in Taiwan originate from Japan unless assembly causes the use to which components are put to become definite and the goods to be given their specific qualities).

20. GATT Basic Instruments and Selected Documents (B.I.S.D.) 37S/132 (1991).

Some have asserted that the European Union employs a double standard when calculating export prices and normal values for dumping law purposes. They claim that the EU has cloaked itself in the technical obscurity of the law so as to systematically inflate normal values and deflate export prices, thereby causing more dumping to be found. Use of asymmetrical methods to reach these determinations has been upheld by the European Court.[21] Additional criticism has been levied against the Commission's refusal to disclose the information upon which it relies in making critical dumping law decisions.[22] Consumer groups have not traditionally been granted access to non-confidential files accumulated by the Commission in antidumping proceedings.[23] However, by amendment,[24] consumers and consumer organizations have been granted the right to inspect all non-confidential information made available to the Commission by any party to an investigation.

§ 6.6　Countervailing Duties

The internal trade problems associated with member state "aids" (subsidies) to enterprises located inside the EU have already been discussed in connection with the Union's competition policy.[1] Many of the same problems re-emerge in the context of the Common Commercial Policy. This time, however, the source of the subsidies are governments located *outside* the Common Market. Many subsidies, especially export subsidies, are treated as an unfair trading practice under the GATT/WTO. As with dumping, there is a separate code which creates the ground rules in this area.[2] This code (as revised after the Uruguay Round) is implemented as a matter of Common Commercial Policy by the EU and therefore parallels similar law in the United States.[3]

The types of "subsidies" subject to "countervailing duties" are in dispute internationally. European Union regulations illustrate what constitutes a countervailable subsidy.[4] Certain domestic manufacturing, production, and transportation subsidies can also be countervailed if they (like export subsidies) threaten material inju-

21. Miniature Bearings, Nippon Seiko v. Council (1987) Eur.Comm.Rep. 1923.

22. *See* Al–Jubail Fertilizer Co. v. Council (1991) Eur.Comm.Rep. 3187 (Case C–49/88).

23. BEUC v. Commission (1991) Eur.Comm.Rep. 5709 (Case C–170/89).

24. Article 2(8) Council Regulation 521/94.

§ 6.6

1. *See* Chapter 5.

2. *See* the Agreement on Interpretation and Application of Articles VI, XVI and XXIII of the GATT (1979) (Subsidies Code). Substantial amendments to this code under the Uruguay Round of GATT negotiations were undertaken, resulting in the 1994 WTO Subsidies Code. EU law conforms to this new Subsidies Code.

3. 19 U.S.C.A. § 1671.

4. Council Regulation 2026/97.

ry to an EU industry. The European Court of Justice has said that the concept of a countervailable subsidy presupposes the grant of an economic advantage through a charge on the public account.[5] For a domestic subsidy to be countervailable, it must have "sectoral specificity" (seek to grant an advantage only to certain firms). For an export subsidy to be countervailable, it must specifically benefit the imported product.[6] As with dumping proceedings, the Commission makes these judgments provisionally and the Council renders final judgment (issued as a customs regulation). The amount of the extra duty corresponds to the amount of the subsidy. Relatively few external subsidy proceedings have been pursued under Union law.

§ 6.7   Trade Relations

Article 302 of the Treaty of Rome gives the Commission the power to represent the Union within the General Agreement on Tariffs and Trade (GATT). This representation affords EU nations much more bargaining power over tariffs and other trade issues with Canada, the United States, and Japan than they ever had individually. The exact extent and delimitation of the Union competences and the competences of the member states were disputed. With regard to the many Uruguay Round agreements, therefore, the European Commission requested the European Court of Justice to render an opinion under Article 300 of the Treaty of Rome[1] to determine whether the Union is competent to conclude the Agreement establishing the World Trade Organization (WTO), in particular as regards the Agreement on Trade in Services (GATS), the Agreement on Trade–Related Aspects of Intellectual Property Rights, including trade in counterfeit goods (TRIPS), and with respect to products and/or services falling within the ECSC and EURATOM Treaties.

United States/EU Trade

Trade between the United States and the European Union is voluminous, roughly in balance and increasingly fractious. While the focal point in recent years has been agricultural trade, especially the problem of export subsidies and nontariff trade barriers (notably Europe's banana quotas, beef hormone bans and freeze on GMO approvals) there are many contentious issues. For example, Airbus subsidies have been said to threaten Boeing, and the single market legislative campaign led to fears concerning the erection of a "Fortress Europe" in banking, insurance, broadcasting and other areas. There is a general concern in North America that Europe is

---

5. FEDIOL v. Commission (1988) Eur.Comm.Rep. 4193.

6. *Id.*

1. Opinion 2/94.

turning inward and protective. A particularly contentious issue has been the field of public procurement, notably the provision of the Utilities Directive[2] which provides for a preference of tenders for supplies which contain less than 50 percent materials originating outside the Union. The dispute between the United States and the European Union has meanwhile been settled in negotiations which led to the conclusion of two agreements[3].

The Union, for its part, has begun imitating the United States' practice of issuing annual reports voicing *its* objections to U.S. trade barriers and unfair practices. Extraterritorial U.S. jurisdiction has been a constant complaint, including the Helms–Burton Cuban LIBERTAD and Iran–Libya Sanctions Act. These reports have also targeted Section 301 of the Trade Act of 1974.[4] The U.S. invoked Section 301 in trade disputes with the EU over the use of animal hormones and EU regulation of oil seeds. The European Union perceives Section 301 to be a unilateral retaliatory mechanism that runs counter to multilateral resolution of trade disputes through the GATT/WTO. This perception has not stopped the Union from partially duplicating this mechanism in EU law protections against "illicit commercial practices."[5] Nevertheless, since the United States has been taking the bulk of its trade disputes to the WTO under its Dispute Settlement Understanding, the Europeans have less to complain about on this score.

Another issue that has been prominently and regularly mentioned is the problem (from the EU perspective) of the diversity of state and local regulation of procurement, product standards, the environment, financial services and taxation. U.S. critics of Europe's legislative diversity could not have said it better. Recent reports by the EU on U.S. trade practices identified major areas of complaint: unilateral U.S. trade legislation; extraterritorial trade law; national security restraints; Buy American policies; import fees, quotas and paperwork; agricultural export subsidies; tax rules on transfer pricing, autos and unitary income taxation; selectively high tariffs; the multiplicity of product standards; services; intellectual property rights; and investment. Perhaps both sides are headed for stronger central government regulation of trade-impacting measures.[6] Each has a lot at stake in trade with the other. The tough question is whether the World Trade Organization dispute resolution procedures can be made to work so as to preserve

2. Article 36, Council Directive 93/38, O.J. L 199/84 (Aug. 9, 1993).

3. Council Decision 93/394, O.J. L 125/54 (May 20, 1993), the Memorandum of Understanding is published in O.J. L 125/2 (May 20, 1993); Commission proposal for a Council Decision concerning the conclusion of an Agreement in the form of an exchange of letters, O.J. C 291/4 (October 19, 1994).

4. 19 U.S.C.A. § 2411 as amended.

5. *See* Section 6.4.

6. *See especially* the discussion of EU product standards and liability law in Chapter 5.

mutually beneficial trade relations between the Union and North America.

Trade relations between the EU and the U.S. have improved in limited ways under the Transatlantic Economic Partnership Program (1995). Nevertheless, deep underlying conflicts remain. It is this author's view that NAFTA and the EU are competing with good reason for possession of the world's largest market. Larger markets bring greater leverage in intergovernmental trade negotiations, economies of scale and improved "terms of trade" (pay less for imports, receive more for exports), and enhanced abilities to exercise global economic leadership. Europe's 2004 expansion from 15 to 25 member states may be matched or bettered by the proposed Free Trade Area of the Americas encompassing 33 nations. And so the struggle for market power will continue.

Japan/EU Trade

The European Union's trade relations with Japan are less voluminous, less in balance and (at least superficially) less fractious than with the United States. Japan runs an annual surplus in its trade with the EU, but the amount is much smaller than the huge surplus it accumulates in trading with the States. Many Europeans speak quietly and with determination about their intent to avoid the "United States example" in their trade relations with Japan. Less quietly, some national governments imposed rigorous quotas on the importation of Japanese autos and instituted demanding local content requirements for Japanese cars assembled in Europe. The Union, for its part, has frequently invoked antidumping proceedings against Japanese goods and demonstrated a willingness to create arcane rules of origin that promote its interests at the expense of the Japanese. At the GATT/WTO level, however, Japan and the EU share common concerns about retaining their agricultural support systems. These concerns place them in opposition to the U.S. and others who seek to liberalize world trade in agricultural products. These differences have been diminished and common positions have been developed in the 1994 WTO Agreement on Agriculture.

§ 6.8 Trade Agreements

Article 300 of the Treaty of Rome establishes the procedures used in the negotiation of most trade agreements with the European Union. Basically, the Commission proposes and then receives authorization from the Council to open negotiations with third countries or within an international organization. When the Commission reaches tentative agreement, conclusion or ratification must take place in the Council after consulting the Parliament. If the Commission alone concludes an agreement, the European Court of Justice will declare void the act whereby the Commission sought to conclude the agreement.[1] The Council votes by qualified majority on Common Commercial Policy agreements.[2] These include most GATT/WTO agreements. The Council votes unanimously on association agreements[3] and on international agreements undertaken via Article 308 (*e.g.,* environmental conventions prior to 1987). The Treaty on European Union amended Article 300 to provide that the Council must also vote unanimously on international agreements covering areas where an unanimous vote is required to adopt internal EU rules.[4] Parliament's role in international agreements was expanded by the TEU. Its consent must now be obtained for association agreements, agreements with important EU budget implications[5] and agreements entailing amendment of legislation adopted under co-decision (Parliamentary veto) procedures.[6] The Council is also authorized to take emergency measures to cut off or reduce trading with other nations for common foreign or security policy reasons.[7]

An opinion of the European Court as to the compatibility with the Treaty of Rome of the proposed agreement and the procedures used to reach it may be obtained in advance at the request of the Commission, Council or a member state. There are no public proceedings when such opinions are sought. Use of this advance ruling procedure may forestall judicial review at a later date of the compatibility of Union agreements with the Treaty of Rome.[8] This lesson was vividly made when the Court of Justice rejected the final draft of the 1991 European Economic Area Agreement between the EU and EFTA because it considered the provisions on judicial control incompatible with the authority of the Union's legal order.[9] This rejection sent the Agreement back for renegotiation and a new set of dispute settlement procedures which subsequently met with ECJ approval.[10]

Trade agreements and other international treaties of the European Union are subject to judicial review by the Court of Justice as "acts" of its institutions.[11] Moreover, such agreements are binding

---

§ 6.8

1. France v. Commission (1994) Eur. Comm.Rep. I–3641 (Case C–327/91) (Agreement between the Commission and the United States regarding the application of their competition laws).

2. Article 300(2), Treaty of Rome.

3. *See* § 6.9.

4. *See* § 2.6.

5. *See* Parliament v. Council (1999) Eur.Comm.Rep. I–4741 (Mauritania fisheries agreement did not have *important* budget implications).

6. *See* §§ 2.2, 2.8.

7. *See* Article 301, Treaty of Rome.

8. *See* ECJ Opinion 1/75 (1975) Eur. Comm.Rep. 1355 (Local Cost Standards).

9. ECJ Opinion 1/91 (1991) Eur. Comm.Rep. 6079.

10. ECJ Opinion 1/92 (1992) Eur. Comm.Rep. 2821.

11. *See* Articles 230, 232 and 234, Treaty of Rome, and Chapter 3; an example of a decision declaring void the

on the member states which must ensure their full implementation.[12] When the European Court holds international agreements of
the Union to be "directly effective" EU law, individuals may rely
upon them in national litigation.[13] The direct effects doctrine has
led to cases where citizens end up enforcing the trade agreements
of the EU despite contrary law of their own or other member state
governments.[14]

ERTA and WTO Agreements Cases

Article 133 of the Treaty of Rome conveys the power to enter
into international commitments to the European Union. This is the
case by implication even when there is no express Treaty authorization to enter into international agreements necessary to achieve
internal Common Market objectives.[15] A well known decision of the
European Court holds the scope of the Union's trade agreements
power to be coextensive with all *effective* surrenders of national
sovereignty accomplished under the Treaty of Rome.[16] Thus, if an
internal economic policy matter is governed by existing EU law, the
external aspects of that policy are (either expressly or *by implication*) exclusively within the Union's competence. More recently, the
Court of Justice revisited the *ERTA* doctrine in an opinion reviewing the Uruguay Round trade agreements. The European Community had long represented the member states in the GATT and
exclusively negotiated these agreements. But the General Agreement on Trade in Services (GATS) and the Agreement on Trade–
Related Aspects of Intellectual Property (TRIPS) raised special
concerns since the Treaty of Rome and *ERTA* were ambiguous as to
whether the Community or the member states or both had the
power to conclude these agreements.

The Court of Justice, in the complex *WTO Agreements* opinion,
ruled that the Community had exclusive power regarding trade in
goods agreements (including agriculture) based on Article 133 authorizing the Common Commercial Policy. While the cross-frontier
supply of services not involving movement of persons also fell under
Article 133, all other aspects of the GATS did not. Regarding
TRIPS, only the provisions dealing with counterfeit goods came
under the Community's exclusive Article 133 authority. Noting that

act whereby the Commission sought to
conclude an agreement is Case C–
327/91, France v. Commission (1994)
Eur.Comm.Rep. I–364.

12. Article 300(2), Treaty of Rome.

13. *See* Chapter 3.

14. Bresciani v. Amministrazione
della Finanze (1976) Eur.Comm.Rep.
129 (Yaoundé Conventions); Hauptzollamt Mainz v. Kupferberg (1982) Eur.

Comm.Rep. 3641 (EC–Portugal Free
Trade Agreement); Eurim–Pharm
GmbH v. Bundesgesundheitsamt (1993)
Eur.Comm.Rep. I–03723 (Case C–
207/91).

15. ECJ Opinion 1/76 (1977) Eur.
Comm.Rep. 741 (Inland Waterways).

16. Commission v. Council (1971)
Eur.Comm.Rep. 263 (the *"ERTA"* decision).

the effective surrender of national sovereignty over intellectual property is not (yet) total and that internal trade in services is not "inextricably linked" to external relations, the Court ruled the competence to conclude GATS and TRIPs was jointly shared by the Community and the member states. Likewise, they share a duty to cooperate within the WTO in the administration of these agreements and disputes relating to them.[17]

Member State Involvement

As a rule, member states may not negotiate trade treaties in EU-occupied fields. They may do so on a transitional basis in areas where the Union lacks authority or (less clearly) has not effectively implemented its authority. For example, in the early 1970s the EU had not developed an effective overall energy policy, although it clearly had competence in the coal and nuclear fields. Thus, the International Energy Agreement achieved through the Organization for Economic Cooperation and Development (OECD) in 1975 after the first oil shocks is not an EU agreement. In contrast, the Union clearly had competence in the field of export credits. OECD arrangements in this area are exclusively the province of the Union with no residual or parallel authority in the member states.[18] Likewise, in 2002 the ECJ ruled that bilateral "open skies" aviation agreement between eight individual member states and the United States were illegal incursions into an exclusively EU domain.

The *ERTA* and to a lesser degree the *WTO* decisions of the European Court, combined with the expanding internal competence of the Union, leaves less and less room for national governments to enter into trade agreements. Several ECJ decisions suggest that the Union's external authority parallels its internal powers even if it has not effectively implemented those powers.[19] However, recognizing the sensitivities involved, "mixed agreements" negotiated by the Commission (acting on a Council mandate) and representatives of the member states are frequently used. Both the Union and the member states are signatories to such accords. This has been done with the "association agreements" authorized by Article 310, certain of the WTO Codes, the Ozone Layer Convention and the Law of the Sea Convention. The Court of Justice has upheld the validity of mixed international agreements and procedures, but suggested that absent special circumstances their use should not occur when the Union's exclusive jurisdiction over external affairs is fully

17. Opinion 1/94 (1994) Eur. Comm.Rep. I–5267 (WTO).

18. ECJ Opinion 1/75 (1975) Eur. Comm.Rep. 1355 (Local Cost Standards).

19. Kramer et al. (1976) Eur. Comm.Rep. 1279 (North Atlantic Fisheries); ECJ Opinion 1/76 (1977) Eur. Comm.Rep. 741 (Inland Waterways).

involved.[20] In other words, mixed procedures should be followed only when the competence to enter into and implement international agreements is in fact shared between the Union and its member states.[21] The Treaty of Nice (2003) makes it clear that trade agreements relating to cultural and audiovisual services, educational services, and social and human health services are shared competences.

Article 307 of the Treaty of Rome indicates that most treaties the member states reached prior to joining the EU continue to be valid even if they impact on areas now governed by Union law. Many bilateral treaties of Friendship, Commerce and Navigation fall within this category despite their impact on immigration, employment and investment opportunities. Member states are, however, required to take all appropriate steps (*e.g.*, upon renewal) to eliminate any incompatibilities between national trade agreements and the Treaty of Rome.[22] Whether prior treaties can be invoked so as to negate or fail to fulfill Treaty of Rome obligations is unclear.[23] Such a dispute between Germany and the Commission concerned the compatibility of the preference-provision in the Utilities Directive[24] for supply contracts with the German–American Treaty of Friendship and Commerce of 1953.[25]

§ 6.9   Association Agreements—Mediterranean Policy, Central and Eastern Europe

Association Agreements

Article 310 of the Treaty of Rome authorizes the Union to conclude association agreements with other nations, regional groups and international organizations. The Council must act unanimously in adopting association agreements. Since the Single European Act of 1987, association agreements also require Parliamentary assent (which it threatened to withhold from renewal of the Israeli–EU association agreement unless better treatment of Palestinian exports to the Union is achieved). The network of trade relations established by Article 238 association agreements covers

20. ECJ Opinion 1/78 (1979) Eur. Comm.Rep. 2871 (Natural Rubber Agreement).

21. See Opinion 2/91 (Convention No. 170 of the ILO).

22. *See generally* Kramer et al. (1976) Eur.Comm.Rep. 1279 (North Atlantic Fisheries); Council Decision 91/167.

23. Compare Re Van Wesemael (1979) Eur.Comm.Rep. 35 (International Labor Organization Convention no ground for member state failure to apply

Union law) and Ministère Public & Anor v. Levy (1993) Eur.Comm.Rep. I–04287 (Case C–158/91) (ILO Convention may take precedence over Community directive on night work by women).

24. Article 36, Council Directive 93/38, O.J. L 199/84 (August 9, 1993).

25. Germany in EC row over US sanctions, Financial Times of 12./13.6.1993; EC hopes Bonn row will fade, Financial Times of 14.6.1993.

much of the globe. Those who are "associated" with the EU usually receive trade and aid preferences which, as a practical matter, discriminate against nonassociates. Arguments about the illegality of such discrimination within the GATT/WTO and elsewhere have typically not prevailed.

Article 310 indicates that association agreements involve "*reciprocal* rights and obligations, common action and special procedures*" (emphasis added). The reciprocity requirement found in Article 238 mirrors GATT law on non-preferential trading and free trade area agreements.[1] European Union association agreements usually establish wide-ranging but hardly reciprocal trade and economic links. Greece for many years prior to membership was an EU associate. Turkey has been an associate since 1963. These two agreements illustrate the use of association agreements to convey high levels of financial, technical and commercial aid as a preliminary to membership. Turkey now has a customs union with Europe. Another type of association agreement links the remaining EFTA nations with the European Union. These agreements originally provided for industrial free trade and symbolize an historic reconciliation of the EU (then EEC) and EFTA trading alliances in 1973. A much broader European Economic Area agreement now governs EU–EFTA trade relations.[2]

Relations between the Union and the EFTA states—with the exception of Switzerland—were put on a new footing with the entry into force of the Agreement on the European Economic Area[3] in 1994. The EEA establishes a free trade area roughly comparable in size to NAFTA[4] and, in addition, provides that the four fundamental freedoms of the internal market of the Union (free movement of goods, persons, services and capital) as well as the competition rules and certain horizontal policies (social policy, consumer protection, environment, statistics and company law) are applied throughout the EEA area.[5] The EFTA states had to adopt the "acquis communautaire", *i.e.* the established EU law in all these areas. A special EFTA Surveillance Authority was set up with powers similar to those of the Commission, and also an EFTA Court, resembling the European Court of Justice. However, the EEA Agreement did not create a customs union, thus there is no common external customs tariff. Excluded are also such sensitive subjects like agriculture, fisheries and economic and monetary policy. The lasting importance of the EEA Agreement is difficult to assess since several EFTA

---

§ 6.9

1. *See* Chapter 1.

2. *See* Chapter 1.

3. O.J. L 1/3 (January 3, 1994).

4. See R. Folsom, *NAFTA and Free Trade in the Americas in a Nutshell.*

5. The EEA area in 1994 comprised the EU and Austria, Finland, Iceland, Norway, Sweden and Liechtenstein.

countries joined the EU in 1995,[6] and it now applies only to Norway, Iceland and Lichtenstein.

Mediterranean Policy

Still another type of association agreement involves pursuit of what the EU refers to as its "Mediterranean Policy." This policy acknowledges the geographic proximity and importance of Mediterranean basin nations to the Union. The Mediterranean is viewed as a European sphere of influence. Most of these association agreements grant trade preferences (including substantial duty free EU entry) and economic aid to Mediterranean nations *without* requiring reciprocal, preferential access for Union goods. Agreements of this type have been concluded with Algeria, Morocco, Tunisia, Egypt, Jordan, Lebanon, Syria, Israel, the former Yugoslavia, Malta and Cyprus. These agreements are not at all uniform. They may be asymmetrical free trade agreements with the final goal of a customs union (Malta, Cyprus), or without such goal (Israel, Maghreb countries) or simple cooperation agreements (e.g. Egypt). In 1995, Europe and these partners declared an intent to create a Mediterranean industrial free trade zone by 2010.

Central and Eastern Europe

Because the former Soviet Union and its European satellites refused for many years to even recognize the European Community (now Union), some bilateral trade and cooperation agreements between those nations and the member states continue in place. It was not until 1988 that official relations between the Union and COMECON were initiated. As more democracy has taken hold, first generation trade and aid ("Partnership and Cooperation") agreements were concluded by the EU with Hungary, Poland, the Czech and Slovak Federal Republic, Bulgaria and nearly every other Central European nation. Similar agreements were concluded with the Baltic states, Slovenia, Albania, Russia, Ukraine and other former Soviet nations. The Union advanced to second generation "association agreements" with some of these countries. These are known as "Europe Agreements." They anticipate substantial adoption of EU law on product standards, the environment, competition, telecommunications, financial services, broadcasting, and a host of other areas. Free movement of workers is not provided. Free trading will emerge over a ten-year period with special protocols on sensitive products like steel, textiles and agricultural goods. More fundamentally, these agreements are clearly focused on the eventual incorporation of these countries into the Union, as many did in 2004 and Romania and Bulgaria expect to do in 2007.

---

6. Finland, Sweden and Austria have done so. This leaves only Iceland, Norway and Liechtenstein as parties to the EEA.

With respect to the former USSR, the basis of the relationship between the EU and the Commonwealth of Independent States initially was the Trade and Cooperation Agreement of 1989 concluded with the Soviet Union. This agreement has been replaced by bilateral Partnership and Cooperation Agreements. The negotiations with Ukraine were concluded in March 1994, with Kazakhstan and Kyrgystan in May 1994, with Russia in June 1994, and with Moldova in July 1994. These new agreements laid down the framework for future commercial and economic cooperation and created a new legal basis for the development of trade and investment links. For example, the agreement with Russia on trade and trade-related issues removed all quotas and other quantitative restrictions on Russian exports to the European Union, with the exception of certain textile and steel products. In 2004, responding to the admission of 10 new EU member states, Russia and the European Union concluded a Partnership agreement. Customs duties on cargo shipments between Russia its Kaliningrad enclave on the Baltic Sea are dropped, tariffs generally lowered, Russian steel quotas increased and EU antidumping duties relaxed. The European Union has also promised to guarantee language rights for the Russian-speaking minorities in Estonia and Latvia.

International Agreements

In addition, the European Union has a host of other association agreements based upon most-favored-nation trading, not preferential access. These include agreements with Sri Lanka, Pakistan, Bangladesh, India, the ASEAN group (Thailand, Singapore, Malaysia, The Philippines, Brunei, and Indonesia), the Andean Pact (Bolivia, Columbia, Ecuador, Venezuela, Peru), Argentina, Uruguay, Brazil and Mexico. In 1990, a Cooperation Agreement was signed with the countries of the Gulf Cooperation Council (GCC): Kuwait, Saudi Arabia, Bahrain, Qatar and the United Arab Emirates. Finally, following the establishment of the MERCOSUR commonmarket by certain South American countries (Brazil, Paraguay, Uruguay and Argentina), the Union has begun discussions with the MERCOSUR countries concerning the conclusion of an agreement providing for a formal relationship and eventually leading to a free trade area. Very significantly, Mexico and the European Union reached a free trade agreement in 2000. Mexico, with its NAFTA membership, thus becomes a production center with duty free access to the world's two largest consumer markets.

§ 6.10   The Lomé/Cotonou Conventions

The Treaty of Rome, in a section entitled the "association of overseas territories and countries," was intended to preserve the special trading and development preferences that came with "colonial" status. In 1957, France, Belgium, Italy and The Netherlands still had a substantial number of these relationships. Article 133 completely abolished (after a transitional period) tariffs on goods coming from associated overseas territories and countries. There is no duty on the part of these regions to reciprocate with duty free access to their markets for EU goods. Although some territories continue to exist (*e.g.*, French territories like Polynesia, New Caledonia, Guadaloupe, Martinique, etc.), most of the once associated overseas colonies are now independent nations. This is true as well for most of the former colonies of Britain, Denmark, Portugal and Spain.

As independence arrived throughout Asia, Africa and elsewhere, new conventions of association were employed by the EU as a form of developmental assistance. The first of these were the Yaoundé Conventions (1964 and 1971) with newly independent French-speaking African states. These conventions were in theory free trade agreements, but the African states could block almost any EU export and the Union in turn could protect itself from agricultural imports that threatened its Common Agricultural Policy. A healthy amount of financial and technical aid from the Union was thrown into the bargain.

Participating ACP States

When Britain joined in 1973, it naturally wished to preserve as many of the Commonwealth trade preferences as it could. The Yaoundé Conventions were already in place favoring former French colonies south of the Sahara. The compromise was the creation of a new convention, the first Lomé Convention (1975), to expand the Yaoundé principles to developing Caribbean and Pacific as well as English-speaking African nations. The fourth Lomé Convention (1990) governed trade and aid between the EU and a large number of African, Caribbean and Pacific (ACP) states. Lomé IV was replaced in 2000 by the Cotonou Agreement, which will operate for 20 years. The Cotonou nations presently include: Angola, Antigua & Barbuda, Bahamas, Barbados, Belize, Benin, Botswana, Burkina Faso, Burundi, Cameroon, Cape Verde, Central African Republic, Chad, Comoros, Congo, Djibouti, Dominica, Dominican Republic, Equatorial Guinea, Eritrea, Ethiopia, Fiji, Gabon, Gambia, Ghana, Grenada, Guinea, Guinea Bissau, Guyana, Haiti, Ivory Coast, Jamaica, Kenya, Kiribati, Lesotho, Liberia, Madagascar, Malawi, Mali, Mauritania, Mauritius, Mozambique, Namibia, Niger, Nigeria, Niue, Palau, Papua New Guinea, Rwanda, St. Christopher & Nevis, St. Lucia, St. Vincent & The Grenadines, Samoa, Sao Tomé & Principe, Senegal, Seychelles, Sierra Leone, Solomon Islands, Somalia, South Africa, Sudan, Suriname, Swaziland, Tanzania, Togo,

Tonga, Trinidad & Tobago, Tuvalu, Uganda, Vanuatu, Zambia and Zimbabwe.

Perhaps the most important feature of this lengthy listing is the developing nations that are *not* Cotonou Convention participants. Unless they fall within the Union's Mediterranean Policy, they are apt to perceive the Lomé/Cotonou Conventions as highly discriminatory against their exports and economic interests.

Contents

Unlike the Yaoundé Conventions, the Lomé Conventions did not create (even in theory) reciprocal free trading relationships. While the Lomé states retained substantial duty free access to the Common Market, the Union obtained no comparable benefit. The Lomé nations did promise not to discriminate in trading among EU countries and to grant each most-favored-nation benefits. This meant, in practice, that they were free to block imports from the EU whenever desired. This one-sided relationship has been continued temporarily under the Cotonou Agreement through 2008. A variety of "development" preferences are also granted by the Union in the Cotonou Convention. These include expensive purchasing obligations on sugar, for example. There is no free movement of persons as between the ACP states and the Union. However, whenever such persons are lawfully resident and working in the other's territories, they must be given national treatment rights.

Most significantly, the Cotonou nations now participate in two innovative EU mechanisms designed to stabilize their agricultural and mineral commodity export earnings. These programs are known as STABEX and MINEX (also known as SYSMIN). STABEX covers (*inter alia*) ground nuts, cocoa, coffee, cotton, coconut, palm, rawhides, leather and wood products, and tea. MINEX deals with copper, phosphates, bauxite, alumina, manganese, iron ore, and tin. These programs are an acknowledgement of the economic dependence of many Lomé nations on commodity exports for very large portions of their hard currency earnings.

Some have argued vigorously that STABEX and MINEX perpetuate rather than relieve this dependence. Both programs provide loans and grants in aid to Lomé nations who have experienced significant declines in export earnings because of falling commodity prices, crop failures and the like. The greater the dependency and decline, the larger the EU financial transfers. In 1989, for example, these amounted to 315 million ECUs. These sums are not, for the most part, tied to reinvestment in the commodity sectors causing their payment, nor to the purchase of Union products or technology. In a world where most development aid is tied (*i.e.*, must usually be spent on the donor's products or projects), STABEX and

MINEX represent a different approach. Many Latin American nations have lobbied the United States to create similar mechanisms for their commodities.

The Lomé IV Convention (1990) added several new features carried over under the Cotonou Agreement (2000). The European Union now financially supports structural adjustments in ACP states, including remedies for balance of payments difficulties, debt burdens, budget deficits, and public enterprises. Cultural and social cooperation, trade in services, and environmental issues are also addressed. For example, an agreement not to ship toxic and radioactive waste was reached. The Convention builds upon earlier provisions by specifying protected human rights such as equal treatment, civil and political liberty, and economic, social and cultural rights. Financial support from the EU is given to ACP nations that promote human rights.

§ 6.11 Duty Free Access to the Common Market

The end-game so far as exporters to the European Union are concerned is unlimited duty free access. Except for raw materials, few North American exports will qualify for such treatment. However, subsidiaries based in developing or EFTA nations may achieve this goal. This is possible because of the Union's adherence to the GSP program, its Mediterranean basin trade agreements, the Lomé Conventions, and the EEA Agreement with certain EFTA countries. It may also be possible to ship goods produced in Central and East European nations duty free into the EU under the "second generation" trade agreements. All of these topics have been previously discussed. There are, of course, exceptions and controls (quotas, NTBs) that may apply under these programs. Nevertheless, the Common Market is so lucrative that careful study of its external trade rules is warranted.

Such studies can realize unusually advantageous trade situations. For example, many developing nations are Lomé Convention participants or GSP beneficiaries. The goods of some of these nations are also entitled to duty free access to the United States market under the U.S. version of the GSP program,[1] the Caribbean Basin Economic Recovery Act (1983),[2] the Andean Trade Preference Act (1991) or various U.S. free trade agreements. A producer strategically located in such a nation (*e.g.*, Jamaica) can have the best of both worlds, duty free access to the European Union and the United States. The same applies for Israel which not only has a free-trade agreement with the Union but also with the United States. Since 2000, this ideal outcome is most importantly available

§ 6.11   **2.** 19 U.S.C.A. § 2701.
1. 19 U.S.C.A. § 2461.

via Mexico, which is a member of NAFTA and has a free trade agreement with the European Union.

§ 6.12   Commercial Agents

Council Directive 86/653 coordinates member state laws regarding self-employed commercial agents. This directive was inspired by existing French and German law. In Denmark and Britain new legislation is required for its implementation. Italy has until 1993 to implement the directive, the U.K. and Ireland until 1994. From a United States perspective, the directive is remarkably protective of the agent. It is particularly significant because many North American firms first do business in Europe through commercial agents. The directive defines a commercial agent as a "self-employed intermediary who has continuing authority to negotiate the purchase or sale of goods on behalf of another person (the principal), or to negotiate and conclude such transactions on behalf of and in the name of that principal."

Directive 86/653 establishes various rights and obligations for commercial agents and principals, *e.g.*, the agent's duty to comply with reasonable instructions and the principal's duty to act in good faith. In the absence of an agreed compensation, customary local practices prevail (and if none, reasonable remuneration). Compensation may apparently be by commission or salary. Compensation rights before and after the effective period of the agency contract are specified. Directive 86/653 also establishes when the agent's commission becomes due and payable, as well as the conditions under which it is extinguishable. For example, the agent is entitled to a compensation on all transactions in which he or she participated. Moreover, transactions that have been concluded during the term of the agreement with third parties the agent previously procured as customers for the principal fall within this rule. The agent is also entitled to a compensation on transactions with customers located in his or her area of responsibility or for whom the agent is an exclusive representative.

Termination Rights

An important element concerns the notice and termination rights of the agent. Agency agreements for fixed periods of time that continue to be performed by both parties upon expiration become contracts for an indefinite period. Minimum termination notice requirements of one month per year of service up to three years, and optional notice requirements up to six months for six years are created. The member states must provide for either a right of indemnification or for damages compensation, which must be claimed within one year of termination. The agency agreement cannot waive or otherwise "derogate" these rights. The indemnity cannot exceed one year's remuneration but does not foreclose damages. The indemnity is payable if the agent has brought in new customers or increased volumes with existing customers to the substantial continuing benefit of the principal and is equitable in light of all circumstances.

The right to damages as a result of termination occurs when the agent is deprived of commissions which would have been earned upon proper performance to the substantial benefit of the principal. The agent may also seek damages relief when termination blocks amortization of the costs and expenses incurred on advice of the principal while performing under the agency contract. The death of the agent triggers these indemnity or compensation rights. They are also payable if the agent must terminate the contract because of age, infirmity or illness causing an inability to reasonably continue service. If an agency agreement chooses non-EU law to govern its terms, this choice of law will not override the agent's mandatory damages remedies.[1] No indemnity or damages may be had under specified circumstances, including when the agent is in default justifying immediate termination under national law. "Restraint of trade" clauses (covenants not to compete) are permissible upon termination to the extent that they are limited to two years, the goods in question and the geographic area and/or customers of the agent. Such clauses can be made a pre-condition to the payment of an indemnity.

Competition Law Applicability

A 1962 Commission Notice announced that agreements with "commercial agents" were outside Article 81(1) of the Rome Treaty and therefore are not subject to Article 81(3) notification.[2] The theory behind exempting commercial agents from EU antitrust law was their "auxiliary function" on behalf of principals who were subject to the law. In *Flemish Travel Agents*,[3] however, the European Court of Justice ruled that the relationship between suppliers and independent commercial agents could present competitive implications under the Treaty of Rome. The 1962 Notice defines "commercial agents" as those who undertake for a specified territory to negotiate or conclude transactions on behalf of an enterprise either in their own name or in the name of that enterprise. The key to distinguishing agents from independent traders who are subject to Article 81 is whether the intermediary assumes any risk in the transaction, including nonpayment, title to a considerable inventory

§ 6.12

1. Ingmar GB v. Eaton Leonard Technologies, 2000 Eur.Comm.Rep. I–9305 (Nov. 9, 2000) (California choice of law clause).

2. 1962 Official Journal 2921; *see* Section 7.9.

3. 1987 Eur.Comm.Rep. 3801.

of products, liability for substantial services to customers, or control over prices or terms of sale. This definition of "commercial agents" has been somewhat narrowed by case law.[4]

In December 1990, the Commission released a draft of a new notice on commercial agency agreements. Under it, the Commission distinguishes between "integrated" agents dependent on the supplier and not generally subject to Article 81, and more independent "unintegrated" agents. An agent is "integrated" if he or she generally devotes at least one-third of the time to the principal and does not handle competing products. Certain restrictions apply even to integrated agents. For example, absolute bans on transactions with customers or suppliers outside designated territories may be prohibited. Unintegrated agents are generally treated as independent traders subject to full review under Article 81.

4. *See* Cooperative Vereniging "Suiker Unie" V.A. v. Commission, 1975 Eur. Comm.Rep. 1663.

Chapter 7

COMPETITION (ANTITRUST) LAW

Table of Sections

---

§ 7.0 Introduction

The primary purpose of competition policy in the European Union is preservation of the trade and other benefits of economic integration. The removal of governmental trade barriers unaccompanied by measures to ensure that businesses do not recreate those barriers would be an incomplete effort. For example, competing enterprises might agree to geographically allocate markets to each other, making the elimination of national tariffs and quotas by the Treaty of Rome irrelevant. Similarly, a dominant enterprise in one state might tie up all important distributors or purchasers of its goods through long-term exclusive dealing contracts. The result could make entry into that market by another business exceedingly difficult. By assisting in the formation and maintenance of an economic union, business competition law is an important component in EU competition policy. It prevents enterprise behavior from becoming a substantial nontariff trade barrier to economic integration.

The secondary purpose of European Union competition policy is not unique to regional integration. This purpose is the attainment of the economic benefits generally thought to accrue in any economy organized on a competitive basis. These benefits are many. Perhaps most important of all, an economy characterized by competitive enterprise answers the questions of economic organization by maximizing the market desires of its human constituents. A genuinely competitive market is responsive to individual choice in a way that acknowledges and promotes diversity. Competition among businesses protects the public interest in having its cumulative demand for goods and services provided at the lowest possible prices and with the greatest possible degree of responsivity to public tastes. It is in this sense that a competitive economy is said to be guided by the principle of "consumer welfare or consumer sovereignty." When, for example, EU law prevents competing enterprises from fixing prices for their goods or prevents a dominant enterprise from charging monopoly prices at the consumers' expense, such law helps to realize the economic benefits of competition within the Euro-economy.

The Maastricht Treaty on European Union added provisions to the Treaty of Rome focused specifically on industrial competitiveness.[1] The Union will promote a system of open and competitive

1. *See* Article 157.

markets by accelerating structural change, encouraging enterprise initiatives, fostering business cooperation and supporting innovation, research and development. However, Article 130 indicates that this authority may not result in "any measure which could lead to a distortion of competition." The concept of nondistorted competition is developed in Section 7.2.

§ 7.1   Coal and Steel Competition Rules

The first body of business competition law was created in the Treaty of Paris establishing the European Coal and Steel Community in 1951. ECSC business competition rules were found largely in Articles 65 and 66 of the Treaty of Paris which expired in 2002 when coal and steel were merged into the Treaty of Rome. Their coverage in this section is primarily of historical and comparative interest.

Restraints on "Normal" Competition

Article 80, which defined "enterprise" for Article 65 and 66 purposes, subjected both public and private coal and steel firms to the rules of ECSC competition law. This was important because many coal and steel businesses in the Union are state-owned. Article 65(1) prohibited and voided business agreements and concerted practices "tending directly or indirectly" to prevent, restrict or distort "normal" competition within the ECSC. Such agreements could not be relied upon before any court or tribunal in the member states. However, certain joint-buying, joint-selling and specialization agreements were, notwithstanding Article 65(1), authorized by the Commission when the conditions of Article 65(2) are met. Authorizations followed when the Commission determined that these agreements:

(1) made a substantial improvement in the production or distribution of coal or steel;

(2) were no more restrictive than necessary to achieve those results;

(3) did not convey power over price, production or marketing of a substantial portion of the products concerned; and

(4) did not shield firms against effective competition in the common coal and steel markets.

Article 65(2) authorizations were valid for limited time periods, subject to conditions and could be revoked.

As a general matter, the coal and steel business competition rules were not been vigorously pursued. However, in 1961 the Commission refused to authorize a joint-selling organization for thirty-five colliery companies operating the great majority of the mines in the Ruhr valley. The organization would have supplied 73 percent of the coal consumed in West Germany and 59 percent of the Union's entire coal sales. These firms had already obtained provisional authorization for three separate joint-selling coal agencies. The Commission, backed by the Court of Justice, found that authorization of a single agency would have conveyed the "power to determine prices" in violation of Article 65(2). The Commission noted that neither cheaper coal nor cheaper fuel oil imports in the past had caused the companies to lower their prices to competitive levels. Included in the Court's opinion is a rare and learned discussion of "pure competition" theory and the "normal" and "imperfect" competitive conditions of oligopoly in the coal sector.[1]

Mergers

Article 66 of the Treaty of Paris established extensive Commission controls over coal and steel "concentrations" (mergers). Merger authorizations were granted when the concentration did not convey the power:

> to determine prices, to control or restrict production or distribution, or to hinder effective competition in a substantial part of the market for [the] products; or to evade the rules of competition instituted under this Treaty.

No merger guidelines or regulations were issued by the Commission under its Article 66 powers.[2] Coal and steel mergers law developed on a case-by-case basis with authorizations frequently granted. Steadily increasing industrial concentration in the coal and steel sectors was given Commission approval. The Commission has thus consistently fostered market structures for coal and steel that may be inimical to effective Common Market competition. The basis for this policy was the belief that larger and, ideally, more efficient Union enterprises were required in order to compete internationally with East Asian and North American firms.

Dominant Firms

Under Article 66(7) the Commission could take action when it found:

> public or private undertakings which, in law or in fact, hold or acquire in the market for [coal or steel] a dominant position shielding them against effective competition in a substantial part of the common market.

§ 7.1

1. Geitling v. High Authority (1962) Eur.Comm.Rep. 83.

2. *Compare* the Commission Regulation on Concentrations under the Treaty of Rome, discussed in § 7.22.

The Commission was ultimately empowered to determine the prices, conditions of sale, production or delivery schedules of a dominant firm. A dominant coal or steel enterprise need not have *abused* its market position to become subject to Commission controls.[3] The existence of the dominant position was enough, although abuse could be a reason for action by the Commission.

Relatively little use was made of Article 66(7) against dominant coal and steel businesses. In 1975, however, the Commission decreed interim measures against the publicly owned National Coal Board of Britain, requiring it to sell coal at a lower, nondiscriminatory price to a private producer of hard coke. The National Coal Board (NCB) held 88 percent of the market for the production of domestic hard coke. The price margin between NCB's coal and hard coke sales was alleged to be insufficient to allow the private firm to operate economically and thus shielded NCB from effective competition.[4]

The Commission exercised exclusive jurisdiction over Articles 65 and 66, subject to an appeal to the European Court of Justice. Since 1989, most of these appeals were lodged with the Court of First Instance. This exclusive jurisdiction prohibited private parties from raising ECSC business competition law issues in national courts. In other words, Articles 65 and 66 were not "directly effective" law.[5] This contrasts sharply with the concurrent jurisdiction of national courts and authorities in many European Community competition law matters. Thus, despite its earlier birth, the facilitating "tending to" language of Article 65, and the broad coverage of Article 66, there was limited case and regulatory development of coal and steel competition law. This is the complete opposite of what has occurred under the Treaty of Rome (below). The utilization by the Commission of some market managing techniques (*e.g.*, occasional price and production controls), the exclusivity of its jurisdiction and (one suspects) the presence of so many publicly owned coal and steel enterprises accounted for this underdevelopment.

§ 7.2   Nondistorted Competition Policy

One of the basic tasks of the European Union as set out in Article 3(g) of the Treaty of Rome is the institution of a "system ensuring that competition in the common market is not distorted." In this regard, the Treaty of Rome appears to reflect a more German perspective on economic organization, whereas the Treaty

---

3. *Compare* Article 82 of the Treaty of Rome discussed in § 7.18.

4. In Re National Carbonising Co. Ltd. (1975) Common Mkt.L.Rep. D82.

5. H.J. Banks & Co. Ltd. v. British Coal Corp. (1994) Eur.Comm.Rep. I–1209 (Case C–128/92). *See also* Chapter 3.

of Paris was more heavily influenced by French views. Distorted competition is a broad English translation for the French concurrence faussée. Nondistorted competition is close to the German concept of funktionsfähiger Wettbewerb, but it is not clear to what extent this concept is a correlative of what Americans call workable or effective competition.[1] There is some suggestion that workable competition is the minimum level required in business competition law analyses.[2]

Nondistorted competition is thus a complex, evolving and distinctly European perspective on economic organization. It includes, for example, the heavy hand of agricultural price regulation and subsidies embodied in the Common Agricultural Policy.[3] Anticompetitive member state regulations, including price rules, are permissible distortions short of requiring or favoring EU competition law violations, reinforcing such violations, or delegations of state economic responsibility to private traders.[4] For example, member states may not approve or require prices fixed in violation of EU competition rules.[5]

Public and private business competition law is only one facet of nondistorted competition policy. Equally, if not at times more important, are a wide range of other Union concerns and decisions including notably state aids (subsidies).[6] Foremost of these concerns has been the implementation and maintenance of the customs union and rights of free movement, which by their very nature promote competition across borders.[7] Indeed, the whole of the single market campaign could be said to underwrite more economic competition within the Union.

Trade treaties and the Common Commercial Policy are another important element in the Union's competition regime since they heavily influence external competitive pressures.[8] Two areas of Union law with specific implications for competition policy are

§ 7.2

1. See the seminal work Clark, Toward a Concept of Workable Competition, 30 Am.Econ.Rev. 241 (1940) and Hoppmann, Workable Competition (Funktionshähiger Wettbewerb) Die Entwicklung einer Idee über die Norm der Wettbewerbspolitik, 102 Zeitschrift des Bernischen Juristenvereins 249 (1966).

2. See Metro SB–Grossmärkte GmbH & Co. KG v. Commission (1977) Eur.Comm.Rep. 1875.

3. See Chapter 5.

4. NV GB–INNO–BM v. Vereniging van de Kleinhandelaars un Tabak (INNO/ATAB) (1977) Eur.Comm.Rep. 2115. See, regarding state prosecutions of price discounters: Ohra (1993) Eur. Comm.Rep. I–5872; Meng (1993) Eur. Comm.Rep. I–5751; Reiff (1993) Eur. Comm.Rep. I–5801. Regarding permissible state pricing rules for lawyers, see Re Manuele Arduino (2002) Eur. Comm.Rep. I–01529 (Case C–35/99).

5. Ahmed Seed Flugreisen v. Zentrale zur Bekämpfung unlauteren Wettbewerbs (1989) Eur.Comm.Rep. 803 (airline pricing).

6. See Section 5.3.

7. See Chapter 4.

8. See Chapter 6.

government subsidies and procurement.[9] In none of these fields of law, however, is there the depth and expansiveness that can be found in businesses competition law. It is very nearly impossible to avoid contact with this law in doing business with the European Union. Hence, business competition rules are often the first encounter that the North Americans have with EU law.

The coverage of competition law that follows is selective. No attempt at a comprehensive survey of this vast field has been made or is possible in a single-volume. The general principles and examples chosen are illustrative of the most common types of legal problems that can be encountered.

§ 7.3 Article 81

Article 81(1) of the Treaty of Rome deals with concerted business practices, business agreements and trade association decisions. Such business activities are deemed incompatible with the Common Market and are prohibited when they have the potential to affect trade between member states *and* have the object or effect of preventing, restricting or distorting competition *within* the Union. The focus of Article 81(1) is thus on cartels. By way of example, Article 81(1) lists certain prohibited activities:

(1) the fixing of prices or trading conditions;

(2) the limitation of production, markets, technical development or investment;

(3) the sharing of markets or sources of supply;

(4) the application of unequal terms to equivalent transactions, creating competitive disadvantages; and

(5) the conditioning of a contract on the acceptance of commercially unrelated additional supplies (tying arrangements).

Article 81(1) has been used to review and challenge a wide range of anticompetitive business activities, some of which are not listed above. These activities include joint buying,[1] joint selling,[2] joint ventures and strategic alliances,[3] and data exchanges[4] among horizontal competitors. They also include an even wider range of

---

9. *See* Chapter 5.

§ 7.3

1. *See Intergroup (SPAR)* Commission Decision 75/482, O.J. L 212/23 (Aug. 9, 1975).

2. *See* Kali & Salz AG v. Commission (1975) Eur.Comm.Rep. 499. *Compare SAFCO,* discussed in Section 7.8.

3. *See AEG/Alcatel,* Commission Decision 90/46, O.J. L. 32/16 (Feb. 3, 1990); *Elopak,* Commission Decision 90/410, O.J. L 209/15 (Aug. 8, 1990); European Night Services v. Commission (1998) Eur.Comm.Rep. II–3141.

4. *See* John Deere Ltd. v. Commission (1998) Eur.Comm.Rep. I–3111.

activities between vertically related suppliers, manufacturers and franchisee/licensee/distributors.[5]

Void Agreements

Article 81(2) voids agreements and decisions prohibited by Article 81(1). Thus the prohibitions of Article 81(1) against anti-competitive activity are absolute and immediately effective under 81(2) without prior judicial or administrative action. The open-ended text of Article 85(1) gives considerable leeway for interpretation and enforcement purposes. It has, for example, been interpreted to cover nonbinding "gentlemen's agreements."[6] Trade association "recommendations" influencing competition are caught.[7] It also generates considerable uncertainty as to the validity of many business agreements, since full market analyses of their competitive and trade impact are often required.[8]

Exemptions

Article 81(3) permits Article 81(1) to be declared inapplicable when agreements, decisions, concerted practices or classes thereof:

(1) contribute to the improvement of the production or distribution of goods, or to the promotion of technical or economic progress; while

(2) reserving to consumers an equitable share of the resulting benefits; and neither

(3) impose any restrictions not indispensable to objectives 1 and 2 (*i.e.,* least restrictive means must be used);[9] nor

(4) make it possible for the businesses concerned to substantially eliminate competition.

The prohibitions of Article 81(1) may be tempered by "declarations of inapplicability" (exemptions) only when the circumstances of Article 81(3) are present. As befits exemptions from broad prohibitions, the terms of 81(3) are more narrow and specific. Article 81(3) and Article 81(1) legal issues are often considered simultaneously in the process of analyzing the market impact of restrictive agreements, decisions and concerted practices. The overall net result resembles the "rule of reason" approach found in United States antitrust law.[10] Since May 1, 2004, Article 81(3) is

---

5. *See* Sections 7.10–7.13.

6. ACF Chemiefarma v. Commission (1970) Eur.Comm.Rep. 661.

7. Verband der Sachversicherer v. Commission (1987) Eur.Comm.Rep. 405; Re ANSEAU–NAVEWA (1983) Eur. Comm.Rep. 3369.

8. *See* Sections 7.15 and 7.17.

9. Grundig, O.J. 1994 L 20/15, 21.

10. See Peeters, The Rule of Reason Revisited: Prohibition on Restraints of Competition in the Sherman Act and the EEC Treaty, 37 Am.J.Comp.L. 521 (1989).

directly effective law, opening up the possibility of its application by national courts and authorities as well as the Commission.

§ 7.4 Regulation 17 and Regulation 1—Commission Investigations, Attorney–Client Privilege, Shared Prosecutorial Powers

In March of 1962 the Council of Ministers adopted Regulation 17 on the basis of proposals from the Commission. Regulation 17 was the major piece of secondary law under Articles 81 and 82. Effective May 1, 2004, Regulation 17 is replaced by Regulation 1/ 2003. These regulations establish the scheme of enforcement for competition law. The Commission, for the most part its Competition Directorate–General, acquires a wide range of powers.

Commission Investigations

The regulations confer investigatory powers in the Commission to conduct general studies into economic sectors and to review the affairs of individual businesses and trade associations. The Commission may investigate in response to a complaint or upon its own initiative. These powers are particularly significant because (except in the case of mergers) notification of restrictive agreements, decisions and practices to the Commission, although at times beneficial, is not mandatory. The Commission may request all information *it* considers necessary, and examine and make copies of record books and business documents. The Commission decides upon whether the information it obtains in competition law investigations and proceedings contains "business secrets" and whether to release that information.[1] However, the Court of Justice has ruled that the Commission must give the information source notice and an opportunity to challenge these decisions.[2]

In conducting its investigations, the Commission may ask for verbal explanations on the spot and have access to and seal off business premises. One author refers to these powers as "dawn raids and other nightmares." Nevertheless, the Court of Justice has affirmed this right of hostile access.[3] Effective May 1, 2004, subject to the issuance of a local court warrant, this right of access extends to private homes, motor vehicles and other personal property of corporate directors, managers and staff. In these matters the Commission acts on its own authority. It must, however, inform mem-

---

§ 7.4

1. *See* Samenwerkende lektriciteitsproduktiebedrijven NV v. Commission (1994) Eur.Comm.Rep. I–01911 (Case C–36/92).

2. AKZO Chemie BV v. Commission (1986) Eur.Comm.Rep. 1965.

3. Hoeschst v. Commission (1987) Eur.Comm.Rep. 1549; Dow Chemical Nederland BV v. Commission (1987) Eur.Comm.Rep. 4367; NV Samenwerkende lectriciteits-produktiebedrijven (SEP) v. Commission (1991) Eur. Comm.Rep. II 649 (Case T–39/90).

ber states prior to taking such steps and may request their assistance. The member states must render assistance when businesses fail to comply with competition law investigations conducted by the Commission. Although the Commission may require production of all necessary information in its competition law investigations, it may not force firms to answer questions which could lead to actual admissions of infringement.[4] Information provided to the Commission as part of an EU competition law investigation may not generally be used by member states to commence enforcement proceedings under their own competition laws.[5]

Businesses involved in the Commission's investigatory process have limited rights to notice and hearing.[6] They do not have access to the Commission's files. Any failure on the part of an enterprise to provide information requested by the Commission or to submit to its investigation can result in the imposition of considerable fines and penalties. For example, the Belgian and French subsidiaries of the Japanese electrical and electronic group, Matsushita, were fined by the Commission for supplying it with false information about whether Matsushita recommended retail prices for its products. These sanctions are civil in nature and run against the corporation, not its directors or management.

The Commission has been increasing the use of its investigatory powers. Several procedural requirements for Commission investigations and hearings have been discussed by the Court of Justice. One notable Court decision upheld the authority of the Commission to conduct searches of corporate offices without notice or warrant when it has reason to believe that pertinent evidence may be lost.[7] Another notable decision permitted a Swiss "whistle blower" who once worked for Hoffmann–La Roche (a defendant in EU competition law proceedings) to sue the Union in tort for disclosure of his identity as an informant.[8]

Attorney-Client Privileges

Written communications with external lawyers licensed in an EU member state undertaken for defense purposes are confidential and need not be disclosed.[9] Written communications with in-house

---

4. Orkem v. Commission (1989) Eur. Comm.Rep. 3283. However, this principle does not necessarily apply to civil proceedings before the courts of the member states. Otto, (1993) Eur. Comm.Rep. I–05683 (Case No. C–60/92). In such cases, the right against self-incrimination depends on national law.

5. Dirección General de Defensa de la Competencia (DGDC) v. Asociación Española de Banca Privada (AEB) & ORS (1992) Eur.Comm.Rep. I–4785 (Case C–67/91).

6. Commission Regulation 99/63. *See generally* Hoffmann–La Roche v. Commission (1979) Eur.Comm.Rep. 461.

7. Re National Panasonic (1980) Eur.Comm.Rep. 2033.

8. Adams v. Commission (1985) Eur. Comm.Rep. 3539.

9. AM & S Europe Ltd. v. Commission (1982) Eur.Comm.Rep. 1575.

lawyers are *not* exempt from disclosure, nor are communications with external *non*-EU counsel.[10] Thus communications with North American attorneys (who are not also EU licensed attorneys) are generally discoverable. For example, shortly after the *AM & S* decision, the Commission obtained in-house counsel documents from John Deere, Inc., a Belgian subsidiary of the United States multinational. These documents were drafted as advice to management on how to avoid EU competition liability for export prohibition restraints. They were used by the Commission to justify the finding of an intentional Article 85 violation and a fine of 2 million ECUs.[11] United States attorneys have followed these developments with amazement and trepidation. Disclaimers of possible nonconfidentiality are one option to consider in dealing with clients on EU law matters. At a minimum, U.S. attorneys ought to advise their clients that the usual rules on attorney-client privilege may not apply.

Shared Powers

Regulation 17 and Regulation 1 envisions significant cooperation between European Union and national authorities in the field of competition law. Effective May 1, 2004, enforcement of Articles 81 and 82 is shared with the competition agencies and national courts of the member states. A new European Competition Network has been established to facilitate cooperative law enforcement and minimize divergent application of competition law principles, with the Commission to act as final arbiter on substantive matters. The principal reason for this sharing of enforcement duties is to allow the Commission to focus its energies on price fixing, cartel arrangements and other serious violations of Articles 81 and 82.

The Commission is not under an affirmative duty to carry out an investigation when a complaint is submitted to it.[12] The Court of First Instance has ruled that the Commission can refuse to pursue a competition law complaint if an adequate remedy is available from a national court.[13] This decision supports the Commission's customary practice of decentralized "subsidiarity" in the competition law field. Of course, subsidiarity carries with it the potential for the inconsistent application of the competition rules. Starting May 1, 2004, national courts may ask the Commission for support regarding Article 81 or 82, with the Commission and national authorities empowered to file opinions with the national courts. Moreover, in all cases affecting member state trade, Regulation 1/ 2003 permits the Commission to issue ex ante binding decisions

10. *Id.*

11. John Deere O.J. 1985 L. 35/58.

12. BEUC v. Commission, (2000) Eur.Comm.Rep. II–00101.

13. Automec SRL v. Commission (1992) Eur.Comm.Rep. II–367.

determining that a particular agreement or practice does not infringe European competition law. Such decisions would preclude different results at the national level.

§ 7.5   Commission Prosecutions and Sanctions

Enforcement Procedures

In addition to its investigatory powers, the Commission determines when violations of the competition law provisions of Article 81 or 82 occur. This is the source of the Commission's power to render enforcement decisions. A regulation limits the time period in which the Commission may render a decision in competition law cases to five years. All Commission decisions, including enforcement decisions and decisions to investigate, fine or penalize must be published and are subject to judicial review. Since 1989, most of these appeals are heard by the Court of First Instance. During interim periods, the Commission has the power to order measures indispensable to its functions.[1] Interim relief should be granted when there is prima facie evidence of an Article 81 or 82 violation and an urgent need to prevent serious and irreparable private damage (or intolerable damage to the public interest).[2] Any measures the Commission takes must, however, be of a temporary and conservatory nature, restricted to what is required in the given situation, and take into account the legitimate interests of the enterprise which is the subject of the interim measures.[3] La Cinq, a private television service twice denied membership in the European Broadcasting Union, successfully met these criteria. The Court of First Instance rebuked the Commission's refusal to grant provisional Article 82 protection.[4] Before deciding that a competition law breach has occurred, the Commission issues a statement of "objections."[5] This statement must reveal which facts the Commission intends to rely upon in reaching a decision that a violation has occurred and be worded with sufficient clarity to enable the parties to know what conduct is being objected to.[6] A hearing can then be requested by the alleged violator(s) or any interested person.[7] These hearings are conducted in private, with separate reviews of complainants and witnesses. The Commission must disclose only those non-confidential documents in its file upon which it intends to rely and are necessary to prepare an adequate defense.[8] The parties

§ 7.5

1. Camera Care v. Commission (1980) Eur.Comm.Rep. 119.

2. Sea Containers v. Stena Sealink, O.J. L 15 (1994) 8, 15 point 56.

3. *Id.*

4. La Cinq v. Commission (1992) Eur.Comm.Rep. II–1.

5. Regulation 99/63, Article 2(4).

6. AEG v. Commission (1983) Eur. Comm.Rep. 3151.

7. Regulation 99/63, Article 7.

8. VBVB and VBBB v. Commission (1984) Eur.Comm.Rep. 19.

generally receive, along with the statement of objections, a list of all the documents in the Commission's possession with an indication of the documents or parts of documents to which they may have access. Among the documents generally regarded as confidential, and therefore inaccessible, are internal Commission documents such as memoranda, drafts and other working papers.[9] After the hearing, the Commission consults with the Advisory Committee on Restrictive Practices and Monopolies, which is composed of one civil servant expert from each member state. The results of this consultation are not made public. Having consulted the Committee, the Commission is then free to render an enforcement decision.

Sanctions

In its enforcement decision, the Commission may require businesses to "cease and desist" their infringing activities. The Commission may not, at least in an Article 81 proceeding, require a violator to contract with the complainant.[10] In practice, this power has sufficed to permit the Commission to order infringing enterprises to come up with their own remedial solutions. However, the Commission may not, at least in Article 81 proceedings, require a violator to contract with the complainant. Daily penalties may be imposed to compel adherence to the order to cease and desist. Commission decisions on violations of Articles 81 and 82 are also accompanied by a capacity to substantially fine any intentionally or negligently infringing enterprise. When appeals are lodged against Commission decisions imposing fines and penalties, payment is suspended but interest is charged and a bank guarantee for the amounts concerned must be provided.[11]

In the early years, fines and penalties actually levied by the Commission were few, relatively small in amount, and frequently reduced on appeal to the Court of Justice. As EU competition law doctrine has become clearer, these trends have all been reversed. In its more recent decisions, the Court has upheld substantial fines and penalties imposed by the Commission in competition law proceedings and recognized their deterrent value.[12] The trend towards larger fines has been confirmed by the Commission in recent cases. The Commission has imposed substantial fines on cartels in the chemicals industry,[13] the cartonboard industry[14] and the steel indus-

---

9. 23rd Report on Competition Policy (1994) point 353.

10. Automec SRL v. Commission (1992) Eur.Comm.Rep. II–367. *Compare* Article 86 Case law on refusals to deal by dominant firms in Section 7.20.

11. Hasselblad v. Commission (1982) Eur.Comm.Rep. 1555.

12. *See* Musique Diffusion Française SA v. Commission (1983) Eur. Comm.Rep. 1825.

13. PVC, O.J. 1994 L 239/14.

14. Cartonboard, O.J. 1994 L 243/1.

try.[15] In 2001, the Commission imposed competition law fines of more than $850 million on European companies for conspiring to fix prices and divide up the vitamins market.

Any complete picture of the development of Article 81 must include the Commission's informal negotiations as well as its decisions to prosecute, exempt or clear infringing activities. Compliance with Articles 81 and 82 is often achieved short of a formal Commission decision. Word of informal file-closings is occasionally revealed. In *Re Eurofima,* for example, the Commission terminated proceedings without issuing a decision. In the process of responding to complaints from suppliers, the Commission was able to secure termination of infringing conduct from Eurofima, the most important buyer of railway rolling stock in the Union. Eurofima also undertook to continue to comply with EU competition law. The Commission announced these results in a press release.[16]

§ 7.6   Individual Exemptions, Negative Clearances and Comfort Letters (Prior to May 1, 2004)

Regulation 17 not only served as the basis for the investigatory and enforcement machinery of EU competition law, but also included the ways of avoiding the application of the law to particular business practices. Until May 1, 2004, businesses could avoid the application of Art. 81(1) to a particular practice if they received an exemption or negative clearance. The basic prerequisite was that the practice be properly notified to the Commission. The Commission could not grant either a negative clearance or exemption until the practice was notified.[1] Once this notification was submitted, the Commission was precluded from imposing fines regarding practices taking place after notification and before the Commission's decision.[2] On the other hand, if the practice was not notified to the Commission and it infringed Article 81(1), fines could be imposed even if the practice hypothetically fulfilled all of the requirements of 81(3).[3]

Individual Exemptions

Under Regulation 17 individual exemptions were granted by the Commission under Article 81(3) for a limited period of time.

15. Steel Beams, O.J. 1994 L 116/1.

16. (1973) Common Mkt.L.Rep. D217.

§ 7.6

1. *See* ECO System/Peugeot, O.J. 1992 L 66/1, 7.

2. An application for negative clearance itself was no protection from fines,

see John Deere, O.J. 1985 L 35/58. However, the general practice was to submit an application for negative clearance along with an application for an exemption under Art. 81(3).

3. Musique Diffusion Française SA v. Commission (1983) Eur.Comm.Rep. 1825, 1902.

They were subject to review on renewal and could be conditioned upon extensive stipulations. Individual exemptions could also be revoked or altered by a subsequent Commission decision. Exempted activities could later be prohibited, when:

(1) the situation changed with respect to a factor essential in the Commission's original decision;

(2) the parties committed a breach of any obligation attached to the exemption;

(3) the original decision was based on false information or obtained fraudulently; or

(4) the parties abused the exemption.

The Commission could revoke its decision with retroactive effect in cases (2), (3) or (4).[4]

Negative Clearances

Regulation 17 permitted businesses in doubt as to the applicability of Article 81(1) to their activities to request a "negative clearance" from the Commission.[5] The Commission granted negative clearances solely on the basis of the factual and legal information then before it. A negative clearance stated that the Commission saw no grounds to intervene under Article 81(1). The Commission's decision could be based on the fact that the relevant agreement, decision or concerted practice did not perceptibly affect trade between member states, or did not perceptibly restrain competition within the Common Market as 81(1) requires. Since negative clearances qualified as decisions in the sense of Article 230 of the Rome Treaty, they were appealable to the Court of First Instance.

There was a critical difference under Regulation 17 between a negative clearance and an individual exemption. The latter admitted an Article 81(1) infringement or potential infringement, but requests a declaration of inapplicability under the special terms of Article 81(3). The former indicated that there was no infringement of 81(1) because of the terms of that Article and the nature of the activities involved. These lines of argument could be and often were pursued simultaneously before the Commission using Form A/B.[6] Only the Commission (not national authorities) could grant individual exemptions and negative clearances.

Procedures

When the Commission intended to grant a negative clearance or an 85(3) individual exemption, it published the "main content"

---

4. Art. 8(3) of Regulation 17.   6. O.J. 1993 L 336/4.
5. Art. 2 of Regulation 17.

of the decision after allowing for protection of legitimate business secrets. After publication, all interested third parties were invited to submit their observations to the Commission prior to its decision. Since important matters could be revealed to competitors and potential litigants, this publication requirement may have chilled business usage of the negative clearance and individual exemption procedures erected under Regulation 17.

When the Commission issued a statement of objections and before an adverse decision was made, the applicant was entitled to a hearing.[7] The Court of Justice held that the Commission had discretion whether to hear oral argument on negative clearance and individual exemption applications.[8] Third parties could have access to the hearing process on showing a legitimate interest. As with enforcement proceedings, the hearing was private and a record was made. The Commission gave written reasons to explain whatever final decision was taken, although the Court of Justice held that the Commission need not discuss every fact or law issue raised during the proceedings.[9] The issuance of an Article 81(3) exemption did not foreclose the possibility of a prosecution under Article 82 since the two provisions of the Rome Treaty concern different types of distortions of competition.[10]

Comfort Letters

In addition to individual exemptions and negative clearances, the Commission increasingly relied on the use of so-called "comfort letters" to close a case. The Commission indicated that it normally dealt with notifications by issuing a comfort letter unless the case was of "particular political, economic or legal significance."[11] This type of decision, which incidentally was not addressed in Regulation 17 but developed as administrative practice, had significant practical importance since it was issued much quicker than an exemption or even a negative clearance.

A comfort letter was issued in response to an application for exemption or negative clearance and it generally stated that based on the facts presented to it the Commission saw no reason to intervene in opposition to the notified practices. Comfort letters were issued only with approval of the parties[12] but because of the time saved, the parties did not generally object. Once the parties received a comfort letter, they typically proceeded to implement

---

7. Hoffmann–La Roche v. Commission (1979) Eur.Comm.Rep. 461.

8. FEDETAB v. Commission (1980) Eur.Comm.Rep. 3125.

9. *Id.*

10. Tetra Pak Rausing SA v. Commission (1990) 2 Eur.Comm.Rep. 309.

11. Notice on cooperation between national courts and the Commission in applying Articles 8[1] and 8[2] of the EEC Treaty, O.J. 1993 C 39/6, 8.

12. 13th Report on Competition Policy (1984) p. 64.

their agreement. In the absence of a change in circumstances, the Commission did not alter its position and was precluded from imposing fines under Regulation 17 since the agreement remained notified. The change of circumstances sufficient to cause the Commission to alter its position did not have to be attributable to the parties. For example, the Commission decided to intervene in a distribution system concerning ice cream for which it had previously issued comfort letters.[13] The Commission based its reasoning not on the fact that the practices of the parties had changed but rather because the circumstances in the market had changed. In this respect, the intervention by the Commission was largely due to complaints made by a competitor of the recipients of the comfort letters.

In addition, the national courts were not bound by the comfort letter.[14] This was one of the primary disadvantages of the comfort letter since they afforded only limited legal certainty against the application of the European and national competition laws by the national courts. Nonetheless, as far as the application of the European competition law was concerned, the Commission called upon the national courts to take the comfort letter into account when deciding whether a particular practice amounts to a restraint of competition.[15]

§ 7.7   Individual Exemptions After May 1, 2004—Marine Paints Example

Effective May 1, 2004, the system of Commission notification to obtain individual exemptions, negative clearances and comfort letters outlined above was abolished. Thereafter, exemptions from Article 81 are primarily of the "group" or "block" type summarized in Section 7.9 below. Member State authorities and courts, in addition to the Commission, have the power to recognize individual Article 81(3) exemptions in appropriate circumstances. See Regulation 1/ 2003 replacing Regulation 17, and the content of Article 81(3) discussed in Section 7.3.

Individual exemptions granted by the Commission under Article 81(3) prior to May 1, 2004 offer guidance to their issuance under Regulation 1. Such grants have stressed the projected advantages of reduced production costs, higher productivity, more effective and less costly activities, and somewhat vague notions of technical and economic progress. Exemptions denied by the Com-

13. Schöller Lebensmittel GmbH & Co., KG,. O.J. 1993 L 183/1; Langnese–Iglo GmbH, O.J. 1993 L 182/19.

14. L'Oréal v. PVBA, (1980) Eur. Comm.Rep. 3775, 3789; Lancôme v. Etos, (1980) Eur.Comm.Rep. 2511, 2533.

15. Notice on cooperation between national courts and the Commission in applying Articles 8[1] and 8[2] of the EEC treaty, O.J.1993 C 39/6, 8.

mission have stressed the likelihood of the alleged benefits occurring under competition anyway, the undesirable protection of national markets and "serious" losses of market competition. As a general rule, the Commission weighs the advantages alleged in favor of the restrictive agreement, decision or practice against the resultant loss of market competition and against the likelihood that competition itself might produce similar advantages. This balancing process is well illustrated by the following example.

Re Transocean Marine Paint

In 1962 the Transocean Marine Paint Association, eighteen medium-sized marine paint manufacturers, sought to develop and market a common brand of standard quality paint. They applied for a negative clearance or, in the alternative, an 81(3) individual exemption for their agreement. Five of the manufacturers were domiciled in the Union. Sales responsibility for this brand was allocated on a territorial basis with commissions payable to offset sales in another member's territory irrespective of that member's services regarding those sales. Prices for the Association's standard paint were set individually. Members of the Association could still sell paints of either higher or lower (but not standard) quality under their own trademarks. Such nonstandard paints could not be imported into the sales territory of another member without its consent.

Since the agreement fell within all the terms of Article 81(1) and was not *de minimis,* the Commission denied the request for a negative clearance. Prior to granting an 81(3) exemption, the Commission required the association to eliminate (as incompatible with Article 81(1)) certain other territorial protection, sales allocation, collective discrimination and price information exchange clauses. The Commission perceived that a common brand of paint would make the Association's product more marketable in the EU and world markets. The availability of standard brand paint in most of the world's shipyards was important because it is apparently desirable for technical reasons to reuse the same marine paints on ships. Moreover, it appears that the marine paint market is quite distinct from the market for paints in general (80 percent of marine paints cannot be used for other purposes). Without citing market shares, the Commission noted that the Association manufacturers faced strong competition within the EU from other large international marine paint companies. Hence, reasoned the Commission, the loss of real or potential competition among medium-sized Association manufacturers was outweighed by the potential increase in EU competition in the standard-quality marine paint market viewed as a whole.

The exemption was subject to conditions requiring the Association to report to the Commission any alterations in its membership, any amendments or additions to their agreement, any relevant board decisions or arbitral awards, and its annual volume of sales and inter-Association deliveries. Issued in June of 1966, the Transocean Marine Paint Association exemption was effective until January of 1973.[1]

On application in 1972 for an extension of the exemption, the Association had grown to twenty in number. Five original members had withdrawn while eight new members had been admitted. Seven of the twenty were based in the enlarged Union. This time the market shares of the Association and its competitors were published. The Association had an expanding 5 to 10 percent of the world marine paint market, 25 percent of which was held by International Red Hand Inc., a nonassociate. From 1966 to 1972 the Association members did well by their standard quality paint. Sales rose from one-third to about three-quarters of the total turnover of the membership. One Far Eastern member accounted for over 60 percent of the Association's turnover. In light of these facts, the Commission declared unjustifiable, in 1973, the Association's territorial consent on nonstandard paint sales and the territorial standard brand sales commission obligations described above. Recision of these terms was ordered by the Commission before it granted the exemption renewal for another six years.[2]

The original 1967 conditions attached to the exemption were retained in 1973 while an additional requirement concerning concentration in the industry was attached. Any new links or changes in existing links by way of common directors or managers, or by way of financial participation between an Association member and another enterprise in the paints sector, were to be reported. The Association appealed the inclusion of this additional condition on procedural grounds. It claimed lack of notice and opportunity to present contrary argument. The Court of Justice agreed with the Association and subsequently annulled this part of the Commission's decision.[3] In a revised monitoring requirement issued in accordance with proper procedures, shareholdings amounting to 25 percent or more of firms in the paint sector doing business in the EU had to be reported.

It is worth noting the extent to which the Commission was able to gradually filter out the most anticompetitive aspects of the Association's agreement. This process has continued over the years

§ 7.7

1. Re Transocean Marine Paint Association (1967) Common Mkt.L.Rep. D9.

2. (1974) Common Mkt.L.Rep. D11.

3. Transocean Marine Paint Association v. Commission (1974) Eur. Comm.Rep. 1063.

as the Commission has periodically renewed the exemption. In December of 1988 the Commission continued the exemption through 1998.[4] Furthermore, while the exempt practices may be illegal under competition laws elsewhere (*e.g.*, under United States antitrust law), individual exemptions do grant immunity under the *Wilhelm* case[5] from the national competition laws of member states.

§ 7.8   "Clearances" After May 1, 2004—SAFCO Example

Regulation 1 does not anticipate use of negative clearances and comfort letters. However, the legal principles previously developed under those procedures are likely to operate to "clear" business practices from potential Article 81(1) liabilities. The SAFCO case detailed below highlights those principles. Negative clearance proceedings did not often involve a full examination of the market impact of a particular business practice. Instead, the Commission focused on the lack of a perceptible effect on trade between member states or on the lack of an appreciable effect on competition in the Common Market. These two legal issues were jointly considered as the SAFCO case illustrates.[1]

Re SAFCO

Seven French producers of preserved vegetables created an exclusive sales agency (SAFCO) to encourage the export of their products to West Germany. They assigned their trademarks to SAFCO for export purposes and could be expelled summarily by the SAFCO Association. Membership in the export association was limited to enterprises with less than five million French francs capital in assets and less than five hundred employees. Admissions' decisions were made secretly. The SAFCO articles of association were transmitted in 1963 to the Commission along with a request for a negative clearance.

Prior to the formation of SAFCO, some of its members had been significantly involved in exports to West Germany. The export association was quite successful and obtained about 2 percent of the German market for preserved vegetables by 1972, the time of the Commission's much delayed decision on the negative clearance request. The Commission acknowledged that while export competition between the French producers was restricted by their agreement, it was not perceptibly restricted. The SAFCO enterprises remained in competition with each other in the French market and

4. Re The Transocean Marine Paint Association (1988) 4 Common Mkt. L.Rep. 674.

5. *See* § 7.25.

§ 7.8

1. SAFCO (1972) Common Mkt. L.Rep. D83.

the preserved vegetable market within the EU and Germany was characterized by numerous products similar in quality and competitive in price. Producers of greatly superior size were competitors of SAFCO. An increasingly integrated and competitive common market for preserved vegetables was apparent. The Commission issued a negative clearance to SAFCO indicating, on the facts and law before it, that there was no necessity for intervention under Article 81(1).

Unlike Article 81(3) exemptions, the Commission cannot issue negative clearances subject to conditions, review and renewal. Although it can negotiate the removal of restrictive clauses prior to issuance, the absence of these important monitoring features makes negative clearances long-term risks as regards competition policy. In SAFCO, the agreement was for ninety-nine years duration. What may not "perceptibly" restrict EU competition or trade in 1963 or 1972 may do so in the future. Suppose SAFCO, through competition or membership expansion, obtains 10 or 20 percent of the German market. Suppose membership denials or dismissals hasten the demise of competitors in the French market. Whether negative clearances are revocable, and if so under what terms and with what effects, are legal questions that remain largely unexplored. The Commission could argue that negative clearances are based strictly on the information before it, and that any significant change of circumstances is cause for revoking the clearance.

§ 7.9 Group Exemptions and Notices

The Commission received an onslaught of negative clearance requests and Article 81(3) notifications in 1962 when Regulation 17 took effect. The vast majority of the business activities involved in this deluge were in the distribution and licensing areas. As a result, the Commission sought and obtained authorization in 1965 from the Council to formulate, for limited time periods, group "declarations of inapplicability" under Article 81(3).[1] These are commonly known as "group or block exemptions." The Council granted this authorization, noting that Article 81(3) allows "classes" of exempt agreements. Group exemptions invite businesses to conform their agreements and behavior to their terms and conditions. In other words, group exemptions rely upon confidential business self-regulation.

Another important indication of permissible business practices are the various notices and guidelines which the Commission has issued. However, in contrast to the group exemptions, these notices are mere policy declarations and have no legally binding effect on the national courts or the European courts. Nonetheless,

---

§ 7.9   **1.** Regulation 19/65.

the notices provide an important indication of the Commission's policy toward certain practices and it is unlikely that the Commission will impose fines on businesses which have relied in good faith on the pronouncements of the Commission in one of its notices.[2] Competition law notices issued by the Commission have concerned agreements of "minor" importance,[3] various "minor" cooperation agreements,[4] exclusive agency contracts,[5] and technology sharing agreements among small and medium-sized businesses.[6] Many business agreements are drafted with the details of these group exemption regulations and policy notices in mind.

After a number of test enforcement decisions and definitive rulings by the Court of Justice, the Commission issued Regulation 67 in 1967. It became the first of a series of group exemptions from Article 85(1). Group exemptions now exist for vertical restraints (including distribution and franchise agreements),[7] vehicle distribution and servicing agreements,[8] production specialization agreements among small firms,[9] research and development agreements among small firms,[10] and technology transfer agreements.[11] In addition there are a number of group exemptions which are directed at specific sectors of the economy. These include most notably the insurance sector[12] and the transport sector.[13]

§ 7.10 Exclusive Dealing and Other Distribution Agreements, The Vertical Restraints Regulation

Regulation 67/67 was replaced in 1983 by Regulation 1983/83 (exclusive distribution) and Regulation 1984/83 (exclusive purchasing).[1] Exclusive dealing agreements ordinarily involve restrictions on manufacturers or suppliers and independent distributors of goods. These restraints concern persons the manufacturer may supply, to whom the manufacturer or distributor may sell, and from whom the distributor may acquire the goods or similar goods. Exclusive dealing agreements should be distinguished from agency

2. In fact, the Commission may be estopped from imposing fines in such cases. *See* Miller v. Commission (1978) Eur.Comm.Rep. 131, 158.

3. 1986 Official Journal C231/2, revised O.J. C 368/07 (Dec. 22, 2001).

4. 1968 Official Journal C75/3.

5. 1962 Official Journal 2921.

6. 61979 Official Journal C1/2.

7. Regulation 2790/99. *See* Section 7.10.

8. Regulation 1400/2002.

9. Regulation 2658/2000.

10. Regulation 2659/2000.

11. Regulation 772/2004. *See* Section 7.11.

12. Regulation 3932/92, replaced by Regulation 358/2003.

13. Regulation 1617/93; Regulation 83/91.

§ 7.10

1. *See* Delimitis v. Henninger Bräu (1991) Eur.Comm.Rep. I–935 (234/89) (Regulation 1984/83 applied extensively to beer-supply agreements).

or consignment agreements where title and most risk remain with the manufacturer until the goods are sold by their retail agents to consumers. The announced EU policy position is that competition law will not require a manufacturer to compete with its agents.[2] Exclusivity in genuine retail agency agreements is therefore legal.[3]

Regulation 67 and its successors may be seen as an excellent example of Commission efforts to employ and develop competition law under Article 81 to serve the goal of economic integration. The formation of absolute territorial trade barriers, similar in impact to national tariffs and quotas that existed prior to the creation of the Common Market, would negate some of the economic benefits of increased trade and economic integration. Yet to prohibit exclusive dealing entirely would deter Common Market sales by national manufacturers. Hence, distributive competition among goods for sale within the EU is encouraged by permitting exclusive dealing agreements between manufacturers and independent distributors *and* by insuring that competition as between exclusive dealers in the same goods is also preserved. It is only *absolute* territorial exclusive dealing that precludes benefit from the group exemption. It is precluded whether achieved by the exercise of national patent, copyright or trademark rights, or simply by contractual restraints between manufacturers and their exclusive dealers. For example, when territorial protection for distributors is obtained by making slight changes to a product's content, this constitutes an Article 81 violation. Manufacturers and distributors may not seek product approvals which effectively divide up the common market in this manner.[4]

According to the Commission, vertical agreements must therefore be examined on two levels:

> Firstly, the exclusive nature of a contractual relationship between a producer and a distributor is viewed as restricting competition, since it limits the parties' freedom of action on the territory covered. Secondly, the agreement may normally be exempted under Article 81(3) of the EC Treaty if it does not contain any provisions that create absolute territorial protection for the distributor or, at any rate, does not objectively have such an effect.[5]

Export bans applied by manufacturers to their EU distributors

---

2. Notice on exclusive agency contracts made with commercial agents, O.J.1962, 2921.

3. *But see* Re Pittsburgh Corning Europe (1973) Common Mkt.L.Rep. D2; Commission Announcement on Exclusive Agency Contracts Made with Commercial Agents, O.J. 1962, 2921.

4. *See* Zera Montedison/Hinkins Staehler, O.J. 1993 L 272/28.

5. 23rd Report on Competition Policy (1994) point 212.

have attracted sizeable fines and penalties under Article 81.[6] This outcome fosters intrabrand competition in ways which have largely been abandoned under United States antitrust law.[7]

Selective Distribution

Another form of distribution which is of practical importance is selective distribution. Although, in contrast to exclusive distribution and exclusive supply agreements, the Commission has not adopted a block exemption for selective distribution agreements,[8] there are certain rules which arise from the Commission's decisions and the case law. A selective distribution system exists where a supplier limits the number of approved distributors of its products based on particular criteria. Whether such a system infringes Article 81(1) depends largely on the criteria used and the justification for not supplying to certain distributors.

Generally, a selective distribution system will not infringe Article 81(1) if it is based on qualitative criteria, these criteria are objectively applied so that any qualifying distributor is admitted to the system, and it does not include any provisions which are likely to prohibit parallel imports.[9] A selective distribution system based on quantitative criteria, on the other hand, will likely infringe Article 81(1)[10] or if the nature of the products is such that a selective distribution system is not necessary.[11] In addition, any particular restraints imposed on the distributors should be examined because they could individually infringe Article 81(1). For example, in the *Grundig* decision, the Commission stated that while the selective distribution system established by Grundig did not in itself infringe Article 81(1), but certain obligations imposed on the dealers did. This included the requirement that retailers carry as complete a selection of the relevant Grundig range as is

---

6. *See, e.g.,* John Deere & Co., 28 O.J. 1985 L 35/58 (fined two million ECU for violation of Article 81(1) for imposing, accepting or practicing bans on the export of its products by dealers or distributors to other member states); Sperry New Holland, a Division of Sperry Corp., 28 O.J. 1985 L 376/21 (fined 750,000 ECU for violation of Article 81(1) for imposing, accepting or practicing a ban on export of SNH products by dealers of distributors to other member states).

7. *Compare* Continental T.V., Inc. v. GTE Sylvania Inc., 433 U.S. 36, 97 S.Ct. 2549, 53 L.Ed.2d 568 (1977); Business Electronics Corp. v. Sharp Electronics Corp., 485 U.S. 717, 108 S.Ct. 1515, 99 L.Ed.2d 808 (1988).

8. The Commission however adopted in 1985 a block exemption applicable to selective distribution systems in the automobile sector, now as amended Regulation 1400/2002.

9. *See* Metro v. Commission, (1977) Eur.Comm.Rep. 1875; AEG v. Commission, (1983) Eur.Comm.Rep. 3151; Hasselblad v. Commission, (1984) Eur. Comm.Rep. 883; Grundig's distribution system, O.J.1994 L 20/15.

10. Ford v. Commission, (1985) Eur. Comm.Rep. 2725; Vichy v. Commission, (1992) Eur.Comm.Rep. II–415; Omega, O.J.1970 L 242/22.

11. Ideal Standard distribution system, O.J.1985 L 20/38; Grohe distribution system, O.J.1985 L 19/17.

necessary for the size of the specialized shop or specialized department and keep adequate stocks of a representative selection of the relevant range, and the requirement that wholesalers carry and stock as far as possible the whole Grundig range.[12]

If the selective distribution system infringes Article 81(1), it will often qualify for an exemption under Article 81(3) unless it includes absolute territorial protection, restricts parallel imports or is used to control prices. The Commission is aware that selective distribution systems can improve the distribution of the goods and that the consumer benefits from the resulting provision of specialist sales and after-sales services. Thus, the Commission is generally receptive to arguments that additional obligations such as those imposed by Grundig are indispensable to the system and therefore exempt under Article 81(3).[13]

Vertical Restraints Regulation

The group exemptions for exclusive dealing, exclusive purchasing and franchise agreements were replaced in 2000 by Regulation 2790/99, known as the vertical restraints regulation. It is accompanied by lengthy vertical restraints guidelines. This regulation and its guidelines are more economic and less formalistic than the predecessors. The efficiency enhancing qualities of intrabrand vertical restraints are recognized. Supply, distribution (including selective distribution) and franchise agreements of firms with less than 30 percent market shares are generally exempt; this is known as a "safe harbor." Companies whose market shares exceed 30 percent may or may not be exempt, depending upon the results of individual competition law reviews. Since 2004, these may be undertaken by the Commission, national competition authorities and national courts. In either case, no vertical agreements containing so-called "hard core restraints" are exempt. These restraints concern primarily resale price maintenance, territorial and customer protection leading to market allocation, and in most instances exclusive dealing covenants that last more than five years.

§ 7.11 Patent Licensing Agreements, The Technology Transfer Regulations

In its seminal 1982 *Maize Seed* judgment, the Court of Justice addressed patent license restrictions under the Union's competition rules.[1] The Commission waited for this judgment before publishing the 1984 group exemption under Article 81(3) for patent licensing

---

12. Grundig's distribution system, O.J.1994 L 20/15, 21 point 35.

13. Grundig's distribution system, O.J.1994 L 20/15, 21.

§ 7.11

1. Nungesser v. Commission (1982) Eur.Comm.Rep. 2015.

agreements. In this case, a research institute financed by the French government (INRA) bred varieties of basic seeds. In 1960, INRA assigned to Kurt Eisele plant breeder's rights for maize seed in the Federal Republic of Germany. Eisele agreed to apply for registration of these rights in accordance with German law. In 1965, a formal agreement was executed by the parties. This agreement consisted of five relevant clauses.

Clause 1 gave Eisele the exclusive rights to "organize" sales of six identified varieties of maize seed propagated from basic seeds provided by INRA. This enabled Eisele to exercise control over distribution outlets. Eisele undertook not to deal in maize varieties other than those provided by INRA. Clause 2 required Eisele to place no restriction on the supply of seed to technically suitable distributors except for rationing in conditions of shortage. The prices charged to the distributors by Eisele were fixed in consultation with INRA, according to a specified formula. Clause 3 obligated Eisele to import from France for sale in Germany at least two-thirds of that territory's requirements for the registered varieties. This restricted Eisele's own production and sale to only one-third of the German market. Clause 4 concerned the protection by Eisele of INRA's proprietary rights, including its trademark, from infringement and granted Eisele the power to take any action to that end. Clause 5 contained a promise by INRA that no exports to Germany of the relevant varieties would take place otherwise than through the agency of Eisele. This meant that INRA would ensure that its French marketing organization would prevent the relevant varieties from being exported to Germany to parallel importers.

In September 1972, it became apparent that dealers in France were selling the licensed varieties of maize seed directly to German traders who were marketing the products in breach of the breeder's rights claimed by Eisele. This resulted in an action by Eisele in the German courts against one of the traders. The parties reached a court approved settlement under which the French trader promised to refrain from offering for sale without permission any variety of maize seed within the rights held by Eisele, and to pay a fine. In February 1974, another breach took place, this time advertising in the German press by a French dealer. In response to threats of legal proceedings, this dealer lodged a complaint with the Commission alleging breach of the Treaty of Rome competition rules.

The Commission considered both the agreement and the settlement to infringe Article 81(1) because they granted an exclusive license and provided absolute territorial protection. The Court of Justice reversed the Commission with respect to exclusivity, but upheld the Commission with respect to absolute territorial protection. The Court drew a distinction between "open" licenses which do not necessarily fall under Article 81(1), and "closed" licenses which do so.

Open license agreements are those which do not involve third parties. In *Maize Seed,* the obligation upon INRA or those deriving rights through INRA to refrain from producing or selling the relevant seeds in Germany was treated as an open license term. The Court held such clauses necessary to the dissemination of new technology inasmuch as potential licensees might otherwise be deterred from accepting the risk of cultivating and marketing new products. The Court defined closed licenses as those involving third parties. Thus, the obligation upon INRA or those deriving rights through INRA to prevent third parties from exporting the seeds into Germany without authorization, Eisele's concurrent use of his exclusive contractual rights, and his breeder's rights, to prevent all imports into Germany or exports to other member states were invalid under Article 85(1).

Patent Licensing Regulation

The Commission adopted in 1984 a patent licensing group exemption regulation under Article 81(3).[2] It acknowledged that patent licensing improves the production of goods and promotes technical progress by allowing licensees to operate with the latest technology. The Commission also believed that patent licensing increases both the number of production facilities and the quantity and quality of goods in the Common Market. Much of its focus concerned territorial restrictions in patent licensing agreements. Specifically, the following clauses were permitted:

(1) restraints on licensors granting rights to other licensees or exploiting the patent in the designated territory during the life of the patent;

(2) restraints on licensee exploitation of the invention in other EU countries to the extent the licensor has parallel patent rights;[3]

(3) restraints on licensee manufacture, use or active selling of the product in territories licensed to others, to the extent the licensor has parallel patent rights;

(4) restraints on licensees intended to keep them from actively or passively selling the product in territories licensed to others for five years after the product is first put on the market, to the extent the licensor has parallel patents; and

2. Commission Regulation 2349/84 as amended by Regulation 151/93, O.J. 1993 L 21/8.

3. Parallel patents are defined in the regulation as covering the same inven-

tion such that the licensor could bring an infringement action against unauthorized activities.

(5) restraints on licensees mandating use of the licensor's trademark on the product.

The distinction between active and passive selling was and remains critical. "Active selling" involves sending agents to call on customers, advertising or creating an office or distribution depot in an EU country other than the licensed territory. "Passive selling" involves responding to unsolicited requests to purchase products from customers outside the licensed territory. Similar regulations governed knowhow licensing.[4]

Transfer of Technology Regulation 240/96

In 1996 the Commission enacted Regulation 240/96 on the application of Article 81(3) of the Rome Treaty to transfer technology agreements. The intention of this Regulation was to combine the existing patent and knowhow block exemptions into a single regulation covering technology transfer agreements, and to simplify and harmonize the rules for patent and knowhow licensing. It contained detailed lists of permitted, permissible and prohibited clauses.

Regulation 240/96 stated that Article 81(1) of the Treaty did not apply to "pure patent and knowhow licensing agreements and missed patent and knowhow licensing agreements," as well as to agreements with ancillary provisions relating to intellectual property other than patents, when only two undertakings are parties and when one or more of eight listed obligations were included. These were obligations of limitation, such as not to license other undertakings to exploit the technology. There were time limits (5 years patents/10 years knowhow) for the exemption of these eight obligations in certain situations. Article 1 was known as the White List. Article 2 allowed technology transfers even when certain clauses existed (17 were listed). These clauses were considered generally not restrictive of competition. There were various obligations on the licensee, such as not divulging knowhow communicated by the licensor. Article 2 was known as the Permissible List.

Article 3 of Regulation 240/96 designated that Articles 1 and 2(2) did not apply when any one of seven obligations were present, such as restricting a party in the determination of prices, competition restrictions, limitations on production quantity, licensee improvement grant-back requirements, etc. Article 3 was known as the Black List. Article 4 carried the scope of the exemption provided for in Articles 1 and 2 to certain other restrictive agreements which were notified to the Commission and received no Commission opposition. Article 4 was known as the Gray List. Regulation 240/96, according to Article 5, did not apply to four classes of agreements, such as most agreements within a joint venture. But

---

4. Commission Regulation 2349/84   and 556/89. *See* Section 7.12.

under Article 5 it did apply to three forms of agreements, including where the licensor is itself a licensee of the technology and was authorized to grant sub-licenses.

The Commission retained power to withdraw benefits of the Regulation 240/96 if in a specific case the exempted agreement was incompatible with the conditions of Article 81(3) of the Treaty. Final articles provided some definitions, a list of what were deemed patents, preservation of confidentiality of information, and the repeal of the two regulations combined in this regulation.

Transfer of Technology Regulation 772/2004

The detailed regulation of technology transfer agreement clauses contained in Regulation 240/96 was replaced by Regulation 772/2004, which applies to patent, know-how and software copyright licensing. The new Regulation distinguishes agreements between those of "competing" and "noncompeting" parties, the latter being treated less strictly than the former. Parties are deemed "competing" if they compete (without infringing each other's IP rights) in either the relevant technology or product market, determined in each instance by what buyers regard as substitutes.[5] If the competing parties have a *combined* market share of 20 percent or less, their licensing agreements are covered by group exemption under Regulation 772/2004.[6] Noncompeting parties, on the other hand, benefit from the group exemption so long as their *individual* market shares do not exceed 30 percent.[7] Agreements initially covered by Regulation 772/2004 that subsequently exceed the "safe harbor" thresholds noted above lose their exemption subject to a two-year grace period.[8] Outside these exemptions, a "rule of reason" approach applies.

Inclusion of certain "hardcore restraints" causes license agreement to lose their group exemption. For competing parties, such restraints include price fixing,[9] output limitations on both parties,[10] limits on the licensee's ability to exploit its own technology,[11] and allocation of markets or competitors (subject to exceptions).[12] Specifically, restraints on active and passive selling by the licensee in a territory reserved for the licensor are allowed, as are active (but not passive) selling restraints by licensees in territories of other licensees.[13] Licensing agreements between noncompeting parties may not contain the "hardcore" restraint of maximum price fixing.[14] Active selling restrictions on licensees can be utilized, along with

5. Regulation 772/2004, Article 1(1)j.

6. *Id.*, Article 3(1).

7. *Id.*, Article 3(2).

8. *Id.*, Article 8(2).

9. *Id.*, Article 4(1)(a).

10. *Id.*, Article 4(1)(b).

11. *Id.*, Article 4(1)(d).

12. *Id.*, Article 4(1)(c).

13. *Id.*, Article 4(1)(c)(iv) and (v).

14. *Id.*, Article 4(2)(a).

passive selling restraints in territories reserved to the licensor or (for two years) another licensee.[15] For these purposes, the competitive status of the parties is decided at the outset of the agreement.[16]

Other license terms deemed "excluded restrictions" also cause a loss of exemption.[17] Such clauses include: (1) mandatory grant-backs or assignments of severable improvements by licensees, excepting nonexclusive license-backs;[18] (2) no-challenges by the licensee of the licensor's intellectual property rights, subject to the licensor's right to terminate upon challenge;[19] and (3) for noncompeting parties, restraints on the licensee's ability to exploit its own technology or either party's ability to carry out research and development (unless indispensable to prevent disclosure of the licensed Know-how).[20]

In all cases, exemption under Regulation 772/2004 may be withdrawn where in any particular case an agreement has effects that are incompatible with Article 81(3).[21]

§ 7.12   Know-how Licensing Agreements

Prior to the 1996 technology transfer regulation (above), there were two group exemptions which applied to know-how licensing agreements. Commission Regulation 2349/84 applied to agreements combining patent and know-how licenses. However, provisions concerning know-how in such mixed agreements were only covered by the group exemption in so far as the licensed patents were necessary for achieving the objects of the licensed technology and as long as at least one of the licensed patents remained in force. In such cases, the "mixed agreement" could qualify for an exemption under Regulation 556/89.

Regulation 556/89 applied to bilateral, pure know-how licensing agreements, bilateral mixed agreements not falling under Regulation 2349/84 and bilateral, pure know-how licensing or mixed agreements containing ancillary provisions relating to trademarks and other intellectual property rights.[1] The concept of know-how was broadly conceived in this regulation to include "a body of technical information that is secret, substantial and identified in any appropriate form."[2] "Secret" meant that the know-how package as a body was not generally known or easily accessible. Each individual component of the know-how did not have to be unknown or unobtainable. "Substantial" meant that the know-how includes

15. *Id.*, Article 4(2)(b).
16. *Id.*, Article 4(3).
17. *Id.*, Article 5.
18. *Id.*, Article 5(1)(a).
19. *Id.*, Article 5(1)(b) and (c).
20. *Id.*, Article 5(2).

21. *Id.*, Article 6.

§ 7.12

1. Art. 1(1) of Regulation 556/89.
2. Art. 1(7)(1) of Regulation 556/89.

important information regarding a manufacturing process, a product or service, or for their development. It excluded information which is trivial. The know-how also had to be useful. Such information was useful if it could be expected to improve the competitive position of the licensee. These approaches, along with the focus on active and passive territorial sales restraints discussed above regarding patent licenses, have largely been retained in Regulations 240/96 and 772/2004. The latter group exemption now regulates both patent licensing and know-how licensing agreements. Its content is detailed in Section 7.11.

§ 7.13 Franchise Agreements

The Pronuptia Case

Prior to its landmark decision in *Pronuptia,*[1] the Commission had never sought to apply Article 81 to franchise agreements. *Pronuptia* arose from the refusal of a franchisee to pay license fees to the franchisor. The distribution of the Pronuptia brand wedding attire in the Federal Republic of Germany was handled by shops operated by the German franchisor and by independent retailers through franchise agreements with that franchisor. The franchisee had obtained franchises for three areas (Hamburg, Oldenburg and Hannover). The franchisor granted the franchisee exclusive rights to market and advertise under the name of "Pronuptia de Paris" in these specific territories. The franchisor promised not to open any shops or provide any goods or services to another person in those territories. The franchisor also agreed to assist the franchisee with business strategies and profitability.

The franchisee agreed to assume all the risk of opening a franchise as an independent retailer. The franchisee also agreed to the following: (1) To sell Pronuptia goods only in the store specified in the contract and to decorate and design the shop according to the franchisor's instructions; (2) to purchase 80 percent of wedding related attire and a proportion of evening dresses from the franchisor, and to purchase the rest of such merchandise only from sellers approved by the franchisor; (3) to pay a one time entrance fee for exclusive rights to the specified territory and a yearly royalty fee of 10 percent of the total sales of Pronuptia and all other products; (4) to advertise only with the franchisor's approval in a method which would enhance the international reputation of the franchise; (5) to make the sale of bridal fashions the franchisee's main business purpose; (6) to consider the retail price recommendations of the

§ 7.13   (1986) Eur.Comm.Rep. 353.

1. Pronuptia de Paris GmbH v.
Pronuptia de Paris Irmgard Schillgallis

franchisor; (7) to refrain from competing directly or indirectly during the contract period or for one year afterward with any Pronuptia store; and (8) to obtain the franchisor's prior approval before assigning the rights and obligations arising under the contract to a third party.

In due course, the case was referred to the European Court of Justice. The Court's judgment concentrates on the crucial issue of whether franchise agreements come within Article 81. The Court draws a preliminary distinction between "distribution" franchises such as Pronuptia as opposed to "service" and "production" franchises. The Court concludes that a franchising system as such does not interfere with competition. Consequently, clauses essential to enable franchising to function are not prohibited. Thus, the franchisor can communicate know-how or assistance and help franchisees apply its methods. The franchisor can take reasonable steps to keep its know-how or assistance from becoming available to competitors. Location clauses forbidding the franchisee during the contract, or for a reasonable time thereafter, from opening a store with a similar or identical object in an area where it might compete with another member of the franchise network were necessary for distribution franchises and therefore permissible. The obligation of the franchisee not to sell a licensed store without prior consent of the franchisor was similarly allowable.

Clauses necessary to preserve the identity and reputation of the franchise network, such as decorations and trademark usage, were upheld. The reputation and identity of the network may also justify a clause requiring the franchisee to sell only products supplied by the franchisor or by approved sources, at least if it would be too expensive to monitor the quality of the stock otherwise. Nevertheless, each franchisee must be allowed to buy from other franchisees. The requirement of uniformity may also justify advertisement approvals by the franchisor, but the franchisee must be allowed to set and advertise resale prices. The Court rejected the view that clauses tending to divide the Common Market between franchisor and franchisee or between franchisees are always necessary to protect the know-how or the identity and the reputation of the network. The location clause in *Pronuptia* was seen as potentially supporting exclusive territories. In combination, location clauses and exclusive territories may divide markets and so restrict competition within the network. Even if a potential franchisee would not take the risk of joining the network by making its own investment because it could not expect a profitable business due to the absence of protection from competition from other franchisees, that consideration (in the Court's view) could be taken into account only under an Article 81(3) individual exemption. The Commission, in fact, ultimately granted such an exemption to Pronuptia.[2]

Franchising Regulation

The Commission, following the European Court of Justice decision in *Pronuptia*,[3] adopted a group exemption regulation for franchise agreements under Article 81(3).[4] Regulation 4087/88 required each franchisee to identify itself as an independent enterprise apart from the trademark/service mark/trade name owner. This disclosure could avoid joint and several franchisor liability for the provision by franchisees of defective goods or services. Regulation 4087/88 defined a "franchise" as a package of industrial or intellectual property rights relating to trademarks, trade names, signs, utility models, designs, copyrights, know-how or patents exploited for the resale of goods or the provision of services to customers.[5] "Franchise agreements" were defined as those in which the franchisor grants the franchisee, in exchange for direct or indirect financial consideration, the right to exploit a franchise so as to market specified types of goods and/or services.[6] A "master franchisee agreement" involved the right to exploit a franchise by concluding franchising agreements with third parties.[7]

Vertical Restraints Regulation

Starting with these basics, Regulation 4087/88 proceeded to detail permitted and prohibited clauses in EU franchise agreements.... This approach remained in force until 2000, when Regulation 2790/99 (the "vertical restraints" group exemption) took over franchise agreements, along with exclusive dealing and other distribution agreements. Regulation 2790/99 is accompanied by lengthy vertical restraints guidelines. This regulation and its guidelines are more economic and less formalistic than the predecessors. Supply and distribution agreements of firms with less than 30 percent market shares are generally exempt; this is known as a "safe harbor." Companies whose market shares exceed 30 percent may or may not be exempt, depending upon the results of individual competition law reviews. In either case, no vertical agreements containing so-called "hard core restraints" are exempt. These restraints concern primarily resale price maintenance, territorial and customer protection leading to market allocation, and in most instances exclusive dealing covenants that last more than five years.

---

2. Re Pronuptia, 30 O.J.Eur.Comm. 39 (L13/1987).

3. Pronuptia de Paris GmbH v. Pronuptia de Paris Irmgard Schillgallis (1986) Eur.Comm.Rep. 353.

4. Regulation 4087/88.

5. *Id.*, Article 1(3)(a).

6. *Id.*, Article 1(3)(b).

7. *Id.*, Article 1(3)(c).

§ 7.14   Article 81—Undertakings and Concerted Practices

Undertakings

There can be no violation of Article 81(1) unless there is an agreement between "undertakings," a decision by an association of undertakings or a concerted practice among undertakings. In other words, unilateral behavior is not caught by Article 81(1).[1]

The term "undertaking" as used in EU competition law refers to every entity engaged in an economic activity, regardless of the legal status of the entity and the way in which it is financed.[2] Thus, partnerships, sole proprietorships and even natural persons may be "undertakings" when they engage in business or commercial activities.[3] However, employees acting in the scope of their employment[4] and public bodies serving exclusively a social function[5] are not considered undertakings. In addition, Article 81 applies to associations of undertakings such as trade and professional associations. The fact that the association itself may not be pursuing a commercial activity—in the sense that it is not profit-oriented—does not mean that it escapes the application of Article 81.[6]

Agreements and Decisions

Article 81 also requires proof of an agreement, decision of an association or a concerted practice. At first glance, one might conclude that Article 81 is much narrower in its sphere of application than Section 1 of the Sherman Act which applies to every contract, combination and conspiracy. However, the application of this requirement by the Commission and Court illustrate that this is not the case. The concept of agreement encompasses not only legally binding contracts, but also oral agreements between undertakings[7] and gentlemen's agreements.[8] According to the Commission: "An agreement within the meaning of Article 81 may exist where the parties reach a common consensus on a plan which limits

§ 7.14

1. *See* Commission v. Bayer AG (2004) Eur.Comm.Rep. I–00000 (Joined Cases C–2/01P and C/3/01P) (unilateral refusal to fill large pharmaceutical orders blocks parallel trade).

2. SAT Fluggesellschaft v. Eurocontrol, (1994) Eur.Comm.Rep. I–43 ¶ 18; Poucet, (1993) Eur.Comm.Rep. I–637 ¶ 17.

3. AOIP/Beyrard, O.J.1976 L 6/8, 12; Vaessen/Moris, O.J.1979 L 19/32, 34; RAI/Unitel, O.J.1978 L 157/39, 40.

4. Suiker Unie v. Commission, (1975) Eur.Comm.Rep. 1663, 2024 ¶ 538.

See also Answer of EC Commission to Question No. 2391/83, O.J.1984 C 222/21.

5. *See e.g.* SAT Fluggesellschaft v. Eurocontrol, (1994) Eur.Comm.Rep. I–43; Poucet, (1993) Eur.Comm.Rep. I–637.

6. Heintz van Landewyck Sàrl v. Commission, (1980) Eur.Comm.Rep. 3125, 3250.

7. Tepea v. Commission, (1978) Eur. Comm.Rep. 1391, 1412.

8. International Chemical Cartel, O.J.1969 L 192/5.

or is likely to limit their commercial freedom by determining the lines of their mutual action or abstention from action in the market."[9] Decisions of an association generally refer to the by-laws, internal statutes, and regulations.[10] However, even recommendations of the associations directed at its members can be considered decisions.[11]

Concerted Practices

If bilateral conduct does not fall under the definition of agreement or decision, the Commission may find that it qualifies as a concerted practice if the conduct has an appreciable restraint on competition. The meaning of concerted practice is critical to Article 81(1). It was included in Article 81 to forestall the possibility of undertakings evading the application of Article 81(1) by colluding in an anticompetitive manner falling short of definite agreement.[12]

The Commission and the Court of Justice considered the concept of a concerted practice extensively in *Imperial Chemical Industries (ICI) v. Commission*.[13] *ICI* involved nearly all the producers of aniline dyes in the EU when it had only six member states. Three industry-wide price increases between 1964 and 1967 took place over the full range of more than 6000 aniline dye products. The Commission, acting on information furnished by trade organizations using dyestuffs, found ten producers of aniline dyes in violation of Article 81(1) by concerting on these price increases. Together they held about 80 percent of the EU aniline dyes market. Proof of the concerted practices tendered by the Commission included: (1) the near identity of the price increases in each country; (2) the uniformity of products covered by the price increases; (3) the exact timing of the increases; (4) the simultaneous dispatch to subsidiaries and representatives of price increase instructions that were nearly identical in form and content; and (5) the existence of informal contacts and occasional meetings between the enterprises concerned. The Commission decided these circumstantial facts warranted its conclusion that a concerted price fixing practice took place.[14]

On appeal, the Court of Justice affirmed. The Court distinguished the concept of concerted practice from an agreement or decision under Article 81(1): "A form of coordination between undertakings which, without going so far as to amount to an

9. PVC, O.J. 1994 L 239/14, 25 point 30.

10. Centraal Bureau voor de Rijwielhandel, O.J.1978 L 20/18 point 18; BPICA, O.J.1977 L 299/18, 23.

11. Verband der Sachversicherer v. Commission, (1987) Eur.Comm.Rep. 405, 454; Heintz van Landewyck Sàrl v.

Commission, (1980) Eur.Comm.Rep. 3125, 3250.

12. PVC, O.J. 1994 L 239/14, 25 point 33.

13. (1972) Eur.Comm.Rep. 619.

14. (1969) Common Mkt.L.Rep. 494.

agreement properly so called, knowingly substitutes a practical cooperation between them for the risks of competition."[15] The Court added that while independent parallel behavior by competitors did not fall within the concept of a concerted practice, the fact of such behavior could be taken as a strong indicator of a concerted practice where it produced market conditions, especially price equilibrium, different from those thought ordinarily to prevail under competition. The cartel's defense of "conscious parallelism" on prices was therefore another piece of evidence affirming the Commission's enforcement decision. The sum total of the evidence on which the Commission relied to find a concerted practice was explicable, in the eyes of the Court, only by convergent intentions of producers to increase prices and avoid competitive conditions in the aniline dyes market.[16]

The impact of the concept of concerted practice in competition law depends on the evidence available to prove cooperative business behavior. Parallel conduct may be relevant to the extent that it is evidence of a concerted practice. Under current law, concerted conduct may be inferred if parallel behaviour exists and contact between the parties is evidenced.[17] As such, whether concerted conduct exists is a question of fact rather than law and has proven useful in combatting cartels. Thus, the mere exchange of information that facilitates price conformity can be sanctioned.[18] In the *Sugar Cartel* case, for example, the Court of Justice reaffirmed *ICI* and then laid down a general warning against competitor cooperation and contact. It held that the EU competition rules inherently require that each undertaking independently determine its activities in the Common Market.[19] Direct or indirect contact with the object or effect of influencing the market conduct of an actual or potential competitor, the disclosure of courses of market conduct of an actual or potential competitor or the disclosure of courses of market conduct intended for adoption by others, is prohibited.[20] But quarterly price announcements, simultaneously released and identical in amount, may not constitute a concerted practice if other plausible explanations exist.[21] Expert testimony suggesting that

---

15. This has become the standard definition of concerted practiced used by the Court and the Commission. *See* Ahlström Oy & ORS v. Commission (1993) Eur.Comm.Rep. I–1307 para. 71; Cartonboard, O.J. 1994 L 243/1, 40 point 126; PVC, O.J. 1994 L 239/14, 25 point 32.

16. ICI v. Commission (1972) Eur. Comm.Rep. 619.

17. Società Italiano Vetro v. Commission, (1992) Eur.Comm.Rep. II–1403;

Åhlström Oy v. Commission, (1993) Eur. Comm.Rep. I–1307.

18. Re Fatty Acids, O.J. 1987 L 3/17.

19. *See also* Cartonboard, O.J. 1994 L 243/1, point 126.

20. Suiker Unie UA v. Commission (1975) Eur.Comm.Rep. 1663.

21. Ahlström Oy & ORS v. Commission (1993) Eur.Comm.Rep. I–1307. (Cases 89/85 et al.).

parallel pricing can be a rational response to market forces may provide the necessary explanation.

However, the Commission believes that oligopolies can be attacked using Article 86 (see Section 7.18) and a theory of collective abuse of a dominant position.[22]

§ 7.15   Article 81—Competitive Impact

Article 81(1) only applies when an agreement, decision or concerted practice has as its object *or* effect the prevention, restriction or distortion of competition within the Common Market. Distinctions can be drawn as between preventing, restraining and distorting competition, but the sweep of this language basically creates a legal and conceptual net in which most activities of competing enterprises may be examined by the Commission. The manner in which the Commission has cut official holes in this net through exemptions and policy announcements has already been discussed. Nevertheless, since there is a sense in which nearly all actions by enterprises affect their competitive position in the marketplace, the language of Article 81 grants expansive administrative power. However, the Court of Justice has imposed a "rule of reason" test when evaluating competitive impact. Only those restraints which are "sufficiently deleterious" to competition in the context in which they appear are prohibited and void.[1]

Restraints of competition by enterprises may take place at different levels of economic activity. Restraints involving competition among firms operating at the same level in the production or distribution process are known as horizontal restraints. Businesses operating at different levels may restrain competition between themselves and third parties. These are known as vertical restraints.

Consten and Grundig Case

In the well known *Grundig* decision, the Court of Justice declined to follow the recommendations of its Advocate General and affirmed that both horizontal and vertical restraints are embraced by Article 81(1).[2] This decision involved a German manufacturer of consumer electronics that established an exclusive dealing agreement with Consten, a French distributor. In other words, *Grundig* was a vertical restraints case. The agreement was made prior to the

22. Re Flat Glass (1990–4) Common Mkt.L.Rep. 535 (Comm. Dec. 89/93).

§ 7.15

1. Société Technique Minière v. Maschinenbau Ulm GmbH (1966) Eur. Comm.Rep. 235; Nungesser v. Commis-

sion (1982) Eur.Comm.Rep. 2015; European Night Services v. Commission (1998) Eur.Comm.Rep. II–3141.

2. Consten and Grundig v. Commission (1966) Eur.Comm.Rep. 299.

adoption of the first group exemption, Regulation 67/67 (see Section 7.9). As part of the agreement, Grundig undertook not to deliver its products directly or indirectly to anyone else in France. Grundig also contracted to similar territorial restraints with its other Common Market dealers outside of France. Consten agreed to sell only in its French territory. The result was that no dealer or wholesaler of Grundig products in the EU could sell outside its contracted territory. To strengthen this absolute pattern of territorial distribution, Grundig assigned the French trademark "GINT" to Consten. GINT was placed on all products delivered to Consten in addition to the usual "GRUNDIG" mark.

When prices in France were 20 to 25 percent above those in Germany, a French firm began competing with Consten by importing Grundig products bearing the GINT mark from a renegade German wholesaler. Consten then sued the importer in the French courts for infringement of GINT and violation of French law on unfair competition. The importer replied that the Grundig–Consten contract and the GINT assignment were void under Articles 81(1) and 81(2). Meanwhile, Grundig notified its series of exclusive dealing agreements to the Commission and sought Article 81(3) exemptions for them. The Cour d'Appel de Paris stayed the proceedings under French law. The Commission found the entire agreement prohibited by Article 81(1) and denied an 81(3) exemption. Although not restrictive of competition between Grundig and Consten, the agreement was restrictive of Consten and third-party sellers of Grundig products. It amounted, the Commission said, to absolute territorial protection in France from the competition of parallel imports of Grundig products. Since, in the Commission's view, the object of the agreement was to restrain competition, an extensive market analysis of its actual competitive impact was not necessary.

The Court of Justice upheld the Commission's position on coverage of vertical restraints by Article 81(1) and on the absence of need for extensive market analysis in this case. However, it partially accepted the argument that, in ascertaining whether competition was restrained under Article 81(1), the Commission ought to have considered the whole of the market for consumer electronics (where Grundig faced strong interbrand competition). Competition within the overall market, it was argued, was increased by the entry of Grundig into France through Consten's exclusive, territorially protected sales. This increase in interbrand competition, the argument continued, outweighed the restrictions on intrabrand competition in Grundig products.

The Court responded to these arguments by holding that only certain clauses of the Grundig–Consten agreement, the absolute territorial protection clause and the GINT assignment, infringed

Article 81(1). Only these clauses were automatically void under Article 85(2). The remainder of the agreement, including the exclusive dealing provisions, was severable and legally binding. Thus, Grundig could enter the French market through an exclusive retailer, but that retailer could not be sheltered from other Grundig sellers in the Common Market. These principles were subsequently incorporated in Regulation 67/67 for which *Grundig* was an important test case. A modified Grundig selective distribution system was subsequently granted an individual exemption by the Commission.[3]

§ 7.16 Market Division and Intellectual Property Rights

In *Grundig,* the Court of Justice affirmed the Commission's remedial order to the parties to refrain from any measure tending to obstruct or impede the acquisition of Grundig products. To reduce the negative impact of national industrial and intellectual property rights on regional trade and competition, the Commission and the Court of Justice have relied on a number of Treaty provisions. In the *Grundig* case, the Court held that Article 81 limitations may be imposed on the exercise or use of national trademark rights. In the Court's opinion, absolute territorial distribution rights are not essential to the protection or benefit sought to be conferred by trademarks. The net result was a Court order prohibiting Consten from exercising its rights under French trademark law to use GINT as a trade and competition barrier.

When used with the object or effect of preventing, restraining or distorting Common Market competition, national industrial and intellectual property rights have generally yielded to the competition law of the European Union.[1] In *Deutsche Grammophon*, for example, results comparable to those in *Grundig* were achieved with copyright-based territorial restraints.[2] When record imports into Germany from the French subsidiary of Deutsche Grammophon caused competition for the parent company, then enjoying lawful resale price maintenance in Germany, it sought infringement protection under German copyright law. Competition law restraints on the exercise (as opposed to the existence) of national copyright rights denied infringement protection. Deutsche Grammophon's German copyright rights were said to be "exhausted" by the sales to its French subsidiary. Dividing up the Common Market was not perceived to be essential to the financial reward and other

3. Official Journal L233/1 (Aug. 30, 1985); Official Journal L20/15 (Jan. 25, 1994).

§ 7.16

1. In addition to the examples discussed here, *see* Herlitz v. Commission, (1994) Eur.Comm.Rep. II–00549 (Case No. T–66/92); Parker Pen v. Commission, (1994) Eur.Comm.Rep. II–00531 (Case No. T–77/92).

2. (1971) Eur.Comm.Rep. 487.

purposes of German copyright. On the other hand, increased intra-brand Deutsche Grammophon sales and price competition was completely compatible with the Treaty of Rome.

Much of the litigation surrounding intellectual property rights in the Common Market has been undertaken in connection with Article 30 and the free movement of goods. As in the competition law area, such rights have generally given way to the Treaty of Rome.[3]

§ 7.17   Articles 81 and 82—Trade Impact

De Minimis Trade Impact

To come within the prohibition of Article 81, an agreement, decision or concerted practice must raise a probability that it will appreciably affect trade between member states.[1] Because of this requirement, it is insufficient to consider the object of restrictive agreements under EU law without also considering their potential trade effects. While in certain cases, such as *Grundig,* it is possible to avoid an extensive market analysis of the competitive impact of restrictive agreements because an intent to restrain competition is clear, analysis of an agreement's *trade* impact is always required. This is doubly true because agreements that affect trade or competition between member states in a *de minimis* fashion are not subject to Article 81(1).

In *Völk v. Vervaecke,* a German manufacturer of washing machines contracted with a Dutch exclusive dealer, Vervaecke. The contract was similar to that of Consten–Grundig and provided for absolute territorial protection. Völk's share of the German washing machine market ranged between 0.20 and 0.05 percent. This time the Court of Justice, on voluntary reference from the Oberlandesgericht in Munich, emphasized the overall product market effect of the restrictive agreement. From that interbrand perspective, the Court advised that the agreement "affect[ed] the market insignificantly" and therefore escaped Article 81(1).[2] This *de minimis* doctrine was developed more fully in subsequent decisions and the Commission's Notice on Agreements of Minor Importance.[3]

Intrastate Trade

In theory, agreements, decisions and concerted practices of a purely national character not affecting trade between member states are outside the scope of Article 81. In practice, however, few

---

3. *See* Chapter 4.

§ 7.17

1. Remia v. Commission (1987) Eur. Comm.Rep. 2545.

2. (1969) Eur.Comm.Rep. 295.

3. Official Journal C231/2 (1986).

national activities of any significance are likely to escape its reach. For example, in the *VCH* case, an entirely national cartel of cement merchants in Holland held a steadily declining two-thirds share of the Dutch retail cement market. The cartel maintained certain fixed and recommended prices and resale conditions as well as a variety of other restraints on competition among its members. Prior to 1967 the merchants' cartel had been exclusively allied with a German, Dutch and Belgian manufacturers' cartel for its supplies. The Commission noted that about one-third of the total sales of cement in Holland were of cheaper products imported from Belgium and West Germany. It held that the merchants' agreement therefore restricted competition within the Common Market and affected trade between member states. In the Commission's view, the agreement inhibited German and Belgian producers from increasing their share of the Dutch cement market. The Commission denied an Article 81(3) individual exemption and a negative clearance for the agreement.

On appeal, the Court of Justice upheld the Commission's decision in all respects.[4] It issued a broad opinion aimed at all restrictive national cartels even when imported products are not involved:

> A restrictive agreement extending to the whole territory of a member state by its very nature consolidates the national boundaries thus hindering the economic interpenetration desired by the Treaty and so protecting national production.

The expansive approach of the Court of Justice to trade impact analysis under Article 81 is also relevant to Article 82 which contains the same language.

§ 7.18 Article 82

Article 82 of the Treaty of Rome prohibits abuse by one or more undertakings of a dominant position within a substantial part of the Common Market insofar as the abuse may affect trade between member states. The existence of a dominant position is not prohibited by European law. Only its abuse is proscribed. Although both Articles 81 and 82 may be applied to the same business practices,[1] they constitute two independent legal instruments addressing different legal situations.[2] Whereas Article 81 is directed at restraints of competition through agreement or concerted practices between undertakings, Article 82 is concerned with restrictive

---

4. VCH v. Commission (1972) Eur. Comm.Rep. 977.

§ 7.18

1. Ahmed Saeed Flugreisen v. Zentrale zur Bekämpfung unlauteren Wett-

bewerbs, (1989) Eur.Comm.Rep. 803, 849 para. 37.

2. Tetra Pak Rausing v. Commission (1990) Eur.Comm.Rep. II–309, II–356 para. 22.

practices arising from the position of the undertaking regardless of the existence of an agreement or concerted practice between undertakings.[3] However, fines for the same conduct under both Articles 81 and 82 will not be permitted by the ECJ.[4]

Article 82 differs fundamentally from Article 81 in other respects. There are no provisions to declare abuses by dominant enterprise(s) automatically void, nor to permit any exemptions from its prohibitions. Thus, under the administrative frameworks of Regulation 17 and Regulation 1, no individual or group exemptions can be granted by the Commission for Article 82 (see Sections 7.6–7.9). The absence of exemptions means that there has been little incentive for dominant firms to notify their abuses to the Commission. Regulations 17 and 1 grant the Commission the same powers with reference to Article 82 as it possesses under Article 81 to obtain information, investigate corporate affairs, render infringement decisions, and fine or penalize offenders.

A few Commission decisions concerning Article 82 have their origins in complaints to the Commission from competitors or those abused. Generally, however, the Commission has acted on its own initiative in Article 82 proceedings. Some of the Commission's decisions have been the subject of appeal to the Court of Justice, which occasionally has received Article 82 issues on reference from national courts under the Article 234 preliminary ruling procedure. A limited number of Article 82 cases have been resolved informally through Commission negotiations. To highlight the more important developments in the interpretation of the language and scope of Article 82, a selection of cases and issues follows.

§ 7.19   Article 82—Dominant Positions

Unless an enterprise or group of enterprises possesses a dominant position within a substantial part of the Common Market, no questions of abuse can arise. A dominant position may exist on either the supply or demand side of the market.[1] An undertaking has a dominant position when it is able to hinder the maintenance of effective competition because it is able to behave to an appreciable extent independently of its competitors, its customers and ultimately of the consumers.[2] In determining the existence of a dominant position, the primary factor is the market share of the undertaking. According to the Court of Justice, save in exceptional

---

3. *Id.*

4. ACF Chemiefarma v. Commission (1970) Eur.Comm.Rep. 661.

§ 7.19

1. Re Eurofima (1973) Common Mkt. L.Rep. D217 (dominant buyer).

2. Bodson v. Pompes Funèbres (1988) Eur.Comm.Rep. 2479, 2514; Société alsacienne et lorraine de télécommunications et d'électronique v. Novasam, (1988) Eur.Comm.Rep. 5987, 6008–9.

circumstances, very large market shares are evidence in themselves of the existence of a dominant position.[3] This is presumptively the case, for example, where the market share is 50 percent or more.[4] The Court has even held that a market share of 40 percent may constitute dominance under Article 82.[5] Such a percentage is well below the threshold market share associated with monopolization cases under Section 2 of the Sherman Antitrust Act. On the other end of the scale, the Court has indicated that a market share of 10 percent would ordinarily rule out the existence of dominance.[6]

Continental Can Case

A celebrated merger case involved Continental Can, a large United States corporation.[7] It is a leading case on the existence of a dominant position under Article 82 law. Evidence of Continental Can's worldwide and German national market strength in the supply of certain metal containers and tops, a concentrated market characterized by ineffective consumers and competitors, and strong technical and financial barriers to entry were sufficient for the Commission to find the existence of a dominant position in certain areas of Germany. In so doing, the Commission stressed that enterprises are in a dominant position:

> when they have the power to behave independently, which puts them in a position to act without taking into account their competitors, purchasers or suppliers ... This power does not necessarily have to derive from an absolute domination ... it is enough that they be strong enough as a whole to ensure to those enterprises an overall independence of behavior, even if there are differences in intensity in their influence on different partial markets.[8]

Power to behave independently of competitors, purchasers or suppliers amounting to a dominant position must be exercisable with reference to the supply or acquisition of particular goods or services, *i.e.,* a market. In *Continental Can* the Commission distinguished between that enterprise's powerful position around the world and in the EU with reference to the generic market for light metal containers, and its dominant position in Germany with reference to the particular markets for preserved meat and shellfish tins and metal caps for glass jars. Thus, initial Commission selec-

---

3. AKZO Chemie v. Commission (1991) Eur.Comm.Rep. 3359 ¶ 60; Hoffmann–La Roche v. Commission, (1979) Eur.Comm.Rep. 461 ¶ 41.

4. AKZO Chemie v. Commission (1991) Eur.Comm.Rep. 3359 ¶ 60.

5. United Brands v. Commission, (1978) Eur.Comm.Rep. 207.

6. Metro v. Commission, (1986) Eur. Comm.Rep. 3021.

7. Europemballage Corporation and Continental Can Co., Inc. v. Commission (1972) Common Mkt.L.Rep. D11 (Commission); (1973) Eur.Comm.Rep. 215 (Court of Justice).

8. *Id.*

tion of the appropriate geographic and product market is the key to its analysis of whether a dominant position exists or not. It is also the key to the utility of its dominant position formula as set out in the *Continental Can* opinion. On such selection hinges the determination of the market power of the enterprise concerned. The broader the market for goods or services is defined (light metal cans versus cans for preserved meat, etc.), the less likely there will be overall independence of behavior from competitors, purchasers or suppliers. The same is true for broader geographic markets selected by the Commission (*e.g.,* the EU versus Germany or parts thereof).

On appeal to the Court of Justice, the Commission's guiding principles for determining the existence of a dominant position under Article 86 were not seriously questioned. The Court did challenge the Commission's delineation of the relevant *product* market and its failure to explain in full how Continental Can had the power to behave independently in the preserved meat, shellfish, and metal top markets. Its German market shares were, by the Commission's calculation, 75, 85, and 55 percent respectively. Regarding the first criticism the Court said:

> The products in question have a special market only if they can be individualized not only by the mere fact that they are used for packaging certain products but also by special production characteristics which give them a specific suitability for this purpose.[9]

In other words the Commission failed to make clear, for the purpose of assessing the existence of a dominant position, why the markets for preserved meat tins, preserved fish tins, and metal tops for glass jars should be treated separately and independently of the general market for light metal containers.

The Commission's failure here overlapped with the Court's second point:

> A dominant position in the market for light metal containers for canned meat and fish cannot be decisive insofar as it is not proved that competitors in other fields but not in the market for light metal containers cannot, by mere adaptation, enter this market with sufficient strength to form a serious counterweight.[10]

The Court felt that the existence or lack of competition from substitute materials such as plastic or glass as well as potential competition from new entrants to the metal container industry or purchasers who might produce their own tins were also aspects of market power insufficiently explored by the Commission. Under the

9. *Id.*

10. *Id.*

Commission's own formula for establishing a dominant position, the Court annulled the decision because it did not "sufficiently explain the facts and appraisals of which it [was] based."

The Court's emphasis in *Continental Can* on "special production characteristics," entry barriers, and potential competition amounted to instructions to the Commission to do its homework a little better in future market power analyses under Article 82. Evaluating potential competition, of course, involves hypothetical calculations with which even an expert Commission would have difficulty. Yet these factors, as well as those considered by the Commission, made up the commercial realities of the German marketplace for canned meat and fish tins and metal tops for glass jars. What is clear from the Court's *Continental Can* opinion is that dominance can be found under Article 82 in sub-product markets such as these, provided the Commission is exhaustive in its research and analysis.

Market Analysis and Dominant Positions

Subsequent opinions of the Court have elaborated upon the product market analysis presented in *Continental Can*. The "interchangeability" of products for specific uses is a critical factor in determining the relevant product market under Article 82.[11] Thus, bananas were a proper product market since their interchangeability with other fresh fruits was limited.[12] And the replacement market for tires (as distinct from original equipment) is another sub-market capable of sustaining a dominant position.[13] In exceptional circumstances, even a brand name product may be the relevant sub-market.[14]

Partial *geographic* markets can also be relevant to Article 82 market power analyses. A dominant position must exist within a "substantial" part of the Common Market. The Commission discussed geographic markets amounting to the whole of Germany in its opinion concerning tins and metal tops. Yet each of these products has different transport costs. The geographic commercial realities of competition in metal tops, given their relatively low level of transport costs, are likely to be much broader than that for tins. The same comparison can be made as between small and large tins. The Court held that the Commission's geographic delineation

---

11. Hoffmann–La Roche v. Commission (1979) Eur.Comm.Rep. 461.

12. United Brands Co. v. Commission (1978) Eur.Comm.Rep. 207.

13. Michelin NV v. Commission (1983) Eur.Comm.Rep. 3461.

14. General Motors Continental NV v. Commission (1975) Eur.Comm.Rep.

1367 (legal monopoly over import certificates for which excessive prices were charged); Hugin Cash Registers Ltd. v. Commission (1979) Eur.Comm.Rep. 1869 (spare parts for brand name product must be supplied to service competitor.)

of the markets for large and small tins in *Continental Can* was at odds with some of its own evidence on their relative transport costs. The commercial realities of potential competition in small tins appeared to go beyond the national boundaries of Germany. Thus the Commission's delineation of the particular geographic markets in *Continental Can* was insufficiently explained and appraised. Later decisions have deferred to the Commission's expertise and discretion in selecting relevant geographic markets. Belgium, Holland, and Southern Germany, for example, have been held substantial parts of the Common Market for Article 82 purposes.[15]

In 1997, the Commission issued a "Notice on the Definition of Relevant Market For Purposes of Community Competition Law."[16] This Notice covers Article 81 and 82 cases, as well as mergers and acquisitions, and takes into account both supply and demand-side substitutability.

When exclusive intellectual property rights are conferred by national states, the question of the existence of a dominant position remains vital. A patent, copyright or trademark for an individual product does not necessarily give an enterprise independent market power.[17] Other patented or nonpatented products of a similar nature may provide effective market competition and thereby protect suppliers and purchasers from abuse. The full market power analysis required in *Continental Can* must be undertaken. Similarly, the absence of patent rights is no barrier to finding a dominant position where know-how and costly and complex technology give former patent holders complete market power.[18]

Collective Dominance

In establishing the existence of a dominant position, the Commission has tended to look at commercial realities not technical legal distinctions. Thus, a dominant position may be collectively held by several otherwise independent undertakings even if these undertakings individually do not have a dominant position. In the *European Sugar Cartel* case, the Commission concluded that two producers of sugar responsible for 85 percent of all the sugar sales in Holland held a dominant position because of the contacts between them.[19] In that case, the two producers had cooperated in the purchase of raw materials, the adoption of production quotas, the

15. Re European Sugar Cartel (1975) Eur.Comm.Rep. 1663.

16. O.J. C 372/5 (Dec. 9, 1997).

17. Parke, Davis v. Probel and Centrafarm (1968) Eur.Comm.Rep. 55; Sirena v. Eda GMBH (1971) Eur.Comm.Rep. 69. *But see* Radio Telefis Eireann v. Commission (Magill TV Guide), 4 Common Mkt.L.Rep. 586 (1991).

18. Commercial Solvents Corp. v. Commission (1973) 12 Common Mkt. L.Rev. D50 (Commission); (1974) Eur. Comm.Rep. 223 (Court of Justice).

19. European Sugar Cartel, O.J.1973 L 140/17 on appeal Suiker Unie v. Commission (1975) Eur.Comm.Rep. 1663.

use of by-products, the pooling of research, advertising and sales promotion, and the unification of prices and terms of sale.

This theory of *collective dominance*, espoused by the Commission in subsequent cases,[20] has been accepted by the Court of Justice. The basic requirement is that the undertakings "be linked in such a way that they adopt the same conduct on the market."[21] In *Società Italiano Vetra SpA*,[22] for example, the Court of First Instance held that there is nothing to prevent two or more independent economic entities from being united by some economic links, and by virtue of that fact, together they hold a dominant position on the market. "This could be the case, for example, where two or more independent undertakings jointly have, through agreements or licenses, a technological lead affording them the power to behave to an appreciable extent independently of their competitors, their customers and ultimately of their consumers."[23]

§ 7.20 Article 82—Abuse

If the existence of a dominant position in the supply or acquisition of certain goods or services within a substantial part of the Common Market has been established, the next issue under Article 82 is whether an abuse or exploitation of that position has occurred.

A dominant firm abuses its position when it engages in conduct that would not be possible in a competitive market.[1] According to the list of examples of abusive practices contained in Article 82, such abuse may, in particular, consist of:

- directly or indirectly imposing unfair purchase or selling prices or other unfair trading conditions;

- limiting production, markets or technical development to the prejudice of consumers;

- applying dissimilar conditions to equivalent transactions with other trading parties, thereby placing them at a competitive disadvantage;

- making the conclusion of contracts subject to acceptance by the other parties of supplementary obligations which, by their nature or according to commercial usage, have no connection with the subject of such contracts.

---

20. *See e.g.* French–West African Shipowners' Committees, O.J.1992 L 134/1.

21. Gemeente Almelo v. Energiebedrijf IJsselmij, (1994) Eur.Comm.Rep. I–01477 (Case No. C–393/92) at ¶ 42.

22. (1992) Eur.Comm.Rep. II–1403.

23. *Id.* at ¶ 358.

§ 7.20

1. Hoffmann–La Roche v. Commission, (1979) Eur.Comm.Rep. 461, 541.

Case Law

In *Commercial Solvents*,[2] the Commission and the Court of Justice found abuse in the activities of the only producer in the world of aminobutanol, a chemical used in the making of the drug ethambutol. Commercial Solvents, a U.S. corporation, sold the chemical in Italy to its subsidiary, Istituto Chemioterapico, which in turn sold it to Zoja, an Italian firm making the drug. After merger negotiations between Istituto and Zoja broke off, Zoja sought but failed to get supplies of the chemical from Istituto. After receiving a complaint from Zoja, the Commission commenced Article 82 infringement proceedings. It eventually held that the *refusal to deal* of Commercial Solvents and Istituto (viewed as one enterprise) amounted to an abuse. Commercial Solvents, through its Italian subsidiary, was ordered to promptly make supplies of aminobutanol available to Zoja at a price no higher than the maximum which it normally charged.

In Re GEMA,[3] the only German authors' and composers' rights licensing society was in possession of a dominant position within a substantial part of the European Community. This dominant position was reinforced by agreements with other societies in the EU granting exclusive rights to the various national markets. The societies were extremely advantageous and profitable to recording artists who otherwise faced formidable, if not impossible, tasks of distributing rights to their copyrighted goods on an individual basis to record manufacturers and other users. These commercial realities reinforced the Commission's conclusion that GEMA's market position was a dominant one. The Commission instituted Article 82 infringement proceedings *sua sponte*. It decided that the imposition of higher license fees on importers of records and tape recorders, compared with fees imposed on German manufacturers, was restrictive of competition between them and therefore an abuse of GEMA's dominant position relative to its purchasers. GEMA similarly abused its dominant position by extending its members' copyrights to noncopyrighted works through a system of package license fees that failed to distinguish between copyrighted and noncopyrighted works. By *discriminating* through loyalty rebates between German users and users from different EU states, GEMA abusively helped to prevent the establishment of a single common market for the supply of recording services. In other words, it also abused its market power concerning potential Union competitors.

GEMA's discrimination against foreign members regarding management positions and a supplementary benefits scheme also constituted abuses of its dominant position. Requirements imposed

---

2. *Id.*

3. (1971) Common Mkt.L.Rep. D35; (1972) Common Mkt.L.Rep. 694.

on members to assign their rights to GEMA for the whole world and all marketing categories were deemed unnecessary to its operation and fell into the same category. GEMA members were also abusively excluded, by their contract terms, from recourse to the courts in the event of disputes as to distribution of GEMA funds. By requiring a six-year term, by obliging assignment of all future works during that six-year period, and by establishing a lengthy period of waiting to be eligible for certain payments, GEMA abused its dominant position through agreements with its supplier-members. By generally curtailing their mobility to join other societies in the Common Market, GEMA inhibited the process of economic integration and the creation of a single market for music publishers.

Many of the abuses found in *GEMA* do not fall under the examples provided by the Treaty terms of Article 82. From this survey of some of the abuses found, it should be apparent that once a dominant position is established the Commission feels free to roam the whole of the behavior of the dominant enterprise. Anti-competitive aspects of contractual and noncontractual relations between GEMA and its members, GEMA's constitution and by-laws, its general commercial practices, and its relations with record manufacturers and users of rights were reviewed and subjected to the Commission's regulation. Another decision in the same industry involves a French society of musical composers' rights.[4]

Hoffmann–La Roche, the large multinational Swiss firm, was fined for abusing its dominant position in seven vitamin markets in the Union. It used a network of *exclusive or preferential supply contracts*, along with loyalty rebates, to reinforce its dominance by cornering retail markets.[5] United Brands, a United States multinational, abused its dominant position in bananas through discriminatory, predatory and excessive pricing in various EU countries. Its abuses also extended to refusals to deal with important past customers and prohibiting the resale of bananas. Abuse is also a legal concept that allows the Commission to review business profits. Taking into account the "high profits" involved, the Commission fined United Brands 1,000,000 ECUs. In the Commission's opinion, this was a "moderate" fine under the circumstances.[6] Tying arrangements may constitute Article 82 abuses.[7]

4. *See* Greenwich Film Production, Paris v. SACEM (1979) Eur.Comm.Rep. 3275. *See generally* regarding copyright abuses, Radio Telefis Eireann v. Commission (Magill TV Guide), 4 Common Mkt.L.Rep. 586 (1991).

5. Hoffmann–La Roche v. Commission (1979) Eur.Comm.Rep. 461.

6. United Brands v. Commission (1978) Eur.Comm.Rep. 207.

7. Tetra Pak International SA v. Commmission (1994) Eur.Comm.Rep. II–7a55 *aff'd* (1996) Eur.Comm.Rep. I–5951.

The Court of Justice has held that *predatory pricing* can constitute an abuse of a dominant position in violation of Article 82. Predatory pricing below average total cost (as well as below average variable cost) may be abusive if undertaken to eliminate a competitor. Regarding the former, pricing below average total cost is thought to be capable of driving out competitors as efficient as the dominant firm but lacking its extensive financial resources.[8] Other types of abuse have included refusal to supply,[9] tying,[10] and fidelity rebates,[11] and using dominance to move into ancillary markets.[12] It is important to note that abuse may exist without any fault of the dominant undertakings. One of the issues in *British Gypsum* was whether BPB, the British holding company of a group that controlled about half of the plasterboard production in the EU, abused its position by making promotional payments to its distributors even though the distributors themselves requested the payments.[13] With reference to the *Hoffmann–La Roche* case noted above,[14] the Court of First Instance held that abuse under Article 82 may occur independent of any fault.

§ 7.21 Articles 81 and 82—Mergers and Acquisitions

In 1965 the Commission announced in a memorandum to the member states that regional concentration ought to be encouraged to achieve efficiency and economies of scale, and to combat competition from large United States and Japanese multinational firms. These rationales have supported a long line of merger approvals by the Commission under its coal and steel concentration controls. It was not until a European merger boom was in progress and extensive studies revealed increasing trends toward industrial concentration that the Commission took action against a merger in *Continental Can*.[1]

Continental Can Case

The Commission decided Continental Can abused its dominant positions in the manufacture of meat and fish tins and metal caps in Germany in only one fashion, by announcing an 80 percent control bid for the only Dutch meat and fish tin company. The

8. *Id*; Akzo Chemie BV v. Commission (1991) Eur.Comm.Rep. I–3359 (Case C–62–86).

9. Boosey & Hawkes, O.J. L 286 (1987) 36 point 19.

10. Gemeente Almelo v. Engiebedrijf Ijsselmij (1994) Eur.Comm.Rep. I–01477 ¶ 44 (Case No. C–393/92).

11. Suiker Unie v. Commission (1975) Eur.Comm.Rep. 1663, 2003; British Gypsum v. Commission (1993) Eur.

Comm.Rep. II–00389 (Case No. T–65/89).

12. Sea Containers v. Stena Sealink, O.J. L 15 (1994) 8, 16; Port of Rodby, O.J. L 55 (1994) 52, 55.

13. (1993) Eur.Comm.Rep. II–4120 (Case No. T–65/89).

14. (1979) Eur.Comm.Rep. 461.

§ 7.21

1. (1972) Common Mkt.L.Rep. D11.

Commission reasoned that Continental Can would strengthen its dominant German market position through this Dutch acquisition, to the detriment of consumers, and that this amounted to an abuse. The Commission emphasized that potential competition between companies located within the Union was to be eliminated. Acting quickly before the merger was a *fait accompli,* the Commission underscored its inability to block proposed mergers. Continental Can was given six months to submit proposals for remedying its Article 82 infringement.

On appeal to the Court of Justice, Continental Can argued that the Commission was acting beyond its powers in attempting to control mergers under Article 82.[2] The Advocate General to the Court concurred. Nevertheless, the Court chose to go beyond the limits of the language of Articles 81 and 82 and interpret them in light of Articles 2 and 3 of the Treaty of Rome. These Articles set out basic tasks and activities. Article 3 calls for the erection of a system of nondistorted competition in the Common Market.

The Court reasoned teleologically that both Articles 81 and 82 were intended to assist in the maintenance of nondistorted competition. If businesses could freely merge and eliminate competition (whereas Article 81 agreements, decisions or concerted practices merely restrict competition), a "breach in the whole system of competition law that could jeopardize the proper functioning of the common market" would be opened.

> There may therefore be abusive behavior if an enterprise in a dominant position strengthens that position so that the degree of control achieved substantially obstructs competition, *i.e.* so that the only enterprises left in the market are those which are dependent on the dominant enterprise with regard to their market behavior.[3]

One problem with relying on Article 82 for control of mergers and acquisitions was the absence of any pre-merger notification system. Once a merger is completed, it is always difficult to persuade a court or tribunal that dissolution is desirable or even possible. The key to effective mergers regulation, as the United States has learned under its Hart–Scott–Rodino pre-merger notification rules,[4] is advance warning and sufficient time to block anticompetitive mergers before they are implemented.

The possibility of using Article 81 against selected mergers was surprisingly dismissed by the Commission in an early 1966 competition policy report.[5] This is because the focus of Article 81 is on

---

2. (1973) Eur.Comm.Rep. 215.

3. *Id.*

4. 15 U.S.C.A. § 18A.

5. Commission Competition Series No. 3, *The Problem of Industrial Con-*

competitive behavior rather than practices which change the structure of the market. However, Article 81 may be applicable to a merger if it has the effect of influencing the competitive behavior of the companies in the relevant market. In 1984, the Commission challenged a tobacco industry acquisition as an unlawful restraint under Article 81(1). The Court of Justice held that Article 81 could be applied to the acquisition by one firm of shares in a competitor if that acquisition could influence the behavior in the marketplace of the companies involved.[6] Likewise, Article 82 could apply if the acquisition resulted in effective control of the target company.[7]

After the ruling of the Court of Justice in *Continental Can,* the Commission submitted a comprehensive mergers' control regulation to the Council for its approval.[8] Nearly twenty years later, a regulation on mergers was finally implemented.

§ 7.22 Commission Regulation of Concentrations (Mergers)

In December of 1989, the Council of Ministers unanimously adopted Regulation 4064/89 on the Control of Concentrations Between Undertakings ("Merger Control Regulation"). This regulation became effective Sept. 21, 1990 and was expanded in scope by amendment in 1997, and significantly revised in 2004. It vests in the Commission the *exclusive* power to oppose large-scale mergers and acquisitions of competitive consequence to the Common Market and the EEA.

Applicability

The Merger Control Regulation applies to concentrations with a Union dimension. The concept of concentration as used in the Merger Control Regulation is based on the notion of a change in control over another undertaking. Such a change in control may exist where two or more previously independent undertakings merge or one or more undertakings acquire, whether by purchase of securities or assets, by contract or by any other means, direct or indirect control of the whole or parts of one or more other undertakings. The most obvious example would be the outright purchase of the share capital of another undertaking.[1]

centration in the Common Market (1966).

6. British American Tobacco Co. Ltd. and R.J. Reynolds Industries, Inc. v. Commission (1987) Eur.Comm.Rep. 4487.

7. *Id.*

8. *See* O.J.1973 C 92/1 and 3rd Report on Competition Policy (1973) point 1.

§ 7.22

1. *See e.g.* AKZO/Nobel Industrier, Comm. Decision of Jan. 10, 1994 (Case No. IV/M390).

A change of control, and hence a concentration, may also exist where joint control is shared by two or more undertakings over another undertaking (*i.e.,* a joint venture). The most obvious example of joint control is where two undertakings each have a 50 percent interest in another undertaking and exercise equal control over it.[2] However, joint control may also exist in the case of a minority investment as long as the minority investor is granted rights going above and beyond its investment so that it is able to exercise control over the major commercial decisions of the joint venture.[3] Not all joint ventures fall under the Merger Control Regulation. In order to qualify as a concentration, the joint venture must fulfill two additional requirements: It must perform all the functions of an autonomous economic entity on a lasting basis and not give rise to the coordination of competitive behavior between the parents themselves or between the parents and the joint venture. Unless both of these conditions are fulfilled, the joint venture will be examined under Article 81 of the Rome Treaty.

To qualify as an autonomous economic entity, the joint venture must act as an independent supplier and buyer on the market. To the extent that the joint venture merely assumes specific duties assigned by its parents, this indicates that it lacks the necessary autonomy.[4] A joint venture which supplies its products or services exclusively to the parent companies will not qualify as a concentrative joint venture.[5] On the other hand, the autonomy of the joint venture will not be contested where the parents merely reserve the right to make certain decisions that are important for the development of the joint venture concerning, for example, major capital investments, increases or decreases of capital and the strategic plan of the company. In addition, the joint venture must not lead to the coordination of the competitive behavior of the parents between themselves or between the parents and the joint venture. The risk of coordination will not generally exist where only one of the parents is active in the market of the joint venture.[6] The risk of coordination of the competitive behavior between the parents and the joint venture is similarly absent when the parents are not active in the market of the joint venture or on neighboring markets (or are active but only to a minor extent).[7]

2. *See e.g.* Pilkington–Techint/SIV, O.J. (1994) L 158/24, 25.

3. *See e.g.* Hoechst/Schering, Comm. Decision of Jan. 6, 1994 (Case No. IV/M392) point 7.

4. Commission notice regarding the concentrative and cooperative operations under Council Regulation (EEC) No 4064/89 on the control of concentrations between undertakings, O.J. (1990) C 203/10 point 16.

5. British Telecom/MCI, Comm. Decision of Sept. 13, 1993 (Case No. IV/M 353) point 6.

6. Ericsson/Kolbe, Comm. Decision of Jan. 22, 1992 (Case No. IV/M133).

7. Mannesmann/Vallourec/Ilva, O.J. (1994) L 102/15 point 11.

EU Dimension

Having qualified as a concentration, the issue then becomes whether it has a Union dimension. According to the Merger Control Regulation, a concentration has a Union dimension when three conditions are fulfilled: (1) the combined aggregate annual world-wide turnover of all the undertakings concerned is more than 5 billion ECU, (2) the aggregate annual Union-wide turnover of each of at least two of the undertakings concerned is more than 250 million ECU, and (3) each of the undertakings involved does not achieve more than two-thirds of its aggregate Union-wide turnover within one and the same Member State. These thresholds were reviewed in 1993, when the Commission declined to lower them because "below this level concentrations would principally have a national impact and, in accordance with the subsidiarity principle, would therefore be better handled at that level."[8] Since 1997, Community-dimension concentrations subject to notification also occur if the enterprises have a combined aggregate world-wide turnover of at least 2.5 billion ECUs *and* they have a combined aggregate turnover of at least 100 million ECUs in at least three member states *and* at least two of the enterprises have at least 25 million ECUs turnover in the same three member states *and* at least two of them have at least 100 million ECUs turnover in the European Community *unless* each of the enterprises achieves more than two-thirds of its aggregate Community-wide turnover in the same member state.

Advance Notice

Parties to a concentration with a Union dimension are under a duty to submit notification to the Commission within one week of the signing of a merger agreement, the acquisition of a controlling interest or the announcement of a takeover bid. The Commission can fine any company failing to notify it as required. The concentration is to be notified using Form CO and must be in one of the official Union languages.[9] This language becomes the language of the proceeding. Form CO is somewhat similar to second request Hart–Scott–Rodino pre-merger notification filings under U.S. antitrust law. However, the extensive need for detailed product and geographic market descriptions, competitive analyses, and information about the parties in Form CO suggests a more demanding submission. Form CO defines a product market as follows:

> A relevant product market comprises all those products and/or services which are regarded as interchangeable or substitutable

8. 23rd Report on Competition Policy (1994) point 46.

9. O.J. 1993 L 336/63.

by the consumer, by reason of the products' characteristics, their prices and their intended use.

Meeting in advance of notification with members of the Commission on an informal basis in order to ascertain whether the "concentration" has a regional dimension and is compatible with the Common Market has become widely accepted. An attempt by minority shareholders to reverse the Commission's failure to review a merger allegedly affecting their interests was denied by the Court of First Instance. The Court held that the shareholders were not directly or individually concerned by the Commission's determination that the merger fell outside the scope of EU regulation of concentrations.[10] Such meetings provide an opportunity to seek waivers from the various requests for information contained in Form CO. Since the Commission is bound by rules of professional secrecy, the substance of the discussions is confidential.

As a general rule, concentrations with a Union dimension cannot be put into effect and fall exclusively within the Commission's domain. The effort here is to create a "one-stop" regulatory system. However, certain exceptions apply so as to allow national authorities to challenge some mergers. The member states can also oppose mergers irrespective of a decision by the Commission under the Merger Control Regulation when their public security is at stake, to preserve plurality in media ownership, when financial institutions are involved or other legitimate interests are at risk.[11] Even if the threshold criteria of the Merger Control Regulation are not met, member states can ask the Commission to investigate mergers that create or strengthen a dominant position in that state.[12] This is known as the "Dutch clause." States that lack national mergers' controls seem likely to do this.[13] Similarly, if the merger only affects a particular market sector or region in one member state, that state may request referral of the merger to it. This is known as the "German clause" reflecting Germany's insistence upon it. It has been sparingly used by the Commission.[14] Since 2004, parties to a merger that is subject to notification in three or more member states may request "one-stop" review by the Commission, which will occur provided no member state objects.

Once a concentration is notified to the Commission, it has one month to decide to investigate the merger. If a formal investigation

10. Zunis Holding S.A. v. Commission (1993) Eur.Comm.Rep. II–01169 (Case T–83/92).

11. The Commission has granted one such 21(3) authorization in IBM France/CGI, Case No. IV/M335, (19.5.93) (concentration involving French defense industry).

12. Article 22(3), Merger Control Regulation.

13. See e.g. British Airways/Dan Air, Case No. IV/M132, (17.2.93).

14. Steetley/Tarmac, Case No. IV/M180, (12.2.1992); McCormick/Ostmann, Case No. IV/330, (6.10.1993).

is commenced, the Commission ordinarily then has four months to challenge or approve the merger. During these months, in most cases, the concentration cannot be put into effect. The parties are precluded from proceeding with the concentration for three weeks after the notification is submitted. However, the Commission may extend the suspension period through a formal decision until it has made a final decision on the merits. The merger is on hold.

Evaluation

The Commission evaluates mergers in terms of their "compatibility" with the Common Market. Prior to May 1, 2004, using language reminiscent of *Continental Can*,[15] the Mergers Regulation stated that if the concentration creates or strengthens a dominant position such that competition is "significantly impeded," it was incompatible. This included dominance not only by a single firm but also joint dominance by more than one firm.[16] The Commission is authorized to consider in its evaluation the interests of consumers and the "development of technical and economic progress." It is uncertain whether economic efficiency arguments fall within this language. A failing company defense has been recognized by the Court of Justice and a 25 percent market share is normally the minimum for purposes of ascertaining the existence of a "dominant position." However, "collective dominance" theories involving duopoly and oligopoly markets have been recognized by the ECJ as valid bases for challenging mergers that may facilitate tacit collusion among leading firms.[17]

Effective May 1, 2004, this test was replaced by a prohibition against mergers that "significantly impede effective competition" by creating or strengthening dominant positions. Thus the new test focuses on effects not dominance. A set of Guidelines on Horizontal Mergers issued by the Commission in 2004 elaborate upon this approach. It is thought that this change will bring EU and U.S. mergers law closer together (the U.S. test is "substantial lessening of competition").

In assessing the merger under the Merger Control Regulation, the Commission can obtain information and records from the parties, and request member states to help with the investigation. In conducting investigations of the undertakings, the Commission is authorized to examine the books and other business records and demand copies, ask for oral explanations on the spot and enter any premises of the undertaking. Fines and penalties back up the

15. *See* § 7.21.

16. *See* Nestlé/Perrier, O.J. 1992 L 356/1; Kali & Salz/MdK/Treuhand, O.J. 1994 L 186/38; Pilkington–Techint/SIV, O.J. 1994 L 158/24.

17. France v. Commission (1998) Eur.Comm.Rep. I–1375 (Kali & Salz); Gencor Ltd. Commission (1999) Eur. Comm.Rep. II–753.

Commission's powers to obtain records and information from the parties. This also applies if the parties give effect to the merger prior to notification or within the first three weeks after its notification. In such cases, the Commission may impose fines not exceeding 10 percent of the aggregate turnover of the undertakings concerned if the parties acted intentionally or negligently.

Approval of the merger may involve modifications of its terms or promises by the parties aimed at diminishing its anticompetitive potential. If the Commission ultimately decides to oppose the merger in a timely manner, it can order its termination by whatever means are appropriate to restore conditions of effective competition (including divestiture, fines or penalties). Such decisions can be appealed to the Court of First Instance since 2002 under "fast track" procedures that limit issues on appeal and promote judicial review within a year. As a practical matter, most merger proposals do not last that long. Hence, a negative Commission decision usually kills the merger.

Case Examples

The first merger actually blocked by the Commission on competition law grounds was the attempted acquisition of a Canadian aircraft manufacturer (DeHaviland—owned by Boeing) by two European companies (Aerospatiale SNI of France and Alenia e Selenia Spa of Italy).[18] Prior to this rejection in late 1991, the Commission had approved over 50 mergers, obtaining modifications in a few instances. The Commission, in the DeHaviland case, took the position that the merger would have created an unassailable dominant position in the world and EU market for turbo prop or commuter aircraft. If completed, the merged entity would have had 50 percent of the world and 67 percent of the Union market for such aircraft.

In contrast, the Commission approved (subject to certain sell-off requirements) the acquisition of Perrier by Nestlé.[19] Prior to the merger, Nestlé, Perrier and BSN controlled about 82 percent of the French bottled water market. Afterwards, Nestlé and BSN each had about 41 percent of the market. The sell-off requirements were thought sufficient by the Commission to maintain effective competition. The case also presents interesting arguments that the Commission, in granting approval, disregarded fundamental workers' social rights. This issue was unsuccessfully taken up on appeal by Perrier's trade union representative.[20]

18. O.J. 1991 L 334/42.

19. O.J. 1992 L 356/1.

20. Comité Central d'Entreprise de la Société Anonyme Vittel & Ors v. Com-

mission (1993) Eur.Comm.Rep. II–01247 (Case T–12/93R).

Even though a merger may create or strengthen a dominant position, the Commission has indicated that it may be willing to approve the merger if the acquired firm would be forced out of the market but for the merger.[21] The requirements of this failing company defense are similar to those under U.S. antitrust law.[22] It must be clear that the acquired undertaking would be forced from the market in the near future but for the merger, the acquiring undertaking would take over the market share of the acquired undertaking if it were indeed forced out of the market, and there is no less anticompetitive alternative. In the *De Havilland* case, the Commission refused to apply the defense since the probability that the acquired firm would be forced out of the market but for the merger was not high enough.[23]

In 1997, the Commission dramatically demonstrated its extra-territorial jurisdiction over the *Boeing–McDonnell Douglas* merger.[24] This merger had already been cleared by the U.S. Federal Trade commission. The European Commission, however, demanded and (at the risk of a trade war) got important concessions from Boeing. These included abandonment of exclusive supply contracts with three U.S. airlines and licensing of technology derived from McDonnell Douglas' military programs at reasonable royalty rates. The Commission's success in this case was widely perceived in the United States as pro-Airbus.

The Commission blocked the MCI Worldcom/Sprint merger in 2001, as did the U.S. Dept. of Justice. Both authorities were worried about the merger's adverse effects on Internet access. For the Commission, this was the first block of a merger taking place outside the EU between two firms established outside the EU. Much more controversy arose when in 2001 the Commission blocked the GE/Honeywell merger after it had been approved by U.S. authorities. The Commission was particularly concerned about the potential for bundling engines with avionics and non-avionics to the disadvantage of rivals.[25] Appeal of this decision is pending. The United States and the EU, in the wake of GE/Honeywell, have agreed to follow a set of "Best Practices" on coordinated timing, evidence gathering, communication and consistency of remedies.

The Court of First Instance overturned a 1999 decision of the European Commission blocking the $1.2 billion merger of Airtours

---

21. Kali & Salz/MdK/Treuhand, O.J. 1994 L 186/38.

22. Citizens Publishing Co. v. United States, 394 U.S. 131, 89 S.Ct. 927, 22 L.Ed.2d 148 (1969); International Shoe Co. v. F.T.C., 280 U.S. 291, 50 S.Ct. 89, 74 L.Ed. 431 (1930).

23. Aérospatiale-Alenia/De Havilland, O.J. 1991 L 334/42.

24. O.J. L 336/16 (Dec. 8, 1997).

25. Case COMP/M.2220 (July 3, 2001).

and First Choice Holidays.[26] The June, 2002 CFI decision was the first reversal of a merger prohibition since the 1990 inception of the review process. The CFI judgment confirmed that transactions can be blocked on collective dominance grounds, but found that the Commission had failed to meet the three conditions for proving collective dominance: (1) each member of the dominant group is able to determine readily how the others are behaving, (2) there is an effective mechanism to prevent group members from departing from the agreed-upon policy, and (3) smaller competitors are unable to undercut that policy.

In June of 2002 the European Court of Justice issued three decisions on the use by member states of so-called "golden shares." Such shares allow governments to retain veto rights with respect to acquisitions of or other significant accumulations in privatized businesses. The court outlawed a golden share decree allowing France to block a foreign takeover of a privatized oil company.[27] The golden share decree created a barrier to the free movement of capital. The court also outlawed a law giving Portugal the ability to block the acquisition of controlling stakes in privatized state companies,[28] but determined as a matter of public interest that Belgium could retain its golden share in recently privatized canal and gas distribution companies.[29]

In October of 2002, acting under its new fast track review procedures, the Court of First Instance overturned two additional mergers decisions of the Commission. In both *Schneider Electric*[30] and *Tetra Laval*[31] the Court found serious errors, omissions and inconsistencies. Credible evidence, not assumptions or "abstract and detached analysis," must be tendered to prove both the strengthening or creation of a dominant position, and the likelihood that the merger will significantly impede competition.

§ 7.23 Articles 81 and 82—Application to Public Enterprises

It is important to keep in mind that the provisions of Articles 81 and 82 apply to both public and private business activities. Despite a noticeable trend toward privatization, many undertakings in Europe are still in the hands of the state. Although the Treaty does not prohibit such state ownership, because of the obvious

26. Airtours v. Commission (2002) Eur.Comm.Rep. II–02585 (Case T–342/99).

27. Commission v. France (2002) Eur.Comm.Rep. I–4781.

28. Commission v. Portugal (2002) Eur.Comm.Rep. I–473.

29. Commission v. Belgium (2002) Eur.Comm.Rep. I–4809.

30. Schneider Electric v. Commission (2002) Eur.Comm.Rep. II–04071 (Cases T–310/01 and T–77/02).

31. Tetra Laval BV v. Commission (2002) Eur.Comm.Rep. II–04381 (Cases T–5/02 and T–80/02).

advantages public undertakings have over private undertakings, it does prohibit the member states from enacting or maintaining in force any measure contrary to the competition rules concerning public undertakings or undertakings to which the member states have granted special or exclusive rights.[1] It is noteworthy that Article 86(1) is directed at the member states and not at the undertakings themselves. These undertakings, even if public, remain subject to the direct application of the competition rules.[2] Moreover, this principle is not limited to the competition rules but applies to all Rome Treaty provisions such as the right of establishment[3] and the free movement of goods.[4]

When Is An Enterprise Public?

The line between public and private undertakings is often the subject of dispute. In general, an undertaking is considered public whenever a member state exerts a controlling influence over it by virtue of their ownership, financial participation or the rules which govern it.[5] The prohibition also applies to undertakings which have been granted special or exclusive rights by the state even if the state itself does not exercise direct control over the undertaking in the form of ownership. For example, Article 86(1) was held applicable to a corporation of navigational pilots exclusively authorized by the Italian state to provide compulsory piloting services in the port of Genoa.[6] Additional examples of undertakings which would fall under that Article would be energy companies, public transport, telecommunication companies and postal services.

Thus the influence of government through subsidies, licensing or regulatory procedures can be important in determining the "public" versus "private" nature of an enterprise. The distinction has legal significance. An enterprise deemed private falls directly in the path of Article 82. An enterprise deemed public may also be subject to Article 86(1) or 86(2) which involve additional considerations. Article 86(2), for example, has its own exempting (and exception to the exemption) language and interpretive difficulties. The Court of Justice has indicated that companies with statutory

---

§ 7.23

1. Article 86(1), Treaty of Rome.

2. See Gemeente Amelo v. Energie-bedrijf (1994) Eur.Comm.Rep. I–1477 (Case No. C–393/92); Sacchi (1974) Eur. Comm.Rep. 409.

3. Article 43 and 52, Treaty of Rome. *See* Greek Insurance, O.J. L 1985 152/25.

4. Article 28, Treaty of Rome. *See* RTT v. GB–Inno–BM (1991) Eur. Comm.Rep. I–5941; Franzen (1997) Eur.

Comm.Rep. I–5909 (Swedish alcohol state monopoly).

5. *See* Art. 2 of Directive 80/723, O.J. 1980 L 195/35 as amended by Commission Directive 93/84, O.J. 1993 L 254/16. However, the definition of public undertaking in the context of this Directive is not necessarily equivalent to that in the context of Art. 82. France v. Commission (1982) Eur.Comm.Rep. 2545.

6. Corsica Ferries v. Corpo dei Piloti del Porto Genova (1994) E.C.R. I–596 (Case No. 18/93).

monopolies that are unwilling or unable to fulfill market demands for their services engage in an unlawful abuse of a dominant position. Indeed, any state grant of exclusive rights that leads to an abuse of a dominant position is unlawful. Despite the uncertainties of the public versus private enterprise distinction drawn in the Treaty of Rome, the attempt at placing all businesses under the rule of competition is nothing less than fundamental.

Services of A General Economic Interest

According to Article 86(2), undertakings, regardless whether private or public, which are entrusted with the operation of services of general economic interest are also subject to the competition rules but only in so far as the application of such rules does not obstruct the performance of the tasks assigned to them.[7] This provision can be seen as an exemption from both the prohibition placed on the member states in Article 86(1) and the competition rules of the Rome Treaty contained in Articles 81 and 82.[8] The basic requirement is that the particular undertaking is entrusted with responsibilities of a general economic interest.

The essential issue in such cases is whether the application of the competition rules to the particular undertaking will undermine its ability to provide the services of a general economic interest with which it is entrusted. The Court has consistently held that such undertakings may be legitimately shielded from competition in one area so that they can achieve higher profits with which to subsidize other less profitable areas.[9] In the *Corbeau* case,[10] for example, the issue was whether a Belgian law granting the public postal services the exclusive right to collect, transport and deliver all mail in Belgium benefitted from Article 86(2) to the extent that it restricted other undertakings from competing in this market. In that case, the applicant was accused of infringing this law because he had established a service in a Belgian city consisting of collecting mail from the home of the sender and delivering it by the next day. The Court held that although the Belgian post office was an undertaking enjoying an exclusive right under Article 86(1), this provision of the Treaty must be read in connection with Article 86(2). Since the Belgian post office was an undertaking entrusted

---

7. *See* Albany International BV and Textile Industry Pension Funds (1999) Eur.Comm.Rep. I–5751 (exclusive pension fund management); Deutsche Post AG v. GZS, Deutsche Post AG v.Citicorp (2000) Eur.Comm.Rep. I–825 (postal monopolies).

8. Gemeente Amelo v. Energiebedrijf (1994) Eur.Comm.Rep. I–1477 (Case No. C–393/92); Corbeau (1993) Eur. Comm.Rep. I–2533 (Case No. C–320/91).

9. *See e.g.* Gemeente Amelo v. Energiebedrijf (1994) Eur.Comm.Rep. I–1477 (Case No. C–393/92); Corbeau (1993) E.C.R. I–2533 (Case No. C–320/91).

10. (1993) E.C.R. I–2533 (Case No. C–320/91. *See* Höfner v. Macrotron GmbH (1991) Eur.Comm.Rep. I–1979 (exclusive employment agency).

with the operation of a service of general economic interest, the question was whether the exclusive rights were necessary for it to adequately exercise this function. The Court held that if the post office were to perform its functions in a profitable manner, it must be able to offset its losses in one sector by its profits in another sector. Otherwise, undertakings would concentrate their business in the profitable sectors and offer lower prices there since they did not have to subsidize their loss making sectors like the undertaking entrusted with the operation of the service of a general economic interest (principle of equalization).

Another issue that has repeatedly arisen in Article 86(2) cases concerns the definition of an undertaking entrusted with the operation of services of a general economic interest. As an exception, this provision is to be interpreted narrowly.[11] Nonetheless, the Commission and Court have held that the provision of energy,[12] telephone[13] and television services[14] are services of a general economic interest. In GEMA, on the other hand, the Commission decided that the only German authors' rights society did not benefit from the exemption provided for in Article 86(2).[15]

Commission Powers

A somewhat unique feature of Article 86(1) and (2) is that the Commission is authorized to adopt directives and decisions necessary to ensure its application.[16] This has proven an effective instrument for the Commission in those sectors which it has decided to liberalize. In 1989, for example, the Commission issued a directive requiring member states to increase competition in the market for telecommunications terminal equipment, including telephones, modems, and telex terminals at a time when these services were primarily in the hands of public monopolies.[17] The Court of Justice has repeatedly confirmed the Commission's broad authority to adopt such directives and decisions[18] despite protestations of certain member states to the contrary.[19] A controversial feature of Article 86 directives is that they bypass the normal legislative procedures, including Parliamentary prerogatives as well as Council enactment.

---

11. BRT v. SABAM (1974) Eur. Comm.Rep. 313 ¶ 19.

12. Gemeente Amelo v. Energiebedrijf (1994) Eur.Comm.Rep. I–1477 (Case No. C–393/92).

13. RTT v. GB–Inno–BM (1991) Eur. Comm.Rep. I–5941.

14. Sacchi (1974) Eur.Comm.Rep. 409.

15. GEMA (1971) Common Mkt. L.Rep. D35.

16. Article 86(3), Treaty of Rome.

17. Commission Directive 88/301, O.J. L 131 (1988) 73. This Directive was subsequently amended by Directive 90/388, O.J. L 192 (1990) 10 and Directive 94/46, O.J. L 268 (1994) 15.

18. *See e.g.* Netherlands and PTT v. Commission (1992) Eur.Comm.Rep. I–565.

19. France v. Commission (1993) Eur.Comm.Rep. I–3283 (Case No. C–325/91); Spain v. Commission (1992) Eur.Comm.Rep. I–5833.

§ 7.24   National Litigation and Remedies for Competition Law Violations

Direct Effect

As primary Union law, Articles 81 and 82 are directly effective in the member states.[1] All regulations, for example, the various group exemption regulations discussed in Section 7.9, are directly applicable law in member states. Directly effective Treaty provisions and directly applicable regulations give individuals within member states (including enterprises) the immediate right to rely on Union law. This means that they may raise competition law issues in private litigation before national courts and tribunals.[2] Indeed, under the supremacy doctrine, they may rely on such law to challenge contradictory national law.[3] The directly effective nature of Articles 81 and 82 and the numerous EU regulations in this area helps to explain the pervasive impact that competition law has had in European business life.

Role of National Courts, Nullification, Damages

Article 81(2) renders agreements which infringe Article 81(1) (or parts thereof) null and void. Since this is a directly effective Treaty provision, the national courts ordinarily enjoin such agreements. This assumes of course that the agreement is not group exempted by the Commission under Article 81(3), which under the 2004 modernization rules can also be applied individually by national authorities and courts.[4] National courts and tribunals may request advice from *the Commission*.[5] Such requests may seek procedural as well as substantive advice. For example, the national courts may inquire whether a case or investigation into the same dispute is pending before the Commission, and how long the Commission will take before acting. They may also consult with the Commission on points of law, e.g. whether the necessary impact on EU trade is present and whether the contested agreement is eligible for an individual exemption under Article 81(3).

National courts can also obtain statistics, market studies and economic analyses from the Commission. All of this information and advice is intended to encourage national courts to efficiently and correctly apply Articles 81 and 82 to disputes coming before them. It is part of a broad policy of decentralized EU competition law enforcement designed to leave the Commission free to pursue

---

§ 7.24

1. Bosch v. deGeus (1962) Common Mkt.L.Rep. 1; Belgische Radio en Televisie v. SABAM (1974) Eur.Comm.Rep. 51.

2. *See* Chapter 3.

3. *See* Chapter 2.

4. *See* Section. 7.7.

5. *See* Commission Press Release IP/92/1107 (Dec. 23, 1992) and Regulation 1/2003.

cases of major importance.[6] National courts need not refer EU competition law questions to the Commission. They may simply rely upon their own analysis of the various group exemption regulations,[7] guidelines and policy notices issued by the Commission under Article 85(3). They may also rely on existing ECJ, CFI and Commission case law.

If the agreement violates European Union competition law, it is up to the national courts to determine the consequences of the nullification of agreements by Article 81(2).[8] This could possibly include an award of damages and legal costs. Article 82 does not contain a provision that is comparable to Article 81(2). Thus the private legal remedies available when a dominant firm abuses its position must be determined strictly under national law. In Britain, for example, the House of Lords has suggested that Article 82 creates "statutory duties," the breach of which permits the recovery of damages under torts principles.[9] As yet, no *European Union* right to damages has been established or recognized for either Articles 81 or 82.

§ 7.25   Conflicts of Competition Law

Wilhelm Case

Conflicts between European Union and national laws governing business competition occur. National competition laws are not preempted by the Treaty of Rome. In *Wilhelm v. Bundeskartellamt,* a conflict of competition laws emerged succinctly before the Court of Justice.[1] Four German producers of dyes were fined by the Bundeskartellamt authorities for price fixing activities under the German Law against Restraints of Competition. The dye producers appealed to the Kartellsenat of the Kammergericht in Berlin. The same 1967 price fixing activities of the four German firms were the subject of parallel competition law proceedings initiated by the Commission under Article 81. Before the Commission rendered its decision, defendants argued that in the light of the possibility of a conflict between EU and German competition law, the Kammergericht could not continue its proceedings. The Kammergericht stayed

---

6. *See* Commission Notice clarifying the application of Community competition law by national courts, 1993 O.J. C239/6.

7. *See* § 7.9.

8. Société de vente de Ciments Bétons v. Kerpen + Kerpen (1983) Eur. Comm.Rep. 4173.

9. Garden Cottage Foods Ltd. v. Milk Marketing Board (1983) 2 All Eng.

Rep. 770, 1984 A.C. 130. For additional discussion *see* Hoskins, Garden Cottage Revisited: The Availability of Damages in the National Courts for Breaches of the EEC Competition Rules, 6 E.C.L.R. 257 (1992).

§ 7.25

1. (1969) Eur.Comm.Rep. 1.

its proceedings and requested a preliminary ruling on that issue from the Court of Justice.

The European Court reviewed Article 83(2)(e) of the Treaty of Rome. This article authorizes the Council to define, by regulation or directive, the relationship between national laws and EU law on business competition. Such Council action has yet to take place, but it is worth noting that the Council could preempt national competition law entirely under this authority. The Court went on to read Article 83 in conjunction with Article 2, which enumerates certain fundamental Union tasks, including the promotion of the harmonious development of economic activities within the Union. Reading Articles 83 and 2 together, while acknowledging that the EU has instituted its own legal order which is integrated into that of its member states, the Court came to the following conclusions:

> In principle the national authorities in competition matters may take proceedings also with regard to situations liable to be the object of the decision of the Commission ... conflicts between the Community rule and the national rules on competition should be resolved by the application of the principle of the primacy of the Community rule ... the application of national law may not prejudice the full and uniform application of the Community law or the effect of acts in implementation of it.[2]

Multiple Liability

Insofar as EU and national laws are in harmony, their simultaneous application can result in multiple liability. In this particular case, the four German firms were fined by the Commission and ordered to cease and desist their price fixing activities. The Kammergericht in Berlin continued to hold its proceedings in abeyance and eventually, after the Commission's decision was rendered, annulled the violations and fines imposed under German competition law on constitutional and evidentiary grounds.

Supremacy

The *Wilhelm* decision reaffirms the supremacy of European Union law in the event of a conflict with national competition law. In such circumstances, litigants can ordinarily invoke EU competition law to nullify national proceedings and liability. Since EU competition law is very extensive, the *Wilhelm* rule of supremacy in the event of conflicts of competition law has wide repercussions. Regulation 1/ 2003 requires national courts and authorities to avoid conflicts of competition law and reaffirms the principal of supremacy. Articles 81 and 82 must be applied concurrently with national

2. *Id.*

law, which cannot bar agreements and practices not prohibited by European law.

International Liability

The *Wilhelm* principles extend to United States antitrust and EU competition law conflicts. For example, one European member of an international price fixing quinine cartel was fined under Article 81.[3] Subsequently, that firm was fined for the same activities by U.S. authorities under federal antitrust law. The price fixer then requested a credit against the EU fines in the amount of the U.S. fines. The Commission denied this request, noting that it had always been aware of the parallel United States proceedings.[4]

§ 7.26   EEA Competition Law

On January 1, 1994, the Agreement on the European Economic Area came into force between the then twelve members of the EU and five of the then seven EFTA states (Austria, Finland, Iceland, Norway, Sweden).[1] Since Austria, Finland and Sweden joined the EU in 1995, the EEA competition law provisions outlined below now apply only to Iceland and Norway. The EEA Agreement does not introduce new substantive competition laws but rather simply adopts the competition law provisions of the Treaty of Rome. In addition, the numerous regulations which form an integral part of the EU competition law system are also adopted by the EEA Agreement. This includes, most notably, the Merger Control Regulation as well as the various group exemptions.[2] For private companies doing business in the EEA, this means essentially that the EEA Agreement does not present a new set of substantive competition law rules which must be observed, but rather geographically extends the application of the existing EU rules.

EFTA Surveillance Authority

Perhaps the most important practical aspect of the EEA Agreement is the creation of an additional competition law authority—the EFTA Surveillance Authority (ESA)—in Europe. The ESA is charged with the enforcement of the EEA competition rules and has enforcement powers equivalent to those enjoyed by the Com-

---

3. Re Quinine Cartel (1969) Common Mkt.L.Rep. D41.

4. Re Boehringer Mannheim (1972) Eur.Comm.Rep. 1281.

§ 7.26

1. O.J. 1994 1/3. Although Switzerland signed the initial Agreement, it failed to ratify it. Because of its close economic integration with Liechtenstein,

the latter also forced to postpone its membership in the EEA. Austria, Finland and Sweden subsequently joined the EU on January 1, 1995. This leaves only Iceland, Norway and potentially Liechtenstein as EEA parties.

2. Annex XIV of the EEA Agreement.

mission.[3] For companies active in Europe, the existence of two competition law authorities presents the practical question of which authority has jurisdiction over a particular business practice. In an attempt to avoid imposing additional compliance burdens on undertakings, the attribution of cases between the Commission and the ESA is based on the "one-stop-shop" principle. This means that a particular case will be attributed to either the Commission or the ESA but not both. Attribution of a particular case depends on the type of restraint at issue. If the restraint is through an agreement, decision or concerted practice—the applicable provision therefore being Article 53 of the EEA Agreement—the ESA has jurisdiction in those cases where only trade between EFTA states is affected. If trade between both the EFTA States and member states of the EU is affected, the ESA has jurisdiction only if the turnover of the undertakings in the territory of the EFTA States represents 33 percent or more of their turnover in the entire EEA.[4] There is one exception to this rule: The EU Commission retains jurisdiction in all cases where trade between member states is affected.[5] If trade between EU Member States is affected but not appreciably, the ESA retains jurisdiction provided the aforementioned 33 percent threshold is met.[6]

If the challenged restraint of trade arises from the abuse of a dominant position—the applicable provision therefore being Article 54 of the EEA Agreement—the authority of the territory where the dominant position exists has jurisdiction. If the dominant position exists in both the territory of the EFTA as well as the European Union, then the ESA has jurisdiction only if the turnover of the undertaking in the area of the EFTA states equals or exceeds 33 percent and if trade between EU member states is not appreciably affected. Otherwise the Commission has jurisdiction.

Finally, if the alleged restraint arises from a concentration—the applicable provision therefore being Article 57 of the EEA Agreement—the EU Commission has exclusive jurisdiction if the concentration has a Union dimension as defined in the Merger Control Regulation.[7] Otherwise, the ESA will be the competent authority if the relevant thresholds identical to those in the Merger

---

3. *See* Agreement between the EFTA States on the Establishment of a Surveillance Authority and a Court of Justice.

4. Art. 56(1)(6) of the EAA Agreement. Articles 2 through 5 of Protocol 22 contain special rules for the determination of the turnover in the context of Art. 56. The concept of turnover corresponds basically with that defined in Art. 5 of the Merger Control Regulation. The determination of turnover in the

cases of distribution and supply agreements between non-competing undertakings or the transfer of technology between such undertakings is governed by special rules contained in Art. 4(1) of Protocol 22 which, in effect, reduces the aggregate turnover of the firms.

5. Art. 56(1)(c), EEA Agreement.

6. Art. 56(3), EEA Agreement.

7. *See* supra § 7.22.

Control Regulation are met in the territory of the EFTA states. In such cases, the undertakings should be aware that jurisdiction by the ESA does not preclude the national competition law authorities of the EU member states from exercising jurisdiction over the same merger.[8]

When the notification or application is sent to the wrong authority, that authority is under the duty to transfer the case to the competent authority.[9] If the notification or application is sent to the wrong authority, the effective date the notification or application is received depends on the type of restraint of trade at issue. For restraints of trade falling under Article 53(1) EEA Agreement, the effective date of notification is the date that the first authority receives it.[10] In the case of a concentration, however, it is the date on which it is received by the competent authority.[11] Although the difference may only be a matter of a day, one should keep this in mind since firms have only one week following the conclusion of the contract leading to the concentration to report to the competent authority.

Cooperation With EU Commission

According to Article 58 of the EEA Agreement, the ESA and Commission are required to cooperate in the implementation and application of the competition law provisions of the EEA Agreement. Regarding agreements in restraint of trade and the abuse of a dominant position, the duties of cooperation exist where the business practice at issue has an effect on trade in the territory of the other competition law authority.[12] In the case of concentrations, the duty to cooperate exists when the combined turnover of the undertakings concerned in the territory of the EFTA states equals 25 percent or more of their total turnover within the territory covered by the EEA Agreement, or each of at least two of the undertakings concerned has a turnover exceeding ECU 250 million in the territory of the EFTA states, or the concentration is liable to create or strengthen a dominant position as a result of which effective competition would be significantly impeded in the territories of the EFTA states or a substantial part thereof.[13]

Although the required cooperation concerns primarily the relationship between the respective competition law authorities (e.g.

---

8. According to Art. 57(2)(b) of the EEA Agreement, the jurisdiction of the ESA is to be exercised "without prejudice to the competence of the EC Member States."

9. Art. 10(2), Protocol 23, EEA Agreement.

10. Art. 11, Protocol 23, EEA Agreement.

11. Art. 11, Protocol 24, EEA Agreement.

12. Art. 1, Protocol 23, EEA Agreement.

13. Art. 2, Protocol 24, EEA Agreement. *See e.g.* Commission Decision of 29 July 1994, Case No.IV/M478, Voith-Sulzer, point 14.

consultation, exchange of administrative letters, etc.), there are several aspects which are of particular interest for firms doing business in the EEA. Perhaps the most significant practical implication of the provisions governing the cooperation between the respective competition law authorities concerns the exchange of information. Since the duty to cooperate requires the authorities to exchange notifications and applications,[14] companies should be aware that in certain cases, the information submitted in conjunction with a notification or application to one of the competition law authorities may fall into the hands of the other competition law authority. Second, the ability of the respective authorities to gain access to information located in the territory of the other authority is substantial. Information requests by the competent authority can be directed to companies situated in the territory of the other authority.[15] If the information is not subsequently provided, the competent authority may request the other authority to undertake an investigation if it deems necessary.[16] Thus, even if information is located outside the territory of the competent authority, it may be still accessed through an investigation undertaken by the authority in that territory.

Finally, if a decision is reached by a competent authority that a particular agreement amounts to a restraint of trade or that a particular business practice is an abuse of a dominant position, and the infringement is not brought to an end, that authority may authorize states within the other territory or request the other authority to authorize states to take appropriate measures "needed to remedy the situation."[17] Decisions of the respective authorities which impose pecuniary obligations on undertakings as a result of a violation of the competition laws, are enforceable in the territory of the other authority.[18]

§ 7.27   The Extraterritorial Reach of Articles 81 and 82

There is a question about the extent to which the competition rules of the European Union extend to activity anywhere in the world, including activity occurring entirely or partly within the territorial limits of the United States or Canada. Decisions by the Commission and the Court of Justice suggest that the territorial reach of Articles 81 and 82 is expanding and may extend to almost any international business transaction.

14. Art. 2, Protocol 23, & Art. 3(1) Protocol 24, EEA Agreement.

15. Art. 8(1), Protocol 23, & Art. 8(2) Protocol 24, EEA Agreement.

16. Art. 8(3), Protocol 23, & Art. 8(4) Protocol 24, EEA Agreement.

17. Art. 55(2), EEA Agreement.

18. Art. 110, EEA Agreement.

For an agreement to be incompatible with the Common Market and prohibited under Article 81(1), it must be "likely to affect trade between Member States" and have the object or effect of impairing "competition within the Common Market." Taken together, these requirements amount to an "effects test" for extraterritorial application of Article 81. This test is similar to that which operates under the Sherman Act of the United States.

Extraterritorial Application

The Court has repeatedly held that the fact that one of the parties to an agreement is domiciled in a third country does not preclude the applicability of Article 81(1).[1] Swiss and British chemical companies, for example, argued that the Commission was not competent to impose competition law fines for acts committed in Switzerland and Britain (before joining the EU) by enterprises domiciled outside the Union even if the acts had effects within the Common Market.[2] Nevertheless, the Court held those companies in violation of Article 81 because they owned subsidiary companies within the Community and controlled their behavior. The foreign parent and its EU subsidiaries were treated as a "single enterprise" for purposes of service of process, judgment, and collection of fines and penalties. In doing so, the Court observed that the fact that a subsidiary company has its own legal personality does not rule out the possibility that its conduct is attributable to the parent company.

The Court has extended its reasoning to the extraterritorial application of Article 82.[3] A United States parent company, for example, was held potentially liable for acquisitions by its EC subsidiary which affected market conditions within the Community.[4] In another decision, the Court held that a Maryland company's refusal to sell its product to a competitor of its affiliate company within the Union was a result of united "single enterprise" action.[5] It proceeded to state that extraterritorial conduct merely having "repercussions on competitive structures" in the Common Market fell within the parameters of Article 82. The Court ordered Commercial Solvents, through its Italian affiliate, to supply the competitor at reasonable prices.

§ 7.27

1. Ahlström v. Commission (1988) Eur.Comm.Rep. 5193; Zinc Producers v. Commission (1984) Eur.Comm.Rep. 1679.

2. See ICI v. Commission (1972) Eur. Comm.Rep. 619.

3. For a discussion of the extraterritorial reach of the Merger Control Regulation, see Montag, Common Market Merger Control of Third–Country Enterprises, Comparative Law Yearbook of International Business 47 (1991).

4. See Europemballage Corp. and Continental Can Co., Inc. v. Commission (1973) Eur.Comm.Rep. 215.

5. See Commercial Solvents Corp. v. Commission (1974) Eur.Comm.Rep. 223.

Wood Pulp Case

In 1988, the Court of Justice widened the extraterritorial reach of Article 81 in a case where wood pulp producers from the U.S., Canada, Sweden and Finland were fined for price fixing activities affecting EU trade and competition. These firms did not have substantial operations within the Union. They were primarily exporters to the Common Market. This decision's utilization of a place of implementation "effects test" is quite similar to that used under the Sherman Act.[6] And the reliance by the U.S. exporters upon a traditional Webb–Pomerene cartel exemptions from United States antitrust law carried no weight in the European Union. The Court has also affirmed the extraterritorial reach of Articles 81 and 82 to airfares in and out of the Union,[7] and the Mergers Regulation (supra) clearly applies to firms located outside the Common Market.

§ 7.28   The Effects Test and Blocking Statutes

It may be a substantial jump to predict that Articles 81 and 82 bear upon a business transaction done in the United States or another non–EU country which merely inures to the competitive disadvantage of a company located within the Common Market. Yet in one of the *Dyestuffs* cases as early as 1969 the Commission took the position that:

> The rules of competition of the Treaty are therefore applicable to all restrictions on competition that produce within the Common Market effects to which Article 81, paragraph 1, applies. There is therefore no need to examine whether the enterprises that originated such restraints of competition have their head office within or outside of the Community.[1]

Although the Court's disposition of the *Dyestuffs* cases did not endorse such reasoning, the Commission has reasserted its "effects test" in subsequent arguments. The Commission's approach merits close consideration if only because the initiation of an Article 81 or 82 inquiry can generate local overhead costs for those involved in EU business transactions. That courts in the United States have also used an "effects test" in connection with the question of the extraterritoriality of American antitrust laws increases the potential for uncertainty and costs in international transactions.[2]

---

6. Woodpulp Producers v. Commission (1988) Eur.Comm.Rep. 5193.

7. Ahmed Saeed Flugreisen v. Zentrale zur Bekämpfung unlauteren Wettbewerbs (1989) Eur.Comm.Rep. 838.

§ 7.28

1. Commission v. I.C.I., 8 Common Mkt.L.Rep. 494 (1969).

2. *See generally* Spencer Weber Waller, International Trade and U.S. Antitrust Law (Supp. 1994).

U.S. Extraterritorial Antitrust

United States courts have long asserted the right to apply the Sherman Antitrust Act to foreign commerce affecting the United States market.[3] In some cases, this approach has been tempered to allow consideration of the interests of comity and foreign countries in the outcome.[4] Sherman Act amendments adopted in 1984 stress the "direct, substantial and reasonably foreseeable" nature of effects on American foreign commerce as a prerequisite to antitrust jurisdiction. Nevertheless, the potential for conflict in this field is enormous. For example, a multinational enterprise (MNE) headquartered in the U.S. but doing business in Europe could be constrained by United States antitrust law from fixing prices, yet permitted by EU competition law under Article 81(3) to do exactly that. Assuming that the price fixing in question has effects in both markets, what course of action is to be followed? There is no easy answer. When the MNE is located within a country other than one of the member states of the EU or the United States, but engages in activity having effects within those markets, the problem potential of extraterritoriality may be even more acute. Reconciling a conflict of antitrust laws applied extraterritorially by these two jurisdictions could become a flashpoint in international business transactions.

The problem becomes all the more apparent when one considers the increasing influence of international trade policy on the application of antitrust laws. For example, the U.S. Department of Justice has indicated that it will take enforcement action against conduct occurring overseas that restrains exports, regardless of whether or not there is direct harm to U.S. consumers, where it is clear that the conduct has a direct, substantial and reasonably foreseeable effect on exports of goods and services from the United States, the conduct infringes U.S. antitrust laws, and the U.S. courts have jurisdiction over the foreign persons or corporations engaged in such conduct.[5] Although the application of this policy has not created any significant problems,[6] the influence of international trade policy on the application of antitrust law does carry the potential of becoming a major issue in relations with foreign countries.

3. *See especially* United States v. Aluminum Co. of America, 148 F.2d 416 (2d Cir. 1945) (L. Hand, J.); Hartford Fire Insurance Co. v. California, 509 U.S. 764, 113 S.Ct. 2891, 125 L.Ed.2d 612 (1993).

4. *See especially* Timberland Lumber Co. v. Bank of America, 549 F.2d 597 (9th Cir. 1976); *Compare* Laker Airways Ltd. v. Sabena, Belgian World Airlines, 731 F.2d 909 (D.C. Cir. 1984); Hartford Fire Insurance Co. v. California, 509 U.S. 764, 113 S.Ct. 2891, 125 L.Ed.2d 612 (1993).

5. Dept. of Justice press release (3 April 1992).

6. *See* United States v. Pilkington, 7 Trade Reg.Rep. (CCH) ¶ 50,758 (1994); United States v. MCI Communications, 7 Trade Reg.Rep. (CCH) ¶ 50,761 (1994).

Blocking Statutes

In the case of antitrust judgments emanating from courts in the United States, most notably the "Uranium Cartel" treble damages litigation of the late 1970s,[7] many nations consider the flashpoint already reached. At least nine nations (Australia, Canada, France, Germany, Netherlands, New Zealand, Philippines, South Africa, and the United Kingdom) have taken retaliatory action by enacting "blocking statutes." In addition, the 41 Commonwealth nations have resolved general support for a position similar to that of the United Kingdom.

The United Kingdom blocking statute is the Protection of Trading Interests Act of 1980.[8] This Act (without specifying American antitrust law) makes it difficult to depose witnesses, obtain documents or enforce multiple liability judgments extraterritorially in the U.K. Violation of the 1980 Act may result in criminal penalties. Furthermore, under the "clawback" provision of the Act, parties with outstanding multiple liabilities in foreign jurisdictions (*e.g.,* United States treble damages defendants) may recoup the punitive element of such awards in Britain against assets of the successful plaintiff. The British Act invites other nations to adopt clawback provisions by offering clawback reciprocity. United States attorneys confronted with a blocking statute need to understand that multiple liability judgments combined with contingency fee arrangements are virtually unknown elsewhere.

Policy Debate

The extensive array of pre-trial discovery mechanisms allowed in U.S. civil litigation rarely, if ever, have a counterpart in foreign law. Discovery subpoenas originating in American litigation are often "shocking" to many foreign defendants. And the U.S. Supreme Court has ruled that use of letters rogatory under the Hague Convention[9] is not obligatory.[10] It is the blocking of discovery that potentially most threatens the extraterritorial application of United States laws, especially antitrust. Since United States courts may sanction parties who in bad faith fail to respond to discovery requests, foreign defendants requesting help from their home governments under blocking statutes are especially at risk. On the other hand, good faith efforts to modify or work around discovery

7. *See* In re Uranium Antitrust Litigation (Westinghouse Electric Corp.) v. Rio Algom Limited, 617 F.2d 1248 (7th Cir. 1980).

8. Reprinted in 21 I.L.M. 834 (1982).

9. Hague Convention on the Taking of Evidence Abroad in Civil or Commercial Matters, 23 U.S.T. 2555, T.A.I.S. No. 7444.

10. Société Nationale Industrielle Aérospatiale v. U.S. District Court, 482 U.S. 522, 107 S.Ct. 2542, 96 L.Ed.2d 461 (1987).

blockades may favor foreign defendants. Such defendants are often caught in a "no win" situation. Either way they will be penalized.

Reasons advanced to support an extraterritorial application of United States antitrust laws are founded on the idea that some extraterritorial extension is necessary to prevent their circumvention by multinational corporations which have the business sagacity to ensure that anticompetitive transactions are consummated beyond the territorial borders of the United States. An extraterritorial extension of antitrust laws can help to protect the export opportunities of domestic firms. Extraterritorial application of the antitrust laws can also help to ensure that the American consumer receives the benefit of competing imports, which in turn may spur complacent domestic industries. The effect of foreign auto imports on the car manufacturers in the United States may be cited as an example. In an increasingly internationalized world, extraterritorial antitrust may merely reflect economic reality.

On the other hand, the British argue that American extraterritoriality permits the U.S. to unjustifiably "mold the international economic and trading world to its own image." In particular, the U.S. "effects" doctrine creates legal uncertainty for international traders, and U.S. courts pay little attention to the competing policies (interests) of other concerned governments. As the House of Lords has stated: "It is axiomatic that in anti-trust matters the policy of one state may be to defend what it is the policy of another state to attack."[11] The British also argue, not without some support, that customary international law does not permit extraterritorial application of national laws.[12] In making this argument, the British have a convenient way of forgetting about the extraterritorial scope of Articles 81 and 82, which are now part of their law. Moreover, in a curious reversal of roles illustrating the extremes of the debate, the British government applied the Protection of Trading Interests Act to block the pursuit of treble damages in *United States* courts by the liquidator of Laker Airways against British Airways and other defendants. A House of Lords decision reversed this ban but retained government restrictions on discovery related to the case.[13]

---

11. Westinghouse Electric Corp. V. Rio Tinto Zinc Corp., 2 W.L.R. 81 (1978).

12. *See* arguments presented by the British government in Hartford Fire Insurance Co. v. California discussed in Reuland, Hartford Fire Insurance Co., Comity and the Extraterritorial Reach of United States Antitrust Laws, 29 Tex. Int'l L.J. 159 (1994) and Brief of the Government of the United Kingdom of Great Britain and Northern Ireland as Amicus Curiae in Société Nationale Industrielle Aérospatiale v. U.S. District Ct., reprinted in 25 I.L.M. 1557 (1986).

13. British Airways Board v. Laker Airways, 3 W.L.R. 413 (1984).

§ 7.29 United States—European Union Cooperation on Antitrust

U.S. Antitrust Cooperation Agreements

Some evidence of international antitrust cooperation is contained in a 1967 recommendation of the OECD which provides for notification of antitrust actions, exchanges of information to the extent that the disclosure is domestically permissible, and where practical, coordination of antitrust enforcement.[1] The OECD resolution served as a model for the 1972 "Antitrust Notification and Consultation Procedure" between Canada and the United States. Following the "Uranium Cartel" litigation, Australia, and the United States reached an Agreement on Cooperation in Antitrust Matters (1982) to minimize jurisdictional conflicts.[2] Australia has taken the position that United States courts are not a proper institution to balance interests of concerned countries within the context of private antitrust litigation. The Agreement on Cooperation provides that when the Government of Australia is concerned with private antitrust proceedings pending in a United States court, the Government of Australia may request the Government of the United States to participate in the litigation. The United States must report to the court on the substance and outcome of consultations with Australia on the matter concerned. In this way, Australia's views and interests in the litigation and its potential outcome are made known to the court. The court is not required to defer to those views, or even to openly consider them. It merely receives the "report." Australia, in turn, has indicated a willingness to be more receptive to discovery requests in U.S. antitrust litigation and to consult before invoking its blocking statute.

Similar arrangements were made in the Memorandum of Understanding Between the U.S. and Canada With Respect to the Application of National Antitrust Laws (1984). No such agreement has been reached with the United Kingdom, with whom the extra-territoriality issue remains contentious, a fact which has led some to wonder whether the United States ought to have its own blocking statute against extraterritorial EU competition law. However, an antitrust cooperation agreement seems more appropriate, and late in 1991 the European Union and the United States reached such an agreement.[3] Comparable agreements between the EU and Canada, and the EU and Japan have been concluded.

§ 7.29

1. In 1986, the OECD issued a similar Recommendation Concerning Cooperation Between Member States on Restrictive Business Practices Affecting International Trade, reprinted in 25 I.L.M. 1629 (1986).

2. Reprinted in 21 I.L.M. 702 (1982).

3. Because the Court of Justice held that the Cooperation Agreement with the United States was void since the Commission did not have the requisite authority to enter into such an agreement, France v. Commission (1994) Eur.

EU—U.S. Cooperation

The U.S.–EU accord commits the parties to notify each other of imminent enforcement action, to share relevant information and consult on potential policy changes. An innovative feature is the inclusion of "comity" principles, each side promising to take the other's interests and requests into account when considering antitrust prosecutions. The agreement has had a significant effect on mergers of firms doing business in North America and the Union. Each side has agreed to notify and consult with the other regarding antitrust matters, including mergers and acquisitions, that "may affect important interests." In its first six months of operation, about 45 notifications were exchanged between the Commission, the U.S. Federal Trade Commission, and the Antitrust Division of the U.S. Justice Department. A large portion of these notifications concerned international mergers and acquisitions. Since both the EU and the U.S. have premerger notification systems,[4] the exchange of such information has increased rapidly. In the first year after the cooperation agreement, U.S. antitrust enforcers sent 37 such notifications to the European Commission and received 15 in return. About 20 percent of all the mergers reviewed by the Commission under its competition law were simultaneously being reviewed by U.S. antitrust authorities, but as Section 7.22 (above) reveals, cooperative review can result in conflicting decisions.

The agreement was prominently used to jointly negotiate a 1994 settlement on restrictive practices of the Microsoft Corporation. Since the Commission has traditionally permitted U.S. lawyers to appear before it on competition law matters, the FTC announced on the same day as the signing of the US–EU antitrust cooperation agreement that EU lawyers would be permitted to appear before it on a reciprocal basis. In the more recent round of public prosecutions of Microsoft focused on Windows as a monopoly, the United States settlement reached in 2001 is less demanding than the Commission judgment of 2004 which requires an unbundling of media playback capabilities. This example reaffirms that transatlantic antitrust "cooperation" need not necessarily result in similar outcomes.

Comm.Rep. I–03641 (Case No. C–327/91), the Commission has recently asked the Council to expressly approve the Agreement.

4. *See* Section 7.22.

Appendix I

CONSOLIDATED VERSION OF THE TREATY ON EUROPEAN UNION

(as amended by the Nice Treaty of 2003)

CONTENTS

II. PROTOCOLS (text not reproduced)

TITLE I
COMMON PROVISIONS

Article 1

By this Treaty, the HIGH CONTRACTING PARTIES establish among themselves a EUROPEAN UNION, hereinafter called 'the Union''.

This Treaty marks a new stage in the process of creating an ever closer union among the peoples of Europe, in which decisions are taken as openly as possible and as closely as possible to the citizen.

The Union shall be founded on the European Communities, supplemented by the policies and forms of cooperation established by this Treaty. Its task shall be to organise, in a manner demonstrating consistency and solidarity, relations between the Member States and between their peoples.

Article 2

The Union shall set itself the following objectives:

— to promote economic and social progress and a high level of employment and to achieve balanced and sustainable development, in particular through the creation of an area without internal frontiers, through the strengthening of economic and social cohesion and through the establishment of economic and monetary union, ultimately including a single currency in accordance with the provisions of this Treaty,

— to assert its identity on the international scene, in particular through the implementation of a common foreign and security policy including the progressive framing of a common defence policy, which might lead to a common defence, in accordance with the provisions of Article 17,

— to strengthen the protection of the rights and interests of the nationals of its Member States through the introduction of a citizenship of the Union,

— to maintain and develop the Union as an area of freedom, security and justice, in which the free movement of persons is assured in conjunction with appropriate measures with respect to external border controls, asylum, immigration and the prevention and combating of crime,

— to maintain in full the *acquis communautaire* and build on it with a view to considering to what extent the policies and forms of cooperation introduced by this Treaty may need to be revised with the aim of ensuring the effectiveness of the mechanisms and the institutions of the Community.

The objectives of the Union shall be achieved as provided in this Treaty and in accordance with the conditions and the timetable set out therein while respecting the principle of subsidiarity as defined in Article 5 of the Treaty establishing the European Community.

Article 3

The Union shall be served by a single institutional framework which shall ensure the consistency and the continuity of the activities carried out in order to attain its objectives while respecting and building upon the *acquis communautaire*.

The Union shall in particular ensure the consistency of its external activities as a whole in the context of its external relations, security, economic and development policies. The Council and the Commission shall be responsible for ensuring such consistency and shall cooperate to this end. They shall ensure the implementation of these policies, each in accordance with its respective powers.

Article 4

The European Council shall provide the Union with the necessary impetus for its development and shall define the general political guidelines thereof.

The European Council shall bring together the Heads of State or Government of the Member States and the President of the Commission. They shall be assisted by the Ministers for Foreign Affairs of the Member States and by a Member of the Commission. The European Council shall meet at least twice a year, under the chairmanship of the Head of State or Government of the Member State which holds the Presidency of the Council.

The European Council shall submit to the European Parliament a report after each of its meetings and a yearly written report on the progress achieved by the Union.

Article 5

The European Parliament, the Council, the Commission, the Court of Justice and the Court of Auditors shall exercise their powers under the conditions and for the purposes provided for, on the one hand, by the provisions of the Treaties establishing the European Communities and of the subsequent Treaties and Acts modifying and supplementing them and, on the other hand, by the other provisions of this Treaty.

Article 6

1. The Union is founded on the principles of liberty, democracy, respect for human rights and fundamental freedoms, and the rule of law, principles which are common to the Member States.

2. The Union shall respect fundamental rights, as guaranteed by the European Convention for the Protection of Human Rights and Funda-

mental Freedoms signed in Rome on 4 November 1950 and as they result from the constitutional traditions common to the Member States, as general principles of Community law.

3. The Union shall respect the national identities of its Member States.

4. The Union shall provide itself with the means necessary to attain its objectives and carry through its policies.

*Article 7**

1. On a reasoned proposal by one third of the Member States, by the European Parliament or by the Commission, the Council, acting by a majority of four fifths of its members after obtaining the assent of the European Parliament, may determine that there is a clear risk of a serious breach by a Member State of principles mentioned in Article 6(1), and address appropriate recommendations to that State. Before making such a determination, the Council shall hear the Member State in question and, acting in accordance with the same procedure, may call on independent persons to submit within a reasonable time limit a report on the situation in the Member State in question.

The Council shall regularly verify that the grounds on which such a determination was made continue to apply.

2. The Council, meeting in the composition of the Heads of State or Government and acting by unanimity on a proposal by one third of the Member States or by the Commission and after obtaining the assent of the European Parliament, may determine the existence of a serious and persistent breach by a Member State of principles mentioned in Article 6(1), after inviting the government of the Member State in question to submit its observations.

3. Where a determination under paragraph 2 has been made, the Council, acting by a qualified majority, may decide to suspend certain of the rights deriving from the application of this Treaty to the Member State in question, including the voting rights of the representative of the government of that Member State in the Council. In doing so, the Council shall take into account the possible consequences of such a suspension on the rights and obligations of natural and legal persons.

The obligations of the Member State in question under this Treaty shall in any case continue to be binding on that State.

4. The Council, acting by a qualified majority, may decide subsequently to vary or revoke measures taken under paragraph 3 in response to changes in the situation which led to their being imposed.

5. For the purposes of this Article, the Council shall act without taking into account the vote of the representative of the government of the Member State in question. Abstentions by members present in

---

* Article amended by the Treaty of Nice.

person or represented shall not prevent the adoption of decisions referred to in paragraph 2. A qualified majority shall be defined as the same proportion of the weighted votes of the members of the Council concerned as laid down in Article 205(2) of the Treaty establishing the European Community.

This paragraph shall also apply in the event of voting rights being suspended pursuant to paragraph 3.

6. For the purposes of paragraphs 1 and 2, the European Parliament shall act by a two-thirds majority of the votes cast, representing a majority of its Members.

* * *

TITLE V
PROVISIONS ON A COMMON FOREIGN
AND SECURITY POLICY

Article 11

1. The Union shall define and implement a common foreign and security policy covering all areas of foreign and security policy, the objectives of which shall be:

— to safeguard the common values, fundamental interests, independence and integrity of the Union in conformity with the principles of the United Nations Charter,

— to strengthen the security of the Union in all ways,

— to preserve peace and strengthen international security, in accordance with the principles of the United Nations Charter, as well as the principles of the Helsinki Final Act and the objectives of the Paris Charter, including those on external borders,

— to promote international cooperation,

— to develop and consolidate democracy and the rule of law, and respect for human rights and fundamental freedoms.

2. The Member States shall support the Union's external and security policy actively and unreservedly in a spirit of loyalty and mutual solidarity.

The Member States shall work together to enhance and develop their mutual political solidarity. They shall refrain from any action which is contrary to the interests of the Union or likely to impair its effectiveness as a cohesive force in international relations.

The Council shall ensure that these principles are complied with.

Article 12

The Union shall pursue the objectives set out in Article 11 by:

— defining the principles of and general guidelines for the common foreign and security policy,

— deciding on common strategies,

— adopting joint actions,

— adopting common positions,

— strengthening systematic cooperation between Member States in the conduct of policy.

Article 13

1. The European Council shall define the principles of and general guidelines for the common foreign and security policy, including for matters with defence implications.

2. The European Council shall decide on common strategies to be implemented by the Union in areas where the Member States have important interests in common.

Common strategies shall set out their objectives, duration and the means to be made available by the Union and the Member States.

3. The Council shall take the decisions necessary for defining and implementing the common foreign and security policy on the basis of the general guidelines defined by the European Council.

The Council shall recommend common strategies to the European Council and shall implement them, in particular by adopting joint actions and common positions.

The Council shall ensure the unity, consistency and effectiveness of action by the Union.

Article 14

1. The Council shall adopt joint actions. Joint actions shall address specific situations where operational action by the Union is deemed to be required. They shall lay down their objectives, scope, the means to be made available to the Union, if necessary their duration, and the conditions for their implementation.

2. If there is a change in circumstances having a substantial effect on a question subject to joint action, the Council shall review the principles and objectives of that action and take the necessary decisions. As long as the Council has not acted, the joint action shall stand.

3. Joint actions shall commit the Member States in the positions they adopt and in the conduct of their activity.

4. The Council may request the Commission to submit to it any appropriate proposals relating to the common foreign and security policy to ensure the implementation of a joint action.

5. Whenever there is any plan to adopt a national position or take national action pursuant to a joint action, information shall be provided in time to allow, if necessary, for prior consultations within the

Council. The obligation to provide prior information shall not apply to measures which are merely a national transposition of Council decisions.

6. In cases of imperative need arising from changes in the situation and failing a Council decision, Member States may take the necessary measures as a matter of urgency having regard to the general objectives of the joint action. The Member State concerned shall inform the Council immediately of any such measures.

7. Should there be any major difficulties in implementing a joint action, a Member State shall refer them to the Council which shall discuss them and seek appropriate solutions. Such solutions shall not run counter to the objectives of the joint action or impair its effectiveness.

Article 15

The Council shall adopt common positions. Common positions shall define the approach of the Union to a particular matter of a geographical or thematic nature. Member States shall ensure that their national policies conform to the common positions.

Article 16

Member States shall inform and consult one another within the Council on any matter of foreign and security policy of general interest in order to ensure that the Union's influence is exerted as effectively as possible by means of concerted and convergent action.

Article 17*

1. The common foreign and security policy shall include all questions relating to the security of the Union, including the progressive framing of a common defence policy, which might lead to a common defence, should the European Council so decide. It shall in that case recommend to the Member States the adoption of such a decision in accordance with their respective constitutional requirements.

The policy of the Union in accordance with this Article shall not prejudice the specific character of the security and defence policy of certain Member States and shall respect the obligations of certain Member States, which see their common defence realised in the North Atlantic Treaty Organisation (NATO), under the North Atlantic Treaty and be compatible with the common security and defence policy established within that framework.

The progressive framing of a common defence policy will be supported, as Member States consider appropriate, by cooperation between them in the field of armaments.

* Article amended by the Treaty of Nice.

2. Questions referred to in this Article shall include humanitarian and rescue tasks, peacekeeping tasks and tasks of combat forces in crisis management, including peacemaking.

3. Decisions having defence implications dealt with under this Article shall be taken without prejudice to the policies and obligations referred to in paragraph 1, second subparagraph.

4. The provisions of this Article shall not prevent the development of closer cooperation between two or more Member States on a bilateral level, in the framework of the Western European Union (WEU) and NATO, provided such cooperation does not run counter to or impede that provided for in this title.

5. With a view to furthering the objectives of this Article, the provisions of this Article will be reviewed in accordance with Article 48.

Article 18

1. The Presidency shall represent the Union in matters coming within the common foreign and security policy.

2. The Presidency shall be responsible for the implementation of decisions taken under this title; in that capacity it shall in principle express the position of the Union in international organisations and international conferences.

3. The Presidency shall be assisted by the Secretary–General of the Council who shall exercise the function of High Representative for the common foreign and security policy.

4. The Commission shall be fully associated in the tasks referred to in paragraphs 1 and 2. The Presidency shall be assisted in those tasks if need be by the next Member State to hold the Presidency.

5. The Council may, whenever it deems it necessary, appoint a special representative with a mandate in relation to particular policy issues.

Article 19

1. Member States shall coordinate their action in international organisations and at international conferences. They shall uphold the common positions in such forums.

In international organisations and at international conferences where not all the Member States participate, those which do take part shall uphold the common positions.

2. Without prejudice to paragraph 1 and Article 14(3), Member States represented in international organisations or international conferences where not all the Member States participate shall keep the latter informed of any matter of common interest.

Member States which are also members of the United Nations Security Council will concert and keep the other Member States fully informed. Member States which are permanent members of the Security Council will, in the execution of their functions, ensure the defence of the positions and the interests of the Union, without prejudice to their responsibilities under the provisions of the United Nations Charter.

Article 20

The diplomatic and consular missions of the Member States and the Commission delegations in third countries and international conferences, and their representations to international organisations, shall cooperate in ensuring that the common positions and joint actions adopted by the Council are complied with and implemented.

They shall step up cooperation by exchanging information, carrying out joint assessments and contributing to the implementation of the provisions referred to in Article 20 of the Treaty establishing the European Community.

Article 21

The Presidency shall consult the European Parliament on the main aspects and the basic choices of the common foreign and security policy and shall ensure that the views of the European Parliament are duly taken into consideration. The European Parliament shall be kept regularly informed by the Presidency and the Commission of the development of the Union's foreign and security policy.

The European Parliament may ask questions of the Council or make recommendations to it. It shall hold an annual debate on progress in implementing the common foreign and security policy.

Article 22

1.   Any Member State or the Commission may refer to the Council any question relating to the common foreign and security policy and may submit proposals to the Council.

2.   In cases requiring a rapid decision, the Presidency, of its own motion, or at the request of the Commission or a Member State, shall convene an extraordinary Council meeting within 48 hours or, in an emergency, within a shorter period.

Article 23*

1.   Decisions under this title shall be taken by the Council acting unanimously. Abstentions by members present in person or represented shall not prevent the adoption of such decisions.

When abstaining in a vote, any member of the Council may qualify its abstention by making a formal declaration under the present subparagraph. In that case, it shall not be obliged to apply the decision, but shall accept that the decision commits the Union. In a spirit of mutual solidarity, the Member State concerned shall refrain from any action likely to conflict with or impede Union action based on that decision and the other Member States shall respect its position. If the members

* Article amended by the Treaty of   Nice.

of the Council qualifying their abstention in this way represent more than one third of the votes weighted in accordance with Article 205(2) of the Treaty establishing the European Community, the decision shall not be adopted.

2.   By derogation from the provisions of paragraph 1, the Council shall act by qualified majority:

—   when adopting joint actions, common positions or taking any other decision on the basis of a common strategy,

—   when adopting any decision implementing a joint action or a common position,

—   when appointing a special representative in accordance with Article 18(5).

If a member of the Council declares that, for important and stated reasons of national policy, it intends to oppose the adoption of a decision to be taken by qualified majority, a vote shall not be taken. The Council may, acting by a qualified majority, request that the matter be referred to the European Council for decision by unanimity.

The votes of the members of the Council shall be weighted in accordance with Article 205(2) of the Treaty establishing the European Community. For their adoption, decisions shall require at least 62 votes in favour, cast by at least 10 members**.

This paragraph shall not apply to decisions having military or defence implications.

3.   For procedural questions, the Council shall act by a majority of its members.

Article 24*

1.   When it is necessary to conclude an agreement with one or more States or international organisations in implementation of this title, the Council may authorise the Presidency, assisted by the Commission as appropriate, to open negotiations to that effect. Such agreements shall be concluded by the Council on a recommendation from the Presidency.

2.   The Council shall act unanimously when the agreement covers an issue for which unanimity is required for the adoption of internal decisions.

3.   When the agreement is envisaged in order to implement a joint action or common position, the Council shall act by a qualified majority in accordance with Article 23(2).

4.   The provisions of this Article shall also apply to matters falling under Title VI. When the agreement covers an issue for which a qualified majority is required for the adoption of internal decisions or

** This subparagraph will be amended on 1 January 2005 in accordance with the Protocol on the enlargement of the European Union (see Annex).

measures, the Council shall act by a qualified majority in accordance with Article 34(3).

5. No agreement shall be binding on a Member State whose representative in the Council states that it has to comply with the requirements of its own constitutional procedure; the other members of the Council may agree that the agreement shall nevertheless apply provisionally.

6. Agreements concluded under the conditions set out by this Article shall be binding on the institutions of the Union.

Article 25*

Without prejudice to Article 207 of the Treaty establishing the European Community, a Political and Security Committee shall monitor the international situation in the areas covered by the common foreign and security policy and contribute to the definition of policies by delivering opinions to the Council at the request of the Council or on its own initiative. It shall also monitor the implementation of agreed policies, without prejudice to the responsibility of the Presidency and the Commission.

Within the scope of this title, this Committee shall exercise, under the responsibility of the Council, political control and strategic direction of crisis management operations.

The Council may authorise the Committee, for the purpose and for the duration of a crisis management operation, as determined by the Council, to take the relevant decisions concerning the political control and strategic direction of the operation, without prejudice to Article 47.

Article 26

The Secretary–General of the Council, High Representative for the common foreign and security policy, shall assist the Council in matters coming within the scope of the common foreign and security policy, in particular through contributing to the formulation, preparation and implementation of policy decisions, and, when appropriate and acting on behalf of the Council at the request of the Presidency, through conducting political dialogue with third parties.

Article 27

The Commission shall be fully associated with the work carried out in the common foreign and security policy field.

Article 27a*

1. Enhanced cooperation in any of the areas referred to in this title shall be aimed at safeguarding the values and serving the interests of the Union as a whole by asserting its identity as a coherent force on the international scene. It shall respect:

* Article amended by the Treaty of   Nice.

— the principles, objectives, general guidelines and consistency of the common foreign and security policy and the decisions taken within the framework of that policy,

— the powers of the European Community, and

— consistency between all the Union's policies and its external activities.

2. Articles 11 to 27 and Articles 27b to 28 shall apply to the enhanced cooperation provided for in this article, save as otherwise provided in Article 27c and Articles 43 to 45.

Article 27b*

Enhanced cooperation pursuant to this title shall relate to implementation of a joint action or a common position. It shall not relate to matters having military or defence implications.

Article 27c*

Member States which intend to establish enhanced cooperation between themselves under Article 27b shall address a request to the Council to that effect.

The request shall be forwarded to the Commission and, for information, to the European Parliament. The Commission shall give its opinion particularly on whether the enhanced cooperation proposed is consistent with Union policies. Authorisation shall be granted by the Council, acting in accordance with the second and third subparagraphs of Article 23(2) and in compliance with Articles 43 to 45.

Article 27d*

Without prejudice to the powers of the Presidency and of the Commission, the Secretary–General of the Council, High Representative for the common foreign and security policy, shall in particular ensure that the European Parliament and all members of the Council are kept fully informed of the implementation of enhanced cooperation in the field of the common foreign and security policy.

Article 27e*

Any Member State which wishes to participate in enhanced cooperation established in accordance with Article 27c shall notify its intention to the Council and inform the Commission. The Commission shall give an opinion to the Council within three months of the date of receipt of that notification. Within four months of the date of receipt of that notification, the Council shall take a decision on the request and on such specific arrangements as it may deem necessary. The decision shall be deemed to be taken unless the Council, acting by a qualified majority within the same period, decides to hold it in abeyance; in that

* Article inserted by the Treaty of   Nice.

case, the Council shall state the reasons for its decision and set a deadline for re-examining it.

For the purposes of this Article, the Council shall act by a qualified majority. The qualified majority shall be defined as the same proportion of the weighted votes and the same proportion of the number of the members of the Council concerned as those laid down in the third subparagraph of Article 23(2).

Article 28

1.   Articles 189, 190, 196 to 199, 203, 204, 206 to 209, 213 to 219, 255 and 290 of the Treaty establishing the European Community shall apply to the provisions relating to the areas referred to in this title.

2.   Administrative expenditure which the provisions relating to the areas referred to in this title entail for the institutions shall be charged to the budget of the European Communities.

3.   Operating expenditure to which the implementation of those provisions gives rise shall also be charged to the budget of the European Communities, except for such expenditure arising from operations having military or defence implications and cases where the Council acting unanimously decides otherwise.

In cases where expenditure is not charged to the budget of the European Communities, it shall be charged to the Member States in accordance with the gross national product scale, unless the Council acting unanimously decides otherwise. As for expenditure arising from operations having military or defence implications, Member States whose representatives in the Council have made a formal declaration under Article 23(1), second subparagraph, shall not be obliged to contribute to the financing thereof.

4.   The budgetary procedure laid down in the Treaty establishing the European Community shall apply to the expenditure charged to the budget of the European Communities.

TITLE VI
PROVISIONS ON POLICE AND JUDICIAL COOPERATION
13 IN CRIMINAL MATTERS

Article 29*

Without prejudice to the powers of the European Community, the Union's objective shall be to provide citizens with a high level of safety within an area of freedom, security and justice by developing common action among the Member States in the fields of police and judicial cooperation in criminal matters and by preventing and combating racism and xenophobia.

* Article amended by the Treaty of Nice.

That objective shall be achieved by preventing and combating crime, organised or otherwise, in particular terrorism, trafficking in persons and offences against children, illicit drug trafficking and illicit arms trafficking, corruption and fraud, through:

— closer cooperation between police forces, customs authorities and other competent authorities in the Member States, both directly and through the European Police Office (Europol), in accordance with the provisions of Articles 30 and 32,

— closer cooperation between judicial and other competent authorities of the Member States including cooperation through the European Judicial Cooperation Unit ("Eurojust"), in accordance with the provisions of Articles 31 and 32,

— approximation, where necessary, of rules on criminal matters in the Member States, in accordance with the provisions of Article 31(e).

Article 30

1. Common action in the field of police cooperation shall include:

(a) operational cooperation between the competent authorities, including the police, customs and other specialised law enforcement services of the Member States in relation to the prevention, detection and investigation of criminal offences;

(b) the collection, storage, processing, analysis and exchange of relevant information, including information held by law enforcement services on reports on suspicious financial transactions, in particular through Europol, subject to appropriate provisions on the protection of personal data;

(c) cooperation and joint initiatives in training, the exchange of liaison officers, secondments, the use of equipment, and forensic research;

(d) the common evaluation of particular investigative techniques in relation to the detection of serious forms of organised crime.

2. The Council shall promote cooperation through Europol and shall in particular, within a period of five years after the date of entry into force of the Treaty of Amsterdam:

(a) enable Europol to facilitate and support the preparation, and to encourage the coordination and carrying out, of specific investigative actions by the competent authorities of the Member States, including operational actions of joint teams comprising representatives of Europol in a support capacity;

(b) adopt measures allowing Europol to ask the competent authorities of the Member States to conduct and coordinate their investigations in specific cases and to develop specific expertise which may be put at the disposal of Member States to assist them in investigating cases of organised crime;

(c) promote liaison arrangements between prosecuting/investigating officials specialising in the fight against organised crime in close cooperation with Europol;

(d) establish a research, documentation and statistical network on cross-border crime.

Article 31*

1. Common action on judicial cooperation in criminal matters shall include:

(a) facilitating and accelerating cooperation between competent ministries and judicial or equivalent authorities of the Member States, including, where appropriate, cooperation through Eurojust, in relation to proceedings and the enforcement of decisions;

(b) facilitating extradition between Member States;

(c) ensuring compatibility in rules applicable in the Member States, as may be necessary to improve such cooperation;

(d) preventing conflicts of jurisdiction between Member States;

(e) progressively adopting measures establishing minimum rules relating to the constituent elements of criminal acts and to penalties in the fields of organised crime, terrorism and illicit drug trafficking.

2. The Council shall encourage cooperation through Eurojust by:

(a) enabling Eurojust to facilitate proper coordination between Member States' national prosecuting authorities;

(b) promoting support by Eurojust for criminal investigations in cases of serious cross-border crime, particularly in the case of organised crime, taking account, in particular, of analyses carried out by Europol;

(c) facilitating close cooperation between Eurojust and the European Judicial Network, particularly, in order to facilitate the execution of letters rogatory and the implementation of extradition requests.

Article 32

The Council shall lay down the conditions and limitations under which the competent authorities referred to in Articles 30 and 31 may operate in the territory of another Member State in liaison and in agreement with the authorities of that State.

Article 33

This title shall not affect the exercise of the responsibilities incumbent upon Member States with regard to the maintenance of law and order and the safeguarding of internal security.

* Article amended by the Treaty of Nice.

Article 34

1.   In the areas referred to in this title, Member States shall inform and consult one another within the Council with a view to coordinating their action. To that end, they shall establish collaboration between the relevant departments of their administrations.

2.   The Council shall take measures and promote cooperation, using the appropriate form and procedures as set out in this title, contributing to the pursuit of the objectives of the Union. To that end, acting unanimously on the initiative of any Member State or of the Commission, the Council may:

(a) adopt common positions defining the approach of the Union to a particular matter;

(b) adopt framework decisions for the purpose of approximation of the laws and regulations of the Member States. Framework decisions shall be binding upon the Member States as to the result to be achieved but shall leave to the national authorities the choice of form and methods. They shall not entail direct effect;

(c) adopt decisions for any other purpose consistent with the objectives of this title, excluding any approximation of the laws and regulations of the Member States. These decisions shall be binding and shall not entail direct effect; the Council, acting by a qualified majority, shall adopt measures necessary to implement those decisions at the level of the Union;

(d) establish conventions which it shall recommend to the Member States for adoption in accordance with their respective constitutional requirements. Member States shall begin the procedures applicable within a time limit to be set by the Council.

Unless they provide otherwise, conventions shall, once adopted by at least half of the Member States, enter into force for those Member States. Measures implementing conventions shall be adopted within the Council by a majority of two thirds of the Contracting Parties.

3.*   Where the Council is required to act by a qualified majority, the votes of its members shall be weighted as laid down in Article 205(2) of the Treaty establishing the European Community, and for their adoption acts of the Council shall require at least 62 votes in favour, cast by at least 10 members.

4.   For procedural questions, the Council shall act by a majority of its members.

Article 35

1.   The Court of Justice of the European Communities shall have jurisdiction, subject to the conditions laid down in this article, to give

---

* This paragraph will be amended on 1 January 2005, in accordance with the   Protocol on the enlargement of the European Union (see Annex).

preliminary rulings on the validity and interpretation of framework decisions and decisions, on the interpretation of conventions established under this title and on the validity and interpretation of the measures implementing them.

2. By a declaration made at the time of signature of the Treaty of Amsterdam or at any time thereafter, any Member State shall be able to accept the jurisdiction of the Court of Justice to give preliminary rulings as specified in paragraph 1.

3. A Member State making a declaration pursuant to paragraph 2 shall specify that either:

(a) any court or tribunal of that State against whose decisions there is no judicial remedy under national law may request the Court of Justice to give a preliminary ruling on a question raised in a case pending before it and concerning the validity or interpretation of an act referred to in paragraph 1 if that court or tribunal considers that a decision on the question is necessary to enable it to give judgment; or

(b) any court or tribunal of that State may request the Court of Justice to give a preliminary ruling on a question raised in a case pending before it and concerning the validity or interpretation of an act referred to in paragraph 1 if that court or tribunal considers that a decision on the question is necessary to enable it to give judgment.

4. Any Member State, whether or not it has made a declaration pursuant to paragraph 2, shall be entitled to submit statements of case or written observations to the Court in cases which arise under paragraph 1.

5. The Court of Justice shall have no jurisdiction to review the validity or proportionality of operations carried out by the police or other law enforcement services of a Member State or the exercise of the responsibilities incumbent upon Member States with regard to the maintenance of law and order and the safeguarding of internal security.

6. The Court of Justice shall have jurisdiction to review the legality of framework decisions and decisions in actions brought by a Member State or the Commission on grounds of lack of competence, infringement of an essential procedural requirement, infringement of this Treaty or of any rule of law relating to its application, or misuse of powers. The proceedings provided for in this paragraph shall be instituted within two months of the publication of the measure.

7. The Court of Justice shall have jurisdiction to rule on any dispute between Member States regarding the interpretation or the application of acts adopted under Article 34(2) whenever such dispute cannot be settled by the Council within six months of its being referred to the Council by one of its members. The Court shall also have jurisdiction to rule on any dispute between Member States and the Commission

regarding the interpretation or the application of conventions established under Article 34(2)(d).

Article 36

1. A Coordinating Committee shall be set up consisting of senior officials. In addition to its coordinating role, it shall be the task of the Committee to:

— give opinions for the attention of the Council, either at the Council's request or on its own initiative,

— contribute, without prejudice to Article 207 of the Treaty establishing the European Community, to the preparation of the Council's discussions in the areas referred to in Article 29.

2. The Commission shall be fully associated with the work in the areas referred to in this title.

Article 37

Within international organisations and at international conferences in which they take part, Member States shall defend the common positions adopted under the provisions of this title.

Articles 18 and 19 shall apply as appropriate to matters falling under this title.

Article 38

Agreements referred to in Article 24 may cover matters falling under this title.

Article 39

1. The Council shall consult the European Parliament before adopting any measure referred to in Article 34(2)(b), (c) and (d). The European Parliament shall deliver its opinion within a time limit which the Council may lay down, which shall not be less than three months. In the absence of an opinion within that time limit, the Council may act.

2. The Presidency and the Commission shall regularly inform the European Parliament of discussions in the areas covered by this title.

3. The European Parliament may ask questions of the Council or make recommendations to it. Each year, it shall hold a debate on the progress made in the areas referred to in this title.

Article 40*

1. Enhanced cooperation in any of the areas referred to in this title shall have the aim of enabling the Union to develop more rapidly into an area of freedom, security and justice, while respecting the powers of the European Community and the objectives laid down in this title.

* Article amended by the Treaty of Nice.

2. Articles 29 to 39 and Articles 40a to 41 shall apply to the enhanced cooperation provided for by this article, save as otherwise provided in Article 40a and in Articles 43 to 45.

3. The provisions of the Treaty establishing the European Community concerning the powers of the Court of Justice and the exercise of those powers shall apply to this article and to Articles 40a and 40b.

Article 40a*

1. Member States which intend to establish enhanced cooperation between themselves under Article 40 shall address a request to the Commission, which may submit a proposal to the Council to that effect. In the event of the Commission not submitting a proposal, it shall inform the Member States concerned of the reasons for not doing so. Those Member States may then submit an initiative to the Council designed to obtain authorisation for the enhanced cooperation concerned.

2. The authorisation referred to in paragraph 1 shall be granted, in compliance with Articles 43 to 45, by the Council, acting by a qualified majority, on a proposal from the Commission or on the initiative of at least eight Member States, and after consulting the European Parliament. The votes of the members of the Council shall be weighted in accordance with Article 205(2) of the Treaty establishing the European Community.

A member of the Council may request that the matter be referred to the European Council. After that matter has been raised before the European Council, the Council may act in accordance with the first subparagraph of this paragraph.

Article 40b*

Any Member State which wishes to participate in enhanced cooperation established in accordance with Article 40a shall notify its intention to the Council and to the Commission, which shall give an opinion to the Council within three months of the date of receipt of that notification, possibly accompanied by a recommendation for such specific arrangements as it may deem necessary for that Member State to become a party to the cooperation in question. The Council shall take a decision on the request within four months of the date of receipt of that notification. The decision shall be deemed to be taken unless the Council, acting by a qualified majority within the same period, decides to hold it in abeyance; in that case, the Council shall state the reasons for its decision and set a deadline for re-examining it.

For the purposes of this Article, the Council shall act under the conditions set out in Article 44(1).

* Article inserted by the Treaty of Nice.

Article 41

1.   Articles 189, 190, 195, 196 to 199, 203, 204, 205(3), 206 to 209, 213 to 219, 255 and 290 of the Treaty establishing the European Community shall apply to the provisions relating to the areas referred to in this title.

2.   Administrative expenditure which the provisions relating to the areas referred to in this title entail for the institutions shall be charged to the budget of the European Communities.

3.   Operating expenditure to which the implementation of those provisions gives rise shall also be charged to the budget of the European Communities, except where the Council acting unanimously decides otherwise. In cases where expenditure is not charged to the budget of the European Communities, it shall be charged to the Member States in accordance with the gross national product scale, unless the Council acting unanimously decides otherwise.

4.   The budgetary procedure laid down in the Treaty establishing the European Community shall apply to the expenditure charged to the budget of the European Communities.

Article 42

The Council, acting unanimously on the initiative of the Commission or a Member State, and after consulting the European Parliament, may decide that action in areas referred to in Article 29 shall fall under Title IV of the Treaty establishing the European Community, and at the same time determine the relevant voting conditions relating to it. It shall recommend the Member States to adopt that decision in accordance with their respective constitutional requirements.

TITLE VII
PROVISIONS ON ENHANCED COOPERATION

Article 43*

Member States which intend to establish enhanced cooperation between themselves may make use of the institutions, procedures and mechanisms laid down by this Treaty and by the Treaty establishing the European Community provided that the proposed cooperation:

(a) is aimed at furthering the objectives of the Union and of the Community, at protecting and serving their interests and at reinforcing their process of integration;

(b) respects the said Treaties and the single institutional framework of the Union;

(c) respects the *acquis communautaire* and the measures adopted under the other provisions of the said Treaties;

* Article amended by the Treaty of Nice.

(d) remains within the limits of the powers of the Union or of the Community and does not concern the areas which fall within the exclusive competence of the Community;

(e) does not undermine the internal market as defined in Article 14(2) of the Treaty establishing the European Community, or the economic and social cohesion established in accordance with Title XVII of that Treaty;

(f) does not constitute a barrier to or discrimination in trade between the Member States and does not distort competition between them;

(g) involves a minimum of eight Member States;

(h) respects the competences, rights and obligations of those Member States which do not participate therein;

(i) does not affect the provisions of the Protocol integrating the Schengen *acquis* into the framework of the European Union;

(j) is open to all the Member States, in accordance with Article 43b.

Article 43a*

Enhanced cooperation may be undertaken only as a last resort, when it has been established within the Council that the objectives of such cooperation cannot be attained within a reasonable period by applying the relevant provisions of the Treaties.

Article 43b*

When enhanced cooperation is being established, it shall be open to all Member States. It shall also be open to them at any time, in accordance with Articles 27e and 40b of this Treaty and with Article 11a of the Treaty establishing the European Community, subject to compliance with the basic decision and with the decisions taken within that framework. The Commission and the Member States participating in enhanced cooperation shall ensure that as many Member States as possible are encouraged to take part.

Article 44**

1. For the purposes of the adoption of the acts and decisions necessary for the implementation of enhanced cooperation referred to in Article 43, the relevant institutional provisions of this Treaty and of the Treaty establishing the European Community shall apply. However, while all members of the Council shall be able to take part in the deliberations, only those representing Member States participating in enhanced cooperation shall take part in the adoption of decisions. The qualified majority shall be defined as the same proportion of the weighted votes and the same proportion of the number of the Council members concerned as laid down in Article 205(2) of the Treaty

---

* Article inserted by the Treaty of Nice.   ** Article amended by the Treaty of Nice.

establishing the European Community, and in the second and third subparagraphs of Article 23(2) of this Treaty as regards enhanced cooperation established on the basis of Article 27c. Unanimity shall be constituted by only those Council members concerned.

Such acts and decisions shall not form part of the Union *acquis*.

2. Member States shall apply, as far as they are concerned, the acts and decisions adopted for the implementation of the enhanced cooperation in which they participate. Such acts and decisions shall be binding only on those Member States which participate in such cooperation and, as appropriate, shall be directly applicable only in those States. Member States which do not participate in such cooperation shall not impede the implementation thereof by the participating Member States.

Article 44a***

Expenditure resulting from implementation of enhanced cooperation, other than administrative costs entailed for the institutions, shall be borne by the participating Member States, unless all members of the Council, acting unanimously after consulting the European Parliament, decide otherwise.

Article 45*

The Council and the Commission shall ensure the consistency of activities undertaken on the basis of this title and the consistency of such activities with the policies of the Union and the Community, and shall cooperate to that end.

TITLE VIII
FINAL PROVISIONS

Article 46*

The provisions of the Treaty establishing the European Community, the Treaty establishing the European Coal and Steel Community and the Treaty establishing the European Atomic Energy Community concerning the powers of the Court of Justice of the European Communities and the exercise of those powers shall apply only to the following provisions of this Treaty:

(a) provisions amending the Treaty establishing the European Economic Community with a view to establishing the European Community, the Treaty establishing the European Coal and Steel Community and the Treaty establishing the European Atomic Energy Community;

(b) provisions of Title VI, under the conditions provided for by Article 35;

*** Article inserted by the Treaty of Nice (former Article 44(2)).   * Article amended by the Treaty of Nice.

(c) provisions of Title VII, under the conditions provided for by Articles 11 and 11a of the Treaty establishing the European Community and Article 40 of this Treaty;

(d) Article 6(2) with regard to action of the institutions, in so far as the Court has jurisdiction under the Treaties establishing the European Communities and under this Treaty;

(e) the purely procedural stipulations in Article 7, with the Court acting at the request of the Member State concerned within one month from the date of the determination by the Council provided for in that Article;

(f) Articles 46 to 53.

Article 47

Subject to the provisions amending the Treaty establishing the European Economic Community with a view to establishing the European Community, the Treaty establishing the European Coal and Steel Community and the Treaty establishing the European Atomic Energy Community, and to these final provisions, nothing in this Treaty shall affect the Treaties establishing the European Communities or the subsequent Treaties and Acts modifying or supplementing them.

Article 48

The government of any Member State or the Commission may submit to the Council proposals for the amendment of the Treaties on which the Union is founded.

If the Council, after consulting the European Parliament and, where appropriate, the Commission, delivers an opinion in favour of calling a conference of representatives of the governments of the Member States, the conference shall be convened by the President of the Council for the purpose of determining by common accord the amendments to be made to those Treaties. The European Central Bank shall also be consulted in the case of institutional changes in the monetary area.

The amendments shall enter into force after being ratified by all the Member States in accordance with their respective constitutional requirements.

Article 49

Any European State which respects the principles set out in Article 6(1) may apply to become a member of the Union. It shall address its application to the Council, which shall act unanimously after consulting the Commission and after receiving the assent of the European Parliament, which shall act by an absolute majority of its component members.

The conditions of admission and the adjustments to the Treaties on which the Union is founded, which such admission entails, shall be the subject of an agreement between the Member States and the applicant State. This agreement shall be submitted for ratification by all the contracting States in accordance with their respective constitutional requirements.

Article 50

1. Articles 2 to 7 and 10 to 19 of the Treaty establishing a Single Council and a Single Commission of the European Communities, signed in Brussels on 8 April 1965, are hereby repealed.

2. Article 2, Article 3(2) and Title III of the Single European Act signed in Luxembourg on 17 February 1986 and in The Hague on 28 February 1986 are hereby repealed.

Article 51

This Treaty is concluded for an unlimited period.

Article 52

1. This Treaty shall be ratified by the High Contracting Parties in accordance with their respective constitutional requirements. The instruments of ratification shall be deposited with the Government of the Italian Republic.

2. This Treaty shall enter into force on 1 January 1993, provided that all the Instruments of ratification have been deposited, or, failing that, on the first day of the month following the deposit of the Instrument of ratification by the last signatory State to take this step.

Article 53

This Treaty, drawn up in a single original in the Danish, Dutch, English, French, German, Greek, Irish, Italian, Portuguese and Spanish languages, the texts in each of these languages being equally authentic, shall be deposited in the archives of the Government of the Italian Republic, which will transmit a certified copy to each of the governments of the other signatory States.

Pursuant to the Accession Treaty of 1994, the Finnish and Swedish versions of this Treaty shall also be authentic.

* * *

Appendix II

CONSOLIDATED VERSION OF THE TREATY ESTABLISHING THE EUROPEAN COMMUNITY

(as amended by the Nice Treaty of 2003)

CONTENTS

---

* Title inserted by the Treaty of Nice.

II. PROTOCOLS (text not reproduced)

PART ONE
PRINCIPLES

Article 1

By this Treaty, the HIGH CONTRACTING PARTIES establish among themselves a EUROPEAN COMMUNITY.

Article 2

The Community shall have as its task, by establishing a common market and an economic and monetary union and by implementing common policies or activities referred to in Articles 3 and 4, to promote throughout the Community a harmonious, balanced and sustainable development of economic activities, a high level of employment and of social protection, equality between men and women, sustainable and non-inflationary growth, a high degree of competitiveness and convergence of economic performance, a high level of protection and improvement of the quality of the environment, the raising of the standard of living and quality of life, and economic and social cohesion and solidarity among Member States.

Article 3

1.   For the purposes set out in Article 2, the activities of the Community shall include, as provided in this Treaty and in accordance with the timetable set out therein:

(a) the prohibition, as between Member States, of customs duties and quantitative restrictions on the import and export of goods, and of all other measures having equivalent effect;

(b) a common commercial policy;

(c) an internal market characterised by the abolition, as between Member States, of obstacles to the free movement of goods, persons, services and capital;

(d) measures concerning the entry and movement of persons as provided for in Title IV;

(e) a common policy in the sphere of agriculture and fisheries;

(f) a common policy in the sphere of transport;

(g) a system ensuring that competition in the internal market is not distorted;

(h) the approximation of the laws of Member States to the extent required for the functioning of the common market;

(i) the promotion of coordination between employment policies of the Member States with a view to enhancing their effectiveness by developing a coordinated strategy for employment;

(j) a policy in the social sphere comprising a European Social Fund;

(k) the strengthening of economic and social cohesion;

(*l*) a policy in the sphere of the environment;

(m) the strengthening of the competitiveness of Community industry;

(n) the promotion of research and technological development;

(*o*) encouragement for the establishment and development of trans-European networks;

(p) a contribution to the attainment of a high level of health protection;

(q) a contribution to education and training of quality and to the flowering of the cultures of the Member States;

(r) a policy in the sphere of development cooperation;

(s) the association of the overseas countries and territories in order to increase trade and promote jointly economic and social development;

(t) a contribution to the strengthening of consumer protection;

(u) measures in the spheres of energy, civil protection and tourism.

2.   In all the activities referred to in this Article, the Community shall aim to eliminate inequalities, and to promote equality, between men and women.

Article 4

1.   For the purposes set out in Article 2, the activities of the Member States and the Community shall include, as provided in this Treaty and in accordance with the timetable set out therein, the adoption of an economic policy which is based on the close coordination of Member States' economic policies, on the internal market and on the definition of common objectives, and conducted in accordance with the principle of an open market economy with free competition.

2.   Concurrently with the foregoing, and as provided in this Treaty and in accordance with the timetable and the procedures set out therein, these activities shall include the irrevocable fixing of exchange rates leading to the introduction of a single currency, the ecu, and the definition and conduct of a single monetary policy and exchange-rate policy the primary objective of both of which shall be to maintain price stability and, without prejudice to this objective, to support the general economic policies in the Community, in accordance with the principle of an open market economy with free competition.

3.   These activities of the Member States and the Community shall entail compliance with the following guiding principles: stable prices,

sound public finances and monetary conditions and a sustainable balance of payments.

Article 5

The Community shall act within the limits of the powers conferred upon it by this Treaty and of the objectives assigned to it therein.

In areas which do not fall within its exclusive competence, the Community shall take action, in accordance with the principle of subsidiarity, only if and in so far as the objectives of the proposed action cannot be sufficiently achieved by the Member States and can therefore, by reason of the scale or effects of the proposed action, be better achieved by the Community.

Any action by the Community shall not go beyond what is necessary to achieve the objectives of this Treaty.

Article 6

Environmental protection requirements must be integrated into the definition and implementation of the Community policies and activities referred to in Article 3, in particular with a view to promoting sustainable development.

Article 7

1. The tasks entrusted to the Community shall be carried out by the following institutions:

— a EUROPEAN PARLIAMENT,

— a COUNCIL,

— a COMMISSION,

— a COURT OF JUSTICE,

— a COURT OF AUDITORS.

Each institution shall act within the limits of the powers conferred upon it by this Treaty.

2. The Council and the Commission shall be assisted by an Economic and Social Committee and a Committee of the Regions acting in an advisory capacity.

Article 8

A European system of central banks (hereinafter referred to as "ESCB") and a European Central Bank (hereinafter referred to as "ECB") shall be established in accordance with the procedures laid down in this Treaty; they shall act within the limits of the powers conferred upon them by this Treaty and by the Statute of the ESCB and of the ECB (hereinafter referred to as "Statute of the ESCB") annexed thereto.

Article 9

A European Investment Bank is hereby established, which shall act within the limits of the powers conferred upon it by this Treaty and the Statute annexed thereto.

Article 10

Member States shall take all appropriate measures, whether general or particular, to ensure fulfilment of the obligations arising out of this Treaty or resulting from action taken by the institutions of the Community. They shall facilitate the achievement of the Community's tasks.

They shall abstain from any measure which could jeopardise the attainment of the objectives of this Treaty.

Article 11*

1.   Member States which intend to establish enhanced cooperation between themselves in one of the areas referred to in this Treaty shall address a request to the Commission, which may submit a proposal to the Council to that effect. In the event of the Commission not submitting a proposal, it shall inform the Member States concerned of the reasons for not doing so.

2.   Authorisation to establish enhanced cooperation as referred to in paragraph 1 shall be granted, in compliance with Articles 43 to 45 of the Treaty on European Union, by the Council, acting by a qualified majority on a proposal from the Commission and after consulting the European Parliament. When enhanced cooperation relates to an area covered by the procedure referred to in Article 251 of this Treaty, the assent of the European Parliament shall be required.

A member of the Council may request that the matter be referred to the European Council. After that matter has been raised before the European Council, the Council may act in accordance with the first subparagraph of this paragraph.

3.   The acts and decisions necessary for the implementation of enhanced cooperation activities shall be subject to all the relevant provisions of this Treaty, save as otherwise provided in this Article and in Articles 43 to 45 of the Treaty on European Union.

Article 11a**

Any Member State which wishes to participate in enhanced cooperation established in accordance with Article 11 shall notify its intention to the Council and to the Commission, which shall give an opinion to the Council within three months of the date of receipt of that notification. Within four months of the date of receipt of that notification, the

---

* Article amended by the Treaty of Nice.   ** Article inserted by the Treaty of Nice (former Article 11(3)).

Commission shall take a decision on it, and on such specific arrangements as it may deem necessary.

Article 12

Within the scope of application of this Treaty, and without prejudice to any special provisions contained therein, any discrimination on grounds of nationality shall be prohibited.

The Council, acting in accordance with the procedure referred to in Article 251, may adopt rules designed to prohibit such discrimination.

Article 13*

1. Without prejudice to the other provisions of this Treaty and within the limits of the powers conferred by it upon the Community, the Council, acting unanimously on a proposal from the Commission and after consulting the European Parliament, may take appropriate action to combat discrimination based on sex, racial or ethnic origin, religion or belief, disability, age or sexual orientation.

2. By way of derogation from paragraph 1, when the Council adopts Community incentive measures, excluding any harmonisation of the laws and regulations of the Member States, to support action taken by the Member States in order to contribute to the achievement of the objectives referred to in paragraph 1, it shall act in accordance with the procedure referred to in Article 251.

Article 14

1. The Community shall adopt measures with the aim of progressively establishing the internal market over a period expiring on 31 December 1992, in accordance with the provisions of this Article and of Articles 15, 26, 47(2), 49, 80, 93 and 95 and without prejudice to the other provisions of this Treaty.

2. The internal market shall comprise an area without internal frontiers in which the free movement of goods, persons, services and capital is ensured in accordance with the provisions of this Treaty.

3. The Council, acting by a qualified majority on a proposal from the Commission, shall determine the guidelines and conditions necessary to ensure balanced progress in all the sectors concerned.

Article 15

When drawing up its proposals with a view to achieving the objectives set out in Article 14, the Commission shall take into account the extent of the effort that certain economies showing differences in development will have to sustain during the period of establishment of the internal market and it may propose appropriate provisions.

* Article amended by Treaty of Nice.

If these provisions take the form of derogations, they must be of a temporary nature and must cause the least possible disturbance to the functioning of the common market.

Article 16

Without prejudice to Articles 73, 86 and 87, and given the place occupied by services of general economic interest in the shared values of the Union as well as their role in promoting social and territorial cohesion, the Community and the Member States, each within their respective powers and within the scope of application of this Treaty, shall take care that such services operate on the basis of principles and conditions which enable them to fulfil their missions.

PART TWO
CITIZENSHIP OF THE UNION

Article 17

1. Citizenship of the Union is hereby established. Every person holding the nationality of a Member State shall be a citizen of the Union. Citizenship of the Union shall complement and not replace national citizenship.

2. Citizens of the Union shall enjoy the rights conferred by this Treaty and shall be subject to the duties imposed thereby.

Article 18*

1. Every citizen of the Union shall have the right to move and reside freely within the territory of the Member States, subject to the limitations and conditions laid down in this Treaty and by the measures adopted to give it effect.

2. If action by the Community should prove necessary to attain this objective and this Treaty has not provided the necessary powers, the Council may adopt provisions with a view to facilitating the exercise of the rights referred to in paragraph 1. The Council shall act in accordance with the procedure referred to in Article 251.

3. Paragraph 2 shall not apply to provisions on passports, identity cards, residence permits or any other such document or to provisions on social security or social protection.

Article 19

1. Every citizen of the Union residing in a Member State of which he is not a national shall have the right to vote and to stand as a candidate at municipal elections in the Member State in which he resides, under the same conditions as nationals of that State. This right shall be exercised subject to detailed arrangements adopted by the

* Article amended by the Treaty of Nice.

Council, acting unanimously on a proposal from the Commission and after consulting the European Parliament; these arrangements may provide for derogations where warranted by problems specific to a Member State.

2. Without prejudice to Article 190(4) and to the provisions adopted for its implementation, every citizen of the Union residing in a Member State of which he is not a national shall have the right to vote and to stand as a candidate in elections to the European Parliament in the Member State in which he resides, under the same conditions as nationals of that State. This right shall be exercised subject to detailed arrangements adopted by the Council, acting unanimously on a proposal from the Commission and after consulting the European Parliament; these arrangements may provide for derogations where warranted by problems specific to a Member State.

Article 20

Every citizen of the Union shall, in the territory of a third country in which the Member State of which he is a national is not represented, be entitled to protection by the diplomatic or consular authorities of any Member State, on the same conditions as the nationals of that State. Member States shall establish the necessary rules among themselves and start the international negotiations required to secure this protection.

Article 21

Every citizen of the Union shall have the right to petition the European Parliament in accordance with Article 194.

Every citizen of the Union may apply to the Ombudsman established in accordance with Article 195.

Every citizen of the Union may write to any of the institutions or bodies referred to in this Article or in Article 7 in one of the languages mentioned in Article 314 and have an answer in the same language.

Article 22

The Commission shall report to the European Parliament, to the Council and to the Economic and Social Committee every three years on the application of the provisions of this part. This report shall take account of the development of the Union.

On this basis, and without prejudice to the other provisions of this Treaty, the Council, acting unanimously on a proposal from the Commission and after consulting the European Parliament, may adopt provisions to strengthen or to add to the rights laid down in this part, which it shall recommend to the Member States for adoption in accordance with their respective constitutional requirements.

PART THREE
COMMUNITY POLICIES

TITLE I
FREE MOVEMENT OF GOODS

Article 23

1. The Community shall be based upon a customs union which shall cover all trade in goods and which shall involve the prohibition between Member States of customs duties on imports and exports and of all charges having equivalent effect, and the adoption of a common customs tariff in their relations with third countries.

2. The provisions of Article 25 and of Chapter 2 of this title shall apply to products originating in Member States and to products coming from third countries which are in free circulation in Member States.

Article 24

Products coming from a third country shall be considered to be in free circulation in a Member State if the import formalities have been complied with and any customs duties or charges having equivalent effect which are payable have been levied in that Member State, and if they have not benefited from a total or partial drawback of such duties or charges.

CHAPTER 1
THE CUSTOMS UNION

Article 25

Customs duties on imports and exports and charges having equivalent effect shall be prohibited between Member States. This prohibition shall also apply to customs duties of a fiscal nature.

Article 26

Common Customs Tariff duties shall be fixed by the Council acting by a qualified majority on a proposal from the Commission.

Article 27

In carrying out the tasks entrusted to it under this chapter the Commission shall be guided by:

(a) the need to promote trade between Member States and third countries;

(b) developments in conditions of competition within the Community in so far as they lead to an improvement in the competitive capacity of undertakings;

(c) the requirements of the Community as regards the supply of raw materials and semi-finished goods; in this connection the Commission shall take care to avoid distorting conditions of competition between Member States in respect of finished goods;

(d) the need to avoid serious disturbances in the economies of Member States and to ensure rational development of production and an expansion of consumption within the Community.

CHAPTER 2
PROHIBITION OF QUANTITATIVE RESTRICTIONS BETWEEN MEMBER STATES

Article 28

Quantitative restrictions on imports and all measures having equivalent effect shall be prohibited between Member States.

Article 29

Quantitative restrictions on exports, and all measures having equivalent effect, shall be prohibited between Member States.

Article 30

The provisions of Articles 28 and 29 shall not preclude prohibitions or restrictions on imports, exports or goods in transit justified on grounds of public morality, public policy or public security; the protection of health and life of humans, animals or plants; the protection of national treasures possessing artistic, historic or archaeological value; or the protection of industrial and commercial property. Such prohibitions or restrictions shall not, however, constitute a means of arbitrary discrimination or a disguised restriction on trade between Member States.

Article 31

1.   Member States shall adjust any State monopolies of a commercial character so as to ensure that no discrimination regarding the conditions under which goods are procured and marketed exists between nationals of Member States.

The provisions of this Article shall apply to any body through which a Member State, in law or in fact, either directly or indirectly supervises, determines or appreciably influences imports or exports between Member States. These provisions shall likewise apply to monopolies delegated by the State to others.

2.   Member States shall refrain from introducing any new measure which is contrary to the principles laid down in paragraph 1 or which restricts the scope of the articles dealing with the prohibition of customs duties and quantitative restrictions between Member States.

3.   If a State monopoly of a commercial character has rules which are designed to make it easier to dispose of agricultural products or obtain

for them the best return, steps should be taken in applying the rules contained in this article to ensure equivalent safeguards for the employment and standard of living of the producers concerned.

TITLE II
AGRICULTURE

Article 32

1. The common market shall extend to agriculture and trade in agricultural products. "Agricultural products" means the products of the soil, of stockfarming and of fisheries and products of first-stage processing directly related to these products.

2. Save as otherwise provided in Articles 33 to 38, the rules laid down for the establishment of the common market shall apply to agricultural products.

3. The products subject to the provisions of Articles 33 to 38 are listed in Annex I to this Treaty.

4. The operation and development of the common market for agricultural products must be accompanied by the establishment of a common agricultural policy.

Article 33

1. The objectives of the common agricultural policy shall be:

(a) to increase agricultural productivity by promoting technical progress and by ensuring the rational development of agricultural production and the optimum utilisation of the factors of production, in particular labour;

(b) thus to ensure a fair standard of living for the agricultural community, in particular by increasing the individual earnings of persons engaged in agriculture;

(c) to stabilise markets;

(d) to assure the availability of supplies;

(e) to ensure that supplies reach consumers at reasonable prices.

2. In working out the common agricultural policy and the special methods for its application, account shall be taken of:

(a) the particular nature of agricultural activity, which results from the social structure of agriculture and from structural and natural disparities between the various agricultural regions;

(b) the need to effect the appropriate adjustments by degrees;

(c) the fact that in the Member States agriculture constitutes a sector closely linked with the economy as a whole.

Article 34

1. In order to attain the objectives set out in Article 33, a common organisation of agricultural markets shall be established.

This organisation shall take one of the following forms, depending on the product concerned:

(a) common rules on competition;

(b) compulsory coordination of the various national market organisations;

(c) a European market organisation.

2. The common organisation established in accordance with paragraph 1 may include all measures required to attain the objectives set out in Article 33, in particular regulation of prices, aids for the production and marketing of the various products, storage and carry-over arrangements and common machinery for stabilising imports or exports.

The common organisation shall be limited to pursuit of the objectives set out in Article 33 and shall exclude any discrimination between producers or consumers within the Community.

Any common price policy shall be based on common criteria and uniform methods of calculation.

3. In order to enable the common organisation referred to in paragraph 1 to attain its objectives, one or more agricultural guidance and guarantee funds may be set up.

Article 35

To enable the objectives set out in Article 33 to be attained, provision may be made within the framework of the common agricultural policy for measures such as:

(a) an effective coordination of efforts in the spheres of vocational training, of research and of the dissemination of agricultural knowledge; this may include joint financing of projects or institutions;

(b) joint measures to promote consumption of certain products.

Article 36

The provisions of the chapter relating to rules on competition shall apply to production of and trade in agricultural products only to the extent determined by the Council within the framework of Article 37(2) and (3) and in accordance with the procedure laid down therein, account being taken of the objectives set out in Article 33.

The Council may, in particular, authorise the granting of aid:

(a) for the protection of enterprises handicapped by structural or natural conditions;

(b) within the framework of economic development programmes.

Article 37

1. In order to evolve the broad lines of a common agricultural policy, the Commission shall, immediately this Treaty enters into force, convene a conference of the Member States with a view to making a comparison of their agricultural policies, in particular by producing a statement of their resources and needs.

2. Having taken into account the work of the Conference provided for in paragraph 1, after consulting the Economic and Social Committee and within two years of the entry into force of this Treaty, the Commission shall submit proposals for working out and implementing the common agricultural policy, including the replacement of the national organisations by one of the forms of common organisation provided for in Article 34(1), and for implementing the measures specified in this title.

These proposals shall take account of the interdependence of the agricultural matters mentioned in this title.

The Council shall, on a proposal from the Commission and after consulting the European Parliament, acting by a qualified majority, make regulations, issue directives, or take decisions, without prejudice to any recommendations it may also make.

3. The Council may, acting by a qualified majority and in accordance with paragraph 2, replace the national market organisations by the common organisation provided for in Article 34(1) if:

(a) the common organisation offers Member States which are opposed to this measure and which have an organisation of their own for the production in question equivalent safeguards for the employment and standard of living of the producers concerned, account being taken of the adjustments that will be possible and the specialisation that will be needed with the passage of time;

(b) such an organisation ensures conditions for trade within the Community similar to those existing in a national market.

4. If a common organisation for certain raw materials is established before a common organisation exists for the corresponding processed products, such raw materials as are used for processed products intended for export to third countries may be imported from outside the Community.

Article 38

Where in a Member State a product is subject to a national market organisation or to internal rules having equivalent effect which affect the competitive position of similar production in another Member State, a countervailing charge shall be applied by Member States to imports of this product coming from the Member State where such organisation or rules exist, unless that State applies a countervailing charge on export.

The Commission shall fix the amount of these charges at the level required to redress the balance; it may also authorise other measures, the conditions and details of which it shall determine.

TITLE III
FREE MOVEMENT OF PERSONS, SERVICES AND CAPITAL

CHAPTER 1
WORKERS

Article 39

1. Freedom of movement for workers shall be secured within the Community.

2. Such freedom of movement shall entail the abolition of any discrimination based on nationality between workers of the Member States as regards employment, remuneration and other conditions of work and employment.

3. It shall entail the right, subject to limitations justified on grounds of public policy, public security or public health:

(a) to accept offers of employment actually made;

(b) to move freely within the territory of Member States for this purpose;

(c) to stay in a Member State for the purpose of employment in accordance with the provisions governing the employment of nationals of that State laid down by law, regulation or administrative action;

(d) to remain in the territory of a Member State after having been employed in that State, subject to conditions which shall be embodied in implementing regulations to be drawn up by the Commission.

4. The provisions of this article shall not apply to employment in the public service.

Article 40

The Council shall, acting in accordance with the procedure referred to in Article 251 and after consulting the Economic and Social Committee, issue directives or make regulations setting out the measures required to bring about freedom of movement for workers, as defined in Article 39, in particular:

(a) by ensuring close cooperation between national employment services;

(b) by abolishing those administrative procedures and practices and those qualifying periods in respect of eligibility for available employment, whether resulting from national legislation or from agreements previously concluded between Member States, the maintenance of which would form an obstacle to liberalisation of the movement of workers;

(c) by abolishing all such qualifying periods and other restrictions provided for either under national legislation or under agreements previously concluded between Member States as imposed on workers of other Member States conditions regarding the free choice of employment other than those imposed on workers of the State concerned;

(d) by setting up appropriate machinery to bring offers of employment into touch with applications for employment and to facilitate the achievement of a balance between supply and demand in the employment market in such a way as to avoid serious threats to the standard of living and level of employment in the various regions and industries.

Article 41

Member States shall, within the framework of a joint programme, encourage the exchange of young workers.

Article 42

The Council shall, acting in accordance with the procedure referred to in Article 251, adopt such measures in the field of social security as are necessary to provide freedom of movement for workers; to this end, it shall make arrangements to secure for migrant workers and their dependants:

(a) aggregation, for the purpose of acquiring and retaining the right to benefit and of calculating the amount of benefit, of all periods taken into account under the laws of the several countries;

(b) payment of benefits to persons resident in the territories of Member States.

The Council shall act unanimously throughout the procedure referred to in Article 251.

Chapter 25
RIGHT OF ESTABLISHMENT

Article 43

Within the framework of the provisions set out below, restrictions on the freedom of establishment of nationals of a Member State in the territory of another Member State shall be prohibited. Such prohibition shall also apply to restrictions on the setting-up of agencies, branches or subsidiaries by nationals of any Member State established in the territory of any Member State.

Freedom of establishment shall include the right to take up and pursue activities as self-employed persons and to set up and manage undertakings, in particular companies or firms within them meaning of the second paragraph of Article 48, under the conditions laid down for its own nationals by the law of the country where such establishment is effected, subject to the provisions of the chapter relating to capital.

Article 44

1. In order to attain freedom of establishment as regards a particular activity, the Council, acting in accordance with the procedure referred to in Article 251 and after consulting the Economic and Social Committee, shall act by means of directives.

2. The Council and the Commission shall carry out the duties devolving upon them under the preceding provisions, in particular:

(a) by according, as a general rule, priority treatment to activities where freedom of establishment makes a particularly valuable contribution to the development of production and trade;

(b) by ensuring close cooperation between the competent authorities in the Member States in order to ascertain the particular situation within the Community of the various activities concerned;

(c) by abolishing those administrative procedures and practices, whether resulting from national legislation or from agreements previously concluded between Member States, the maintenance of which would form an obstacle to freedom of establishment;

(d) by ensuring that workers of one Member State employed in the territory of another Member State may remain in that territory for the purpose of taking up activities therein as self-employed persons, where they satisfy the conditions which they would be required to satisfy if they were entering that State at the time when they intended to take up such activities;

(e) by enabling a national of one Member State to acquire and use land and buildings situated in the territory of another Member State, in so far as this does not conflict with the principles laid down in Article 33(2);

(f) by effecting the progressive abolition of restrictions on freedom of establishment in every branch of activity under consideration, both as regards the conditions for setting up agencies, branches or subsidiaries in the territory of a Member State and as regards the subsidiaries in the territory of a Member State and as regards the conditions governing the entry of personnel belonging to the main establishment into managerial or supervisory posts in such agencies, branches or subsidiaries;

(g) by coordinating to the necessary extent the safeguards which, for the protection of the interests of members and other, are required by Member States of companies or firms within the meaning of the second paragraph of Article 48 with a view to making such safeguards equivalent throughout the Community;

(h) by satisfying themselves that the conditions of establishment are not distorted by aids granted by Member States.

Article 45

The provisions of this chapter shall not apply, so far as any given Member State is concerned, to activities which in that State are connected, even occasionally, with the exercise of official authority.

The Council may, acting by a qualified majority on a proposal from the Commission, rule that the provisions of this chapter shall not apply to certain activities.

Article 46

1. The provisions of this chapter and measures taken in pursuance thereof shall not prejudice the applicability of provisions laid down by law, regulation or administrative action providing for special treatment for foreign nationals on grounds of public policy, public security or public health.

2. The Council shall, acting in accordance with the procedure referred to in Article 251, issue directives for the coordination of the abovementioned provisions.

Article 47

1. In order to make it easier for persons to take up and pursue activities as self-employed persons,the Council shall, acting in accordance with the procedure referred to in Article 251, issue directives for the mutual recognition of diplomas, certificates and other evidence of formal qualifications.

2. For the same purpose, the Council shall, acting in accordance with the procedure referred to in Article 251, issue directives for the coordination of the provisions laid down by law, regulation or administrative action in Member States concerning the taking-up and pursuit of activities as self-employed persons. The Council, acting unanimously throughout the procedure referred to in Article 251, shall decide on directives the implementation of which involves in at least one Member State amendment of the existing principles laid down by law governing the professions with respect to training and conditions of access for natural persons. In other cases the Council shall act by qualified majority.

3. In the case of the medical and allied and pharmaceutical professions, the progressive abolition of restrictions shall be dependent upon

coordination of the conditions for their exercise in the various Member States.

Article 48

Companies or firms formed in accordance with the law of a Member State and having their registered office, central administration or principal place of business within the Community shall, for the purposes of this Chapter, be treated in the same way as natural persons who are nationals of Member States.

"Companies or firms" means companies or firms constituted under civil or commercial law, including cooperative societies, and other legal persons governed by public or private law, save for those which are non-profit-making.

CHAPTER 3
SERVICES

Article 49

Within the framework of the provisions set out below, restrictions on freedom to provide services within the Community shall be prohibited in respect of nationals of Member States who are established in a State of the Community other than that of the person for whom the services are intended.

The Council may, acting by a qualified majority on a proposal from the Commission, extend the provisions of the Chapter to nationals of a third country who provide services and who are established within the Community.

Article 50

Services shall be considered to be "services" within the meaning of this Treaty where they are normally provided for remuneration, in so far as they are not governed by the provisions relating to freedom of movement for goods, capital and persons.

"Services" shall in particular include:

(a) activities of an industrial character;

(b) activities of a commercial character;

(c) activities of craftsmen;

(d) activities of the professions.

Without prejudice to the provisions of the chapter relating to the right of establishment, the person providing a service may, in order to do so, temporarily pursue his activity in the State where the service is provided, under the same conditions as are imposed by that State on its own nationals.

Article 51

1. Freedom to provide services in the field of transport shall be governed by the provisions of the title relating to transport.

2. The liberalisation of banking and insurance services connected with movements of capital shall be effected in step with the liberalisation of movement of capital.

Article 52

1. In order to achieve the liberalisation of a specific service, the Council shall, on a proposal from the Commission and after consulting the Economic and Social Committee and the European Parliament, issue directives acting by a qualified majority.

2. As regards the directives referred to in paragraph 1, priority shall as a general rule be given to those services which directly affect production costs or the liberalisation of which helps to promote trade in goods.

Article 53

The Member States declare their readiness to undertake the liberalisation of services beyond the extent required by the directives issued pursuant to Article 52(1), if their general economic situation and the situation of the economic sector concerned so permit.

To this end, the Commission shall make recommendations to the Member States concerned.

Article 54

As long as restrictions on freedom to provide services have not been abolished, each Member State shall apply such restrictions without distinction on grounds of nationality or residence to all persons providing services within the meaning of the first paragraph of Article 49.

Article 55

The provisions of Articles 45 to 48 shall apply to the matters covered by this chapter.

CHAPTER 4
CAPITAL AND PAYMENTS

Article 56

1. Within the framework of the provisions set out in this chapter, all restrictions on the movement of capital between Member States and between Member States and third countries shall be prohibited.

2. Within the framework of the provisions set out in this chapter, all restrictions on payments between Member States and between Member States and third countries shall be prohibited.

Article 57

1. The provisions of Article 56 shall be without prejudice to the application to third countries of any restrictions which exist on 31 December 1993 under national or Community law adopted in respect of the movement of capital to or from third countries involving direct investment—including in real estate—establishment, the provision of financial services or the admission of securities to capital markets.

2. Whilst endeavouring to achieve the objective of free movement of capital between Member States and third countries to the greatest extent possible and without prejudice to the other chapters of this Treaty, the Council may, acting by a qualified majority on a proposal from the Commission, adopt measures on the movement of capital to or from third countries involving direct investment— including investment in real estate—establishment, the provision of financial services or the admission of securities to capital markets. Unanimity shall be required for measures under this paragraph which constitute a step back in Community law as regards the liberalisation of the movement of capital to or from third countries.

Article 58

1. The provisions of Article 56 shall be without prejudice to the right of Member States:

(a) to apply the relevant provisions of their tax law which distinguish between taxpayers who are not in the same situation with regard to their place of residence or with regard to the place where their capital is invested;

(b) to take all requisite measures to prevent infringements of national law and regulations, in particular in the field of taxation and the prudential supervision of financial institutions, or to lay down procedures for the declaration of capital movements for purposes of administrative or statistical information, or to take measures which are justified on grounds of public policy or public security.

2. The provisions of this chapter shall be without prejudice to the applicability of restrictions on the right of establishment which are compatible with this Treaty.

3. The measures and procedures referred to in paragraphs 1 and 2 shall not constitute a means of arbitrary discrimination or a disguised restriction on the free movement of capital and payments as defined in Article 56.

Article 59

Where, in exceptional circumstances, movements of capital to or from third countries cause, or threaten to cause, serious difficulties for the operation of economic and monetary union, the Council, acting by a qualified majority on a proposal from the Commission and after consulting the ECB, may take safeguard measures with regard to third countries for a period not exceeding six months if such measures are strictly necessary.

Article 60

1. If, in the cases envisaged in Article 301, action by the Community is deemed necessary, the Council may, in accordance with the procedure provided for in Article 301, take the necessary urgent measures on the movement of capital and on payments as regards the third countries concerned.

2. Without prejudice to Article 297 and as long as the Council has not taken measures pursuant to paragraph 1, a Member State may, for serious political reasons and on grounds of urgency, take unilateral measures against a third country with regard to capital movements and payments. The Commission and the other Member States shall be informed of such measures by the date of their entry into force at the latest.

The Council may, acting by a qualified majority on a proposal from the Commission, decide that the Member State concerned shall amend or abolish such measures. The President of the Council shall inform the European Parliament of any such decision taken by the Council.

TITLE IV
VISAS, ASYLUM, IMMIGRATION AND OTHER POLICIES RELATED TO FREE MOVEMENT OF PERSONS

Article 61

In order to establish progressively an area of freedom, security and justice, the Council shall adopt:

(a) within a period of five years after the entry into force of the Treaty of Amsterdam, measures aimed at ensuring the free movement of persons in accordance with Article 14, in conjunction with directly related flanking measures with respect to external border controls, asylum and immigration, in accordance with the provisions of Article 62(2) and (3) and Article 63(1)(a) and (2)(a), and measures to prevent and combat crime in accordance with the provisions of Article 31(e) of the Treaty on European Union;

(b) other measures in the fields of asylum, immigration and safeguarding the rights of nationals of third countries, in accordance with the provisions of Article 63;

(c) measures in the field of judicial cooperation in civil matters as provided for in Article 65;

(d) appropriate measures to encourage and strengthen administrative cooperation, as provided for in Article 66;

(e) measures in the field of police and judicial cooperation in criminal matters aimed at a high level of security by preventing and combating crime within the Union in accordance with the provisions of the Treaty on European Union.

Article 62

The Council, acting in accordance with the procedure referred to in Article 67, shall, within a period of five years after the entry into force of the Treaty of Amsterdam, adopt:

1. measures with a view to ensuring, in compliance with Article 14, the absence of any controls on persons, be they citizens of the Union or nationals of third countries, when crossing internal borders;

2. measures on the crossing of the external borders of the Member States which shall establish:

(a) standards and procedures to be followed by Member States in carrying out checks on persons at such borders;

(b) rules on visas for intended stays of no more than three months, including:

    (i) the list of third countries whose nationals must be in possession of visas when crossing the external borders and those whose nationals are exempt from that requirement;

    (ii) the procedures and conditions for issuing visas by Member States;

    (iii) a uniform format for visas;

    (iv) rules on a uniform visa;

3. measures setting out the conditions under which nationals of third countries shall have the freedom to travel within the territory of the Member States during a period of no more than three months.

Article 63

The Council, acting in accordance with the procedure referred to in Article 67, shall, within a period of five years after the entry into force of the Treaty of Amsterdam, adopt:

1. measures on asylum, in accordance with the Geneva Convention of 28 July 1951 and the Protocol of 31 January 1967 relating to the status of refugees and other relevant treaties, within the following areas:

(a) criteria and mechanisms for determining which Member State is responsible for considering an application for asylum submitted by a national of a third country in one of the Member States,

(b) minimum standards on the reception of asylum seekers in Member States,

(c) minimum standards with respect to the qualification of nationals of third countries as refugees,

(d) minimum standards on procedures in Member States for granting or withdrawing refugee status;

2. measures on refugees and displaced persons within the following areas:

(a) minimum standards for giving temporary protection to displaced persons from third countries who cannot return to their country of origin and for persons who otherwise need international protection,

(b) promoting a balance of effort between Member States in receiving and bearing the consequences of receiving refugees and displaced persons;

3. measures on immigration policy within the following areas:

(a) conditions of entry and residence, and standards on procedures for the issue by Member States of long-term visas and residence permits, including those for the purpose of family reunion,

(b) illegal immigration and illegal residence, including repatriation of illegal residents;

4. measures defining the rights and conditions under which nationals of third countries who are legally resident in a Member State may reside in other Member States.

Measures adopted by the Council pursuant to points 3 and 4 shall not prevent any Member State from maintaining or introducing in the areas concerned national provisions which are compatible with this Treaty and with international agreements.

Measures to be adopted pursuant to points 2(b), 3(a) and 4 shall not be subject to the five-year period referred to above.

Article 64

1. This title shall not affect the exercise of the responsibilities incumbent upon Member States with regard to the maintenance of law and order and the safeguarding of internal security.

2. In the event of one or more Member States being confronted with an emergency situation characterised by a sudden inflow of nationals of third countries and without prejudice to paragraph 1, the Council may, acting by qualified majority on a proposal from the Commission, adopt provisional measures of a duration not exceeding six months for the benefit of the Member States concerned.

Article 65

Measures in the field of judicial cooperation in civil matters having cross-border implications, to be taken in accordance with Article 67 and in so far as necessary for the proper functioning of the internal market, shall include:

(a) improving and simplifying:

— the system for cross-border service of judicial and extrajudicial documents,

— cooperation in the taking of evidence,

— the recognition and enforcement of decisions in civil and commercial cases, including decisions in extrajudicial cases;

(b) promoting the compatibility of the rules applicable in the Member States concerning the conflict of laws and of jurisdiction;

(c) eliminating obstacles to the good functioning of civil proceedings, if necessary by promoting the compatibility of the rules on civil procedure applicable in the Member States.

Article 66

The Council, acting in accordance with the procedure referred to in Article 67, shall take measures to ensure cooperation between the relevant departments of the administrations of the Member States in the areas covered by this title, as well as between those departments and the Commission.

Article 67*

1. During a transitional period of five years following the entry into force of the Treaty of Amsterdam, the Council shall act unanimously on a proposal from the Commission or on the initiative of a Member State and after consulting the European Parliament.

2. After this period of five years:

— the Council shall act on proposals from the Commission; the Commission shall examine any request made by a Member State that it submit a proposal to the Council,

— the Council, acting unanimously after consulting the European Parliament, shall take a decision with a view to providing for all or parts of the areas covered by this title to be governed by the procedure referred to in Article 251 and adapting the provisions relating to the powers of the Court of Justice.

3. By derogation from paragraphs 1 and 2, measures referred to in Article 62(2)(b) (i) and (iii) shall, from the entry into force of the Treaty of Amsterdam, be adopted by the Council acting by a qualified majority on a proposal from the Commission and after consulting the European Parliament.

4. By derogation from paragraph 2, measures referred to in Article 62(2)(b) (ii) and (iv) shall, after a period of five years following the entry into force of the Treaty of Amsterdam, be adopted by the Council acting in accordance with the procedure referred to in Article 251.

5. By derogation from paragraph 1, the Council shall adopt, in accordance with the procedure referred to in Article 251:

— the measures provided for in Article 63(1) and (2)(a) provided that the Council has previously adopted, in accordance with paragraph

---

* Article amended by the Treaty of Nice.

1 of this article, Community legislation defining the common rules and basic principles governing these issues,

— the measures provided for in Article 65 with the exception of aspects relating to family law.

Article 68

1. Article 234 shall apply to this title under the following circumstances and conditions: where a question on the interpretation of this title or on the validity or interpretation of acts of the institutions of the Community based on this title is raised in a case pending before a court or a tribunal of a Member State against whose decisions there is no judicial remedy under national law, that court or tribunal shall, if it considers that a decision on the question is necessary to enable it to give judgment, request the Court of Justice to give a ruling thereon.

2. In any event, the Court of Justice shall not have jurisdiction to rule on any measure or decision taken pursuant to Article 62(1) relating to the maintenance of law and order and the safeguarding of internal security.

3. The Council, the Commission or a Member State may request the Court of Justice to give a ruling on a question of interpretation of this title or of acts of the institutions of the Community based on this title. The ruling given by the Court of Justice in response to such a request shall not apply to judgments of courts or tribunals of the Member States which have become *res judicata*.

Article 69

The application of this title shall be subject to the provisions of the Protocol on the position of the United Kingdom and Ireland and to the Protocol on the position of Denmark and without prejudice to the Protocol on the application of certain aspects of Article 14 of the Treaty establishing the European Community to the United Kingdom and to Ireland.

TITLE V
TRANSPORT

Article 70

The objectives of this Treaty shall, in matters governed by this title, be pursued by Member States within the framework of a common transport policy.

Article 71

1. For the purpose of implementing Article 70, and taking into account the distinctive features of transport, the Council shall, acting in accordance with the procedure referred to in Article 251 and after

consulting the Economic and Social Committee and the Committee of the Regions, lay down:

(a) common rules applicable to international transport to or from the territory of a Member State or passing across the territory of one or more Member States;

(b) the conditions under which non-resident carriers may operate transport services within a Member State;

(c) measures to improve transport safety;

(d) any other appropriate provisions.

2. By way of derogation from the procedure provided for in paragraph 1, where the application of provisions concerning the principles of the regulatory system for transport would be liable to have a serious effect on the standard of living and on employment in certain areas and on the operation of transport facilities, they shall be laid down by the Council acting unanimously on a proposal from the Commission, after consulting the European Parliament and the Economic and Social Committee. In so doing, the Council shall take into account the need for adaptation to the economic development which will result from establishing the common market.

Article 72

Until the provisions referred to in Article 71(1) have been laid down, no Member State may, without the unanimous approval of the Council, make the various provisions governing the subject on 1 January 1958 or, for acceding States, the date of their accession less favourable in their direct or indirect effect on carriers of other Member States as compared with carriers who are nationals of that State.

Article 73

Aids shall be compatible with this Treaty if they meet the needs of coordination of transport or if they represent reimbursement for the discharge of certain obligations inherent in the concept of a public service.

Article 74

Any measures taken within the framework of this Treaty in respect of transport rates and conditions shall take account of the economic circumstances of carriers.

Article 75

1. In the case of transport within the Community, discrimination which takes the form of carriers charging different rates and imposing different conditions for the carriage of the same goods over the same transport links on grounds of the country of origin or of destination of the goods in question shall be abolished.

2. Paragraph 1 shall not prevent the Council from adopting other measures pursuant to Article 71(1).

3. The Council shall, acting by a qualified majority on a proposal from the Commission and after consulting the Economic and Social Committee, lay down rules for implementing the provisions of paragraph 1.

The Council may in particular lay down the provisions needed to enable the institutions of the Community to secure compliance with the rule laid down in paragraph 1 and to ensure that users benefit from it to the full.

4. The Commission shall, acting on its own initiative or on application by a Member State, investigate any cases of discrimination falling within paragraph 1 and, after consulting any Member State concerned, shall take the necessary decisions within the framework of the rules laid down in accordance with the provisions of paragraph 3.

Article 76

1. The imposition by a Member State, in respect of transport operations carried out within the Community, of rates and conditions involving any element of support or protection in the interest of one or more particular undertakings or industries shall be prohibited, unless authorised by the Commission.

2. The Commission shall, acting on its own initiative or on application by a Member State, examine the rates and conditions referred to in paragraph 1, taking account in particular of the requirements of an appropriate regional economic policy, the needs of underdeveloped areas and the problems of areas seriously affected by political circumstances on the one hand, and of the effects of such rates and conditions on competition between the different modes of transport on the other.

After consulting each Member State concerned, the Commission shall take the necessary decisions.

3. The prohibition provided for in paragraph 1 shall not apply to tariffs fixed to meet competition.

Article 77

Charges or dues in respect of the crossing of frontiers which are charged by a carrier in addition to the transport rates shall not exceed a reasonable level after taking the costs actually incurred thereby into account.

Member States shall endeavour to reduce these costs progressively.

The Commission may make recommendations to Member States for the application of this article.

Article 78

The provisions of this title shall not form an obstacle to the application of measures taken in the Federal Republic of Germany to the extent that such measures are required in order to compensate for the economic disadvantages caused by the division of Germany to the economy of certain areas of the Federal Republic affected by that division.

Article 79

An Advisory Committee consisting of experts designated by the governments of Member States shall be attached to the Commission. The Commission, whenever it considers it desirable, shall consult the Committee on transport matters without prejudice to the powers of the Economic and Social Committee.

Article 80

1. The provisions of this title shall apply to transport by rail, road and inland waterway.

2. The Council may, acting by a qualified majority, decide whether, to what extent and by what procedure appropriate provisions may be laid down for sea and air transport.

The procedural provisions of Article 71 shall apply.

TITLE VI
COMMON RULES ON COMPETITION, TAXATION AND APPROXIMATION OF LAWS

CHAPTER 1
RULES ON COMPETITION

SECTION 1
RULES APPLYING TO UNDERTAKINGS

Article 81

1. The following shall be prohibited as incompatible with the common market: all agreements between undertakings, decisions by associations of undertakings and concerted practices which may affect trade between Member States and which have as their object or effect the prevention, restriction or distortion of competition within the common market, and in particular those which:

(a) directly or indirectly fix purchase or selling prices or any other trading conditions;

(b) limit or control production, markets, technical development, or investment;

(c) share markets or sources of supply;

(d) apply dissimilar conditions to equivalent transactions with other trading parties, thereby placing them at a competitive disadvantage;

(e) make the conclusion of contracts subject to acceptance by the other parties of supplementary obligations which, by their nature or according to commercial usage, have no connection with the subject of such contracts.

2. Any agreements or decisions prohibited pursuant to this article shall be automatically void.

3. The provisions of paragraph 1 may, however, be declared inapplicable in the case of:

— any agreement or category of agreements between undertakings,

— any decision or category of decisions by associations of undertakings,

— any concerted practice or category of concerted practices,

which contributes to improving the production or distribution of goods or to promoting technical or economic progress, while allowing consumers a fair share of the resulting benefit, and which does not:

(a) impose on the undertakings concerned restrictions which are not indispensable to the attainment of these objectives;

(b) afford such undertakings the possibility of eliminating competition in respect of a substantial part of the products in question.

Article 82

Any abuse by one or more undertakings of a dominant position within the common market or in a substantial part of it shall be prohibited as incompatible with the common market in so far as it may affect trade between Member States.

Such abuse may, in particular, consist in:

(a) directly or indirectly imposing unfair purchase or selling prices or other unfair trading conditions;

(b) limiting production, markets or technical development to the prejudice of consumers;

(c) applying dissimilar conditions to equivalent transactions with other trading parties, thereby placing them at a competitive disadvantage;

(d) making the conclusion of contracts subject to acceptance by the other parties of supplementary obligations which, by their nature or according to commercial usage, have no connection with the subject of such contracts.

Article 83

1. The appropriate regulations or directives to give effect to the principles set out in Articles 81 and 82 shall be laid down by the Council, acting by a qualified majority on a proposal from the Commission and after consulting the European Parliament.

2. The regulations or directives referred to in paragraph 1 shall be designed in particular:

(a) to ensure compliance with the prohibitions laid down in Article 81(1) and in Article 82 by making provision for fines and periodic penalty payments;

(b) to lay down detailed rules for the application of Article 81(3), taking into account the need to ensure effective supervision on the one hand, and to simplify administration to the greatest possible extent on the other;

(c) to define, if need be, in the various branches of the economy, the scope of the provisions of Articles 81 and 82;

(d) to define the respective functions of the Commission and of the Court of Justice in applying the provisions laid down in this paragraph;

(e) to determine the relationship between national laws and the provisions contained in this section or adopted pursuant to this article.

Article 84

Until the entry into force of the provisions adopted in pursuance of Article 83, the authorities in Member States shall rule on the admissibility of agreements, decisions and concerted practices and on abuse of a dominant position in the common market in accordance with the law of their country and with the provisions of Article 81, in particular paragraph 3, and of Article 82.

Article 85

1. Without prejudice to Article 84, the Commission shall ensure the application of the principles laid down in Articles 81 and 82. On application by a Member State or on its own initiative, and in cooperation with the competent authorities in the Member States, which shall give it their assistance, the Commission shall investigate cases of suspected infringement of these principles. If it finds that there has been an infringement, it shall propose appropriate measures to bring it to an end.

2. If the infringement is not brought to an end, the Commission shall record such infringement of the principles in a reasoned decision. The Commission may publish its decision and authorise Member States to take the measures, the conditions and details of which it shall determine, needed to remedy the situation.

Article 86

1. In the case of public undertakings and undertakings to which Member States grant special or exclusive rights, Member States shall neither enact nor maintain in force any measure contrary to the rules contained in this Treaty, in particular to those rules provided for in Article 12 and Articles 81 to 89.

2.   Undertakings entrusted with the operation of services of general economic interest or having the character of a revenue-producing monopoly shall be subject to the rules contained in this Treaty, in particular to the rules on competition, in so far as the application of such rules does not obstruct the performance, in law or in fact, of the particular tasks assigned to them. The development of trade must not be affected to such an extent as would be contrary to the interests of the Community.

3.   The Commission shall ensure the application of the provisions of this Article and shall, where necessary, address appropriate directives or decisions to Member States.

SECTION 2
AIDS GRANTED BY STATES

Article 87

1.   Save as otherwise provided in this Treaty, any aid granted by a Member State or through State resources in any form whatsoever which distorts or threatens to distort competition by favouring certain undertakings or the production of certain goods shall, in so far as it affects trade between Member States, be incompatible with the common market.

2.   The following shall be compatible with the common market:

(a) aid having a social character, granted to individual consumers, provided that such aid is granted without discrimination related to the origin of the products concerned;

(b) aid to make good the damage caused by natural disasters or exceptional occurrences;

(c) aid granted to the economy of certain areas of the Federal Republic of Germany affected by the division of Germany, in so far as such aid is required in order to compensate for the economic disadvantages caused by that division.

3.   The following may be considered to be compatible with the common market:

(a) aid to promote the economic development of areas where the standard of living is abnormally low or where there is serious underemployment;

(b) aid to promote the execution of an important project of common European interest or to remedy a serious disturbance in the economy of a Member State;

(c) aid to facilitate the development of certain economic activities or of certain economic areas, where such aid does not adversely affect trading conditions to an extent contrary to the common interest;

(d) aid to promote culture and heritage conservation where such aid does not affect trading conditions and competition in the Community to an extent that is contrary to the common interest;

(e) such other categories of aid as may be specified by decision of the Council acting by a qualified majority on a proposal from the Commission.

Article 88

1. The Commission shall, in cooperation with Member States, keep under constant review all systems of aid existing in those States. It shall propose to the latter any appropriate measures required by the progressive development or by the functioning of the common market.

2. If, after giving notice to the parties concerned to submit their comments, the Commission finds that aid granted by a State or through State resources is not compatible with the common market having regard to Article 87, or that such aid is being misused, it shall decide that the State concerned shall abolish or alter such aid within a period of time to be determined by the Commission.

If the State concerned does not comply with this decision within the prescribed time, the Commission or any other interested State may, in derogation from the provisions of Articles 226 and 227, refer the matter to the Court of Justice direct.

On application by a Member State, the Council may, acting unanimously, decide that aid which that State is granting or intends to grant shall be considered to be compatible with the common market, in derogation from the provisions of Article 87 or from the regulations provided for in Article 89, if such a decision is justified by exceptional circumstances. If, as regards the aid in question, the Commission has already initiated the procedure provided for in the first subparagraph of this paragraph, the fact that the State concerned has made its application to the Council shall have the effect of suspending that procedure until the Council has made its attitude known.

If, however, the Council has not made its attitude known within three months of the said application being made, the Commission shall give its decision on the case.

3. The Commission shall be informed, in sufficient time to enable it to submit its comments, of any plans to grant or alter aid. If it considers that any such plan is not compatible with the common market having regard to Article 87, it shall without delay initiate the procedure provided for in paragraph 2. The Member State concerned shall not put its proposed measures into effect until this procedure has resulted in a final decision.

Article 89

The Council, acting by a qualified majority on a proposal from the Commission and after consulting the European Parliament, may make any appropriate regulations for the application of Articles 87 and 88 and may in particular determine the conditions in which Article 88(3) shall apply and the categories of aid exempted from this procedure.

CHAPTER 2
TAX PROVISIONS

Article 90

No Member State shall impose, directly or indirectly, on the products of other Member States any internal taxation of any kind in excess of that imposed directly or indirectly on similar domestic products.

Furthermore, no Member State shall impose on the products of other Member States any internal taxation of such a nature as to afford indirect protection to other products.

Article 91

Where products are exported to the territory of any Member State, any repayment of internal taxation shall not exceed the internal taxation imposed on them whether directly or indirectly.

Article 92

In the case of charges other than turnover taxes, excise duties and other forms of indirect taxation, remissions and repayments in respect of exports to other Member States may not be granted and countervailing charges in respect of imports from Member States may not be imposed unless the measures contemplated have been previously approved for a limited period by the Council acting by a qualified majority on a proposal from the Commission.

Article 93

The Council shall, acting unanimously on a proposal from the Commission and after consulting the European Parliament and the Economic and Social Committee, adopt provisions for the harmonisation of legislation concerning turnover taxes, excise duties and other forms of indirect taxation to the extent that such harmonisation is necessary to ensure the establishment and the functioning of the internal market within the time limit laid down in Article 14.

CHAPTER 3
APPROXIMATION OF LAWS

Article 94

The Council shall, acting unanimously on a proposal from the Commission and after consulting the European Parliament and the Economic and Social Committee, issue directives for the approximation of such laws, regulations or administrative provisions of the Member States as directly affect the establishment or functioning of the common market.

Article 95

1. By way of derogation from Article 94 and save where otherwise provided in this Treaty, the following provisions shall apply for the achievement of the objectives set out in Article 14. The Council shall, acting in accordance with the procedure referred to in Article 251 and after consulting the Economic and Social Committee, adopt the measures for the approximation of the provisions laid down by law, regulation or administrative action in Member States which have as their object the establishment and functioning of the internal market.

2. Paragraph 1 shall not apply to fiscal provisions, to those relating to the free movement of persons nor to those relating to the rights and interests of employed persons.

3. The Commission, in its proposals envisaged in paragraph 1 concerning health, safety, environmental protection and consumer protection, will take as a base a high level of protection, taking account in particular of any new development based on scientific facts. Within their respective powers, the European Parliament and the Council will also seek to achieve this objective.

4. If, after the adoption by the Council or by the Commission of a harmonisation measure, a Member State deems it necessary to maintain national provisions on grounds of major needs referred to in Article 30, or relating to the protection of the environment or the working environment, it shall notify the Commission of these provisions as well as the grounds for maintaining them.

5. Moreover, without prejudice to paragraph 4, if, after the adoption by the Council or by the Commission of a harmonisation measure, a Member State deems it necessary to introduce national provisions based on new scientific evidence relating to the protection of the environment or the working environment on grounds of a problem specific to that Member State arising after the adoption of the harmonisation measure, it shall notify the Commission of the envisaged provisions as well as the grounds for introducing them.

6. The Commission shall, within six months of the notifications as referred to in paragraphs 4 and 5, approve or reject the national provisions involved after having verified whether or not they are a means of arbitrary discrimination or a disguised restriction on trade between Member States and whether or not they shall constitute an obstacle to the functioning of the internal market.

In the absence of a decision by the Commission within this period the national provisions referred to in paragraphs 4 and 5 shall be deemed to have been approved.

When justified by the complexity of the matter and in the absence of danger for human health, the Commission may notify the Member State concerned that the period referred to in this paragraph may be extended for a further period of up to six months.

7. When, pursuant to paragraph 6, a Member State is authorised to maintain or introduce national provisions derogating from a harmonisation measure, the Commission shall immediately examine whether to propose an adaptation to that measure.

8. When a Member State raises a specific problem on public health in a field which has been the subject of prior harmonisation measures, it shall bring it to the attention of the Commission which shall immediately examine whether to propose appropriate measures to the Council.

9. By way of derogation from the procedure laid down in Articles 226 and 227, the Commission and any Member State may bring the matter directly before the Court of Justice if it considers that another Member State is making improper use of the powers provided for in this Article.

10. The harmonisation measures referred to above shall, in appropriate cases, include a safeguard clause authorising the Member States to take, for one or more of the non-economic reasons referred to in Article 30, provisional measures subject to a Community control procedure.

Article 96

Where the Commission finds that a difference between the provisions laid down by law, regulation or administrative action in Member States is distorting the conditions of competition in the common market and that the resultant distortion needs to be eliminated, it shall consult the Member States concerned.

If such consultation does not result in an agreement eliminating the distortion in question, the Council shall, on a proposal from the Commission, acting by a qualified majority, issue the necessary directives. The Commission and the Council may take any other appropriate measures provided for in this Treaty.

Article 97

1. Where there is a reason to fear that the adoption or amendment of a provision laid down by law, regulation or administrative action may cause distortion within the meaning of Article 96, a Member State desiring to proceed therewith shall consult the Commission. After consulting the Member States, the Commission shall recommend to the States concerned such measures as may be appropriate to avoid the distortion in question.

2. If a State desiring to introduce or amend its own provisions does not comply with the recommendation addressed to it by the Commission, other Member States shall not be required, pursuant to Article 96, to amend their own provisions in order to eliminate such distortion. If the Member State which has ignored the recommendation of the Commission causes distortion detrimental only to itself, the provisions of Article 96 shall not apply.

TITLE VII
ECONOMIC AND MONETARY POLICY

CHAPTER 1
ECONOMIC POLICY

Article 98

Member States shall conduct their economic policies with a view to contributing to the achievement of the objectives of the Community, as defined in Article 2, and in the context of the broad guidelines referred to in Article 99(2). The Member States and the Community shall act in accordance with the principle of an open market economy with free competition, favouring an efficient allocation of resources, and in compliance with the principles set out in Article 4.

Article 99

1. Member States shall regard their economic policies as a matter of common concern and shall coordinate them within the Council, in accordance with the provisions of Article 98.

2. The Council shall, acting by a qualified majority on a recommendation from the Commission, formulate a draft for the broad guidelines of the economic policies of the Member States and of the Community, and shall report its findings to the European Council.

The European Council shall, acting on the basis of the report from the Council, discuss a conclusion on the broad guidelines of the economic policies of the Member States and of the Community.

On the basis of this conclusion, the Council shall, acting by a qualified majority, adopt a recommendation setting out these broad guidelines. The Council shall inform the European Parliament of its recommendation.

3. In order to ensure closer coordination of economic policies and sustained convergence of the economic performances of the Member States, the Council shall, on the basis of reports submitted by the Commission, monitor economic developments in each of the Member States and in the Community as well as the consistency of economic policies with the broad guidelines referred to in paragraph 2, and regularly carry out an overall assessment.

For the purpose of this multilateral surveillance, Member States shall forward information to the Commission about important measures taken by them in the field of their economic policy and such other information as they deem necessary.

4. Where it is established, under the procedure referred to in paragraph 3, that the economic policies of a Member State are not consistent with the broad guidelines referred to in paragraph 2 or that they risk jeopardising the proper functioning of economic and monetary

union, the Council may, acting by a qualified majority on a recommendation from the Commission, make the necessary recommendations to the Member State concerned. The Council may, acting by a qualified majority on a proposal from the Commission, decide to make its recommendations public.

The President of the Council and the Commission shall report to the European Parliament on the results of multilateral surveillance. The President of the Council may be invited to appear before the competent committee of the European Parliament if the Council has made its recommendations public.

5. The Council, acting in accordance with the procedure referred to in Article 252, may adopt detailed rules for the multilateral surveillance procedure referred to in paragraphs 3 and 4 of this Article.

Article 100*

1. Without prejudice to any other procedures provided for in this Treaty, the Council, acting by a qualified majority on a proposal from the Commission, may decide upon the measures appropriate to the economic situation, in particular if severe difficulties arise in the supply of certain products.

2. Where a Member State is in difficulties or is seriously threatened with severe difficulties caused by natural disasters or exceptional occurrences beyond its control, the Council, acting by a qualified majority on a proposal from the Commission, may grant, under certain conditions, Community financial assistance to the Member State concerned. The President of the Council shall inform the European Parliament of the decision taken.

Article 101

1. Overdraft facilities or any other type of credit facility with the ECB or with the central banks of the Member States (hereinafter referred to as "national central banks") in favour of Community institutions or bodies, central governments, regional, local or other public authorities, other bodies governed by public law, or public undertakings of Member States shall be prohibited, as shall the purchase directly from them by the ECB or national central banks of debt instruments.

2. Paragraph 1 shall not apply to publicly owned credit institutions which, in the context of the supply of reserves by central banks, shall be given the same treatment by national central banks and the ECB as private credit institutions.

Article 102

1. Any measure, not based on prudential considerations, establishing privileged access by Community institutions or bodies, central governments, regional, local or other public authorities, other bodies governed

* Article amended by the Treaty of Nice.

by public law, or public undertakings of Member States to financial institutions, shall be prohibited.

2. The Council, acting in accordance with the procedure referred to in Article 252, shall, before 1 January 1994, specify definitions for the application of the prohibition referred to in paragraph 1.

Article 103

1. The Community shall not be liable for or assume the commitments of central governments, regional, local or other public authorities, other bodies governed by public law, or public undertakings of any Member State, without prejudice to mutual financial guarantees for the joint execution of a specific project. A Member State shall not be liable for or assume the commitments of central governments, regional, local or other public authorities, other bodies governed by public law, or public undertakings of another Member State, without prejudice to mutual financial guarantees for the joint execution of a specific project.

2. If necessary, the Council, acting in accordance with the procedure referred to in Article 252, may specify definitions for the application of the prohibition referred to in Article 101 and in this Article.

Article 104

1. Member States shall avoid excessive government deficits.

2. The Commission shall monitor the development of the budgetary situation and of the stock of government debt in the Member States with a view to identifying gross errors. In particular it shall examine compliance with budgetary discipline on the basis of the following two criteria:

(a) whether the ratio of the planned or actual government deficit to gross domestic product exceeds a reference value, unless:

— either the ratio has declined substantially and continuously and reached a level that comes close to the reference value,

— or, alternatively, the excess over the reference value is only exceptional and temporary and the ratio remains close to the reference value;

(b) whether the ratio of government debt to gross domestic product exceeds a reference value, unless the ratio is sufficiently diminishing and approaching the reference value at a satisfactory pace.

The reference values are specified in the Protocol on the excessive deficit procedure annexed to this Treaty.

3. If a Member State does not fulfil the requirements under one or both of these criteria, the Commission shall prepare a report. The report of the Commission shall also take into account whether the government deficit exceeds government investment expenditure and take into account all other relevant factors, including the medium-term economic and budgetary position of the Member State.

The Commission may also prepare a report if, notwithstanding the fulfilment of the requirements under the criteria, it is of the opinion that there is a risk of an excessive deficit in a Member State.

4. The Committee provided for in Article 114 shall formulate an opinion on the report of the Commission.

5. If the Commission considers that an excessive deficit in a Member State exists or may occur, the Commission shall address an opinion to the Council.

6. The Council shall, acting by a qualified majority on a recommendation from the Commission, and having considered any observations which the Member State concerned may wish to make, decide after an overall assessment whether an excessive deficit exists.

7. Where the existence of an excessive deficit is decided according to paragraph 6, the Council shall make recommendations to the Member State concerned with a view to bringing that situation to an end within a given period. Subject to the provisions of paragraph 8, these recommendations shall not be made public.

8. Where it establishes that there has been no effective action in response to its recommendations within the period laid down, the Council may make its recommendations public.

9. If a Member State persists in failing to put into practice the recommendations of the Council, the Council may decide to give notice to the Member State to take, within a specified time limit, measures for the deficit reduction which is judged necessary by the Council in order to remedy the situation.

In such a case, the Council may request the Member State concerned to submit reports in accordance with a specific timetable in order to examine the adjustment efforts of that Member State.

10. The rights to bring actions provided for in Articles 226 and 227 may not be exercised within the framework of paragraphs 1 to 9 of this Article.

11. As long as a Member State fails to comply with a decision taken in accordance with paragraph 9, the Council may decide to apply or, as the case may be, intensify one or more of the following measures:

— to require the Member State concerned to publish additional information, to be specified by the Council, before issuing bonds and securities,

— to invite the European Investment Bank to reconsider its lending policy towards the Member State concerned,

— to require the Member State concerned to make a non-interest-bearing deposit of an appropriate size with the Community until the excessive deficit has, in the view of the Council, been corrected,

— to impose fines of an appropriate size.

The President of the Council shall inform the European Parliament of the decisions taken.

12.   The Council shall abrogate some or all of its decisions referred to in paragraphs 6 to 9 and 11 to the extent that the excessive deficit in the Member State concerned has, in the view of the Council, been corrected. If the Council has previously made public recommendations, it shall, as soon as the decision under paragraph 8 has been abrogated, make a public statement that an excessive deficit in the Member State concerned no longer exists.

13.   When taking the decisions referred to in paragraphs 7 to 9, 11 and 12, the Council shall act on a recommendation from the Commission by a majority of two thirds of the votes of its members weighted in accordance with Article 205(2), excluding the votes of the representative of the Member State concerned.

14.   Further provisions relating to the implementation of the procedure described in this article are set out in the Protocol on the excessive deficit procedure annexed to this Treaty.

The Council shall, acting unanimously on a proposal from the Commission and after consulting the European Parliament and the ECB, adopt the appropriate provisions which shall then replace the said Protocol.

Subject to the other provisions of this paragraph, the Council shall, before 1 January 1994, acting by a qualified majority on a proposal from the Commission and after consulting the European Parliament, lay down detailed rules and definitions for the application of the provisions of the said Protocol.

CHAPTER 2
MONETARY POLICY

Article 105

1.   The primary objective of the ESCB shall be to maintain price stability. Without prejudice to the objective of price stability, the ESCB shall support the general economic policies in the Community with a view to contributing to the achievement of the objectives of the Community as laid down in Article 2. The ESCB shall act in accordance with the principle of an open market economy with free competition, favouring an efficient allocation of resources, and in compliance with the principles set out in Article 4.

2.   The basic tasks to be carried out through the ESCB shall be:

—   to define and implement the monetary policy of the Community,

—   to conduct foreign-exchange operations consistent with the provisions of Article 111,

—   to hold and manage the official foreign reserves of the Member States,

—   to promote the smooth operation of payment systems.

3. The third indent of paragraph 2 shall be without prejudice to the holding and management by the governments of Member States of foreign-exchange working balances.

4. The ECB shall be consulted:

— on any proposed Community act in its fields of competence,

— by national authorities regarding any draft legislative provision in its fields of competence, but within the limits and under the conditions set out by the Council in accordance with the procedure laid down in Article 107(6).

The ECB may submit opinions to the appropriate Community institutions or bodies or to national authorities on matters in its fields of competence.

5. The ESCB shall contribute to the smooth conduct of policies pursued by the competent authorities relating to the prudential supervision of credit institutions and the stability of the financial system.

6. The Council may, acting unanimously on a proposal from the Commission and after consulting the ECB and after receiving the assent of the European Parliament, confer upon the ECB specific tasks concerning policies relating to the prudential supervision of credit institutions and other financial institutions with the exception of insurance undertakings.

Article 106

1. The ECB shall have the exclusive right to authorise the issue of banknotes within the Community. The ECB and the national central banks may issue such notes. The banknotes issued by the ECB and the national central banks shall be the only such notes to have the status of legal tender within the Community.

2. Member States may issue coins subject to approval by the ECB of the volume of the issue. The Council may, acting in accordance with the procedure referred to in Article 252 and after consulting the ECB, adopt measures to harmonise the denominations and technical specifications of all coins intended for circulation to the extent necessary to permit their smooth circulation within the Community.

Article 107

1. The ESCB shall be composed of the ECB and of the national central banks.

2. The ECB shall have legal personality.

3. The ESCB shall be governed by the decision-making bodies of the ECB which shall be the Governing Council and the Executive Board.

4. The Statute of the ESCB is laid down in a Protocol annexed to this Treaty.

5. Articles 5.1, 5.2, 5.3, 17, 18, 19.1, 22, 23, 24, 26, 32.2, 32.3, 32.4, 32.6, 33.1(a) and 36 of the Statute of the ESCB may be amended by the Council, acting either by a qualified majority on a recommendation from the ECB and after consulting the Commission or unanimously on a proposal from the Commission and after consulting the ECB. In either case, the assent of the European Parliament shall be required.

6. The Council, acting by a qualified majority either on a proposal from the Commission and after consulting the European Parliament and the ECB or on a recommendation from the ECB and after consulting the European Parliament and the Commission, shall adopt the provisions referred to in Articles 4, 5.4, 19.2, 20, 28.1, 29.2, 30.4 and 34.3 of the Statute of the ESCB.

Article 108

When exercising the powers and carrying out the tasks and duties conferred upon them by this Treaty and the Statute of the ESCB, neither the ECB, nor a national central bank, nor any member of their decision-making bodies shall seek or take instructions from Community institutions or bodies, from any government of a Member State or from any other body. The Community institutions and bodies and the governments of the Member States undertake to respect this principle and not to seek to influence the members of the decision-making bodies of the ECB or of the national central banks in the performance of their tasks.

Article 109

Each Member State shall ensure, at the latest at the date of the establishment of the ESCB, that its national legislation including the statutes of its national central bank is compatible with this Treaty and the Statute of the ESCB.

Article 110

1. In order to carry out the tasks entrusted to the ESCB, the ECB shall, in accordance with the provisions of this Treaty and under the conditions laid down in the Statute of the ESCB:

— make regulations to the extent necessary to implement the tasks defined in Article 3.1, first indent, Articles 19.1, 22 and 25.2 of the Statute of the ESCB and in cases which shall be laid down in the acts of the Council referred to in Article 107(6),

— take decisions necessary for carrying out the tasks entrusted to the ESCB under this Treaty and the Statute of the ESCB,

— make recommendations and deliver opinions.

2. A regulation shall have general application. It shall be binding in its entirety and directly applicable in all Member States.

Recommendations and opinions shall have no binding force.

A decision shall be binding in its entirety upon those to whom it is addressed.

Articles 253, 254 and 256 shall apply to regulations and decisions adopted by the ECB.

The ECB may decide to publish its decisions, recommendations and opinions.

3. Within the limits and under the conditions adopted by the Council under the procedure laid down in Article 107(6), the ECB shall be entitled to impose fines or periodic penalty payments on undertakings for failure to comply with obligations under its regulations and decisions.

Article 111*

1. By way of derogation from Article 300, the Council may, acting unanimously on a recommendation from the ECB or from the Commission, and after consulting the ECB in an endeavour to reach a consensus consistent with the objective of price stability, after consulting the European Parliament, in accordance with the procedure in paragraph 3 for determining the arrangements, conclude formal agreements on an exchange-rate system for the ecu in relation to non-Community currencies. The Council may, acting by a qualified majority on a recommendation from the ECB or from the Commission, and after consulting the ECB in an endeavour to reach a consensus consistent with the objective of price stability, adopt, adjust or abandon the central rates of the ecu within the exchange-rate system. The President of the Council shall inform the European Parliament of the adoption, adjustment or abandonment of the ecu central rates.

2. In the absence of an exchange-rate system in relation to one or more non-Community currencies as referred to in paragraph 1, the Council, acting by a qualified majority either on a recommendation from the Commission and after consulting the ECB or on a recommendation from the ECB, may formulate general orientations for exchange-rate policy in relation to these currencies. These general orientations shall be without prejudice to the primary objective of the ESCB to maintain price stability.

3. By way of derogation from Article 300, where agreements concerning monetary or foreign exchange regime matters need to be negotiated by the Community with one or more States or international organisations, the Council, acting by a qualified majority on a recommendation from the Commission and after consulting the ECB, shall decide the arrangements for the negotiation and for the conclusion of such agreements. These arrangements shall ensure that the Community expresses a single position. The Commission shall be fully associated with the negotiations.

* Article amended by the Treaty of Nice.

Agreements concluded in accordance with this paragraph shall be binding on the institutions of the Community, on the ECB and on Member States.

4. Subject to paragraph 1, the Council, acting by a qualified majority on a proposal from the Commission and after consulting the ECB, shall decide on the position of the Community at international level as regards issues of particular relevance to economic and monetary union and on its representation, in compliance with the allocation of powers laid down in Articles 99 and 105.

5. Without prejudice to Community competence and Community agreements as regards economic and monetary union, Member States may negotiate in international bodies and conclude international agreements.

CHAPTER 3
INSTITUTIONAL PROVISIONS

Article 112

1. The Governing Council of the ECB shall comprise the members of the Executive Board of the ECB and the Governors of the national central banks.

2. (a) The Executive Board shall comprise the President, the Vice–President and four other members.

   (b) The President, the Vice–President and the other members of the Executive Board shall be appointed from among persons of recognised standing and professional experience in monetary or banking matters by common accord of the governments of the Member States at the level of Heads of State or Government, on a recommendation from the Council, after it has consulted the European Parliament and the Governing Council of the ECB.

   Their term of office shall be eight years and shall not be renewable.

   Only nationals of Member States may be members of the Executive Board.

Article 113

1. The President of the Council and a member of the Commission may participate, without having the right to vote, in meetings of the Governing Council of the ECB.

The President of the Council may submit a motion for deliberation to the Governing Council of the ECB.

2. The President of the ECB shall be invited to participate in Council meetings when the Council is discussing matters relating to the objectives and tasks of the ESCB.

3. The ECB shall address an annual report on the activities of the ESCB and on the monetary policy of both the previous and current year to the European Parliament, the Council and the Commission, and also to the European Council. The President of the ECB shall present this report to the Council and to the European Parliament, which may hold a general debate on that basis.

The President of the ECB and the other members of the Executive Board may, at the request of the European Parliament or on their own initiative, be heard by the competent committees of the European Parliament.

Article 114

1. In order to promote coordination of the policies of Member States to the full extent needed for the functioning of the internal market, a Monetary Committee with advisory status is hereby set up.

It shall have the following tasks:

— to keep under review the monetary and financial situation of the Member States and of the Community and the general payments system of the Member States and to report regularly thereon to the Council and to the Commission,

— to deliver opinions at the request of the Council or of the Commission, or on its own initiative for submission to those institutions,

— without prejudice to Article 207, to contribute to the preparation of the work of the Council referred to in Articles 59, 60, 99(2), (3), (4) and (5), 100, 102, 103, 104, 116(2), 117(6), 119, 120, 121(2) and 122(1),

— to examine, at least once a year, the situation regarding the movement of capital and the freedom of payments, as they result from the application of this Treaty and of measures adopted by the Council; the examination shall cover all measures relating to capital movements and payments; the Committee shall report to the Commission and to the Council on the outcome of this examination.

The Member States and the Commission shall each appoint two members of the Monetary Committee.

2. At the start of the third stage, an Economic and Financial Committee shall be set up. The Monetary Committee provided for in paragraph 1 shall be dissolved.

The Economic and Financial Committee shall have the following tasks:

— to deliver opinions at the request of the Council or of the Commission, or on its own initiative for submission to those institutions,

— to keep under review the economic and financial situation of the Member States and of the Community and to report regularly thereon to the Council and to the Commission, in particular on financial relations with third countries and international institutions,

— without prejudice to Article 207, to contribute to the preparation of the work of the Council referred to in Articles 59, 60, 99(2), (3), (4) and (5), 100, 102, 103, 104, 105(6), 106(2), 107(5) and (6), 111, 119, 120(2) and (3), 122(2), 123(4) and (5), and to carry out other advisory and preparatory tasks assigned to it by the Council,

— to examine, at least once a year, the situation regarding the movement of capital and the freedom of payments, as they result from the application of this Treaty and of measures adopted by the Council; the examination shall cover all measures relating to capital movements and payments; the Committee shall report to the Commission and to the Council on the outcome of this examination.

The Member States, the Commission and the ECB shall each appoint no more than two members of the Committee.

3.   The Council shall, acting by a qualified majority on a proposal from the Commission and after consulting the ECB and the Committee referred to in this Article, lay down detailed provisions concerning the composition of the Economic and Financial Committee. The President of the Council shall inform the European Parliament of such a decision.

4.   In addition to the tasks set out in paragraph 2, if and as long as there are Member States with a derogation as referred to in Articles 122 and 123, the Committee shall keep under review the monetary and financial situation and the general payments system of those Member States and report regularly thereon to the Council and to the Commission.

Article 115

For matters within the scope of Articles 99(4), 104 with the exception of paragraph 14, 111, 121, 122 and 123(4) and (5), the Council or a Member State may request the Commission to make a recommendation or a proposal, as appropriate. The Commission shall examine this request and submit its conclusions to the Council without delay.

CHAPTER 4
TRANSITIONAL PROVISIONS

Article 116

1.   The second stage for achieving economic and monetary union shall begin on 1 January 1994.

2.   Before that date:

(a) each Member State shall:

— adopt, where necessary, appropriate measures to comply with the prohibitions laid down in Article 56 and in Articles 101 and 102(1),

— adopt, if necessary, with a view to permitting the assessment provided for in subparagraph (b), multiannual programmes intended to ensure the lasting convergence necessary for the achievement of economic and monetary union, in particular with regard to price stability and sound public finances;

(b) the Council shall, on the basis of a report from the Commission, assess the progress made with regard to economic and monetary convergence, in particular with regard to price stability and sound public finances, and the progress made with the implementation of Community law concerning the internal market.

3. The provisions of Articles 101, 102(1), 103(1) and 104 with the exception of paragraphs 1, 9, 11 and 14 shall apply from the beginning of the second stage.

The provisions of Articles 100(2), 104(1), (9) and (11), 105, 106, 108, 111, 112, 113 and 114(2) and (4) shall apply from the beginning of the third stage.

4. In the second stage, Member States shall endeavour to avoid excessive government deficits.

5. During the second stage, each Member State shall, as appropriate, start the process leading to the independence of its central bank, in accordance with Article 109.

Article 117

1. At the start of the second stage, a European Monetary Institute (hereinafter referred to as "EMI") shall be established and take up its duties; it shall have legal personality and be directed and managed by a Council, consisting of a President and the Governors of the national central banks, one of whom shall be Vice–President.

The President shall be appointed by common accord of the governments of the Member States at the level of Heads of State or Government, on a recommendation from the Council of the EMI, and after consulting the European Parliament and the Council. The President shall be selected from among persons of recognised standing and professional experience in monetary or banking matters. Only nationals of Member States may be President of the EMI. The Council of the EMI shall appoint the Vice–President.

The Statute of the EMI is laid down in a Protocol annexed to this Treaty.

2. The EMI shall:

— strengthen cooperation between the national central banks,

— strengthen the coordination of the monetary policies of the Member States, with the aim of ensuring price stability,

— monitor the functioning of the European Monetary System,

— hold consultations concerning issues falling within the competence of the national central banks and affecting the stability of financial institutions and markets,

— take over the tasks of the European Monetary Cooperation Fund, which shall be dissolved; the modalities of dissolution are laid down in the Statute of the EMI,

— facilitate the use of the ecu and oversee its development, including the smooth functioning of the ecu clearing system.

3. For the preparation of the third stage, the EMI shall:

— prepare the instruments and the procedures necessary for carrying out a single monetary policy in the third stage,

— promote the harmonisation, where necessary, of the rules and practices governing the collection, compilation and distribution of statistics in the areas within its field of competence,

— prepare the rules for operations to be undertaken by the national central banks within the framework of the ESCB,

— promote the efficiency of cross-border payments,

— supervise the technical preparation of ecu banknotes.

At the latest by 31 December 1996, the EMI shall specify the regulatory, organisational and logistical framework necessary for the ESCB to perform its tasks in the third stage. This framework shall be submitted for decision to the ECB at the date of its establishment.

4. The EMI, acting by a majority of two thirds of the members of its Council, may:

— formulate opinions or recommendations on the overall orientation of monetary policy and exchange-rate policy as well as on related measures introduced in each Member State,

— submit opinions or recommendations to governments and to the Council on policies which might affect the internal or external monetary situation in the Community and, in particular, the functioning of the European Monetary System,

— make recommendations to the monetary authorities of the Member States concerning the conduct of their monetary policy.

5. The EMI, acting unanimously, may decide to publish its opinions and its recommendations.

6. The EMI shall be consulted by the Council regarding any proposed Community act within its field of competence.

Within the limits and under the conditions set out by the Council, acting by a qualified majority on a proposal from the Commission and after consulting the European Parliament and the EMI, the EMI shall be consulted by the authorities of the Member States on any draft legislative provision within its field of competence.

7. The Council may, acting unanimously on a proposal from the Commission and after consulting the European Parliament and the EMI, confer upon the EMI other tasks for the preparation of the third stage.

8. Where this Treaty provides for a consultative role for the ECB, references to the ECB shall be read as referring to the EMI before the establishment of the ECB.

9. During the second stage, the term "ECB" used in Articles 230, 232, 233, 234, 237 and 288 shall be read as referring to the EMI.

Article 118

The currency composition of the ecu basket shall not be changed.

From the start of the third stage, the value of the ecu shall be irrevocably fixed in accordance with Article 123(4).

Article 119

1. Where a Member State is in difficulties or is seriously threatened with difficulties as regards its balance of payments either as a result of an overall disequilibrium in its balance of payments, or as a result of the type of currency at its disposal, and where such difficulties are liable in particular to jeopardise the functioning of the common market or the progressive implementation of the common commercial policy, the Commission shall immediately investigate the position of the State in question and the action which, making use of all the means at its disposal, that State has taken or may take in accordance with the provisions of this Treaty. The Commission shall state what measures it recommends the State concerned to take.

If the action taken by a Member State and the measures suggested by the Commission do not prove sufficient to overcome the difficulties which have arisen or which threaten, the Commission shall, after consulting the Committee referred to in Article 114, recommend to the Council the granting of mutual assistance and appropriate methods therefor.

The Commission shall keep the Council regularly informed of the situation and of how it is developing.

2. The Council, acting by a qualified majority, shall grant such mutual assistance; it shall adopt directives or decisions laying down the conditions and details of such assistance, which may take such forms as:

(a) a concerted approach to or within any other international organisations to which Member States may have recourse;

(b) measures needed to avoid deflection of trade where the State which is in difficulties maintains or reintroduces quantitative restrictions against third countries;

(c) the granting of limited credits by other Member States, subject to their agreement.

3. If the mutual assistance recommended by the Commission is not granted by the Council or if the mutual assistance granted and the measures taken are insufficient, the Commission shall authorise the State which is in difficulties to take protective measures, the conditions and details of which the Commission shall determine.

Such authorisation may be revoked and such conditions and details may be changed by the Council acting by a qualified majority.

4. Subject to Article 122(6), this article shall cease to apply from the beginning of the third stage.

Article 120

1. Where a sudden crisis in the balance of payments occurs and a decision within the meaning of Article 119(2) is not immediately taken, the Member State concerned may, as a precaution, take the necessary protective measures. Such measures must cause the least possible disturbance in the functioning of the common market and must not be wider in scope than is strictly necessary to remedy the sudden difficulties which have arisen.

2. The Commission and the other Member States shall be informed of such protective measures not later than when they enter into force. The Commission may recommend to the Council the granting of mutual assistance under Article 119.

3. After the Commission has delivered an opinion and the Committee referred to in Article 114 has been consulted, the Council may, acting by a qualified majority, decide that the State concerned shall amend, suspend or abolish the protective measures referred to above.

4. Subject to Article 122(6), this article shall cease to apply from the beginning of the third stage.

Article 121

1. The Commission and the EMI shall report to the Council on the progress made in the fulfilment by the Member States of their obligations regarding the achievement of economic and monetary union. These reports shall include an examination of the compatibility between each Member State's national legislation, including the statutes of its national central bank, and Articles 108 and 109 of this Treaty and the Statute of the ESCB. The reports shall also examine the achievement of a high degree of sustainable convergence by reference to the fulfilment by each Member State of the following criteria:

— the achievement of a high degree of price stability; this will be apparent from a rate of inflation which is close to that of, at most, the three best performing Member States in terms of price stability,

— the sustainability of the government financial position; this will be apparent from having achieved a government budgetary position without a deficit that is excessive as determined in accordance with Article 104(6),

— the observance of the normal fluctuation margins provided for by the exchange-rate mechanism of the European Monetary System, for at least two years, without devaluing against the currency of any other Member State,

— the durability of convergence achieved by the Member State and of its participation in the exchange-rate mechanism of the European Monetary System being reflected in the long-term interest-rate levels.

The four criteria mentioned in this paragraph and the relevant periods over which they are to be respected are developed further in a Protocol annexed to this Treaty. The reports of the Commission and the EMI shall also take account of the development of the ecu, the results of the integration of markets, the situation and development of the balances of payments on current account and an examination of the development of unit labour costs and other price indices.

2. On the basis of these reports, the Council, acting by a qualified majority on a recommendation from the Commission, shall assess:

— for each Member State, whether it fulfils the necessary conditions for the adoption of a single currency;

— whether a majority of the Member States fulfils the necessary conditions for the adoption of a single currency,

and recommend its findings to the Council, meeting in the composition of the Heads of State or Government. The European Parliament shall be consulted and forward its opinion to the Council, meeting in the composition of the Heads of State or Government.

3. Taking due account of the reports referred to in paragraph 1 and the opinion of the European Parliament referred to in paragraph 2, the Council, meeting in the composition of the Heads of State or Government, shall, acting by a qualified majority, not later than 31 December 1996:

— decide, on the basis of the recommendations of the Council referred to in paragraph 2, whether a majority of the Member States fulfils the necessary conditions for the adoption of a single currency,

— decide whether it is appropriate for the Community to enter the third stage,

and if so:

— set the date for the beginning of the third stage.

4. If, by the end of 1997, the date for the beginning of the third stage has not been set, the third stage shall start on 1 January 1999. Before

1 July 1998, the Council, meeting in the composition of the Heads of State or Government, after a repetition of the procedure provided for in paragraphs 1 and 2, with the exception of the second indent of paragraph 2, taking into account the reports referred to in paragraph 1 and the opinion of the European Parliament, shall, acting by a qualified majority and on the basis of the recommendations of the Council referred to in paragraph 2, confirm which Member States fulfil the necessary conditions for the adoption of a single currency.

Article 122

1.   If the decision has been taken to set the date in accordance with Article 121(3), the Council shall, on the basis of its recommendations referred to in Article 121(2), acting by a qualified majority on a recommendation from the Commission, decide whether any, and if so which, Member States shall have a derogation as defined in paragraph 3 of this Article. Such Member States shall in this Treaty be referred to as "Member States with a derogation".

If the Council has confirmed which Member States fulfil the necessary conditions for the adoption of a single currency, in accordance with Article 121(4), those Member States which do not fulfil the conditions shall have a derogation as defined in paragraph 3 of this Article. Such Member States shall in this Treaty be referred to as "Member States with a derogation".

2.   At least once every two years, or at the request of a Member State with a derogation, the Commission and the ECB shall report to the Council in accordance with the procedure laid down in Article 121(1). After consulting the European Parliament and after discussion in the Council, meeting in the composition of the Heads of State or Government, the Council shall, acting by a qualified majority on a proposal from the Commission, decide which Member States with a derogation fulfil the necessary conditions on the basis of the criteria set out in Article 121(1), and abrogate the derogations of the Member States concerned.

3.   A derogation referred to in paragraph 1 shall entail that the following articles do not apply to the Member State concerned: Articles 104(9) and (11), 105(1), (2), (3) and (5), 106, 110, 111, and 112(2)(b). The exclusion of such a Member State and its national central bank from rights and obligations within the ESCB is laid down in Chapter IX of the Statute of the ESCB.

4.   In Articles 105(1), (2) and (3), 106, 110, 111 and 112(2)(b), 'Member States' shall be read as "Member States without a derogation".

5.   The voting rights of Member States with a derogation shall be suspended for the Council decisions referred to in the articles of this Treaty mentioned in paragraph 3. In that case, by way of derogation from Articles 205 and 250(1), a qualified majority shall be defined as two thirds of the votes of the representatives of the Member States without a derogation weighted in accordance with Article 205(2), and

unanimity of those Member States shall be required for an act requiring unanimity.

6. Articles 119 and 120 shall continue to apply to a Member State with a derogation.

Article 123*

1. Immediately after the decision on the date for the beginning of the third stage has been taken in accordance with Article 121(3), or, as the case may be, immediately after 1 July 1998:

— the Council shall adopt the provisions referred to in Article 107(6),

— the governments of the Member States without a derogation shall appoint, in accordance with the procedure set out in Article 50 of the Statute of the ESCB, the President, the Vice–President and the other members of the Executive Board of the ECB. If there are Member States with a derogation, the number of members of the Executive Board may be smaller than provided for in Article 11.1 of the Statute of the ESCB, but in no circumstances shall it be less than four.

As soon as the Executive Board is appointed, the ESCB and the ECB shall be established and shall prepare for their full operation as described in this Treaty and the Statute of the ESCB. The full exercise of their powers shall start from the first day of the third stage.

2. As soon as the ECB is established, it shall, if necessary, take over tasks of the EMI. The EMI shall go into liquidation upon the establishment of the ECB; the modalities of liquidation are laid down in the Statute of the EMI.

3. If and as long as there are Member States with a derogation, and without prejudice to Article 107(3) of this Treaty, the General Council of the ECB referred to in Article 45 of the Statute of the ESCB shall be constituted as a third decision-making body of the ECB.

4. At the starting date of the third stage, the Council shall, acting with the unanimity of the Member States without a derogation, on a proposal from the Commission and after consulting the ECB, adopt the conversion rates at which their currencies shall be irrevocably fixed and at which irrevocably fixed rate the ecu shall be substituted for these currencies, and the ecu will become a currency in its own right. This measure shall by itself not modify the external value of the ecu. The Council, acting by a qualified majority of the said Member States, on a proposal from the Commission and after consulting the ECB, shall take the other measures necessary for the rapid introduction of the ecu as the single currency of those Member States. The second sentence of Article 122(5) shall apply.

5. If it is decided, according to the procedure set out in Article 122(2), to abrogate a derogation, the Council shall, acting with the unanimity

* Article amended by the Treaty of Nice.

of the Member States without a derogation and the Member State concerned, on a proposal from the Commission and after consulting the ECB, adopt the rate at which the ecu shall be substituted for the currency of the Member State concerned, and take the other measures necessary for the introduction of the ecu as the single currency in the Member State concerned.

Article 124

1. Until the beginning of the third stage, each Member State shall treat its exchange-rate policy as a matter of common interest. In so doing, Member States shall take account of the experience acquired in cooperation within the framework of the European Monetary System (EMS) and in developing the ecu, and shall respect existing powers in this field.

2. From the beginning of the third stage and for as long as a Member State has a derogation, paragraph 1 shall apply by analogy to the exchange-rate policy of that Member State.

TITLE VIII
EMPLOYMENT

Article 125

Member States and the Community shall, in accordance with this title, work towards developing a coordinated strategy for employment and particularly for promoting a skilled, trained and adaptable workforce and labour markets responsive to economic change with a view to achieving the objectives defined in Article 2 of the Treaty on European Union and in Article 2 of this Treaty.

Article 126

1. Member States, through their employment policies, shall contribute to the achievement of the objectives referred to in Article 125 in a way consistent with the broad guidelines of the economic policies of the Member States and of the Community adopted pursuant to Article 99(2).

2. Member States, having regard to national practices related to the responsibilities of management and labour, shall regard promoting employment as a matter of common concern and shall coordinate their action in this respect within the Council, in accordance with the provisions of Article 128.

Article 127

1. The Community shall contribute to a high level of employment by encouraging cooperation between Member States and by supporting and, if necessary, complementing their action. In doing so, the competences of the Member States shall be respected.

2. The objective of a high level of employment shall be taken into consideration in the formulation and implementation of Community policies and activities.

Article 128

1. The European Council shall each year consider the employment situation in the Community and adopt conclusions thereon, on the basis of a joint annual report by the Council and the Commission.

2. On the basis of the conclusions of the European Council, the Council, acting by a qualified majority on a proposal from the Commission and after consulting the European Parliament, the Economic and Social Committee, the Committee of the Regions and the Employment Committee referred to in Article 130, shall each year draw up guidelines which the Member States shall take into account in their employment policies. These guidelines shall be consistent with the broad guidelines adopted pursuant to Article 99(2).

3. Each Member State shall provide the Council and the Commission with an annual report on the principal measures taken to implement its employment policy in the light of the guidelines for employment as referred to in paragraph 2.

4. The Council, on the basis of the reports referred to in paragraph 3 and having received the views of the Employment Committee, shall each year carry out an examination of the implementation of the employment policies of the Member States in the light of the guidelines for employment. The Council, acting by a qualified majority on a recommendation from the Commission, may, if it considers it appropriate in the light of that examination, make recommendations to Member States.

5. On the basis of the results of that examination, the Council and the Commission shall make a joint annual report to the European Council on the employment situation in the Community and on the implementation of the guidelines for employment.

Article 129

The Council, acting in accordance with the procedure referred to in Article 251 and after consulting the Economic and Social Committee and the Committee of the Regions, may adopt incentive measures designed to encourage cooperation between Member States and to support their action in the field of employment through initiatives aimed at developing exchanges of information and best practices, providing comparative analysis and advice as well as promoting innovative approaches and evaluating experiences, in particular by recourse to pilot projects.

Those measures shall not include harmonisation of the laws and regulations of the Member States.

Article 130

The Council, after consulting the European Parliament, shall establish an Employment Committee with advisory status to promote coordination between Member States on employment and labour market policies. The tasks of the Committee shall be:

— to monitor the employment situation and employment policies in the Member States and the Community,

— without prejudice to Article 207, to formulate opinions at the request of either the Council or the Commission or on its own initiative, and to contribute to the preparation of the Council proceedings referred to in Article 128.

In fulfilling its mandate, the Committee shall consult management and labour.

Each Member State and the Commission shall appoint two members of the Committee.

TITLE IX
COMMON COMMERCIAL POLICY

Article 131

By establishing a customs union between themselves Member States aim to contribute, in the common interest, to the harmonious development of world trade, the progressive abolition of restrictions on international trade and the lowering of customs barriers.

The common commercial policy shall take into account the favourable effect which the abolition of customs duties between Member States may have on the increase in the competitive strength of undertakings in those States.

Article 132

1. Without prejudice to obligations undertaken by them within the framework of other international organisations, Member States shall progressively harmonise the systems whereby they grant aid for exports to third countries, to the extent necessary to ensure that competition between undertakings of the Community is not distorted.

On a proposal from the Commission, the Council shall, acting by a qualified majority, issue any directives needed for this purpose.

2. The preceding provisions shall not apply to such a drawback of customs duties or charges having equivalent effect nor to such a repayment of indirect taxation including turnover taxes, excise duties and other indirect taxes as is allowed when goods are exported from a Member State to a third country, in so far as such a drawback or repayment does not exceed the amount imposed, directly or indirectly, on the products exported.

Article 133*

1. The common commercial policy shall be based on uniform principles, particularly in regard to changes in tariff rates, the conclusion of tariff and trade agreements, the achievement of uniformity in measures of liberalisation, export policy and measures to protect trade such as those to be taken in the event of dumping or subsidies.

2. The Commission shall submit proposals to the Council for implementing the common commercial policy.

3. Where agreements with one or more States or international organisations need to be negotiated, the Commission shall make recommendations to the Council, which shall authorise the Commission to open the necessary negotiations. The Council and the Commission shall be responsible for ensuring that the agreements negotiated are compatible with internal Community policies and rules.

The Commission shall conduct these negotiations in consultation with a special committee appointed by the Council to assist the Commission in this task and within the framework of such directives as the Council may issue to it. The Commission shall report regularly to the special committee on the progress of negotiations.

The relevant provisions of Article 300 shall apply.

4. In exercising the powers conferred upon it by this Article, the Council shall act by a qualified majority.

5. Paragraphs 1 to 4 shall also apply to the negotiation and conclusion of agreements in the fields of trade in services and the commercial aspects of intellectual property, in so far as those agreements are not covered by the said paragraphs and without prejudice to paragraph 6.

By way of derogation from paragraph 4, the Council shall act unanimously when negotiating and concluding an agreement in one of the fields referred to in the first subparagraph, where that agreement includes provisions for which unanimity is required for the adoption of internal rules or where it relates to a field in which the Community has not yet exercised the powers conferred upon it by this Treaty by adopting internal rules.

The Council shall act unanimously with respect to the negotiation and conclusion of a horizontal agreement insofar as it also concerns the preceding subparagraph or the second subparagraph of paragraph 6.

This paragraph shall not affect the right of the Member States to maintain and conclude agreements with third countries or international organisations in so far as such agreements comply with Community law and other relevant international agreements.

6. An agreement may not be concluded by the Council if it includes provisions which would go beyond the Community's internal powers, in particular by leading to harmonisation of the laws or regulations of the

* Article amended by the Treaty of Nice.

Member States in an area for which this Treaty rules out such harmonisation.

In this regard, by way of derogation from the first subparagraph of paragraph 5, agreements relating to trade in cultural and audiovisual services, educational services, and social and human health services, shall fall within the shared competence of the Community and its Member States. Consequently, in addition to a Community decision taken in accordance with the relevant provisions of Article 300, the negotiation of such agreements shall require the common accord of the Member States. Agreements thus negotiated shall be concluded jointly by the Community and the Member States.

The negotiation and conclusion of international agreements in the field of transport shall continue to be governed by the provisions of Title V and Article 300.

7. Without prejudice to the first subparagraph of paragraph 6, the Council, acting unanimously on a proposal from the Commission and after consulting the European Parliament, may extend the application of paragraphs 1 to 4 to international negotiations and agreements on intellectual property in so far as they are not covered by paragraph 5.

Article 134

In order to ensure that the execution of measures of commercial policy taken in accordance with this Treaty by any Member State is not obstructed by deflection of trade, or where differences between such measures lead to economic difficulties in one or more Member States, the Commission shall recommend the methods for the requisite cooperation between Member States. Failing this, the Commission may authorise Member States to take the necessary protective measures, the conditions and details of which it shall determine.

In case of urgency, Member States shall request authorisation to take the necessary measures themselves from the Commission, which shall take a decision as soon as possible; the Member States concerned shall then notify the measures to the other Member States. The Commission may decide at any time that the Member States concerned shall amend or abolish the measures in question.

In the selection of such measures, priority shall be given to those which cause the least disturbance of the functioning of the common market.

TITLE X
CUSTOMS COOPERATION

Article 135

Within the scope of application of this Treaty, the Council, acting in accordance with the procedure referred to in Article 251, shall take measures in order to strengthen customs cooperation between Member States and between the latter and the Commission. These measures shall not concern the application of national criminal law or the national administration of justice.

TITLE XI
SOCIAL POLICY, EDUCATION, VOCATIONAL TRAINING AND YOUTH

CHAPTER 1
SOCIAL PROVISIONS

Article 136

The Community and the Member States, having in mind fundamental social rights such as those set out in the European Social Charter signed at Turin on 18 October 1961 and in the 1989 Community Charter of the Fundamental Social Rights of Workers, shall have as their objectives the promotion of employment, improved living and working conditions, so as to make possible their harmonisation while the improvement is being maintained, proper social protection, dialogue between management and labour, the development of human resources with a view to lasting high employment and the combating of exclusion.

To this end the Community and the Member States shall implement measures which take account of the diverse forms of national practices, in particular in the field of contractual relations, and the need to maintain the competitiveness of the Community economy.

They believe that such a development will ensue not only from the functioning of the common market, which will favour the harmonisation of social systems, but also from the procedures provided for in this Treaty and from the approximation of provisions laid down by law, regulation or administrative action.

Article 137*

1. With a view to achieving the objectives of Article 136, the Community shall support and complement the activities of the Member States in the following fields:

(a) improvement in particular of the working environment to protect workers' health and safety;

(b) working conditions;

(c) social security and social protection of workers;

(d) protection of workers where their employment contract is terminated;

(e) the information and consultation of workers;

* Article amended by the Treaty of Nice.

(f) representation and collective defence of the interests of workers and employers, including co-determination, subject to paragraph 5;

(g) conditions of employment for third-country nationals legally residing in Community territory;

(h) the integration of persons excluded from the labour market, without prejudice to Article 150;

(i) equality between men and women with regard to labour market opportunities and treatment at work;

(j) the combating of social exclusion;

(k) the modernisation of social protection systems without prejudice to point (c).

2.   To this end, the Council:

(a) may adopt measures designed to encourage cooperation between Member States through initiatives aimed at improving knowledge, developing exchanges of information and best practices, promoting innovative approaches and evaluating experiences, excluding any harmonisation of the laws and regulations of the Member States;

(b) may adopt, in the fields referred to in paragraph 1(a) to (i), by means of directives, minimum requirements for gradual implementation, having regard to the conditions and technical rules obtaining in each of the Member States. Such directives shall avoid imposing administrative, financial and legal constraints in a way which would hold back the creation and development of small and medium-sized undertakings.

The Council shall act in accordance with the procedure referred to in Article 251 after consulting the Economic and Social Committee and the Committee of the Regions, except in the fields referred to in paragraph 1(c), (d), (f) and (g) of this article, where the Council shall act unanimously on a proposal from the Commission, after consulting the European Parliament and the said Committees. The Council, acting unanimously on a proposal from the Commission, after consulting the European Parliament, may decide to render the procedure referred to in Article 251 applicable to paragraph 1(d), (f) and (g) of this article.

3.   A Member State may entrust management and labour, at their joint request, with the implementation of directives adopted pursuant to paragraph 2.

In this case, it shall ensure that, no later than the date on which a directive must be transposed in accordance with Article 249, management and labour have introduced the necessary measures by agreement, the Member State concerned being required to take any necessary measure enabling it at any time to be in a position to guarantee the results imposed by that directive.

4.   The provisions adopted pursuant to this article:

— shall not affect the right of Member States to define the fundamental principles of their social security systems and must not significantly affect the financial equilibrium thereof,

— shall not prevent any Member State from maintaining or introducing more stringent protective measures compatible with this Treaty.

5. The provisions of this article shall not apply to pay, the right of association, the right to strike or the right to impose lock-outs.

Article 138

1. The Commission shall have the task of promoting the consultation of management and labour at Community level and shall take any relevant measure to facilitate their dialogue by ensuring balanced support for the parties.

2. To this end, before submitting proposals in the social policy field, the Commission shall consult management and labour on the possible direction of Community action.

3. If, after such consultation, the Commission considers Community action advisable, it shall consult management and labour on the content of the envisaged proposal. Management and labour shall forward to the Commission an opinion or, where appropriate, a recommendation.

4. On the occasion of such consultation, management and labour may inform the Commission of their wish to initiate the process provided for in Article 139. The duration of the procedure shall not exceed nine months, unless the management and labour concerned and the Commission decide jointly to extend it.

Article 139*

1. Should management and labour so desire, the dialogue between them at Community level may lead to contractual relations, including agreements.

2. Agreements concluded at Community level shall be implemented either in accordance with the procedures and practices specific to management and labour and the Member States or, in matters covered by Article 137, at the joint request of the signatory parties, by a Council decision on a proposal from the Commission.

The Council shall act by qualified majority, except where the agreement in question contains one or more provisions relating to one of the areas for which unanimity is required pursuant to Article 137(2). In that case, it shall act unanimously.

Article 140

With a view to achieving the objectives of Article 136 and without prejudice to the other provisions of this Treaty, the Commission shall

---

* Article amended by the Treaty of   Nice.

encourage cooperation between the Member States and facilitate the coordination of their action in all social policy fields under this chapter, particularly in matters relating to:

— employment,

— labour law and working conditions,

— basic and advanced vocational training,

— social security,

— prevention of occupational accidents and diseases,

— occupational hygiene,

— the right of association and collective bargaining between employers and workers.

To this end, the Commission shall act in close contact with Member States by making studies, delivering opinions and arranging consultations both on problems arising at national level and on those of concern to international organisations.

Before delivering the opinions provided for in this article, the Commission shall consult the Economic and Social Committee.

Article 141

1.   Each Member State shall ensure that the principle of equal pay for male and female workers for equal work or work of equal value is applied.

2.   For the purpose of this article, "pay" means the ordinary basic or minimum wage or salary and any other consideration, whether in cash or in kind, which the worker receives directly or indirectly, in respect of his employment, from his employer.

Equal pay without discrimination based on sex means:

(a) that pay for the same work at piece rates shall be calculated on the basis of the same unit of measurement;

(b) that pay for work at time rates shall be the same for the same job.

3.   The Council, acting in accordance with the procedure referred to in Article 251, and after consulting the Economic and Social Committee, shall adopt measures to ensure the application of the principle of equal opportunities and equal treatment of men and women in matters of employment and occupation, including the principle of equal pay for equal work or work of equal value.

4.   With a view to ensuring full equality in practice between men and women in working life, the principle of equal treatment shall not prevent any Member State from maintaining or adopting measures providing for specific advantages in order to make it easier for the underrepresented sex to pursue a vocational activity or to prevent or compensate for disadvantages in professional careers.

Article 142

Member States shall endeavour to maintain the existing equivalence between paid holiday schemes.

Article 143

The Commission shall draw up a report each year on progress in achieving the objectives of Article 136, including the demographic situation in the Community. It shall forward the report to the European Parliament, the Council and the Economic and Social Committee.

The European Parliament may invite the Commission to draw up reports on particular problems concerning the social situation.

Article 144*

The Council, after consulting the European Parliament, shall establish a Social Protection Committee with advisory status to promote cooperation on social protection policies between Member States and with the Commission. The tasks of the Committee shall be:

— to monitor the social situation and the development of social protection policies in the Member States and the Community,

— to promote exchanges of information, experience and good practice between Member States and with the Commission,

— without prejudice to Article 207, to prepare reports, formulate opinions or undertake other work within its fields of competence, at the request of either the Council or the Commission or on its own initiative.

In fulfilling its mandate, the Committee shall establish appropriate contacts with management and labour.

Each Member State and the Commission shall appoint two members of the Committee.

Article 145

The Commission shall include a separate chapter on social developments within the Community in its annual report to the European Parliament.

The European Parliament may invite the Commission to draw up reports on any particular problems concerning social conditions.

CHAPTER 2
THE EUROPEAN SOCIAL FUND

Article 146

In order to improve employment opportunities for workers in the internal market and to contribute thereby to raising the standard of

* Article amended by the Treaty of Nice.

living, a European Social Fund is hereby established in accordance with the provisions set out below; it shall aim to render the employment of workers easier and to increase their geographical and occupational mobility within the Community, and to facilitate their adaptation to industrial changes and to changes in production systems, in particular through vocational training and retraining.

Article 147

The Fund shall be administered by the Commission.

The Commission shall be assisted in this task by a Committee presided over by a Member of the Commission and composed of representatives of governments, trade unions and employers' organisations.

Article 148

The Council, acting in accordance with the procedure referred to in Article 251 and after consulting the Economic and Social Committee and the Committee of the Regions, shall adopt implementing decisions relating to the European Social Fund.

CHAPTER 3
EDUCATION, VOCATIONAL TRAINING AND YOUTH

Article 149

1. The Community shall contribute to the development of quality education by encouraging cooperation between Member States and, if necessary, by supporting and supplementing their action, while fully respecting the responsibility of the Member States for the content of teaching and the organisation of education systems and their cultural and linguistic diversity.

2. Community action shall be aimed at:

— developing the European dimension in education, particularly through the teaching and dissemination of the languages of the Member States,

— encouraging mobility of students and teachers, by encouraging *inter alia*, the academic recognition of diplomas and periods of study,

— promoting cooperation between educational establishments,

— developing exchanges of information and experience on issues common to the education systems of the Member States,

— encouraging the development of youth exchanges and of exchanges of socioeducational instructors,

— encouraging the development of distance education.

3. The Community and the Member States shall foster cooperation with third countries and the competent international organisations in the field of education, in particular the Council of Europe.

4. In order to contribute to the achievement of the objectives referred to in this Article, the Council:

— acting in accordance with the procedure referred to in Article 251, after consulting the Economic and Social Committee and the Committee of the Regions, shall adopt incentive measures, excluding any harmonisation of the laws and regulations of the Member States,

— acting by a qualified majority on a proposal from the Commission, shall adopt recommendations.

Article 150

1. The Community shall implement a vocational training policy which shall support and supplement the action of the Member States, while fully respecting the responsibility of the Member States for the content and organisation of vocational training.

2. Community action shall aim to:

— facilitate adaptation to industrial changes, in particular through vocational training and retraining,

— improve initial and continuing vocational training in order to facilitate vocational integration and reintegration into the labour market,

— facilitate access to vocational training and encourage mobility of instructors and trainees and particularly young people,

— stimulate cooperation on training between educational or training establishments and firms,

— develop exchanges of information and experience on issues common to the training systems of the Member States.

3. The Community and the Member States shall foster cooperation with third countries and the competent international organisations in the sphere of vocational training.

4. The Council, acting in accordance with the procedure referred to in Article 251 and after consulting the Economic and Social Committee and the Committee of the Regions, shall adopt measures to contribute to the achievement of the objectives referred to in this article, excluding any harmonisation of the laws and regulations of the Member States.

TITLE XII
CULTURE

Article 151

1. The Community shall contribute to the flowering of the cultures of the Member States, while respecting their national and regional diver-

sity and at the same time bringing the common cultural heritage to the fore.

2.   Action by the Community shall be aimed at encouraging cooperation between Member States and, if necessary, supporting and supplementing their action in the following areas:

— improvement of the knowledge and dissemination of the culture and history of the European peoples,

— conservation and safeguarding of cultural heritage of European significance,

— non-commercial cultural exchanges,

— artistic and literary creation, including in the audiovisual sector.

3.   The Community and the Member States shall foster cooperation with third countries and the competent international organisations in the sphere of culture, in particular the Council of Europe.

4.   The Community shall take cultural aspects into account in its action under other provisions of this Treaty, in particular in order to respect and to promote the diversity of its cultures.

5.   In order to contribute to the achievement of the objectives referred to in this Article, the Council:

— acting in accordance with the procedure referred to in Article 251 and after consulting the Committee of the Regions, shall adopt incentive measures, excluding any harmonisation of the laws and regulations of the Member States. The Council shall act unanimously throughout the procedure referred to in Article 251,

— acting unanimously on a proposal from the Commission, shall adopt recommendations.

TITLE XIII
PUBLIC HEALTH

Article 152

1.   A high level of human health protection shall be ensured in the definition and implementation of all Community policies and activities.

Community action, which shall complement national policies, shall be directed towards improving public health, preventing human illness and diseases, and obviating sources of danger to human health. Such action shall cover the fight against the major health scourges, by promoting research into their causes, their transmission and their prevention, as well as health information and education.

The Community shall complement the Member States' action in reducing drugs-related health damage, including information and prevention.

2. The Community shall encourage cooperation between the Member States in the areas referred to in this Article and, if necessary, lend support to their action.

Member States shall, in liaison with the Commission, coordinate among themselves their policies and programmes in the areas referred to in paragraph 1. The Commission may, in close contact with the Member States, take any useful initiative to promote such coordination.

3. The Community and the Member States shall foster cooperation with third countries and the competent international organisations in the sphere of public health.

4. The Council, acting in accordance with the procedure referred to in Article 251 and after consulting the Economic and Social Committee and the Committee of the Regions, shall contribute to the achievement of the objectives referred to in this article through adopting:

(a) measures setting high standards of quality and safety of organs and substances of human origin, blood and blood derivatives; these measures shall not prevent any Member State from maintaining or introducing more stringent protective measures;

(b) by way of derogation from Article 37, measures in the veterinary and phytosanitary fields which have as their direct objective the protection of public health;

(c) incentive measures designed to protect and improve human health, excluding any harmonisation of the laws and regulations of the Member States.

The Council, acting by a qualified majority on a proposal from the Commission, may also adopt recommendations for the purposes set out in this article.

5. Community action in the field of public health shall fully respect the responsibilities of the Member States for the organisation and delivery of health services and medical care. In particular, measures referred to in paragraph 4(a) shall not affect national provisions on the donation or medical use of organs and blood.

TITLE XIV
CONSUMER PROTECTION

Article 153

1. In order to promote the interests of consumers and to ensure a high level of consumer protection, the Community shall contribute to protecting the health, safety and economic interests of consumers, as well as to promoting their right to information, education and to organise themselves in order to safeguard their interests.

2. Consumer protection requirements shall be taken into account in defining and implementing other Community policies and activities.

3.   The Community shall contribute to the attainment of the objectives referred to in paragraph 1 through:

(a) measures adopted pursuant to Article 95 in the context of the completion of the internal market;

(b) measures which support, supplement and monitor the policy pursued by the Member States.

4.   The Council, acting in accordance with the procedure referred to in Article 251 and after consulting the Economic and Social Committee, shall adopt the measures referred to in paragraph 3(b).

5.   Measures adopted pursuant to paragraph 4 shall not prevent any Member State from maintaining or introducing more stringent protective measures. Such measures must be compatible with this Treaty. The Commission shall be notified of them.

TITLE XV
TRANS–EUROPEAN NETWORKS

Article 154

1.   To help achieve the objectives referred to in Articles 14 and 158 and to enable citizens of the Union, economic operators and regional and local communities to derive full benefit from the setting-up of an area without internal frontiers, the Community shall contribute to the establishment and development of trans-European networks in the areas of transport, telecommunications and energy infrastructures.

2.   Within the framework of a system of open and competitive markets, action by the Community shall aim at promoting the interconnection and interoperability of national networks as well as access to such networks. It shall take account in particular of the need to link island, landlocked and peripheral regions with the central regions of the Community.

Article 155

1.   In order to achieve the objectives referred to in Article 154, the Community:

— shall establish a series of guidelines covering the objectives, priorities and broad lines of measures envisaged in the sphere of trans-European networks; these guidelines shall identify projects of common interest,

— shall implement any measures that may prove necessary to ensure the interoperability of the networks, in particular in the field of technical standardisation,

— may support projects of common interest supported by Member States, which are identified in the framework of the guidelines referred to in the first indent, particularly through feasibility studies, loan guarantees or interest-rate subsidies; the Community may also contribute, through the Cohesion Fund set up pursuant to Article 161, to the financing of specific projects in Member States in the area of transport infrastructure.

The Community's activities shall take into account the potential economic viability of the projects.

2. Member States shall, in liaison with the Commission, coordinate among themselves the policies pursued at national level which may have a significant impact on the achievement of the objectives referred to in Article 154. The Commission may, in close cooperation with the Member State, take any useful initiative to promote such coordination.

3. The Community may decide to cooperate with third countries to promote projects of mutual interest and to ensure the interoperability of networks.

Article 156

The guidelines and other measures referred to in Article 155(1) shall be adopted by the Council, acting in accordance with the procedure referred to in Article 251 and after consulting the Economic and Social Committee and the Committee of the Regions.

Guidelines and projects of common interest which relate to the territory of a Member State shall require the approval of the Member State concerned.

TITLE XVI
INDUSTRY

Article 157*

1. The Community and the Member States shall ensure that the conditions necessary for the competitiveness of the Community's industry exist.

For that purpose, in accordance with a system of open and competitive markets, their action shall be aimed at:

— speeding up the adjustment of industry to structural changes,

— encouraging an environment favourable to initiative and to the development of undertakings throughout the Community, particularly small and medium-sized undertakings,

— encouraging an environment favourable to cooperation between undertakings,

— fostering better exploitation of the industrial potential of policies of innovation, research and technological development.

2. The Member States shall consult each other in liaison with the Commission and, where necessary, shall coordinate their action. The

* Article amended by the Treaty of Nice.

Commission may take any useful initiative to promote such coordination.

3. The Community shall contribute to the achievement of the objectives set out in paragraph 1 through the policies and activities it pursues under other provisions of this Treaty. The Council, acting in accordance with the procedure referred to in Article 251 and after consulting the Economic and Social Committee, may decide on specific measures in support of action taken in the Member States to achieve the objectives set out in paragraph 1.

This title shall not provide a basis for the introduction by the Community of any measure which could lead to a distortion of competition or contains tax provisions or provisions relating to the rights and interests of employed persons.

TITLE XVII
ECONOMIC AND SOCIAL COHESION

Article 158

In order to promote its overall harmonious development, the Community shall develop and pursue its actions leading to the strengthening of its economic and social cohesion.

In particular, the Community shall aim at reducing disparities between the levels of development of the various regions and the backwardness of the least favoured regions or islands, including rural areas.

Article 159*

Member States shall conduct their economic policies and shall coordinate them in such a way as, in addition, to attain the objectives set out in Article 158. The formulation and implementation of the Community's policies and actions and the implementation of the internal market shall take into account the objectives set out in Article 158 and shall contribute to their achievement. The Community shall also support the achievement of these objectives by the action it takes through the Structural Funds (European Agricultural Guidance and Guarantee Fund, Guidance Section; European Social Fund; European Regional Development Fund), the European Investment Bank and the other existing Financial Instruments.

The Commission shall submit a report to the European Parliament, the Council, the Economic and Social Committee and the Committee of the Regions every three years on the progress made towards achieving economic and social cohesion and on the manner in which the various means provided for in this Article have contributed to it. This report shall, if necessary, be accompanied by appropriate proposals.

If specific actions prove necessary outside the Funds and without prejudice to the measures decided upon within the framework of the

* Article amended by the Treaty of Nice.

other Community policies, such actions may be adopted by the Council acting in accordance with the procedure referred to in Article 251 and after consulting the Economic and Social Committee and the Committee of the Regions.

Article 160

The European Regional Development Fund is intended to help to redress the main regional imbalances in the Community through participation in the development and structural adjustment of regions whose development is lagging behind and in the conversion of declining industrial regions.

Article 161*

Without prejudice to Article 162, the Council, acting unanimously on a proposal from the Commission and after obtaining the assent of the European Parliament and consulting the Economic and Social Committee and the Committee of the Regions, shall define the tasks, priority objectives and the organisation of the Structural Funds, which may involve grouping the Funds. The Council, acting by the same procedure, shall also define the general rules applicable to them and the provisions necessary to ensure their effectiveness and the coordination of the Funds with one another and with the other existing Financial Instruments.

A Cohesion Fund set up by the Council in accordance with the same procedure shall provide a financial contribution to projects in the fields of environment and trans-European networks in the area of transport infrastructure.

From 1 January 2007, the Council shall act by a qualified majority on a proposal from the Commission after obtaining the assent of the European Parliament and after consulting the Economic and Social Committee and the Committee of the Regions if, by that date, the multiannual financial perspective applicable from 1 January 2007 and the Interinstitutional Agreement relating thereto have been adopted. If such is not the case, the procedure laid down by this paragraph shall apply from the date of their adoption.

Article 162

Implementing decisions relating to the European Regional Development Fund shall be taken by the Council, acting in accordance with the procedure referred to in Article 251 and after consulting the Economic and Social Committee and the Committee of the Regions.

With regard to the European Agricultural Guidance and Guarantee Fund, Guidance Section, and the European Social Fund, Articles 37 and 148 respectively shall continue to apply.

* Article amended by the Treaty of Nice.

TITLE XVIII
RESEARCH AND TECHNOLOGICAL DEVELOPMENT

Article 163

1. The Community shall have the objective of strengthening the scientific and technological bases of Community industry and encouraging it to become more competitive at international level, while promoting all the research activities deemed necessary by virtue of other chapters of this Treaty.

2. For this purpose the Community shall, throughout the Community, encourage undertakings, including small and medium-sized undertakings, research centres and universities in their research and technological development activities of high quality; it shall support their efforts to cooperate with one another, aiming, notably, at enabling undertakings to exploit the internal market potential to the full, in particular through the opening-up of national public contracts, the definition of common standards and the removal of legal and fiscal obstacles to that cooperation.

3. All Community activities under this Treaty in the area of research and technological development, including demonstration projects, shall be decided on and implemented in accordance with the provisions of this title.

Article 164

In pursuing these objectives, the Community shall carry out the following activities, complementing the activities carried out in the Member States:

(a) implementation of research, technological development and demonstration programmes, by promoting cooperation with and between undertakings, research centres and universities;

(b) promotion of cooperation in the field of Community research, technological development and demonstration with third countries and international organisations;

(c) dissemination and optimisation of the results of activities in Community research, technological development and demonstration;

(d) stimulation of the training and mobility of researchers in the Community.

Article 165

1. The Community and the Member States shall coordinate their research and technological development activities so as to ensure that national policies and Community policy are mutually consistent.

2. In close cooperation with the Member State, the Commission may take any useful initiative to promote the coordination referred to in paragraph 1.

Article 166

1.   A multiannual framework programme, setting out all the activities of the Community, shall be adopted by the Council, acting in accordance with the procedure referred to in Article 251 after consulting the Economic and Social Committee.

The framework programme shall:

— establish the scientific and technological objectives to be achieved by the activities provided for in Article 164 and fix the relevant priorities,

— indicate the broad lines of such activities,

— fix the maximum overall amount and the detailed rules for Community financial participation in the framework programme and the respective shares in each of the activities provided for.

2.   The framework programme shall be adapted or supplemented as the situation changes.

3.   The framework programme shall be implemented through specific programmes developed within each activity. Each specific programme shall define the detailed rules for implementing it, fix its duration and provide for the means deemed necessary. The sum of the amounts deemed necessary, fixed in the specific programmes, may not exceed the overall maximum amount fixed for the framework programme and each activity.

4.   The Council, acting by a qualified majority on a proposal from the Commission and after consulting the European Parliament and the Economic and Social Committee, shall adopt the specific programmes.

Article 167

For the implementation of the multiannual framework programme the Council shall:

— determine the rules for the participation of undertakings, research centres and universities,

— lay down the rules governing the dissemination of research results.

Article 168

In implementing the multiannual framework programme, supplementary programmes may be decided on involving the participation of certain Member States only, which shall finance them subject to possible Community participation.

The Council shall adopt the rules applicable to supplementary programmes, particularly as regards the dissemination of knowledge and access by other Member States.

Article 169

In implementing the multiannual framework programme, the Community may make provision, in agreement with the Member States concerned, for participation in research and development programmes undertaken by several Member States, including participation in the structures created for the execution of those programmes.

Article 170

In implementing the multiannual framework programme the Community may make provision for cooperation in Community research, technological development and demonstration with third countries or international organisations.

The detailed arrangements for such cooperation may be the subject of agreements between the Community and the third parties concerned, which shall be negotiated and concluded in accordance with Article 300.

Article 171

The Community may set up joint undertakings or any other structure necessary for the efficient execution of Community research, technological development and demonstration programmes.

Article 172

The Council, acting by qualified majority on a proposal from the Commission and after consulting the European Parliament and the Economic and Social Committee, shall adopt the provisions referred to in Article 171.

The Council, acting in accordance with the procedure referred to in Article 251 and after consulting the Economic and Social Committee, shall adopt the provisions referred to in Articles 167, 168 and 169. Adoption of the supplementary programmes shall require the agreement of the Member States concerned.

Article 173

At the beginning of each year the Commission shall send a report to the European Parliament and to the Council. The report shall include information on research and technological development activities and the dissemination of results during the previous year, and the work programme for the current year.

TITLE XIX
ENVIRONMENT

Article 174

1. Community policy on the environment shall contribute to pursuit of the following objectives:

— preserving, protecting and improving the quality of the environment,

— protecting human health,

— prudent and rational utilisation of natural resources,

— promoting measures at international level to deal with regional or
worldwide environmental problems.

2. Community policy on the environment shall aim at a high level of
protection taking into account the diversity of situations in the various
regions of the Community. It shall be based on the precautionary
principle and on the principles that preventive action should be taken,
that environmental damage should as a priority be rectified at source
and that the polluter should pay.

In this context, harmonisation measures answering environmental
protection requirements shall include, where appropriate, a safeguard
clause allowing Member States to take provisional measures, for non-
economic environmental reasons, subject to a Community inspection
procedure.

3. In preparing its policy on the environment, the Community shall
take account of:

— available scientific and technical data,

— environmental conditions in the various regions of the Community,

— the potential benefits and costs of action or lack of action,

— the economic and social development of the Community as a whole
and the balanced development of its regions.

4. Within their respective spheres of competence, the Community and
the Member States shall cooperate with third countries and with the
competent international organisations. The arrangements for Community cooperation may be the subject of agreements between the Community and the third parties concerned, which shall be negotiated and
concluded in accordance with Article 300.

The previous subparagraph shall be without prejudice to Member
States' competence to negotiate in international bodies and to conclude
international agreements.

Article 175*

1. The Council, acting in accordance with the procedure referred to in
Article 251 and after consulting the Economic and Social Committee
and the Committee of the Regions, shall decide what action is to be
taken by the Community in order to achieve the objectives referred to
in Article 174.

* Article amended by the Treaty of Nice.

2. By way of derogation from the decision-making procedure provided for in paragraph 1 and without prejudice to Article 95, the Council, acting unanimously on a proposal from the Commission and after consulting the European Parliament, the Economic and Social Committee and the Committee of the Regions, shall adopt:

(a) provisions primarily of a fiscal nature;

(b) measures affecting:

— town and country planning,

— quantitative management of water resources or affecting, directly or indirectly, the availability of those resources,

— land use, with the exception of waste management;

(c) measures significantly affecting a Member State's choice between different energy sources and the general structure of its energy supply.

The Council may, under the conditions laid down in the first subparagraph, define those matters referred to in this paragraph on which decisions are to be taken by a qualified majority.

3. In other areas, general action programmes setting out priority objectives to be attained shall be adopted by the Council, acting in accordance with the procedure referred to in Article 251 and after consulting the Economic and Social Committee and the Committee of the Regions.

The Council, acting under the terms of paragraph 1 or paragraph 2 according to the case, shall adopt the measures necessary for the implementation of these programmes.

4. Without prejudice to certain measures of a Community nature, the Member States shall finance and implement the environment policy.

5. Without prejudice to the principle that the polluter should pay, if a measure based on the provisions of paragraph 1 involves costs deemed disproportionate for the public authorities of a Member State, the Council shall, in the act adopting that measure, lay down appropriate provisions in the form of:

— temporary derogations, and/or

— financial support from the Cohesion Fund set up pursuant to Article 161.

Article 176

The protective measures adopted pursuant to Article 175 shall not prevent any Member State from maintaining or introducing more stringent protective measures. Such measures must be compatible with this Treaty. They shall be notified to the Commission.

TITLE XX
DEVELOPMENT COOPERATION

Article 177

1.   Community policy in the sphere of development cooperation, which shall be complementary to the policies pursued by the Member States, shall foster:

— the sustainable economic and social development of the developing countries, and more particularly the most disadvantaged among them,

— the smooth and gradual integration of the developing countries into the world economy,

— the campaign against poverty in the developing countries.

2.   Community policy in this area shall contribute to the general objective of developing and consolidating democracy and the rule of law, and to that of respecting human rights and fundamental freedoms.

3.   The Community and the Member States shall comply with the commitments and take account of the objectives they have approved in the context of the United Nations and other competent international organisations.

Article 178

The Community shall take account of the objectives referred to in Article 177 in the policies that it implements which are likely to affect developing countries.

Article 179

1.   Without prejudice to the other provisions of this Treaty, the Council, acting in accordance with the procedure referred to in Article 251, shall adopt the measures necessary to further the objectives referred to in Article 177. Such measures may take the form of multiannual programmes.

2.   The European Investment Bank shall contribute, under the terms laid down in its Statute, to the implementation of the measures referred to in paragraph 1.

3.   The provisions of this Article shall not affect cooperation with the African, Caribbean and Pacific countries in the framework of the ACP–EC Convention.

Article 180

1.   The Community and the Member States shall coordinate their policies on development cooperation and shall consult each other on their aid programmes, including in international organisations and during international conferences. They may undertake joint action. Member States shall contribute if necessary to the implementation of Community aid programmes.

2. The Commission may take any useful initiative to promote the coordination referred to in paragraph 1.

Article 181

Within their respective spheres of competence, the Community and the Member States shall cooperate with third countries and with the competent international organisations. The arrangements for Community cooperation may be the subject of agreements between the Community and the third parties concerned, which shall be negotiated and concluded in accordance with Article 300.

The previous paragraph shall be without prejudice to Member States' competence to negotiate in international bodies and to conclude international agreements.

TITLE XXI*
ECONOMIC, FINANCIAL AND TECHNICAL COOPERATION WITH THIRD COUNTRIES

Article 181a

1. Without prejudice to the other provisions of this Treaty, and in particular those of Title XX, the Community shall carry out, within its spheres of competence, economic, financial and technical cooperation measures with third countries. Such measures shall be complementary to those carried out by the Member States and consistent with the development policy of the Community.

Community policy in this area shall contribute to the general objective of developing and consolidating democracy and the rule of law, and to the objective of respecting human rights and fundamental freedoms.

2. The Council, acting by a qualified majority on a proposal from the Commission and after consulting the European Parliament, shall adopt the measures necessary for the implementation of paragraph 1. The Council shall act unanimously for the association agreements referred to in Article 310 and for the agreements to be concluded with the States which are candidates for accession to the Union.

3. Within their respective spheres of competence, the Community and the Member States shall cooperate with third countries and the competent international organisations. The arrangements for Community cooperation may be the subject of agreements between the Community and the third parties concerned, which shall be negotiated and concluded in accordance with Article 300.

The first subparagraph shall be without prejudice to the Member States' competence to negotiate in international bodies and to conclude international agreements.

* Title added by the Treaty of Nice.

PART FOUR
ASSOCIATION OF THE OVERSEAS COUNTRIES AND TERRITORIES

Article 182

The Member States agree to associate with the Community the non-European countries and territories which have special relations with Denmark, France, the Netherlands and the United Kingdom. These countries and territories (hereinafter called the "countries and territories") are listed in Annex II to this Treaty.

The purpose of association shall be to promote the economic and social development of the countries and territories and to establish close economic relations between them and the Community as a whole.

In accordance with the principles set out in the preamble to this Treaty, association shall serve primarily to further the interests and prosperity of the inhabitants of these countries and territories in order to lead them to the economic, social and cultural development to which they aspire.

Article 183

Association shall have the following objectives.

1. Member States shall apply to their trade with the countries and territories the same treatment as they accord each other pursuant to this Treaty.

2. Each country or territory shall apply to its trade with Member States and with the other countries and territories the same treatment as that which it applies to the European State with which is has special relations.

3. The Member States shall contribute to the investments required for the progressive development of these countries and territories.

4. For investments financed by the Community, participation in tenders and supplies shall be open on equal terms to all natural and legal persons who are nationals of a Member State or of one of the countries and territories.

5. In relations between Member States and the countries and territories the right of establishment of nationals and companies or firms shall be regulated in accordance with the provisions and procedures laid down in the Chapter relating to the right of establishment and on a non-discriminatory basis, subject to any special provisions laid down pursuant to Article 187.

Article 184

1. Customs duties on imports into the Member States of goods originating in the countries and territories shall be prohibited in conformity with the prohibition of customs duties between Member States in accordance with the provisions of this Treaty.

2. Customs duties on imports into each country or territory from Member States or from the other countries or territories shall be prohibited in accordance with the provisions of Article 25.

3. The countries and territories may, however, levy customs duties which meet the needs of their development and industrialisation or produce revenue for their budgets.

The duties referred to in the preceding subparagraph may not exceed the level of those imposed on imports of products from the Member State with which each country or territory has special relations.

4. Paragraph 2 shall not apply to countries and territories which, by reason of the particular international obligations by which they are bound, already apply a non-discriminatory customs tariff.

5. The introduction of or any change in customs duties imposed on goods imported into the countries and territories shall not, either in law or in fact, give rise to any direct or indirect discrimination between imports from the various Member States.

Article 185

If the level of the duties applicable to goods from a third country on entry into a country or territory is liable, when the provisions of Article 184(1) have been applied, to cause deflections of trade to the detriment of any Member State, the latter may request the Commission to propose to the other Member States the measures needed to remedy the situation.

Article 186

Subject to the provisions relating to public health, public security or public policy, freedom of movement within Member States for workers from the countries and territories, and within the countries and territories for workers from Member States, shall be governed by agreements to be concluded subsequently with the unanimous approval of Member States.

Article 187

The Council, acting unanimously, shall, on the basis of the experience acquired under the association of the countries and territories with the Community and of the principles set out in this Treaty, lay down provisions as regards the detailed rules and the procedure for the association of the countries and territories with the Community.

Article 188

The provisions of Articles 182 to 187 shall apply to Greenland, subject to the specific provisions for Greenland set out in the Protocol on special arrangements for Greenland, annexed to this Treaty.

PART FIVE
INSTITUTIONS OF THE COMMUNITY

TITLE I
PROVISIONS GOVERNING THE INSTITUTIONS

CHAPTER 1
THE INSTITUTIONS

SECTION 1
THE EUROPEAN PARLIAMENT

Article 189*

The European Parliament, which shall consist of representatives of the peoples of the States brought together in the Community, shall exercise the powers conferred upon it by this Treaty.

The number of Members of the European Parliament shall not exceed 732.

Article 190*

1. The representatives in the European Parliament of the peoples of the States brought together in the Community shall be elected by direct universal suffrage.

2.** The number of representatives elected in each Member State shall be as follows:

Belgium	25
Denmark	16
Germany	99
Greece	25
Spain	64
France	87
Ireland	15
Italy	87
Luxembourg	6
Netherlands	31
Austria	21
Portugal	25
Finland	16
Sweden	22
United Kingdom	87.

In the event of amendments to this paragraph, the number of representatives elected in each Member State must ensure appropriate repre-

---

* Article amended by the Treaty of Nice.

** This paragraph will be amended, on 1 January 2004, in accordance with the

Protocol on the enlargement of the European Union (see the end of this publication).

sentation of the peoples of the States brought together in the Community.

3. Representatives shall be elected for a term of five years.

4. The European Parliament shall draw up a proposal for elections by direct universal suffrage in accordance with a uniform procedure in all Member States or in accordance with principles common to all Member States.

The Council shall, acting unanimously after obtaining the assent of the European Parliament, which shall act by a majority of its component members, lay down the appropriate provisions, which it shall recommend to Member States for adoption in accordance with their respective constitutional requirements.

5. The European Parliament, after seeking an opinion from the Commission and with the approval of the Council acting by a qualified majority, shall lay down the regulations and general conditions governing the performance of the duties of its Members. All rules or conditions relating to the taxation of Members or former Members shall require unanimity within the Council.

Article 191*

Political parties at European level are important as a factor for integration within the Union. They contribute to forming a European awareness and to expressing the political will of the citizens of the Union.

The Council, acting in accordance with the procedure referred to in Article 251, shall lay down the regulations governing political parties at European level and in particular the rules regarding their funding.

Article 192

In so far as provided in this Treaty, the European Parliament shall participate in the process leading up to the adoption of Community acts by exercising its powers under the procedures laid down in Articles 251 and 252 and by giving its assent or delivering advisory opinions.

The European Parliament may, acting by a majority of its Members, request the Commission to submit any appropriate proposal on matters on which it considers that a Community act is required for the purpose of implementing this Treaty.

Article 193

In the course of its duties, the European Parliament may, at the request of a quarter of its Members, set up a temporary Committee of Inquiry to investigate, without prejudice to the powers conferred by this Treaty on other institutions or bodies, alleged contraventions or maladministration in the implementation of Community law, except

*Article amended by the Treaty of   Nice.

where the alleged facts are being examined before a court and while the case is still subject to legal proceedings.

The temporary Committee of Inquiry shall cease to exist on the submission of its report.

The detailed provisions governing the exercise of the right of inquiry shall be determined by common accord of the European Parliament, the Council and the Commission.

Article 194

Any citizen of the Union, and any natural or legal person residing or having its registered office in a Member State, shall have the right to address, individually or in association with other citizens or persons, a petition to the European Parliament on a matter which comes within the Community's fields of activity and which affects him, her or it directly.

Article 195

1. The European Parliament shall appoint an Ombudsman empowered to receive complaints from any citizen of the Union or any natural or legal person residing or having its registered office in a Member State concerning instances of maladministration in the activities of the Community institutions or bodies, with the exception of the Court of Justice and the Court of First Instance acting in their judicial role.

In accordance with his duties, the Ombudsman shall conduct inquiries for which he finds grounds, either on his own initiative or on the basis of complaints submitted to him direct or through a Member of the European Parliament, except where the alleged facts are or have been the subject of legal proceedings. Where the Ombudsman establishes an instance of maladministration, he shall refer the matter to the institution concerned, which shall have a period of three months in which to inform him of its views. The Ombudsman shall then forward a report to the European Parliament and the institution concerned. The person lodging the complaint shall be informed of the outcome of such inquiries.

The Ombudsman shall submit an annual report to the European Parliament on the outcome of his inquiries.

2. The Ombudsman shall be appointed after each election of the European Parliament for the duration of its term of office. The Ombudsman shall be eligible for reappointment.

The Ombudsman may be dismissed by the Court of Justice at the request of the European Parliament if he no longer fulfils the conditions required for the performance of his duties or if he is guilty of serious misconduct.

3. The Ombudsman shall be completely independent in the performance of his duties. In the performance of those duties he shall neither seek nor take instructions from any body. The Ombudsman may not,

during his term of office, engage in any other occupation, whether gainful or not.

4. The European Parliament shall, after seeking an opinion from the Commission and with the approval of the Council acting by a qualified majority, lay down the regulations and general conditions governing the performance of the Ombudsman's duties.

Article 196

The European Parliament shall hold an annual session. It shall meet, without requiring to be convened, on the second Tuesday in March.

The European Parliament may meet in extraordinary session at the request of a majority of its Members or at the request of the Council or of the Commission.

Article 197

The European Parliament shall elect its President and its officers from among its Members.

Members of the Commission may attend all meetings and shall, at their request, be heard on behalf of the Commission.

The Commission shall reply orally or in writing to questions put to it by the European Parliament or by its Members.

The Council shall be heard by the European Parliament in accordance with the conditions laid down by the Council in its Rules of Procedure.

Article 198

Save as otherwise provided in this Treaty, the European Parliament shall act by an absolute majority of the votes cast.

The Rules of Procedure shall determine the quorum.

Article 199

The European Parliament shall adopt its Rules of Procedure, acting by a majority of its Members.

The proceedings of the European Parliament shall be published in the manner laid down in its Rules of Procedure.

Article 200

The European Parliament shall discuss in open session the annual general report submitted to it by the Commission.

Article 201

If a motion of censure on the activities of the Commission is tabled before it, the European Parliament shall not vote thereon until at least three days after the motion has been tabled and only by open vote.

If the motion of censure is carried by a two-thirds majority of the votes cast, representing a majority of the Members of the European Parliament, the Members of the Commission shall resign as a body. They shall continue to deal with current business until they are replaced in accordance with Article 214. In this case, the term of office of the Members of the Commission appointed to replace them shall expire on the date on which the term of office of the Members of the Commission obliged to resign as a body would have expired.

SECTION 2
THE COUNCIL

Article 202

To ensure that the objectives set out in this Treaty are attained the Council shall, in accordance with the provisions of this Treaty:

— ensure coordination of the general economic policies of the Member States,

— have power to take decisions,

— confer on the Commission, in the acts which the Council adopts, powers for the implementation of the rules which the Council lays down. The Council may impose certain requirements in respect of the exercise of these powers. The Council may also reserve the right, in specific cases, to exercise directly implementing powers itself. The procedures referred to above must be consonant with principles and rules to be laid down in advance by the Council, acting unanimously on a proposal from the Commission and after obtaining the opinion of the European Parliament.

Article 203

The Council shall consist of a representative of each Member State at ministerial level, authorised to commit the government of that Member State.

The office of President shall be held in turn by each Member State in the Council for a term of six months in the order decided by the Council acting unanimously.

Article 204

The Council shall meet when convened by its President on his own initiative or at the request of one of its Members or of the Commission.

Article 205*

1. Save as otherwise provided in this Treaty, the Council shall act by a majority of its Members.

---

* This Article will be amended, on 1 January 2005, in accordance with the Protocol on the enlargement of the European Union (see the end of this publication).

2. Where the Council is required to act by a qualified majority, the votes of its Members shall be weighted as follows:

Belgium	5
Denmark	3
Germany	10
Greece	5
Spain	8
France	10
Ireland	3
Italy	10
Luxembourg	2
Netherlands	5
Austria	4
Portugal	5
Finland	3
Sweden	4
United Kingdom	10.

For their adoption, acts of the Council shall require at least:

— 62 votes in favour where this Treaty requires them to be adopted on a proposal from the Commission,

— 62 votes in favour, cast by at least 10 members, in other cases.

3. Abstentions by Members present in person or represented shall not prevent the adoption by the Council of acts which require unanimity.

Article 206

Where a vote is taken, any Member of the Council may also act on behalf of not more than one other member.

Article 207**

1. A committee consisting of the Permanent Representatives of the Member States shall be responsible for preparing the work of the Council and for carrying out the tasks assigned to it by the Council. The Committee may adopt procedural decisions in cases provided for in the Council's Rules of Procedure.

2. The Council shall be assisted by a General Secretariat, under the responsibility of a Secretary–General, High Representative for the common foreign and security policy, who shall be assisted by a Deputy Secretary–General responsible for the running of the General Secretariat. The Secretary–General and the Deputy Secretary–General shall be appointed by the Council acting by a qualified majority.

The Council shall decide on the organisation of the General Secretariat.

3. The Council shall adopt its Rules of Procedure.

For the purpose of applying Article 255(3), the Council shall elaborate in these Rules the conditions under which the public shall have access to Council documents. For the purpose of this paragraph, the Council

** Article amended by the Treaty of   Nice.

shall define the cases in which it is to be regarded as acting in its legislative capacity, with a view to allowing greater access to documents in those cases, while at the same time preserving the effectiveness of its decision-making process. In any event, when the Council acts in its legislative capacity, the results of votes and explanations of vote as well as statements in the minutes shall be made public.

Article 208

The Council may request the Commission to undertake any studies the Council considers desirable for the attainment of the common objectives, and to submit to it any appropriate proposals.

Article 209

The Council shall, after receiving an opinion from the Commission, determine the rules governing the committees provided for in this Treaty.

*Article 210**

The Council shall, acting by a qualified majority, determine the salaries, allowances and pensions of the President and Members of the Commission, and of the President, Judges, Advocates–General and Registrar of the Court of Justice and of the Members and Registrar of the Court of First Instance. It shall also, again by a qualified majority, determine any payment to be made instead of remuneration.

SECTION 3
THE COMMISSION

Article 211

In order to ensure the proper functioning and development of the common market, the Commission shall:

— ensure that the provisions of this Treaty and the measures taken by the institutions pursuant thereto are applied,

— formulate recommendations or deliver opinions on matters dealt with in this Treaty, if it expressly so provides or if the Commission considers it necessary,

— have its own power of decision and participate in the shaping of measures taken by the Council and by the European Parliament in the manner provided for in this Treaty,

— exercise the powers conferred on it by the Council for the implementation of the rules laid down by the latter.

* Article amended by the Treaty of Nice.

Article 212

The Commission shall publish annually, not later than one month before the opening of the session of the European Parliament, a general report on the activities of the Community.

Article 213

1.* The Commission shall consist of 20 Members, who shall be chosen on the grounds of their general competence and whose independence is beyond doubt.

The number of Members of the Commission may be altered by the Council, acting unanimously.

Only nationals of Member States may be Members of the Commission.

The Commission must include at least one national of each of the Member States, but may not include more than two Members having the nationality of the same State.

2. The Members of the Commission shall, in the general interest of the Community, be completely independent in the performance of their duties.

In the performance of these duties, they shall neither seek nor take instructions from any government or from any other body. They shall refrain from any action incompatible with their duties. Each Member State undertakes to respect this principle and not to seek to influence the Members of the Commission in the performance of their tasks.

The Members of the Commission may not, during their term of office, engage in any other occupation, whether gainful or not. When entering upon their duties they shall give a solemn undertaking that, both during and after their term of office, they will respect the obligations arising therefrom and in particular their duty to behave with integrity and discretion as regards the acceptance, after they have ceased to hold office, of certain appointments or benefits. In the event of any breach of these obligations, the Court of Justice may, on application by the Council or the Commission, rule that the Member concerned be, according to the circumstances, either compulsorily retired in accordance with Article 216 or deprived of his right to a pension or other benefits in its stead.

Article 214*

1. The Members of the Commission shall be appointed, in accordance with the procedure referred to in paragraph 2, for a period of five years, subject, if need be, to Article 201.

Their term of office shall be renewable.

* This paragraph will be amended, on 1 January 2005, and thereafter when the Union comprises 27 Member States in accordance with the Protocol on the enlargement of the European Union (see the end of this publication).

* Article amended by the Treaty of Nice.

2. The Council, meeting in the composition of Heads of State or Government and acting by a qualified majority, shall nominate the person it intends to appoint as President of the Commission; the nomination shall be approved by the European Parliament.

The Council, acting by a qualified majority and by common accord with the nominee for President, shall adopt the list of the other persons whom it intends to appoint as Members of the Commission, drawn up in accordance with the proposals made by each Member State.

The President and the other Members of the Commission thus nominated shall be subject as a body to a vote of approval by the European Parliament. After approval by the European Parliament, the President and the other Members of the Commission shall be appointed by the Council, acting by a qualified majority.

Article 215*

Apart from normal replacement, or death, the duties of a Member of the Commission shall end when he resigns or is compulsorily retired.

A vacancy caused by resignation, compulsory retirement or death shall be filled for the remainder of the Member's term of office by a new Member appointed by the Council, acting by a qualified majority. The Council may, acting unanimously, decide that such a vacancy need not be filled.

In the event of resignation, compulsory retirement or death, the President shall be replaced for the remainder of his term of office. The procedure laid down in Article 214(2) shall be applicable for the replacement of the President.

Save in the case of compulsory retirement under Article 216, Members of the Commission shall remain in office until they have been replaced or until the Council has decided that the vacancy need not be filled, as provided for in the second paragraph of this Article.

Article 216

If any Member of the Commission no longer fulfils the conditions required for the performance of his duties or if he has been guilty of serious misconduct, the Court of Justice may, on application by the Council or the Commission, compulsorily retire him.

Article 217*

1. The Commission shall work under the political guidance of its President, who shall decide on its internal organisation in order to ensure that it acts consistently, efficiently and on the basis of collegiality.

* Article amended by the Treaty of Nice.

* Article amended by the Treaty of Nice.

2. The responsibilities incumbent upon the Commission shall be structured and allocated among its Members by its President. The President may reshuffle the allocation of those responsibilities during the Commission's term of office. The Members of the Commission shall carry out the duties devolved upon them by the President under his authority.

3. After obtaining the approval of the College, the President shall appoint Vice–Presidents from among its Members.

4. A Member of the Commission shall resign if the President so requests, after obtaining the approval of the College.

Article 218

1. The Council and the Commission shall consult each other and shall settle by common accord their methods of cooperation.

2. The Commission shall adopt its Rules of Procedure so as to ensure that both it and its departments operate in accordance with the provisions of this Treaty. It shall ensure that these Rules are published.

Article 219*

The Commission shall act by a majority of the number of Members provided for in Article 213.

A meeting of the Commission shall be valid only if the number of Members laid down in its Rules of Procedure is present.

SECTION 4
THE COURT OF JUSTICE

Article 220*

The Court of Justice and the Court of First Instance, each within its jurisdiction, shall ensure that in the interpretation and application of this Treaty the law is observed.

In addition, judicial panels may be attached to the Court of First Instance under the conditions laid down in Article 225a in order to exercise, in certain specific areas, the judicial competence laid down in this Treaty.

Article 221*

The Court of Justice shall consist of one judge per Member State.

The Court of Justice shall sit in chambers or in a Grand Chamber, in accordance with the rules laid down for that purpose in the Statute of the Court of Justice.

---

* Article amended by the Treaty of Nice.

When provided for in the Statute, the Court of Justice may also sit as a full Court.

Article 222*

The Court of Justice shall be assisted by eight Advocates–General. Should the Court of Justice so request, the Council, acting unanimously, may increase the number of Advocates–General.

It shall be the duty of the Advocate–General, acting with complete impartiality and independence, to make, in open court, reasoned submissions on cases which, in accordance with the Statute of the Court of Justice, require his involvement.

Article 223*

The Judges and Advocates–General of the Court of Justice shall be chosen from persons whose independence is beyond doubt and who possess the qualifications required for appointment to the highest judicial offices in their respective countries or who are jurisconsults of recognised competence; they shall be appointed by common accord of the governments of the Member States for a term of six years.

Every three years there shall be a partial replacement of the Judges and Advocates–General, in accordance with the conditions laid down in the Statute of the Court of Justice.

The Judges shall elect the President of the Court of Justice from among their number for a term of three years. He may be re-elected.

Retiring Judges and Advocates–General may be reappointed.

The Court of Justice shall appoint its Registrar and lay down the rules governing his service.

The Court of Justice shall establish its Rules of Procedure. Those Rules shall require the approval of the Council, acting by a qualified majority.

Article 224*

The Court of First Instance shall comprise at least one judge per Member State. The number of Judges shall be determined by the Statute of the Court of Justice. The Statute may provide for the Court of First Instance to be assisted by Advocates–General.

The members of the Court of First Instance shall be chosen from persons whose independence is beyond doubt and who possess the ability required for appointment to high judicial office. They shall be appointed by common accord of the governments of the Member States for a term of six years. The membership shall be partially renewed every three years. Retiring members shall be eligible for reappointment.

The Judges shall elect the President of the Court of First Instance from among their number for a term of three years. He may be re-elected.

* Article amended by the Treaty of Nice.

The Court of First Instance shall appoint its Registrar and lay down the rules governing his service.

The Court of First Instance shall establish its Rules of Procedure in agreement with the Court of Justice. Those Rules shall require the approval of the Council, acting by a qualified majority.

Unless the Statute of the Court of Justice provides otherwise, the provisions of this Treaty relating to the Court of Justice shall apply to the Court of First Instance.

Article 225*

1. The Court of First Instance shall have jurisdiction to hear and determine at first instance actions or proceedings referred to in Articles 230, 232, 235, 236 and 238, with the exception of those assigned to a judicial panel and those reserved in the Statute for the Court of Justice. The Statute may provide for the Court of First Instance to have jurisdiction for other classes of action or proceeding.

Decisions given by the Court of First Instance under this paragraph may be subject to a right of appeal to the Court of Justice on points of law only, under the conditions and within the limits laid down by the Statute.

2. The Court of First Instance shall have jurisdiction to hear and determine actions or proceedings brought against decisions of the judicial panels set up under Article 225a.

Decisions given by the Court of First Instance under this paragraph may exceptionally be subject to review by the Court of Justice, under the conditions and within the limits laid down by the Statute, where there is a serious risk of the unity or consistency of Community law being affected.

3. The Court of First Instance shall have jurisdiction to hear and determine questions referred for a preliminary ruling under Article 234, in specific areas laid down by the Statute.

Where the Court of First Instance considers that the case requires a decision of principle likely to affect the unity or consistency of Community law, it may refer the case to the Court of Justice for a ruling.

Decisions given by the Court of First Instance on questions referred for a preliminary ruling may exceptionally be subject to review by the Court of Justice, under the conditions and within the limits laid down by the Statute, where there is a serious risk of the unity or consistency of Community law being affected.

Article 225a**

The Council, acting unanimously on a proposal from the Commission and after consulting the European Parliament and the Court of Justice

---

* Article amended by the Treaty of Nice.

** Article inserted by the Treaty of Nice.

or at the request of the Court of Justice and after consulting the European Parliament and the Commission, may create judicial panels to hear and determine at first instance certain classes of action or proceeding brought in specific areas.

The decision establishing a judicial panel shall lay down the rules on the organisation of the panel and the extent of the jurisdiction conferred upon it.

Decisions given by judicial panels may be subject to a right of appeal on points of law only or, when provided for in the decision establishing the panel, a right of appeal also on matters of fact, before the Court of First Instance.

The members of the judicial panels shall be chosen from persons whose independence is beyond doubt and who possess the ability required for appointment to judicial office. They shall be appointed by the Council, acting unanimously.

The judicial panels shall establish their Rules of Procedure in agreement with the Court of Justice. Those Rules shall require the approval of the Council, acting by a qualified majority.

Unless the decision establishing the judicial panel provides otherwise, the provisions of this Treaty relating to the Court of Justice and the provisions of the Statute of the Court of Justice shall apply to the judicial panels.

Article 226

If the Commission considers that a Member State has failed to fulfil an obligation under this Treaty, it shall deliver a reasoned opinion on the matter after giving the State concerned the opportunity to submit its observations.

If the State concerned does not comply with the opinion within the period laid down by the Commission, the latter may bring the matter before the Court of Justice.

Article 227

A Member State which considers that another Member State has failed to fulfil an obligation under this Treaty may bring the matter before the Court of Justice.

Before a Member State brings an action against another Member State for an alleged infringement of an obligation under this Treaty, it shall bring the matter before the Commission.

The Commission shall deliver a reasoned opinion after each of the States concerned has been given the opportunity to submit its own case and its observations on the other party's case both orally and in writing.

If the Commission has not delivered an opinion within three months of the date on which the matter was brought before it, the absence of such opinion shall not prevent the matter from being brought before the Court of Justice.

Article 228

1. If the Court of Justice finds that a Member State has failed to fulfil an obligation under this Treaty, the State shall be required to take the necessary measures to comply with the judgment of the Court of Justice.

2. If the Commission considers that the Member State concerned has not taken such measures it shall, after giving that State the opportunity to submit its observations, issue a reasoned opinion specifying the points on which the Member State concerned has not complied with the judgment of the Court of Justice.

If the Member State concerned fails to take the necessary measures to comply with the Court's judgment within the time limit laid down by the Commission, the latter may bring the case before the Court of Justice. In so doing it shall specify the amount of the lump sum or penalty payment to be paid by the Member State concerned which it considers appropriate in the circumstances.

If the Court of Justice finds that the Member State concerned has not complied with its judgment it may impose a lump sum or penalty payment on it.

This procedure shall be without prejudice to Article 227.

Article 229

Regulations adopted jointly by the European Parliament and the Council, and by the Council, pursuant to the provisions of this Treaty, may give the Court of Justice unlimited jurisdiction with regard to the penalties provided for in such regulations.

Article 229a*

Without prejudice to the other provisions of this Treaty, the Council, acting unanimously on a proposal from the Commission and after consulting the European Parliament, may adopt provisions to confer jurisdiction, to the extent that it shall determine, on the Court of Justice in disputes relating to the application of acts adopted on the basis of this Treaty which create Community industrial property rights. The Council shall recommend those provisions to the Member States for adoption in accordance with their respective constitutional requirements.

Article 230**

The Court of Justice shall review the legality of acts adopted jointly by the European Parliament and the Council, of acts of the Council, of the

* Article inserted by the Treaty of Nice.   ** Article amended by the Treaty of Nice.

Commission and of the ECB, other than recommendations and opinions, and of acts of the European Parliament intended to produce legal effects vis-à-vis third parties.

It shall for this purpose have jurisdiction in actions brought by a Member State, the European Parliament, the Council or the Commission on grounds of lack of competence, infringement of an essential procedural requirement, infringement of this Treaty or of any rule of law relating to its application, or misuse of powers.

The Court of Justice shall have jurisdiction under the same conditions in actions brought by the Court of Auditors and by the ECB for the purpose of protecting their prerogatives.

Any natural or legal person may, under the same conditions, institute proceedings against a decision addressed to that person or against a decision which, although in the form of a regulation or a decision addressed to another person, is of direct and individual concern to the former.

The proceedings provided for in this article shall be instituted within two months of the publication of the measure, or of its notification to the plaintiff, or, in the absence thereof, of the day on which it came to the knowledge of the latter, as the case may be.

Article 231

If the action is well founded, the Court of Justice shall declare the act concerned to be void.

In the case of a regulation, however, the Court of Justice shall, if it considers this necessary, state which of the effects of the regulation which it has declared void shall be considered as definitive.

Article 232

Should the European Parliament, the Council or the Commission, in infringement of this Treaty, fail to act, the Member States and the other institutions of the Community may bring an action before the Court of Justice to have the infringement established.

The action shall be admissible only if the institution concerned has first been called upon to act. If, within two months of being so called upon, the institution concerned has not defined its position, the action may be brought within a further period of two months.

Any natural or legal person may, under the conditions laid down in the preceding paragraphs, complain to the Court of Justice that an institution of the Community has failed to address to that person any act other than a recommendation or an opinion.

The Court of Justice shall have jurisdiction, under the same conditions, in actions or proceedings brought by the ECB in the areas falling within the latter's field of competence and in actions or proceedings brought against the latter.

Article 233

The institution or institutions whose act has been declared void or whose failure to act has been declared contrary to this Treaty shall be required to take the necessary measures to comply with the judgment of the Court of Justice.

This obligation shall not affect any obligation which may result from the application of the second paragraph of Article 288.

This article shall also apply to the ECB.

Article 234

The Court of Justice shall have jurisdiction to give preliminary rulings concerning:

(a) the interpretation of this Treaty;

(b) the validity and interpretation of acts of the institutions of the Community and of the ECB;

(c) the interpretation of the statutes of bodies established by an act of the Council, where those statutes so provide.

Where such a question is raised before any court or tribunal of a Member State, that court or tribunal may, if it considers that a decision on the question is necessary to enable it to give judgment, request the Court of Justice to give a ruling thereon.

Where any such question is raised in a case pending before a court or tribunal of a Member State against whose decisions there is no judicial remedy under national law, that court or tribunal shall bring the matter before the Court of Justice.

Article 235

The Court of Justice shall have jurisdiction in disputes relating to compensation for damage provided for in the second paragraph of Article 288.

Article 236

The Court of Justice shall have jurisdiction in any dispute between the Community and its servants within the limits and under the conditions laid down in the Staff Regulations or the Conditions of employment.

Article 237

The Court of Justice shall, within the limits hereinafter laid down, have jurisdiction in disputes concerning:

(a) the fulfilment by Member States of obligations under the Statute of the European Investment Bank. In this connection, the Board of Directors of the Bank shall enjoy the powers conferred upon the Commission by Article 226;

(b) measures adopted by the Board of Governors of the European Investment Bank. In this connection, any Member State, the Commission or the Board of Directors of the Bank may institute proceedings under the conditions laid down in Article 230;

(c) measures adopted by the Board of Directors of the European Investment Bank. Proceedings against such measures may be instituted only by Member States or by the Commission, under the conditions laid down in Article 230, and solely on the grounds of non-compliance with the procedure provided for in Article 21(2), (5), (6) and (7) of the Statute of the Bank;

(d) the fulfilment by national central banks of obligations under this Treaty and the Statute of the ESCB. In this connection the powers of the Council of the ECB in respect of national central banks shall be the same as those conferred upon the Commission in respect of Member States by Article 226. If the Court of Justice finds that a national central bank has failed to fulfil an obligation under this Treaty, that bank shall be required to take the necessary measures to comply with the judgment of the Court of Justice.

Article 238

The Court of Justice shall have jurisdiction to give judgment pursuant to any arbitration clause contained in a contract concluded by or on behalf of the Community, whether that contract be governed by public or private law.

Article 239

The Court of Justice shall have jurisdiction in any dispute between Member States which relates to the subject matter of this Treaty if the dispute is submitted to it under a special agreement between the parties.

Article 240

Save where jurisdiction is conferred on the Court of Justice by this Treaty, disputes to which the Community is a party shall not on that ground be excluded from the jurisdiction of the courts or tribunals of the Member States.

Article 241

Notwithstanding the expiry of the period laid down in the fifth paragraph of Article 230, any party may, in proceedings in which a regulation adopted jointly by the European Parliament and the Council, or a regulation of the Council, of the Commission, or of the ECB is at issue, plead the grounds specified in the second paragraph of Article 230 in order to invoke before the Court of Justice the inapplicability of that regulation.

Article 242

Actions brought before the Court of Justice shall not have suspensory effect. The Court of Justice may, however, if it considers that circumstances so require, order that application of the contested act be suspended.

Article 243

The Court of Justice may in any cases before it prescribe any necessary interim measures.

Article 244

The judgments of the Court of Justice shall be enforceable under the conditions laid down in Article 256.

Article 245*

The Statute of the Court of Justice shall be laid down in a separate Protocol.

The Council, acting unanimously at the request of the Court of Justice and after consulting the European Parliament and the Commission, or at the request of the Commission and after consulting the European Parliament and the Court of Justice, may amend the provisions of the Statute, with the exception of Title I.

SECTION 5
THE COURT OF AUDITORS

Article 246

The Court of Auditors shall carry out the audit.

Article 247*

1. The Court of Auditors shall consist of one national from each Member State.

2. The Members of the Court of Auditors shall be chosen from among persons who belong or have belonged in their respective countries to external audit bodies or who are especially qualified for this office. Their independence must be beyond doubt.

3. The Members of the Court of Auditors shall be appointed for a term of six years. The Council, acting by a qualified majority after consulting the European Parliament, shall adopt the list of Members drawn up in accordance with the proposals made by each Member State. The term of office of the Members of the Court of Auditors shall be renewable.

---

* Article amended by the Treaty of Nice.   * Article amended by the Treaty of Nice.

They shall elect the President of the Court of Auditors from among their number for a term of three years. The President may be re-elected.

4. The Members of the Court of Auditors shall, in the general interest of the Community, be completely independent in the performance of their duties.

In the performance of these duties, they shall neither seek nor take instructions from any government or from any other body. They shall refrain from any action incompatible with their duties.

5. The Members of the Court of Auditors may not, during their term of office, engage in any other occupation, whether gainful or not. When entering upon their duties they shall give a solemn undertaking that, both during and after their term of office, they will respect the obligations arising therefrom and in particular their duty to behave with integrity and discretion as regards the acceptance, after they have ceased to hold office, of certain appointments or benefits.

6. Apart from normal replacement, or death, the duties of a Member of the Court of Auditors shall end when he resigns, or is compulsorily retired by a ruling of the Court of Justice pursuant to paragraph 7.

The vacancy thus caused shall be filled for the remainder of the Member's term of office.

Save in the case of compulsory retirement, Members of the Court of Auditors shall remain in office until they have been replaced.

7. A Member of the Court of Auditors may be deprived of his office or of his right to a pension or other benefits in its stead only if the Court of Justice, at the request of the Court of Auditors, finds that he no longer fulfils the requisite conditions or meets the obligations arising from his office.

8. The Council, acting by a qualified majority, shall determine the conditions of employment of the President and the Members of the Court of Auditors and in particular their salaries, allowances and pensions. It shall also, by the same majority, determine any payment to be made instead of remuneration.

9. The provisions of the Protocol on the privileges and immunities of the European Communities applicable to the Judges of the Court of Justice shall also apply to the Members of the Court of Auditors.

Article 248*

1. The Court of Auditors shall examine the accounts of all revenue and expenditure of the Community. It shall also examine the accounts of all revenue and expenditure of all bodies set up by the Community in so far as the relevant constituent instrument does not preclude such examination.

* Article amended by the Treaty of Nice.

The Court of Auditors shall provide the European Parliament and the Council with a statement of assurance as to the reliability of the accounts and the legality and regularity of the underlying transactions which shall be published in the *Official Journal of the European Union*. This statement may be supplemented by specific assessments for each major area of Community activity.

2. The Court of Auditors shall examine whether all revenue has been received and all expenditure incurred in a lawful and regular manner and whether the financial management has been sound. In doing so, it shall report in particular on any cases of irregularity.

The audit of revenue shall be carried out on the basis both of the amounts established as due and the amounts actually paid to the Community.

The audit of expenditure shall be carried out on the basis both of commitments undertaken and payments made.

These audits may be carried out before the closure of accounts for the financial year in question.

3. The audit shall be based on records and, if necessary, performed on the spot in the other institutions of the Community, on the premises of any body which manages revenue or expenditure on behalf of the Community and in the Member States, including on the premises of any natural or legal person in receipt of payments from the budget. In the Member States the audit shall be carried out in liaison with national audit bodies or, if these do not have the necessary powers, with the competent national departments. The Court of Auditors and the national audit bodies of the Member States shall cooperate in a spirit of trust while maintaining their independence. These bodies or departments shall inform the Court of Auditors whether they intend to take part in the audit.

The other institutions of the Community, any bodies managing revenue or expenditure on behalf of the Community, any natural or legal person in receipt of payments from the budget, and the national audit bodies or, if these do not have the necessary powers, the competent national departments, shall forward to the Court of Auditors, at its request, any document or information necessary to carry out its task.

In respect of the European Investment Bank's activity in managing Community expenditure and revenue, the Court's rights of access to information held by the Bank shall be governed by an agreement between the Court, the Bank and the Commission. In the absence of an agreement, the Court shall nevertheless have access to information necessary for the audit of Community expenditure and revenue managed by the Bank.

4. The Court of Auditors shall draw up an annual report after the close of each financial year. It shall be forwarded to the other institutions of the Community and shall be published, together with the

replies of these institutions to the observations of the Court of Auditors, in the *Official Journal of the European Union*.

The Court of Auditors may also, at any time, submit observations, particularly in the form of special reports, on specific questions and deliver opinions at the request of one of the other institutions of the Community.

It shall adopt its annual reports, special reports or opinions by a majority of its Members. However, it may establish internal chambers in order to adopt certain categories of reports or opinions under the conditions laid down by its Rules of Procedure.

It shall assist the European Parliament and the Council in exercising their powers of control over the implementation of the budget.

The Court of Auditors shall draw up its Rules of Procedure. Those rules shall require the approval of the Council, acting by a qualified majority.

CHAPTER 2
PROVISIONS COMMON TO SEVERAL INSTITUTIONS

Article 249

In order to carry out their task and in accordance with the provisions of this Treaty, the European Parliament acting jointly with the Council, the Council and the Commission shall make regulations and issue directives, take decisions, make recommendations or deliver opinions.

A regulation shall have general application. It shall be binding in its entirety and directly applicable in all Member States.

A directive shall be binding, as to the result to be achieved, upon each Member State to which it is addressed, but shall leave to the national authorities the choice of form and methods.

A decision shall be binding in its entirety upon those to whom it is addressed.

Recommendations and opinions shall have no binding force.

Article 250

1. Where, in pursuance of this Treaty, the Council acts on a proposal from the Commission, unanimity shall be required for an act constituting an amendment to that proposal, subject to Article 251(4) and (5).

2. As long as the Council has not acted, the Commission may alter its proposal at any time during the procedures leading to the adoption of a Community act.

Article 251

1. Where reference is made in this Treaty to this Article for the adoption of an act, the following procedure shall apply.

2. The Commission shall submit a proposal to the European Parliament and the Council.

The Council, acting by a qualified majority after obtaining the opinion of the European Parliament:

— if it approves all the amendments contained in the European Parliament's opinion, may adopt the proposed act thus amended,

— if the European Parliament does not propose any amendments, may adopt the proposed act,

— shall otherwise adopt a common position and communicate it to the European Parliament. The Council shall inform the European Parliament fully of the reasons which led it to adopt its common position. The Commission shall inform the European Parliament fully of its position.

If, within three months of such communication, the European Parliament:

(a) approves the common position or has not taken a decision, the act in question shall be deemed to have been adopted in accordance with that common position;

(b) rejects, by an absolute majority of its component members, the common position, the proposed act shall be deemed not to have been adopted;

(c) proposes amendments to the common position by an absolute majority of its component members, the amended text shall be forwarded to the Council and to the Commission, which shall deliver an opinion on those amendments.

3. If, within three months of the matter being referred to it, the Council, acting by a qualified majority, approves all the amendments of the European Parliament, the act in question shall be deemed to have been adopted in the form of the common position thus amended; however, the Council shall act unanimously on the amendments on which the Commission has delivered a negative opinion. If the Council does not approve all the amendments, the President of the Council, in agreement with the President of the European Parliament, shall within six weeks convene a meeting of the Conciliation Committee.

4. The Conciliation Committee, which shall be composed of the Members of the Council or their representatives and an equal number of representatives of the European Parliament, shall have the task of reaching agreement on a joint text, by a qualified majority of the Members of the Council or their representatives and by a majority of the representatives of the European Parliament. The Commission shall take part in the Conciliation Committee's proceedings and shall take all the necessary initiatives with a view to reconciling the positions of the European Parliament and the Council. In fulfilling this task, the Conciliation Committee shall address the common position on the basis of the amendments proposed by the European Parliament.

5. If, within six weeks of its being convened, the Conciliation Committee approves a joint text, the European Parliament, acting by an absolute majority of the votes cast, and the Council, acting by a qualified majority, shall each have a period of six weeks from that approval in which to adopt the act in question in accordance with the joint text. If either of the two institutions fails to approve the proposed act within that period, it shall be deemed not to have been adopted.

6. Where the Conciliation Committee does not approve a joint text, the proposed act shall be deemed not to have been adopted.

7. The periods of three months and six weeks referred to in this Article shall be extended by a maximum of one month and two weeks respectively at the initiative of the European Parliament or the Council.

Article 252

Where reference is made in this Treaty to this Article for the adoption of an act, the following procedure shall apply.

(a) The Council, acting by a qualified majority on a proposal from the Commission and after obtaining the opinion of the European Parliament, shall adopt a common position.

(b) The Council's common position shall be communicated to the European Parliament. The Council and the Commission shall inform the European Parliament fully of the reasons which led the Council to adopt its common position and also of the Commission's position.

   If, within three months of such communication, the European Parliament approves this common position or has not taken a decision within that period, the Council shall definitively adopt the act in question in accordance with the common position.

(c) The European Parliament may, within the period of three months referred to in point (b), by an absolute majority of its component Members, propose amendments to the Council's common position. The European Parliament may also, by the same majority, reject the Council's common position. The result of the proceedings shall be transmitted to the Council and the Commission.

   If the European Parliament has rejected the Council's common position, unanimity shall be required for the Council to act on a second reading.

(d) The Commission shall, within a period of one month, re-examine the proposal on the basis of which the Council adopted its common position, by taking into account the amendments proposed by the European Parliament.

   The Commission shall forward to the Council, at the same time as its re-examined proposal, the amendments of the European Parliament which it has not accepted, and shall express its opinion on them. The Council may adopt these amendments unanimously.

(e) The Council, acting by a qualified majority, shall adopt the proposal as re-examined by the Commission.

Unanimity shall be required for the Council to amend the proposal as re-examined by the Commission.

(f) In the cases referred to in points (c), (d) and (e), the Council shall be required to act within a period of three months. If no decision is taken within this period, the Commission proposal shall be deemed not to have been adopted.

(g) The periods referred to in points (b) and (f) may be extended by a maximum of one month by common accord between the Council and the European Parliament.

Article 253

Regulations, directives and decisions adopted jointly by the European Parliament and the Council, and such acts adopted by the Council or the Commission, shall state the reasons on which they are based and shall refer to any proposals or opinions which were required to be obtained pursuant to this Treaty.

Article 254*

1. Regulations, directives and decisions adopted in accordance with the procedure referred to in Article 251 shall be signed by the President of the European Parliament and by the President of the Council and published in the *Official Journal of the European Union*. They shall enter into force on the date specified in them or, in the absence thereof, on the 20th day following that of their publication.

2. Regulations of the Council and of the Commission, as well as directives of those institutions which are addressed to all Member States, shall be published in the *Official Journal of the European Union*. They shall enter into force on the date specified in them or, in the absence thereof, on the 20th day following that of their publication.

3. Other directives, and decisions, shall be notified to those to whom they are addressed and shall take effect upon such notification.

Article 255

1. Any citizen of the Union, and any natural or legal person residing or having its registered office in a Member State, shall have a right of access to European Parliament, Council and Commission documents, subject to the principles and the conditions to be defined in accordance with paragraphs 2 and 3.

2. General principles and limits on grounds of public or private interest governing this right of access to documents shall be deter-

---

* Article amended by the Treaty of   Nice.

mined by the Council, acting in accordance with the procedure referred to in Article 251 within two years of the entry into force of the Treaty of Amsterdam.

3. Each institution referred to above shall elaborate in its own Rules of Procedure specific provisions regarding access to its documents.

Article 256

Decisions of the Council or of the Commission which impose a pecuniary obligation on persons other than States, shall be enforceable.

Enforcement shall be governed by the rules of civil procedure in force in the State in the territory of which it is carried out. The order for its enforcement shall be appended to the decision, without other formality than verification of the authenticity of the decision, by the national authority which the government of each Member State shall designate for this purpose and shall make known to the Commission and to the Court of Justice.

When these formalities have been completed on application by the party concerned, the latter may proceed to enforcement in accordance with the national law, by bringing the matter directly before the competent authority.

Enforcement may be suspended only by a decision of the Court of Justice. However, the courts of the country concerned shall have jurisdiction over complaints that enforcement is being carried out in an irregular manner.

CHAPTER 3
THE ECONOMIC AND SOCIAL COMMITTEE

Article 257*

An Economic and Social Committee is hereby established. It shall have advisory status.

The Committee shall consist of representatives of the various economic and social components of organised civil society, and in particular representatives of producers, farmers, carriers, workers, dealers, craftsmen, professional occupations, consumers and the general interest.

Article 258*

The number of members of the Economic and Social Committee shall not exceed 350.

The number of members of the Committee shall be as follows:

Belgium	12
Denmark	9
Germany	24
Greece	12

* Article amended by the Treaty of Nice.

Spain	21
France	24
Ireland	9
Italy	24
Luxembourg	6
Netherlands	12
Austria	12
Portugal	12
Finland	9
Sweden	12
United Kingdom	24.

The members of the Committee may not be bound by any mandatory instructions. They shall be completely independent in the performance of their duties, in the general interest of the Community.

The Council, acting by a qualified majority, shall determine the allowances of members of the Committee.

Article 259*

1. The members of the Committee shall be appointed for four years, on proposals from the Member States. The Council, acting by a qualified majority, shall adopt the list of members drawn up in accordance with the proposals made by each Member State. The term of office of the members of the Committee shall be renewable.

2. The Council shall consult the Commission. It may obtain the opinion of European bodies which are representative of the various economic and social sectors to which the activities of the Community are of concern.

Article 260

The Committee shall elect its chairman and officers from among its members for a term of two years.

It shall adopt its Rules of Procedure.

The Committee shall be convened by its chairman at the request of the Council or of the Commission. It may also meet on its own initiative.

Article 261

The Committee shall include specialised sections for the principal fields covered by this Treaty.

These specialised sections shall operate within the general terms of reference of the Committee. They may not be consulted independently of the Committee.

Subcommittees may also be established within the Committee to prepare on specific questions or in specific fields, draft opinions to be submitted to the Committee for its consideration.

* Article amended by the Treaty of Nice.

The Rules of Procedure shall lay down the methods of composition and the terms of reference of the specialised sections and of the subcommittees.

Article 262

The Committee must be consulted by the Council or by the Commission where this Treaty so provides. The Committee may be consulted by these institutions in all cases in which they consider it appropriate. It may issue an opinion on its own initiative in cases in which it considers such action appropriate.

The Council or the Commission shall, if it considers it necessary, set the Committee, for the submission of its opinion, a time limit which may not be less than one month from the date on which the chairman receives notification to this effect. Upon expiry of the time limit, the absence of an opinion shall not prevent further action.

The opinion of the Committee and that of the specialised section, together with a record of the proceedings, shall be forwarded to the Council and to the Commission.

The Committee may be consulted by the European Parliament.

CHAPTER 4
THE COMMITTEE OF THE REGIONS

Article 263*

A committee, hereinafter referred to as "the Committee of the Regions", consisting of representatives of regional and local bodies who either hold a regional or local authority electoral mandate or are politically accountable to an elected assembly, is hereby established with advisory status.

The number of members of the Committee of the Regions shall not exceed 350.

The number of members of the Committee shall be as follows:

Belgium	12
Denmark	9
Germany	24
Greece	12
Spain	21
France	24
Ireland	9
Italy	24
Luxembourg	6
Netherlands	12
Austria	12
Portugal	12
Finland	9
Sweden	12

* Article amended by the Treaty of Nice.

United Kingdom   24.

The members of the Committee and an equal number of alternate members shall be appointed for four years, on proposals from the respective Member States. Their term of office shall be renewable. The Council, acting by a qualified majority, shall adopt the list of members and alternate members drawn up in accordance with the proposals made by each Member State. When the mandate referred to in the first paragraph on the basis of which they were proposed comes to an end, the term of office of members of the Committee shall terminate automatically and they shall then be replaced for the remainder of the said term of office in accordance with the same procedure. No member of the Committee shall at the same time be a Member of the European Parliament.

The members of the Committee may not be bound by any mandatory instructions. They shall be completely independent in the performance of their duties, in the general interest of the Community.

Article 264

The Committee of the Regions shall elect its chairman and officers from among its members for a term of two years.

It shall adopt its Rules of Procedure.

The Committee shall be convened by its chairman at the request of the Council or of the Commission. It may also meet on its own initiative.

Article 265

The Committee of the Regions shall be consulted by the Council or by the Commission where this Treaty so provides and in all other cases, in particular those which concern cross-border cooperation, in which one of these two institutions considers it appropriate.

The Council or the Commission shall, if it considers it necessary, set the Committee, for the submission of its opinion, a time limit which may not be less than one month from the date on which the chairman receives notification to this effect. Upon expiry of the time limit, the absence of an opinion shall not prevent further action.

Where the Economic and Social Committee is consulted pursuant to Article 262, the Committee of the Regions shall be informed by the Council or the Commission of the request for an opinion. Where it considers that specific regional interests are involved, the Committee of the Regions may issue an opinion on the matter.

The Committee of the Regions may be consulted by the European Parliament.

It may issue an opinion on its own initiative in cases in which it considers such action appropriate.

The opinion of the Committee, together with a record of the proceedings, shall be forwarded to the Council and to the Commission.

CHAPTER 5
THE EUROPEAN INVESTMENT BANK

Article 266*

The European Investment Bank shall have legal personality.

The members of the European Investment Bank shall be the Member States.

The Statute of the European Investment Bank is laid down in a Protocol annexed to this Treaty. The Council acting unanimously, at the request of the European Investment Bank and after consulting the European Parliament and the Commission, or at the request of the Commission and after consulting the European Parliament and the European Investment Bank, may amend Articles 4, 11 and 12 and Article 18(5) of the Statute of the Bank.

Article 267

The task of the European Investment Bank shall be to contribute, by having recourse to the capital market and utilising its own resources, to the balanced and steady development of the common market in the interest of the Community. For this purpose the Bank shall, operating on a non-profit-making basis, grant loans and give guarantees which facilitate the financing of the following projects in all sectors of the economy:

(a) projects for developing less-developed regions;

(b) projects for modernising or converting undertakings or for developing fresh activities called for by the progressive establishment of the common market, where these projects are of such a size or nature that they cannot be entirely financed by the various means available in the individual Member States;

(c) projects of common interest to several Member States which are of such a size or nature that they cannot be entirely financed by the various means available in the individual Member States.

In carrying out its task, the Bank shall facilitate the financing of investment programmes in conjunction with assistance from the Structural Funds and other Community Financial Instruments.

TITLE II
FINANCIAL PROVISIONS

Article 268

All items of revenue and expenditure of the Community, including those relating to the European Social Fund, shall be included in estimates to be drawn up for each financial year and shall be shown in the budget.

* Article amended by the Treaty of Nice.

Administrative expenditure occasioned for the institutions by the provisions of the Treaty on European Union relating to common foreign and security policy and to cooperation in the fields of justice and home affairs shall be charged to the budget. The operational expenditure occasioned by the implementation of the said provisions may, under the conditions referred to therein, be charged to the budget.

The revenue and expenditure shown in the budget shall be in balance.

Article 269

Without prejudice to other revenue, the budget shall be financed wholly from own resources.

The Council, acting unanimously on a proposal from the Commission and after consulting the European Parliament, shall lay down provisions relating to the system of own resources of the Community, which it shall recommend to the Member States for adoption in accordance with their respective constitutional requirements.

Article 270

With a view to maintaining budgetary discipline, the Commission shall not make any proposal for a Community act, or alter its proposals, or adopt any implementing measure which is likely to have appreciable implications for the budget without providing the assurance that that proposal or that measure is capable of being financed within the limit of the Community's own resources arising under provisions laid down by the Council pursuant to Article 269.

Article 271

The expenditure shown in the budget shall be authorised for one financial year, unless the regulations made pursuant to Article 279 provide otherwise.

In accordance with conditions to be laid down pursuant to Article 279, any appropriations, other than those relating to staff expenditure, that are unexpended at the end of the financial year may be carried forward to the next financial year only.

Appropriations shall be classified under different chapters grouping items of expenditure according to their nature or purpose and subdivided, as far as may be necessary, in accordance with the regulations made pursuant to Article 279.

The expenditure of the European Parliament, the Council, the Commission and the Court of Justice shall be set out in separate parts of the budget, without prejudice to special arrangements for certain common items of expenditure.

Article 272

1. The financial year shall run from 1 January to 31 December.

2. Each institution of the Community shall, before 1 July, draw up estimates of its expenditure. The Commission shall consolidate these estimates in a preliminary draft budget. It shall attach thereto an opinion which may contain different estimates.

The preliminary draft budget shall contain an estimate of revenue and an estimate of expenditure.

3. The Commission shall place the preliminary draft budget before the Council not later than 1 September of the year preceding that in which the budget is to be implemented.

The Council shall consult the Commission and, where appropriate, the other institutions concerned whenever it intends to depart from the preliminary draft budget.

The Council, acting by a qualified majority, shall establish the draft budget and forward it to the European Parliament.

4. The draft budget shall be placed before the European Parliament not later than 5 October of the year preceding that in which the budget is to be implemented.

The European Parliament shall have the right to amend the draft budget, acting by a majority of its Members, and to propose to the Council, acting by an absolute majority of the votes cast, modifications to the draft budget relating to expenditure necessarily resulting from this Treaty or from acts adopted in accordance therewith.

If, within 45 days of the draft budget being placed before it, the European Parliament has given its approval, the budget shall stand as finally adopted. If within this period the European Parliament has not amended the draft budget nor proposed any modifications thereto, the budget shall be deemed to be finally adopted.

If within this period the European Parliament has adopted amendments or proposed modifications, the draft budget together with the amendments or proposed modifications shall be forwarded to the Council.

5. After discussing the draft budget with the Commission and, where appropriate, with the other institutions concerned, the Council shall act under the following conditions:

(a) the Council may, acting by a qualified majority, modify any of the amendments adopted by the European Parliament;

(b) with regard to the proposed modifications:

— where a modification proposed by the European Parliament does not have the effect of increasing the total amount of the expenditure of an institution, owing in particular to the fact that the increase in expenditure which it would involve would be expressly compensated by one or more proposed modifications correspondingly reducing expenditure, the Council may, acting by a qualified majority, reject the proposed modification. In the absence of a decision to reject it, the proposed modification shall stand as accepted,

— where a modification proposed by the European Parliament has the effect of increasing the total amount of the expenditure of an institution, the Council may, acting by a qualified majority, accept this proposed modification. In the absence of a decision to accept it, the proposed modification shall stand as rejected,

— where, pursuant to one of the two preceding subparagraphs, the Council has rejected a proposed modification, it may, acting by a qualified majority, either retain the amount shown in the draft budget or fix another amount.

The draft budget shall be modified on the basis of the proposed modifications accepted by the Council.

If, within 15 days of the draft being placed before it, the Council has not modified any of the amendments adopted by the European Parliament and if the modifications proposed by the latter have been accepted, the budget shall be deemed to be finally adopted. The Council shall inform the European Parliament that it has not modified any of the amendments and that the proposed modifications have been accepted.

If within this period the Council has modified one or more of the amendments adopted by the European Parliament or if the modifications proposed by the latter have been rejected or modified, the modified draft budget shall again be forwarded to the European Parliament. The Council shall inform the European Parliament of the results of its deliberations.

6. Within 15 days of the draft budget being placed before it, the European Parliament, which shall have been notified of the action taken on its proposed modifications, may, acting by a majority of its Members and three fifths of the votes cast, amend or reject the modifications to its amendments made by the Council and shall adopt the budget accordingly. If within this period the European Parliament has not acted, the budget shall be deemed to be finally adopted.

7. When the procedure provided for in this Article has been completed, the President of the European Parliament shall declare that the budget has been finally adopted.

8. However, the European Parliament, acting by a majority of its Members and two thirds of the votes cast, may, if there are important reasons, reject the draft budget and ask for a new draft to be submitted to it.

9. A maximum rate of increase in relation to the expenditure of the same type to be incurred during the current year shall be fixed annually for the total expenditure other than that necessarily resulting from this Treaty or from acts adopted in accordance therewith.

The Commission shall, after consulting the Economic Policy Committee, declare what this maximum rate is as it results from:

— the trend, in terms of volume, of the gross national product within the Community,

— the average variation in the budgets of the Member States, and

— the trend of the cost of living during the preceding financial year.

The maximum rate shall be communicated, before 1 May, to all the institutions of the Community. The latter shall be required to conform to this during the budgetary procedure, subject to the provisions of the fourth and fifth subparagraphs of this paragraph.

If, in respect of expenditure other than that necessarily resulting from this Treaty or from acts adopted in accordance therewith, the actual rate of increase in the draft budget established by the Council is over half the maximum rate, the European Parliament may, exercising its right of amendment, further increase the total amount of that expenditure to a limit not exceeding half the maximum rate.

Where the European Parliament, the Council or the Commission consider that the activities of the Communities require that the rate determined according to the procedure laid down in this paragraph should be exceeded, another rate may be fixed by agreement between the Council, acting by a qualified majority, and the European Parliament, acting by a majority of its Members and three fifths of the votes cast.

10. Each institution shall exercise the powers conferred upon it by this article, with due regard for the provisions of the Treaty and for acts adopted in accordance therewith, in particular those relating to the Communities' own resources and to the balance between revenue and expenditure.

Article 273

If, at the beginning of a financial year, the budget has not yet been voted, a sum equivalent to not more than one twelfth of the budget appropriations for the preceding financial year may be spent each month in respect of any chapter or other subdivision of the budget in accordance with the provisions of the Regulations made pursuant to Article 279; this arrangement shall not, however, have the effect of placing at the disposal of the Commission appropriations in excess of one twelfth of those provided for in the draft budget in course of preparation.

The Council may, acting by a qualified majority, provided that the other conditions laid down in the first subparagraph are observed, authorise expenditure in excess of one twelfth.

If the decision relates to expenditure which does not necessarily result from this Treaty or from acts adopted in accordance therewith, the Council shall forward it immediately to the European Parliament;

within 30 days the European Parliament, acting by a majority of its Members and three fifths of the votes cast, may adopt a different decision on the expenditure in excess of the one twelfth referred to in the first subparagraph. This part of the decision of the Council shall be suspended until the European Parliament has taken its decision. If within the said period the European Parliament has not taken a decision which differs from the decision of the Council, the latter shall be deemed to be finally adopted.

The decisions referred to in the second and third subparagraphs shall lay down the necessary measures relating to resources to ensure application of this Article.

Article 274

The Commission shall implement the budget, in accordance with the provisions of the regulations made pursuant to Article 279, on its own responsibility and within the limits of the appropriations, having regard to the principles of sound financial management. Member States shall cooperate with the Commission to ensure that the appropriations are used in accordance with the principles of sound financial management.

The regulations shall lay down detailed rules for each institution concerning its part in effecting its own expenditure.

Within the budget, the Commission may, subject to the limits and conditions laid down in the regulations made pursuant to Article 279, transfer appropriations from one chapter to another or from one subdivision to another.

Article 275

The Commission shall submit annually to the Council and to the European Parliament the accounts of the preceding financial year relating to the implementation of the budget. The Commission shall also forward to them a financial statement of the assets and liabilities of the Community.

Article 276

1. The European Parliament, acting on a recommendation from the Council which shall act by a qualified majority, shall give a discharge to the Commission in respect of the implementation of the budget. To this end, the Council and the European Parliament in turn shall examine the accounts and the financial statement referred to in Article 275, the annual report by the Court of Auditors together with the replies of the institutions under audit to the observations of the Court of Auditors, the statement of assurance referred to in Article 248(1), second subparagraph and any relevant special reports by the Court of Auditors.

2. Before giving a discharge to the Commission, or for any other purpose in connection with the exercise of its powers over the implementation of the budget, the European Parliament may ask to hear the

Commission give evidence with regard to the execution of expenditure or the operation of financial control systems. The Commission shall submit any necessary information to the European Parliament at the latter's request.

3. The Commission shall take all appropriate steps to act on the observations in the decisions giving discharge and on other observations by the European Parliament relating to the execution of expenditure, as well as on comments accompanying the recommendations on discharge adopted by the Council.

At the request of the European Parliament or the Council, the Commission shall report on the measures taken in the light of these observations and comments and in particular on the instructions given to the departments which are responsible for the implementation of the budget. These reports shall also be forwarded to the Court of Auditors.

Article 277

The budget shall be drawn up in the unit of account determined in accordance with the provisions of the regulations made pursuant to Article 279.

Article 278

The Commission may, provided it notifies the competent authorities of the Member States concerned, transfer into the currency of one of the Member States its holdings in the currency of another Member State, to the extent necessary to enable them to be used for purposes which come within the scope of this Treaty. The Commission shall as far as possible avoid making such transfers if it possesses cash or liquid assets in the currencies which it needs.

The Commission shall deal with each Member State through the authority designated by the State concerned. In carrying out financial operations the Commission shall employ the services of the bank of issue of the Member State concerned or of any other financial institution approved by that State.

Article 279*

1. The Council, acting unanimously on a proposal from the Commission and after consulting the European Parliament and obtaining the opinion of the Court of Auditors, shall:

(a) make Financial Regulations specifying in particular the procedure to be adopted for establishing and implementing the budget and for presenting and auditing accounts;

(b) lay down rules concerning the responsibility of financial controllers, authorising officers and accounting officers, and concerning appropriate arrangements for inspection.

* Article amended by the Treaty of Nice.

From 1 January 2007, the Council shall act by a qualified majority on a proposal from the Commission and after consulting the European Parliament and obtaining the opinion of the Court of Auditors.

2.   The Council, acting unanimously on a proposal from the Commission and after consulting the European Parliament and obtaining the opinion of the Court of Auditors, shall determine the methods and procedure whereby the budget revenue provided under the arrangements relating to the Community's own resources shall be made available to the Commission, and determine the measures to be applied, if need be, to meet cash requirements.

Article 280

1.   The Community and the Member States shall counter fraud and any other illegal activities affecting the financial interests of the Community through measures to be taken in accordance with this article, which shall act as a deterrent and be such as to afford effective protection in the Member States.

2.   Member States shall take the same measures to counter fraud affecting the financial interests of the Community as they take to counter fraud affecting their own financial interests.

3.   Without prejudice to other provisions of this Treaty, the Member States shall coordinate their action aimed at protecting the financial interests of the Community against fraud. To this end they shall organise, together with the Commission, close and regular cooperation between the competent authorities.

4.   The Council, acting in accordance with the procedure referred to in Article 251, after consulting the Court of Auditors, shall adopt the necessary measures in the fields of the prevention of and fight against fraud affecting the financial interests of the Community with a view to affording effective and equivalent protection in the Member States. These measures shall not concern the application of national criminal law or the national administration of justice.

5.   The Commission, in cooperation with Member States, shall each year submit to the European Parliament and to the Council a report on the measures taken for the implementation of this article.

PART SIX
GENERAL AND FINAL PROVISIONS

Article 281

The Community shall have legal personality.

Article 282

In each of the Member States, the Community shall enjoy the most extensive legal capacity accorded to legal persons under their laws; it may, in particular, acquire or dispose of movable and immovable property and may be a party to legal proceedings. To this end, the Community shall be represented by the Commission.

Article 283

The Council shall, acting by a qualified majority on a proposal from the Commission and after consulting the other institutions concerned, lay down the Staff Regulations of officials of the European Communities and the Conditions of employment of other servants of those Communities.

Article 284

The Commission may, within the limits and under conditions laid down by the Council in accordance with the provisions of this Treaty, collect any information and carry out any checks required for the performance of the tasks entrusted to it.

Article 285

1. Without prejudice to Article 5 of the Protocol on the Statute of the European System of Central Banks and of the European Central Bank, the Council, acting in accordance with the procedure referred to in Article 251, shall adopt measures for the production of statistics where necessary for the performance of the activities of the Community.

2. The production of Community statistics shall conform to impartiality, reliability, objectivity, scientific independence, cost-effectiveness and statistical confidentiality; it shall not entail excessive burdens on economic operators.

Article 286

1. From 1 January 1999, Community acts on the protection of individuals with regard to the processing of personal data and the free movement of such data shall apply to the institutions and bodies set up by, or on the basis of, this Treaty.

2. Before the date referred to in paragraph 1, the Council, acting in accordance with the procedure referred to in Article 251, shall establish an independent supervisory body responsible for monitoring the application of such Community acts to Community institutions and bodies and shall adopt any other relevant provisions as appropriate.

Article 287

The members of the institutions of the Community, the members of committees, and the officials and other servants of the Community shall be required, even after their duties have ceased, not to disclose information of the kind covered by the obligation of professional secrecy, in particular information about undertakings, their business relations or their cost components.

Article 288

The contractual liability of the Community shall be governed by the law applicable to the contract in question.

In the case of non-contractual liability, the Community shall, in accordance with the general principles common to the laws of the Member States, make good any damage caused by its institutions or by its servants in the performance of their duties.

The preceding paragraph shall apply under the same conditions to damage caused by the ECB or by its servants in the performance of their duties.

The personal liability of its servants towards the Community shall be governed by the provisions laid down in their Staff Regulations or in the Conditions of employment applicable to them.

Article 289

The seat of the institutions of the Community shall be determined by common accord of the governments of the Member States.

Article 290*

The rules governing the languages of the institutions of the Community shall, without prejudice to the provisions contained in the Statute of the Court of Justice, be determined by the Council, acting unanimously.

Article 291

The Community shall enjoy in the territories of the Member States such privileges and immunities as are necessary for the performance of its tasks, under the conditions laid down in the Protocol of 8 April 1965 on the privileges and immunities of the European Communities. The same shall apply to the European Central Bank, the European Monetary Institute, and the European Investment Bank.

Article 292

Member States undertake not to submit a dispute concerning the interpretation or application of this Treaty to any method of settlement other than those provided for therein.

Article 293

Member States shall, so far as is necessary, enter into negotiations with each other with a view to securing for the benefit of their nationals:

— the protection of persons and the enjoyment and protection of rights under the same conditions as those accorded by each State to its own nationals,

* Article amended by the Treaty of Nice.

— the abolition of double taxation within the Community,

— the mutual recognition of companies or firms within the meaning of the second paragraph of Article 48, the retention of legal personality in the event of transfer of their seat from one country to another, and the possibility of mergers between companies or firms governed by the laws of different countries,

— the simplification of formalities governing the reciprocal recognition and enforcement of judgments of courts or tribunals and of arbitration awards.

Article 294

Member States shall accord nationals of the other Member States the same treatment as their own nationals as regards participation in the capital of companies or firms within the meaning of Article 48, without prejudice to the application of the other provisions of this Treaty.

Article 295

This Treaty shall in no way prejudice the rules in Member States governing the system of property ownership.

Article 296

1. The provisions of this Treaty shall not preclude the application of the following rules:

(a) no Member State shall be obliged to supply information the disclosure of which it considers contrary to the essential interests of its security;

(b) any Member State may take such measures as it considers necessary for the protection of the essential interests of its security which are connected with the production of or trade in arms, munitions and war material; such measures shall not adversely affect the conditions of competition in the common market regarding products which are not intended for specifically military purposes.

2. The Council may, acting unanimously on a proposal from the Commission, make changes to the list, which it drew up on 15 April 1958, of the products to which the provisions of paragraph 1(b) apply.

Article 297

Member States shall consult each other with a view to taking together the steps needed to prevent the functioning of the common market being affected by measures which a Member State may be called upon to take in the event of serious internal disturbances affecting the maintenance of law and order, in the event of war, serious international tension constituting a threat of war, or in order to carry out obligations it has accepted for the purpose of maintaining peace and international security.

Article 298

If measures taken in the circumstances referred to in Articles 296 and 297 have the effect of distorting the conditions of competition in the common market, the Commission shall, together with the State concerned, examine how these measures can be adjusted to the rules laid down in the Treaty.

By way of derogation from the procedure laid down in Articles 226 and 227, the Commission or any Member State may bring the matter directly before the Court of Justice if it considers that another Member State is making improper use of the powers provided for in Articles 296 and 297. The Court of Justice shall give its ruling in camera.

Article 299

1. This Treaty shall apply to the Kingdom of Belgium, the Kingdom of Denmark, the Federal Republic of Germany, the Hellenic Republic, the Kingdom of Spain, the French Republic, Ireland, the Italian Republic, the Grand Duchy of Luxembourg, the Kingdom of the Netherlands, the Republic of Austria, the Portuguese Republic, the Republic of Finland, the Kingdom of Sweden and the United Kingdom of Great Britain and Northern Ireland.

2. The provisions of this Treaty shall apply to the French overseas departments, the Azores, Madeira and the Canary Islands.

However, taking account of the structural social and economic situation of the French overseas departments, the Azores, Madeira and the Canary Islands, which is compounded by their remoteness, insularity, small size, difficult topography and climate, economic dependence on a few products, the permanence and combination of which severely restrain their development, the Council, acting by a qualified majority on a proposal from the Commission and after consulting the European Parliament, shall adopt specific measures aimed, in particular, at laying down the conditions of application of the present Treaty to those regions, including common policies.

The Council shall, when adopting the relevant measures referred to in the second subparagraph, take into account areas such as customs and trade policies, fiscal policy, free zones, agriculture and fisheries policies, conditions for supply of raw materials and essential consumer goods, State aids and conditions of access to structural funds and to horizontal Community programmes.

The Council shall adopt the measures referred to in the second subparagraph taking into account the special characteristics and constraints of the outermost regions without undermining the integrity and the coherence of the Community legal order, including the internal market and common policies.

3. The special arrangements for association set out in part four of this Treaty shall apply to the overseas countries and territories listed in Annex II to this Treaty.

This Treaty shall not apply to those overseas countries and territories having special relations with the United Kingdom of Great Britain and Northern Ireland which are not included in the aforementioned list.

4.   The provisions of this Treaty shall apply to the European territories for whose external relations a Member State is responsible.

5.   The provisions of this Treaty shall apply to the Åland Islands in accordance with the provisions set out in Protocol 2 to the Act concerning the conditions of accession of the Republic of Austria, the Republic of Finland and the Kingdom of Sweden.

6.   Notwithstanding the preceding paragraphs:

(a) this Treaty shall not apply to the Faeroe Islands;

(b) this Treaty shall not apply to the sovereign base areas of the United Kingdom of Great Britain and Northern Ireland in Cyprus;

(c) this Treaty shall apply to the Channel Islands and the Isle of Man only to the extent necessary to ensure the implementation of the arrangements for those islands set out in the Treaty concerning the accession of new Member States to the European Economic Community and to the European Atomic Energy Community signed on 22 January 1972.

Article 300*

1.   Where this Treaty provides for the conclusion of agreements between the Community and one or more States or international organisations, the Commission shall make recommendations to the Council, which shall authorise the Commission to open the necessary negotiations. The Commission shall conduct these negotiations in consultation with special committees appointed by the Council to assist it in this task and within the framework of such directives as the Council may issue to it.

In exercising the powers conferred upon it by this paragraph, the Council shall act by a qualified majority, except in the cases where the first subparagraph of paragraph 2 provides that the Council shall act unanimously.

2.   Subject to the powers vested in the Commission in this field, the signing, which may be accompanied by a decision on provisional application before entry into force, and the conclusion of the agreements shall be decided on by the Council, acting by a qualified majority on a proposal from the Commission. The Council shall act unanimously when the agreement covers a field for which unanimity is required for the adoption of internal rules and for the agreements referred to in Article 310.

By way of derogation from the rules laid down in paragraph 3, the same procedures shall apply for a decision to suspend the application of an agreement, and for the purpose of establishing the positions to be

* Article amended by the Treaty of   Nice.

adopted on behalf of the Community in a body set up by an agreement, when that body is called upon to adopt decisions having legal effects, with the exception of decisions supplementing or amending the institutional framework of the agreement.

The European Parliament shall be immediately and fully informed of any decision under this paragraph concerning the provisional application or the suspension of agreements, or the establishment of the Community position in a body set up by an agreement.

3. The Council shall conclude agreements after consulting the European Parliament, except for the agreements referred to in Article 133(3), including cases where the agreement covers a field for which the procedure referred to in Article 251 or that referred to in Article 252 is required for the adoption of internal rules. The European Parliament shall deliver its opinion within a time limit which the Council may lay down according to the urgency of the matter. In the absence of an opinion within that time limit, the Council may act.

By way of derogation from the previous subparagraph, agreements referred to in Article 310, other agreements establishing a specific institutional framework by organising cooperation procedures, agreements having important budgetary implications for the Community and agreements entailing amendment of an act adopted under the procedure referred to in Article 251 shall be concluded after the assent of the European Parliament has been obtained.

The Council and the European Parliament may, in an urgent situation, agree upon a time limit for the assent.

4. When concluding an agreement, the Council may, by way of derogation from paragraph 2, authorise the Commission to approve modifications on behalf of the Community where the agreement provides for them to be adopted by a simplified procedure or by a body set up by the agreement; it may attach specific conditions to such authorisation.

5. When the Council envisages concluding an agreement which calls for amendments to this Treaty, the amendments must first be adopted in accordance with the procedure laid down in Article 48 of the Treaty on European Union.

6. The European Parliament, the Council, the Commission or a Member State may obtain the opinion of the Court of Justice as to whether an agreement envisaged is compatible with the provisions of this Treaty. Where the opinion of the Court of Justice is adverse, the agreement may enter into force only in accordance with Article 48 of the Treaty on European Union.

7. Agreements concluded under the conditions set out in this Article shall be binding on the institutions of the Community and on Member States.

Article 301

Where it is provided, in a common position or in a joint action adopted according to the provisions of the Treaty on European Union relating to the common foreign and security policy, for an action by the Community to interrupt or to reduce, in part or completely, economic relations with one or more third countries, the Council shall take the necessary urgent measures. The Council shall act by a qualified majority on a proposal from the Commission.

Article 302

It shall be for the Commission to ensure the maintenance of all appropriate relations with the organs of the United Nations and of its specialised agencies.

The Commission shall also maintain such relations as are appropriate with all international organisations.

Article 303

The Community shall establish all appropriate forms of cooperation with the Council of Europe.

Article 304

The Community shall establish close cooperation with the Organisation for Economic Cooperation and Development, the details of which shall be determined by common accord.

Article 305

1.   The provisions of this Treaty shall not affect the provisions of the Treaty establishing the European Coal and Steel Community, in particular as regards the rights and obligations of Member States, the powers of the institutions of that Community and the rules laid down by that Treaty for the functioning of the common market in coal and steel.

2.   The provisions of this Treaty shall not derogate from those of the Treaty establishing the European Atomic Energy Community.

Article 306

The provisions of this Treaty shall not preclude the existence or completion of regional unions between Belgium and Luxembourg, or between Belgium, Luxembourg and the Netherlands, to the extent that the objectives of these regional unions are not attained by application of this Treaty.

Article 307

The rights and obligations arising from agreements concluded before 1 January 1958 or, for acceding States, before the date of their accession, between one or more Member States on the one hand, and one or more third countries on the other, shall not be affected by the provisions of this Treaty.

To the extent that such agreements are not compatible with this Treaty, the Member State or States concerned shall take all appropriate steps to eliminate the incompatibilities established. Member States shall, where necessary, assist each other to this end and shall, where appropriate, adopt a common attitude.

In applying the agreements referred to in the first paragraph, Member States shall take into account the fact that the advantages accorded under this Treaty by each Member State form an integral part of the establishment of the Community and are thereby inseparably linked with the creation of common institutions, the conferring of powers upon them and the granting of the same advantages by all the other Member States.

Article 308

If action by the Community should prove necessary to attain, in the course of the operation of the common market, one of the objectives of the Community, and this Treaty has not provided the necessary powers, the Council shall, acting unanimously on a proposal from the Commission and after consulting the European Parliament, take the appropriate measures.

Article 309*

1.   Where a decision has been taken to suspend the voting rights of the representative of the government of a Member State in accordance with Article 7(3) of the Treaty on European Union, these voting rights shall also be suspended with regard to this Treaty.

2.   Moreover, where the existence of a serious and persistent breach by a Member State of principles mentioned in Article 6(1) of the Treaty on European Union has been determined in accordance with Article 7(2) of that Treaty, the Council, acting by a qualified majority, may decide to suspend certain of the rights deriving from the application of this Treaty to the Member State in question. In doing so, the Council shall take into account the possible consequences of such a suspension on the rights and obligations of natural and legal persons.

The obligations of the Member State in question under this Treaty shall in any case continue to be binding on that State.

3.   The Council, acting by a qualified majority, may decide subsequently to vary or revoke measures taken in accordance with paragraph 2 in response to changes in the situation which led to their being imposed.

4.   When taking decisions referred to in paragraphs 2 and 3, the Council shall act without taking into account the votes of the representative of the government of the Member State in question. By way of

---

* Article amended by the Treaty of   Nice.

derogation from Article 205(2) a qualified majority shall be defined as the same proportion of the weighted votes of the members of the Council concerned as laid down in Article 205(2).

This paragraph shall also apply in the event of voting rights being suspended in accordance with paragraph 1. In such cases, a decision requiring unanimity shall be taken without the vote of the representative of the government of the Member State in question.

Article 310

The Community may conclude with one or more States or international organisations agreements establishing an association involving reciprocal rights and obligations, common action and special procedure.

Article 311

The protocols annexed to this Treaty by common accord of the Member States shall form an integral part thereof.

Article 312

This Treaty is concluded for an unlimited period.

FINAL PROVISIONS

Article 313

This Treaty shall be ratified by the High Contracting Parties in accordance with their respective constitutional requirements. The Instruments of ratification shall be deposited with the Government of the Italian Republic.

This Treaty shall enter into force on the first day of the month following the deposit of the Instrument of ratification by the last signatory State to take this step. If, however, such deposit is made less than 15 days before the beginning of the following month, this Treaty shall not enter into force until the first day of the second month after the date of such deposit.

Article 314

This Treaty, drawn up in a single original in the Dutch, French, German, and Italian languages, all four texts being equally authentic, shall be deposited in the archives of the Government of the Italian Republic, which shall transmit a certified copy to each of the Governments of the other signatory States.

Pursuant to the Accession Treaties, the Danish, English, Finnish, Greek, Irish, Portuguese, Spanish and Swedish versions of this Treaty shall also be authentic.

* * *

ANNEX II
OVERSEAS COUNTRIES AND TERRITORIES

to which the provisions of part four of the Treaty apply

— Greenland

— New Caledonia and Dependencies

— French Polynesia

— French Southern and Antarctic Territories

— Wallis and Futuna Islands

— Mayotte

— Saint Pierre and Miquelon

— Aruba

— Netherlands Antilles:

    — Bonaire

    — Curaçao

    — Saba

    — Sint Eustatius

    — Sint Maarten

— Anguilla

— Cayman Islands

— Falkland Islands

— South Georgia and the South Sandwich Islands

— Montserrat

— Pitcairn

— Saint Helena and Dependencies

— British Antarctic Territory

— British Indian Ocean Territory

— Turks and Caicos Islands

— British Virgin Islands

— Bermuda.

* * *

PROTOCOL
ON THE ENLARGEMENT OF
THE EUROPEAN UNION

THE HIGH CONTRACTING PARTIES

HAVE AGREED UPON the following provisions, which shall be annexed to the Treaty on European Union and to the Treaties establishing the European Communities:

Article 1
Repeal of the Protocol on the institutions

The Protocol on the institutions with the prospect of enlargement of the European Union, annexed to the Treaty on European Union and to the Treaties establishing the European Communities, is hereby repealed.

Article 2
Provisions concerning the European Parliament

1. On 1 January 2004 and with effect from the start of the 2004 to 2009 term, in Article 190(2) of the Treaty establishing the European Community and in Article 108(2) of the Treaty establishing the European Atomic Energy Community, the first subparagraph shall be replaced by the following:

'The number of representatives elected in each Member State shall be as follows:

Belgium	22
Denmark	13
Germany	99
Greece	22
Spain	50
France	72
Ireland	12
Italy	72
Luxembourg	6
Netherlands	25
Austria	17
Portugal	22
Finland	13
Sweden	18
United Kingdom	72'.

2. Subject to paragraph 3, the total number of representatives in the European Parliament for the 2004 to 2009 term shall be equal to the number of representatives specified in Article 190(2) of the Treaty establishing the European Community and in Article 108(2) of the Treaty establishing the European Atomic Energy Community plus the number of representatives of the new Member States resulting from the accession treaties signed by 1 January 2004 at the latest.

3. If the total number of members referred to in paragraph 2 is less than 732, a pro rata correction shall be applied to the number of representatives to be elected in each Member State, so that the total number is as close as possible to 732, without such a correction leading

to the number of representatives to be elected in each Member State being higher than that provided for in Article 190(2) of the Treaty establishing the European Community and in Article 108(2) of the Treaty establishing the European Atomic Energy Community for the 1999 to 2004 term.

The Council shall adopt a decision to that effect.

4. By way of derogation from the second paragraph of Article 189 of the Treaty establishing the European Community and from the second paragraph of Article 107 of the Treaty establishing the European Atomic Energy Community, in the event of the entry into force of accession treaties after the adoption of the Council decision provided for in the second subparagraph of paragraph 3 of this Article, the number of members of the European Parliament may temporarily exceed 732 for the period for which that decision applies. The same correction as that referred to in the first subparagraph of paragraph 3 of this Article shall be applied to the number of representatives to be elected in the Member States in question.

Article 3
**Provisions concerning the weighting of
votes in the Council**

1. On 1 January 2005:

(a) in Article 205 of the Treaty establishing the European Community and in Article 118 of the Treaty establishing the European Atomic Energy Community:

(i) paragraph 2 shall be replaced by the following:

'2. Where the Council is required to act by a qualified majority, the votes of its members shall be weighted as follows:

Belgium	12
Denmark	7
Germany	29
Greece	12
Spain	27
France	29
Ireland	7
Italy	29
Luxembourg	4
Netherlands	13
Austria	10
Portugal	12
Finland	7
Sweden	10
United Kingdom	29

Acts of the Council shall require for their adoption at least 169 votes in favour cast by a majority of the members where this Treaty requires them to be adopted on a proposal from the Commission.

In other cases, for their adoption acts of the Council shall require at least 169 votes in favour, cast by at least two-thirds of the members.';

(ii) the following paragraph 4 shall be added:

'4. When a decision is to be adopted by the Council by a qualified majority, a member of the Council may request verification that the Member States constituting the qualified majority represent at least 62% of the total population of the Union. If that condition is shown not to have been met, the decision in question shall not be adopted.'

(b) In Article 23(2) of the Treaty on European Union, the third subparagraph shall be replaced by the following text:

'The votes of the members of the Council shall be weighted in accordance with Article 205(2) of the Treaty establishing the European Community. For their adoption, decisions shall require at least 169 votes in favour cast by at least two thirds of the members. When a decision is to be adopted by the Council by a qualified majority, a member of the Council may request verification that the Member States constituting the qualified majority represent at least 62% of the total population of the Union. If that condition is shown not to have been met, the decision in question shall not be adopted.'

(c) In Article 34 of the Treaty on European Union, paragraph 3 shall be replaced by the following:

'3. Where the Council is required to act by a qualified majority, the votes of its members shall be weighted as laid down in Article 205(2) of the Treaty establishing the European Community, and for their adoption acts of the Council shall require at least 169 votes in favour, cast by at least two thirds of the members. When a decision is to be adopted by the Council by a qualified majority, a member of the Council may request verification that the Member States constituting the qualified majority represent at least 62% of the total population of the Union. If that condition is shown not to have been met, the decision in question shall not be adopted.'

2. At the time of each accession, the threshold referred to in the second subparagraph of Article 205(2) of the Treaty establishing the European Community and in the second subparagraph of Article 118(2) of the Treaty establishing the European Atomic Energy Community shall be calculated in such a way that the qualified majority threshold expressed in votes does not exceed the threshold resulting from the table in the Declaration on the enlargement of the European Union, included in the Final Act of the Conference which adopted the Treaty of Nice.

Article 4
Provisions concerning the Commission

1. On 1 January 2005 and with effect from when the first Commission following that date takes up its duties, Article 213(1) of the Treaty establishing the European Community and Article 126(1) of the Treaty establishing the European Atomic Energy Community shall be replaced by the following:

'1. The Members of the Commission shall be chosen on the grounds of their general competence and their independence shall be beyond doubt.

The Commission shall include one national of each of the Member States.

The number of Members of the Commission may be altered by the Council, acting unanimously.'

2. When the Union consists of 27 Member States, Article 213(1) of the Treaty establishing the European Community and Article 126(1) of the Treaty establishing the European Atomic Energy Community shall be replaced by the following:

'1. The Members of the Commission shall be chosen on the grounds of their general competence and their independence shall be beyond doubt.

The number of Members of the Commission shall be less than the number of Member States. The Members of the Commission shall be chosen according to a rotation system based on the principle of equality, the implementing arrangements for which shall be adopted by the Council, acting unanimously.

The number of Members of the Commission shall be set by the Council, acting unanimously.'

This amendment shall apply as from the date on which the first Commission following the date of accession of the 27th Member State of the Union takes up its duties.

3. The Council, acting unanimously after signing the treaty of accession of the 27th Member State of the Union, shall adopt:

— the number of Members of the Commission,

— the implementing arrangements for a rotation system based on the principle of equality containing all the criteria and rules necessary for determining the composition of successive colleges automatically on the basis of the following principles:

(a) Member States shall be treated on a strictly equal footing as regards determination of the sequence of, and the time spent by, their nationals as Members of the Commission; consequently, the difference between the total number of terms of office held by nationals of any given pair of Member States may never be more than one;

(b) subject to point (a), each successive college shall be so composed as to reflect satisfactorily the demographic and geographical range of all the Member States of the Union.

4. Any State which accedes to the Union shall be entitled, at the time of its accession, to have one of its nationals as a Member of the Commission until paragraph 2 applies.

*

Table of Cases

G

H

*

Index

References are to Sections

---

†